To Jagodan,

For 16 wonderful

*Volumes in the series Music in American Life
are listed at the end of this book.*

America's Music

Gilbert Chase

America's Music
From the Pilgrims to the Present

Revised Third Edition

With a Foreword by Richard Crawford
and a Discographical Essay by William Brooks

University of Illinois Press
Urbana and Chicago

This book is printed on acid-free paper.

Library of Congress Cataloging-in-Publication Data

Chase, Gilbert, 1906–
   America's music, from the pilgrims to the present.

   (Music in American life)
   "American music on record, by William Brooks": p.
   Bibliography: p.
   Includes index.
   1. Music—United States—History and criticism.
I. Title.   II. Series.
ML200.C5   1987   781.773   86-30795
ISBN 0-252-00454-X

To Kathleen

Contents

Part Three: Toward a Composite Culture

Part Four: America and the World

Foreword

Richard Crawford

In 1955, in the introduction to the first edition of *America's Music,* Gilbert Chase wrote: "By *America's Music* I mean the music made or continuously used by the people of the United States, people who have come from many parts of the earth to build a new civilization and to create a new society in a new world, guided by ideals of human dignity, freedom, and justice."[1] Implicit in these patriotic words are two perceptions that break sharply with earlier histories of music in the United States: first, that the key to American music lies in the nature of American society and, second, that a historian can hope to do justice to the subject only by studying the musics of all Americans. So convincingly did Chase's book illustrate these perceptions that they have shaped historical views of American music ever since.

Two generations before *America's Music* appeared on the scene, pioneering American music historian Oscar G. Sonneck had noted that when an American writes about music, he usually "does not feel himself as an American at all, but as a European." He continued: "Musically his country interests him and exists for him only in so far as it has participated and is participating in the council of nations governing the world of music."[2] Today, it might seem that an American writing American music history could hardly avoid doing so *as* an American. But, in fact, so firm were the barriers in and before Sonneck's day that he was the first even to hint that the subject might be approached from anything but a European angle.

Before Sonneck's time most American writers on music, including historians, were teachers or critics engaged in what they considered missionary work: the fostering of the European art of music as it had been transplanted to American shores. Musically speaking, America for them, as for European musicians, was a somewhat backward province—an outpost of European settlement on a faraway continent. The central drama of American music history, they believed, was the growth in America of cultivated music making in the European mold. The burgeoning of music education, conservatories, and concert life and the founding of choral societies, orchestras, and opera companies were, in their eyes, all signs of musical progress— signals that European emulation was proceeding apace.

For the generation of historians who wrote just before World War I, a new phase of American musical achievement seemed at hand. In their teleological view of history, the time was finally ripe for American composers to seize the nation's musical destiny from the hands of educators and performers. A generation of native-born composers had already shown that Americans could master the Old World craft of composition. Now it was time for a decisive breakthrough: for Americans to begin to compose large-scale works—symphonies, perhaps even operas—that were not only technically sound but artistically inspired and distinctively national in flavor. When that happened, these historians believed, the United States, having achieved creative particularity within a European framework, would begin to be accepted into the community of Western nations whose musical accomplishments deserved international respect.[3]

Fundamental to this view of American music history was the belief that, rather than a unique entity, the United States was simply one among many Western nations. From that belief another followed: that the writing of American music history was chiefly a matter of tracing *continuities* that linked American musical life with that of Europe.

During the thirty-nine years that passed between Sonneck's statement and the publication of Chase's book, little changed in the field of American music history. John Tasker Howard's *Our American Music* (1931; rev. ed., 1939; 3d ed., 1946; 3d ed., with supplementary chapters, 1954; 4th ed., 1965), the only general history of the subject written between 1916 and 1955, did wear the trappings of a new approach. For Howard claimed as his subject "the music that has been written in this country,"[4] and he gave American composers the central place in his narrative. Yet the landscape in which Howard set these composers differed hardly at all from that of his predecessors. Howard cast his work in three parts, which he called "Euterpe in the Wilderness" (1620–1800), "Euterpe Clears the Forest" (1800–1860), and "Euterpe Builds Her American Home" (1860–1931). The story of progress told by earlier historians is here captured in a metaphor. Euterpe, one of the nine Greek muses, arrives from the Old World and, finding a desolate wilderness, sets to work until she has tamed it, then settles in for a permanent stay. Old World cultivation struggles with New World crudeness and eventually civilizes it. Howard's choice of Euterpe in the wilderness as his underlying myth corresponded to his own musical preferences, which were those of a music lover steeped in the ethos of the Euro-American concert hall of his day and noticeably uneasy in the presence of American musical vernaculars. The composers he considered most significant were those whose allegiance to Euterpe, the Old World muse, was strongest. A European view still ruled American music historiography, even at mid-century.

Enter Chase. We pick up his career in 1940 when, in his early thirties, with some experience as a music critic behind him, he was appointed to the staff of the Library of Congress's Music Division as a Latin American specialist. "My desk happened to face a portrait of Oscar G. Sonneck," he later wrote, and "the example of his industry, erudition, and enthusiasm could not fail to impress me profoundly."[5] Sonneck never wrote a general history of American music. But between 1905 and 1915 he published five books about eighteenth-century American secular music. Based upon meticulous documentary research, Sonneck's works revealed, in full detail, a musical tradition whose existence earlier historians had barely suspected. In an address to the Music Teachers' National Association in 1916, Sonneck set down some ideas about how the history of American music should be written. "The interests of a historian of music and musical life," he advised, "are not and ought not to remain confined to matters of musical esthetics or technique."[6] These words made a deep impression on Chase when he read them many years later. They helped him to form his own idea of the music historian's role: "It is the historian's task to study and interpret what *was*—the values and events and cultural configurations of a given time and place—not what he regards as valuable or beautiful or edifying in terms of his own cultural time-space niche."[7]

Chase's job at the Library of Congress also brought him into contact with the Archive of American Folk Song, which was both a repository of recordings and a center visited by many "folklorists and folk singers." Listening to these recordings and talking with the people who made and studied them helped Chase eventually "to recognize the underlying unity of Negro music in the New World," and he found himself "absorbed by the whole fascinating process of the development of musical culture in the Americas."[8] It was about this time that Charles Seeger, working in Washington with the Federal Music Project (1938–41) and then as chief of the Pan-American Union's music division (1941–55), began to publish his theoretical studies of musicology, which insisted on the significance of folk music. Seeger's agenda for musicology included the study of "the field of music as a whole," an acceptance of the idea "of music as a social and cultural function," and a study of "the relationships between written and unwritten" musics.[9]

Seeger's ideas fit perfectly with Chase's studies of Spanish and Latin American music, where folk genres were so obviously prominent and significant. In his first book, *The Music of Spain* (New York, 1941), Chase urged historians to "look beyond the conventional periphery of the church, the concert hall and the opera house" and to seek out "the sum total of musical experience in its full range of social and human values." He continued: "This can only be embraced by including every manifestation of the musical instinct among human beings, not only in its aspect of genuine folk music, but also in such hybrid manifestations as urban street music and popular theatrical music."[10]

"My own work in American music," Chase later wrote, "owes its initial impetus to the example of Oscar Sonneck in history and the influence of Charles Seeger in theory."[11] During his three-year stay at the Library of Congress, this Latin American specialist's interests were drawn more and more toward the music of his own country, as the work of his two intellectual mentors helped him to begin to sense the richness of the musical history of the United States. Chase made a crucial connection between Sonneck's emphasis on "documentation" and Seeger's on "theory." He saw that the two intersected in their fundamental concern for "the sociocultural foundations of music."[12] Thus, rather than opposing, they could complement each other. Certainly, Chase drew upon both in his own work. Under Sonneck's influence he accepted the task of setting down "what *was*" in the American musical past, regardless of enduring popularity or aesthetic worth by present-day standards. Under Seeger's he widened the horizon to include all kinds of American music making, written and oral. Having enlarged his grasp of both past and present, he found further inspiration in a statement made by composer Arthur Farwell in 1914 about the future of American music. Declaring that American music was more a matter of "prophecy" than of history, Farwell had explained: "What a new world, with new processes and new ideals, will do with the tractable and still unformed art of music; what will arise from the contact of this art with our unprecedented democracy—these are the questions of deepest import in our musical life in the United States."[13]

All three of these approaches—those of the "exegetes"[14] Sonneck and Seeger, who sought to "show the way" through fresh observation, and of

Farwell, who labored as a composer, critic, publisher, and municipal employee to close the gap between the concert hall and the mass of the American people—seemed to undermine the importance of American music's continuities with Europe. The three perspectives combined to bring a flood of new data into the study of American music—data that, irrelevant from earlier viewpoints, now demanded consideration.

At least one more influence, albeit a negative one, must also have worked on Chase when he was writing *America's Music* in the 1940s and early 1950s, and that was Howard's *Our American Music*. The signs are clear that Chase wrote not only to bring his fresh, new ideas to light but also to overturn Howard's view of the subject. His comments on Howard's history leave no doubt that Howard's outlook—too genteel and "respectable" for Chase's taste—triggered much of the emotional energy that invigorates Chase's account.[15] Howard fit Sonneck's description of an American who wrote "as a European." As for Chase himself, the writings of Sonneck, Seeger, and Farwell had led him to believe that earlier historians had taken too narrow a view of American music. Under their influence and galled by the knowledge that Howard's unmethodical, browsing chronicle was the only general account available, he found a way to approach the history of American music as an American.

Chase's *America's Music* is a landmark in American musical historiography because its author was the first general historian of the subject to recognize American music as a unique phenomenon that demanded to be studied as such. Contrary to most received opinion, Chase had come to understand American music as not simply another branch of European music but something new and different under the sun. Where his predecessors, anticipating the arrival on these shores of a kind of cosmopolitan millennium, thought they could detect a pattern of advancing gentility, he saw that trend as just one among many. The American musical landscape, for him, could be resolved into no distinct pattern. Rather, it was an arena in which a vast congeries of individuals and groups had made music according to their own needs and tastes—much of it potentially significant, and little of it fully explainable by reference to European practices and standards. The essence of American musical life for Chase lay not only in those branches that emulated Old World models but also in the complexity and disorderedness of the whole—in short, in the *discontinuities* of the New World's musical life with the Old. It is precisely in the author's perception of America's *difference* from Europe that the viewpoint of *America's Music* is rooted.

It is one thing to propose a new approach to a subject and quite another to put one successfully into practice—especially when it encompasses a much broader range than its predecessors. The writing of history poses challenges in methodology and research. But, however well these may be met, the ultimate challenge for the historian is literary. Unless he or she can write something that readers will read, historiographical visions will count for little. *America's Music* is a book that has been read and understood. Its premises have been widely accepted, leaving their mark on all later histories of American music and making earlier efforts seem rather old-fashioned.[16] If impact, influence, and respect are measures of success in the field, then *America's Music* has already been a success. But now, at the age of eighty, Chase has returned to the arena with a new edition of *America's Music*. While covering much of the same territory as earlier editions, *America's Music,* revised third edition, is actually a new book—one that has been entirely rethought and rewritten, and one that reflects the author's continued involvement with the subject and his intellectual preoccupations since the mid-1950s.

Tracing the differences between the revised third edition of *America's Music* and its earlier incarnations would be an interesting exercise in itself. But surely more to the point for readers of this volume is the question of what kind of book they hold in their hands. After some four decades of grappling seriously with the subject—of listening, of attending concerts and the theater, of reading in history and historiography and musicology and especially anthropology, of writing on American music and musicians and methodology, and of interpreting and reinterpreting all of this experience—what kind of portrait of America's music does Gilbert Chase present?

The short answer to that question is that Chase perceives music as a cultural statement. Pieces of music express and embody the maker's oneness with a particular American cultural strain—a strain that might be anything from an ethnic group, to a religious outlook, to an approach to musical composition. Thus, music itself is not Chase's chief concern but rather the attitudes and conditions that bring music into being. "The task of the cultural historian," Chase has written, "is not to get inside a piece of music with a microscope (otherwise known as theoretical analysis), but to account for the kinds of human behavior that produce this or that type of musical expression."[17] One suspects that Chase would agree with Clifford Geertz's Weberian description of man as "an animal suspended in webs of significance he himself has spun," with culture being those webs, and the analysis of culture being an "interpretive" search for "meaning."[18]

Chase's choice of domain reinforces his democratic predilection for judging as equally worthy of respect all of the cultural strains that lie behind American musical styles. Styles are introduced chiefly as extensions of human outlooks and needs rather than as aesthetic or technical modes of musical expression. Thus, while an aesthetic approach would invoke the faculty of critical judgment, Chase's cultural perspective calls upon the author's capacity for empathy. Just as the Declaration of Independence, the Constitution, and the Bill of Rights proclaim the political equality of all Americans, Chase's cultural perspective recognizes no hierarchy of importance between, for example, a symphony, a minstrel song, and a tribal chant. Chase would be the first to distinguish among the impulses that animate these genres: the wish to create an elaborate, self-contained musical structure; to produce a diverting item of popular entertainment; to manifest a belief about man's spiritual existence upon the earth. Nevertheless, it is the essence of his method to consider each on its own terms, to respect the motives behind each, to recognize each as a response to particular human circumstances, and to welcome all three, and many more, as partners in the vast and complex enterprise of making America's music.

Here, perhaps, is the ultimate key to understanding Chase's achievement in *America's Music,* revised third edition. He writes, most of all, to celebrate American musical pluralism: the coexistence of many different kinds of music in this land of "people who have come from many parts of the earth to build a new civilization." Choosing American musical traditions that seem to make distinctive cultural statements, he describes each empathetically. Thomas Carlyle once wrote of Mohammed that, while not recommending that his readers become Mohammedans, "I mean to say all the good of him I justly can. It is the way to get at his secret."[19] In much the same way, Chase seeks to enter into the motives and beliefs of each of his subjects, either making their case for them or letting them make it in their own words. In this trait can be seen the triumph of the cultural approach over the aesthetic in Chase's own mind.[20] America's music, in his view, is a counterpoint of ideas, trends, voices, and sounds, issuing from many different layers of society, each distinct and eloquent in its own right, and each free to accept or resist outside influences.

It follows naturally from Chase's perspective that he finds many kinds of relationships among the disparate strains that make up American music's pluralism. He especially relishes some of the apparently incongruous juxtapositions that have marked American musical life. He claims William Walker's *Southern Harmony* as "a true musical democracy" because it includes tunes by composers as dissimilar as Walker himself, Lowell Mason, Billings, and Handel (p. 175). He praises Gottschalk as a man who managed to endure "the vicissitudes of a traveling salesman while holding his head high as an artist" (p. 292). Of vaudeville, he recalls: "For a quarter you could also bask in the splendor of a gorgeous 'palace' " (p. 364). And a 1982 folk festival becomes, in his view, a paradigm of American ethnic diversity—its featured performer, a Jewish-American singer of Yiddish and Russian song, joined in the festival by "Israeli, Greek, Scottish and Laotian folk dance groups, an Irish accordionist, a Scottish bagpiper, a Chinese folk singer, a Polish polka band, and Greek bouzouki players" (p. 484). In *America's Music,* revised third edition, such a gathering—which took place, incidentally, in the blues-saturated city of Memphis—comes to seem a normal American happenstance.

The coexistence of so many different musics in America threatens the purity of all of them. Chase applauds the attempts of American Indian tribes to maintain indigenous songs and styles, even though their original contexts have long ago disappeared and the dominant culture threatens to engulf them (chapter 22). Yet the nation's true musical vitality, he proposes, flows from the dynamism that has constantly brought new musical contexts to the fore, blending and transforming older styles and genres to fit the new circumstances. By the 1840s, for example, religion, commerce, and musical artistry were already interacting to spawn some unusual progeny. Thomas Commuck, a Narragansett Indian, chose the proper psalmodist Thomas Hastings to harmonize some sacred tunes he had composed, publishing them as *Indian Melodies* (New York, 1845) (p. 144). In 1846 a few Shaker apostates from Canterbury, New Hampshire, were observed in a theater, presenting their community's distinctive religious rituals for pay in public: singing, dancing, and speaking in unknown tongues (p. 210). By that time it was also common practice among evangelical Protestants to add short refrains and fervent expostulations to solemn standard hymns by Watts and Wesley, turning them into rollicking revival songs that then circulated orally at religious camp meetings and in print through published tunebooks (pp. 197–98). And, after the Civil War, Negro spirituals, collected from the mouths of ex-slaves, were written down, harmonized, and made into artistic choral music for the concert stage (chapter 12). The popularity of nineteenth-century parlor songs was reflected in the number of arrangements they received. Stephen Foster's "Oh! Susanna" appeared in at least twenty different printed settings during its first three years in print. Since then, Chase notes, Foster's best-known melodies "have been 'transformed' countless times and in far-ranging contexts, from the hurdy-gurdy barrel organ to the brass band, from the fiddle to the electronic synthesizer, from classical to 'pop,' and from jazz to 'rock.' " Such "transformations," he writes, "as in the mythology of ancient Greece . . . are a symbol of immortality" (p. 264).

It is hardly surprising that interaction, change, blending, and juxtaposition dominate Chase's account of American music in the twentieth century, and that he gives special attention to musicians and genres that most directly reflect these processes. George Ives's "many-sided, pluralistic view of music" is noted, and Charles Ives's "alienation" from the professional world of music is tied to his belief in an "inclusive" aesthetic stance, contradicting the professional world's "exclusive" one (pp. 430, 440). Henry Cowell's San Francisco boyhood, spent in the company of both Chinese opera and Irish folksongs, is praised as "beneficial" in its promotion of "uninhibited exploration" in the composer's "formative years" (p. 456). Soprano Eva Gauthier's 1923 song recital, accompanied by George Gershwin, is deemed "an important event in America's musical history" for its breaking down of "cult barriers" (p. 475). B. B. King's 1970s style is identified as a "new synthesis of blues, gospel, and jazz" (p. 503). Jazz's gradual assimilation of "all the compositional forms of world music" (p. 523) is said to mark its transformation from American entertainment to a global form of musical expression. And Bob Dylan's ability to bridge the gap "between beat bohemianism and the radical counter culture" (p. 627) of the 1960s helped to make a mass movement out of what had been a somewhat esoteric sensibility. Ives, Cowell, Gershwin, King, Dylan, and others who have united musical practices and techniques that were previously separate occupy starring roles in *America's Music,* revised third edition. Chase admires purity and consistency where he finds them—as in his sympathetic treatment of the serialism of Babbitt and Wuorinen in the chapter on "Creative Systems" (chapter 32) and his praise for the "strong and fierce" singing of Aretha Franklin and her backup groups, based upon "decades of gospel technique" (p. 630). But for him the hearty hybrids that American musicians have so prodigiously created are the strongest and most distinctive products of American musical pluralism.

An author who embraces pluralism and diversity with Chase's enthusiasm invests in richness at the expense of order. If many different kinds of music—all, in principle, equal in human value and worthy of the historian's attention—have coexisted in the United States, how can they be incorporated into a single, coherent narrative? In his earliest article on historiography, drafted the year after *America's Music* first appeared, Chase recognized the problem.[21] As he was often to do again in the future, he found help among the anthropologists. Historians of music, he wrote, have generally taken a "diachronic" view of time, which considers phenomena sequentially, in the order in which events in their development have occurred. The diachronic view is ideal for tracing the history of a single idiom, Chase noted. But it is confounded by the concurrence of several. Where two or more equally important kinds of music do coexist, time is better thought of spatially, or "synchronically." A synchronic view of time allows the writer to study the events of a particular era or place together, juxtaposing accounts of many different musics, just as they live side by side in real life. American music's long history, Chase knew, needed to be studied diachronically, but its diversity demanded synchronic treatment. Only by mastering both concepts of time and interweaving them, he concluded, could he, as a historian of American music, do full justice to his subject.

The idea that, in Siegfried Kracauer's words, "works of art occupy positions in time that do not depend wholly on chronology,"[22] helped during the 1960s to show Chase that a synchronic view of time was one of the keys to the vision of music history he was developing. Not only do old works and new coexist in time, he recognized, influencing each other's reception, but unremembered composers and works from the past may also be revived and take on new life and new meanings in a different present—a fact that may remain hidden from a diachronic view of time.

In an article published in 1981, Chase cited some examples. The music of Anthony Philip Heinrich (1781–1861), largely ignored in his own day and then forgotten for a century after his death, had recently begun to be resurrected by young performers "brought up with the works of Ives, Satie, Debussy, [and] Cage." To the ears of these musicians and some of their listeners, Heinrich's music sounded not like "the work of a deluded amateur but the logical result of an approach to composition radically different from all his contemporaries"—a composer "one hundred years ahead of his time."[23] A synchronic view of time, recognizing that Heinrich's music might enjoy a vigorous afterlife in the present or future, thus convinced Chase to give "the loghouse composer of Kentucky" an entire chapter in *America's Music,* revised third edition, even though he had received only passing mention in earlier editions. William Billings (1746–1800) was another case in point. Within a few years of his death, a shift in taste had purged his music from the tunebooks of his native New England. But during the nineteenth and twentieth centuries, three groups brought it back to life, each for its own reasons: shape-note tunebook compilers and singers who continued to perform unaccompanied psalmody in the rural South well into the present century; northern advocates of the revival of "ancient" New England psalmody, beginning in the 1830s and including "Father" Robert Kemp and his "Old Folks" concert troupe; and urban and academic choral singers since the 1930s, in search of authentic American music from the past.[24] These and other examples of how musical significance can elude the temporal net sparked Chase's determination to find a structure for *America's Music,* revised third edition, in which "the manifold spaces of time" (Kracauer's phrase) could be more faithfully revealed.

As Chase notes, the format of any book gives a reader a sense of moving forward in time, so an author who wants to counteract that illusion must "break up the obvious temporal order whenever feasible."[25] In *America's Music,* revised third edition, Chase accomplishes this in several ways. First, in the ordering of his chapters he bucks diachronic sequence and from the beginning plunges his readers into historical time that is more spatial than linear. Chase explains: "After my first two chapters ['The Musical Puritans' and 'Conflict and Reform'] one would normally expect the chapter on the early New England 'tunesmiths.' . . . Instead we pass on to 'Dissenters and Minority Sects,' 'The African Presence,' 'Gentleman Amateurs,' ['European Professionals']—and *then* pick up . . . Billings and company."[26]

Second, his focus shifts from chapter to chapter, according to the subject. Chapters 18–24, for example, cover roughly the period 1865–1920. In them Chase describes, in turn, the founding and growth of an institution (Tin Pan Alley), a group of composers for the concert hall (the so-called Boston Classicists), the progress of another institution (the Broadway stage), another group of concert composers (later New Englanders), an ethnic group (American Indians), a musical genre (ragtime), and a composer (Charles Ives). While no unifying thread could survive such abrupt changes of subject, the descriptive depth of these chapters taken together creates its own sense of vivid complexity.

Finally, even within chapters, Chase plays freely with time when the situation seems to demand it. Chapter 34, for example, starts in the 1920s with early country music and carries the subject up to bluegrass in the 1940s and 1950s. Then, after speculating on just who "the folk" are in twentieth-century industrial America, Chase doubles back to the 1930s and 1940s to pick up the beginnings of urban folk music, tracing its links with social protest into the 1960s. Without transition Mahalia Jackson follows on the heels of Joan Baez, and black "soul" music is traced from the 1950s into the 1970s. Finally, a paragraph on the electric guitar leads to the beginnings in the 1950s of rock and roll, the ultimate blend of elements from all the foregoing, and a survey of some of its more diverse branches into the 1980s. Through this kind of crosscutting, Chase provides glimpses of the independent workings of four different popular forms *and* of interactions between them. Floating free of strict diachronic time, he can suggest the dense complementarity of popular music's recent past while still preserving for each genre some of the breathing room that it enjoyed in "the manifold spaces of time" in which it first flourished. Here, as in his playing with the time-space continuum at other levels, he follows his democratic, pluralistic view of America's music.

In the fall of 1958, as a student at the University of Michigan, I took my first (and only) academic course in American music. The teacher was H. Wiley Hitchcock. The textbook was *America's Music*. I remember well two things about my reactions then to Chase's book. First, its human dimension—Chase's deft vignettes of the people who had made America's music and his own presence as a guide who was continually popping up to give his opinion on this matter or that—made it far more pleasurable to read than the books for my other courses. Second, by challenging the aura of genteel respectability that, in those days and to a neophyte, seemed sometimes to pervade musicology, it hinted that perhaps musicology could stretch itself to catch more of the directness of the music-making spirit itself. I am happy to report that in *America's Music*, revised third edition, the human dimension remains intact and fresh. Moreover, with the genteel outlook fading gradually into the past, Chase now challenges his readers to recognize its virtues and to reconcile them with the obvious ones of more informal kinds of American music. A whole generation of students was once called by Gilbert Chase to the study of America's music. That his voice, tuned now to a deepened, renewed point of view, is now calling another generation to the same task is a tribute both to his own remarkable intellectual stamina and to the inexhaustible vitality of his subject.

Notes

1. Gilbert Chase, *America's Music: From the Pilgrims to the Present* (New York: McGraw-Hill, 1955), p. xxi.

2. Oscar G. Sonneck, "The History of Music in America, a Few Suggestions," in Sonneck, *Miscellaneous Studies in the History of Music* (New York: Macmillan, 1921), p. 330; reprinted from *Papers and Proceedings of the Music Teachers' National Association* (1916).

3. Frédéric Louis Ritter, *Music in America* (1883; rev. ed., New York: Scribner, 1890), was the first general history of American music, followed by W. S. B. Mathews, ed., *A Hundred Years of Music in America* (Chicago: G. L. Howe, 1889). Ritter said very little about American composers of his day; Mathews believed that "a school of national music . . . different from that of Europe" lay in America's future (p. 636). Between 1904 and 1915 three new general histories appeared. Louis C. Elson, *The History of American Music* (New York: Macmillan, 1904; rev. ed., 1915; rev. ed., 1925), gave American composers of concert music a prominent place, occupying nearly half the book. W. L. Hubbard, ed., *History of American Music* (Toledo: Irving Squire, 1908), began with a section on the Boston circle of composers by George W. Chadwick, one of its most prominent members. In Arthur Farwell and W. Dermot Darby, eds., *Music in America* (New York: National Society of Music, 1915), Farwell, himself an ardent nationalist, wrote several chapters on his fellow modern American composers, as well as an introduction that, many years later, was to inspire Chase's own work.

4. John Tasker Howard, *Our American Music: Three Hundred Years of It* (New York: Thomas Y. Crowell Co., 1931), p. vii.

5. Chase, *America's Music,* pp. xix–xx.

6. See Sonneck, "History of Music in America," p. 342. Chase has often quoted these words or the idea behind them. See, for example, "The Significance of Oscar Sonneck: A Centennial Tribute," in William Lichtenwanger, ed., *Oscar Sonneck and American Music* (Urbana: University of Illinois Press, 1983), p. 207; "American Music and American Musicology," *Journal of Musicology* 1 (1982): 59; and "The Shape of Time in America's Music," *Journal of American Culture* 4, no. 4 (1981): 95.

7. Gilbert Chase, "American Musicology and the Social Sciences," in Barry S. Brook, Edward O. D. Downes, and Sherman Van Solkema, eds., *Perspectives in Musicology* (New York: W. W. Norton and Co., 1972), p. 221.

8. Chase, *America's Music,* p. xx.

9. Seeger's agenda was published under the title "Folk Music as a Source of Social History," in Caroline F. Ware, ed., *The Cultural Approach to History* (New York: Columbia University Press, 1940). See Chase, "American Musicology and the Social Sciences," pp. 215–16.

10. Gilbert Chase, *The Music of Spain* (New York: W. W. Norton and Co., 1941), p. 17; quoted in part in Chase, "A Dialectical Approach to Music History," *Ethnomusicology* 2 (Jan. 1958): 3, an abridged version of a paper read at the annual meeting of the American Musicological Society, Urbana, Ill., Dec. 30, 1956.

11. Chase, "American Musicology and the Social Sciences," p. 221.

12. Chase, "American Music and American Musicology," p. 59.

13. Arthur Farwell, introduction to *Music in America,* p. vii. Although the book was published in 1915, Farwell's introduction was dated August 1914.

14. Chase, "American Music and American Musicology," p. 59.

15. In the first edition of *America's Music,* Chase reviewed Howard's book in a paragraph, noting Howard's approval of Ethelbert Nevin's "The Rosary" as "an almost perfect work of art" and Carleton Sprague Smith's comment that Howard's approach to music history was "highly respectable." He then burst out: "My own approach to America's music is not at all respectable—my bête noire is the genteel tradition, and I take my stand with that Connecticut Yankee, Charles Ives, whose most damning adjective is said to be 'nice' " (p. xvii).

16. Several major histories of American music have followed Chase. Wilfrid Mellers, *Music in a New Found Land: Themes and Developments in the History of American Music* (New York: Alfred A. Knopf, 1966), declares Chase's book to be "admirable" (p. xiii) and, following his example, emphasizes jazz and the most distinctively American twentieth-century music. H. Wiley Hitchcock, *Music in the United States: A Historical Introduction* (Englewood Cliffs, N.J.: Prentice-Hall, 1969; 2d ed., 1974), counts Chase and his book among his deepest influences (p. [x]). Charles Hamm, *Music in the New World* (New York: W. W. Norton and Co., 1983), acknowledges *America's Music* for setting "new standards of scope, scholarship and writing style against which every subsequent history of American music has had to be measured." And he adds: "Every student and scholar of the subject is indebted to this landmark book, in countless ways" (p. ix).

17. Chase, "The Shape of Time," p. 104.

18. Clifford Geertz, *The Interpretation of Cultures* (New York: Basic Books, 1973), p. 5.

19. Thomas Carlyle, *On Heroes, Hero-Worship and the Heroic in History* (Lincoln: University of Nebraska Press, [1966]), p. 43; reprinted from *The Works of Thomas Carlyle,* vol. 5 (London: Chapman and Hall, 1904).

20. See n. 15 above for Chase's condemnation of the genteel tradition as his bête noire. Certainly, he made no effort to disguise his distaste for nineteenth-century sentimentality in the first and second editions of *America's Music. America's Music,* revised third edition, however, has no bête noire. While it is clear enough, for example, that Chase's emotional sympathies lie more with shape-note singers than with Thomas Hastings, the man who dubbed their musical notation "buckwheat notes," he keeps his opinions under wraps to the point where even the earnest Dr. Hastings's ideas receive an unprejudiced hearing. In *America's Music,* revised third edition, Chase can quote Charles Ives's antiprofessional diatribes without joining in on the attacks himself. To borrow a phrase he uses more than once, he has set aside the "either/or" dichotomy in favor of "both/and."

21. See Chase, "Dialectical Approach."

22. Vincent Duckles, "Musicology at the Mirror: A Prospectus for the History of Musical Scholarship," in Brook et al., eds., *Perspectives in Musicology,* p. 37.

23. Chase, "The Shape of Time," p. 97.

24. Ibid., pp. 97ff.

25. Ibid., p. 102.

26. Ibid., pp. 102–3.

Acknowledgments

I became involved with *America's Music* a long time ago (1955, 1966), and from the beginning my aim has been to present "the music made or continuously used by the people of the United States, people who have come from many parts of the earth to build a new civilization and to create a new society in a new world, guided by ideals of human dignity, freedom, and justice."

As I neared my eightieth year, I decided to publish my last revision of *America's Music* with the University of Illinois Press. Most important for me was the opportunity to work with Judith McCulloh, whose excellence as editor and scholar I had long admired. What she has done for me during these years will be remembered for the rest of my life.

My wife, Kathleen, has been a delight to work with in every way. Her invaluable assistance and the importance of her contribution to *America's Music* cannot be overstated.

Richard Crawford has provided an excellent foreword to *America's Music,* third revised edition—the best that I have ever had. I am delighted with his presentation of the contexts and aims of my earlier work. No one has summarized them better.

William Brooks's discographical essay, "American Music on Record," is an extremely valuable addition to this study. He writes that *"America's Music* is devoted in part to elucidating the ways in which the *interactions* between different genres and traditions have generated the American musical experience" and succinctly reviews the current state of recordings within the categories of concert ("art") music, folk music, commercial music (blues, pop, rock, country, etc.), and jazz. I am grateful for his excellent presentation.

Finally, we have the highly important work of Aaron Appelstein, who, as assistant editor, copyedited the manuscript with great diligence and distinction.

PART ONE

From Colony to Republic

Chapter 1

The Musical Puritans

We refreshed ourselves with singing of psalms . . . there being
many of our congregation very expert in music.
—Edward Winslow, on the departure of the Pilgrims from Leyden,
in *Hypocrisie Unmasked* (London, 1646)

The Puritans who settled in New England have been held up to posterity
as haters of music, so that the dawn of America's musical heritage was long
darkened by this sinister shadow. The music historian Frédéric L. Ritter,
writing in 1883, combined ignorance with prejudice when he wrote, "The
Puritans, who landed at Plymouth Rock, brought with them their psalm-
tunes and their hatred of secular music."[1] He was right on the first count,
wrong on the second.

It is true that the so-called Pilgrims—actually a separatist Puritan
sect—were psalm singers both by ordinance and predilection, as were
many other dissenting Protestant sects, both in Great Britain and on the
Continent. The only sort of "secular music" that they "hated"—more correctly, "deplored"—was that which they had good reason to believe was in-
imical to morality.

But this was by no means a uniquely Puritanical attitude. During the
reign of Queen Elizabeth, an Anglican psalter titled *Psalmes of David in English Metre* appeared in England with the admonition, "Very mete to be
used of all sorts of people privat[e]ly for their godly solace and comfort, laying aparte all ungodly songes & ballades, which tende only to the nor-
ishing of vice, and corrupting of youth."[2] That was precisely the Puritan attitude toward vocal music.

It is also true that the early Puritans objected to the use of musical instruments in churches, as well as to an elaborate vocal liturgy, because they
associated these with the "Romish" ritual that they strongly repudiated.
But music per se, sacred or secular, they did not condemn or renounce.

While insisting on the importance of skill in singing, Cotton Mather,

in his *Directions for a Candidate of the Ministry,* took what may be fairly regarded as a permissive view of playing an instrument for personal recreation:

> For MUSIC, I know not what well to say.—Do as you please. If you *Fancy* it,
> I don't *Forbid* it. Only do not for the sake of it, Alienate your Time too much,
> from those that are more Important Matters. It may be so, that you may serve
> your GOD the better, for the Refreshment of *One that can play well on an In-*
> *strument.* However, to accomplish yourself at *Regular Singing,* is a thing that
> will be of *Daily Use* to you. For I would not have a Day pass without *Singing,*
> but so as at the same time to *make a Melody in your Heart unto the Lord;* . . .[3]

As we shall see later, the Puritan clergy took the lead in improving the
quality of congregational singing in New England. The Puritan attitude
toward music was *not* antagonistic or intolerant, but it *was* moralistic in
principle. Obviously, to sing bawdy songs was regarded as wrong, and
the use of music as an incentive to wanton or lascivious dancing was
strongly condemned.

The moralistic attitude toward music was by no means peculiar to the
Puritans. This view was expressed, for example, by the famous London music publisher John Playford (1623–86), who issued many widely used and
often reprinted collections of sacred and secular music that became well
known in America. He wrote in his *An Introduction to the Skill of Musick*
that "the first and chief Use of *Musick* is for the Service and Praise of God,
whose Gift it is. The second Use is for the Solace of Men [i.e., mankind],
which as it is agreeable unto Nature, so it is allowed by God, as a temporal
Blessing to recreate and cheer Men after long study and weary labour in
their Vocations."[4]

After lamenting that "our late and Solemn Musick, both Vocal and Instrumental, is now justled out of Esteem by the New Corants and Jiggs of
Foreigners" (a theme upon which every age has made its variations),
Playford quotes from Owen Feltham's *Resolves:* "I believe it [music] is an
helper both to Good and Evil, and will therefore honour it when it *moves*
to *Virtue,* and shall beware of it when it would *flatter* into *Vice.*"[5] No better
statement of the Puritan attitude toward music could be found; yet it was
stated by a writer who was not a Puritan.

Music was loved and skillfully practiced by that band of Separatists
whom we call Pilgrims. The founder of the Separatist sect was a certain
Robert Browne, known to be very fond of music and reputed to be an accomplished lutenist. One of the Pilgrim Fathers, Edward Winslow, has left

us an account of the Pilgrims' departure from Holland, when they took leave of their exiled brethren: "They that stayed at Leyden feasted us that were to go at our pastor's house, [it] being large; where we refreshed ourselves, after tears, with singing of Psalms, making joyful melody in our hearts as well as with the voice, there being many of our congregation very expert in music; and indeed it was the sweetest melody that ever mine ears heard."[6]

Among the 400 volumes in the personal library of William Brewster, one of the original Pilgrim Fathers, was a celebrated musical work by one of the most notable composers of the Elizabethan period, Richard Allison (or Alison). The title is worth quoting in full: *The Psalmes of David in Meter, the plaine Song beeing the common tunne to be sung and plaide upon the Lute, Orpharyon, Citterne, or Base Violl, severally or altogether, the singing part to be either Tenor or Treble to the Instrument, according to the nature of the voyce, or for fowre voyces: With tenne short Tunnes in the end, to which for the most part all the Psalmes may be usually sung, for the use of such as are of mean skill, and whose leysure least serveth to practize* (London, 1599). The elaborate title page is an informative commentary on musical practice of the period, and it indicates that Allison's book may have been used for a wide variety of musical purposes, ranging from concerted vocal and instrumental performance to the simplest psalmody. Although the Plymouth settlers were certainly among those "whose leysure least serveth to practize," we know from Winslow's testimony that not all were "such as are of mean skill." Whatever use Brewster and his fellow colonists may have made of Allison's volume, the work forms a direct link with the vocal and instrumental music of Elizabethan England.

It was Oscar Sonneck who first expressed skepticism about the "mysterious motives prompting Providence to send to our shores out of all the millions who inhabited Europe just those few thousand beings who had no music in their souls."[7] Recent research and a more objective view have fully justified his skepticism. At this point it would be well to ask ourselves, What sort of people were the early New England colonists? The first and most important answer is that they were of many sorts.

We tend to think of the Plymouth settlers as a homogeneous group of strict Calvinists, believers in the harsh doctrine of predestination—as some indeed were. But let us look at the colonists who sailed from Plymouth, England, on the *Mayflower,* on July 22, 1620. The Separatists who had taken refuge in Holland did not like the idea of remaining there permanently, yet they could not prudently return to England. America was the obvious alternative, but establishing a colony was basically a capitalistic enterprise. In this instance, a group of London merchants provided the initial capital and thus had a say in the conduct of the venture. They chose, for example, the colonists who were to join the small band of Pilgrims from Leyden. The *Mayflower,* in addition to its crew of 48, carried 101 passengers. "Of the latter, fifty-six were adults, fourteen were servants and hired artisans (not Separatists), and thirty-one were children, of whom at least seven belonged neither to the passengers nor to any English Separatists, but were probably waifs and idlers."[8] Most of the passengers had lower-middle-class backgrounds. They were a cross section of average humanity.

After the first settlers of Plymouth had proved their ability to survive, colonists began to arrive from all parts of England. The majority were not religiously motivated. They sought an opportunity to prosper in a new land, in spite of its dangers and hardships. Soon Plymouth Colony had sixteen towns or villages (other than Plymouth), the whole maintained by a basically agricultural economy that required hard and constant labor. More than one historian has commented on its lack of intellectual and artistic culture, attributing this to the alleged narrowness and religious prejudice of the Calvinists. A more liberal view is that "Plymouth was, until its merger with Massachusetts in 1692, a backwater, its people quiet and basically conservative, seldom rising above the ordinary round of daily work."[9] As we shall see, there were exceptions to this general pattern.

Music figured prominently in the religious observances of the early Plymouth Colony settlers, and the Ainsworth Psalter provided a primary source for the singing of psalms among them. Officially titled *The Book of Psalmes: Englished Both in Prose and Metre,* it went through six editions, the last in 1690. Its compiler was the English scholar and linguist Henry Ainsworth, who first published it in Amsterdam in 1612, for the benefit of the exiled Separatists who had taken refuge in Holland. The title page has a quotation from the Bible (*Ephesians* 5): "Be ye filled with the Spirit: speaking to your selves in Psalms, and hymns, and spiritual Songs: singing & making melodie in your hart to the Lord."

The melodies, for one voice only, were printed in the customary diamond-shaped notes of the period and without bar lines. There are thirty-nine different tunes, concerning which Ainsworth writes: "Tunes for the Psalmes, I find none set of God: so that e[a]ch people is to use the most grave, decent, and comfortable manner of singing that they know. . . . The singing notes therefore I have most taken frō our former Englished psalms, when they wil fit the mesure of the verse: and for the other long verses I have also taken (for the most part) the gravest and easiest tunes of the French and Dutch psalmes."

Obviously, a particular tune could be used for several different psalms, and Ainsworth included varied metrical versions of all the 150 psalms from the Old Testament; indeed, "one of the most striking things about Ainsworth's psalter is the variety and number of poetic meters into which he translated the psalms: no fewer than sixteen different metrical schemes are employed. . . ."[10] These range from the four-line stanza of Common Meter to the twelve-line stanza of Long Particular Double Meter! The most frequently used, by far, is Common Meter Doubled, which occurs forty-three times. Although Long Meter rates only ten tunes, it is of special interest because of the association with Psalm 100, which was to become widely popular in New England. The pattern is that of a four-line stanza with eight syllables per line, as follows:

> Showt to Jehovah, al the earth.
> Serv ye Jehovah with gladnes;
> before him come with singing-merth.
> Know, that Jehovah he God is.

And as it appears with the music in the Ainsworth Psalter:

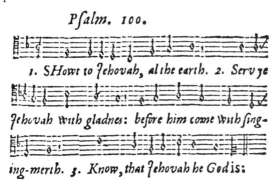

The source of the tune has been identified as the Anglo-Genevan Psalter of 1561, and it also appeared in the French Psalter of 1562. One of the best known of all hymn tunes, it continued to appear with various texts in modern hymnals for Protestant churches; but it is most generally associated with Thomas Ken's Doxology for Morning and Evening Hymns (version of 1709), as "Praise God, from Whom All Blessings Flow."[11]

The early New England settlers really believed in coming before Him "with singing-merth." Quoting Saint James the Apostle, they proclaimed,

"If any be merry, let him sing psalms." Shakespeare, in *The Winter's Tale,* has a character say, "But one Puritan amongst them, and he sings psalms to hornpipes." (The hornpipe was a lively sailors' dance.)

The Puritan John Cotton, in his *Singing of Psalmes a Gospel-Ordinance,* reacted strongly to the enemies of Puritanism, as in this combination of ridicule and scorn: "And they be Cathedrall Priests of an Antichristian spirit, that have scoffed at Puritan-Ministers, as calling the People to sing one of *Hopkins* Jiggs, and so hop into the Pulpit."[12]

The Plymouth colonists continued to use the Ainsworth Psalter until 1692, when the Old Colony merged with the larger and more powerful Massachusetts Bay Colony, of which Boston was the principal city.

We can assume, on the basis of Winslow's testimony and the musical character of the Ainsworth Psalter, that there was, at least within the first generation of the Separatist group, a nucleus sufficiently adept in music to be able to read notes, to cope with lengthy melodies and varied meters, and to sing correctly as a group.

However, to argue that the early New England settlers were of average musicality is not to claim expertise for the majority. In a community that might include indentured servants, artisans, tradesmen, merchants, farmers, soldiers, mariners (one wonders what they did with the "waifs and idlers"!), as well as educated clergymen and some ladies and gentlemen of cultivated taste, it would be unrealistic to prescribe or expect a uniform and stable standard of congregational singing.

We should also bear in mind that the basic organization of the Calvinistic-Puritanical churches was *congregational,* which meant that each church was independent and autonomous. Church membership depended on complex points of theology, but once admitted, members were expected to act as a group and to participate as a body in the established modes of worship. These included—not as a matter of choice but (in the words of John Cotton) as a "Gospel-Ordinance"—the singing of all the Psalms of David in a prescribed order throughout the year.

Changing patterns of colonial society in New England precluded a continuation of the musical expertise vaunted by Winslow. The increasing heterogeneity of the population and its dispersion in semirural communities throughout the colony were important factors in eroding uniform standards of psalm singing.

Indicative of the trend was the abandonment of the Ainsworth Psalter, with its often difficult tunes and complex meters. Salem, for example, which had close relations with Plymouth, had adopted Ainsworth for a time. But in May 1667 the congregation voted to discontinue its use, alleging "the difficulty of the tunes, and that we could not sing them so well as formerly." In 1685 Plymouth itself began to retrench. On May 17 of that year, "the Elders stayed the chh after the publick worship was ended & moved to sing Psal: 130: in another Translation, because in Mr Ainsworths Translation which wee sang, the tune was soe difficult few could follow it, the chh readily consented thereunto."[13] Finally, in August 1692, after objection had been made that "many of the Psalmes in Mr Ainsworths Translation which wee now sung had such difficult tunes as none in the church could sett," the Plymouth congregation accepted the proposal that "when the Tunes were difficult in our Translation, wee should sing the Psalmes now in use in the neighbour-churches in the Bay."[14] The process was simply one of democratization.

The Massachusetts Bay colonists very soon became dissatisfied with the Sternhold and Hopkins Psalter because they considered the translations not sufficiently faithful to the original. Consequently, a group of New England divines prepared a new version, which was printed in Cambridge, Massachusetts, in 1640, as *The Whole Booke of Psalmes Faithfully Translated into English Metre*. Commonly known as the Bay Psalm Book, it was the first book printed in the English colonies of North America and held sway for several generations (the twenty-sixth edition appeared at Boston in 1744).

No music was included in early editions of the Bay Psalm Book, but an "Admonition to the Reader" contained instructions regarding the tunes to which psalms in various meters might be sung: "The verses of these psalmes may be reduced to six kindes, the first whereof may be sung in very neere forty common tunes; as they are collected out of our chief musicians by Thomas Ravenscroft." This shows that the Puritans were acquainted with the best musical publications of their time. Ravenscroft's *The Whole Booke of Psalmes, with the Hymnes Evangelicall, and Songs Spirituall* (London, 1621) contains four-part settings by such prominent composers as Thomas Morley, Thomas Tallis, Giles Farnaby, John Dowland, John Farmer, Michael Cavendish, Richard Allison, and Ravenscroft himself.

But matters of artistic appreciation are one thing, practical realities are another. The Puritan elite might admire the four-part settings by these composers, yet the basic question remained: what could the *people* sing in church? From what has been said in this chapter, one answer can be deduced: the people could, and would, sing mostly psalm tunes with four-line stanzas—the easiest ones to learn and remember.¹⁵ These included the popular jog-trot ballad stanza alternating lines of eight and six syllables:

> The Lord to mee a shepheard is,
> want therefore shall not I.
> He in the folds of tender grasse,
> doth cause me downe to lie.

Yet the improvement of psalmody, in one way or another, was much in the minds of the Congregational clergy. While the versions in the Bay Psalm Book may have been "faithful" to King David, they were far from polished and not particularly apt for singing. Hence it was decided (in the words of Cotton Mather) "that a little more of Art was to be employ'd upon them." As a result, the third edition appeared in 1651, and with a new title: *The Psalms, Hymns and Spiritual Songs of the Old and New Testament Faithfully Translated into English Metre for the Use, Edification, and Comfort of the Saints in Publick and Private, Especially in New England.* In this definitive form the work came to be known as the New England Psalm Book. But it still lacked music. As far as is known, the first edition to contain a selection of tunes was the ninth, printed in 1698. Thirteen tunes in two parts were included in a section at the end, with instructions for singing. The tunes are those known as "Oxford," "Litchfield," "Low-Dutch," "York," "Windsor," "Cambridge," "St. David's," "Martyrs," "Hackney," and tunes identified with Psalms 100, 115, 119, and 148.

The tunes were taken from Playford's *Introduction to the Skill of Musick,* mainly the eleventh edition of 1687. (One wonders why they bypassed his *Whole Book of Psalms, with the Usual Spiritual Songs,* 1673; twenty editions to 1757.) The instructions for singing came from the same source, but apparently from earlier editions. It is interesting that the letters *FSLM,* standing for the "fasola" notation, are placed directly under the notes of the psalm tunes, a device also used by Playford in the sixth edition of his work (1672). As we shall see, the fasola notation was to have a long and fruitful tradition in America's music.

In summary, the replacement of the Sternhold and Hopkins Psalter by the Bay Psalm Book had the effect of reducing the number of tunes and meters in general use in New England—a trend also emphasized by the disuse of the Ainsworth Psalter. But this was due to sociocultural factors rather than to any musical prejudice on the part of the Puritans.

THE

VVHOLE

BOOKE OF PSALMES
Faithfully
TRANSLATED *into* ENGLISH
Metre.

Whereunto is prefixed a difcourfe declaring not only the lawfullnes, but alfo
the neceffity of the heavenly Ordinance
of finging Scripture Pfalmes in
the Churches of
God.

Coll. III.
Let the word of God dwell plenteoufly in
you, in all wifdome, teaching and exhort-
ing one another in Pfalmes, Himnes, and
fpirituall Songs, finging to the Lord with
grace in your hearts.

Iames V.
If any be afflicted, let him pray, and if
any be merry let him fing pfalmes.

Imprinted
1640

Bay Psalm Book (1640), title page.

Recent research by Barbara Lambert, covering the first hundred years of the Massachusetts Bay Colony (1630–1731) and concentrating on the Boston area, indicates that the use of musical instruments was much more widespread than has been supposed. Data drawn from household inventories of deceased residents of Suffolk County, which then included Boston and several surrounding towns, reveals that colonists, both Anglicans and Congregationalists, from all walks of life owned musical instruments. The variety of occupations represented is surprising: "three doctors, one brickburner, one carpenter, seven merchants, one farmer, five mariners, one tailor, one printer, one shipwright, one housewright, one ironmonger and cooper, two taverners, one baker, one Governor, and two clergymen." Lambert rightly remarks: "The old idea that a taste and talent for making music could not have existed in the colonies except among a small and exclusive group attached to the Old World, should begin to fade in the light of new evidence."[16]

The favorite keyboard instrument of that time was the virginals (they came in pairs, hence the plural designation). Thirteen virginals are listed in the inventories. Another preferred instrument, recorded in equal quantity, was the cittern, a plucked string instrument shaped like a lute but with a flat back like that of the guitar and strung with wire rather than with gut strings. The lute, a costly and delicate instrument requiring frequent tuning and much care, does not appear in the inventories. One authority (Thomas Mace) recommended that the lute "should be kept between blankets in a well-aired bed"—adding, however, that it was a good idea "not to tumble back on top of it." On the other hand, "the cittern kept excellently in tune for weeks on end and when not in use could be hung on the wall." What's more, "it was small, robustly made and cheap, and its wire strings rarely broke."[17] It could be played either with a plectrum or with the fingers and was good for strumming. No wonder it was so popular! The guitar, with gut strings, was still a novelty among English-speaking people, and only four are listed in the inventories.

The principal bowed string instruments were the viol and the violin. Two treble viols, four bass viols, and one of unspecified size are cited. The bass viol was a versatile instrument that could be used for a variety of purposes. Nine violins are listed in the Boston inventories, including "two Trible Violins" owned by Governor Burnet and "a Violin with Case" owned by the taverner William Bryant.

The difference between owning a violin and a fiddle is illustrated by one Samuel Kendall (d. 1711), whose inventory lists "one fiddle." In 1705 Kendall was summoned before the Select Men, charged with having lately kept "bad orders in his House: they [the Select Men] are of Opinion that he is not a Suitable person to be admitted to keep a Tavern in this Town." A violin kept "In ye Parlor" of a respectable home was a sign of gentility, but a fiddle kept in a disorderly house was the Devil's instrument. Finally, wind instruments were in the minority. Five fifes and about the same number of flutes are listed, together with three trumpets, one double "Courtell" (an early type of bassoon), and a "mock trumpet" (early soprano clarinet).

By the second decade of the eighteenth century, we find advertisements for teaching to play musical instruments. In April 1716 an advertisement in the *Boston Weekly News-Letter* announced the arrival from London of "a choice collection of Musickal Instruments, consisting of Flageolets, Flutes, Haut-Boys, Bass-Viols, Violins, Bows, Strings, Reeds for Haut-Boys, Books of instruction for all these instruments, Books of Ruled Paper." These were to be sold "at the Dancing School of Mr. Enstone in Sudbury Street near the Orange Tree, Boston." Moreover, "any person may have all Instruments of Musick mended, or Virginalls and Spinnets Strung and Tuned at a reasonable Rate, and likewise may be taught to Play on any of these instruments above mention'd; dancing taught by a true and easier method than has been heretofore." In 1713 a Mr. George Brownell, at his house in Wing's Lane, taught "Dancing, Treble Violin, Flute, Spinnet, &c."[18]

No less an authority than the Reverend Increase Mather informs us that about this time Boston was swept by what he calls "the Dancing Humour." The important question, he explains,

> is not, Whether People of Quality may not Employ a Dancing-Master, with due Circumstances of Modesty to instruct their Children how to carry themselves handsomely, in company? But, whether the Dancing Humour, as it now prevails, and especially in *Balls,* or in circumstances that Lead the Young People of both Seces, unto great Liberties with one another, be not a *Vanity* forbidden by the Rules of Christianity? And, if it be so, Whether Vertuous and Prudent Parents, will not upon Second Thoughts be very cautious, how far they expose their Children to the Temptations of such a *Vanity?*[19]

But it was not only a Puritan minister who had misgivings about exposing children to such a "Vanity." A more mundane view, involving such matters as needless expenses and distraction from domestic duties, was expressed by a Boston tradesman who opposed his wife's wish to send their adolescent daughter to dancing school:

> I tell thee Wife; once more, I'll have her bred
> To Book'ry, Cook'ry, Thimble, Needle, Thread,
> First teach her these, and then the pritty Fool,
> Shall jigg her Crupper at the dancing School.[20]

Meanwhile, public performance of instrumental music was gaining ground in Boston, and the first concert known to have been advertised in a colonial newspaper was announced in the *Boston Gazette* of February 2, 1729, as "a Concert of Music Performed on sundry Instruments, at the Dancing School in King-Street."

We know that music acquired considerable importance at Harvard College (founded in 1636). In 1720 Thomas Symmes published an essay on "Singing by Note," or the skill of reading musical notation. He stated that the theory of music was "studied, known and approv'd of in our *College,* for many Years after its first Founding." "This is evident," he added, "from the Musical *Theses,* which were formerly Printed, and from some Writings containing some *Tunes,* with Directions for *Singing by Note,* as they are now Sung; and these [tunes] are yet in Being, tho' of more than *Sixty Years* standing; besides no Man that Studied *Music,* as it is treated of by *Alsted, Playford* and others, could be ignorant of it."[21]

Symmes also drew on personal recollection to confirm that instruction in "Singing by Note" was obtainable at Harvard: "My Father [class of 1657] learnt it at College; and I can Sing a Tune he learnt me by Note, when I was a Child, and I have now in my study, Tunes prick'd with his own Hand, and I can't be more sure of any thing of that nature, than of this, that he highly approved of it, & greatly delighted in it."[22]

When Symmes mentions Playford we can assume that he refers to his *An Introduction to the Skill of Musick,* a do-it-yourself instruction book addressed to "all Lovers and Practitioners of Musick." First published in London in 1654, it went through many editions (the nineteenth appeared in 1730) and was well known in America. The thirteenth edition included such popular tunes as "The King's Delight," "John Come Kiss Me," and "The Lark." With this and other collections, plenty of "household" music, both vocal and instrumental, was available to the colonists.

There is ample evidence that secular songs and ballads circulated widely in New England, both in the oral tradition and in printed form. Often both traditions were combined, as in the highly popular "broadside ballads" printed on single sheets and often hawked by peddlers in the streets. It was generally indicated that the words were to be sung to some familiar tune, perhaps a traditional melody or a current "pop" tune from a successful ballad opera or the like.

We have direct evidence that some of these broadside ballads were known to students of divinity at Harvard College. John Cotton, for example, had a son born on the voyage to America (aptly named Seaborn Cotton) who in due course went to Harvard. While there, he found time to copy out in his commonplace book the words of several broadside ballads such as "The Lovesick Maid; or, Cordelia's Lamentation for the Absence of Her Gerhard" and "The Last Lamentation of the Languishing Squire; or, Love Overcomes All Things."

Benjamin Franklin, in a letter to his brother Peter, refers to "some country girl in the heart of Massachusetts, who has never heard any other than psalm tunes or *Chevy Chace,* the *Children in the Wood,* the *Spanish Lady,* and such old simple ditties"—mentioning in a single breath three of the most famous English ballads! Judging by their durability, we can hardly say that a country girl in New England was culturally underprivileged in her choice of ballads.[23]

On the other hand, Cotton Mather, in his diary of September 27, 1713, viewed with alarm the popularity of broadside ballads and songs: "I am informed that the Minds and Manners of many People about the Countrey are much corrupted, by foolish Songs and Ballads which by the Hawkers and Pedlars carry into all parts of the Countrey. By way of Antidote, I would procure poetical Composures full of Piety, and such as may have a Tendency to advance Truth and Goodness, to be published, and scattered into all Corners of the Land."[24]

Symmes was perhaps more realistic when he proposed as an antidote the satisfaction of learning to sing proper songs and psalms in "singing societies" and improvised "singing schools." We shall see how this worked out in the course of the next chapter.

We turn now to the use of musical instruments in the churches of New England. The Eminent Thomas Brattle, treasurer of Harvard College, had a small English chamber organ, which at his death in 1713 he bequeathed to the Brattle Square Church in Boston, of which he was one of the founders. He specified that within a year of his decease the church must "procure a sober person that can play skillfully thereon with a loud noise." But the church was evidently more Puritanical than its founder, for his executors were informed that "they did not think it proper" to use the organ "in the public worship of God."[25] Thereupon it was offered to, and accepted by, the King's Chapel, which was the Church of England.

Still to come were the first organs built especially for church use, and we are told that "the first organ actually designed for church use" was installed at Trinity Church in Newport, Rhode Island, in 1733. By 1744 the Anglican Trinity Church of Boston had "the first two-manual organ in Boston—possibly the first organ in the city actually built expressly as a church instrument" with thirteen stops.[26]

For practical reasons, including the cost of an organ and the difficulty of finding a resident organist, a number of country churches toward the end of the century began to use various portable instruments to accompany congregational singing. Foremost among these was the so-called church bass, with three to five strings, colloquially known as "God's fiddle" to distinguish it from the "Devil's fiddle" (i.e., the violin).

According to Barbara Owen: "The first church basses were imported, but soon many were being produced in Boston. By the turn of the century New Hampshire had become a center for making these instruments. The "bass fiddle" was a convenient instrument for many small churches: portable, relatively unobtrusive, and easily learned by any amateur with a musical bent. Many churches later added other instruments—German flute, clarinet, violin, bassoon, cornet, ophicleide, trombone; whatever was available—and the church band was born."[27]

During the eighteenth century, taverns became increasingly numerous in colonial America, and each could have had for its sign a fiddle and a flowing bowl. In 1746 a certain Captain Francis Goelet of New York went to Boston on business and was invited to a turtle dinner for forty gentlemen, with singing and many toasts. The company, he wrote in his diary, was "Exceeding Merry untill 3 a Clock in the morning, from whence Went upon the Rake, Going past the Commons in our way Home, Surprised a Compy [company of] Country Young Men and Women with a Violin, at a Tavern Dancing and making Merry. Upon our Ent'g the House the Young Women Fled, We took Possession of the Room hav'g the Fidler and the Young Man with us with the Keg of Sugar'd Dram, we were very merry. . . ."[28]

It is very unlikely that these merrymakers were Puritans, but that the latter were not above frivolity is attested by an entry in Cotton Mather's diary of 1711 that complained about "a Number of young People, of both Sexes, belonging, many of them, to my Flock, who have had on Christmas-night, this last Week, a Frolick, a revelling Feast, and Ball. . . ."[29]

By the end of the seventeenth century the power and influence of the

Puritan ministry had been greatly diminished. Cotton Mather, for example, declared "the peculiar Spirit, and Error of the Time, to be *Indifferency in Religion*" and bemoaned that "the two comprehensive points of our corruption, are an Ambition of saecular *Grandeur,* and an Affection for sensual *Pleasures.*"[30]

Finally, by the mid-eighteenth century, Boston was no longer a Puritan city in the usual sense of that term. It had become a thriving seaport, a center of commerce and culture that comprised a very mixed population. Balladry and bawdiness, fiddling and frolic, dancing and drinking were "sensual *Pleasures*" that went along with the "saecular *Grandeur*" of official pomp, handsome houses, costly carriages, fine clothes, and the possession of musical instruments (especially the high-class harpsichord and the fashionable viol). Eventually, many Bostonians would come to understand that the Art of Music was most apt for combining sensual Pleasure with formal Grandeur.

Notes

1. Frédéric Louis Ritter, *Music in America,* p. 6. (Complete citations for abbreviated references in the footnotes may be found in the Bibliography.)
2. *Psalmes of David in English Metre, by Thomas Sternhold and Others,* [comp. John Day?] (London, 1560).
3. Cotton Mather, *Manuductio ad Ministerium* (Boston, 1726), p. 57.
4. John Playford, *An Introduction to the Skill of Musick* (London, 1655), as quoted in the twelfth edition of 1694, p. 39.
5. Ibid., p. 45.
6. Edward Winslow, *Hypocrisie Unmasked* (London, 1646); quoted in Waldo Selden Pratt, *The Music of the Pilgrims,* p. 6.
7. Oscar G. Sonneck, *Early Concert-Life in America,* p. 7.
8. Sydney E. Ahlstrom, *A Religious History of the American People,* pp. 137–38.
9. Darrett B. Rutman, *Husbandmen of Plymouth,* p. 63.
10. Lorraine Inserra and H. Wiley Hitchcock, *The Music of Henry Ainsworth's Psalter,* p. 19.
11. In *A Manual of Prayers for the Use of the Scholars of Winchester College, and All Other Devout Christians* . . . (London, 1709).
12. John Cotton, *Singing of Psalmes a Gospel-Ordinance* (London, 1647), p. 61.
13. *Publications of the Colonial Society of Massachusetts: Collections,* vol. 22, *Plymouth Church Records, 1620–1859,* pt. 1, p. 160.
14. Ibid., pp. 277–78.
15. Irving Lowens, "The Bay Psalm Book in 17th-Century New England," in Lowens, *Music and Musicians in Early America,* pp. 30–33.
16. Barbara Lambert, "The Musical Puritans," p. 69.

17. Quotations from Thurston Dart, "The Cittern and Its English Music," pp. 46–63.

18. Lambert, "The Musical Puritans," p. 74.

19. Increase Mather, "A Cloud of Witnesses; Darting Out Light upon a CASE, too Unseasonably made Seasonable to be Discoursed on" (Boston, n.d.), p. 1.

20. Quoted in Carl Bridenbaugh, *Cities in Revolt*, p. 149.

21. Thomas Symmes, *The Reasonableness of Regular Singing; or, Singing by Note* (Boston, 1720), p. 6.

22. Ibid., p. 38.

23. For a history of these ballads and their tunes, see Claude M. Simpson, *The British Broadside Ballad and Its Music*, pp. 232, 250, 391.

24. *Diary of Cotton Mather* 2:242.

25. Barbara Owen, *The Organ in New England*, p. 3.

26. Ibid., pp. 6, 9.

27. Ibid., p. 5.

28. Bridenbaugh, *Cities in Revolt*, pp. 165–66.

29. *Diary of Cotton Mather* 2:146.

30. Ibid., pp. 16, 451.

Chapter 2
Conflict and Reform

Be sure, 'Tis not a meer Noise in the *Throat,* that will be
a *Singing* acceptable unto GOD.
—Cotton Mather, *The Accomplished Singer* (Boston, 1721)

It is important to understand the conditions under which psalm singing developed in early New England and to comprehend, in particular, the diver-
gent and conflicting cultural pressures that led to a confrontation between
the zealous reformers who advocated what they called "Regular Singing"
and the people who preferred their own "Common Way" of singing. The
reformers, most of whom were clergymen educated at Harvard, held that
the "usual way of singing" practiced by the populace was an abomination
to the Lord and an offense to persons of cultivated tastes. But the people
clung tenaciously to their own way, handed down through generations by
oral tradition. They obviously cherished what the reformers condemned;
hence, they were "very loath to part with it."

Each side was strongly convinced of the superior merit of its kind of
singing. There is no evidence, however, that those who adhered to the
Common Way endeavored to impose their convictions on others. They
simply wished to be left alone, to sing as they pleased. The reformers, on
the other hand, maintained that Regular Singing was "the Only True Way
of Singing the Songs of the Lord." But they were not simply advocating a
musical reform; they also asserted that their "Only True Way" was indeed
God's Truth, ordained by Divine Rule.

The Reverend Nathaniel Chauncey, one of the most vociferous reformers, argued strongly for this dogmatic premise in his pamphlet *Regular Singing Defended.*[1] Since Man is incapable of discerning how to worship
God in a becoming manner, it is truly a great favor that God gives to Man
the needful directions. Hence, instead of following the "Traditions of
Men," mankind should heed "the Mind and Will of GOD." Indeed, to reject Divine Truth "is a great Sin," as we are told by Jeremiah (8:9): "Lo,

they have rejected the Word of the Lord." Wherefore there is "an Obligation lying on Man" to observe and follow the directions of the Lord in all
matters of worship, including the singing of psalms and spiritual songs.[2]

Chauncey defines "the matter of Controversy" regarding the manner
of singing psalms in the form of a question: "Whether in Singing the
Songs of the LORD, we ought to proceed by a certain Rule, or to do it in
any Loose, Defective, Irregular way, that this, or that People, have Accustomed themselves unto?"[3]

That "certain Rule," as we have noted, is identified with the Divine
Will of God; the "Irregular way" with the "Traditions of Men." The latter
is further defined as proceeding from "the influence and power of Custom." A powerful influence indeed, for not only does it sway "a multitude
of Persons," but it induces them to cling to it tenaciously despite God's
Will and the arguments of the learned clergy. As a consequence, not only is
this custom-bound multitude living in sin, it is also making bad sounds:

> The Rule being neglected as useless, the Performance is very mean. . . . It is as
> flat Drink, compared with that which is lively, brisk and full of Spirit. . . .
> [However, Chauncey does *not* recommend drinking stronger spirits as a rem-
> edy.] Many are found so under the influence and power of Custom, that they
> account the common performance to be better, than any Reformation can
> make it; and are therefore, so far, from hearkning to any proposals for a Refor-
> mation, that the Proposal meets with not only Rejection, but very fierce
> Opposition. . . . And some, are ready to Lavish away as much Zeal, as tho'
> there were an attempt to pluck away a Fundamental Article in Religion. . . .[4]

The common people expressed their convictions by singing and maintaining a cherished custom; they did not publish sermons and tracts in defense of their practice. Thus, the written accounts are definitely one-sided.
In 1721, for example, Rev. Thomas Walter wrote, "I have observed in many
Places, one Man is upon this Note, while another is a Note before him,
which produces something so hideous and disorderly as is beyond Expression bad."[5] Until recently, historians of America's music seized upon such
polemical tirades to condemn the Common Way of psalmody as deplor-
ably uncouth. The procedure is about the same as that of a writer who
would base the biography of a politician on the campaign speeches of his
opponents.

Once we accept the premise that the advocates of Regular Singing are
polemical writers, combining acquired aesthetic standards with a class-
conscious culture and a dogmatic theology, we are in a position to extract
some objective data from their polemics. Take, for example, the following

passage from a tract by Rev. Cotton Mather: "It has been found . . . in some of our Congregations, that in length of Time, their *singing* has degenerated, into an *Odd Noise,* that has had more of what we want a Name for, than any *Regular Singing* in it. . . . And they must have Strange Notations of the Divine SPIRIT, and of His Operations, who shall imagine, that the Delight which their *Untuned Ears* take in an *Uncouth Noise,* more than in a *Regular Singing,* is any *Communion* with Him."⁶ One has to admire the superb assurance of the Puritan divine: that he alone is privy to the musical tastes of God!

We cannot, of course, blame the New England reformers for being ignorant of cultural anthropology, ethnomusicology, and the modern science of folklore. But we could blame ourselves for not using the hindsight afforded by these social sciences to elucidate the significance of the Common Way of psalmody. Even from such a biased statement as Mather's, we can extract some objective information: the process has been going on for a long time and thus qualifies as a *tradition;* the singers take "delight" in their traditional manner of singing, as the folk have done for generations. They had no sense of being "uncouth" in their custom—any more than do the millions of people who speak a language colloquially rather than grammatically.

One of the most active and influential leaders of the reform movement, Rev. Thomas Walter (1696–1725), asserted—doubtless to enhance his authority—that he was familiar with the common or country way of singing, and he described himself as one "who can sing all the various Twistings of the old Way, and that too according to the *Genius* of most of the Congregations." The last phrase is significant, for it indicates that each congregation had its idiosyncrasies within the common tradition. The reformers are informants in spite of themselves. In arguing for the suppression of traits he considered objectionable, Walter tells us what those traits were:

> The Omission of those unnatural Quaverings and Turnings, will serve to prevent all that Discord and lengthy Tediousness which is so much a Fault in our singing of Psalms. For much time is taken up in shaking out these Turns and Quavers; and besides, no two Men in the Congregation quaver alike, or together; which sounds in the Ears of a good Judge, like *Five Hundred* different Tunes roared out at the same time, whose perpetual interferings with one another, perplexed Jars, and unmeasured Periods, would make a Man wonder at the false Pleasure which they conceive in that which good Judges of Musick and Sounds, cannot bear to hear.⁷

Walter assumes that the pleasure is "false" because it conflicted with the cultural standards of his class and therefore did not please *him*. He is, in short, a prototype of the critic for whom anything that is different is damned.

Nevertheless, Walter is a useful informant. He charges, for example, that "our tunes are, for want of a standard to appeal to in all our Singing, left to the Mercy of every unskilful Throat to chop and alter, twist and change, according to their infinitely divers and no less odd Humours and Fancies. . . ." The argument is that a single standard should replace infinite diversity. (There is, perhaps, an analogy here with the rigidity of Puritan theology.) Walter goes on to deplore the fact that "our Tunes have passed thro' strange *Metamorphoses* . . . since their first Introduction into the World."[8] By this statement, taken out of context, Walter would qualify as a perceptive folklorist, for in the process of oral transmission, many folk tunes and styles *do* undergo a series of metamorphoses.

Defending the Regular Way of psalmody, Walter writes, "And this I am sure of, we sing them [the tunes] as they are pricked down, and I am sure the Country People do not."[9] Of course they do not! We are talking about the difference between a written and an oral tradition—between Singing by Note and Singing by Custom.

Walter's reference to "the Country People" emphasizes the contrast between rural and urban, but we know from various sources that the separation was not absolute. John Adams noted in his diary (August 21, 1774) that at a church in New York City the singing was "in the *Old Way*, as we call it—all the drawling, quavering, Discord in the World."[10] Yet the "Old Way" was more deeply rooted and persistent in rural areas.

The Reverend Thomas Symmes, in a pamphlet titled *The Reasonableness of Regular Singing; or, Singing by Note*, has this to say: "Now, *Singing by Note* is giving every *Note* it's proper *Pitch*, and *Turning* the Voice in it's proper Place, and giving to every *Note* it's true *Length* and *Sound*, &c. Whereas, the *Usual Way* varies much from this: In it, some *Notes* are sung too *high*, others too *low*, and most too *long*, and many *Turnings of*, or *Flourishes with* the Voice (as they call them) are made where they should *not* be, and some are wanting where they should have been."[11]

Symmes's conclusion both confirms and condemns the function of oral tradition: "Your *Usual Way* of Singing is handed down by *Tradition* only, and whatsoever is only so conveyed down to us, it is a thousand to one if it be not miserably corrupted. . . ." In another pamphlet, *Utile Dulci; or, A*

Joco-Serious Dialogue concerning Regular Singing, he adopts the objection-and-answer method, putting the objections into the mouth of a rural parishioner, with the answers given by the minister. (The latter continually refers to the Common Way adherents as "A.R.S.'s," meaning antiregular singers—a pun doubtless more relished by the Harvard graduates than by their country cousins.) In the course of the dialogues the minister takes up the objection that psalm tunes sung in the Regular Way are more like "song-tunes" (i.e., secular songs) than are those sung according to the Common Way. Here is part of his answer: "And further I affirm, the *most* of the *Psalm-Tunes*, as Sung in the *Usual way*, are much more like *Song*-Tunes, than as Sung by *Rule*; because you've more *Supernumerary* Notes & Turnings of the voice in your way, than in ours. An Ingenious Gentleman, who has prick'd *Canterbury*, as some of *you* Sing it, finds (as I remember) no less than 150 Notes, in that Tune, in *your* way, whereas in our's, there are but 30."[12]

Regrettably, Symmes failed to print the tune of "Canterbury" as "prick'd" (notated) by his enterprising friend, but the latter deserves an accolade as perhaps the first "scientific" musical folklorist of North America. The whole point of the story is that the Common Way singers were allegedly more lavish with their interpolated notes than were the Regulars.

Here we face a paradox. The New England reformers regarded themselves as musically sophisticated because they knew how to read notes and to sing "by Rule," without excessive ornamentation. Yet ornamentation—often lavish if not excessive—was recognized in Europe as a skill that enhanced both vocal and instrumental melody. In the seventeenth and eighteenth centuries singers probably rarely executed a solo part as it was written. That the practice of ornamentation was applied to psalmody is attested in both oral tradition and printed sources.

Nicholas Temperley has called attention to *A New and Easie Method to Learn to Sing by Book* (London, 1686), which contains both a plain and an ornamented version of the tune for Psalm 25 ("Southwell"):[13]

Plain and ornamented versions of tune for Psalm 25 ("Southwell")

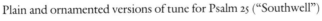

Another publication cited by Temperley, John Chetham's *A Book of Psalmody* (London, 1718), gives an ornamented version of the tune for Psalm 4 ("Coleshill"):

Plain and ornamented versions of tune for Psalm 4 ("Coleshill")

According to a comment by Chetham, "Those Psalms which the Clark gives out Line by Line, are generally sung in these Tunes [i.e., ornamented]; which is call'd the Old way of Singing."[14] Whatever the "Old Way" of psalm singing may have been in New England, it definitely had British antecedents.

What about the practice of "lining out" to which Chetham refers? Its original purpose is explained in the ordinances of the Westminster Assembly of Divines (London, 1644), which recommended its adoption in English churches: "For the present, where many in the Congregation cannot read, it is convenient that the Minister, or some other fit person appointed

by him . . . do reade the Psalme, line by line, before the singing thereof."[15]
This statement contains the seeds of a controversy that has persisted for
more than three centuries.

In 1724 the *New England Courant* published a satirical letter ridiculing
the defects of the Common Way of psalmody, written by a correspondent
who signed himself "Jeoffry Chanticleer" and was probably James Franklin, half-brother of Benjamin. As usual with such denunciations, this one
conveys some useful information concerning both the manner of "setting"
the tune and of singing in an unorthodox manner:

> The same person who sets the Tune, and guides the Congregation in Sing-
> ing, commonly reads the Psalm, which is a Task so few are capable of per-
> forming well, that in Singing two or three Staves the Congregation falls
> from a cheerful Pitch to downright *Grumbling,* and then some to relieve
> themselves mount an Eighth [octave] above the rest, others perhaps a
> Fourth or Fifth, by which means the Singing appears to be rather a con-
> fused Noise, made up of *Reading, Squeaking* and *Grumbling,* than a decent
> and orderly part of God's Worship.[16]

Translating this into unpolemical language, we get an aural image of a
successive lowering of pitch among the main body of the congregation carrying the tune, while other voices sing above it at intervals of a fourth, a
fifth, or an octave. For the sake of analogy with another oral tradition, this
may be compared with an account by the English writer John Spencer
Curwen concerning "two old ladies in the North of England, who were
noted among their friends for their power of improvising a high part
above the melody of the tune." The custom, Curwen adds, was common,
"and it was always considered a sign of musicianship to be able to sing this
part."[17] This last remark should be emphasized, for it underlines the point
we want to make throughout this chapter: that what is considered bad
taste, incorrect practice, or even "a confused Noise" by the conventional
standards of one class or culture group may be regarded as a sign of
musicianship and a source of pride in another tradition. The ethnologist,
in studying different cultures, frequently has occasion to corroborate this
pattern.

According to Curwen, congregational singing in English parish
churches during the eighteenth century "was a string of grace-notes, turns,
and other embellishments."[18] This is exactly what Symmes, Walter,
Chauncey, and other early New England writers tell us about the demotic
psalmody of that region—except that their statements are encrusted with

polemical verbiage, which has to be cleared away in order to obtain an objective view.

Although Curwen was writing in the 1870s, he interviewed informants whose memory and experience reached back to the early decades of the century and who spoke of traditional practices handed down from an earlier generation. One informant states that "in his early days, when the melody leaped a third, the women invariably added the intervening note; and if it leaped more than a third, they glided up or down, *portamento*, giving the next note in anticipation." Another informant confirmed the common use of appoggiaturas and gliding from one note to another. Curwen also was told of a congregation in which the men "sing the air through the tune until they get to the end, and then, if the melody ends low, they will scale up in falsetto to the higher octave, and thus make harmony at the cadence."[19]

Curwen's informant also told him that "in the old times the people liked the tunes pitched high; the women especially enjoyed screaming out high G. It made the psalmody more brilliant and far-sounding."[20] It should be observed that in those days it was the men, not the women, who carried the "tune" or principal melody; hence, the screaming on high notes may have been a compensatory means of feminine self-assertion.

As no objective accounts of the Common Way of psalmody in early New England have come down to us, our only recourse for elucidating its character is to bring together the *specific* traits mentioned by the polemical reformers and compare them with the objective reports of analogous oral traditions that have been documented elsewhere, beginning with England and Scotland. But first, something needs to be said about the confusing and often misunderstood practice of lining out.

In 1647 John Cotton stated that "where all have books and can reade, or else can say the *Psalme* by heart, it were needlesse there to reade each line of the *Psalme* before hand in order to singing [*sic*]." But where this is not the case, "it will be a necessary helpe, that the words of the Psalme be openly read before hand, line after line, or two lines together, that so they who want [i.e., lack] either books or skill to reade, may know what is to be sung, and joyne with the rest in the dutie of singing."[21] In other words, lining out was *not* a mandatory or standard procedure in psalmody but an optional practice to be adopted under special circumstances.

Almost a century later, according to Cotton Mather's *Ratio Disciplinae Fratrum* (1726), the practice of reading line by line appears to have been widespread. Yet the usage was still contingent, not mandatory: "In some [churches] the Assembly being furnished with *Psalm-Books,* they sing without the stop of Reading between every Line."²² Again, the point to be emphasized is that the practice of "Reading between every Line" was an *ad hoc* expedient, depending on the degree of illiteracy in the congregation, and not an inherent factor of early New England psalmody. In certain situations, however, lining out became a vital and intrinsic element of demotic psalmody. The crucial factor was the transition from reading to melodic vocalization. To illustrate this development we turn first to the highlands of Scotland.

In the mid-seventeenth century the Scottish church accepted lining out reluctantly, under a directive from the Westminster Assembly. Yet 100 years later, when attempts were made to abolish the practice, great resentment arose among the people, and in some parishes the custom was not abandoned until well into the nineteenth century. According to Curwen, " 'Lining-out,' which had at first been resented as a concession to illiterate England, was clung to as a vital principle."²³ What had happened to transform lining out from an alien imposition to "a vital principle," to which the people clung tenaciously? The tradition of Gaelic psalmody will help us to elucidate this question.

Again, Curwen is our informant. Writing at a time when Gaelic psalmody could still be heard in Highland parishes in much the same manner as it was 100 years earlier, he summarized its main features as follows: "There are five tunes—French, Martyrs, Stilt (or York), Dundee, and Elgin—which are the traditional melodies used for the Psalms. These have been handed down from generation to generation, amplified by endless grace notes, and altered according to the fancy of every precentor. When used, they are sung so slowly as to be beyond recognition. . . . Each parish and each precentor had differences of detail, for the variations were never written or printed, but were handed down by tradition."²⁴ Is this not, in all essential points, a counterpart of the Common Way of psalmody in early New England as described by Symmes and his colleagues?

To further illustrate the vital principle of Gaelic psalmody we turn to Dr. Joseph Mainzer's monograph *Gaelic Psalm Tunes of Ross-shire* (Edinburgh, 1844), in which he collected vestiges of the traditional psalmody that had been handed down through many generations. In this tradition, *vocally inflected lining out becomes integral to the style.* The precentor gives out one line at a time, chanting it on the tonic or dominant, according to the key of the tune. The dominant is preferred, but if it is too high or too low for the voice, the tonic is taken. The chant is not always on a monotone: it often touches the tone next above. The congregation then sings the line *with much elaboration of the melody.* Here is an example as collected by Mainzer:[25]

French Tune

Variant of French Tune

The people who clung to what Thomas Walter called "the Uncertain and doubtful Conveyance of *Oral Tradition*" simply did what millions have done since mankind first began to make music. The written tradition has been but a small part of the world's music.

With regard to lining out *as a musical style,* there is evidence that it has persisted in various subcultures to the last quarter of the twentieth century. To begin with, the American music historian George Hood stated in 1846 that lining out still prevailed "over three-fourths of the territory of the United States."[26] However much lining out may have declined since that time, it still lingers in pockets of resistance to modern "progress"—a boon to the cultural historian in search of a presumably vanished past.

Thanks to the research and fieldwork of William H. Tallmadge (including several hundred transcriptions), we can now trace the survival of lining out and embellished psalmody or hymnody among American religious communities in the southern Appalachians. His fieldwork was done among Regular, Primitive, and United Baptists in the mountain areas of eastern Kentucky and western North Carolina and Virginia. In referring to the practice that immediately concerns us, Tallmadge uses the term "lining":

> One might imagine that lining would consist of the precentor singing a line of a hymn followed by the congregation echoing what they have just heard. While such a method may have occurred somewhere at some time, it does not happen that way in live tradition, nor have I ever come across any descriptive material which indicated that such was ever the case. A little analysis will indicate the impracticality of such literal lining.
>
> The lining method implies a prior knowledge of the tune on the part of the singers; consequently, the concern of the precentor is with the text, not the tune. That being true, he chants the lines rapidly so as not to break the continuity of the on-going tune any more than necessary. He also ends his chant on a tone that will assist the singers in pitching the first tone of their response. Literal lining (the echo effect) would, of course, hinder the singers from finding their first tone, as the last pitch of the precentor would only coincidentally assist the singers in their response; furthermore, if literal lining ever occurred it would have been deadly dull, since a hymn of ten verses would take twice as long to sing.[27]

Referring to the Regular Baptists of eastern Kentucky, among whom the lining tradition was strong, Tallmadge explains that the deacon or minister, "after introducing the first line of melody and text at a regular tempo and being joined at once by the congregation, chants the following line of text rather rapidly on tonic and dominant tones with a few ornamental flourishes." Moreover, "Sometimes there is a close melodic relationship between the lining and subsequent singing, but more often the melodic relationship is quite distant."[28] Here is an example from Tallmadge's collection, as sung by a preacher and his congregation at Jackson, Kentucky, in 1968:[29]

"Ye Nations All"

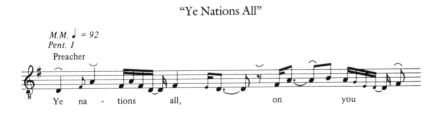

As Tallmadge observes, "Lining hymns have a basic beat; however, the beat is entirely free of strict metronomic regularity." It is the hymn text that "dictates the rhythmic structure of the melody. . . ."[30] Whatever the specific traits might be, they were a product of oral tradition, which is both retentive and transformational, with an inherent capacity for developing consistent stylistic features.

The New England musical reformers were neither folklorists nor professors of popular culture; they could only regard singing "by Custom" as a deplorable aberration. As educated clergymen they were painfully aware that such practices were contrary to the "Art of Musick" that they had studied at Harvard. Chauncey, after appealing to the authority of Holy Scripture, eventually brought his argument around to what he well knew was the crux of the matter: singing by Rule instead of by Custom: "For it is to be Remembered, that our Singing was Originally by Rule. . . . Every Song that we Sing, was Originally Composed by the Art of Musick; and Directions given us to Sing the Tunes by."[31]

Chauncey repeatedly hammers home the necessity of Rule, the need for a Standard whereby to distinguish Well Doing from Ill Doing. He even argues that "unless there be a certain Rule to proceed by in Singing, there can be no Singing at all." That is to say, if singing is not ruled by the Art and Skill of Musick, then it does not merit the name of singing.

Taken on their own terms, the reformers cannot be faulted. Their position was analogous to that of grammarians arguing for the necessity of correct grammar and syntax. The total collapse of grammatical syntax (not to speak of spelling) in American verbal usage of the twentieth century demonstrates that what prevails in a culture is the voice of the people, not the teaching of pedagogues. Nevertheless, the New England reformers constituted a highly educated enclave that was able to exert considerable pressure on its immediate milieu.

In pursuing their aims the reformers displayed exemplary zeal, industry, and skill, in a confrontation that was often acrimonious. The best of them avoided vituperation in favor of reason and persuasion. Theology and forensics were reinforced by manuals of musical instruction. Theory and argument were supported by practical measures such as that described in the *New England Courant* of March 5, 1722: "On Thursday last in the Afternoon, a Lecture was held at the New Brick Church [Boston], by the Society for Promoting Regular Singing in the Worship of God. The Rev. Thomas Walter of Roxbury preach'd an excellent Sermon on that Occasion, *The Sweet Psalmist of Israel*. The Singing was perform'd in Three Parts (according to Rule) by about Ninety Persons skill'd in that Science, to the great Satisfaction of a Numerous Assembly there Present."[32]

Forming a Society for the Promotion of Regular Singing meant *organization*—generally the key to victory, cultural as well as political. Americans have always been organizers and promoters. In the campaign for musical reform, ideas and projects were put forward persuasively. Symmes, for example, argued for another institution to promote Regular Singing:

> Q. 9. *WOULD it not greatly tend to the promoting* [of] *Singing Psalms*, if Singing Schools *were promoted?* Would not this be a Conforming to *Scripture Pattern?* Have we not as much need of them as GOD's People of Old? Have we any Reason to expect to be inspired with the Gift of *Singing*, any more than that of *Reading?* or to attain it without the use of suitable Means, any more than they of Old, when *Miracles, Inspirations,* &c. were common? Where would be the *Difficulty,* or what the *Disadvantages,* if People that want [i.e., lack] *Skill* in *Singing,* would procure a *Skilfull Person* to *Instruct* them, and meet *Two* or *Three* Evenings in the Week, from *Five* or *six* a Clock, to *Eight,* and spend the Time in Learning to Sing? Would not this be an innocent and profitable *Recreation,* and would it not have a Tendency (if prudently managed) to prevent the unprofitable *Expence* of Time on *other Occasions?* Has it

not a Tendency to divert Young People (who are most proper to learn) from Learning *Idle, Foolish,* yea, *pernicious Songs* and *Ballads,* and banish all such *Trash* from their Minds? . . . Are not they very unwise who plead against Learning to Sing by Rule, when they can't learn to Sing at all, unless they learn by Rule? Has not the grand *Enemy of Souls* a hand in this, who prejudices them against the Means of Singing?[33]

In this Argument by Question, Symmes goes beyond the "God is on our side" theme and tries to clinch the matter by suggesting that those who reject Regular Singing are ensnared by the archfiend, Satan. Symmes was indeed a master of polemics; yet it might be an exaggeration to claim that he turned the tide toward Singing by Rule. The sociocultural configuration of New England had developed to a point where the cultivated tradition would inevitably predominate over the demotic substratum.

The formation of singing schools and the promotion of singing societies went forward apace and complemented each other, each having the same basic purpose. The diaries of two eminent Bostonians confirm the success of these enterprises (both refer to the same occasion, on March 16, 1721). From the diary of Cotton Mather: "In the Evening I preached unto a large Auditory, where a Society of persons learning to Sing, began a quarterly solemnity. . . ."[34] From the diary of Samuel Sewall: "At night Dr. Mather preaches in the School-House to the young Musicians, from Rev. 14. 3—no man could learn that Song.—House was full, and the Singing extraordinarily Excellent, such as had hardly been heard before in Boston."[35]

The Boston Society for Regular Singing held weekly meetings for instruction. Every three months there was the "solemnity" mentioned by Mather, consisting of a public concert together with a sermon or lecture for the occasion. During the 1720s many such "Singing Lectures" began to be held in New England towns.

Obviously, instruction books were needed for acquiring the skill of Singing by Note, and there were English antecedents for such books. *A New and Easie Method to Learn to Sing by Book* (London, 1686), for example, was described by an American scholar as "the first work which displays the principal characteristics of the eighteenth-century tune-book; i.e., a set of musical instructions combined with a collection of harmonized psalm tunes."[36] The New England reformers were quick to offer their own manuals for the local market. The *Boston News-Letter* of January 2/9, 1721, carried the following advertisement: "A Small Book containing 20 Psalm Tunes, with Directions how to Sing them, contrived in the most easy Method ever yet Invented, for the ease of Learners, whereby even Children, or People of the meanest Capacities, may come to Sing them by Rule. . . . To be Sold by Samuel Gerrish, Bookseller, near the Brick Church in Cornhill."

Later advertisements give the complete title of this American tunebook and the name of its author: *A Very Plain and Easy Introduction to the Art of Singing Psalm Tunes . . . By the Rev. Mr. John Tufts.* The author was a Harvard graduate who drew on Ravenscroft and Playford for his musical theory, and who used letters instead of notes for his tunes: *F* for *fa*, *S* for *sol*, *L* for *la*, *M* for *mi.* The time value of a note was indicated by punctuation: a letter standing alone was equal to a quarter note; followed by a period it equaled a half note; and followed by a colon, a whole note. Tufts claimed to have introduced an "easy method of singing by letters instead of notes," but this method was not widely adopted. Nevertheless, his little book went into eleven editions by 1744, so it must have had some influence.[37]

The year 1721 was evidently a turning point in the movement for Regular Singing. In addition to Tufts's, there was Rev. Thomas Walter of Roxbury's publication, *The Grounds and Rules of Musick Explained; or, An Introduction to the Art of Singing by Note,* which went through at least six editions, the last in 1764. It was highly regarded and had a wide influence. It was also the first music book to be printed with bar lines in the British colonies of North America. The printer was James Franklin of Boston, in whose shop Benjamin Franklin worked for a time as apprentice.

In spite of scattered pockets of resistance and much heated debate in some congregations, most of the principal towns in New England had accepted Regular Singing by 1750. With the growth of singing societies and singing schools, however, there was increasing emphasis on the social aspects of what we would now call "community singing." Since many singing schools were held in taverns or rented rooms, they tended to acquire a more secular orientation. Moreover, beginning in the last decades of the eighteenth century, public funds for singing schools were often provided by towns, thus diminishing ecclesiastical influence. The prevalence of young people in the classes also contributed to emphasizing the social aspect.

It should be understood that singing schools were not institutional. They had no designated buildings, no permanent staff, and no fixed terms. Singing-school masters were generally itinerant and often self-taught. Armed with a strong voice, some rudiments of music theory, and a tunebook, they solicited patronage in towns, villages, and countryside.

When they had obtained a sufficient number of pupils, they would set up their "school" in any available locale such as a tavern or church and remain there for a designated period that might last several weeks, holding sessions on specified days and at specified hours.

In larger cities singing-school masters solicited the patronage of "Ladies and Gentlemen," as indicated by the following advertisement in the *Pennsylvania Gazette* (1760): "Notice is hereby given that the Singing-School lately kept in the Rooms over Mr. William's School in Second Street [Philadelphia], will again be opened on Monday Evening, the 3d of November next, at the same Place, where the ART OF PSALMODY will be taught, as usual, in the best Manner, on Monday and Friday Evenings, from Six to Eight. And that, if any Number of Ladies and Gentlemen incline to make up an exclusive Set, to Sing on two other Nights, they may be gratified by making Application in time."

It would be a distortion to assume that singing schools flourished only during the eighteenth century and only in New England. During the nineteenth century they were widespread in the rural South and Midwest, and in many communities from Maine to Texas, they continued well into the twentieth century.

In 1841 Moses Cheney (1776–1856), who became a singing master himself, wrote an account of his first singing-school experience as a boy of twelve living in New Hampshire. After the master had taught and rehearsed the basic elements, he said, "Come boys, you must rise and fall the notes [i.e., go up and down the scale] first, and then the gals must try." Each pupil had to try it alone, beginning with the oldest. Since Cheney was the youngest, he had time to observe the proceedings (which often caused "great fits of laughing") and to decide on a strategy:

> Now my eyes were fixed on the Master's mouth, if possible to learn the names of the notes before he came to me. . . . it came to my mind that I could mimic every beast, and bird, and thing . . . and it was no more to mimic my master than it was anything else. . . . I had only time to draw a long breath, and blow out the flutter of my heart, when the master came to me. "Well my lad, will you try?" "Yes sir." I looked him in the mouth, and as he spoke a note, so did I, both up and down. . . . The master turned away, saying, "this boy will make a singer." I felt well enough.[38]

The story ends on a typical note of Yankee self-reliance and will to succeed: "When he left us, he [the singing master] gave me his singing book and wooden pitch-pipe, and told me to believe I was the best singer in the world, and then I should never be afraid to sing anywhere."

THE
Grounds and Rules
OF
MUSICK
Explained : Or,
An *Introduction* to the Art of Singing
by NOTE.
Fitted to the meaneft Capacities.

By THOMAS WALTER, M. A.

Recommended by feveral MINISTERS.

The Second Edition.

Let every thing that hath Breath Praife the Lord, Pfal. 150. 6.

BOSTON: Printed by B.Green, for S.Gerrifh, near the Brick Meeting-Houfe in Cornhill. 1723

Title page and two psalm tunes from Thomas Walter, *The Grounds and Rules of Musick Explained; or, An Introduction to the Art of Singing by Note,* 2d ed. (1723).

Notes

1. Nathaniel Chauncey, *Regular Singing Defended and Proved to Be the Only True Way of Singing the Songs of the Lord* (New London, 1728).

2. Ibid., pp. 1–8.

3. Ibid., p. 10.

4. Ibid., pp. 11–12.

5. Thomas Walter, *The Grounds and Rules of Musick Explained; or, An Introduction to the Art of Singing by Note* (Boston, 1721), p. 4.

6. Cotton Mather, *The Accomplished Singer* (Boston, 1721), p. 22.

7. Walter, *The Grounds and Rules*, p. 5.

8. Ibid., pp. 3–4.

9. Ibid., p. 10.

10. *Diary and Autobiography of John Adams* 2:104.

11. Thomas Symmes, *The Reasonableness of Regular Singing; or, Singing by Note* (Boston, 1720), p. 10.

12. Thomas Symmes, *Utile Dulci; or, A Joco-Serious Dialogue concerning Regular Singing* (Boston, 1723), pp. 44–45.

13. Nicholas Temperley, "The Old Way of Singing," pp. 525–26.

14. Ibid., pp. 526–27.

15. Ibid., p. 532.

16. *New England Courant*, Feb. 17/24, 1724; quoted in Henry Wilder Foote, *Three Centuries of American Hymnody*, pp. 377–78.

17. John Spencer Curwen, *Studies in Worship Music*, p. 67.

18. Ibid., p. 66.

19. Ibid., pp. 66–67.

20. Ibid., p. 66.

21. John Cotton, *Singing of Psalmes a Gospel-Ordinance* (London, 1647), p. 62.

22. Cotton Mather, *Ratio Disciplinae Fratrum* (Boston, 1726), p. 52.

23. Curwen, *Studies in Worship Music*, p. 142.

24. Ibid., pp. 145–46.

25. The "French Tune" and its variant setting are given in Alan C. Buechner, "Yankee Singing Schools and the Golden Age of Choral Music in New England, 1760–1800," after p. 52.

26. George Hood, *History of Music in New England*, p. 200.

27. William H. Tallmadge, "Baptist Monophonic and Heterophonic Hymnody in Southern Appalachia," pp. 110–11.

28. Ibid., p. 111.

29. Ibid., p. 121.

30. Ibid., p. 116.

31. Chauncey, *Regular Singing Defended*, p. 31.

32. Quoted in Foote, *Three Centuries of American Hymnody*, p. 104.

33. Symmes, *The Reasonableness of Regular Singing*, p. 20.

34. *Diary of Cotton Mather* 2:608.

35. *Diary of Samuel Sewall, 1674–1729* 2:976.

36. Allen Britton, "Theoretical Introductions in American Tune-Books to 1800," p. 45.

37. See Irving Lowens, "John Tufts's *Introduction to the Singing of Psalm-Tunes* (1721–1744): The First American Music Textbook," in Lowens, *Music and Musicians in Early America,* pp. 39–57.

38. Moses Cheney, "Letter to Friend Mason," *Musical Visitor* 2, no. 17 (Dec. 1, 1841): 132–33, and no. 18 (Jan. 1, 1842): 139–40; quoted in Buechner, "Yankee Singing Schools," p. 136.

Chapter 3

Dissenters and Minority Sects

Likewise in Amerikay
Shines the glorious Gospel-Day.
—Joseph Humphreys, in Cennick,
Sacred Hymns (Bristol, 1743)

The trend toward nonconformity and innovation in religious worship was prevalent throughout the eighteenth century. For example, the nonconformist English divine Dr. Isaac Watts (1674–1748) strongly objected to the old, strict, metrical psalmody and even protested (in the preface to his *Hymns and Spiritual Songs,* London, 1707) against the very contents of the psalms: "Some of 'em are almost opposite to the Spirit of the Gospel: Many of them foreign to the State of the New-Testament, and widely different from the present Circumstances of Christians."

On the other side, those who clung to the old metrical psalmody, as opposed to the new hymns, were convinced that the word of God was being impiously replaced by "man-made" concoctions. Actually, a few hymns had been included in the appendixes of English psalters as early as the sixteenth century. The first supplement to Tate and Brady's *New Version of the Psalms* (London, 1700) included three hymns for Holy Communion, two for Easter, and the familiar Christmas hymn beginning "While shepherds watched their flocks by night," based on a passage from Luke (2:8–14). Other hymns followed, but it was in the early decades of the eighteenth century that the hymns of Dr. Watts swept like a flood over England and quickly spread to the North American colonies.

The influence of Dr. Watts in America was enormous. The first American edition of his *Hymns and Spiritual Songs* (undated, but identified as the "7th ed.") was published in Boston, perhaps as early as 1720. An extant edition (now in the Newberry Library) was printed by Benjamin Franklin in Philadelphia in 1741. But Watts's hymns and paraphrases of the psalms were well known and greatly admired before these American editions appeared. As early as 1711 Benjamin Colman of Boston wrote to Cotton Mather: "Mr. Watts is a great Master in Poetry, and a burning Light and Ornament of the Age. . . . You will forgive me that I emulate, and have dar'd to attempt to imitate, his Muse in the Inclosed. . . ."[1]

There were many other imitators of Watts in America, among them that precocious literary ornament of New England, Dr. Mather Byles, hailed by a contemporary as "Harvard's honour and New England's hope." In his early youth he penned these admiring verses:

> What Angel strikes the trembling Strings;
> And whence the golden Sound!
> Or is it Watts—or Gabriel sings
> From yon celestial Ground?

Watts did not entirely discard the psalms; he selected those he considered most appropriate for Christian worship and paraphrased them freely. In 1719 he brought out *The Psalms of David Imitated,* which ten years later was also printed by Franklin in Philadelphia. The "System of Praise" of Dr. Watts continued to gain favor in the British colonies. But when the American War of Independence broke out, it became necessary to emend certain passages in which he alluded to British sovereignty and the glory of British arms. In 1784 the ingenious Mr. Joel Barlow of Connecticut was appointed to "accommodate" the psalm versions of Dr. Watts for American usage. Barlow, a laborious poet and a member of the "Hartford Wits," aroused some opposition by making too free with Dr. Watts, for which he was censured by a fellow rhymester:

> You've proved yourself a sinful cre'tur;
> You've murdered Watts, and spoilt the metre;
> You've tried the Word of God to alter,
> And for your pains deserve a halter.

But the alteration of "the Word of God" had gone too far to be halted even by threats of a halter. Paraphrases of the psalms became so free that they could scarcely be distinguished from the new hymnody that proliferated in the English-speaking world. Timothy Dwight, president of Yale College, paraphrased a portion of Psalm 137 and produced what proved to be a favorite hymn:

> I love thy kingdom, Lord,
> The house of thine abode,
> The Church our blest Redeemer saved
> With his own precious blood.

The blood of the Redeemer was to be a recurrent theme of evangelical hymnody, and thence of the revival spirituals and gospel hymns ("Are you washed in the blood of the Lamb?").

Dwight was commissioned to prepare another "accommodation" of Watts, which he did with a considerable injection of patriotic zeal. There is more of General Washington than of King David in his version of Psalm 18:

> When, fir'd to rage, against our nation rose
> Chiefs of proud name, and bands of haughty foes,
> He train'd our hosts to fight, with arms array'd,
> With health invigor'd, and with bounty fed,
> Gave us his chosen chief our sons to guide,
> Heard every prayer, and every want supplied.
> He gave their armies captive to our hands,
> Or sent them frustrate to their native lands.

Such paraphrases of scripture, sometimes with local or topical allusions, were frequently set to music by early New England composers. But that is another chapter of our story; for now we return to the spread of evangelical hymnody and, in particular, to the extraordinary impetus it received from the work of the Wesleys, John and Charles.

In 1735 Governor Oglethorpe of Georgia was in England seeking ways to strengthen the recently founded colony. Appreciating the importance of religion as a stabilizing factor in a new settlement, he invited a serious-minded young minister, John Wesley, to accompany him to Georgia. Wesley and his younger brother Charles were then active in Oxford as members of a group variously known as the Holy Club, the Bible Moths, and the Methodists (because they studied methodically—a strange innovation at the university!). They accepted Oglethorpe's invitation and embarked on the *Simmonds*, bound for Savannah.

On board were twenty-six Moravian missionaries, members of a persecuted German Protestant sect. They were enthusiastic hymn singers, and their hymnody made a deep impression on the Wesleys. Once, during a severe storm that terrified most of the passengers, the Moravians calmly stood on the deck singing their hymns, unperturbed by the towering waves. John Wesley began at once to study their hymns, as attested by an entry in his journal for October 27, 1735: "Began Gesang Buch"[22]—referring to *Das Gesang-Buch der Gemeine in Herrnhut,* the principal hymnal of the Moravian Brethren in their central community at Herrnhut.

When their ship sailed into the Savannah River, John Wesley was pleasantly surprised by "the pines, palms, and cedars running in rows along the shore," making "an exceeding beautiful prospect, especially to us who did not expect to see the bloom of spring in the depth of winter."[3] The admiration was not all one-sided, for during his sojourn in Savannah, John Wesley evidently made an impression on a niece of the town's chief magistrate. The young Methodist, however, balked at matrimony and departed a free man.

Wesley's aim was to spread the gospel in the colonies, and especially to apply the power of hymnody in this endeavor. In 1737 he published in "Charles-Town," South Carolina, *A Collection of Psalms and Hymns* (texts only), important especially as containing his first translations of the German hymns that so deeply stirred him.

After his return to England in 1738, John Wesley frequented meetings of the Moravian Brethren in London, whose leader was his former shipboard acquaintance, Peter Böhler. This association resulted in a crucial religious experience for Wesley—a revelation and conversion that occurred during a reading of Luther's preface to the Epistle to the Romans: "About a quarter before nine, while he was describing the change which God works in the heart through faith in Christ, I felt my heart strangely warmed. I felt I did trust in Christ, Christ alone, for salvation; and an assurance was given me that He had taken away *my* sins, even *mine,* and saved *me* from the law of sin and death."[4]

This could be taken as the basic text, the gospel, as it were, for the whole movement of evangelical revivalism, with its emphasis on direct salvation through faith in Christ; the conviction of salvation as an emotional, personal experience; and the feeling of elation from the taking away of sin. The keynote themes of conversion and salvation, counteracting the terrors of sin and death, with a consequent feeling of intense elation, constitute the vital core of revival hymnody. The gospel of the Wesleys and their cohorts has been described as " the intensely individualistic proclamation of a way of escape for the soul from eternal damnation. The test of conversion was an emotional reaction rather than an intellectual acceptance of a creedal statement. . . ."[5]

What came to be known as the Great Awakening was a popular mass movement sparked by the powerful oratory of preachers such as John Wesley, George Whitefield, and Jonathan Edwards of New England, whose sermon *The Reality of Spiritual Light* touched off the emotional Northampton revival of 1735. Shortly thereafter, George Whitefield, leader of the Calvinist Methodists, made the first of his several journeys to America and aroused tremendous enthusiasm by his preaching. The power of Whitefield's appeal may be measured by the effect he had on Benjamin Franklin when Whitefield preached in Philadelphia. Intending at first to give only a few coppers for the collection, Franklin (noted for his thriftiness) ended by pouring out all the money he had in his pockets.

While powerful preaching could be effective, Wesley also emphasized the importance of hymnody. He and his brother Charles wrote the words of a great many hymns that were published in various collections. The first to appear with music was *A Collection of Tunes . . . As They Are Commonly Sung at the Foundery* (London, 1742), generally known as the Foundery Collection. (The Methodists had acquired for their meetings a building formerly used for casting canon; hence they called their meetinghouse the Foundery.) It was followed in 1746 by *Hymns on the Great Festivals and Other Occasions,* containing twenty-four tunes by a German musician residing in London, John Frederick Lampe. This included hymns that eventually became part of America's folklore and that oral tradition has kept alive through the centuries. One of these is "Ah, Lovely Appearance of Death," which evidently exerted a morbid fascination.[6] Here is the original version in Lampe's ornamental style (which also had its popular appeal):

"Ah, Lovely Appearance of Death"

Probably about 1760 Thomas Butts, a friend of the Wesleys, published his *Harmonia Sacra,* containing hymns with both words and tunes, many of the latter in florid style. It proved popular but did not entirely meet the approval of John Wesley, who evidently felt that embellished hymnody was getting out of hand. Hence it was not long before Wesley expressly forbade the use of "vain repetitions" in congregational singing. He also denounced florid melodies and fuging tunes as no better than "Lancashire hornpipes"—curiously reminiscent of the attacks on Puritan psalm tunes as "Geneva Jigs"!

In an effort to impose his own standards of congregational hymnody, Wesley in 1761 brought out the *Select Hymns, with Tunes Annext: Designed Chiefly for Use of the People Called Methodists,* with a selection of tunes and directions for singing. His precepts included singing the tunes "exactly as printed"—which assumes that most of his followers could read music, a situation hardly to be expected. Another precept was to "sing in tune"—also desirable, but unrealistic. In short, in spite of his immense contribution to popular evangelical hymnody, Wesley's conservatism in musical practice could not keep pace with the immense surge of revivalism that was to sweep over America soon after his death. As summarized by Benson, "The entire course of Methodist Episcopal Hymnody may be viewed as a continuous effort to keep the Church on a level sufficiently described as Wesleyan, and a failure to cooperate therein on the part of a considerable section of the people who preferred the plane of the Revival Hymn and the popular Spiritual Song."[7]

Besides Dr. Watts and the Wesleys, two other English hymn writers left a lasting impression on American popular hymnody during this period: John Cennick (1718–55) and John Newton (1725–1807). The former was a Quaker who became a follower of John Wesley and later (in 1745) joined the Moravian Brethren. His first publication, *Sacred Hymns for the Children of God* (London, 1741), was followed by *Sacred Hymns for the Use of Religious Societies, Generally Composed in Dialogues* (Bristol, 1743). (Hymns in dialogue form were to become popular in the camp-meeting revivals.) The importance of Cennick, in the words of G. P. Jackson, is that he "was destined to become the real founder of folky religious song in the rebellious eighteenth century movement."[8] Typical of his style is "Jesus My All to Heaven Is Gone," which (again quoting Jackson) "was to become one of the most widely sung religious lyrics among the country folk of America during the entire 200 years . . . since it appeared."[9] The fundamental simplicity of the message is what came across and endured:

I'll tell to all poor sinners round
What a dear Saviour I have found;
I'll point to thy redeeming blood
And say, behold the way to God.

The "dialogues" mentioned in Cennick's second collection were sung antiphonally by men and women who, at this time and for about 100 years thereafter, sat on opposite sides of the meetinghouse (sometimes they used a "double-deck" meetinghouse, with the women below and the men above).

John Newton was a rather wild character who went to sea at the age of eleven, was flogged as a deserter from the Royal Navy, became servant to a slave dealer in Africa, and before long was in the slave trade himself. While acting as captain of a slave ship, he was converted by reading Thomas à Kempis (*On the Imitation of Christ*), and soon afterward he came under the influence of Wesley and Whitefield, leading to his ordination as curate of Olney in 1764. Together with the unfortunate poet William Cowper, he undertook a remarkable collection, published in three books as *Olney Hymns* (London, 1779). Of its 280 hymn texts, all but 68 were written by Newton. The "old African blasphemer" (as he called himself) drew largely on his own experience in wrestling with sin and being snatched from damnation into eternal salvation; hence, the strong personal appeal and emotional impact of his hymns.

Without dwelling on details of multiple sectarianism and doctrinal difference that characterized the popular religious movements of the eighteenth century, we may simply observe that this religious discord—through what might be called a process of collective individualism—proliferated into a large number of dissenting groups, many of them offshoots of the major denominations. The Baptists, for example, split into New Lights, Free Willers, and Separatists, while the Presbyterians divided into Old Side and New Side, the latter going strongly for revivalism.

Although dissenters were often denounced and deplored, they had a sturdy defender in the Reverend Samuel Davies, a staunch upholder of religious toleration. The prevailing climate of acrimony and hostility may be gathered from Davies's *Impartial Trial Impartially Tried* (Williamsburg, 1748): "Tho' the pulpits around us, I am told, ring with exclamatory harangues, accusations, arguments, railings, warnings, etc., etc., etc., against New-Lights, Methodists, Enthusiasts, Deceivers, Itinerants, Pretenders, etc., etc., etc., yet I never design to prostitute mine to such mean purposes."[10]

The repeated "etceteras" speak more eloquently than anything else in this passage. Let it also be noted that the Methodists, however they may have been regarded by the Establishment, were no fly-by-night offshoot, but a thriving and influential denomination, which in 1784 separated from the Church of England and thereafter had an important role in the spread of revivalism and the development of American hymnody—as did the Baptists and (to a lesser degree) the Presbyterians.

In many ways the most remarkable minority sect was that of the Shakers, whose formal designation was United Society of Believers in Christ's Second Coming. The sect originated in Manchester, England, with a group known as the Shaking Quakers, under the leadership of Ann Lee, who soon became known to her followers as "Mother Ann." Born to a poor family, she endured as a girl the hardship of toiling in a local cotton factory. Her parents forced her into marriage with a blacksmith, to whom she bore four children who died in infancy. As a result she came to regard sexual intercourse as the root of all evil, and she imposed the rule of celibacy upon her followers. For this antisocial doctrine, together with charges of disturbing the Sabbath, she went to jail in 1772. Pious churchgoers may also have looked askance at the "dancing ecstasy" by which Mother Ann's followers expressed their joy in salvation.

Like many others who looked to the New World for a better fortune, Mother Ann had thoughts that turned toward America, and she informed her followers that a divine power directed them to seek that Promised Land. Fortunately for them, heavenly inspiration was bolstered with ready cash from a well-to-do member of the group, and in 1774 nine Shaker pilgrims sailed for America, exhorted and led by the indomitable Mother Ann.

It was not a propitious moment for a mystifying English group to arrive in the colonies, where anti-British sentiment was widespread. Hence the small group of Shakers endured persecution, including imprisonment as "pacifists"—tantamount to treason in that turbulent atmosphere. Nevertheless they persevered, soon adding many members to their fold and establishing settlements that eventually would reach from Maine to Kentucky. Until 1794 all Shaker communities were located in New York and New England; after 1806 they spread to Ohio, Kentucky, and Indiana.

After the death of Mother Ann in 1784, the administrative organization of the Shakers was carried on even more systematically by leaders such as James Whittaker and Joseph ("Father") Meacham. Doubtless in deference to the memory of Mother Ann, the doctrine of equal status for men and women was observed, and a second "Mother"—Lucy Wright (1760–1821)—succeeded Meacham and did much to develop Shaker communities in the Midwest.

But the spirit and influence of Mother Ann lived on, as did many elements of Shaker rituals that were believed to have been revealed to her in visions: the ritual dances and holy exercises that had such an enduring effect and the songs that were to make the Shakers so important in the vast panorama of America's music. The Shakers believed that they were engaged in a holy war against the devil and the flesh, and that the spirit of Mother Ann would bring them victory in this conflict. They expressed these beliefs in one of their songs:

> I will be like Mother,
> *I'll war, I'll war, I'll war* the flesh,
> And overcome and conquer and reign with my Mother.

Singing, dancing, shaking, running, leaping—all these were means whereby the Shakers expressed the joy of their religious faith and their victory over the flesh and the devil. Mother Ann firmly believed in the corporeal reality of the devil. "The devil is a real being," she said, "as real as a bear. I know, for I have seen him and fought with him." The Shaker rituals were for real; we shall encounter them again when we come to the nineteenth-century revival hymns and spiritual songs in chapter 11.

Besides the predominantly Anglo-Celtic movements of religious dissent, various minority sects from continental Europe also established themselves in America. Although they remained relatively self-contained and isolated from popular mass movements, they nevertheless were part of the American cultural experience. Chronological priority belongs to the Mennonites (followers of Menno Simon), who came from Switzerland and the German Palatinate and immigrated to America between 1683 and 1748. The first group came to Pennsylvania and settled in Germantown, near Philadelphia. Their pastor was Willem Rittinghuysen, great-grandfather of the celebrated astronomer and mathematician David Rittenhouse (the name having become thus "Americanized"). In 1770 they built a stone church, which is still in use. They used a hymnbook originally printed in Schaffhausen in 1583 and reprinted in Germantown in 1742 with the title *Der Ausbund: Das ist etliche schöne christliche Lieder* (many later editions). In religious beliefs the Mennonites were related to the Dunkers or German Baptists, but they practiced baptism by affusion, not by immersion. They were opposed to instrumental music in church worship.

In 1694 a group of German Pietists, under the leadership of Johannes Kelpius, came to Pennsylvania and soon settled on the banks of the Wissahickon River, not far from Philadelphia—hence becoming known as the Hermits or the Mystics of the Wissahickon. Kelpius, besides dabbling in oriental lore and cabalistic philosophy, was somewhat of a musician and hymn writer. He was only twenty-one when he set sail for America with about forty followers, some of whom were musicians, as we gather from his account of the voyage: "We had also prayer meetings and sang hymns of praise and joy, several of us accompanying on instruments that we brought from London."[11] It is believed that these instruments may also have been used at the ordination of Justus Falckner as pastor of the Gloria Dei Church on November 23, 1703—for which occasion the Mystics of the Wissahickon provided music with viols, hautboys, trumpets, and kettledrums.

The church already had an organ, sent from Germany in response to a plea from Falckner, whose letter shows the importance he attached to music in promoting missionary work:

> It would not only attract and civilize the wild Indian, but it would do much good in spreading the Gospel truths among the sects and others by attracting them. . . . Thus a well-sounding organ would perhaps prove of great profit, to say nothing of the fact that the Indians would come running from far and near to listen to such unknown melody, and upon that account might become willing to accept our language and teaching, and remain with people who had such agreeable things; for they are said to come ever so far to listen to one who plays even upon a reed pipe (*rohr-pfeiffe*): such an extraordinary love have they for any melodious and ringing sound.[12]

The Gloria Dei Church in Philadelphia, of which Falckner became pastor, was built by Swedish Lutherans who had first settled on the Delaware River in 1638. Falckner was a German Lutheran from Saxony, educated at the universities of Leipzig and Halle. He wrote several hymn texts, of which the best known is "Rise, Ye Children of Salvation," sung to the tune of "Meine Hoffnung."

Magister Johannes Kelpius, leader of the Wissahickon Hermits, has been put forward by some writers as the first Pennsylvanian composer, based on his supposed authorship of some hymn tunes in a manuscript collection titled "The Lamenting Voice of the Hidden Love, at the Time

When She Lay in Misery & Forsaken; and Oprest by the Multitude of Her Enemies. Composed by One in Kumber . . . Pennsylvania in America 1705."[13] (*Kumber* [or *cumber*] is an obsolete English word for *distress*.) Kelpius may have written the text, but there is no valid evidence that he wrote the music, most of which is taken from identifiable German sources. The English translations of the hymns in this remarkable collection have been attributed to Dr. Christopher Witt, who migrated from England to America in 1704 and joined the Mystics of the Wissahickon. He was a portrait painter and an amateur musician who is said to have built a pipe organ for his own use—supposedly the first private organ in the North American colonies.

An extraordinary musical enterprise was that of the Ephrata Cloister, or the Community of the Solitary, established on the Cocalico River in 1720, in what is now Lancaster County, Pennsylvania. They were Seventh-day Baptists under the leadership of Conrad Beissel and Peter Miller, who strongly believed in music as essential to worship. Moreover, they developed their own musical system and homespun hymnody, based on "Beissel's Dissertation on Harmony."[14] In this curiously quaint and original treatise, Beissel divided the notes of the scale into two categories: notes belonging to the common chord he termed *masters;* all remaining notes he called *servants.* In his metrical system he simply followed the rhythm of the words, giving accented syllables longer note values and unaccented syllables shorter ones. In setting texts to music, he provided that the accent should always fall on a "master" note, while the "servants" took care of the unaccented syllables. With the help of chord tables for all the keys, composing hymns became an easy and popular occupation for members of the Ephrata Cloister. They were no less enthusiastic in singing what they had invented, and they had a repertory of nearly 1,000 hymns. They also had a variety of musical instruments, including the violin.

A visitor to the Ephrata Cloister in 1753 observed that many of the "younger sisters are mostly employed in drawing. A part of them are just now constantly employed in copying musical note books for themselves and the brethren."[15] These hand-copied songbooks were beautifully illuminated. Printed hymnals were also used, several of which were printed by Benjamin Franklin in the 1730s. But the main body of Ephrata hymnody was contained in a compilation titled *Das Gesang der einsamen und verlassenen Turtel-Taube, nemlich der christlichen Kirche* (Song of the lonely and forsaken turtle dove, namely the Christian Church), more familiarly known as the *Turtle-Taube.* The first printed edition of this work is

Earliest Ephrata music, manuscript hymnbook, ca. 1735.

stamped Ephrata, 1747, but there is also a magnificent manuscript copy, with some 750 hymns, dating from 1746. The latter was at one time in the possession of Franklin, who took it to England and lent it to the Lord Mayor of London in 1775. (Eventually it was acquired by the Library of Congress.) Beissel's last collection of hymns, *Paradisisches Wunder-Spiel* (Paradisiacal wonder music, Ephrata, 1754), was partly handwritten and partly printed.

Artistically, none of the religious minorities that settled in America approached the musical achievement of the Unitas Fratrem, more commonly known as the Moravian Church. Founded in 1457, it flourished in Moravia, Bohemia, and Poland, until disrupted by persecution during the seventeenth century. In 1722 a remnant of Moravians settled in Saxony under the protection of Count Nikolaus Ludwig von Zinzendorf, and thereafter the church grew and prospered. Zinzendorf wrote many hymn texts and edited collections of hymns that were widely used, including the *Gesang-Buch der Gemeine in Herrnhut,* previously mentioned as having influenced the Wesleys. The Moravians, like the Wesleys, were much concerned with missionary work, and after their initial efforts in Georgia failed, they decided to move on to Pennsylvania. There, in 1741, under the leadership of Zinzendorf, they established on the banks of the Lehigh River a settlement called Bethlehem. Soon joined by other Moravian Church members from Europe, the settlement flourished and became especially known for its music—a reputation that it retains to the present day, largely because of its prestigious Bach festivals.

Shortly after the founding of Bethlehem, a group of Moravians went to North Carolina, where they established several settlements, of which the most important was Salem (now Winston-Salem). There they built churches equipped with organs and zealously cultivated both sacred and secular music, vocal and instrumental. They were especially partial to trombones, which they performed in choirs (soprano, alto, tenor, bass), and which they used both on festive occasions and for the sad duty of announcing a death in the community. For the latter it was customary to have the players stationed on the roof of a building so that they could be heard far and wide. Concerning this practice, there is a legend that during the French and Indian War a group of Indian warriors planned a surprise attack on one of the Moravian settlements. As they awaited the coming of darkness, they heard the sound of a trombone choir, and thinking that this strange noise from on high must be the voice of the Great Spirit warning them away, they gave up the attack and fled.

The Moravians were deeply concerned with missionary work among the Indians (as well as among the Negroes), and in 1763 they published a collection of hymns in the language of the Delaware Indians. In 1803 one of their missionaries, David Zeisberger, published in Philadelphia *A Collection of Hymns for the Use of the Christian Indians of the Mission of the United Brethren in North America.*

In addition to their vast repertory of hymnody (containing many tunes of popular origin), the Moravians cultivated secular "art" music as both performers and composers. One of their most important musicians was Johann Friedrich Peter (1746–1813). Born in Holland to German parents, Peter joined the Bethlehem settlement in 1770 and brought with him manuscript copies that he had made of music by many prominent European composers such as C. F. Abel, Johann Christoph Friedrich Bach, and Johann Stamitz. He also copied several scores by Franz Joseph Haydn, who strongly influenced his style of composition.

Peter was active at several Moravian settlements but did his most important work at Bethlehem and Salem. He went to Salem in 1780 and for ten years gave great impetus to the musical activity of that community, particularly by establishing and directing its Collegium Musicum (founded in 1786). He built up a vast collection of musical scores and parts, so that the repertory of the Collegium totaled some 500 works, including chamber music, symphonies, anthems, and oratorios. Most of the music was from the early classical period, with Haydn and Mozart well represented.

It was during his stay in Salem, in 1789, that Peter composed six quintets for two violins, two violas, and cello, upon which his reputation as an instrumental composer chiefly rests. All but one are in three movements. There is a curious discrepancy between the virtuosity required by the violin and first viola parts and the lack of technical difficulty in the second viola and cello parts. This was probably to make the music fit the skills of available performers. The quintets reveal considerable harmonic freedom and boldness in modulation, and at times they are even brilliant in execution.

Peter also composed sacred music, including more than 100 anthems and arias, mostly with instrumental accompaniment. Typical are the anthem "It Is a Precious Thing," for soprano, baritone, mixed chorus, and string orchestra (1772), and the aria "The Lord Is in His Holy Temple," for baritone (or soprano) and string orchestra (1786). The latter was written in Salem, presumably for that town's leading soprano, Catherine Leinbach, who became the composer's wife and accompanied him when he returned to Bethlehem in 1790.

John Antes (1740–1811) was the first native-born American among the early Moravian composers. However, although he was born and raised in Pennsylvania, he spent his adult life in Germany, Egypt (as a missionary), and England. In Egypt, where he went in 1769, he suffered hardship, peril, and cruel punishment because of his missionary activities. In England, where he lived from 1781, pursuing various occupations, he composed arias, anthems, chorales, and three trios for two violins and cello, which rank with the best music of the Moravian pioneers. Although he regarded himself as an amateur or dilettante, Antes was a capable musician and a gifted composer. He is well remembered for the soprano aria "Go, Congregation, Go!" and the anthem for mixed chorus and string orchestra "Surely He Has Borne Our Griefs" (text from Isaiah 54:4–5).

The roster of Moravian composers in America is impressive. Besides those already mentioned, the list includes Johannes Herbst (1735–1812), Jeremiah Dencke (1725–95), Simon Peter (1743–1819), David Moritz Michael (1751–1827), Georg Gottfried Müller (1762–1821), Johann Christian Bechler (1784–1857), Peter Wolle (1792–1871), Francis F. Hagen (1815–1907), and Edward W. Leinbach (1823–1901). Thus for more than a century and a half there was an unbroken tradition, with a cohesion and continuity unmatched in the annals of American musical composition.

The industry and dedication of the Moravians in preserving and handing down to posterity the immense holdings of their musical archives is also impressive. Bishop Johannes Herbst, besides writing more than 100 hymns, formed an immense manuscript collection of music during his stay in the Moravian settlement of Lancaster, Pennsylvania, from 1787 to 1811. In the latter year he went as bishop to Salem, bringing his collection with him. At his death it was deposited in the church archives, and in 1977 the entire contents, totaling 11,447 pages, was made available on microfiche and rollfilm.[16] While a number of Moravian composers are represented, the bulk of the music is by European composers whose works were regularly performed at settlements such as Bethlehem, Lancaster, and Salem. The last-named, in the course of time, has become the chief center for the preservation of a Moravian musical heritage, largely through the dedicated efforts of the Moravian Music Foundation. Among the fifty-eight composers whose works are included in the Herbst collection are C. P. E. Bach, Gluck, Grétry, Handel, Hasse, and Haydn, along with other less famous names. Among the Moravians, Herbst and J. F. Peter are well represented.

Although the Moravians did not participate in the War of Independence because bearing arms was contrary to their religious convictions, they responded enthusiastically when Governor Martin of North Carolina issued the following proclamation, dated "the 18th day of June in the year 1783":

> Whereas the honorable the General Assembly have by a Resolution of both Houses recommended to me to appoint the fourth of July next being the anniversary of the declaration of the American Independence, as a Day of Solemn Thanksgiving to Almighty God, for the many most glorious interpositions of his Providence manifested in a great and signal manner in behalf of these United States. . . . For conducting them gloriously and triumphantly through a just and necessary War, and putting an end to the calamities thereof by the restoration of Peace. . . . And for all other divine favors bestowed on the Inhabitants of the United States and this in particular.
>
> In conformity with the pious intentions of the Legislature I have thought proper to issue this my Proclamation directing that the said 4th Day of July next be observed as above, hereby strictly commanding and enjoining all the Good Citizens of this State to set apart the said Day from bodily labour, and employ the same in devout and religious exercises. . . .[17]

Besides the desire to identify themselves fully with their adopted land, the Moravians in Salem must have welcomed the tone of religious piety in the governor's proclamation. As far as the records reveal, they were the only community to respond with a formally organized and impressive program of celebration. In keeping with both the governor's admonitions and their own convictions, the day-long program they presented consisted of "devout and religious exercises," with the main music offering described as a "Psalm of Joy" ("Freudenpsalm"—all the texts were sung in German). J. F. Peter took the initiative in preparing the program and conducted the vocal and instrumental performers in *A Psalm of Joy,* which consisted of seventeen numbers, including chorales, anthems, and recitatives. Most of these were traditional, some were of unknown authorship, and several were by Moravian composers.[18]

After this joyous celebration, which is believed to be the first formal celebration of Independence Day, the music was returned to the Salem archives, where it remained for the next 183 years, unperformed. In the words of Karl Kroeger:

> By then everything but the fact that the celebration had taken place was forgotten. In 1966 as a part of the festivities of the 200th anniversary of the Founding of Salem, it was decided to try to reconstruct the Fourth of July celebration. . . . Starting with only the words, the young musicologist Marilyn P. Gombosi located, authenticated, and pieced together anthems, chorales, and solos until the whole Psalm stood complete and performable. It

turned out to be a beautifully constructed and dramatically moving cantata of praise and thanksgiving that is as appropriate to be performed today as it was nearly 200 years ago.[19]

By this time the Moravian Music Foundation, through its concerts (many of them conducted by Thor Johnson, 1913–75), publications, research projects, and recordings, had firmly established the prestige of the Moravian pioneer enterprise as a significant contribution to America's musical heritage.

Notes

1. *Diary of Cotton Mather* 2:169.
2. *Journal of the Rev. John Wesley* 1:114.
3. Ibid., p. 146.
4. Ibid., pp. 475–76.
5. Thomas Cuming Hall, *The Religious Background of American Culture*, p. 154.
6. For a version of this hymn (also known as "Over the Corpse of a Believer") as sung "by a deacon and deaconess of the Hard-Shell Baptists in Clay, County, Ky., in 1937," see John Avery Lomax and Alan Lomax, *Our Singing Country*, pp. 38–39.
7. Louis F. Benson, *The English Hymn*, p. 285.
8. George Pullen Jackson, *White and Negro Spirituals*, p. 19.
9. Ibid., p. 20.
10. Quoted in George H. Bost, "Samuel Davies," p. 185.
11. Quoted in *Church Music and Musical Life in Pennsylvania* 1:11.
12. Quoted in ibid., p. 173.
13. Ibid., pp. 21–165; reproduced in facsimile, including an English translation by Dr. Christopher Witt.
14. Beissel's short treatise forms part of the *Vorrede* (preface) to *Das Gesang der einsamen und verlassenen Turtel-Taube, nemlich der christlichen Kirche* (Ephrata, 1747). The title "dissertation on harmony" first appears in an English translation of the preface, found in Julius F. Sachse, *Music of the Ephrata Cloister*.
15. *Church Music and Musical Life in Pennsylvania* 2:40.
16. A combined project of University Music Editions and the Moravian Music Foundation.
17. Marilyn Gombosi, *A Day of Solemn Thanksgiving*, p. 17.
18. The music and texts (German with English translations) are reproduced in ibid.
19. Karl Kroeger, liner notes to *A Psalm of Joy*, Moravian Music Foundation MMF 001.

Chapter 4
The African Presence

... if the Negro represents, or is symbolic of, something in
and about the nature of American culture, this certainly should
be revealed by his characteristic music.
—LeRoi Jones, *Blues People* (1963)

From the early seventeenth century, African presence made itself felt in
North America through "the peculiar institution" of chattel slavery that
provided the economic basis for several of the newly established colonies.
Dutch ships landed a few Africans in Virginia as early as 1619, and thereafter the slave trade grew rapidly. By 1727 there were more than 75,000 Africans in the North American British colonies, and by 1790 there were more
than ten times that number in the United States. By 1800 there were over a
million blacks, who formed nearly 19 percent of the population. Of these,
more than 100,000 were free—a significant fact to bear in mind. Such was
the inevitable growth of a socioeconomic system that was to have a profound effect on the history and culture of the American nation.

To speak of "African" music as a whole is a tremendous oversimpli-
fication. A recent book on the music of Africa lists 137 different ethnic
groups occupying that vast continent—and the list is not exhaustive! To
generalize, therefore, is to oversimplify a highly complex situation. Nevertheless, our purpose is to summarize the basic traits of traditional African
music in a broad cultural context, with emphasis on the period pertaining
to the institution of slavery in America.

Although some slaves were taken from East Africa (Mozambique in
particular), most slaves shipped to the New World came from the coastal
area of West Africa, from Angola to the Ivory Coast, including Nigeria,
Dahomey (now Benin), and the western Congo (now Zaire). This region was mainly inhabited by the Ashanti, Dahomean, Yoruba, Bini, and
Congo tribes. Most of the African cultural retentions in America can be

traced to these linguistic groups. It should be noted, however, that there was a great deal of cultural interaction in the music and dance of black Africa, including a significant input from the Islamic cultures of the Mediterranean.

Song was the characteristic musical expression of black Africa. There were songs for every occasion: marriages and funerals, ceremonies and festivals, love and war, work and worship. The African expressed all feelings through song, taunting enemies or rivals with songs of derision, propitiating the deities with a ritual of sacred songs and dances. Singing accompanied labor in the fields, on the rivers, in the household, and in communal tasks. The many dances—social, ceremonial, ritualistic, warlike—were usually accompanied by singing, as well as by the ubiquitous battery of drum and other percussive instruments providing a strong and complex rhythmic foundation.

The alternation between solo and chorus is a fundamental trait of West African singing. This is the "call-and-response" type of song that has been carried over into Afro-American music. As Richard Waterman writes:

> While antiphonal song-patterning, whereby a leader sings phrases which alternate with phrases sung by a chorus, is known all over the world, nowhere else is this form so important as in Africa, where almost all songs are constructed in this manner. A peculiarity of the African call-and-response pattern, found but infrequently elsewhere, is that the chorus phrase regularly commences while the soloist is still singing; the leader, on his part, begins his phrase before the chorus has finished. This phenomenon is quite simply explained in terms of the African musical tradition of the primacy of rhythm. The entrance of the solo or the chorus part on the proper beat of the measure is the important thing, not the effects attained through antiphony or polyphony. Examples of call-and-response music in which the solo part, for one reason or another, drops out for a time, indicate clearly that the chorus part, rhythmical and repetitive, is the mainstay of the songs and the one really inexorable component of their rhythmic structure. The leader, receiving solid rhythmic support from the metrically accurate, rolling repetition of phrases by the chorus, is free to embroider as he will.[1]

Certain peculiarities of intonation and of melodic practice in African song were long regarded by outsiders as "weird," a characterization on which W. E. Ward elaborates: "The 'weird' intervals are most noticeable at the beginning and end of the tune or of a phrase. Now it is at these places that the African, instead of endeavouring to end or begin his phrase on a pure note as any European singer would, allows himself to slide on to the note or down from it. It seems to be left to the individual to decide the range of the slide, and whether to approach the note from above or below. A final note is always quitted in a downward slide."[2]

Rejecting the hypothesis of an "African" scale of fractional or microtonal intervals, Ward believes that "African melodies are essentially diatonic in structure, modified by a liberal, and unregulated, use of portamento" (i.e., sliding from one note to another).[3] Waterman also asserts the diatonic character of the African scale and remarks that "the tendency toward variable intonation of the third and seventh of the scale has occasionally been noted in West African music."[4] The diatonic scale with ambiguous intonation of the third and seventh degrees—usually somewhat flattened—is the so-called blues scale of American popular music.

A fundamental trait of African music is to have several rhythms going on simultaneously. Every piece of African music has at least two or three rhythms, sometimes four or five. A frequent combination is with two percussion parts, one of which may be the clapping of hands, and one vocal part with its own metrical pattern. Often there are several metrical patterns in the percussion, played by drums of different sizes. Confusion is avoided by a fundamental underlying beat that never varies. If there are several drums, this regular beat is played by the largest drum. The diverse rhythms of all the other instruments must coincide on the first beat of the fundamental rhythm. Rhythm in African music, therefore, is conceived as a combination of time patterns that coincide at a given moment.

In a recording of Gold Coast drums with gong, the following combination of rhythms appear, with the basic beat of the drum in 3/4 and that of the gong in 6/8 (in the background a second drum is heard in another rhythm, with what Waterman describes as "a fluttering beat in 12/8 time"— a rhythmic pattern frequently found in African music):[5]

The following example of an African song with accompaniment of hand clapping will further illustrate some of the varied rhythmical patterns of this music:[6]

The "metronome sense" is cited by Waterman as crucial for the understanding of African music:

> From the point of view of the listener, it entails habits of conceiving any music as structured along a theoretical framework of beats regularly spaced in time and of co-operating in terms of overt or inhibited motor behavior with the pulses of this metric pattern whether or not the beats are expressed in actual melodic or percussion tones. Essentially, this simply means that African music, with few exceptions, is to be regarded as music for the dance, although the "dance" involved may be entirely a mental one. Since this metronome sense is of such basic importance, it is obvious that the music is conceived and executed in terms of it; it is assumed without question or consideration to be part of the perceptual equipment of both musicians and listeners and is, in the most complete way, taken for granted. When the beat is actually sounded, it serves as a confirmation of this subjective beat.[7]

A grasp of this fundamental concept underlying the traditional values of African music enables us to understand how and why the Afro-American influence has had such a tremendous impact on the dance music of the Western world.

Notwithstanding the differences in the concept of rhythm that have been pointed out, there is a basis of unity between African and European music. The diatonic scale is common to both systems, as well as an elementary concept of harmony. Some significant differences, however, have been pointed out by J. H. Kwabena Nketia:

> In African musical practice, the areas of tolerance of pitch variation for particular steps of the scale are much larger than those of traditions that base their music on a fixed pitch. . . . The structure of melodies built out of these scales is based on the controlled use of selected interval sequences. Thinking in

terms of these sequences, which reflect melodic processes rather than the scales as constructs, gives one a greater insight into the usages that guide performers, for the patterns formed by these sequences are used in creating new songs or for varying existing materials when the situation demands it.[8]

These practices and patterns are clearly reflected in Afro-American music, from work songs and spirituals to blues and jazz.

Black Africans were brought to America for the purpose of enforced labor. That truism is stated to remind the reader of what is equally obvious: that the desire to sing while working was a prime impulse for the growth of Afro-American folksong. In spite of the horrible and cruel conditions under which the blacks were transported to America, it was not in the interest of the slave traders to let their human cargo pine and die. Hence, to improve morale and spirit, singing and dancing were imposed on the miserable captives. In 1700 Thomas Starks of London directed the captain of the *Africa* to take on a cargo of 450 slaves, and he added a typical admonition: "Make your Negroes cheerful and pleasant makeing them dance at the Beating of your Drum, etc." It was said that "slave captains preferred happy tunes"—perhaps so as not to be reminded of the suffering they inflicted—and "frequently would resort to whips to exact their preference."

While European instruments such as bagpipes and fiddles were often carried on board for compulsory recreation, some slavers acquired native African instruments for this purpose—not out of consideration but because they might be more effective. Here is an account from 1801: "In the intervals between their meals they [the slaves] are encouraged to divert themselves with music and dancing; for which purpose such rude and uncouth instruments as are used in Africa, are collected for their departure. . . ."[9] The writer, of course, scorned a description of such "rude and uncouth instruments." Another chronicler, however, was a little more specific: "Their music, upon these occasions, consists of a drum, sometimes with only one head; and when that is worn out, they do not scruple to make use of the bottom of one of the tubs. . . . The poor wretches are frequently compelled to sing also; but when they do so, their songs are generally, as may naturally be expected, melancholy lamentations of their exile from their native country."[10]

The blacks in the New World would have ample occasion for cultivating many other "songs of sorrow" for generations to come. But nothing could destroy their ingenuity and persistence in retaining vital aspects of their African heritage and in adapting these to the harsh conditions of their new environment. In no aspect was this persistent ingenuity and creative transformation more evident than in the scope and power of Afro-American music.

Thomas Jefferson, in his *Notes on the State of Virginia,* expressed admiration for the musical gifts of the Negroes and added that "the instrument proper to them is the Banjar, which they brought hither from Africa. . . ."[11] That was but one of the many names for the instrument that came to be known in America as the banjo; but all the variants point to a common African origin: banza, bangil, banjer, bangelo, banjor, bangoe, banshaw, etc. The one exception appears to be "merry-wang," by which name the instrument was known in Jamaica. It would be a wise scholar indeed who could tell a merry-wang from a banshaw.

In 1620 an English sea captain, Richard Jobson, was sent to Africa by a London trading company to explore the region of the Gambra River. Three years later he published an account of his travels, including a description of African musical instruments and their use on ceremonial occasions. "There is without doubt," he wrote, "no people on the earth more naturally affected to the sound of musicke than these people." He goes on to describe an instrument "which is most common in use," and that appears to be a prototype of the banjar. "[It] is made of a great gourd, and a necke thereunto fastened, resembling in some sort, our Bandora; but they have no manner of fret, and the strings are such as the place yeeldes or their invention can attaine to make, being very unapt to yeeld a sweete and musicall sound, notwithstanding with pinnes they winde and bring to agree in tunable notes, having not above sixe strings upon their greatest [largest] instrument."[12]

There are many descriptions of the banjar-banjo in the New World, all agreeing on the main features while differing slightly in details of construction and the materials used. It was this flexibility (and resourcefulness) in construction that facilitated the widespread use of the banjo among blacks in America, for they could use whatever materials were at hand to serve the purpose. The most common procedure was to take a large gourd or calabash, scoop out the seeds, and cut the bowl away so as to make it level with a long handle or neck that was attached to it. Over the bowl, tightly stretched, was some kind of animal skin, dried or tanned; in North America this was usually coonskin. Four strings, made of any suitable material at hand, were passed over the bridge, placed near the center of the drum-head, and attached to the neck at various points to produce different pitches. According to Jefferson, the banjar of his day was tuned to correspond with the four lower strings of the guitar: E–A–d–g. It was played by plucking or strumming with the fingers.

The banjo will reappear frequently in the course of America's music, for it has never ceased to have an important role, from the plantation to the minstrel show, from ragtime to jazz, from folk music to bluegrass. It has had its influence on art music, too, beginning with Heinrich's *Negro's Banjo Quickstep* and Gottschalk's *The Banjo*. It was a seedbed for countless syncopated tunes that would be heard around the world.

Drums, of course, have always been important in the music of Africa; and had their use not been prohibited in the British colonies of North America, they would certainly have provided a continuous and conspicuous retention of African traditions in the United States—as was the case, notably, in Brazil and in the French and Spanish West Indies. This is not to say that African traditions in drumming have not had a significant influence in North America, but rather that—unlike the banjo, which has had an unbroken continuity throughout our history—Afro-American drumming styles did not make their full impact until the rise of jazz in the first decades of the twentieth century.

In the British colonies of North America, the use of drums by slaves was forbidden because drumming could signal uprisings and other disturbances. But in Louisiana, and particularly New Orleans, with its Franco-Hispanic cultural heritage and large influx of "persons of color" from the West Indies, public dancing by blacks, accompanied by singing and African-type instruments, including drums, was tolerated at least through the early decades of the nineteenth century.

According to the general custom, Sunday was when blacks could assemble in New Orleans for their dances and festivities in public places. At first the levee appears to have been the favorite place for blacks to congregate. A visitor in 1799, strolling on the edge of town, saw "vast numbers of negro slaves, men, women, and children, assembled together on the levee . . . dancing, in large rings."[13] In 1808 a traveler, Christian Schultz, caught sight of "twenty different dancing groups," which he described as follows: "They have their own national music, consisting for the most part of a long kind of narrow drum of various sizes, from two to eight feet in length, three or four of which make a band. The principal dancers or leaders are dressed in a variety of wild and savage fashions, always ornamented with a number of the tails of the smaller wild beasts. . . ."[14]

Because Schultz writes of this gathering as taking place in the rear of the city, he was probably referring to Congo Square (originally called Circus Square) at Rampart and Orleans streets, on the edge of the old French Quarter or *Vieux Carré*. By a law passed in 1817, public dancing by blacks was restricted to Congo Square on Sundays before sundown, under police supervision. While the civil authorities were concerned about maintaining law and order (openly flouted by most inhabitants), the ecclesiastical authorities did not oppose dancing on Sunday, for the Catholic church was liberal in this respect.

The architect and engineer Benjamin Henry Latrobe, who visited New Orleans in 1819, has left us the following account of dancing in Congo Square:

> In going up St. Peters Street & approaching the common I heard a most extraordinary noise, which I supposed to proceed from some horse mill, the horses trampling on a wooden floor. I found, however, on emerging from the houses onto the Common, that it proceeded from a crowd of 5 or 600 persons assembled in an open space or public square. I went to the spot & crowded near enough to see the performance. All those who were engaged in the business seemed to be *blacks*. I did not observe a dozen yellow faces. They were formed into circular groupes in the midst of four of which, which I examined (but there were more of them), was a ring, the largest not 10 feet in diameter. In the first were two women dancing. They held each a coarse handkerchief extended by the corners in their hands, & *set* to each other in a miserably dull & slow figure, hardly moving their feet or bodies. The music consisted of two drums and a stringed instrument. An old man sat astride of a cylindrical drum about a foot in diameter, & beat it with incredible quickness with the edge of his hand & fingers. The other drum was an open staved thing held between the knees & beaten in the same manner. They made an incredible noise. The most curious instrument, however, was a stringed instrument which no doubt was imported from Africa. On the top of the finger board was the rude figure of a man in a sitting posture, & two pegs behind him to which the strings were fastened. The body was a calabash. It was played upon by a very little old man, apparently 80 or 90 years old.
>
> The women squalled out a burthen to the playing at intervals, consisting of two notes, as the negroes, working in our cities, respond to the song of their leader. Most of the circles contained the same sort of dancers. One was larger, in which a ring of a dozen women walked, by way of dancing, round the music in the center. But the instruments were of a different construction. One, which from the color of the wood seemed new, consisted of a block cut into something of the form of a cricket bat with a long & deep mortice down the center. This thing made a considerable noise, being beaten lustily on one side by a short stick. In the same orchestra was a square drum, looking like a stool, which made an abominably loud noise; also a calabash with a round

hole in it, the hole studded with brass nails, which was beaten by a woman with two short sticks.

A man sung an uncouth song to the dancing which I suppose was in some African language, for it was not French, & the women screamed a detestable burthen on one single note. The allowed amusements of Sunday have, it seems, perpetuated here those of Africa among its inhabitants. I have never seen anything more brutally savage, and at the same time dull & stupid, than this whole exhibition. Continuing my walk about a mile along the canal, & returning after Sunset near the same spot, the noise was still heard. There was not the least disorder among the crowd, nor do I learn on enquiry, that these weekly meetings of the negroes have ever produced any mischief.[15]

In spite of its obvious cultural (rather than racial) prejudice, Latrobe's account is valuable for its recognition of the African character of the dancing, singing, and instruments he sketched as a trained artist. Latrobe's observations are all the more important because they were made at the moment when the Africanism of the Congo Square festivities was about to be diluted by various developments, such as growing opposition from civic leaders and the increasing Americanization of New Orleans, including an influx of acculturated blacks from other parts of the United States.

Dancing in Congo Square was sporadic after 1820. When occasionally revived, as on a Sunday in June 1845, its character had changed, as indicated by a reporter who wrote of "regular Ethiopian Breakdowns" and such songs as "Hey Jim Along Josey" and "Get Along Home You Yellow Gals."[16] This smacks less of Africa than of American minstrelsy.

French travelers of the eighteenth century, in particular, have left us detailed descriptions of African dances and drums that were prevalent in the West Indies, whence they were in all probability transmitted to Louisiana. The Dominican monk Jean-Baptiste Labat published in 1724 his *Nouveau voyage aux isles de l'Amérique,* referring to his experiences during the years 1693–1705. Writing of the blacks in the French Antilles, he remarks: "The dance is their favorite passion; I do not believe that there is any people in the world who are more fond of it than they."[17]

Labat goes on to say that the dance which pleases them most is the *calenda,* from the coast of Guinea, which was accompanied by drums made from hollowed tree trunks, with one end open and the other covered with the skin of a sheep or goat (with the hair removed, and smoothed like parchment). The larger drum was three to four feet long and fifteen or sixteen inches in diameter. The smaller, called *baboula,* was approximately the same length, with a diameter of eight to nine inches. The players held the drums between their legs, or sat on top of them, and struck them with their fingers. The large drum kept a steady and measured beat, while the *baboula* produced a fast and irregular beat. It was also loud and high-pitched. The dancers and spectators (who might alternate) reinforced the ensemble with hand clapping and singing.

Labat also describes another dance of African origin, attributed to the blacks of the Congo, but to which he gives no name. The dancers, both men and women, form a circle and, without budging from their places, do nothing but raise their feet and strike them on the ground in a kind of ca-dence, while keeping their bodies in a half-bowed position facing each other. Meanwhile they mumble the words of a story that one of the com-pany is telling, to which they reply at intervals with a chorus, while the on-lookers clap their hands. Labat comments: "Cette danse n'a rien qui choque la pudeur [like the indecent *calenda!*], mais aussi elle est très-peu di-vertissante."[18] Evidently it never occurred to him that this ceremony might have a religious significance for black Africans—hence was not meant to en-tertain a French friar.

What Labat described was an African circle dance of the type that came to be called "ring shout" in North America, in which the "shouters" moved in a circle with a shuffling step. Something like this is alluded to by Labat when he remarks that "les Negres Mines dansent en tournant en rond, le visage hors du cercle qu'ils décrivent."[19] That is, the participants moved in a circle while facing outward.

The character of the "ring shout" could be modified by circumstances. For example, when straitlaced masters in North America forbade their slaves to dance, the latter would move as fast as they could in the "ring shout" and still give the appearance that they were not dancing.

The French writer and statesman Moreau de Saint-Méry, who spent some time in the West Indies as well as in the United States, gave consider-able attention to African dances and instruments in a descriptive work about the island colony of Santo Domingo, published in Philadelphia in 1797. In some instances he follows Labat so closely that one is tempted to suspect pla-giarism; however, he supplies additional information. He writes, for exam-ple, about a dance of African origin, the *chica,* which he says is called the *calenda* in the Windward Islands and the *congo* in Cayenne.

If the same dance has different names in different places, this obvi-ously complicates the task of knowing what dance is meant when it is men-tioned without description. From early accounts it appears that *calenda* (or *kalenda*) was a generic term for either the dance or the assembly of dancers. Later the name was attached to this or that dance by various writers. Moreau de Saint-Méry, for example, thus describes the *calenda:*

> The dancers, male and female, always equal in number, come to the middle of a circle . . . and they begin to dance. Each male dancer chooses a partner to cut a figure before her. This . . . consists of a movement in which each foot is successively thrust forward and then backward, while rapidly striking the ground, now with the toe, now with the heel, in a manner somewhat similar to that of the *Anglaise* [heel-and-toe step]. The dancer turns on himself or around his partner, who turns also, and changes place while waving the two ends of a handkerchief that she holds. The dancer alternately raises and lowers his arms while keeping the elbows near the body and the hand almost closed. This dance, to which the play of the eyes is anything but foreign, is lively and animated, and an exact timing lends it real grace.[20]

Again the observer insists on the importance of *timing*. In this connection it is interesting to compare what an African scholar of our time writes about this aspect of music and the dance in Africa: "So much in African music depends on coming in or leaving off at the right moment or maintaining the values of durational units that a sense of time is not only desirable but absolutely necessary. This sense of time is closely linked with the dance, with the concept of the beat as a regulative factor in songs in strict rhythm."[21]

Moreau de Saint-Méry's descriptions are important not only for their authentic historical context, but also because of the notoriety and influence they have acquired in the musical history of the United States through the use made of them by the Louisiana writer George W. Cable in his too-often-quoted article "The Dance in Place Congo."[22] Because Cable does not mention his sources, the uninformed reader is unaware that what he is reading is either lifted verbatim from Moreau de Saint-Méry or is embroidered or paraphrased for literary (and sensational) effect. Cable aimed to titillate the sedate readers of the *Century Magazine,* not to write history (his forte was fiction).

Nevertheless, there is authentic evidence from other sources that the *bamboula, calenda, congo,* and *counjai* were danced in Louisiana and in other parts of the United States at least until the 1820s. But the eyewitness accounts are factual and descriptive, hence have not achieved the notoriety of Cable's fictionized hodgepodge.

Along with drums (when permitted), a wide variety of improvised percussion instruments, and the basic banjar, blacks in America used an assortment of traditional instruments such as the quills (a kind of panpipe); the notched gourd with a scraper (similar to the *güiro*); the jawbone of a horse or an ass, scraped with a wire or a stick to make the teeth rattle; and a dried gourd filled with pebbles or seeds, used as a rattle attached to a stick. The resourcefulness and ingenuity of the blacks in improvising sound-makers from almost any material at hand are proverbial. I myself, while living in New Orleans, have often been treated to a fascinating rhythmic toccata performed by a black expert slapping his shoe-shining rag on leather.

The poet-musician Sidney Lanier (1842–81), who was born and raised in the South, has left us a firsthand account of the intricacy of rhythmic patterns used by the blacks:

> Perhaps the very earliest form of marking-off rhythms is . . . the "patting" of the Southern negroes. This method of indicating rhythms merely with the interplay of strokes between hands and thighs, feet and floor, is capable of a considerable degree of complexity; and I remember when a boy among the Southern plantations to have seen negroes excited to a frenzy of delight in dancing to no other music than that purely rhythmical form of it afforded by the patting of hands and feet. [The so-called "patting juba."] The degree of what musicians call "attack," and the intensity of a certain fiery indescribable spirit . . . which these strange people exhibit in their patting dances by a lightwood fire when the day's work is done, would be, I think, almost incredible to one who has never seen them.[23]

Moreau de Saint-Méry describes (almost verbatim) the same types of drums mentioned by Labat, but he also mentions the so-called thumb piano, a plucked idiophone known in Africa as *mbira* or *sanza*, which has been documented in North America. As for European instruments, he writes that the violin was the favorite of the blacks and that many of them are good violinists because they have such a fine ear: "Most of them learn to play by ear, quickly memorizing any tune they hear." They also mastered such European instruments as the clarinet, oboe, and French horn.

Because we have stressed percussive or plucked instruments, it should not be supposed that wind instruments were unknown in Africa. They were, on the contrary, very important; but in America horns and trumpets were forbidden to the slaves for the same reason as drums: they were regarded as too suitable for signaling and calling to arms. Exception was made, however, for trusted household slaves, who played for private dances and public balls and often brought extra income to their masters.

We read, for instance, of the black musician Sy Gilliat, who as the body servant to Lord Botecourt, governor of Virginia, also served as the of-

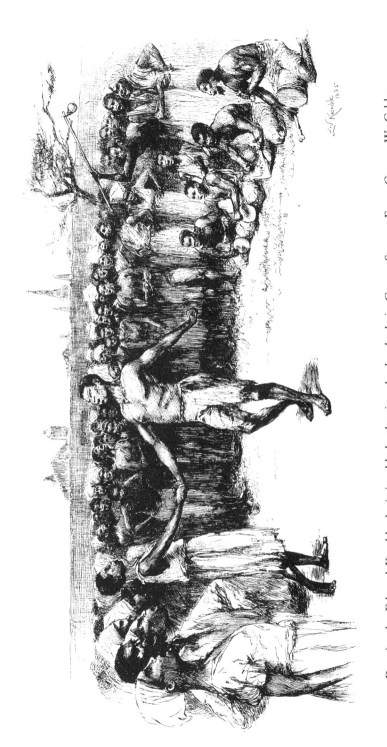

Drawing by Edward Kemble depicting blacks dancing the *bamboula* in Congo Square. From George W. Cable, "Creole Slave Dances: The Dance in Place Congo," *Century Illustrated Monthly Magazine* (Feb. 1886).

ficial fiddler at state balls in Williamsburg. His dress included an embroidered silk coat and vest of faded lilac, silk stockings, and shoes with large buckles. He also wore a powdered wig, and his manners were said to be "as courtly as his dress."²⁴ Another black musician, known as "London Brigs," who became Gilliat's assistant after the capital was moved to Richmond, was reputed to be equally skillful on the flute and the clarinet: "All sorts of capers were cut to the music of Si. Gilliat's fiddle, and the flute or clarionet of his blacker comrade, London Brigs. Contra dances followed and sometimes a congo, or a hornpipe; and when 'the music grew fast and furious' . . . a jig would wind up the evening."²⁵

Mention of the *congo* as a social dance in colonial Richmond arouses our curiosity and also points to a gap in our knowledge of what influence the music and dancing of blacks may have had upon white society in eighteenth-century America. Further research might indicate a continuity from the *congo* to the cakewalk and thence to the whole sequence of social dances in duple time, with and without syncopation, that proliferated in the early decades of the twentieth century, dances such as the Turkey Trot, Charleston, and Lindy Hop. We know that by the early nineteenth century many blacks had become adept at dancing the jig with their own improvisations and variations. There was certainly a process of acculturation that still needs to be investigated and documented.²⁶ In our present state of knowledge we can scarcely even look through a keyhole, so to speak, to see what "sorts of capers were cut" in American ballrooms when the black fiddler's music "grew fast and furious."

Another clue to follow up would be the remarks made by an observer in 1818 about the celebrated bandleader and composer Frank Johnson (1792–1844), "a descendant of Africa," who was much in demand to provide music for the ballrooms of white society, from New York to Virginia: "In fine, he is the leader of the band at all balls, public and private; . . . inventor-general of cotillions; to which add, a remarkable taste in distorting a sentimental, simple, and beautiful song, into a reel, jig, or country dance."²⁷

While slave owners were concerned that the blacks should not rise up in rebellion, missionaries were concerned that they should not go down to Hell. To lead them to Heaven it was essential to rid them of their "heathen" beliefs and practices, and the singing of psalms and hymns was found to be especially effective for this purpose.

In this Christian enterprise the missionaries generally had little support from the slave owners. The Reverend Samuel Davies, Presbyterian evangelist and champion of religious tolerance, who was active in Virginia during the 1750s, deplored "the almost universal neglect of the many thousands of slaves . . . [who] generally continue heathens in a Christian country."[28] These conditions were to change gradually, through the efforts of zealous missionaries and increasing cooperation from slave owners.

In 1755 Davies wrote to a friend in London, telling of his work among the blacks and asking for books, especially Bibles and Watts's psalms and hymns: "They are exceedingly delighted with Watts's *Songs,* and I cannot but observe, that the negroes, above all of the human species I ever knew, have the nicest ear for music. They have a kind of ecstatic delight in psalmody; nor are there any books they so soon learn, or take so much pleasure in, as those used in that heavenly part of divine worship."[29]

As we shall observe in later chapters, the blacks absorbed these elements of eighteenth-century Anglo-American psalmody and hymnody while retaining many vocal traits from their African heritage. There was, to begin with, a considerable similarity between the lining out practice of demotic psalmody in America and the overlapping leader-and-chorus patterns of African song. Thus, there was both assimilation and transformation in the development of a distinctive Afro-American style of religious singing.

Folklorist Alan Lomax, discussing "The Homogeneity of African-Afro-American Musical Style," writes as follows: "In spite of the fact that blacks in the American colonies learned the various musical languages of their masters, they always adapted these novel musical devices to their ongoing black African stylistic practices. . . . Afro-American music, considered as a whole, is a sub-system of a continental Black African style tradition that seems to be one of the most ancient, consistent, and fertile of world musical families."[30] The vital African elements in America's music indeed bear witness to the fertile impact of a deeply rooted tradition.

Notes

1. Richard A. Waterman, "African Influence on the Music of the Americas," in *Acculturation in the Americas,* ed. Sol Tax, p. 214.
2. William E. Ward, "Music of the Gold Coast," p. 707.
3. Ibid.
4. Waterman, "African Influence," pp. 214–15.
5. Richard A. Waterman, "Laboratory Notes on Tribal, Folk and Cafe Music

70 *America's Music*

of West Africa," *Tribal, Folk and Cafe Music of West Africa,* ed. Arthur S. Alberts, with texts and commentaries by Melville J. Herskovits, Duncan Emrich, Richard A. Waterman, and Marshall W. Stearns (New York: Field Recordings, 1950), p. 7.

6. Nicholas Ballanta-Taylor, *Saint Helena Island Spirituals,* p. x.

7. Waterman, "African Influence," p. 211.

8. J. H. Kwabena Nketia, *The Music of Africa,* p. 147.

9. Bryan Edwards, *The History, Civil and Commercial, of the British Colonies in the West Indies . . .,* 2 vols. (London: printed for J. Stockdale, 1793–1801), 2:116; quoted in Dena J. Epstein, *Sinful Tunes and Spirituals,* p. 14.

10. Alexander Falconbridge, *An Account of the Slave Trade on the Coast of Africa* (London, 1788); quoted in Epstein, *Sinful Tunes and Spirituals,* p. 14.

11. Thomas Jefferson, *Notes on the State of Virginia,* p. 288 n. 10.

12. Richard Jobson, *The Golden Trade; or, A Discovery of the River Gambra . . .* (London, 1623); quoted in Eileen Southern, ed., *Readings in Black American Music,* pp. 1–2.

13. Quoted in Epstein, *Sinful Tunes and Spirituals,* p. 84.

14. Christian Schultz, *Travels on an Inland Voyage* 2:197.

15. Benjamin Henry Latrobe, *Impressions Respecting New Orleans,* pp. 49–51.

16. Henry A. Kmen, "The Roots of Jazz and the Dance in Place Congo," p. 11.

17. Jean-Baptiste Labat, *Nouveau voyage aux isles de l'Amérique* 2:51–52: "La danse est leur passion favorite, je ne croi[s] pas qu'il y ait Peuple au monde qui y soit plus attaché qu'eux."

18. Ibid. 2:53.

19. Ibid.

20. [Médéric Louis Elie] Moreau de Saint-Méry, *Description topographique, physique, civile, politique et historique de la partie française de l'Isle Saint-Domingue* 1:45. (Author's translation)

21. J. H. Kwabena Nketia, *African Music in Ghana,* p. 87.

22. George W. Cable, "Creole Slave Dances: The Dance in Place Congo; with Arrangements of Creole Music by H. E. Krehbiel, Miss M. L. Bartlett, and John A. Broekhoven," *Century Illustrated Monthly Magazine* (Feb. 1886), pp. 517–32. Reproduced in Bernard Katz, ed., *The Social Implications of Early Negro Music,* pp. 31–47. Also includes "Creole Slave Songs," pp. 47–68 (text and music).

23. Sidney Lanier, *The Science of English Verse,* p. 247. Lanier also quotes the following from Shakespeare's *A Midsummer Night's Dream:* "I have a reasonable good ear in music: let's have the tongs and bones" (act 4, sc. 1).

24. Samuel Mordecai, *Virginia, Especially Richmond, in By-Gone Days,* p. 352.

25. Ibid., pp. 251–52

26. See Marshall W. Stearns and Jean Stearns, *Jazz Dance,* chap. 4, "The Patter of Diffusion," pp. 25–32.

27. Robert Waln [Peter Atall, Esq.], *The Hermit in America on a Visit to Philadelphia* (Philadelphia, 1819); quoted in Eileen Southern, *The Music of Black Americans,* p. 113.

28. William Henry Foote, *Sketches of Virginia, Historical and Biographical,* p. 292.

29. Quoted in *The Journal of the Rev. John Wesley* 4:125–26. See also *Letters from*

the Rev. *Samuel Davies and Others; Shewing the State of Religion in Virginia, South Carolina, &c., Particularly among the Negroes* (London: J. and W. Oliver, 1761); and Foote, *Sketches of Virginia, Historical and Biographical,* p. 286.

30. Alan Lomax, "The Homogeneity of African-Afro-American Musical Style," in *Afro-American Anthropology,* ed. Whitten and Szwed, p. 181.

Chapter 5

Gentlemen Amateurs

They would talk of nothing but high life, and high-lived company;
with other fashionable topics, such as pictures, taste, Shakespeare
and the musical glasses.
—Oliver Goldsmith, *The Vicar of Wakefield* (1761)

On October 11, 1760, the *South Carolina Gazette* carried the announcement
of "A Concert of Vocal and Instrumental Music" to be given in Charleston
with the assistance of "the Gentlemen who are the best Performers, both in
Town and Country." In the eighteenth century professional musicians
were not considered gentlemen. Hence this announcement, like many others of similar tenor that appeared in newspapers throughout the colonies,
refers to the participation of those "gentlemen amateurs" who practiced
music because they loved it and who played in public because in those days
there were not enough professional musicians in any American community
to make up a "full band." As a rule they played in semiprivate subscription
concerts such as those sponsored by the St. Cecilia Society of Charleston,
but when a worthy member of the musical profession gave a public "benefit" concert—that is, according to the custom of those times, a concert for
his own benefit—then the Gentlemen from Town and Country rallied gal-
lantly to his assistance with their fiddles, flutes, and hautboys. French
horns, clarinets, and even an occasional bassoon were not unknown; but
these were not regarded as particularly genteel instruments.

That the gentlemen amateurs had no prejudice against performing in
the theater is indicated by the following announcement in the *Pennsylvania
Gazette* of Philadelphia for November 30, 1769: "The Orchestra, on Opera
Nights, will be assisted by some musical Persons, who as they have no
View but to contribute to the Entertainment of the Public, certainly claim
a Protection from any Manner of Insult." This implies that the professionals, who were paid for their pains, had no recourse save to suffer the abuse
of the public if their efforts failed to please, while the amateurs claimed im-

munity from criticism by virtue of their voluntary service. Besides, *they* were Gentlemen—that is to say, social aristocrats.

In modern English-American dictionaries, *aristocrat* is defined as a member of the nobility or aristocracy. But the common secondary definition is more to our purpose: a person having the tastes, opinions, manners, and other characteristics of an upper class. This goes back to the Greek root, *aristos*, meaning "best" or "noblest." In the eighteenth century—and indeed ever since the Renaissance—this ideal was embodied in the concept of the "gentleman." It was an ideal consciously and deliberately cultivated, and many times defined and elaborated in treatises that were read by those whose economic and social situation permitted them to aspire to emulate the model with distinction. Such a work was Henry Peacham's *The Compleat Gentleman* (London, 1622), which included music, along with drawing, painting, heraldry, cosmography, and mathematics, as recommended studies.

While there were undoubtedly some "gentlemen" among the New England colonists, it was in the colonies to the south that the socioeconomic structure nurtured the growth of a hereditary ruling class, based on ownership of land and supported by the institution of chattel slavery. The landowning "aristocracy" of the South was not drawn from British nobility but consisted chiefly of self-made entrepreneurs who gained their fortunes through a combination of acumen, enterprise, and vested privilege. The English "country gentleman" served as a model for the landed gentry of the colonies. Wealth and property provided the foundation, and politics the chief mode of public activity, with learning, the "polite" arts, dancing, and other forms of sociability as the principal amenities of such a privileged mode of existence. Whatever the type of activity, the fundamental concept was that of *aristos:* the best that money could buy for a cultivated taste to enjoy.

William Byrd the younger (1674–1744) of Westover in Virginia, posthumously famous for his "Secret Diary" and his immense library, inherited from his father vast properties that he continually enlarged. In 1717 he listed his holdings as 43,000 acres and 220 slaves. An avid book collector, he had a library containing more than 3,600 titles, of which some 300 were in Greek and Latin. (Only Cotton Mather's library in Boston was of comparable size.) It included various music collections as well as Italian and English operas.[1] But there are very few references to music in his diary ("secret" because he wrote it in code). He mentions that he and his wife attended sessions held by the singing master of their church, in order to learn the "new way" of singing psalms.

Although the catalogue of William Byrd's library does not mention Playford, copies of his *Brief Introduction to the Skill of Musick* were in the libraries of two other Virginia gentlemen: Edmund Berkeley of Middlesex County and Ralph Wormeley II of "Rosegill" on the Rappahannock. The catalogue of Wormeley's library also lists "Experiments in Consort," without further identification.

A truly dedicated musical amateur among the landed gentry of Virginia was Councillor Robert Carter of Nomini Hall, grandson of Robert "King" Carter who left an estate of about 300,000 acres and 1,000 Negro slaves. Philip Vickers Fithian, who was a tutor at Nomini Hall, has left us an account of Carter's musical interests and accomplishments: "He has a good Ear for Music, a vastly delicate Taste: and keeps good Instruments, he has here at Home a *Harpsichord, Forte-Piano, Harmonica, Guittar* & *German Flutes,* & at Williamsburg, has a good *Organ,* he himself also is indefatigable in the Practice."[2]

Lest the mention of "Harmonica" evoke an unseemly image of Mr. Carter playing the mouth organ, let me explain that this was, according to a description in the councillor's notebook, an instrument invented by Mr. B. Franklin of Philadelphia, "being the musical glasses without water, framed into a complete instrument capable of thorough bass and never out of tune." We shall hear more about this wonderful invention. For the moment, simply pause to contemplate the edifying spectacle of a country squire who keeps "good instruments" as one might keep good horses, and who is as familiar with a "thorough bass" as with a thoroughbred. He is, moreover, reputed to have "a vastly delicate Taste"—than which there could be no higher compliment to a gentleman of the eighteenth century. Good taste was the touchstone of the age.

We take for granted the good taste of our colonial ancestors in architecture and interior decoration because we are familiar with the incontestable beauty of the homes, churches, and public buildings of that period. But until lately we were sadly ignorant about the musical taste of our eighteenth-century forebears because it was attested only by musty newspaper files, library inventories, and documental archives. Some time ago, however, the Williamsburg Festival Concerts revived the musical elegance and sophistication of that colonial capital, which knew the music of the best European composers such as Handel, Hasse, Vivaldi, Corelli, Galuppi, Pugnani, Boccherini, Rameau, Arne, Stamitz, the "London" Bach, and many others.[3]

Young Thomas Jefferson, while studying law at the College of Wil-

A Musical Gathering. Photo courtesy of the Nassau County Museum, Long Island, N.Y. (Museum Services Division, Department of Recreation and Parks).

liam and Mary in Williamsburg, belonged to the intimate circle of Governor Francis Fauquier, of whom he later wrote: "[The governor] was musical also, being a good performer, and associated me with two or three other amateurs in his weekly concerts."[4] Jefferson himself played the violin, and Robert Carter was the harpsichordist at these private concerts. Another music lover and good violinist was Lieutenant Governor John Penn of Pennsylvania, who gave private chamber music concerts at his home in Philadelphia every Sunday during the season. With his friend Francis Hopkinson, he was one of the chief promoters of musical activity in Philadelphia.

While there may have been more gentlemen of leisure in the South, there were musical amateurs everywhere, including New York and Boston. Both as performers and patrons, their role in the development of America's musical life was important.

Among the devotees of music none was more ardent than Thomas Jefferson, and none felt more keenly than he the deterioration in American musical activity during the Revolutionary War. Patriot though he was, he must have looked back wistfully on those halcyon days when, as a crony of Francis Fauquier, he joined in the governor's chamber music concerts. We know by his own confession that he gazed with intense longing upon the greener pastures of European musical life. In 1778 he wrote to a friend (probably a Frenchman), saying: "If there is a gratification which I envy any people in this world, it is your country its music."[5] Years later, when his diplomatic mission to France enabled him to savor this gratification at firsthand, he repeated the thought in a letter to Charles Bellini, a professor at the College of William and Mary, dated Paris, September 30, 1785: "Were I to proceed to tell you how much I enjoy their architecture, sculpture, painting, music, I should want words. It is in these arts they shine. The last of them particularly is an enjoiment, the deprivation of which with us, cannot be calculated. I am almost ready to say it is the only thing which from my heart I envy them, and which in spight of all the authority of the decalogue, I do covet."[6]

Can this passage be reconciled with the view that musical life in early America was not as crude and primitive as it has generally been depicted? I think it can. The concert programs so painstakingly unearthed and assembled by Sonneck prove that the music of the best European composers of that time was known and performed in America. But it would be hazardous to claim that the performances were on a par with the best that could be heard in Europe. Jefferson was thinking of Europe's finest: the Paris Opéra, the "Concerts Spirituels," and the English oratorio performances. Only the best, and a great deal of it, would satisfy his passion for music.

Had Jefferson been able to carry out a cherished idea, he would have created a small musical world of his own at Monticello. In the letter of 1778 from which I have already quoted, he outlined an ingenious scheme for providing himself with a private musical establishment somewhat after the manner of the European nobility:

> The bounds of an American fortune will not admit the indulgence of a domestic band of musicians, yet I have thought that a passion for music might be reconciled with that economy which we are obliged to observe. I retain for instance among my domestic servants a gardener . . . a weaver . . . a cabinet maker . . . and a stone cutter . . . to which I would add a vigneron. In a country where like yours music is cultivated and practised by every class of men I suppose there might be found persons of those trades who could perform on the French horn, clarinet or hautboy & bassoon, so that one might have a band of two French horns, two clarinets & hautboys and a bassoon, without enlarging their domestic expenses.[7]

Nothing seems to have come of the scheme, but the letter leaves no doubt that Jefferson knew what he wanted. He was not exaggerating when, in the same letter, he referred to music as "this favorite passion of my soul." The truth is that the father of American democracy was an aristocrat in his musical tastes. He courted the Muse like a *grand seigneur*.

Even though Jefferson's economic situation did not permit the luxury of a household "band," he compensated for this lack by performing frequently on the violin and by encouraging his womenfolk to make music for the household on the various keyboard instruments he bought for them, including harpsichords and pianos. He took intense interest in the mechanical and technical details of these instruments and acquired considerable expertise in their maintenance and repair. He also delighted in gadgetry and inventions of every kind. When he heard that a craftsman in Philadelphia had built a portable grand piano, he immediately ordered one for Monticello, only to learn that it was more portable than playable.

Jefferson accumulated a remarkably large and varied musical library that included theoretical, didactic, and historical works, as well as operas, cantatas, sacred music, song collections, and a quantity of instrumental music by composers such as Corelli, Vivaldi, Pergolesi, Gasparini, Handel,

Haydn, Stamitz, Boccherini, Giardini, and Pugnani. There was also a considerable amount of popular music such as ballad operas, two books of "Drinking Songs," country dances, and collections of "English, Scotch & Irish Airs."[8] Jefferson enjoyed playing fiddle tunes that he no doubt picked up by ear from country dances.

Among Jefferson's letters from Paris is one to Francis Hopkinson, dated July 6, 1785, which casts a sidelight on the musical inclinations of two prominent Philadelphians: "I communicated to Doctr. Franklin your idea of Mesmerising the Harpsichord. He has not tried it, probably because his affairs have been long packed & packing, as I do not play on that instrument I cannot try it myself. The Doctr. carries with him a pretty little instrument. It is the sticcado, with glass bars instead of wooden ones, and with keys applied to it. It's principal defect is the want of extent, having but three octaves. I wish you could exercise your ingenuity to give it an upper and lower octave. . . ."[9] These Americans of the eighteenth century were always exercising their ingenuity on something or other!

The reference to "Mesmerising the Harpsichord" concerns Hopkinson's improved method for "quilling" the harpsichord—a very ingenious device. The "pretty little instrument" that Dr. Franklin carried about with him was a sort of glass dulcimer, usually called "sticcado-pastorale." James Woodforde, in his *Diary of a Country Parson*, wrote that it looked, when covered, "like a working Box for Ladies."[10] So, what Dr. Franklin carried around in Paris was not necessarily a dispatch box full of state papers.

Franklin also played the guitar, the harp, and the violin. While living in London he offered his services as guitar teacher to the mother of Leigh Hunt, the English poet and essayist. He was also fond of singing in congenial company and was especially partial to Scotch songs. He tells us of one, "The Old Man's Wish," that he sang "a thousand times in his singing days."

It was as an inventor that Franklin made the greatest impression on musical circles in both Europe and America. On April 19, 1762, the *New-York Mercury* carried the following news item: "In the *Bristol Journal* [i.e., Bristol, England] we find advertised 'The celebrated Glassy-chord invented by Mr. Franklin, of Philadelphia, who has greatly improved the Musical Glasses, and formed them into a compleat Instrument . . . capable of a thorough Bass, and never out of tune."

The use of musical glasses was known to the Persians as early as the fourteenth century and may have spread to Europe from the Near East. A work published in Nuremberg in 1677 mentions "making a cheerful wine-music" by stroking the rims of partially filled glasses with a moistened finger. In the 1740s an Irishman named Richard Pockrich (or Puckeridge) began giving concerts on the musical glasses with much success until, in 1759, both he and his "angelick organ" (as he called it) perished in a London fire.[11]

A similar set of musical glasses was then reconstructed by E. H. Delaval, whom Franklin heard at a London performance in 1761. Writing to his Italian friend Padre Beccaria, Franklin states that Delaval's instrument was "the first I saw or heard." And he continues: "Being charmed by the sweetness of its tones, and the music he produced from it, I wished only to see the glasses disposed in a more convenient form, and brought together in a narrower compass, so as to admit of a greater number of tones, and all within reach of hand to a person sitting before the instrument. . . ." Instead of having the glasses contain varying quantities of water to produce a variety of pitches, Franklin had them made of different sizes and used only the bowls, without the stems. He placed the glasses on a horizontal rod or spindle that was rotated by a foot action, in much the same manner as a spinning wheel. The instrument, he wrote, "is played upon by sitting before the middle of the set of glasses as before the keys of a harpsichord, turning them with the foot [pedal], and wetting them now and then with a spunge and clean water."[12]

Although the instrument was at first called "glassy-chord," Franklin preferred to give it a more euphonious name—"armonica"—in honor, he said, of the musical Italian language. But in English an aspirate was more comfortable, hence it became known as the "glass harmonica."

Its European success was tremendous, especially as performed by Marianne Davies in concerts with her sister Cecilia, a singer. In the summer of 1773 Leopold Mozart wrote from Vienna: "Do you know that Herr von Mesmer plays Miss Davies's harmonica unusually well? . . . Wolfgang too has played upon it. How I should like to have one!" According to A. Hyatt King, "There seems little doubt that Mesmer used his mastery of the highly emotional tones of the harmonica to induce a receptive state in his patients."[13] (Mesmer was the exponent of "animal magnetism," or hypnotism.) The glass harmonica appears to have had an extraordinary physiological effect. Its tone could unnerve the strongest man and cause women to faint. Franklin, however, appeared to be immune: he must have had nerves of iron.

In 1791, the year after Franklin's death and the last of his own life, Mozart, inspired by the playing of a blind girl named Marianne Kirckgassner, composed the lovely Quintet (Adagio and Rondo) for Harmonica, Flute, Oboe, Viola, and Cello (K. 617), as he had earlier written an Adagio for harmonica solo (K. 356). Many other composers, including Beethoven and Schumann, succumbed to its charms. The glass harmonica appealed strongly to the Romantic temperament and inspired poets such as Goethe, Schiller, and Wieland.

As a musical inventor, Benjamin Franklin was not without honor in his own country. To show what impression the glass harmonica made on his countrymen, let us return to Nomini Hall, the Virginia home of Councillor Robert Carter, and read Philip Vickers Fithian's description of a certain winter evening in that gentleman's household in the year 1773: "Evening Mr Carter spent in playing on the Harmonica; It is the first time I have heard the Instrument. The Music is charming! . . . The Notes are clear and inexpressibly Soft, they swell, and are inexpressibly grand; & either it is because the sounds are new, and therefore please me, or it is the most captivating Instrument I have Ever heard."[14]

In our own time Franklin's invention has continued to interest a number of musicians. In 1956, for example, the famous organist E. Power Biggs (1906–79), who was born in England but became an American citizen in 1938, performed on a reconstructed model of the original glass harmonica and did much to make the instrument known to his many fans.

Franklin, although many-sided, was no mere dabbler. His interest in music was neither casual nor superficial. Proof of his original thinking on musical subjects is afforded by two of his letters, one to the philosopher Lord Kames of Edinburgh, the other to his brother Peter Franklin (both written from London). In the letter to Lord Kames, dated June 2, 1765, Franklin wrote (in part):[15]

> In my Passage to America, I read your excellent Work, the Elements of Criticism, in which I found great Entertainment, much to admire, and nothing to reprove. I only wish'd you had examin'd more fully the Subject of Music, and demonstrated that the Pleasure Artists feel in hearing much of that compos'd in the modern Taste, is not the natural Pleasure arising from Melody or Harmony of Sounds, but of the same kind with the Pleasure we feel on seeing the surprizing Feats of Tumblers and Rope Dancers, who execute difficult Things. For my part, I take this to be really the Case and suppose it the Reason why those who being unpractis'd in Music, and therefore unacquainted with those Difficulties, have little or no Pleasure in hearing this Music. Many Pieces of it are mere Compositions of Tricks. I have sometimes at a Concert attended by a common Audience plac'd myself so as to see all their Faces, and

observ'd no Signs of Pleasure in them during the Performance of much that was admir'd by the Performers themselves; while a plain old Scottish Tune, which they disdain'd and could scarcely be prevail'd on to play, gave manifest and general Delight. . . .

The Connoisseurs in modern Music will say I have no Taste, but I cannot help adding, that I believe our Ancestors in hearing a good Song, distinctly articulated, sung to one of those Tunes and accompanied by the Harp, felt more real Pleasure than is communicated by the generality of modern Operas, exclusive of that arising from the Scenery and Dancing. Most Tunes of late Composition, not having the natural Harmony united with their Melody, have recourse to the artificial Harmony of a Bass and other accompanying Parts. This Support, in my Opinion, the old Tunes do not need, and are rather confus'd than aided by it. Whoever has heard James Oswald[16] play them on his Violoncello, will be less inclin'd to dispute this with me. I have more than once seen Tears of Pleasure in the Eyes of his Auditors; and yet I think even his Playing those Tunes would please more, if he gave them less modern Ornament.

The letter to his older brother Peter tells us more about Franklin's attitude toward that "modern music" whose artificialities he deplored and derided—not sparing even the venerated Handel:[17]

Dear Brother,

I like your ballad, and think it well adapted for your purpose of discountenancing expensive foppery, and encouraging industry and frugality. If you can get it generally sung in your country, it may probably have a good deal of the effect you hope and expect from it. But as you aimed at making it general, I wonder you chose so uncommon a measure in poetry, that none of the tunes in common use will suit it. Had you fitted it to an old one, well known, it must have spread much faster than I doubt it will do from the best new tune we can get compos'd for it. I think too, that if you had given it to some country girl in the heart of the Massachusets, who has never heard any other than psalm tunes, or *Chevy Chace,* the *Children in the Wood,* the *Spanish Lady* and such old simple ditties, but has naturally a good ear, she might more probably have made a pleasing popular tune for you, than any of our masters here, and more proper for your purpose, which would best be answered, if every word could as it is sung be understood by all that hear it, and if the emphasis you intend for particular words could be given by the singer as well as by the reader; much of the force and impression of the song depending on those circumstances. . . .

A modern song, on the contrary, neglects all the proprieties and beauties of common speech, and in their place introduces its *defects* and *absurdities* as so many graces. I am afraid you will hardly take my word for this, and therefore I must endeavour to support it by proof. Here is the first song I lay my hand on. It happens to be a composition of one of our greatest masters, the ever famous Handel. . . . It is called, *The additional* FAVOURITE *Song in Judas*

Maccabeus.[18] Now I reckon among the defects and improprieties of common speech the following, viz.

1. *Wrong placing the accent or emphasis,* by laying it on words of no importance, or on the wrong syllables.
2. *Drawling;* or extending the sounds of words or syllables beyond their natural length.
3. *Stuttering;* or making many syllables of one.
4. *Unintelligibleness;* the result of the three foregoing united.
5. *Tautology;* and
6. *Screaming,* without cause.

For the *wrong placing of the accent, or emphasis,* see it on the word *their* instead of being on the word *vain.*

And on the word *from,* and the wrong syllable *like.*

For the *Drawling,* see the last syllable of the word *wounded.*

And in the syllable *wis,* and the word *from,* and syllable *bove*

For the *Stuttering*, see the words *ne'er relieve*, in

Ma - gick   Charms can   *ne'er   re - lieve*   you

Here are four syllables made of one, and eight of three; but this is moderate. I have seen in another song that I cannot now find, seventeen syllables made of three, and sixteen of one; the latter I remember was the word *charms; viz. Cha, a, a, a, a, a, a, a, a, a, a, a, a, a, a, arms.* Stammering with a witness! . . .

In a postscript, Franklin concludes with a couple of trenchant sentences: "If ever it was the ambition of musicians to make instruments that should imitate the human voice, that ambition seems now reversed, the voice aiming to be like an instrument. Thus wigs were first made to imitate a good natural head of hair; but when they became fashionable, though in unnatural forms, we have seen natural hair dressed to look like wigs."

It is a rule of history that trivial things attached to famous persons acquire an importance inconsistent with their intrinsic value. This is the case with a very odd composition for string quartet, attributed to Franklin on the basis of a manuscript discovered in 1941 at the Bibliothèque Nationale in Paris, bearing the inscription: *Quartetto a 3 Violini con Violoncello Del Sigre Benjamin Francklin.*[19] It consists of five very short movements, all in the key of F major: Introduction (Allegro), Minuet, Capriccio, another Minuet, and Siciliano [*sic*]. The performance time is about six minutes. That it was written for three violins and cello instead of the usual quartet combination of two violins, viola, and cello is the least of its oddities. The strangest feature is that it was written entirely for open strings, which would require no fingering by the performers, and it employed a method of tuning called *scordatura*—normally used only for special effects.

The plot thickens when we learn that six other versions or copies of the quartet have been found in various European archives—all attributed to well-known composers![20] But no one has explained why any composer would *want* to write such a work. The possibility arises that Franklin may have indulged in a prank with this piece. E. Power Biggs implies as much when he remarks that it "displays an amusing combination of musical skill, practical sense, and humor" and that it was written with "tongue in cheek."

Whatever the circumstances and the opinions, Franklin's fame and well-publicized musical interests appear to have carried the day, as we find his dubious quartet (actually a miniature suite) included in a record album titled *The Early String Quartet in the U.S.A.*, along with works by Mason, Griffes, Foote, Chadwick, Hadley, and Loeffler. That Franklin's piece is the only "early" work in the collection (historically speaking) makes it all the more evident that his name was the main attraction.

In a letter to Mary Stevenson written from Philadelphia in 1763, Franklin wrote: "After the first Cares of the Necessaries of Life are over, we shall come to think of the Embellishments. Already some of our young Geniuses begin to lisp Attempts at Painting, Poetry, and Musick."[21] We now meet one of these "young Geniuses" who lisped elegantly in all three arts.

While visiting relatives in England in September 1766, a young lawyer from Philadelphia named Francis Hopkinson attended a performance of Handel's *Messiah* at Gloucester. Although he was afflicted by a large and painful boil, he felt no pain during the concert. He even did not perceive that the boil had broken while at the concert, even though, as he told his friend Thomas Jefferson long afterward, had he been alone in his chamber he "should have cried out with Anguish." And in a speculative vein he added, "May not the Firmness of Martyrs be accounted for on the same principle?"

Whatever Hopkinson may have thought about the "Firmness of Martyrs," there can be no question about his belief in the Power of Music, for he repeatedly proved it both by word and deed. Some seven years before his English journey he had written a "Prologue in Praise of Music," in which these lines occur:

> Such pow'r hath music o'er the human soul,
> Music the fiercest passions can controul.
> Touch the nice springs that sway a feeling heart,
> Sooth ev'ry grief, and joy to joy impart.
> Sure virtue's friends and music are the same,
> And blest that person is that owns the sacred flame.

At the age of seventeen, when he began to take up the study of the harpsichord, he wrote an "Ode on Music" that reveals his enthusiasm for the "divine art":

> Hark! Hark! the sweet vibrating lyre
> Sets my attentive soul on fire;
> Thro' all my frame what pleasures thrill,

> Whilst the loud treble warbles shrill,
> And the more slow and solemn bass,
> Adds charms to charm and grace to grace.

A poem titled "Description of a Church" describes the effect that an organ had on him:

> Hail heav'n born music! by thy pow'r we raise
> Th' uplifted soul to arts of highest praise:
> Oh! I would die with music melting round,
> And float to bliss upon a sea of sound.

The final couplet almost matches the emotional mysticism of Fray Luis de León—and this from the pen of an eighteenth-century American lawyer, businessman, and public official![22]

This was the Age of Reason and Good Taste, but it was also the Age of Sentiment and Enthusiasm. A "rational" man like Hopkinson could indulge his sensibilities to the full while keeping a firm hand on practical matters. Although as a poet he wrote about music like an enthusiast (which in eighteenth-century parlance meant a "crackpot"), he could also class it with "reading, walking, riding, . . . drawing &ca." as agreeable pastimes that "season the Hours with calm and rational Pleasure."[23] If Hopkinson let himself go in his feelings toward music, it was precisely because he considered it a "calm and rational pleasure" that even in its most ecstatic moments would not lead him from the path of Virtue and Reason. It thus contrasted with those moral dangers that he mentions in a letter to his mother from London: "You can have no Idea of the many powerful Temptations, that are continually thrown out here to decoy unwary Youth into Extravagance & Immorality."[24]

The reader, now well acquainted with the habits of the gentleman amateur, will not be too surprised at finding a Philadelphia lawyer playing the harpsichord and dabbling in verse, or even trying his hand at painting, which was Hopkinson's third avocation. Born in Philadelphia on September 21, 1737, son of a distinguished father and a pious mother, Francis Hopkinson graduated from the College of Philadelphia, was admitted to the bar, and became prominent in the political, religious, educational, and artistic life of his native city. A staunch patriot, he cast his fortune and the power of his pen with the cause of the American Revolution and was a delegate to the Continental Congress and a signer of the Declaration of Independence. In 1779 he was appointed Judge of the Admiralty from Pennsylvania, and he took an active part in the Constitutional Convention of 1787, influencing its decisions with a humorous political pamphlet titled *The History of a New Roof*. During the war he wrote his famous satirical poem "The Battle of the Kegs," which became immensely popular. It was set to music and widely sung.

John Adams met Hopkinson in the studio of the artist Charles Willson Peale in Philadelphia in 1776 and wrote about the meeting to his wife: "He is one of your pretty, little curious, ingenious men. His head is not bigger than a large apple. I have not met with anything in natural history more amusing and entertaining than his personal appearance, yet he is genteel and well bred, and is very social."[25] Adams envied the leisure and tranquillity of mind that enabled Hopkinson to "amuse" himself with "those elegant and ingenious arts of painting, sculpture, statuary, architecture, and music."

In this view Hopkinson appears as a dilettante, seeking pleasure and distraction by cultivating the "polite arts." But this underestimates his many-sided musical activities and, above all, their *public* dimension, which distinguishes him from most other musical amateurs among the landed gentry—including Jefferson, whose musical activities were essentially personal and domestic. Hopkinson represents a new breed of gentleman amateur that was emerging from the ranks of upper-middle-class urban society and that during, and especially after, the Revolution, began to exert leadership in cultural as well as political and economic affairs.

When Hopkinson's "Ode on Music" was published in the *American Magazine* of Philadelphia in October 1757, the following remark was included: "Written at Philadelphia by a young Gentleman of 17, on his beginning to learn the Harpsichord." There were several professional musicians from Europe active in Philadelphia with whom he might have studied, among them Charles Love and John Palma. It is highly probable that his principal teacher was the English organist James Bremner, for he became proficient on the organ as well as the harpsichord. He also may have studied theory with Bremner, with whom, in any event, he formed a close friendship, and with whom he was later associated in organizing public subscription concerts in Philadelphia.

In 1759 Hopkinson began to copy out in a large book, in his neat and methodical manner, a collection of songs, operatic airs, cantatas, anthems, hymns, and duets by various celebrated European composers, including Handel, Pergolesi, Purcell, and Arne. The completed collection contained over 100 pieces in a volume of more than 200 pages, and scattered among them were six songs signed with the initials "F. H." The first of these is

Francis Hopkinson. Photo courtesy of the Music Division, The New York Public Library at Lincoln Center, Astor, Lenox and Tilden Foundations.

"My Days Have Been So Wondrous Free" (a setting of Thomas Parnell's "Love and Innocence"), which has attained a somewhat unwarranted notoriety as the first secular song composed by an American. The others are "The Garland," "Oh! Come to Mason Borough's Grove," "With Pleasures Have I Past [*sic*] My Days," "The Twenty-third Psalm," and "An Anthem from the 114th Psalm." All of them are written in two parts—the ubiquitous eighteenth-century "treble and bass." The common procedure was for the accompanist to fill in the harmony at the harpsichord.

The inclusion of the psalm and anthem in this collection points to Hopkinson's lifelong interest in church music. There is strong evidence that he was the compiler of *A Collection of Psalm Tunes, with a Few Anthems and Hymns . . .*, which was published in Philadelphia in 1763 for the United Churches of Christ Church and St. Peter's Church. Hopkinson served as organist at Christ Church during the absence of James Bremner, and he instructed the children of the two churches in "the art of psalmody." In 1786 he wrote *A Letter to the Rev. Dr. White, Rector of Christ Church and St. Peter's on the Conduct of Church Organs,* which contains some interesting observations on "the application of instrumental music to purposes of piety." Arguing for the dignity of church music, he writes, "It is as offensive to hear lilts and jigs from a church organ, as it would be to see a venerable matron frisking through the public street with all the fantastic airs of a *columbine*."[26]

At the beginning of the 1780s, American independence hung in the balance. Even with vigorous support from the French, victory seemed illusive. In Philadelphia the French ambassador, Chevalier de la Luzerne, was very active in aiding the American cause, and by the spring of 1781 he was evidently optimistic. This was displayed when, on March 21, he sponsored the performance at his residence of a musical work titled for the occasion *America Independent: An Oratorical Entertainment.* His confidence was justified, for in October of that year Cornwallis surrendered at Yorktown.

Some two months later (on December 19, 1781) the following notice appeared in the *Freeman's Journal* of Philadelphia:

> On Tuesday evening of the 11th inst. his Excellency the Minister of France, who embraces every opportunity to manifest his respect to the worthies of America, and politeness to its inhabitants, entertained his Excellency General Washington, and his lady, the lady of General Greene and a very polite circle of gentlemen and ladies with an elegant Concert, in which the following *Oratorio* composed and set to music by a gentleman whose taste in the polite arts

is well known, was introduced, and afforded the most sensible pleasure: the *Temple of Minerva,* An Oratorical Entertainment. . . .[27]

The "gentleman" in question was of course Francis Hopkinson, and the work performed was simply a revised version of *America Independent.* We must remember that Hopkinson was a signer of the Declaration of Independence, and what he presents to us is in the form of an allegory, with the Genius of America and the Genius of France invoking the aid and guidance of Minerva, goddess of wisdom, in bringing honor, virtue, and prosperity to the new nation. While the earlier version concludes with a hymn to "Great Minerva! Pow'r divine," the later libretto substitutes a chorus of acclamation for General Washington:

> Fill the golden trump of Fame,
> Through the world his worth proclaim;
> Let rocks, and hills, and vales, resound,
> He comes, he comes, with conquest crown'd.
> Hail Columbia's god-like son!
> Hail the glorious WASHINGTON!

This was sung to "An Air by Handel." Musically, the work was a pastiche, with borrowings from Michael and Thomas Arne, Henry Carey, and Handel. The phrase "composed and set to music" meant that the gentleman in question had written the libretto and set it to preexisting music—a fairly common practice at the time.[28]

Hopkinson was a rather prolific poet in both lyrical and satirical verse, much of which was set to preexisting music. But he also wrote the words and music for more than a dozen songs, of which eight were published in a collection discrepantly titled *Seven Songs for the Harpsichord or Forte Piano* (Philadelphia, 1788).

On October 23, 1788, Hopkinson wrote to his friend Thomas Jefferson: "I have amused myself with composing Six easy & simple Songs for the Harpsichord—Words & Music all my own. The Music is now engraving. When finished, I will do myself the Pleasure of sending a Copy to Miss Jefferson. The best of them is that they are so easy that any Person who can play at all may perform them without much Trouble, & I have endeavour'd to make the Melodies pleasing to the untutored Ear."[29] The work was published before the end of the year and was advertised as follows in the *Pennsylvania Packet:* "These songs are composed in an easy, familiar style, intended for young Practitioners on the *Harpsichord* or *Forte-*

Piano, and is the first Work of this kind attempted in the United States."[30]

The letter to Jefferson mentions six songs, the title of the book is *Seven Songs,* and the collection actually contains eight, with the last song bearing a note that it was added after the title page was engraved. Here are the complete contents (the titles consisting of first lines):

1. Come, fair Rosina, come away
2. My Love is gone to the sea
3. Beneath a weeping willow's shade
4. Enraptur'd I gaze when my Delia is by
5. See down Maria's blushing cheek
6. O'er the hills far away, at the birth of the morn
7. My gen'rous heart disdains
8. The travellor benighted and lost

Hopkinson dedicated the volume to George Washington in a letter from which we quote the passage wherein he claims credit for being the first native American composer: "However small the Reputation may be that I shall derive from this Work, I cannot, I believe, be refused the Credit of being the first Native of the United States who has produced a Musical Composition. If this attempt should not be too severely treated, others may be encouraged to venture on a path, yet untrodden in America, and the Arts in succession will take root and flourish amongst us."[31]

How can we account for Hopkinson's claims to priority, when by 1788 so many pieces by American composers had long been published? Until recently it was assumed that he based his claim on the song "My Days Have Been So Wondrous Free," presumably dating from 1759 but never published in his lifetime. That assumption has been challenged on the ground that if he had considered that song so important for establishing his priority, he surely would have published it.

Another hypothesis, proposed by a historian, is that Hopkinson's *Seven Songs* justifies his claim to be "the first Native of the United States who has produced a Musical Composition," because it was in the year of its publication, 1788, that the United States of America actually became a political entity.[32] At the Constitutional Convention in 1787 it was agreed (Article VII) that the Constitution would be put into effect when nine states had approved it. New Hampshire, on June 21, 1788, became the ninth state to ratify, and on July 2 the Constitution was officially adopted. Politically involved, and moreover a Philadelphia lawyer, Hopkinson might very likely have based his claim to priority on such a legal distinction.

There remains, however, another angle to consider. As Richard Crawford has pointed out, the second edition of *The Worcester Collection of Sacred Harmony* appeared in August 1788, with several new pieces by American composers; and in that year (probably in September) the *Federal Harmony* was published in Boston, with eight new sacred pieces, three of them later attributed to Oliver Holden. Thus, as Crawford observes, Hopkinson's claim "is better understood as a response to the 1788 ratification of the Constitution of the United States than as evidence of the disjunction of American sacred and secular music of that time."[33] His view is that Hopkinson did not regard psalm tunes and anthems as "musical compositions" in the sense of musical works of art. Hence, "the significance of Hopkinson's claim is that he considered himself America's first native composer of *art* music."[34]

The reader now has a choice of several explanations. I shall say only that the hypothesis of a priority based on "My Days Have Been So Wondrous Free" seems very weak; that the postratification hypothesis seems quite plausible; and that the hypothesis of nonrecognition of psalm tunes and anthems as "musical compositions" may be valid but is nonetheless deplorable in its implications.

If the dedication of *Seven Songs* to General Washington reveals the public/political aspect of Hopkinson's character, a letter he wrote to Jefferson, dated December 21, 1788, reveals the personal/domestic aspect:

> I wrote to you three or four weeks ago, & now I take the Opportunity by Mr. Govr. Morris of sending you a small Package of News Papers, Pamphlets, & amongst which is a Work of my own just published. I beg Miss Jefferson's Acceptance of a Copy, and wish it may be to her Taste. It is a Book of Songs which I composed, occasionally, for my Daughters, who play & sing them very well. The last Song, if play'd very slow, and sung with Expression, is forcibly pathetic—at least in my Fancy. Both Words & Music were the Work of an hour in the Heights of a Storm. But the Imagination of an Author who composes from the Heart rather than his Head, is always more heated than he can expect his Readers to be.[35]

That at least one listener found this song "forcibly pathetic" is indicated by Jefferson's reply: "Accept my thanks . . . and my daughter's for the book of songs. I will not tell you how much they have pleased us, nor how well the last of them merits praise for its pathos, but relate a fact only, which is that while my elder daughter was playing it on the harpsichord, I happened to look toward the fire, & saw the younger one all in tears. I asked her if she was sick? She said 'no; but the tune was so mournful.' "[36]

We have here a foretaste of the "parlor songs" of the genteel tradition, in which the operative criterion was not high art but pathos—play it "very slow," and sing it "with Expression." At what point did pathos turn into bathos?

It is high time to evaluate Francis Hopkinson's place in America's musical history in terms other than those of an ambiguous and inconsequential chronological priority. Nor is the quality of his compositions essentially at issue. He was a gifted amateur who cultivated the "polite arts" as an avocation. His importance in the cultural history of the United States resides in his public promotion of the fine arts, particularly music, in the transitional period from colony to nationhood. He combined his literary and musical talents in the cause of American independence. He participated, conspicuously and effectively, in the musical life of the largest and most important American city of his time. Poet, musician, artist, humanist, lawyer, statesman, patriot—America may well remember him with pride.

Jefferson, Franklin, and Hopkinson represent a Golden Age of American culture, when men of affairs, successful in business, in the professions, and in the conduct of government, thought it no shame not only to love music and practice it in private, but also to make public their love of the "Divine Art." In helping to create a nation that recognized man's inalienable right to the pursuit of happiness, they did not overlook the aid and comfort that music can give in this unceasing quest.

Notes

1. The library is catalogued in *The Writings of Colonel William Byrd*, pp. 413–43.
2. *Journal & Letters of Philip Vickers Fithian*, p. 30.
3. John W. Molner, "Art Music in Colonial Virginia," in *Art and Music in the South*, ed. Francis B. Simkins, pp. 63–108; and Maurer Maurer, "The Library of a Colonial Musician, 1755," pp. 39–52.
4. Helen Cripe, *Thomas Jefferson and Music*, p. 14.
5. *The Writings of Thomas Jefferson* 2:158.
6. *The Papers of Thomas Jefferson* 8:659.
7. *The Writings of Thomas Jefferson* 2:159.
8. For Jefferson's music catalogue of 1783 and collections of Jefferson family music, see Cripe, *Thomas Jefferson and Music*, pp. 97–128.
9. Quoted in Oscar G. Sonneck, *Francis Hopkinson . . . and James Lyon*, p. 67.
10. *The Diary of a Country Parson, the Reverend James Woodforde* 1:235.
11. See A. Hyatt King, "The Musical Glasses and Glass Harmonica," pp. 99, 101–2.

12. The letter to Beccaria, dated July 13, 1762, is quoted in the *Complete Works of Benjamin Franklin* 3:198–204; see especially pp. 199–200, 203.

13. King, "The Musical Glasses and Glass Harmonica," pp. 109–10.

14. *Journal & Letters of Philip Vickers Fithian*, p. 37.

15. The letter is printed in its entirety, with documentation, in the *Papers of Benjamin Franklin* 12:158–65.

16. James Oswald (d. 1769) was a Scottish musician who settled in London ca. 1741–42.

17. *Papers of Benjamin Franklin* 11:538–43.

18. The Israelitish Woman's aria, "Wise Men Flatt'ring May Deceive Us," act 2 of *Judas Maccabeus.*

19. First published in a transcription by Guillaume de Van, *Benjamin Franklin: Quatuor pour trois violons et violoncelle* (Paris: Odette Lieutier, 1946).

20. See M. E. Grenander, "Reflections on the String Quartet(s) Attributed to Franklin," pp. 73–87; and W. Thomas Marrocco, "The String Quartet Attributed to Benjamin Franklin," pp. 477–85.

21. *Papers of Benjamin Franklin* 10:233.

22. The three poems cited above are quoted in full in Sonneck, *Francis Hopkinson . . . and James Lyon,* pp. 3–5.

23. Quoted in George E. Hastings, *The Life and Works of Francis Hopkinson,* p. 146.

24. Quoted in ibid., pp. 144–45.

25. Sonneck, *Francis Hopkinson . . . and James Lyon,* p. 9.

26. Ibid., pp. 59–62, especially p. 62.

27. Quoted in ibid., p. 106.

28. See Gillian B. Anderson, " 'The Temple of Minerva' and Francis Hopkinson," pp. 166–77; and idem, " 'Samuel the Priest Gave Up the Ghost' and *The Temple of Minerva,*" pp. 493–516.

29. Quoted in Hastings, *The Life and Works of Francis Hopkinson,* pp. 436–37.

30. Quoted in ibid., p. 437.

31. The dedication is quoted in Sonneck, *Francis Hopkinson . . . and James Lyon,* p. 113.

32. Kenneth Silverman, *A Cultural History of the American Revolution,* p. 673 n. 1 (to chap. 48).

33. Richard Crawford, "Music of Pre-Twentieth-Century America," *Musical Quarterly* 68 (1982): 257 n. 2.

34. Richard Crawford, "Introduction" to Sonneck, *Francis Hopkinson . . . and James Lyon,* p. xii. Sonneck (pp. 78–79) went out on a limb by categorically declaring that "Francis Hopkinson was the first native American composer of songs of whom we know, and his song 'My Days Have Been so Wondrous Free' is the earliest secular American composition extant, dating back to 1759."

35. Quoted in Sonneck, *Francis Hopkinson . . . and James Lyon,* p. 115.

36. Ibid.

Chapter 6

European Professionals

The promptness of this young country in those sciences
which were once thought peculiar only to riper age,
has already brought upon her the eyes of the world.
—William Selby, advertisement for *The New Minstrel* (1782)

On the last Sunday of August 1757, a tall, thin man, about sixty years of age,
rode on a small white horse rapidly along a road in Westmoreland County,
Virginia. A glance inside his saddlebags would have revealed an assortment
of musical instruments, including a violin, a German flute, an oboe, and a
bassoon. A glimpse into his mind would have revealed that his chief concerns were to place as much distance as possible between himself and Stratford, the home of Philipp Ludwell Lee, Esquire, and to reach a town
whose inhabitants would appreciate the talents of a versatile fellow like
himself, skilled in the "polite arts" of music, dancing, and fencing.

Meanwhile the master of Stratford was in a rage over the theft of his
prize bassoon, "made by Schuchart." Going to his desk, he wrote an advertisement to appear in the principal colonial newspapers: "Run away from
the Subscriber [i.e., the undersigned], at Stratford, in Westmoreland
County . . . Charles *Love* . . . he professes Musick, Dancing, fencing and
plays exceedingly well on the Violin and all Wind Instruments; *he stole
when he went away, a very good Bassoon, made by Schuchart,* which he carried
with him. . . . It is supposed he will make towards Charlestown in South
Carolina.'"[1] This, together with a description of the said Love and the offer
of a handsome reward for his apprehension, drew public attention to Mr.
Lee's deplorable loss.

Apart from his larcenous propensities, Charles Love was typical of the
professional musicians who emigrated to the North American colonies and
sought their fortune, for better or for worse, in the New World. Versatile
and resourceful they had to be to survive in a pioneer society in which the
"polite arts" had yet to win a secure place. Few of them could earn a living

solely by music; dancing and fencing might help as remunerative sidelines. Herman Zedwitz, "violin teacher just from Europe," had a chimney-sweeping business in New York. Giovanni Gualdo was a wine dealer in Philadelphia as well as a music teacher, concert manager, performer, and composer. William Selby, organist and composer, sold groceries and liquor in Boston during the Revolution. The flutist and composer William Young, who settled in Philadelphia, was made so desperate by mounting debts that in a fit of rage he killed the constable his creditors had sent to arrest him.

In spite of all hazards, European musicians came to America in growing numbers. Before the Revolution, Charleston, South Carolina (then called Charlestown), was a chief point of attraction. This was because, in the words of Edmund Burke, it "approached more nearly to the social refinement of a great European capital" than any other American city. Music was, of course, an indispensable ingredient of this "social refinement."

The oldest musical society in North America, the St. Cecilia Society, was founded in Charleston in 1762. It combined private subscription concerts with the most elegant and exclusive social amenities. Some of its activities are recorded in the journal of Josiah Quincy of Boston, who visited the southern metropolis in 1773. Describing a dinner with the Sons of St. Patrick, he writes: "While at dinner six violins, two hautboys and bassoon, with a hand-taber beat excellently well. After dinner six French horns in concert—most surpassing musick. Two solos on the French horn by one who is said to blow the finest horn in the world: he has fifty guineas for the season from the St. Cecilia Society."[2]

To Josiah Quincy's journal we turn again for a priceless vignette of eighteenth-century colonial music and manners, as he recounts his impressions of a fashionable concert in Charleston:

> The musick was good. The two bass-viols and French horns were grand. One Abbercrombie, a Frenchman just arrived, played a first fiddle and solo incomparably, better than any one I ever heard. . . . Abbercrombie can't speak a word of English and has a salary of 500 guineas a year from the St. Cecilia Society. . . . Here was upwards of two hundred fifty ladies, and it was called no great show. . . . In loftiness of head-dress these ladies stoop to the daughters of the North: in richness of dress surpass them: in health and floridity of countenance veil [bow] to them: in taciturnity during the performances greatly before our ladies: in noise and flirtations after the music is over pretty much on a par. . . . The gentlemen many of them dressed with richness and elegance uncommon with us—many with swords on. We had two Macaronis present— just arrived from London.[3]

The last two sentences provide a poignant insight into southern colonial culture, which was based on an aristocracy of wealth supported by the slave labor of the plantations. Why would a serious and sensible man like Quincy mention a couple of mincing fops—the two "Macaronis"—in his description of the concert? Simply because they had "just arrived from London" and therefore set the ultimate stamp of *bon ton* upon the event. They brought the latest gossip from the Pall Mall coffeehouses, reports of the latest hit show at Drury Lane, news of the latest scandal at court—just as Monsieur Abbercrombie brought the latest musical fashions from Paris.

Concerts had been given in Charleston long before the founding of the St. Cecilia Society. In 1737 a concert was announced "for the Benefit of Mr. *Theodore Pachelbel,*" with the following significant notice: "N.B. As this is the first time the said Mr. Pachelbel has attempted anything of this kind in a publick Manner in this Province, he thinks proper to give Notice that there will be sung a *Cantata* suitable to the Occasion."[4] The cantata is not further identified, but it very probably was composed by Pachelbel, who was a well-schooled composer of superior ability. There exists an admirable Magnificat by him, for eight voices with organ accompaniment.

Pachelbel was a son of the famous Nuremberg organist and composer Johann Pachelbel. He was born in 1690, emigrated to America at the age of forty-three, and became organist at Trinity Church in Newport, Rhode Island. In January 1736 he gave the first documented concert in New York. The following year he was in Charleston, where he died in 1750. His career indicates that even in the early decades of the eighteenth century America was attracting some distinguished musicians from the Old World.

After the Revolution the focus of America's concert life shifted northward, to cities such as Philadelphia, New York, and Boston. Philadelphia, in particular, became the leading cultural center of the new Republic. A French observer, Moreau de Saint-Méry, declared that there were more beautiful women in Philadelphia than anywhere else in the world, and this pulchritude was matched by an impressive array of talent: the city was full of lawyers, physicians, scientists, philosophers, writers, and artists. In spite of the Quakers, the city was lively, and following the repeal of a municipal law that banned theatrical performances between 1779 and 1789, Philadelphia emerged as the leading center for musical theater in the United States. Theater-lovers derived encouragement from the example of George Washington, who never missed an opportunity to attend a play or a concert.

In June 1787 Washington was in Philadelphia as a delegate to the Constitutional Convention. His diary reveals that on June 12 he attended a concert for the benefit of Mr. Alexander Reinagle, a musician from England who had recently established himself in Philadelphia. The program began with an overture by Johann Christian Bach (the "London" Bach) and ended with two compositions by Reinagle: a sonata for the pianoforte and an overture "in which is introduced a Scotch Strathspey."[5] Whatever Washington thought of the music, he must have been impressed by Reinagle's skill and commanding presence at the pianoforte. In fact, he later engaged Reinagle as music teacher for his adopted daughter, Nelly Custis.

These two men, the soldier and the musician, had much in common: each was a leader in his field, a man of character and integrity who commanded respect. Reinagle conducting an orchestra was a counterpart of Washington commanding an army. And often an eighteenth-century theater could be almost as dangerous as a battlefield.

When George Washington, as president, attended the theater in Philadelphia (the nation's capital from 1790 to 1800), some measure of order was enforced by a military guard, with a soldier posted at each entrance and four in the gallery—where trouble was most likely to break out. That part of the house was always crowded, and the rowdy element found safety in numbers. The "gods" of the gallery, as they were called, would hurl bottles and glasses, as well as apples, nuts, and vegetables, onto the stage and into the orchestra. When political feelings ran high, riots might ensue. No one obeyed the no-smoking signs, and in defiance of the regulations, liquor was brought into the house and liberally imbibed. In some theaters it was customary for the loose women of the town to use the best boxes in the theater to pursue their professional trade, until (in 1795) management exasperatedly decreed that "no persons of notorious ill fame will be suffered to occupy any seat in a box where places are already taken."[6]

As musical director of the New Theatre on Chestnut Street, Reinagle reigned like a monarch over the unruly mobs. According to a contemporary account:

Who that only once saw old manager Reinagle in his official capacity, could ever forget his dignified *personne*. He presided at the pianoforte, looking the very personification of the patriarch of music—investing the science of harmonic sounds, as well as the dramatic school, with a moral influence reflecting and adorning its salutary uses with high respectability and polished manners. His appearance was of the reverend and impressive kind, which at once inspired the universal respect of the audience. Such was Reinagle's imposing appearance that it awed the disorderly of the galleries, or the fop of annoying propensities and impertinent criticism of the box lobby, into decorum. . . . It was truly inspiring to behold the polished Reinagle saluting from his seat (before the grand square pianoforte in the orchestra) the highest respectability of the city, as it entered into the boxes to take seats. It was a scene before the curtain that suggested a picture of the master of private ceremonies receiving his invited guests at the fashionable drawing-room. Mr. Reinagle was a gentleman and a musician.[7]

While it was taken for granted that a gentleman might be an amateur musician, it was very difficult for a professional musician to be recognized as a gentleman. Reinagle was indeed a rara avis. Let it also be remarked that he was not "old" at the time, but in his forties, and he died at the age of fifty-three, having spent slightly less than half his life in America. He was born in England of German parentage and was active in the cosmopolitan musical life of London, where he came under the spell of Johann Christian Bach, the clever and fashionable "Music Master in the Queen's Household," who wrote easy keyboard pieces "such as ladies can execute with little trouble" and graceful sonatas for piano or harpsichord with violin accompaniment. Reinagle also visited Carl Philipp Emanuel Bach (who was then regarded as the "great" Bach) in Hamburg and was deeply impressed.

Although he enjoyed a good professional standing in London, Reinagle found the competition extremely keen, and America beckoned as the land of opportunity. So in 1786 he sailed for New York, where he set up a studio and offered lessons on the pianoforte, harpsichord, and violin. The response was not encouraging, for at that time New York was a thriving commercial center, not an artistic one. Hearing that prospects were more favorable in Philadelphia, Reinagle moved once more, and this time luck and opportunity were on his side. A quarrel among three of his European colleagues—Henri Capron, William Brown, and John Bentley—had forced the discontinuation of the City Concerts. Reinagle immediately took the situation in hand. Effecting a reconciliation between Capron and Brown (Bentley conveniently left for New York), he revived the City Concerts with himself as principal manager and featured performer. His superior abilities were at once recognized, and he thenceforth had a decisive role in the musical life of Philadelphia.

In 1792, when the actor and impresario Thomas Wignell formed a new theatrical company in Philadelphia, Reinagle was appointed its musical director. While Wignell traveled abroad to recruit a company of actors and singers, Reinagle supervised the construction of the New Theatre on Chestnut Street, a large, handsome, and ornate building that came to be regarded as one of the seven wonders of America. It was customary for theatrical companies to include in their repertory not only spoken drama but also plays interspersed with musical numbers, ballets, pantomimes, scenic extravaganzas (or "panoramas"), and—most popular of all—the "ballad operas," which combined dialogue with singing (a famous example is *The Beggar's Opera,* a big hit in America). The Chestnut Street company was no exception.

After a long delay, caused by the terrible epidemic of yellow fever that ravaged Philadelphia, the New Theatre formally opened on February 17, 1794, with a performance of Samuel Arnold's opera *The Castle of Andalusia.* Thereafter Reinagle was kept busy arranging and adapting musical works for the theater and writing music for operas and pantomimes. Variety was the keynote of the repertory, ranging from a historical tragedy in five acts (*Pizarro; or, The Spaniards in Peru*) to a frothy musical farce (*The Repentant Seducer*).

Two of the librettos for which Reinagle composed the music were written by a remarkable woman, Mrs. Susannah Haswell Rowson (1762–1828), famous both as actress and author. Besides poems and songs, she wrote the celebrated novel *Charlotte Temple* (1791), one of the earliest and most successful to be published in America. Born in Portsmouth, England (also the birthplace of Reinagle), she spent part of her childhood in America, where her father was stationed with the British army. She married a musician and was herself musically gifted as a singer and a performer on the harpsichord and guitar. Her engagement as a singer for Wignell's company brought her back to America, where she continued to star until her retirement in 1793. She wrote several plays, including *Slaves in Algiers* (1794), described as "a play interspersed with Songs," and a comic opera, *The Volunteers,* that dealt with a national theme. (The libretto is lost, but a copy of the vocal score is in the Library of Congress.) Reinagle composed the music for both works.

Before taking leave of Reinagle, something should be said about his nontheatrical compositions. In London he had written *Six Sonatas for the Pianoforte or Harpsichord, with an Accompaniment for Violin,* which reveal the influence of Johann Christian Bach. In America he composed, among many smaller pieces and songs, the *Concerto on the Improved Pianoforte with*

Additional Keys (1794) and four attractive sonatas for piano that were never published in his lifetime.[8]

Of special historical significance is a publication by Reinagle that appeared in August 1787, titled *A Selection of the Most Favorite Scots Tunes with Variations for the Piano Forte or Harpsichord* (Philadelphia: printed for the author). This was printed "from the first plates on which music was stamped in America, the punching having been done by John Aitken." Aitken was a Scottish metalsmith who had settled in Philadelphia at about the same time as Reinagle, with whom he formed a close association. Reinagle urged him to take up musical engraving and assisted him in this successful enterprise, so that from 1787 to 1793 Aitken had a monopoly over this business in America. During this period he produced twenty-one publications, including nine by Reinagle as well as two arrangements by Reinagle of songs by John Hook and Charles Dibdin.[9]

One of the musicians associated with Reinagle in the City Concerts of Philadelphia was the German-born organist, harpsichordist, pianist, and composer John Christopher Moller (1755–1803), who emigrated to America in 1790 and soon settled in Philadelphia. In 1791 he opened a "Musical Academy" for instruction in piano and voice. Among his pupils were Maria Jefferson and Eleanor (called "Nelly") Custis, a granddaughter of Martha Washington by her first marriage. By 1793 Moller and Henri Capron, a cellist and composer of French origin, formed a partnership to teach and publish music. Their first publication, consisting of "monthly numbers," was advertised in March 1793: "MUSIC. The great scarcity of well adapted music for the pianoforte or harpsichord and particularly of songs, has induced the subscribers [i.e., the undersigned] to publish by subscription in monthly numbers, all the newest vocal and instrumental music, and most favourite songs, duets, catches and glees—as also by permission of the author, a set of canzonetti, composed by a lady in Philadelphia."[10]

Three features of this advertisement are worth noting: (1) emphasis on the "newest" music as a counterpart to the latest fashions that the middle class was eager to keep up with, (2) the appeal of "social" music such as catches and glees that were popular with everyone, and (3) the enticing novelty of a "lady" composer who preferred to remain anonymous—as custom and propriety required well into the nineteenth century (this did not apply to actresses like Mrs. Rowson). Guessing the lady's identity was no doubt part of the attraction.

In spite of these well-calculated come-ons, *Moller & Capron's Monthly*

The Chestnut Street Theatre in Philadelphia (interior and exterior views).

Numbers did not prosper: only four issues are known to have appeared. Perhaps the publishers made a mistake by featuring too much of their own music, including a sinfonia by Moller. Not until the fourth number did they present the work of a well-known European composer, an overture by Giovanni Martini (composer of the perennially popular "Plaisir d'amour"). Nevertheless, Moller and Capron did publish, separately, several instrumental and vocal works, and their pioneer enterprise helped to make Philadelphia an important center for the printing of music. In 1794 the business was sold to George Willig, and Moller moved to New York, where he remained until his death, very active in a wide range of musical undertakings. (These, nevertheless, did not always save him from "laboring under some pecuniary embarrassment.") He often appeared as a performer on Franklin's glass harmonica.

Frequently associated with Reinagle as a composer for the New Theatre was his older friend and former teacher, Rayner Taylor (1747–1825).[11] Trained in the king's singing school as one of the boys of the Chapel Royal, he was for a time musical director of Sadler's Wells Theatre in London. Coming to America in 1792, he appeared in Baltimore as "music professor, organist and teacher of music in general." He also appeared in the less dignified role of theatrical entertainer, presenting a type of musical skit called "olio." Moving to Philadelphia soon afterward, he became organist at St. Peter's Church, without renouncing his theatrical high jinks—a further proof of eighteenth-century tolerance.

Rayner Taylor appears to have been a rare blend of erudition and clownishness. He was reputed to be the finest organist in America, famous for his masterly improvisations. According to Reinagle, his extemporizing on the organ was "equal to the skill and powers of Bach himself"—meaning of course C. P. E. Bach. John R. Parker, who often heard him play, wrote of his "never failing strain of harmony and science. . . . His ideas flowed with wonderful freedom in all the varieties of plain chant, imitation and fugue." Parker also mentions the "shelves groaning under manuscript files of overtures, operas, anthems, glees, &c."—for which there was evidently little demand. In spite of his extraordinary skill and industry, Taylor achieved no other material recompense than "the drudgery of teaching and a scanty organ salary."[12]

Had Rayner Taylor lived in the twentieth century, he might well have made a fortune as the Anglo-American Victor Borge. To quote Parker again:

Sometimes among particular friends he would in perfect playfulness sit down to the piano forte and extemporize an Italian opera, giving no bad specimen, though a highly caricatured one, of that fashionable entertainment. The overture, the recitative, songs and dialogue, by singing alternately in the natural and falsetto voice were all the thought of the moment, as well as the words which were nothing but a sort of gibberish with Italian terminations. Thus would he often in sportive mood throw away ideas sufficient to establish a musical fame.[13]

Because Taylor lived long before the invention of the phonograph, we never will be able to recapture the first, fine, careless rapture of those impromptu entertainments. But we can at least revive and perform his music without necessarily waiting for the next centennial celebration. Actually, the bicentennial sparked a Rayner Taylor revival with a spirited performance by the New York After Dinner Opera Company of his jovial ballad opera *Buxom Joan* (1801).

Benjamin Carr (1768–1831) was one of the most productive, energetic, and successful of the post-Revolution musicians who came to America from England. Arriving in New York in 1793, he was soon followed by his brother Thomas and his father, Joseph Carr. They became very successful as music publishers and dealers, with stores in Philadelphia, Baltimore, and New York. Benjamin Carr made his American debut as a singer and quickly won popular favor in ballad operas. But his most important contributions to America's musical life were as composer, arranger, organist, pianist, and, above all, as publisher and editor. He edited the *Musical Journal* (founded by his father) and published *Carr's Musical Miscellany in Occasional Numbers.*

The Carrs imported the best vocal and instrumental music from Europe but did not neglect local talent. The first issue of *The Gentleman's Amusement,* which they published in Philadelphia (1793), included "The President's March" by Philip Phile, which was to become one of the most popular and enduring of all American patriotic tunes.

Phile, presumably of German origin, was active in Philadelphia from about 1784 and is credited with having written "The President's March" for the inauguration of President Washington in 1789. As Irving Lowens has remarked, "One provocative aspect of cultural dynamics on the American scene during the 1790s was an unusually close interaction between music and politics, with the theater serving as catalyst."[14] The transformation of "The President's March" into a patriotic song with political implications illustrates this interaction. Phile's march was taken up by the Federalists as their rallying tune, but to make it more effective it needed a text.

In response to this "partisan public demand," Joseph Hopkinson (son of Francis Hopkinson) wrote some patriotic verses, beginning with "Hail! Columbia, happy land," and including a chorus that began: "Firm united let us be, rallying round our Liberty."[15] The partisan implication was made clear when the first edition of the song, published by Carr as "The favorite new Federal Song, Adapted to the Federal March" (1798), included a medallion portrait of President Adams with the inscription, "Behold the Chief who now commands!" (the opening line of the fourth stanza).

"Hail Columbia," as it soon came to be known, was sung for the first time by Gilbert Fox at the New Theatre in Philadelphia on the night of April 25, 1798, with immense success. According to Mrs. John Adams, "The whole . . . Audience broke forth in the Chorus whilst the thunder from their Hands was incessant, and at the close they rose, gave 3 Huzzas, that you might have heard a mile. . . ."[16] At the second performance, two days later, the enthusiasm was even greater. Naturally, the Republican papers blasted it as "ridiculous bombast" and "vilest adulation." With or without words, Philip Phile's tune has remained one of the most popular and enduring patriotic airs of the United States—even though the name of the obscure emigrant who wrote it is seldom remembered.

When launching his weekly *Musical Journal* (1800), Benjamin Carr announced that he would draw on "a regular supply of new music from Europe and the assistance of Men of Genius in the Country" (i.e., the United States). This sums up his constructive policy of striking a fair balance between foreign imports and national products. The phrase "Men of Genius" should not be interpreted as flattery, for it then meant talent and skill rather than great inspiration.

That Carr was a composer of considerable competence is indicated by his extant music, including selections from his opera *The Archers; or, The Mountaineers of Switzerland,* produced in New York in 1796. The libretto deals with the story of William Tell. The two existing musical numbers are the graceful Rondo from the Overture and the song "Why, Huntress, Why?" The latter could be said to touch upon a theme of today's movement for "women's liberation." Walter's daughter, Rudolpha, urges that she and her "fifty virtuous maidens" be allowed to fight along with the men. But does she really mean it when she promises that after victorious combat she and her maidens will resume their meek, submissive manners? In any case, it is at this point that Walter protectively sings, "Why,

Huntress, why wilt thou thy life expose? . . ." At the end it is Rudolpha who sings in praise of patriotism.

The author of the libretto of *The Archers* was William Dunlap (1766–1859), a versatile American humanist, active not only as playwright and librettist but also as theater manager and historian, poet, novelist, and painter. He probably would have agreed with the critic who wrote, apropos of the New York premiere of *The Archers,* "Our stage should represent to us the superior excellence of those manners which result from strict morality and the proper exercise of our political principles. . . ."[17] Dunlap's libretto contains at least one political allusion: "In federal bonds united we are safe."

The story of William Tell evidently appealed to the emigrant composers, probably because it gave them an opportunity to do some musical flagwaving for their adopted country. For example, in 1794 James Hewitt wrote the music for an opera titled *The Patriot; or, Liberty Asserted,* in which Tell was the hero and presumably a surrogate for Washington.

James Hewitt (1770–1827), son of a captain in the British Royal Navy, was one of the most distinguished and influential musicians who emigrated to America. At the age of twenty-two, having established an excellent reputation in London as violinist and director of music at the court of George III, he decided to try his fortune in America. He was accompanied by several musicians, including the Belgian violinist and composer Jean Gehot, who had played with him in "Professional Concerts under the direction of Haydn, Pleyel, etc." Soon after arriving in New York in 1792, they gave a concert that included Gehot's *Overture in Twelve Movements, Expressive of a Voyage from England to America* and Hewitt's *Overture in Nine Movements, Expressive of a Battle.* Thus they catered to the vogue for descriptive "program" music, which favored battle pieces in particular.

Hewitt later responded to this fashion by composing (in 1797) a sonata for piano titled *The Battle of Trenton* and dedicated to George Washington. He undertook to depict episodes such as "The Army in Motion," "Attack-Cannons-Bombs," "Flight of the Hessians," "General Confusion," "Trumpets of Victory," and "General Rejoicing." He also managed to bring in the ubiquitous "Yankee Doodle." This piece has enjoyed a posthumous popularity not accorded to Hewitt's more "serious" sonatas.

Hewitt's position in New York was comparable to that of Reinagle in Philadelphia: he organized subscription concerts, appeared as performer and conductor, and was the principal composer and arranger for the Old American Company, which produced operas and plays with incidental music. He also bought the New York branch of Carr's music store and publishing house. He conducted performances of theater music, too—which had its professional hazards, as illustrated by the premiere of his opera *Tammany; or, The Indian Chief*, with libretto by Mrs. Anna Julia Hatton, a local bluestocking. This is considered to be the first American opera on an Indian subject. It ran into a political snag when the New York Tammany Society, an anti-Federalist stronghold, sponsored its premiere by the Old American Opera Company (March 3, 1794). Feelings ran so high that Hewitt, who conducted, was verbally abused and got a knock or two. It was customary for the public to demand—often with noisy and rowdy insistence—whatever musical numbers they wanted the pit orchestra to play. Hewitt was perhaps slow or reluctant to respond, for a newspaper report on the "disturbance" stated that it "commenced upon an *individual*, poor Hewitt, the leader of the band, and a very respectable and inoffensive character."

Hewitt became even more "respectable," and more prominent socially, when he married a young lady from a wealthy family, Eliza King, who was educated in Paris and achieved some reputation as an author. He became so class-conscious that he objected when his son John Hill Hewitt wanted to make music his profession.[18] As we shall see in chapter 9, young Hewitt eventually defied his father's prejudice and had a long and productive musical career. Curiously, Hewitt senior did not object when his daughter Sophia became an accomplished concert pianist and married a professional violinist. Was there a double standard?

In 1811 Hewitt moved to Boston with his family and continued to give concerts, but his rivals were so strongly entrenched that he never became a dominant figure there. His last years were spent in New York, where, separated from his wife, he died in poverty.

No account of professional musical activity in Boston should fail to mention the English organist, choirmaster, and composer William Selby (ca. 1738–98), who arrived in 1771 and managed to survive the Revolution, having been appointed organist at Trinity Church in 1776. In April 1782 he organized and directed an impressive concert of sacred music, which included selections "from the Oratorios of Mr. Stanly [*sic*], Mr. Smith, and the late celebrated Mr. Handel. . . ." In his concerts he welcomed the assistance of a "Society of Gentlemen" for the instrumental parts. It has been said that Selby gave to Boston "performances on a level unequaled by any previously heard in America."[19]

Two years before the death of Selby the musical life of Boston was enhanced by the arrival of the versatile Dutch organist, violinist, and composer Peter Albrecht van Hagen (ca. 1750–1803), who had first emigrated to Charleston in 1774. From 1789 until his departure for Boston in 1796, he was active in New York as performer and (from 1793) as director of the Old City Concerts. He also advertised that he was prepared to give instruction on the "violin, harpsichord, tenor [viola], violoncello, German flute, clarinet, bassoon, and singing"—a one-man musical conservatory! For instructing singers he may have been assisted by his wife, who was a trained vocalist. A son, Peter Albertus, became active as violinist, teacher, and composer.[20]

In Boston, van Hagen became musical director of the Federal Theatre (1797–1800) and wrote the music for some "musical dramas" performed there. (Boston by this time had two theaters—the other was the Haymarket Theatre.) In 1798 father and son (they now called themselves "von" Hagen) established a "Musical Magazine and Warehouse," for the sale of sheet music and instruments, as well as some publishing. Among their publications was "A new patriotic song," titled "Adams & Washington." It expressed a time of warlike tension between the United States and France, as indicated by the defiant tone of the first stanza:

> Columbia's brave friends with alertness advance,
> Her rights to support in defiance of France . . .
> To volatile fribbles we never will yield,
> While John's at the helm, and George rules the field.

Another widely popular song that they advertised was "Adams and Liberty," with words by Thomas Paine, sung to the tune of "To Anacreon in Heaven," which later was used for "The Star-Spangled Banner" (1814). Also included in the list was "The Ladies Patriotic Song," to the tune of "Washington's March at the Battle of Trenton."[21] The first line is "Columbians arise, independence proclaim"—which could readily be converted to a feminist rallying song. Not to be outdone in patriotism, the elder von Hagen composed "A Funeral Dirge on the Death of General Washington As Sung at the Stone Chapel" (where he was the organist). Upon the death of Peter Albrecht von Hagen in 1803, the family's influence and prosperity were eclipsed by the activities of more successful rivals.

The man who assumed a dominant position in the musical life of Boston was Johann Christian Gottlieb Graupner (1767–1836), who was of German origin and trained as an oboist. From 1788 he was active in London,

and in 1795 he went to Charleston to begin his American career. There he
met and married the English singer Catherine Comerford Hillier (or
Hellyer), and after touring for a time, they settled in Boston in 1797, where
Graupner was engaged as oboist in the orchestra of the Federal Street Theatre. But his talent, versatility, and enterprise carried him far beyond the orchestra. His wife, too, was a prestigious artist, and within a very short time
they became leading luminaries in Boston musical life.

In 1810 the *Boston Gazette* informed its readers that Mrs. Graupner's
benefit concerts were "annually attended by the most brilliant and respectable circles of the community." Here was the difference between Boston society and that of Charleston: in the latter it sufficed to be brilliant; in the
former, respectability was also required. In New York it was sufficient to
be successful; in Philadelphia the aim was to be brilliant, respectable, *and*
successful.

Let it also be recorded, as a noteworthy novelty, that on December 30,
1799, Mrs. Graupner sang a sentimental ballad titled "I Sold a Guiltless Negro Boy" (also known as "The Negro Boy"). The opening lines are as follows:

> When thirst of gold enslaves the mind
> And selfish view alone bears sway,
> Man turns a savage to his kind,
> And blood and rapine mark his sway.

The last couplet is:

> Forgive the wretch, that for a toy,
> Could sell a helpless Negro boy!

This was published in the *American Musical Miscellany* (Northampton,
Mass., 1798). Whether its primary intent was to move the emotions or to
condemn the institution of slavery, it could be taken as a harbinger of the
antislavery songs and tracts that would eventually proliferate in New England.

Graupner, for his part, was active and industrious in many pursuits.
He taught piano, oboe, and almost any other instrument that anyone
might want to learn, often beginning his lessons as early as 6:00 A.M. He
opened a music store and established a music-publishing business (including his own compositions). In 1810 he was a principal founder of the Philharmonic Society, which continued until 1824 and was the first semiprofessional orchestra in Boston. He also had a decisive role in founding the

Boston Handel and Haydn Society, which was eventually to become a prestigious and permanent feature of Boston's musical life, with ramifications that spread its influence far and wide (see chapter 8). The society was officially constituted on April 13, 1815. It was essentially an association of amateurs for the purpose of performing mostly sacred music, featuring the oratorios of Handel and Haydn, and Graupner was the only professional among its founding members. (The first president, Thomas Smith Webb, was a manufacturer of cotton goods.)

In 1801 Graupner joined forces with the Italian composer Filippo Trajetta (Anglicized as Philip Traetta, 1777–1854) and the versatile French musician Francis Mallet (1750–1834) in establishing a musical academy or conservatory. Trajetta was active in Boston, Charleston, New York, and Philadelphia. His cantata, "Peace" (*Jubilate*), written to celebrate peace with England after the War of 1812, was performed by the Handelian Society of New York in 1815. He also composed popular topical pieces, including "Commodore Decatur's Turkish March" (1817). Mallet had come to America with Lafayette and had settled in Boston about 1795. The joint enterprise of these three musicians began promisingly but soon collapsed when Graupner's partners proved unreliable. Graupner's own musical activities continued to be successful and productive, especially in performing, publishing, and teaching. His *Rudiments of the Art of Playing on the Piano Forte* appeared in 1806 and was reissued in 1819, 1825, and 1827. We may well agree with the historian of music in Boston who wrote: "For twenty-five years, or the first quarter of the century, Graupner remained the unquestioned leader of all musical forces, and the most esteemed musical scholar of the town."[22]

The pioneer European professional of Boston, William Selby, will provide a coda for this chapter. The *Boston Evening Post* of February 2, 1782, carried an advertisement for the publication (in monthly installments and by subscription) of various instrumental pieces that he had composed. But he did not regard this merely as a routine business transaction, for he included a manifesto of confidence in the artistic potential of the fledgling nation:

> At this age of general civilization, at this area [*sic*] of the acquaintance with a nation far gone in politeness and fine arts—even the stern patriot and lover of his country's glory, might be addressed on the present subject with not less propriety than the man of elegance and taste.
> The promptness of this young country in those sciences which were once thought peculiar only to riper age, has already brought upon her the eyes of the world. . . .

And shall those arts which make her happy, be less courted than those arts which have made her great? Why may she not be "In song unequall'd as unmatch'd in war"?[23]

Although Selby's hopes of publishing this collection by subscription were ultimately thwarted, he was not embittered, nor did he turn against his adopted country. He continued to develop the musical potential of his community with undiminished zeal.

With varying degrees of success or disappointment, of fulfillment or frustration, the professional musicians from abroad who entrusted their fate to the United States of America reshaped not only their own destiny but also the entire course of organized musical activity in their adopted land. Whatever prejudices or misconceptions they may have held in any given situation, their continuous role has been fundamentally constructive.

Notes

1. *Pennsylvania Gazette*, Oct. 6, 1757; quoted in Oscar G. Sonneck, *Francis Hopkinson . . . and James Lyon*, p. 25 n.

2. "Journal of Josiah Quincy, Junior, 1773," p. 451.

3. Ibid., pp. 441–42.

4. *South Carolina Gazette*, Oct. 29–Nov. 5, 1737; quoted in Oscar G. Sonneck, *Early Concert-Life in America*, p. 13.

5. See Sonneck, *Early Concert-Life in America*, p. 132.

6. Oscar G. Sonneck, *Early Opera in America*, pp. 119, 120, 121.

7. Charles Durang, *History of the Philadelphia Stage between the Years 1749 and 1855*, comp. Thompson Westcott (Philadelphia: University of Pennsylvania Library, 1868); quoted in Sonneck, *Early Opera in America*, pp. 118–19.

8. Ernst C. Krohn, "Alexander Reinagle as Sonatist," pp. 140–49.

9. For the Aitken-Reinagle connection, see Richard J. Wolfe, *Early American Music Engraving and Printing*, pp. 113–20.

10. *Federal Gazette* (Philadelphia), Mar. 13, 1793; as quoted in ibid., pp. 217–18.

11. On the correct spelling of Taylor's name, see Victor Fell Yellin, "Rayner Taylor," p. 49.

12. John Rowe Parker, *Musical Biography*, p. 181.

13. Ibid., p. 182.

14. Irving Lowens, *Music and Musicians in Early America*, p. 89.

15. Vera Brodsky Lawrence, *Music for Patriots, Politicians, and Presidents*, p. 142.

16. Ibid.

17. New York *Diary*, Apr. 20, 1796; quoted in Julian Mates, *The American Musical Stage before 1800*, p. 223.

18. Coy Elliott Huggins, "John Hill Hewitt," p. 11.

19. David McKay, "William Selby, Musical Emigré in Colonial Boston," pp. 613, 615, 617.

20. In most reference works the son's name is listed as Peter Albrecht, but the correct form is Peter Albertus.

21. Oscar G. Sonneck, *A Bibliography of Early Secular American Music*, p. 452, states that "Washington's March at the Battle of Trenton" was "possibly composed by Francis Hopkinson."

22. H. Earle Johnson, *Musical Interludes in Boston*, p. 191.

23. Advertisement, *Boston Evening Post,* Feb. 2, 1782; quoted in Sonneck, *A Bibliography of Early Secular American Music*, p. 293.

Chapter 7

American Pioneers

Our Country is made up of the small fry. Give me a seine
Of small meshes.
—Mason L. ("Parson") Weems, letter to Mathew Carey (March 25, 1809)

The native-born American musician in the eighteenth century occupied a precarious situation between the privileged status of the gentleman amateur and the acknowledged competence of the professional emigrant. Salaried positions in church or theater were almost invariably filled by foreign musicians. Our musical pioneers—largely self-taught empiricists with more zeal than skill—could scarcely compete with the professionals on their own ground. Nevertheless, by their energy and enthusiasm, and the frequent success of a good tune, they managed to stake out an area for themselves. Even if it seldom provided a satisfactory income, it enabled them to supply with considerable effectiveness a large portion of the country's rapidly growing musical needs. Being mostly "small fry," they knew how to make a "seine of small meshes" to catch their own kind.

As Balzac remarked in a conversation: "To live in a material way one must work—one must be a sower, a reaper, a spinner, a weaver, a carpenter, a mason, a blacksmith, a wheelwright. . . . The rest is luxury—luxury of the mind, of genius, of reason." Although Balzac doubtless did not have America especially in mind, his remarks are particularly applicable to the young nation that emerged from the American Revolution. The main difference from the European scene was that in America a carpenter, a mason, or a blacksmith could aspire to that "luxury of the mind" that involved self-education through reading, discussion, observation, and the cultivation of latent talents.

The question was, if touched by "the sacred flame," how far should a carpenter or a blacksmith let it carry him from the material realities of life—to what heights, or to what depths? Take the case of Jacob Kimball, a blacksmith of Topsfield, Massachusetts. Old Jake had some musical ability.

No doubt he sang at his forge, and surely it was a proud day for him when he was "chosen to set ye psalms, and to sit in ye elders' seat"¹ in the local church. Thus on the Sabbath and on meeting days he enjoyed the prestige of setting "ye psalms"—but the rest of the time he stuck to his smithy.

The blacksmith of Topsfield had a son, Jacob Kimball, Jr., who was fortunate enough to attend Harvard College, where he prepared himself for the practice of law. What an opportunity, in a democratic land, for the next generation to advance in professional and social status! But what had been a mild disposition in the father became a powerful urge in the son. On December 7, 1795, William Bentley of Salem wrote in his diary: "Found Mr. Kimball, the celebrated musician, at his father's. It is his purpose to establish himself in the law in Maine." So Jacob, Jr., aged thirty-five, was already known as a celebrated musician—no doubt from his publication, *The Rural Harmony* (Boston, 1793), which contained seventy-one original compositions "for the use of singing schools and singing assemblies." Whatever "purpose" he may have had to concentrate on, law was soon abandoned in favor of music—with the result that instead of spending his last years in a comfortable town house, he ended his days at the almshouse in Topsfield.²

Let us call the roll of these native musical pioneers, for names convey something of the character and background of the bearers. Among them are Supply Belcher, Asahel Benham, William Billings, Bartholomew Brown, Amos Bull, Amos Doolittle, Ezekiel Goodale, Oliver Holden, Jeremiah Ingalls, Stephen Jenks, Thomas Loud, Justin Morgan, Daniel Read, Timothy Swan, Abraham Wood—solid yeoman names, smacking of useful trades and manual occupations. The records confirm this. Although they were generally mobile and versatile, it is recorded that at one time or another Belcher was a tavern keeper, Billings a tanner, Bull a storekeeper, Doolittle a silversmith, Holden a carpenter, Ingalls a cooper, Morgan a horse breeder (his breed is still famous), Read a combmaker, and Wood a fuller (or dresser) of cloth.

Their lives, however, were not necessarily bounded by the trades to which they were apprenticed. Being Americans in a democratic society, they were able to climb as high on the social and economic ladder as their enterprise and energy could take them, and several became substantial citizens. Belcher, for example, became a justice of the peace and a member of the Massachusetts legislature, while Holden was a real estate operator and a member of the Massachusetts House of Representatives. Billings had plenty of enterprise and energy, but no talent for rising economically from his humble origins.

Although New Englanders dominate the scene during this period, we cannot overlook the contribution of James Lyon (1735–94), born in Newark, New Jersey. In 1759 he graduated from the College of New Jersey with a bachelor of arts degree, having composed the music for a commencement ode on that occasion. He then went to Philadelphia, where he shared the musical honors with Francis Hopkinson at a public commencement program given by the College of Pennsylvania on May 23, 1761. The *Pennsylvania Gazette* reported that the event took place "before a vast Concourse of People of all Ranks," and "there was performed in the Forenoon an elegant *Anthem* composed by James LYON, A.M. of New Jersey College [later Princeton University], and in the Afternoon an *Ode* . . . written and set to Music in a very grand and masterly Taste by Francis Hopkinson, Esq. A.M. of the College of this City."[3] Note that Hopkinson gets lavish praise, while Lyon, an outsider and newcomer, reaps only a trite "elegant."

Shortly after his arrival in Philadelphia, Lyon issued proposals for the publication of a music collection containing compositions by himself and others: "URANIA, or a choice Collection of Psalm-Tunes, Anthems and Hymns from the most approv'd authors, with some entirely new. . . . The whole adapted to the Use of Churches and Private Families. . . ." It was published in 1761, with subsequent editions in 1767 and 1773, and was intended "to spread the Art of Psalmody, in its Perfection, thro' our American Colonies." The intention no doubt held good after independence, and the collection was liberally dedicated to "the clergy of every denomination in America."[4]

Lyon's musical reputation was greatly enhanced by the success of *Urania*, as we gather from an entry in the diary of Philip Vickers Fithian, dated April 22, 1774: "Rode to the Stage early for the Papers thence I went Mr Hunters where I met with that great master of music, Mr *Lyon*. . . ." Fithian adds, "He is about publishing a new Book of Tunes which are to be chiefly of his own Composition."[5] (This was evidently never published.)

Besides the six pieces by Lyon included in *Urania*, several others appeared in various American collections before 1807. The last of these, Elias Mann's *Massachusetts Collection of Sacred Harmony*, included the "Anthem on Friendship." As summarized by Richard Crawford: "Lyon possessed certain innate musical gifts. . . . But what stood beyond his knowledge was the system of functional harmony—of established chord connections—

rooted in the principles of thoroughbass."⁶ He was, in short, a pioneer in a new land, operating anachronistically.

Nevertheless, at a concert in Philadelphia in 1786 an anthem by Lyon was performed on the same program with music by Handel—an indication that our ancestors were willing to combine admiration for the great European masters with recognition of native efforts.

But, even at best, the situation of America's musical pioneers was difficult. They could not live on praise, and their principal economic base— teaching singing schools and selling tunebooks—was generally precarious. The career of William Billings illustrates the vicissitudes, for he ended his life in poverty and was buried in a pauper's grave.

William Billings was born in Boston on October 7, 1746. He probably had no formal schooling after the age of fourteen, when his father, a shopkeeper, died. As a youth he was apprenticed to the tanner's trade, and as far as the official records indicate, a tanner he remained to the end of his days. He did, however, have some minor municipal appointments, including "sealer of Leather." He took some lessons in music from a member of the New South Church choir but was mainly self-taught in theory and composition. He tells us that he had "read several Author's Rules on Composition," but he did not always choose to follow the rules. As he wrote in his introduction to *The New-England Psalm-Singer:*

> Perhaps it may be expected by some, that I should say something concerning the Rules for composition; to these I answer that *Nature is the best Dictator,* for all the hard dry studied Rules that ever was prescribed, will not enable any Person to form an Air. . . . It must be Nature, Nature must lay the Foundation, Nature must inspire the Thought. . . . For my own Part, as I don't think myself confin'd to any Rules for Composition, laid down by any that went before me, neither should I think (were I to pretend to lay down Rules) that any who came after me were any ways obligated to adhere to them, any further than they should think proper. So in fact, I think it best for every *Composer* to be his own *Carver.*⁷

This statement has a defiant ring and therefore has been interpreted as a distinctly personal "declaration of independence." Billings was indeed the first American composer to emphasize strongly a creative independence and to flaunt his personal idiosyncrasies in both his music and (especially) his published writings.⁸

Billings began his activities as a singing-school master during the 1760s, and in 1770, at the age of twenty-four, he published his first tunebook, *The New-England Psalm-Singer; or, American Chorister, Contain-ing a Number of Psalm-Tunes, Anthems and Canons, in Four and Five Parts.* (The frontispiece was engraved by Paul Revere.) Of this book it has been rightly said:

> It would be difficult to find another single publication in the history of Ameri-can music—in the history of western music, for that matter—whose priority in its tradition is more conspicuous than that of Billings's collection. . . . Tak-ing *Urania*'s half-dozen American-composed tunes, and adding tunes from other American compilations . . . it appears that roughly a dozen American-composed psalm tunes were published before 1770. Billings's *New-England Psalm-Singer,* with its one hundred twenty-odd original compositions in-creased that figure tenfold. It was the first published compilation of entirely American music: moreover, it was the first tunebook produced by a single American composer.[9]

It should also be noted that on the title page Billings conspicuously identi-fies himself as "A Native of Boston, in New-England." True, it is a regional identification; but then, we were not yet the United States of America. When that time came, Billings fully rose to the occasion.

Billings was evidently dissatisfied with some of the pieces in his first book, for when he published his second collection, *The Singing Master's As-sistant* (Boston, 1778), he wrote disparagingly of its predecessor as "this in-fant production of my own Numb-Skull." But for the new volume he is full of zest and exuberant pride: "Welcome; thrice welcome; thou legiti-mate offspring of my brain, go forth my little Book, go forth and immortal-ize the name of your Author; may your sale be rapid and may you speedily run through ten thousand Editions, may you be a welcome guest in all companies and what will add tenfold to thy dignity, may you find your way into the Libraries of the Learned."[10]

What is remarkable in this spirited passage is its comprehensive scope in a truly democratic context. In spite of his humble origins, his lack of edu-cational advantages, and his financial difficulties, Billings was imbued with a strong conviction of his own worth and of his ability to please not only the "small fry" but also the "learned" gentry—among whom he did indeed find many friends and admirers of his music.

Although the title page describes it as "an abridgement from the New-England Psalm-Singer," the *Singing Master's Assistant* actually contains a large number of new tunes by Billings. Its popularity was extraordinary: not only did it go into four editions within the decade, but more than a third of the tunes were reprinted in other collections. No wonder it was nicknamed "Billings's Best"! Four other collections by Billings followed: *Music in Miniature* (Boston, 1779), *The Psalm-Singer's Amusement* (Boston, 1781), *The Suffolk Harmony* (Boston, 1786), and *The Continental Harmony* (Boston, 1794).

No tune by Billings is more famous than "Chester," which first appeared in *The New-England Psalm-Singer,* with words that reflect the growing tension between the North American colonies and Great Britain:

> Let tyrants shake their iron rod,
> and Slav'ry clank her galling chains;
> We fear them not, we trust in God,
> New England's God forever reigns.

The text was by Billings, who lost no opportunity to express his patriotic fervor as an American—although physical handicaps had disqualified him from military service. A contemporary described him as "somewhat deformed in person, blind with one eye, one leg shorter than the other, one arm somewhat withered. . . ."[11]

When the Revolutionary War broke out, "Chester" was adopted as a stirring march tune by the New England regiments and was also widely sung with additional defiant stanzas by Billings that appeared in *The Singing Master's Assistant.*

Billings and his contemporary tunesmiths wrote mostly unaccompanied vocal music, usually in four parts, with a preponderance of religious texts. The prevailing types were the plain tune, the fuging tune (a colloquialism for "fuguing"), the set piece, and the anthem. The first was the most common and the simplest, consisting of syllabic settings of metrical verse (sacred or secular). The second has been described as "An Anglo-American psalm tune or hymn tune which contains one or more groups of contrapuntal voice entries involving textual overlap." Furthermore: "A typical American fuging-tune of the late 18th or early 19th century contains two sections, with the second repeated. The first section normally proceeds in block chords to a cadence. The second begins with overlapping contrapuntal entries, each voice singing the same text if not precisely the same subject; chordal texture is usually restored before the concluding cadence."[12]

The thousands of people who sang fuging tunes with great gusto, because they were exciting as each voice entered in succession, knew nothing, of course, about "chordal texture"—but they relished the ensuing results. Typical fuging tunes by Billings are "North Providence," "Kittery," and "Creation."

The set piece and the anthem were extended and varied in form and texture. Billings briefly described the anthem as "a divine song, generally in prose."[13] The set piece, often dealing with a particular event or occasion, is a "through-composed" setting of several stanzas of verse. The anthem was the most elaborate type of composition available to musicians of the tunebook tradition, and Billings distinguished himself in this form, of which he wrote over forty. Among the most remarkable are "Lamentation over Boston" (about the British occupation of that city), "I Am the Rose of Sharon" (from the Song of Solomon), and "Easter Anthem" (1795 revision), beginning with "The Lord is risen indeed!" Here a strong, surging rhythm contributes to the general effect of jubilant exultation, heightened by the frequent ejaculation, "Hallelujah!" Rhetorically, the anthem employs the device of interrogation and affirmation. One after another the various voices ask, "And did he rise?"—and the full choir peals out, "Hear it ye nations, hear it, O ye dead, He rose, He rose, He rose, he burst the bars of death." Now it is the risen Christ who affirms His Ascension: "Then I rose, then first humanity triumphant past [passed] the chrystal ports of light." Here Billings creates a vivid impression of this image, declaiming the text in successive eighth notes while the four-part choir sings on a full triad. We can certainly endorse a comment of the writer in the *Columbian Magazine* of April 1788: "Mr. *Billings'* music is in general well adapted to the subject to which it is applied"—a bit stuffy, but well intentioned.[14]

For contrasting examples of humor and versatility, we can turn to pieces such as "Jargon" and "Modern Music." The former was prompted by criticism that accused Billings of using only consonant intervals in his music. In the words of a later writer: "This roused up the temper of our hero, and he concluded to give them discords enough at one dose to satisfy the most craving appetite. He accordingly composed the tune Jargon, in which after the first chord every step is discordant to the last degree."[15] Billings was no believer in halfway measures!

"Modern Music," which appeared appropriately in *The Psalm-Singer's Amusement,* is a good-natured spoof of the fashionable desire to be up-to-date. It begins by announcing:

> We are met for a concert of modern invention,
> To tickle the ear is our present intention.

This delightfully entertaining piece is but one more example of the variety of Billings's output, not only in music but also in poetry and prose.

Frontispiece and title page to William Billings, *The Continental Harmony* (1794).

After 1790 Billings, with a large family to support, fell on hard times, and his star was waning. He died on September 26, 1800, and we do not know for certain where he was buried.[16] His only monument was the music, the verve, and the vivid image that he left to posterity.

Francis Hopkinson, describing some of the differences in American and European ways of living, remarked that in Europe one could get any kind of work done by a specialist, but the average American was accustomed to do everything himself, from building a house to pulling a tooth. Supply Belcher (1751–1836) was of this sturdy, self-reliant breed. After attending a singing school in his native town of Stoughton, where he kept a tavern, he moved to Maine with his family. There, in Farmington, he taught school, led the church choir, and in his leisure time wrote music that he hoped would be "ornamental to civilization." He published only one tunebook, *The Harmony of Maine* (Boston, 1794), which included the usual psalm and hymn tunes, with a number of fuging pieces and several anthems, notably "An Anthem for Easter." While most are in the usual four parts (treble, tenor, counter, bass), several are in three parts, with the tenor on the upper staff—which meant that the topmost voice carried the main melody, as later became the general practice.

Belcher's tunes are characterized by their variety and inventiveness, as well as their freshness and melodic appeal, often akin to folksong. His book has an unusual number of secular songs, of which several evoke the charms of nature, as with "Invitation," celebrating the arrival of spring. He was partial to vivacious melodies and lively rhythms, expressed as notably in the piece titled "Jubilant" and marked *Vigoroso* (leading to *Fortissimo!*), with the added impact of fuging entries.

Belcher's close contemporary Daniel Read (1757–1836) was also from Massachusetts, but instead of moving northward he went to Connecticut, eventually settling in New Haven. There he courted Jerusha Sherman, whose father, said Read, "would not consent to her marriage with me, because I was guilty of the unpardonable crime of poverty."[17] Nevertheless, Daniel wed his Jerusha, four offspring were born (one christened George Frederick Handel!), and the *paterfamilias* did his best to overcome the stigma of poverty. Although he tried various business ventures, he was determined to make music his chief concern—and in fact did very well with the selling of tunebooks.

Read's first publication bore a significantly comprehensive title: *The*

American Singing Book; or, A New and Easy Guide to the Art of Psalmody, Devised for the Use of Singing Schools in America (New Haven, 1785; four other editions to 1795). Besides the double emphasis on "America," the title reminds us that the term *psalmody* no longer had a primary religious connotation but was basically identified with the singing societies and so-called schools that were springing up everywhere.

Read carried on an extensive correspondence that illuminates many of the difficulties with which tunebook compilers and publishers had to contend, such as the pirating of material by rivals. When preparing the third edition of *The Columbian Harmonist* in 1807 (originally issued in three separate parts, 1793–95; fourth edition 1810), Read set forth his criteria of selection: "You will observe my governing principles in the choice of tunes is like that of the Vicar of Wakefield in the choice of a wife, not so much for any glossy outside, or superficial appearance as for those intrinsic properties which induce me to believe that they will *wear well*. At the same time remembering that as the Collection is for the use of the public, the public opinion is always to be respected."[18]

That Read had the gift for turning out tunes that would "wear well" is demonstrated by the widespread acceptance of his pieces, such as the fuging tune "Sherburne" (a setting of Nahum Tate's Christmas hymn, "While shepherds watch'd their flocks by night"). Others include "Amity" (Psalm 133, after Watts), "Russia" ("My spirit looks to God alone"), and "Windhan" ("Broad is the road that leads to death"). Their popularity is attested by their continuous appearance in the "shape-note" tunebooks of the twentieth century and reprinted editions until the present.

Read's many-sided activities included issuing, in collaboration with Amos Doolittle, the *American Musical Magazine,* which appeared in twelve numbers (1786–87)— "the earliest musical periodical published in the English-speaking colonies." The previously mentioned *Columbian Harmonist* included pieces by both American and English composers, old and new.

The trend toward the secularization of tunebooks that began with Billings continued into the nineteenth century, although many tunebook titles were designed to straddle the fence between sacred and secular usage, as in *The Christian Harmony; or, Songsters Companion* (Exeter, N.H., 1805). This was the work of Jeremiah Ingalls (1764–1828), a native of Massachusetts, who settled in Newbury, Vermont, where he kept a tavern, presided as deacon of the Congregational Church, directed the choir, taught singing school, and worked at various times as a cooper and farmer. He married in

1791 and fathered several children. The following anecdote illustrates how the pull between sacred and secular could affect even a pious family:

> His children were musical and his sons could play clarinet, bassoon, flute, and violin, and they would often practice for hours, the old man leading the band with his bass viol [which he would also use in church]. One Sunday they were having an excellent time performing anthems, and after a while the youngsters started a secular piece, the father with composure joining in. From that they went on until they found themselves furiously engaged in a boisterous march, in the midst of which the old gentleman stopped short, exclaiming, "Boys, this won't do. Put away these corrupt things and take your Bibles."[19]

This anecdote is pointed up by the fact that Ingalls's *Christian Harmony* contains many lively tunes, obviously taken from songs or dances, as settings for sacred texts. In fact, one of the songs makes a plea for the use of secular tunes in sacred music. It is titled "Innocent Sounds," and the second stanza develops the idea of recovering the "innocent sounds" that have been misused for carnal pleasures:

> Who, on the part of God, will rise,
> Innocent sounds recover;
> Fly on the prey and seize the prize,
> Plunder the carnal lover;
> Strip him of every moving strain,
> Of every melting measure;
> Music in virtue's cause retain,
> Risk the holy pleasure.

Ingalls himself did a rather effective job of "plundering the carnal lover," judging by the large number of tunes in *The Christian Harmony* that are reminiscent of English, Irish, and Scottish folksongs and dances. The anonymous "Redeeming Love" is a typical example.

Ingalls's most popular tune is "Northfield," a fuging piece that has been a favorite of rural singers for many generations. The following anecdote is told about the origin of this tune:

> Returning from fishing one rainy day, he [Ingalls] laid down before the fire to get dry, and impatient at the slow progress of dinner began to sing a parody to a well-known hymn [by Dr. Watts]:

> > "How long, my people, Oh! how long
> > Shall dinner hour delay?
> > Fly swifter round, ye idle maids,
> > And bring a dish of tea."

"Why, Jerry," said his wife, "that's a grand tune." "So it is," replied the man of song; "I'll write it down." And dinner waited the completion of "North-field."[20]

But in the early decades of the nineteenth century, very few of the "taste makers" in American musical composition would agree that "Northfield" was indeed "a grand tune." This was the beginning of the era of "progressive improvement" that would dominate the new century. Fuging tunes (also called "fuges") were the special targets of disapproval. As Elias Mann wrote in his introduction to *The Massachusetts Collection* (Boston, 1807): "In this collection will be found none of those wild fuges, the rapid and confused movements, which have so long been the disgrace of Congregational psalmody, and the contempt of the judicious and taste-ful amateur."

Oliver Holden, in *The Worcester Collection of Sacred Harmony*, 8th ed. (Boston, 1803), tried to be more impartial in his judgment: "It is indeed to be lamented that among *so many* American authors [i.e., composers], so lit-tle can be found well written, or well adapted to sacred purposes; but it is disingenuous and impolitic to throw that little away, while our country is in a state of progressive improvement." The basic issue, then, appears to be whether or not the early native pioneers were capable of being assimilated into the prevailing current of "progressive improvement." On this issue the prevailing opinion was negative.

For a strong statement on this point we turn to *An Essay on Music* (Boston, 1808) by the distinguished educator John Hubbard:

Almost every pedant, after learning his eight notes, has commenced author. With a genius, sterile as the deserts of Arabia, he has attempted to rival the great masters of music. On the leaden wings of dullness, he has attempted to soar into those regions of science, never penetrated but by real genius. From such distempered imagination, no regular productions can be expected. The unhappy writers, after torturing every note in the octave, have fallen into oblivion, and have generally outlived their insignificant works.[21]

This was obviously intended as a scathing rejection of Billings and his ilk. But how did the trend toward "progressive improvement" affect those native pioneers whose musical careers extended into the nineteenth cen-tury?

Let us take, for example, the career of Andrew Law (1749–1821), who stood somewhat higher in the social scale than most of his fellow tunebook compilers and composers. A grandson of Governor Law of Connecticut, he received a master's degree from Rhode Island College, studied divinity privately, began preaching in 1777, and was ordained to the ministry ten years later. By that time he had already been active as an itinerant singing master, having evidently prepared himself as a self-taught musician while still at college. Definitely opting for music as a career, he compiled and published in December 1778 his first tunebook, *The Select Harmony,* advertised as "A Collection of Psalm-Tunes and Anthems, from the most celebrated authors in Great Britain and America." (Note the precedence of Britain; perhaps a matter of prestige in this climate of Europeanization?) An enlarged edition appeared the following year; the third and final edition was published in 1812. As Richard Crawford states, "Law was to devote the remainder of his life to convincing the American people that their native sacred music was crude and inferior and that it must be replaced with European-style music."[22]

The question arises, Where does that leave Law himself as a native American composer? To begin with, he was much less important as a composer than as a compiler of tunebooks, promoter of singing schools, and organizer of musical events. Hitherto the best-known tunes attributed to him have been "Archdale" and "Bunker Hill" (the former appeared in two different versions: in the *Art of Singing,* pt. 2, *Christian Harmony,* Cheshire, Conn., 1794; and *The Harmonic Companion,* Philadelphia, 1807). The catch is that recent research by Crawford (Law's most authoritative biographer) indicates there are no solid grounds for attributing either of these tunes to Andrew Law. Crawford has traced "Archdale" to the English composer Edward Harwood, while the only evidence connecting Law with "Bunker Hill" is that he included it in *A Select Number of Plain Tunes* (Cheshire, Conn., 1781). The text is from a poem, "The American Hero," by Nathaniel Niles, and according to a Connecticut historian: "This poem first appeared in print in the Connecticut Gazette, Feb. 2, 1776, but dated Norwich, 1775. It had been circulated and sung in private and patriotic meetings, before it was printed, the music being composed by one of the author's friends." Further information concerning the writer of the music is provided in a footnote: "This is supposed to have been Col. Absalom Peters, of Lebanon, who was at that time a young man giving lessons to the choirs in Norwich as a singing-master."[23]

Law is perhaps best remembered for having introduced what he called "a new Plan of printing Music." This consisted in using, instead of the customary rounded notes, characters of four different shapes: diamond, square, oval, and triangle. No staff lines were used, the pitches being indicated by the relative positions of the "shape notes." This innovation, for which Law had obtained a government patent in May 1802, first appeared in *The Musical Primer* (*Art of Singing,* 3rd ed., pt. 3, 1803), with an introductory essay titled "A View of the new Plan of printing Music, and of the new Method of teaching the Art of Singing." Law expended much energy and effort during the next ten years promoting his new method of notation, but with very poor success.

The fact is that his invention had been anticipated by two singing-school masters, William Smith and William Little, who in 1798 copyrighted a book titled *The Easy Instructor.* Although evidently not published until 1801, in Philadelphia, it appeared two years earlier than Law's book and thus had a head start. Its success was immediate. Smith and Little's system had the advantage of retaining staff lines, thus facilitating sight-reading. As we shall observe in chapter 10, their shape-note system (with subsequent variants) had an enduring impact throughout large areas of the United States.

Before taking leave of Law, we should add that he was active in promoting singing schools far beyond New England—from New York and New Jersey to Pennsylvania, and southward to the Carolinas. He made special efforts to expand the tunebook market westward, particularly to Pittsburgh, about which his brother William wrote enthusiastically, "[It] is the key to Canetuck, Tenesee, and Ohio States."[24] Law, however, drew back from that venture, and it was left to others to open the western territory for singing schools and tunebooks.

New England contemporaries honored Law particularly as an advocate of "progressive improvement." In the words of an obituary notice, "To his correct taste and scientific improvements may be ascribed much of that decent, solemn and chaste style of singing so noticeable in so many of the American churches."[25] In this view he can be regarded as a precursor of Lowell Mason.

Oliver Holden (1765–1844), whose remarks on "progressive improvement" were previously quoted, is remembered chiefly as composer of the tune "Coronation," a setting of Edward Perronet's hymn "All Hail the Power of Jesus' Name." His first important book, *The Union Harmony* (Boston, 1793), was followed by *The Massachusetts Compiler* (Boston, 1795), in which he collaborated with Samuel Holyoke and Hans Gram. The latter was a professional musician of Danish origin, active in Boston, and it is no doubt because of his influence that this work has been regarded as the most up-to-date manual of music theory published in America until that time.

Holden also edited the sixth, seventh, and eighth editions of *The Worcester Collection of Sacred Harmony* (Boston, 1797, 1800, 1803), one of the most important and widely used tunebooks of that period. In 1803 he brought out *The Charlestown Collection of Sacred Songs.* The aim, in his own words, was to compose "music in a style suited to the solemnity of sacred devotion."[26]

Statements such as the foregoing help to explain the breach between the advocates of "progressive improvement" and those who remained faithful to the lively fuging tunes and varied set pieces of the early pioneers. As previously remarked, the earlier tunebooks were meant primarily for social recreation; the later compilations tended to emphasize the "solemnity" of religious observance. A comparison might be made with the controversy over Regular Singing versus the Common Way that preceded the rise of singing schools. In both debates the result was similar: the fuging tunes and the Common Way of singing moved into the hinterland, while the European-oriented tunebooks and hymns predominated in the urban-industrial centers. (As we shall see, there was never a total separation but rather a pattern of prevalence and ascendancy, according to social and economic factors.)

The trend toward instrumental music was also characteristic of this transitional period. Samuel Holyoke (1762–1820), who played the clarinet, directed an amateur performing group in Salem called the Instrumental Club. The group's activity led to the publication of *The Instrumental Assistant,* in two volumes (Exeter, N.H., 1800, 1807)—"the first comprehensive instrumental manual and collection of traditional music for band instruments published in America."[27]

The blind composer Oliver Shaw (1779–1848) was also partial to instrumental music. Besides being an accomplished organist, he studied piano and various other instruments with Gottlieb Graupner in Boston. Indicative of the growing interest in instrumental music was a compilation that he published in Providence in 1818: *Sacred Melodies, Selected from Haydn, Mozart, Beethoven, and Others, with Several Original Compositions, Arranged with an Accompaniment for the Pianoforte or Organ.*

Shaw also published *A Plain Introduction to the Art of Playing the Piano; to Which Is Added a Selection of Progressive Airs, Songs, etc.* (Dedham, 1811); and a collection titled *For the Gentlemen: A Favorite Selection of Instrumental Music . . . Consisting Principally of Marches, Airs, Minuets, etc.* Writ-

ten Chiefly in Four Parts, viz. 2 Clarionettes, Flute and Bassoon, or 2 Violins, Flute and Violincello . . . (Dedham, 1807). Shaw also wrote many marches, among them "Bonaparte's Grand March" and "General Bates' Quick March." As a prominent performer and a prolific and versatile composer, Shaw merits wider recognition than he has received thus far.

Shaw was, of course, committed to the "better music" movement, and in 1816 he and several associates founded in Providence, Rhode Island, the Psallonian Society, "for the purpose of improving themselves in the knowledge and practice of sacred music and inculcating a more correct taste in the choice and performance of it."[28] The society flourished for sixteen years, with Shaw presiding over and conducting most of its concerts, which featured music by eminent European composers from Handel to Mendelssohn.

Within forty years of the Declaration of Independence, the "native American" trend of the early pioneers was in decline, overshadowed by the inevitable advance of "progressive improvement," with its increasing allegiance to accredited culture as represented by the European masters.

Nevertheless, it would be a myopic view to see the native pioneers and their homespun music as disappearing from the theater of history. What we are witnessing is simply a change of scene; another act is about to unfold. True, the native pioneers no longer occupy center stage, applauded by polite society and supported by cultivated audiences eager to display their refined tastes. They are moving toward the hinterlands and the frontiers. They are going toward the people—in the countryside, on the farms, and in the burgeoning towns of the Midwest. History consists of exits and entrances; the native pioneers will hold the stage again—yea, in the very heart of Boston itself!

Notes

1. Frank J. Metcalf, *American Writers and Compilers of Sacred Music*, p. 111.
2. Ibid., pp. 112, 113.
3. *Pennsylvania Gazette*, May 28, 1761; quoted in Oscar G. Sonneck, *Francis Hopkinson . . . and James Lyon*, p. 128.
4. Sonneck, *Francis Hopkinson . . . and James Lyon*, pp. 134–47, especially pp. 135, 139.
5. *Journal & Letters of Philip Vickers Fithian*, p. 101.
6. Richard Crawford, preface to James Lyon, comp., *Urania*, p. xiii.
7. William Billings, *New-England Psalm-Singer* (Boston, 1770), pp. 19–20;

quoted in David McKay and Richard Crawford, *William Billings of Boston*, pp. 53–55.

8. For Billings's tunebooks and published writings, see Hans Nathan, *William Billings: Data and Documents*.

9. McKay and Crawford, *William Billings of Boston*, p. 41.

10. Quoted in ibid., p. 81.

11. Nathaniel D. Gould, *History of Church Music in America*, p. 46; quoted in ibid., p. 35.

12. Richard Crawford, "Fuging-tune," *The New Grove Dictionary of Music and Musicians* 7:9.

13. William Billings, *The Continental Harmony* (Boston, 1794), p. xxxii; quoted in McKay and Crawford, *William Billings of Boston*, p. 95.

14. *The Columbian Magazine; or, Monthly Miscellany* (Philadelphia), Apr. 1788, pp. 212–13; quoted in McKay and Crawford, *William Billings of Boston*, p. 155.

15. Nahum Mitchell, "William Billings," *Musical Reporter*, no. 7 (1841): 350–51; quoted in McKay and Crawford, *William Billings of Boston*, pp. 82–83.

16. It has been generally assumed that Billings was buried in an unmarked grave in Boston Common. But according to a resolution of the Town Council on Nov. 6, 1795, it was decreed that no new graves should be opened in the Common after May 1, 1796. See Nathan, *William Billings: Data and Documents*, p. 46.

17. Quoted in Metcalf, *American Writers and Compilers of Sacred Music*, p. 95.

18. From letter no. 894 to Ezra Read, dated Nov. 28, 1806; quoted in Irving Lowens, *Music and Musicians in Early America*, p. 170.

19. Metcalf, *American Writers and Compilers of Sacred Music*, p. 123.

20. Frederic P. Wells, *History of Newbury, Vermont*, p. 581.

21. Quoted in Richard Crawford, *Andrew Law, American Psalmodist*, p. 183 n. 33.

22. Ibid., p. 105. The advertisement for *The Select Harmony* appeared in the New London *Connecticut Gazetteer* on July 10, 1777. It is quoted in ibid., p. 110.

23. Frances Manwaring Caulkins, *History of Norwich, Connecticut*, pp. 470–71.

24. Quoted in Crawford, *Andrew Law, American Psalmodist*, p. 195.

25. *Connecticut Courant* (Hartford), July 17, 1821; quoted in ibid., p. 247.

26. From preface to *The Charlestown Collection of Sacred Songs*; quoted in Metcalf, *American Writers and Compilers of Sacred Music*, p. 128.

27. Alan C. Buechner, brochure notes to *The New England Harmony*, Folkways FA 2377, p. 27.

28. Quoted in Metcalf, *American Writers and Compilers of Sacred Music*, p. 181. Also see Joyce Mangler Carlson, "Early Music in Rhode Island, V: Oliver Shaw and the Psallonian Society," pp. 35–50.

PART TWO

The People and the Nation

Chapter 8
Progress, Profit, and Uplift

The dream of my life was to be a musician. . . . I was going
where the air was filled with music, and pent-up desires and
ambitions could have unlimited freedom.
—George F. Root, *The Story of a Musical Life* (1891)

During the first half of the nineteenth century, the pattern of music as "big
business" began to take shape in the United States. American musicians
were making money from their publications, as they profited from American methods of mass production and distribution, including high-pressure
promotion and sensational advertising. When the ex-blacksmith Isaac
Baker Woodbury brought out his collection of sacred music, *The Dulcimer*,
an advertisement in *Dwight's Journal of Music* screamingly proclaimed:

125,000 Copies in Two Seasons!
Live Music Book!
The Dulcimer

The sacred-music collections of Lowell Mason topped them all. His
Carmina Sacra (in various editions) sold 500,000 copies between 1841 and
1858. Another of Mason's collections, *The Hallelujah*, sold 150,000 copies in
five years. To our struggling musical pioneers such as Billings or Kimball,
the idea of making $100,000 from a collection of sacred music, as Mason
did, would have seemed fantastic.

For the music business of the United States during the first half of the
nineteenth century, two facts stand out. One is that the leading musical impresario of the period was also a pioneer of the circus and freak sideshow,
the great master of ballyhoo—that sensational showman, Phineas Taylor
Barnum. The other is that the most influential and financially successful
musical leader of the period, Lowell Mason, was a prototype of the self-
made American businessman.

Contemporary accounts agree that Mason was shrewd in his business dealings; he was "a manager of men, an organizer of movements." He also had "huge industry" and "great ability, penetrating foresight, splendid ideas." He had a "commanding personality" and "a remarkable degree of personal magnetism." He was "a clear-sighted, practical man, just the leader the American people could then understand, and be willing to follow." He was "a man of strong and impressive individuality, a virile nature in which an iron will was coupled with a gentle and tender heart."[1] Although the last-mentioned quality is not usually associated with big business, we may at least give Mason the benefit of the doubt.

Lowell Mason was born in Medfield, Massachusetts, on January 8, 1792, and grew up in the tradition of the New England singing school. His grandfather, Barachias Mason, had been a singing-school master as well as a school teacher. His father, who was town treasurer and a member of the state legislature, also sang in the church choir and played several instruments. As a boy, Lowell attended the singing school of Amos Albee, compiler of *The Norfolk Collection of Sacred Harmony* (Dedham, Mass., 1805), and later received musical instruction from the celebrated blind composer and organist Oliver Shaw. He learned to play organ, flute, clarinet, and various other instruments.

In 1812 Mason accompanied the Medford organ builder George Whitefield Adams to Savannah, where he took a job as clerk in a bank (he was a prudent young man). At the same time he took lessons in music from Frederick L. Abel, a professional musician recently arrived from Germany. Thanks to his professional training, Mason was appointed organist and choirmaster of the Independent Presbyterian Church in Savannah and also began to compose hymns and anthems. In 1817 he married Abigail Gregory, of Westboro, Massachusetts.

Although not yet fully determined to make music his career, he decided to compile a collection of sacred music. In it he included some of his own tunes, as well as melodies from instrumental compositions by Handel, Mozart, Beethoven, and other European composers, adapted to familiar hymns and arranged for three or four voices "with a figured base [*sic*] for the organ or pianoforte." Having completed this work, he sought a publisher in Philadelphia and elsewhere, but without success. Then he met Dr. George K. Jackson, organist of the Handel and Haydn Society of Boston, who took an interest in the compilation and recommended that the society sponsor its publication—with several of his own compositions included. Thus was born the famous *Boston Handel and Haydn Society Collection of Church Music*, which went to press in 1821 and was copyrighted the following year. Dr. Jackson, whose opinion carried much weight, endorsed it "as much the best book of the kind I have seen published in this country."[2]

Lowell Mason's name did not appear as editor, although he was mentioned in the preface. In later years Mason gave this explanation for the omission of his name on the title page: "I was then a bank officer in Savannah and did not wish to be known as a musical man, and I had not the least thought of making music my profession."[3] The success of this collection soon made him change his mind. The book went through twenty-two editions and brought handsome profits both to its compiler and the Handel and Haydn Society, to which it gave financial stability.

Mason returned to Savannah; but in 1826 he was in Boston to deliver a lecture on church music, and a year later he was persuaded to settle in Boston as choirmaster of Dr. Lyman Beecher's church on Hanover Street. (This church was destroyed by fire soon afterward, and a new one was built on Bowdoin Street.) Mason also took a temporary job as bank teller; he was not yet convinced that music could be made to pay. But his star was obviously rising. Before the year was over he was elected president of the Handel and Haydn Society—an office held until 1832, when he resigned in order to devote more time to teaching music to children. In 1829 he brought out the *Juvenile Psalmist; or, The Child's Introduction to Sacred Music,* followed a year or two later by the *Juvenile Lyre; or, Hymns and Songs, Religious, Moral, and Cheerful . . . for the Use of Primary and Common Schools.* This, he claimed, was "the first school songbook published in this country." It is pleasant to note that cheerfulness was encouraged.

Mason believed, and preached, that all schoolchildren should be taught to sing, just as they were taught to read. Due to his persistent efforts, the Boston School Committee in 1838 authorized the introduction of music as a branch of instruction in the city schools. Mason administered this activity and thus became the first superintendent of music in an American public school system. He continued in this post until 1845, when he was forced out by political intrigue.

Meanwhile, in 1833 Mason had taken the initiative in founding the Boston Academy of Music, whose far-reaching aims included vocal instruction for adults and children (the latter free of charge), teacher-training methods, sacred music performance, lectures, and publications. Of the latter, the most successful was the *Manual of the Boston Academy of Music* (Boston, 1834).

To succeed in his ventures, Mason had to strike a balance between the familiar and the innovative. Public taste was generally conservative; yet it

also was attracted by novelty, especially if linked to the idea of progress—
of being "up-to-date." Mason's skill in achieving this balance is illustrated
in his preface to the tenth edition (1831) of *The Boston Handel and Haydn Society Collection of Church Music:*

> The several later editions of this work have presented an almost uniform ap-
> pearance. . . . It is obvious, however, from the progressive nature of science
> and taste, in respect to music as well as other subjects, that this uniformity can-
> not be, and ought not to be perpetual. Within the last few years, much atten-
> tion has been directed to the subject, and, as was to be expected, great im-
> provement has been made, not only in the manner of performing psalm and
> hymn tunes, but also in their composition.
>
> Is it to be supposed that in psalmody, science and taste have accom-
> plished all that they can accomplish? And is it desirable that all attempts at im-
> provement should be checked? This is impracticable if it were desirable. . . .
>
> Unless, therefore, it be maintained that the present psalm and hymn
> tunes cannot be improved, and that no better can be substituted in their stead,
> or else, that bad tunes are as valuable as good ones, there may be as valid rea-
> sons, founded in public utility, for introducing alterations into text books of
> psalmody, as for introducing alterations into text books on arithmetic or
> grammar.

Mason gives an indication of what he means by "bad" tunes when he
states that he has reduced the number of "imitative and fugueing pieces"
and kept down the proportion of "light pieces" in deference to "the good
sense and improved taste of the public" (a touch of flattery there!). As we
shall see, there was still a large public ready and eager to enjoy the fuging
pieces of the early New England singing-school masters.

Nevertheless, the forces of progress and uplift were closing ranks, as
indicated by a review of the new edition of the *Handel and Haydn Collection* that appeared in the *New Haven Chronicle:* "A book so valuable must
become the standard of music in our churches, since its harmony and style
are fixed on the immovable basis of science and correct taste." We have
here an assertion of the classical concept of inherent and immutable aesthetic values, grafted onto the scientific rationalism of the Enlightenment.
In this view, progressive improvement could continue indefinitely, provided it built on the firm foundation of science.

For Lowell Mason and his associates, going back to the music of the
New England pioneers represented an aesthetic retrogression. To counteract this backward trend it was necessary to present the music of prestigious
European composers such as Beethoven, Cherubini, Handel, Haydn, Mozart, Palestrina, Schubert, and Weber—all of whom figure in Mason's 1850

collection of church music, *The New Carmina Sacra,* published under the auspices of the Boston Academy of Music.

As stated on the elaborately descriptive title page, this collection comprised "the Most Popular Psalm and Hymn Tunes in General Use, Together with a Great Variety of New Tunes, Chants, Sentences, Motetts, and Anthems; Principally by Distinguished European Composers. . . ." Once again, "made in Europe" was the mark of distinction in music for American consumption, as it would continue to be throughout the nineteenth century. Yet Mason was more of an opportunist than a propagandist. He aimed at "improving" public taste, but not at the cost of losing a potential market. In *The New Carmina Sacra,* Mason yielded to market demands by including tunes by such native pioneers as William Billings, Daniel Read, and Oliver Holden. His concession, however, had its price. The "Most Popular Psalm and Hymn Tunes" of the early American singing-school masters were presented in altered form, reharmonized in accordance with modern "scientific" criteria. The banner of progress persisted in leading the way.

Mason and his colleagues confronted competition from an unexpected source. Although the early tunesmiths were no longer in the front line, they still had a considerable following. The Boston Handel and Haydn Society had its popular counterpart in the Boston Billings and Holden Society, founded in the 1830s through the efforts of "many respectable singers and musicians, partly for amusement, and partly for the purpose of reviving old associations, and giving an opportunity to the curious who had a desire to hear the tunes sung by their fathers and mothers . . . and [to] others who really preferred them."[4]

The society also aimed to present this music in its original character, instead of in the "improved" versions favored by Mason and his associates. For this purpose it published in 1836 *The Billings and Holden Collection of Ancient Psalmody,* on the principle that these tunes "must be republished as originally written, or the elderly and middle-aged must be deprived of the satisfaction and delight they have heretofore experienced."[5] This may be an early example of musical consideration for the benefit of "senior citizens."

Similar considerations of authenticity and nostalgia prompted a later publication, *Ancient Harmony Revived* (Hallowell, Maine, and Boston, 1847), so that the movement was evidently gaining momentum. In fact, the 1850s brought an extraordinary impetus to the revival of the old tunes, demonstrating that "although singing-school music had been depreciated by the musical establishment, it still commanded wide affection and respect among ordinary people."⁶ An enterprising shoe merchant from Wellfleet, Massachusetts, by the name of Robert Kemp—soon to be widely known as "Father Kemp"—had the idea of organizing "Old Folks Concerts" as a professional venture, with the performers dressed in eighteenth-century costumes. The programs actually mixed old hymn tunes with patriotic and popular songs of a later period. But they emphasized the singing-school tradition sufficiently to attract and delight large audiences, as well as to arouse the ire of the Masons, who denounced the music as "trash" and the performances as "uncouth." Billings, they declared, "knew about as much of the laws of harmony and musical composition as did Maezel's automaton trumpeter."⁷ Nevertheless, the Old Folks Concerts flourished well into the 1860s and reached millions of people in many parts of the nation.

Whereas the emphasis of the Old Folks Concerts was on entertainment, the emphasis of the choirs trained by Lowell Mason and his colleagues was on aesthetic edification. Both indicated a trend toward the secularization of religious music (which had actually begun in the eighteenth century), inasmuch as the character or quality of the performance became the main attraction. Mason and his emulators drew extensively on secular melodies by well-known (and sometimes obscure) European composers for their settings of religious texts. This was analogous to, at a more sophisticated level, the "borrowing" of secular folk tunes by the early singing-school composers.

With respect to performance, quality counted more than content. For Mason, as for McLuhan a century later, the medium was the message. Lowell Mason trained his choir at Dr. Lyman Beecher's church in Boston to such a point of excellence that it drew nationwide attention and admiration. A contemporary wrote: "Pilgrimages were made from all parts of the land to hear the wonderful singing. Clergymen who attended ministerial gatherings in Boston carried home with them oftentimes quite as much musical as spiritual inspiration."⁸ The choir loft had become a national shrine.

An interesting feature of Mason's musical arrangements is the interpolation of "Hallelujah" refrains, which he called "codas." In the preface to *The New Carmina Sacra,* Mason states:

> The Codas added to many of the tunes form quite a new feature in a book of this kind, and it is hoped they may add interest to the performance of psalmody. Although they are called codas, yet they are not designed for the close, merely, but may be introduced before the first stanza, or between the stanzas of a hymn, as may be appropriate. In the singing schools and choir

Lowell Mason. Photo courtesy of the Music Division, The New York Public Library at Lincoln Center, Astor, Lenox and Tilden Foundations.

meetings, they may always be sung, but in public worship the propriety of singing them must depend upon the circumstances of the occasion, hymn, &c. The hymns in which these Hallelujahs may with propriety be introduced, are more numerous than may be at first supposed; for under what circumstances does not the devout heart say, "Praise the Lord?"

Here is an example of Mason's "coda," showing only the rhythmic pattern:

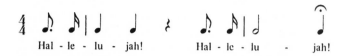

Although Mason claimed that this was "quite a new feature" in collections of sacred music, the "Hallelujah" refrain had been a feature of revival hymnody for several decades before the publication of *The New Carmina Sacra*. We may conjecture that Mason borrowed this popular device as an added attraction for his collection. It would never do to let the competition have a monopoly of the more obvious joys of hymn singing. Let it also be noted that one of Mason's most successful collections was called *The Hallelujah*. First published in Boston and New York in 1854, it reached a third edition in 1882. It was deliberately modeled on the old singing-school tunebooks, including a section on "musical notation in a nutshell: a brief course for singing schools; intended for skillful teachers and apt pupils." The singing schools certainly did not disappear with the eighteenth century; we shall have ample evidence of that in a later chapter ("The Fasola Folk").

During half a century (1822–72) Lowell Mason edited or compiled, alone or in collaboration with others, a huge quantity of sacred (and some secular) music collections. His industry, initiative, and perseverance were extraordinary. His role in the development of music education in America cannot be overestimated. Yet his organizational and didactic activities by no means overshadowed his great and enduring success as a composer of hymns. We need only mention such perennial favorites as "Nearer My God to Thee" ("Bethany"), "From Greenland's Icy Mountains" ("Missionary Hymn"), "My Faith Looks Up to Thee" ("Olivet"), "Work, for the Night Is Coming" ("Diligence"), "When I Survey the Wondrous Cross" ("Hamburg"), and "Watchman, Tell Us of the Night" ("Watchman").

Outdoing Lowell Mason in longevity and rivaling him in productivity, influence, and success was his older contemporary and colleague,

Thomas Hastings (1784–1872). An account that credits him with having written 1,000 hymn tunes is probably exaggerated. Whatever the number, only one remains widely known, "Rock of Ages, Cleft for Me" (tune name, "Toplady"), while three are frequently used: "Ortonville," "Retreat," and "Zion." He is said to have written 600 hymn texts, many of them set to music by European composers, and he compiled and published upward of twenty collections, also collaborating on several others. His *Dissertation on Musical Taste* (Albany, 1822; rev. 2d ed., New York, 1853) was influential in its time.

Although Hastings was born in Washington, Connecticut, where his father was a physician, the family moved to western New York (Oneida County) when he was twelve. The move was made in winter, with sleighs and ox-drawn sleds, and in their new home the family faced pioneer conditions, with farm fields only partially cleared and much of the area surrounded by deep woods. While his father continued to practice medicine *cum* farming, young Thomas decided he wanted to be a musician, which, in that environment, meant self-help and strong determination.

From a musical treatise acquired at a local auction, Hastings learned the rudiments. After mastering all the tunes in an old book of psalmody, and having served his apprenticeship in the choir of the village church, he felt ready to begin his professional career. True, for him there was no primrose path to success, no Boston Handel and Haydn Society to boost his prospects. But he was industrious and dedicated, ambitious and high-minded, and he saw a great need for spreading musical education among the people. So he eventually became the eminent Dr. Thomas Hastings, with an honorary doctorate from New York University—a taste maker whose word was respected, a musical magnate whose books sold in the hundreds of thousands.

Hastings's first and most famous collection, *Musica Sacra,* was published in Utica in 1815, with ten editions and reprints to 1831. Described as a "Collection of Psalm Tunes, Hymns, and Set Pieces" (shades of Billings and company!), it ranged from familiar psalm tunes of the colonial period to selections from Handel's *Messiah.* Two years later he brought out a small collection titled *Flute Melodies* (Utica, 1817/22), containing airs, duets, cotillions, waltzes, marches, and other pieces for the German flute and flageolet. Hastings's attitude toward secular music, as we shall see, was narrow but not negative: its "proper" function was to provide good tunes for sacred texts.

By about 1817 Hastings was devoting much time and effort to promot-

ing singing schools in New York State. His efforts even included an advertising campaign. Writing to his brother in 1817 about publicity, he remarked, "I wish that the advertisement may have as conspicuous a place in
the paper and an inviting caption but nothing that shall be deemed inconsistent with the strictest principles of modesty." He wanted to do "business
in the Auburn style"—genteel and dignified.[9]

Although Hastings is seldom given credit for possessing a sense of humor, a letter describing the first meeting of his singing school in Troy reveals that he did not lack this quality: "Last Monday I met the school for
the first time, when lo, a marvelous company of aged men, batchellors and
boys, old women, staid dames and saplings were assembled. . . . And there
right merrily was to be heard forth issuing from the vocal bundles of their
faces the true-blue 'nasal twang,' the Screatch *Owle squeak*, the *whippoor-
will's* and blackbird's descant, and the bullfrog's gutteral bellow—all in a
dispot [*sic*] uniform pace of movement."[10]

Nevertheless, he was a strict disciplinarian, brooking no nonsense
from young or old, dames or misses, grey-beards or saplings. Besides, he
was preparing for bigger things: before long he was to be the leading
trainer and director of church choirs in the great metropolis of New York
City. With a steady output of tunebooks for adults and children, with his
journalistic outlets as editor of the *Western Recorder* in Utica and later the
Musical Magazine in New York (1835–37), his participation in musical conventions, and his lecture tours, he was widely recognized by the 1830s as a
leading figure in the musical life of the nation.

Hastings took the initiative in founding the New York Academy of Sacred Music (1835), which in 1840 sponsored his highly popular collection
The Sacred Lyre. Although titles were becoming fancier and more sophisticated in their appeal to cultivated urban users, Hastings's first collaboration with William B. Bradbury resulted in a book called simply *The
Psalmodist* (New York, 1844). This "retrogression" was corrected not long
after 1847, the year Bradbury went to Germany to study with such prestigious teachers as Moritz Hauptmann and Ignaz Moscheles. Two years later he returned with trunks full of German music, much of which was used
in the next Bradbury-Hastings opus, stylishly titled *The Mendelssohn Collection* (New York, 1849). But the cultural ambivalence (and Yankee shrewd-
ness) that persisted in this era of "progressive improvement" is revealed in
the subtitle: *Hastings and Bradbury's Third Book of Psalmody*.

The collection did in fact include some "old tunes . . . which are gen-

erally sung in congregational singing." However, in spite of this concession to the taste of the "old folks," the editors made a special plea for the superiority of German music, with its "many beautiful melodies" capable of
providing "the most interesting and delightful part of the worship."[11]

Hastings noted with satisfaction that, five months after its publication, *The Mendelssohn Collection* had sold "near 28,000 copies" and that it
was "ahead of its predecessors in the same line; and is also ahead of Mason's last book."[12] Although Mason and Hastings collaborated on several
collections, there was much rivalry between them, and more than a little
jealousy on Hastings's part. Competition was as keen in the sacred music
business as in any other aspect of American industry.

We have mentioned Hastings's ambivalence concerning secular music, and, in view of his role as a would-be taste maker, his views on this subject deserve further comment. In his preface to *The Oriental Glee & Anthem Book* (New York, 1861), to which he contributed twenty-five pieces,
Hastings wrote: "Secular compositions are as necessary in music, perhaps,
as is prose or poetry. The exclusive use of sacred pieces for aesthetic purposes, has a tendency to their desecration. Hence the necessity for lighter
compositions."[13] This resembles the old argument that prostitutes should
be tolerated in order to preserve the chastity of virtuous women.

We have reason to believe that Hastings took a rather dim view of
"aesthetic purposes" on the whole—as we may gather from his *Dissertation
on Musical Taste*, first published in 1822 and extensively revised in 1853. He
regards music as a language of *feeling*, which is to be judged by its *influence*
on the listener rather than by any intrinsic stylistic quality or formal structure. While acknowledging a need for "the preservation of grammatical cor-
rectness in musical composition," he insists on the priority of affective values: "When we say that a composition is merely correct, we virtually affirm
that it is insipid, or destitute of meaning; but when we speak of it as grave
or facetious; descriptive, or impassioned; and when we pronounce it to be
tender, soothing, lofty, sublime or beautiful, we then evidently allude to
ideas of a higher nature."[14]

While granting that it was possible to associate "aesthetic considerations with devotional sentiments,"[15] he felt strongly that the latter should
take precedence, and he was "not willing to acknowledge excellence in any
music of this kind, any further than it can be made to subserve the great
ends of religious edification."[16] It has been rightly observed that Hastings's
judgment of music was "Puritanical"—in the strict doctrinal meaning of

the term. His statement that secular music could be countenanced as long as it was "not incompatible with other duties and obligations"[17] is Puritan dogma verbatim.

The paradox remains that the collections of "sacred music" compiled by Hastings are full of secular melodies. To cite one example, the hymn text "Gently, Lord, O Gently Lead Us" is set to a tune based on "Batti, batti, o bel Masetto," from Mozart's *Don Giovanni*. The explanation is probably that he was not averse to secularity per se, provided it was put to good use. What did concern him greatly were the *associations* of secular tunes. He evidently rejected the notion that a tune might be divorced from its familiar text as a popular song or ballad. He regarded such associations as ineradicable contamination; hence his vehement repudiation of "unchaste" tunes. He deplored the "multitude of insipid, vulgar, and profane melodies"[18] that were given further currency in many collections of sacred music, such as Joshua Leavitt's *Christian Lyre*. He protested vigorously against such travesties as changing the line in a song about George Washington ("Saw ye not my hero George?") into a hymn beginning "Saw ye not my Saviour?" Unlike the old adage about not letting the devil have all the best tunes, he wanted none of the devil's doing, "after he has used it up, and trodden it under foot."[19]

With regard to the melodies of the great (and small) European masters, it was a different matter. Hastings favored instrumental music because it carried no overt associations; songs and arias were admissible, provided the words bore no profane or "vulgar" connotations. Besides, the risk of contamination was less because of their relative unfamiliarity—unlike the songs of Stephen Foster, which circulated in every household and even found their way into Sunday schools! As Hastings became increasingly concerned with music instruction for children, especially in Sunday schools (a very large market), he was adamant in holding out against their contamination by popular melodies. Although he bravely held his finger in the dike, he was unable to stem the rising flood of "vulgar" tunes.

Hastings, together with Timothy Mason, had taken a hand in compiling an extremely successful collection called *The Shawm* (New York, 1853), which was, however, chiefly the work of George F. Root and William B. Bradbury. According to an advertisement in 1855, "89,000 copies were sold within a year of publication, a number unequaled by any previous similar publication." It also had the distinction of bringing together four of the most prominent tunebook compilers and music educators of this period.

Timothy Mason (brother of Lowell) was active in the Midwest, where he published *Mason's Juvenile Harp* (Cincinnati, 1845), "containing a large number of new and beautiful melodies and hymns, *selected and translated from the German. . . .*" (Italics added.) George F. Root (of whom much more will be said in the next chapter) was associated with Lowell Mason in various educational activities and vied with him in the sale of edifying song collections. *The Silver Lute* (Chicago, 1862), intended for day schools, sold more than 100,000 copies, and *The Prize* (Chicago, 1870), for Sunday schools, did even better. Concerning *The Triumph* (Chicago, 1868), Root informs us that it "sold ninety thousand copies the first year, at a profit to us [the firm of Root and Cady] of thirty thousand dollars." Quite a profitable triumph!

As music educator, Root had assisted Lowell Mason at the Boston Academy of Music, and in 1853 they organized the first Normal Musical Institute for music teachers in New York, with Hastings and Bradbury as members of the faculty. Its impact was nationwide, as students came from every part of the United States. In 1856 the activities of the institute were transferred to North Reading, Massachusetts, where it became—in the words of Root—"a great school in a small town." Among its admirers and supporters were Henry Ward Beecher and his sister Harriet Beecher Stowe, the famous writer, both of whom "attended the afternoon chorus and glee singing, which they greatly enjoyed."[20] The institute was dissolved in 1859, as its leading members went their separate ways. But the idea of training music teachers through Normal Institutes and periodic conventions prospered and expanded in the years to come.

One of the music educators whom we have mentioned, William B. Bradbury (1816–68), was also a highly successful compiler and promoter of sacred music. From 1841 to 1867 he turned out, on average, two music books each year. Among the most popular was *The Jubilee* (New York, 1858), which reportedly sold over 250,000 copies. Another, *The Golden Chain* (New York, 1861), was so successful that it drew severe attacks from his competitors, who claimed that it was full of errors. Doctored up by Bradbury's friend, Dr. Hastings, it brought in a golden harvest. Bradbury's music books were estimated to have sold over two million copies. As a composer of hymns, he is remembered chiefly for "He Leadeth Me" and "Sweet Hour of Prayer."

One of the most successful song collections of this period was *The Dulcimer; or, The New York Collection of Sacred Music* (New York, 1850), edited by Isaac B. Woodbury (1819–58). Born in Beverly, Massachusetts, his first occupation was that of blacksmith. But he also studied music in Boston from the age of thirteen and learned to play the violin. In 1838 he went to Europe for further study in London and Paris, after which he taught music in Boston for six years. Later he traveled throughout New England with the Bay State Glee Club and organized the New Hampshire and Vermont Musical Association, which he directed. From 1849 he was active in New York as a choirmaster and as editor of the *Musical Review*. Plagued by ill health, he went south in 1858, hoping to recuperate. He got as far as Columbia, South Carolina, where he died, leaving a wife and six small children.

Covering the eastern seaboard from Vermont to South Carolina, Woodbury published two collections especially designed for southern use: *The Harp of the South* (1853) and *The Casket* (Charleston, S.C., 1855), the latter sponsored by the southern Baptist Society. He also brought out *Woodbury's Self-Instructor in Musical Composition and Thorough-Bass* (Boston, 1849), catering to the American appetite for self-instruction. This was an appropriate gesture from a one-time blacksmith who became a successful composer, not only of hymn tunes but also of secular songs that enjoyed wide popularity.

Among so many celebrated and successful champions of progress and profit, let us note a less conspicuous individual, who in his own way aspired to better things. His name was Thomas Commuck, a Narragansett Indian, who in order to make his way in the world, "commenced trying to learn, scientifically, the art of singing." He also devised some tunes and asked Hastings to harmonize them. The eminent Doctor of Music complied, and together they published *Indian Melodies . . . Harmonized by Thomas Hastings* (New York, 1845).

The melodies were "Indian" in name only, for they were composed by this "son of the forest" as settings for psalms and hymns, to which were given "the names of Indian chiefs, Indian females, Indian names of places, &c." An "Old Indian Hymn" had the following explanation: "The Narragansett Indians have a tradition, that the following tune was heard in the air by them, and other tribes bordering on the Atlantic coast, many years before the arrival of the whites in America; and that on their first visiting a church in Plymouth Colony, after the settlement of that place by the whites, the same tune was sung while performing divine service, and the Indians knew it as well as the whites. The tune is therefore preserved among them to this day, and is sung to the words here set."[21] The words are as follows:

My soul doth magnify the Lord,
My spirit doth rejoice
In God my Saviour, and my God;
I hear a joyful voice.
Hallelujah, Hallelujah,
Hosanna, Hosanna!

Surely we must seek far to find another such instance of extraterrestrial acculturation!

Notes

1. Quotations cited in Arthur Lowndes Rich, *Lowell Mason,* pp. 106–7.
2. Lowell Mason, comp., *The Boston Handel and Haydn Society Collection of Church Music,* p. vi.
3. Frank J. Metcalf, *American Writers and Compilers of Sacred Music,* p. 212.
4. Nathaniel D. Gould, *History of Church Music in America,* p. 190; quoted in Judith T. Steinberg [Judith Tick], "Old Folks Concerts and the Revival of New England Psalmody," p. 603.
5. Ibid.
6. Ibid., p. 605.
7. *New York Musical Review and Gazette,* June 12, 1858; quoted in ibid., p. 611 n. 23.
8. Theodore F. Seward, *The Educational Work of Dr. Lowell Mason* (n.p., 1879), p. 9; quoted in Rich, *Lowell Mason,* p. 12.
9. Letter from Thomas Hastings to Eurotas Hastings, dated Auburn, N.Y., Sept. 28, 1817; quoted in James Edward Dooley, "Thomas Hastings," p. 28.
10. Letter from Thomas Hastings to Eurotas Hastings, dated June 23, 1819; quoted in Dooley, "Thomas Hastings," p. 33.
11. *The Mendelssohn Collection* (New York, 1849), p. 637; quoted in Dooley, "Thomas Hastings," p. 99.
12. Letter from Thomas Hastings to Eurotas Hastings, dated New York, Jan. 19, 1850; quoted in Dooley, "Thomas Hastings," pp. 99–100.
13. T. J. Cook and T. E. Perkins, *The Oriental Glee & Anthem Book* (New York, 1861), p. 627; quoted in Dooley, "Thomas Hastings," p. 114.
14. Thomas Hastings, *Dissertation on Musical Taste,* 2d rev. ed., p. 132; quoted in Dooley, "Thomas Hastings," p. 123.
15. Thomas Hastings, *The History of Forty Choirs* (New York, 1853), p. 230; quoted in Dooley, "Thomas Hastings," p. 129.
16. Hastings, *Dissertation on Musical Taste,* p. 245; quoted in Dooley, "Thomas Hastings," p. 129.
17. Hastings, *Dissertation on Musical Taste,* p. 264; quoted in Dooley, "Thomas Hastings," p. 130.

18. Thomas Hastings and Lowell Mason, *Spiritual Songs* . . . (Utica, 1832), p. 637; quoted in Dooley, "Thomas Hastings," pp. 158–59.

19. *Proceedings of the American Musical Convention* (New York: Saxton and Miles, 1845), pp. 71–72; quoted in Dooley, "Thomas Hastings," p. 160.

20. George Frederick Root, *The Story of a Musical Life*, pp. 107, 110.

21. Quoted in Robert Stevenson, *Protestant Church Music*, p. 9. See also J. Vincent Higginson, *Hymnody in the American Indian Missions*.

Chapter 9

The Genteel Tradition

I would ask if there are not words in the Anglo-Saxon language
that can be associated so as to express what is, in the supreme
affectation of fashionable parlance, termed "soirée musicale."
—John Hill Hewitt, *Shadows on the Wall* (1877)

Nothing could be more elegant than to refer to a concert as a *soirée
musicale*. These two words were fragrant with the aristocratic aroma of a
Parisian salon, redolent of an elite society in which celebrated artists min-
gled with the representatives of rank and wealth. They disguised the obvious fact that the performing musicians were professionals who hoped to
make money from their concerts. Could such a distinguished personage as
the Baron Rudolph, self-styled pianist to His Majesty the Emperor of Russia, be concerned with vulgar pecuniary consideration when, in 1839, he
gave a recital that attracted the cream of New York society? Or could one
place on the crude level of commercial entertainment the *soirées musicales*
presented in the same year by the eminent maestro Charles Edward Horn
and his accomplished wife? The programs offered by Mr. and Mrs. Horn
featured vocal selections from the most celebrated European composers of
the day, among whom Mr. Horn might include himself, for he had
achieved considerable success in England before migrating to America in
1833. Moreover, some of these *soirées* were graced by the participation of
two of the most prominent English ballad composers and singers of that
time—Mr. Joseph Knight and Mr. Henry Russell—both of whom were
bent on elevating the musical taste of Americans, much to the benefit of
their bank accounts.

In this endeavor they had plenty of competition. Two distinguished
opera singers from England, Anna and Arthur Seguin, offered a series of
recitals featuring selections from Italian operas. Those who favored this
truly fashionable type of musical entertainment were also regaled with operatic selections by such artistes as Madame Alboni, Madame Vellani, Si-

gnora Marconcelli, and Signore Rapetti. It should be noted that Italian opera, in particular, besides catering to the elite, also had gained wide popular acceptance in America, especially in the context of "favorite airs."[1]

About this time the Irish composer and violinist William Vincent Wallace and his wife were also concertizing in America. Some years later Wallace made a gallant musical offering to the ladies of America in the form of *Six valses élégantes* for piano—further inscribed as *Fleurs musicales, offertes aux dames d'Amérique*. The elegance of the French language, the exquisite gallantry of the gesture, the beautiful bouquet of flowers depicted on the cover, the facile charm of the music—everything about this offering reflected the fashionable gentility that was spreading like a veneer over American society.

There was, however, a considerable cultural crossover during this period of transition and assimilation. High-class connections were touted along with popular entertainment, as in the following notice that appeared in the *Public Ledger* of Philadelphia (December 28, 1838):

> MUSICAL SOIREE! *Vocal and Instrumental*, at the Grand Saloon of the Philadelphia Museum. . . . Frank Johnson will give Musical Soirees . . . commencing at 7 o'clock precisely, on the plan of those held at Musard's Rooms, at Paris, where the Music, being of a popular and varied character, and the fee of admission moderate, thousands assemble nightly, to pass an hour or two in the enjoyment of an intellectual source of amusement, and a social promenade. The selections of Music performed will be those brought before the nobility and gentry at F. Johnson's Concerts in London, last winter, and received with distinguished applause.

The juxtapositional enticements cleverly blend sociability and amusement with high-class qualities, in which pleasure becomes "intellectual," while the music to be performed is noted for having been previously received with "distinguished" applause by the English "nobility and gentry." The *"PROGRAMME of THIS Evening's Performances"* includes a "Grand Symphony," followed by a "Solo on the Kent Bugle," with Frank Johnson performing "The Light of Other Days Is Faded," by the Irish singer and composer Michael William Balfe, from his opera *The Maid of Artois* (1836). Other operatic numbers included Bellini's "Tue [*sic*] Vedrai Sventurata, with introduction and embellishments, on the Cornet à Piston, from the Opera of the Pirate—by F. Johnson," and "Quadrilles, from Fra Diavolo," Auber's popular *opéra-comique*. A "Quadrille Parisien" gave another touch of Paris to the Philadelphians in search of pleasure combined with "class."

As we shall see later (chapter 17), Frank Johnson and his band provided a great deal of high-class pleasure for people in both America and Europe, and many of his own compositions contributed to the prestige of the genteel tradition.[2]

When it came to cultural diffusion, mobility and variety were the keynotes. When elegant feminine fingers ceased to pluck the harp strings, the brass bands and the cornet soloist were ready for anything from polkas to operatic arias. Where the parlor piano left off, the hurdy-gurdy street organ took over. A song intended for the parlor would appear in a minstrel show, or vice versa. For instance, H. S. Thompson's sentimental ballad "Lilly Dale" (1852) became a favorite blackface number, featured by "the romantic balladeer, usually a tenor, who sang sentimental love songs that provided an outlet for tender emotions and a chance for the ladies in the audience to sigh, to weep, or to do both."[3]

When it came to playing on the heartstrings, there were no class barriers or social distinctions. The theme of the dear, departed maiden was the touchstone of the nineteenth century. If "Lilly Dale" wrung the hearts of minstrel-show audiences, she also provided a delicious sensation of sadness for more genteel listeners, who sighed with pleasure whenever a fashionable pianist—or an accomplished young lady—played Sigmund Thalberg's elegant variations titled *Lilly Dale: Air américain varié pour le piano*. (Thalberg was an eminent piano virtuoso and composer who toured the United States in 1856.)

The omnipresent theme of the dear, departed maiden reappears in a very genteel song that has antecedents in minstrelsy. It is found in a collection titled *National Melodies of America* by the English composer previously mentioned, Charles E. Horn, with texts by the facile poet and journalist George Pope Morris. The song is actually a slightly altered version of an old-time minstrel tune, "Long Time Ago," which was popularized by Thomas "Daddy" Rice (see chapter 13, p. 236). Here is a stanza of the Horn-Morris song, with the vocal melody only:

"On the Lake Where Droop'd the Willow"

Dwelt   a maid,   be - loved   and   cher -ish'd,   By   high   and_   low;

But,   with au -tumn's   leaf,   she per -ish'd,   Long   time_ a   -   go!

When Edgar Allan Poe formulated his famous dictum that the most poetic subject was the death of a beautiful young woman, he stated an aesthetic principle that prevailed as a cliché of the genteel tradition. The maid who dwelt on or near the lake and "perish'd with the autumn's leaf" in Morris's lyric was a literary cousin (perhaps twice removed) of Poe's "rare and radiant maiden whom the angels named Lenore." To that ephemeral family Stephen Foster added many names, from "Gentle Annie" and "Eulalie" to "Gentle Lena Clare" and "Laura Lee." This was a way of being sentimentally romantic while skirting sexual taboo. As Richard Jackson observes, "The great majority of Foster's ladies are either asleep or dead."[4] Both situations were regarded as perfectly proper, but the latter was edifyingly definitive.

We tend to put musical types into separate compartments with specific labels such as "parlor songs," "household music," "minstrel melodies," and so forth, as though they were utterly distinct and unrelated. We tend to emphasize *categories* rather than *situations*. This may do well enough for scholarly classification but not for the sociocultural context of actual experience. We know, for example, that Foster's so-called plantation melodies were as popular on the minstrel stage as they were welcome in the parlor. Any sentimental song with a sufficient number of high notes would find a lyric tenor in blackface ready to give it an "Ethiopian" presentation.

Nelson Kneass (1823–68) is an example of a composer and performer who made the transition from "art" music to minstrelsy and enjoyed considerable success in both fields. In 1843, for example, a newspaper account tells of a concert at which "an orchestra rendered selections from Auber, Bellini, Beethoven, Kneass, Messemer, Balfe, Bishop, and Musard." The following year he was with a group of singers in New York who presented "sentimental or comic tunes, rendered singly or in vocal combination," performing with great success both at the Broadway Concert Hall and the fashionable Vauxhall Gardens.[5] Thereafter he turned to blackface minstrelsy, specializing in operatic burlesques with his own "Ethiopian Troupe."

Most pertinent to our present topic is an 1850 publication titled *Melodies of the New Orleans Serenaders Operatic Troupe,* naming a popular company with which Kneass was performing. The collection included many genteel gems such as "I Hear the Hoofs; or, The Lost Child," "The Haunted Well," "Rosa Clare," and "Thou Art Gone from My Gaze." As Ernst Krohn observes: "The predominance of romantic ballads is remarkable."[6] It was also typical.

Kneass, like Foster, wrote both comical and sentimental songs. Among the latter are "My Canoe Is on the Ohio," "Gently Down the Stream," "Deep in a Shady Dell," and "How Swift the Blissful Moments Pass!" His biggest and most lasting success was with "Ben Bolt; or, Oh! Don't You Remember." The ballad text was written by Thomas Dunn English and first appeared in the *New-York Mirror* of September 2, 1843. Its blend of romantic sentiment and mysterious menace prompted several musical settings; the one by Kneass, published by W. C. Peters (Louisville, 1848), proved to be the most enduring. (Kneass, however, was accused of plagiarizing the tune.) "Ben Bolt" also became a favorite theme for elaborate piano transcriptions, notably the *Fantasy on Ben Bolt* by William Vincent Wallace and a set of variations by Charles Grobe (1850). It also received wide literary fame when it was featured as a kind of *leitmotiv* in the sensational novel *Trilby* (1894) by the English author George du Maurier (1834–96).

In the period with which we are dealing, histrionic projection—expression, diction, gesture—was a very important factor in the performance of songs. As one impresario stated, "Highly musical attainments are not so essential as expression, feeling, and vivacity."[7] According to a contemporary witness, for example, the professional singer and parlor-song interpreter Clara Fisher Maeder "not only sings it [the song], but acts it in the most arch and spirited or tender and impressive manner. Her face is a mirror where every sentiment of humor or feeling expressed in the verse is reflected."[8] The emphasis is on the "verse," which served as a kind of scenario for the singer, and "singing in character" was the desired achievement, often enhanced by appropriate costuming. Nicholas Tawa observes that "there is also ample evidence that not only a song's key and accompaniment but also its melody, dynamics, and expressive indications could be altered."[9] The utmost effectiveness in a particular situation appears to have been the chief criterion.

The English composer, singer, pianist, and writer Henry Russell (1812–1900), who spent the years 1833–41 in America, obtained tremendous success with his vivid and emotional interpretations of sentimental songs and dramatic ballads. Russell himself commented that "the orator Clay was the direct cause of my taking to the composition of descriptive songs." It seems that Clay deeply impressed Russell by the musical quality of his speaking voice. "Why," Russell asked himself, "if Henry Clay could create such an impression by his distinct enunciation of every word, should it not be possible for me to make music the vehicle of grand thoughts and noble sentiments, to speak to the world through the power of poetry and song!"[10] Why not, indeed! Except that Russell was not a Longfellow—or even a James Russell Lowell. But he had the good sense to turn to some well-known poets of his generation, including George Pope Morris, whom we have already met as a pillar of the genteel tradition. The fact that a contemporary satirist had referred to Morris as "A household poet, whose domestic muse / Is soft as milk, and sage as Mother Goose" evidently did not deter Russell, who sensed the pathetic possibilities of the household poet's heartrending ballad "Woodman! Spare That Tree!" which he immediately set to music. It was an instant success and remains a classic of the genteel tradition. Russell states that it never failed to work on the emotions of an audience. On one occasion a dignified gentleman stood up and in a very agitated voice asked, "Was the tree spared, sir?" When Russell replied that it was, the man heaved a heartfelt sigh of relief and exclaimed, "Thank God for that!"[11]

In contrast to the sentimental song was the dramatic or "descriptive" narrative ballad that aimed to stir the emotions with a blending of pity and terror. Russell achieved a sensational success in this genre with "The Ship on Fire," set to a text by Charles MacKay. Here the household muse is abandoned in favor of an all-out combination of bombast and bathos, with an elaborate piano accompaniment full of runs, tremolos, octaves, and arpeggios. The first threat is that of shipwreck by an approaching hurricane:

> A young mother knelt in the cabin below,
> And pressing her babe to her bosom of snow,
> She pray'd to her God 'mid the hurricane wild—
> "O Father; have mercy; look down on my child!"

The storm passes away, and terror is succeeded by joy; the mother sings a sweet song to her babe as she rocks it to rest; the husband sits beside her, and they dream of the cottage where they will live when their roaming is finished.

> O, gently the ship glided over the sea . . .

(here the music fades to a *pianissimo* cadence). But now thunderous octaves strike an ominous warning of impending disaster. "Hark! what was that— Hark, hark to the shout,—FIRE!" The young wife is shaken with terror:

> She flew to her husband, she clung to his side,
> Oh there was her refuge what e'er might betide.

Fire! Fire! Raging above and below. The smoke, in thick wreaths, mounts higher and higher (furious octave runs in the piano accompaniment, *fortissimo*). There's no remedy save to lower the boat.

> Cold, cold was the night as they drifted away,
> And mistily dawn'd o'er their pathway the day.

Then suddenly, oh joy!

> "Ho, a sail, ho! a sail!" cried the man o'er the lea.

The chords of the accompaniment take on a solemn and joyous grandiosity: "Thank God, thank God, we're sav'd."[12]

The imminent perils of a sea voyage were very much in the minds of Americans during the nineteenth century; hence, it is not surprising that poets and composers made the most of this theme. In 1858 the Boston firm of Oliver Ditson and Company published a cantata for mixed voices titled *The Burning Ship*, with music by Benjamin Franklin Baker (1811–89) and text by Howard M. Ticknor. Baker, a New Englander, was active as a church singer, music educator, and composer—especially of cantatas.

The Burning Ship adheres to the standard formula, beginning with hope and confidence, changing to dire peril, and concluding with a rescue and general rejoicing. The music serves its purpose without being of any particular distinction. Such cantatas were evidently the genteel tradition's mode of purging the soul through pity and terror—but with an obligatory happy ending. While attractive maidens might better be consigned to the tomb, a mother and babe merited salvation by the power of God.

That the performance of such relatively ambitious works was not limited to the major urban centers is indicated by the following concert notice:

CONCERT

PROGRAMME OF CONCERT TO BE GIVEN BY THE
VOCAL CLASS IN ROCHESTER, VT.,
WEDNESDAY Eve., Feb'y 17, 1869,
AT THE UNIVERSALIST CHURCH.

CHARACTERS

Captain of Ship, ... Mr. W. Ford.
Mate of Ship, ... Mr. H. Hodgkins.
Lady and Child, ... Miss Ella Hubbard.
Crew and Sailors are represented by the Class.

The program of the Rochester concert was actually in two parts, the second consisting of miscellaneous numbers and a whistling solo. The aim was to please as many different tastes as possible, as indicated by the following list:

Part Second

1. Solo and Chorus—Devotion—Solo .... Miss Ellen Packard
2. Song—Will ye nae come back again .... Miss Jennie Hubbard
3. Song—Not for Joseph .... Scott Hubbard
4. Te sol quest annima, a Tersetta .. Mr. H. Hodgkins, Mrs. E. Hodgkins
5. Solo and Chorus—Welcome May—Solo .... Miss E. Matthews
6. Song and Chorus—Come in and Shut the Door—Song .. Miss J. Ashley
7. Let the Eagle Scream .... By the younger members of the Class
8. Song—Walking down Broadway .... Miss Ellen Packard
9. Song and Chorus—Let the dead and beautiful rest
       Song by Miss Addie Campbell, Sop., Miss Lena Campbell, Alto
10. Anthem—Hear us our Heavenly Father
11. Solo and Chorus—Marseilles Hymn—Solo .... Mr. H. Lesure
12. Bird Carol. Whistling Solo
13. Anthem—God of Israel—Solo .... Miss Lizzie Buck

The Universalist Church of Rochester, Vermont, was thus the center for a musical program of wide diversity and scope, all evidently presented by local talent.

As we have noted, the genteel tradition was by no means exclusively linked to "high society" but was also an aspiration of the middle class. Such was the case with George Frederick Root, whom we previously met as an associate of Lowell Mason. He regarded himself as a composer of and for the people, and his aim was to write the kind of music they wanted. The mark that he set for himself is delineated in the following statement: "It is easy to write correctly a simple song, but so to use the material of which such a song must be made that it will be received and live in the hearts of the people is quite another matter."[13] When one of his best-known songs, "The Hazel Dell," was published in 1852, Root rejoiced that it at once "began the run which was not to end until the boys whistled it and the hand organs played it from Maine to Georgia." To which he added, "No ambition for a song-writer could go higher than that."[14]

Another big success in the sentimental mood was "Rosalie, the Prairie Flower," who lived "On the distant prairie,/Where the heather wild,/In its quiet beauty lived and smiled." Of course, in keeping with the genteel tradition, Rosalie had to die, and the angels "gently bore her, robed in spotless white,/To their blissful home of light."

But at this stage of his career, Root still felt constrained by the "better music" complex. He confessed that he still "shared the feeling that was around me [the Lowell Mason circle] in regard to that grade of music"— he evidently was ashamed of it. As a result, he signed many of his early songs with the pseudonym "G. Friederich Wurzel" (a German pun on *Root*). But later, as he "went more among the people of the country," he "saw these things in a truer light" and was "thankful when I could write something that all the people would sing." He also tells us that he was influenced by Foster's "wonderful melodies," which succeeded in being popular while remaining genteel.[15]

The sentimental songs of Root are less known today, but he made his enduring mark for posterity with four of the most successful and best-remembered songs of the Civil War: "Just before the Battle, Mother," "The Vacant Chair," "Tramp, Tramp, Tramp (or the Prisoner's Hope)," and especially "The Battle Cry of Freedom" (1862), which for a time rivaled the popularity and prestige of "Hail Columbia" and "The Star-Spangled Banner" (the latter not being the official national anthem until 1931). His gospel hymn "The Shining Shore" has also endured.

Thanks to his highly successful professional career, not only as a prolific and versatile composer but also as a music educator and publisher, Root's musical activities were far-ranging. In 1850–51 he was in Paris, where he studied singing and attended concerts. He heard Rossini's *Stabat Mater* "in the Italian Opera-house" and went to a concert of orchestral works by Berlioz (who conducted). The composer's physical appearance evidently impressed him more than the music, for he wrote that Berlioz's "pale, wild face, surmounted by shaggy locks, black as night, haunted me for months."[16] His religious affiliation prevented him from hearing operas, but during a stay in London he had his fill of oratorios.

This whiff of the grand tradition at close range may have prompted Root to compose his most ambitious work, *Belshazzar's Feast; or, The Fall of Babylon* (1860), a "Dramatic Cantata in Ten Scenes." One of the numbers is "The National Anthem of the Babylonians," which must have required considerable imagination. The cantata appears to have been written in contradiction to Root's principle of not aiming too high, for he overshot the mark by a wide margin. Writing a "Dramatic Cantata" may also have been a substitution for the opera that his religion did not sanction.

Root was on firmer ground when he decided to concentrate on what he called "cantatas for the people," which he began to write in the 1850s, commencing with *The Flower Queen, Daniel,* and *The Haymakers.* According to his general scheme, these represented the "juvenile, scriptural, and secular" types. Many others followed in his long and prolific career, but the one that stands out is *The Haymakers* (1857), subtitled *An Operatic Cantata.* Evidently, this was as near as he could venture toward opera.

In composing *The Haymakers,* Root displayed no delusions of grandeur. He chose a pastoral theme in a familiar rural setting that recalled his boyhood background. The principal characters are the farmer, his two daughters, a dairymaid, and two male farmhands (one for each daughter!). A city "slicker" gets short shrift in the plot. The choral complement includes a "Semi-Chorus of Mowers" (men's voices), a "Semi-Chorus of Spreaders" (women's voices), and the "Full Chorus of Haymakers."[17]

In keeping with the pastoral tradition (which goes back to ancient times), rural life and its labors are idealized. For dramatic effect, the menace of a thunderstorm is introduced; but a rainbow appears, and the finale is a hymn of gratitude and rejoicing. The music is unpretentiously mellifluous, often spirited in the choral numbers, and conventionally ingratiating in the solo songs. There is a diversity of familiar styles, from urban gospel hymns and church music to genteel popular songs and imitations of operatic *bel canto*—the latter reflecting the widespread Italian influence on America's music.

As Root tells us in his memoirs: "This cantata was published in 1857, and began to be sung immediately. During the following year I conducted it twenty times in Boston and the neighboring cities."[18] Concurrently it was announced that a Boston publisher was offering "Selections from the Operatic Cantata of the Haymakers." Soon afterward (January 1860) it was repeatedly performed with great success and enthusiastic reviews in Chicago. An item in the *Chicago Press and Tribune* (January 12, 1860) reveals the importance given to the "moral" factor:

The operatic cantata of the "Haymakers" . . . bids fair to create as much of a furor here as it did in Boston. And there are good reasons why it should. Though as a musical production it is less difficult than the more pretentious works of Foreign composers, it contains much that compares favorably with them. . . . But as we have before hinted, its chief excellence consists in the naturalness and success with which it gives expression, not to the exaggerated, violent and often baleful passions common to the Italian Opera, but the healthy sentiments of home and every day life. Mr. Root deserves credit for having struck out a new path in this respect. He has dared to appeal only to such sentiments as find their appropriate place at every happy farm fireside, and eschew all those intoxicating passions that excite only to harm.[19]

When Root was on a visit to England in 1886, he was told by a choral conductor in London: "I have given your cantatas a great deal for many years; indeed, one of them has been more remunerative than any other work of the kind that I have ever had to do with—I mean 'The Haymakers.' I have given it seventeen times."[20] Nearly a century later it would be revived with fond remembrance, notably at the University of Michigan in Ann Arbor.

In 1858 Root's older brother, E. T. Root, in partnership with C. M. Cady, established in Chicago the music-publishing firm of Root and Cady, which enjoyed a flourishing business until hit by the havoc of the great fire of 1871. George Root joined the firm in 1859, continuing to write songs while working as a partner. In his autobiography he recalls that one day, soon after the beginning of the Civil War,

a quiet and rather solemn-looking young man, poorly clad, was sent up to my room from the store with a song for me to examine. I looked at it and then at him in astonishment. It was "Kingdom Coming,"—elegant in manuscript, full of bright, good sense and comical situations in its "darkey" dialect—the words fitting the melody almost as aptly and neatly as Gilbert fits Sullivan— the melody decidedly good and taking, and the whole exactly suited to the times. "Did you write this—words and music?" I asked. A gentle "Yes" was the answer. "What is your business, if I may inquire?" "I am a printer." "Would you rather write music than set type?" "Yes." "Well, if this is a specimen of what you can do, I think you may give up the printing business." He liked that idea very much, and an arrangement with us was soon made. He needed some musical help that I could give him, and we needed just such songs as he could write. . . . This was Henry C. Work, whose principal songs while he was with us were "Kingdom Coming," "Babylon is Fallen," "Wake, Nicodemus," "Ring the Bell, Watchman," "Song of a Thousand Years," "Marching Thro' Georgia," and "Come Home, Father."[21]

Root adds that Work was "a slow, pains-taking writer, being from one to three weeks upon a song; but when the work was done it was like a piece of fine mosaic, especially in the fitting of words to music."[22]

Henry Clay Work (1832–84) was born in Connecticut but spent part of his boyhood in Illinois, where his father, an ardent abolitionist, had migrated. In 1845 the family returned to Connecticut. Young Work, like his father, was an active abolitionist. He also championed the cause of temperance and wrote the classic song of that movement, "Come Home, Father." Even more heartrending was the pathetic tearjerker "Lillie of the Snow-Storm," about a drunkard who drives his wife and little daughter out into a raging storm, where they perish.

Work's output covered a large variety of topics, from minstrel-show numbers such as "Wake, Nicodemus" (1864) to songs of the Civil War, most notably "Marching through Georgia" (1864). Concerning the latter, he wrote in 1889 that it was "more played and sung at the present time than any other song of the war." It remains his most famous song, often quoted in military marches.

In keeping with the tendency of the time, he wrote a number of sentimental ballads that achieved great popularity, in some cases almost worldwide. The most famous and enduring of all is "Grandfather's Clock" (1876), dedicated "To my Sister Lizzie," with the customary form of "Song and Chorus." The burden of the latter is as follows:

> Ninety years, without slumbering (tick, tick, tick, tick),
> His life-seconds numbering (tick, tick, tick, tick),
> It stopp'd short—never to go again—
> When the old man died.[23]

Other ballads of sorrowful sentiment are "Phantom Footsteps" and "The Ship That Never Returned." As an antidote to the usual unhappy endings, there is "Nellie Lost and Found." And "Kingdom Coming" (1862) presented his spirited version of emancipation, to which he was so strongly committed.[24]

Another composer who wrote most of his song texts was John Hill Hewitt (1801–90)—actually a poet in his own right, with a considerable literary reputation. As previously noted, his father, the English composer James Hewitt, had married an American lady with high social pretensions and consequently regarded music as professionally unsuitable for a male offspring. After several fruitless apprenticeships, young Hewitt entered the military academy at West Point, where he studied music with the bandmaster, Richard S. Willis. His involvement in the cadet rebellion of 1820 and other imprudent behavior forced him to leave the academy without graduating. Thereafter he earned a living in various ways: as actor, private tutor, school teacher, journalist, director of musical societies, theater manager, literary author, and, last but not least, as a prolific composer of some 300 songs, as well as piano pieces, cantatas, operas, operettas, and what his biographer calls "miscellaneous compositions."[25] In spite of such industry and the wide popularity of some of the songs, Hewitt found that music as a profession did not pay. "The publisher pockets all," he declared, "and gets rich on the brains of the poor fool who is chasing that *ignis fatuus,* reputation."[26]

Most of Hewitt's varied career was in the South, mainly in Georgia, Virginia, and South Carolina, although he eventually settled in Baltimore. When the Civil War broke out, he quickly became the "Bard of the Confederacy," thereby achieving the peak of his musical and poetic prestige. He had previously made his reputation with two highly popular songs, "The Minstrel's Return from the War" and "The Knight of the Raven Black Plume," both dating from the 1820s.

During the Civil War, Hewitt published nineteen songs, of which the most successful were "Rock Me to Sleep, Mother," "Somebody's Darling," and especially "All Quiet along the Potomac Tonight," one of the most popular songs of the war, both in the South and in the North. Hewitt wrote only the music for these songs. He did, however, write the words, but not the music, for "The Soldier's Farewell; or, The South Shall Yet Be Free," adapted to the French air "Partant pour la Syrie."

Although Hewitt's sentimental/romantic songs and ballads were typical of the genteel tradition, his personal attitude was ambivalent and at times hostile. He particularly disliked what he regarded as the affectation of upper-class society, which made a show of admiring Italian vocal music. He also resented being regarded as a mere entertainer or dependent. This comes out clearly in his account of a dinner party at the home of a wealthy South Carolina planter. At first he was in a state of euphoria: "I found the company everything I could have wished for. The ladies were bright and beautiful, and the gentlemen . . . full of that genial hilarity and warmth of heart so peculiar to Southerners. The dinner was sumptuous, the wit brilliant, and the conversation edifying."[27]

But after dinner it was another story; scarcely had he lighted his cigar and addressed himself to a bottle of "sparkling sherry" when he was informed by a servant that the ladies desired his company in the parlor. They wanted some music, so "I played and sang for an hour, while they conversed on trifling topics—the fashions of the day, the wedding of a mutual friend, the style of the dresses there exhibited. . . . My mortification did not end with a solo or two or a ballad, for one of the heiresses proposed a quadrille, which was heartily agreed to by all but myself. I played, of course, for I was determined to do my best to prove myself a gentleman. . . ."[28]

A fruitless endeavor, alas! The social label for an American musician of the early nineteenth century was still "The Entertainer"—especially in the class-conscious society of the South. And, of course, if the gentlemen paid the piper, the ladies called the tune.

A number of women were also calling the tune in musical composition during this period, chiefly (but not exclusively) with songs of the "parlor" type. They were definitely moving toward creative "emancipation" in music, literature, and the arts, as well as female assertion in other areas.

We turn first to Marion Dix Sullivan, who came from New England and acquired her surname by marrying a Mr. J. W. Sullivan of Boston in 1825. Her productive decades were the 1840s and 1850s, when she brought out two very successful collections: *Juniata Ballads* (Boston, 1855) and *Bible Songs* (Boston, 1856). Her biggest and most enduring success was with "The Blue Juniata" (1844), which Judith Tick aptly describes as "one of the most popular parlor songs of the nineteenth century [and] the first composition by an American woman to become a commercial hit song."[29] It was, moreover, "anthologized in countless collections" well into the twentieth century (e.g., *Heart Songs,* New York, 1909, for an early starter).[30]

Sullivan's songs embraced a wide range of topics, from "We Cross the Prairies as of Old" (1854) and "Oh! Boatman, Row Me O'er the Stream" (a sacred song—1846) to "The Field of Monterey," a ballad of the Mexican-American War that ended in 1848. She wrote the words for all her songs.

Augusta Browne (1821–82) came to America from Ireland and is definitively distinguished as "the most prolific woman composer in America before 1870."[31] According to a contemporary reference work: "Her productions, which are in all styles—fantasies, airs variés, waltzes, songs sacred and secular—number about 200; and many of them, such as the brilliant romance 'La Brise dans les Feuillage' [*sic*], 'Airs a la Russe,' 'National Bouquets,' and various songs have gained great popularity."[32]

Browne considered herself as participating in a "refined intellectual society," so we may think of her as pertaining to the upper stratum of the genteel tradition, but with a strongly assertive sense of women's importance, creatively and socially. She was a frequent contributor to the many periodicals that catered to women, such as *Godey's Lady's Book* and the *Columbian Lady's and Gentleman's Magazine*. In the latter she published one of her most impressive songs, "Wake, Lady Mine" (1845), which she placed in the category of "parlor arias," as contrasted with the more common ballads. She also wrote a song about the Mexican war, "The Warlike Dead in Mexico" (1848), marked by a passionate intensity of feeling.

Faustina Hasse Hodges (1822–95) was the daughter of a professional musician from England, by whom she was well trained, especially as a pianist. She achieved an impressive professional career both as performer and composer, and at least two of her songs, "Dreams" and "The Rose-Bush" (both from 1859), had a wide commercial success. Hodges's *cantabile* piano textures and independent piano accompaniments are much richer than the average parlor song, and as Tick observes, her "familiarity with 'recondite forms of classic art' is apparent in her skillful assimilation of German and Italian song styles."[33] An example is the parlor ballad "Still O'er the Waters" (1852), described as a "Nocturne with or without words for the Piano Forte."

Also of professional stature was Jane Sloman, active as concert pianist, vocalist, and composer. She, too, was of English origin (born in 1824) and began her career in the United States at the age of seventeen. Her songs, which included well-known works such as "Roll On, Silver Moon," "Forget Thee," and "The Maiden's Farewell," were well received. She also composed a feminist ballad, "I'll Make Him Speak Out," dedicated "to the ladies." As she expressed it, "Are women's hearts playthings to be broken by boys?"

In 1839, while Baron Rudolph de Fleur and other fashionable musicians from Europe were entertaining the elite of American society, the Baptist meetinghouse in Milford, New Hampshire, was packed by local folk who had come to hear a concert of hymns, anthems, and glees by members of the Hutchinson family, whose numerous members had been established in the community for several generations. It was Thanksgiving Day, and the singing Hutchinsons had every reason to be thankful, for they were received with warm applause and were given every indication that their vocal talents had been fully appreciated. After another successful concert at nearby Lynn, they were sufficiently encouraged to consider a professional career. For that, said John Hutchinson, "We need more discipline and more culture."[34] So several of the brothers went to Boston and called on

Dr. Lowell Mason, who recommended that they acquire his latest singing book and expressed no further interest in their project. They then approached another eminent leader of musical culture in Boston, Professor George James Webb, who received them most courteously and advised them to join the chorus of the Handel and Haydn Society. At this point the brothers evidently decided that what they needed was less culture and more discipline.

Renting a room in Boston, they began to practice and rehearse a varied repertory: sacred and secular, serious and comic, sentimental and political. To support themselves they took whatever odd jobs they could get. For John, who worked for a grocer, the most repugnant chore was "to tend bar and sell liquor by the glass" (it was then customary to dispense liquor, mostly rum, in grocery stores).[35] The Hutchinson's repugnance for liquor endured and placed them among the leading champions of temperance, particularly with their famous song "King Alcohol." For them, music was not simply entertainment but also a means of moral uplift, social reform, political action, and general edification—which nevertheless did not exclude a sense of humor. And it was possible to advocate a worthy cause with a song that proved to be a smashing success, as the Hutchinsons did with Henry Russell's "The Maniac."[36]

Russell claimed that he wrote this song to expose the abuses of asylums for the insane, but its immediate effect was to work on the emotions of the audience. John Hutchinson was quick to see its possibilities and invested his last dollar plus twelve and a half cents for express postage to order a copy of "The Maniac" from the publisher. Seldom if ever has such a modest investment proved so remunerative. While two of the brothers played a prelude on violin and cello, John would sit in a chair behind them, raising his hair on end with the fingers of each hand. Then he would stand up, "with the expression of vacancy inseparable from mania," and proceed with the gruesome performance, to the horror and delight of the audience.[37]

The national and international success of the Hutchinson Family Singers was achieved when three of the sons were joined by their sister Abby in 1842, when she was only eleven. This charming feminine image had its immediate effect in genteel circles. Nathaniel Parker Willis, influential critic of the *New York Home Journal,* praised the quartet as "a nest of brothers with a sister in it" (eventually she flew the nest and married a wealthy broker).[38] George P. Morris became their "dear friend" and provided them with several lyrics, including that nostalgic tug at the heartstrings "My Mother's Bible":

This book is all that's left me now,
Tears will unbidden start;
With faltering lip and throbbing brow,
I press it to my heart.

Through Morris, they met Henry Russell, who said to them, "I think you are the best singers in America."[39] His song "The Gambler's Wife" gave Abby a chance to shine as soloist and to wring tears from the audience with her pathetic description of the poor, lonely, deserted wife. Meanwhile they had set to music Longfellow's "Excelsior," and one of the brothers called on the great man to request that he write an introduction for this number ("he gladly complied with our request," wrote John).[40] Thus, true to the message of *excelsior* ("more lofty; still higher; ever upward"—as defined by Noah Webster), the singing Hutchinsons, without abandoning their grass roots, were rapidly ascending to the higher spheres of genteel culture.

When the Hutchinsons gave their first concert at the Broadway Tabernacle of New York, they were introduced by the celebrated preacher Dr. Lyman Beecher, and their program was announced as having pleased "fashionable audiences in Boston." For an enthusiastic audience of 3,600 they sang such favorite numbers as "King Alcohol," "We Are Happy and Free," "We Have Come from the Mountains," and their theme song, "The Old Granite State" (to the tune of that rousing revival hymn "The Old Churchyard").[41]

The Hutchinson family members were numerous and prolific, and at various times there were several "Hutchinson Family Singers" on the road. They had some competition, notably from the Baker Family of New Hampshire, whose leader, John C. Baker, wrote sentimental and topical songs such as "The Happiest Time Is Now," "Where Can the Soul Find Rest?" and "The Inebriate's Lament." But no other group was as internationally famous and controversial as the Hutchinsons.

The basic symbol of sociocultural mobility in the genteel tradition is probably that of the "Grecian Bend"—an extraordinary fad, which flourished circa 1858–69. It became indeed a national craze, extending from the elite to the lowly, from the parlor to the levee. Musically and pictorially the Grecian Bend appeared in sheet-music editions, with the customary cover illustrations, and in both vocal and instrumental versions—the latter including galops, mazurkas, waltzes, and marches. These were published or sold in all the principal cities, from Boston to Galveston, Philadelphia to St. Louis, and Chicago to Louisville. Most covers featured a fashionable female with a minuscule parasol, high-heeled gaiters, and a prominent bustle. There were exceptions, notably a cover of "The Original Grecian Bend: A Grand March, by George B. Wilson, Esq.," which shows a gentleman with an enormous mustache, a small hat, and high-heeled shoes, bending forward with uplifted coattails and holding at arm's length a long boot.[42] The message, we gather, is "We can do it too"—with the implication, "How ridiculous"!

As evidence of the wide sociocultural spread of the Grecian Bend fad, we find among the many rhymes that the roustabouts improvised for their working songs as they loaded or unloaded cargo on the river packets, the following couplet:

> I'm goin' to ship on the Eagle Tender,
> Buy my wife a Grecian Bender.

The second line was obviously chosen because it rhymed with the name of the steamboat, but it also shows that the notion was very much in the air— from the city sidewalks to the river docks.

There appears to be a pattern of female assertion and male reaction in the social symbolism of the Grecian Bend. For the women, it was evidently a matter of "doing their own thing" and telling the men to mind *their* own business. Take, for example, "The Girl with the Grecian Bend," song and dance, words and music by James W. Long (Louisville, Ky., 1868). In the second stanza the gent explains his attempt to assist a high-heeled young lady, presumably in danger of falling on her face. His offer of help is snappily refused:

> She call'd me a brute and said I was not polite
> And that my ways I'd better amend,
> The hump-tilt and toeing she assur'd me was right,
> Like any other Grecian Bend.

The final stanza facetiously justifies this feminine reaction as motivated by the frustration of being excluded from forms of behavior and achievement available to men:

> Girls can't get drunk, nor fight the tiger like men,
> They at the club can't meet a friend,
> Can't bet on horses, nor can they play base ball,
> So let them sport their Grecian Bend.

So, by this gracious concession, *he* is being a "good sport."

"The Famous Grecian Bend," song and chorus, words by Martin

The Hutchinson Family as depicted on the sheet-music cover to "The Old Granite State" (1843).

"The Famous Grecian Bend" (1868).

Meyer, music by John Molter (Chicago, 1868), takes the cake for its illustration showing the tiniest parasol and the largest bustle that have come to my attention. The third stanza brings a black miss into the picture:

> "Miss. Dinah Snow," of sable hue,
> In festive style arrayed,
> Came loit'ring down the avenue,
> The Grecian she displayed;
> Accosting her, in sportive mood,
> She thus to me appeals,
> "I carry, sir, the 'Grecian Bend'
> to balancy my heels."

Another Grecian Bend, song and chorus, is described as a "Comic Song for Gentlemen with Male Chorus, Ad. Lib. [and] Music by J. Offenbach (Air, 'O Grecian People'), Words by George Cooper, Arr^d and adapt^d by W. D. Raphaelson" (New York: J. L. Peters, 1869). It helpfully combines a fashion note with the vaunted democracy of the Bender fad:

> The mistress and the servant,
> To please us condescend;
> For there's the Cook, on Sunday,
> She flings the "Grecian Bend!"
> But don't go on a "bender"
> And swing the "Grecian Bend!"

Considering the slang meaning of *bender* as "a drinking spree," the image of a female "swinger" certainly lurks behind the lyrics. Moral: whatever Santayana may have said on the subject, never underestimate the social impact of the "Genteel Tradition!"

Notes

1. See Charles Hamm, *Yesterdays,* chap. 4, " 'Hear Me, Norma'; or, Bel Canto Comes to America—Italian Opera as Popular Song."
2. For Frank (Francis) Johnson (1792–1844), including a list of his compositions, see Richard J. Wolfe, *Secular Music in America, 1801–1825,* pp. 451–55.
3. Robert C. Toll, *Blacking Up,* p. 53.
4. *Stephen Foster Song Book,* ed. Richard Jackson, p. 175.
5. Ernst C. Krohn, "Nelson Kneass," pp. 20, 21.
6. Ibid., pp. 25–27.
7. Letter from Richard Peters, Jr., to Francis Courtenay Wemyss, June 19, 1877, in Wemyss, *Twenty-six Years of the Life of an Actor and Manager,* vol. 1 (New York,

1847), p. 125; quoted in Nicholas E. Tawa, "The Performance of Parlor Songs in America, 1790–1860," p. 72.

8. William Cox, from the appendix to Clara Fisher Maeder, *Autobiography,* ed. Douglas Taylor (New York, 1897), p. 133; quoted in Tawa, "The Performance of Parlor Songs in America, 1790–1860," p. 76.

9. Tawa, "The Performance of Parlor Songs in America, 1790–1860," p. 76.

10. Henry Russell, *Cheer! Boys, Cheer!* p. 61.

11. Ibid., p. 193.

12. "The Ship on Fire" was a favorite number and a great success of the Hutchinson Family Singers. Their leader, John W. Hutchinson, was the soloist, with brothers Judson and Asa playing the accompaniment. John claimed to have sung it at least 500 times. See John Wallace Hutchinson, *Story of the Hutchinsons* 1:328–31.

13. George Frederick Root, *The Story of a Musical Life,* p. 97.

14. Ibid., p. 89.

15. Ibid., p. 83.

16. Ibid., p. 68.

17. For a comprehensive history and analysis of *The Haymakers,* see Herbert Holl, "Some Versions of Pastoral in American Music," pp. 73–115.

18. Root, *The Story of a Musical Life,* pp. 113–14.

19. Quoted in Holl, "Some Versions of Pastoral in American Music," p. 101.

20. Root, *The Story of a Musical Life,* p. 186.

21. Ibid., pp. 137–38.

22. Ibid., p. 138.

23. For an authentic contemporary sheet-music publication of "Grandfather's Clock," as a "Song and Chorus," see Richard Jackson, comp., *Popular Songs of Nineteenth-Century America,* pp. 76–79. The cover also indicates versions for piano and for guitar.

24. "Kingdom Coming" and "Grandfather's Clock," with thirteen other songs by Work, are recorded on *Who Shall Rule This American Nation? Songs of the Civil War Era by Henry Clay Work,* with historical notes by Jon Newsom, Nonesuch H-71317; performed by Joan Morris, mezzo-soprano, Clifford Jackson, baritone, William Bolcom, pianist and conductor, and the Camerata Chorus of Washington.

25. See "Catalog of Musical Works," in Coy Elliott Huggins, "John Hill Hewitt," pp. 142–68.

26. John Hill Hewitt, *Shadows on the Wall,* p. 66.

27. Ibid., pp. 93–94.

28. Ibid., pp. 95–96.

29. Judith Tick, *American Women Composers before 1870,* p. 146.

30. Ibid., pp. 146 and 263 n. 11.

31. Ibid., p. 150.

32. John W. Moore, *Appendix to Encyclopedia of Music* (Boston: Oliver Ditson, 1875), p. 22; cited in ibid. Although Moore lists 200 works by Browne, Tick notes that only "about a quarter of her total output has been located to date."

33. Tick, *American Women Composers before 1870,* p. 163.

34. Hutchinson, *Story of the Hutchinsons* 1:37.

35. Ibid., p. 39.

36. "The Maniac" is included on a recording of songs by Henry Russell that also presents "The Ship on Fire," "The Old Arm Chair," "A Life on the Ocean Wave," and "Woodman! Spare That Tree!" See *An Evening with Henry Russell,* Nonesuch H-71338; performed by Clifford Jackson, baritone, and William Bolcom, piano.

37. Hutchinson, *Story of the Hutchinsons* 2:294.

38. Ibid. 1:46.

39. Quoted in Philip D. Jordan, *Singin' Yankees,* p. 78.

40. Hutchinson, *Story of the Hutchinsons* 1:91.

41. A recording of "The Old Granite State," along with "King Alcohol" and other numbers by the Hutchinson Family Singers, is included on a three-record album titled *Homespun America* (Vox SVBX 5309), which presents a wide variety of mid-nineteenth-century vocal and instrumental music.

42. "Published Expressly for GEORGE B. WILSON ESQ. and dedicated to his numerous PATRONS.—Washington City, D.C. Published by JOHN F. ELLIS, 306 Penna². Ave. Piano & Music Store."

Chapter 10

The Fasola Folk

O, tell me young friends, While the morning's fair and cool,
O, where, tell me, where Shall I find your singing school.
You'll find it under the tall oak, where the leaves do shake and blow,
You'll find a half hundred asinging faw, sol, faw.
—"Singing School," by J. H. Moss, in *The Social Harp* (1855)

In an earlier chapter ("American Pioneers") we mentioned that about 1800 both Andrew Law and two singing-school masters, Smith and Little, published tunebooks using various shapes to indicate the notes of the scale, which from about 1650 had been represented by the syllables *do, re, mi, fa, sol, la, si* (or *ti*). But in England and America a simplified system was also used, discarding the first three syllables and designating the seven notes of the diatonic scale as follows: *fa-sol-la-fa-sol-la-mi*. In the method of Smith and Little, *fa* was represented by a right-angled triangle, *sol* by a round note, *la* by a square, and *mi* by a diamond shape, each with a stem, thus:

$$\triangleright \quad \rho \quad \sqcap \quad \diamondsuit$$

The shape-note tunebook by Smith and Little, *The Easy Instructor,* caught on immediately and went through many editions between 1801 and 1831. The shape notes were often called "buckwheat notes" (from the diamond *mi*), although the supercilious Dr. Thomas Hastings referred to them as "dunce notes." But they came to designate an immense repertory of semifolk music (mostly, but not exclusively, religious) and a distinctive style of singing that has endured for many generations and has experienced in recent decades a remarkable revival. This style is now generally known as Sacred Harp singing, after the most widely used shape-note tunebook, *The Sacred Harp* (1844).

The term *fasola folk,* then, is simply one way of referring to the (mostly) rural singers, tunebook compilers, and singing-school teachers of the South and Midwest, who carried on the tradition of music for the people established by the native pioneers in New England. Much of the music was indeed drawn from early New England tunebooks. An intermediate point for this transition appears to have been Harrisburg, Pennsylvania, where an enterprising publisher named John Wyeth (1770–1858) issued two influential collections similarly titled the *Repository of Sacred Music* (1810) and the *Repository of Sacred Music, Part Second* (1813). Employing the shape-note system used by Smith and Little in *The Easy Instructor*, Wyeth also borrowed many tunes from that collection, as well as from Read's *Columbian Harmonist* (New Haven, 1793–95) and the celebrated *Worcester Collection of Sacred Harmony* (Worcester, 1786). He included hymns, anthems, and fuging tunes by composers such as Billings, Holden, Holyoke, Ingalls, Kimball, Morgan, and Read—all names that appear repeatedly in southern shape-note tunebooks.[1]

The first of the southern tunebook compilers who claims our attention is Ananias Davisson (1780–1859), an elder of the Presbyterian church. He established himself as a singing-school master in the Shenandoah Valley of Virginia, near Harrisonburg, and was for a time also active in Knoxville, Tennessee. His shape-note tunebook, *Kentucky Harmony* (1816), was published in Harrisonburg, Virginia, and went through many editions. Irving Lowens reports that Davisson borrowed fifteen tunes from Wyeth's *Repository of Sacred Music, Part Second*, although, "curiously enough, three of these are claimed as his own compositions."[2] Authorship was not taken too seriously in the rural South.

The 144 tunes in the *Kentucky Harmony* are written in four-part harmony, and in his instructions on singing Davisson writes: "The bass stave is assigned to the gravest voices of men, and the tenor to the highest. The counter to the lowest voices of the Ladies, and the treble to the highest of Ladies' voices."[3] The custom of giving the principal melody to the tenors prevailed for a long time, but it should be remarked that in the fasola tradition composers and arrangers tried to make each voice as independent and as interesting as they knew how. They aimed at true part singing rather than harmonized melody. We should also observe that many of the shape-note tunebooks favored the more characteristic three-voiced texture, with the "air" in the middle part.

In 1820 Davisson published a *Supplement to the Kentucky Harmony*, proudly placing after his name the initials A. K. H.—"Author of Kentucky Harmony." He claimed authorship of eleven tunes, besides six written in collaboration. But the question of authorship is not of paramount importance in this rural context. Many of the tunes had prototypes in folksongs and traditional ballads. The shape-note compilers were craftsmen rather than creators. When they arranged a preexisting tune, they felt entitled to claim it as their own work.

Whatever hand Davisson may have had in shaping the twenty-six tunes of his nominal authorship, his real importance resides in having compiled and published tunebooks that served as a source for American demotic hymnody, upon which later compilers would draw freely.

Here we should note, parenthetically, the following comment by Dorothy Horn concerning a basic trait of the fasola tradition: "The most obvious advantage of a shape-note notation is that it dispenses with the whole wearisome business of learning key signatures, thus removing one hurdle in the teaching of sight-singing. Obviously, if one knows the shape for the keynote, a signature is unnecessary."[4] A limiting factor, however, is that "shapes have never been devised for chromatic inflections; in consequence, modulations, altered chords, and the harmonic and melodic forms of the minor are impossible. The singers don't mind, and the music doesn't seem to suffer much."[5] We are reminded of Alexander Pope's immortal line: "Where ignorance is bliss, 'tis folly to be wise."

Although most of the fasola compilers and composers had rural or semirural backgrounds and activities, there were exceptions that created a sort of sociocultural hierarchy in the movement. For example, the Reverend James P. Carrell [or Carroll] (1787–1854), of Lebanon, Virginia, became a Methodist minister, clerk of the county court, and a substantial citizen, owning farmlands and slaves. No doubt this comparatively elevated status prompted him to make his publications as correct and dignified as possible. In his preface to *The Virginia Harmony* (Winchester, 1831), he states that the editors have passed by many of the light airs to be found in several of the recent publications . . . and, with the exception of a few pieces, have confined themselves chiefly to the plain psalmody of the most eminent composers."[6] Yet he was entirely loyal to the fasola system, extolling in his "Rudiments of Music" the advantages of the four-shape notes, which he calls "patent" notes, "on account of their author's having obtained a patent for the invention."[7]

Carrell affixed his name to seventeen tunes in *The Virginia Harmony*, including "The Dying Penitent," which is particularly interesting as a specimen of the American religious ballad stemming from British folksong. Eight other religious songs by Carrell were reprinted in various collections by other compilers, indicating that he continued to enjoy some regional reputation as a composer.

An incident that occurred in Ohio will serve to illustrate the growing acceptance of the shape-note system—as well as to indicate some contrary factors. This involved Lowell Mason and his brother Timothy B. Mason, when they presented *The Sacred Harp; or, Eclectic Harmony,* published in 1834 by the firm of Truman and Smith in Cincinnati. It was thus described: "A Collection of Church Music Consisting of a Great Variety of Psalm and Hymn Tunes, Anthems, Sacred Songs and Chants, Original and Selected: Including Many New and Beautiful Subjects from the Most Eminent Composers, Harmonized and Arranged Expressly for This Work." (In all, 128 tunes were presented.)[8]

The Masons aimed to do away with fasola singing and shape notes, and they wrote a preface attacking these methods: "By pursuing the common method of only *four* syllables, singers are almost always superficial. It is therefore recommended to all who wish to be thorough, to pursue the system of seven syllables, disregarding the different forms of the notes."[9] But the publishers were the first to disregard the admonitions of the Mason brothers, and *The Sacred Harp* was printed with shape notes and an explanation that this was done "under the belief that it will prove much more acceptable to a majority of singers in the West and South."[10] The Masons retorted that the publishers had "Printed in patent notes contrary to the wishes of the Authors" (p. iv). As we shall see, the Masons had a point with respect to using only four syllables to represent seven notes.

In 1825 William Moore of Wilson County, Tennessee, brought out his *Columbian Harmony,* printed in Cincinnati. In his "General Observations" he admonished the singers: "Nothing is more disgusting in singers than affected quirks, and ostentatious parade, endeavoring to overpower other voices by the strength of their own, or officiously assisting other parts while theirs is silent."[11] Once again (as with the early New England reformers) denunciation and confirmation are synonymous. We learn from Moore how the fasola singers enjoyed themselves in singing. And they are still doing the same today. Emulating the forces of Nature, they abhor a vacuum in any vocal part.

Moore claimed authorship of eighteen songs in *Columbian Harmony,* including "Sweet Rivers," an example of the "crossing over Jordan" theme that is so frequent in American revival hymnody. The tune is also typical of this tradition.

Another Tennessee collection is William Caldwell's *Union Harmony,* printed in Maryville in 1837 and including forty-two tunes that the compiler assigns to himself. He admits, however, that many of these are not entirely original, but because he has harmonized them, he claims them as his own. He furthermore states in his preface that "many of the airs which the author has reduced to system [i.e., notated] and harmonized, have been selected from the unwritten music in general use in the Methodist Church, others from the Baptist and many more from the Presbyterian taste."[12] This is an interesting statement, for it confirms the existence of a body of "unwritten music"—that is, music transmitted by oral tradition—among the three principal dissenting churches of the early nineteenth century.

It would, nevertheless, be misleading to equate "unwritten music" with what later became known to scholars as folk music. The designation "unwritten" tells us nothing about the *source* of the music, only about its *situation* in a particular cultural and temporal context. The tunes could have come from a variety of printed sources: broadsides, ballad operas, periodicals, any number of popular song collections or tunebooks. Wheeler Gillet of Baltimore, who published *The Virginia Sacred Minstrel* in 1817, found fault with less fastidious compilers who brought out "trifling and doleful ditties, patched up from old Love Songs."[13] Any tune that circulated in oral tradition, whatever its printed source, was fair game for the free-lance compiler. And a tune was judged by its attraction, not by its antecedents.

We turn now to a book of exceptional interest and importance: *The Southern Harmony*, compiled by William Walker (1809–75) and published in 1835 (printed for the author in New Haven, Conn.). "Singin' Billy" Walker, as he was familiarly called, was the son of poor parents who settled near Spartanburg, South Carolina, when he was eighteen years old. He had only a rudimentary education but early in life was imbued with an ambition "to perfect the vocal modes of praise." According to a quaint account in Landrum's *History of Spartanburg County:* "From the deep minstrels of his own bosom he gathered and arranged into meter and melody a wonderful book suitably adapted to the praise and glory of God. . . . Notwithstanding some depreciation by the press, he adhered to his original system [i.e., shape notes], and his reputation for attainments in his science soon spread all through the South and Southwest. Everywhere his popularity as a music teacher went and his work received a most popular indorsement."[14]

This "wonderful book," *The Southern Harmony,* went into five editions, the last in 1854, and Walker stated in the preface to his *Christian Harmony* that 600,000 copies were sold. The original edition contained 209 songs, of which 25 were claimed by Walker as composer. In later editions he attributed other songs to himself, making a total of 40. In the preface to the first edition, he wrote: "I have composed the parts to a great many good airs (which I could not find in any publication, nor in manuscript), and assigned my name as the author. I have also composed several tunes wholly, and inserted them in this work, which also bear my name."[15] Hence Walker appears to have been more of an arranger than a composer. In one tune, however, titled "French Broad," Walker was careful to explain in a footnote: "This song was composed by the Author, in the fall of 1831, while travelling over the mountains, on French Broad River, in North Carolina and Tennessee."[16] No French connection there!

The title page of *The Southern Harmony* announced "A Choice Collection of Tunes, Hymns, Psalms, Odes, and Anthems; Selected from the Most Eminent Authors in the United States"—to whose company, incidentally, Handel was admitted, as well as the eccentric Billings, the eminent Lowell Mason, and the self-made tunesmith "Singin' Billy" Walker: a true musical democracy.

William Walker had been assisted in compiling *The Southern Harmony* by his brother-in-law Benjamin Franklin White (1800–1879), but when the book appeared, the latter received no credit for his collaboration. The story goes that White, in a huff, left Spartanburg and settled with his family in Hamilton, Georgia, where he taught singing schools and began to gather songs for a new collection. The result was the most famous, most influential, and most enduring of all shape-note tunebooks, *The Sacred Harp*, printed in Philadelphia in 1844. On the title page the name E. J. King appears as coauthor, but little is known about him, while B. F. White achieved immediate prominence. According to White's biographer, Joe James, "he never used his talent as a musician to make money," and his purpose was to bring good music to all religious denominations, even though he himself was a Missionary Baptist.[17] White became president of the Southern Musical Convention, founded in 1845, and was also associated with the Chattahoochee Musical Convention, founded in 1852. These conventions brought together the fasola people for annual "singings" that lasted several days (a custom still maintained in some sections of the South). In most areas where this traditional style persists it is called Sacred Harp singing.

In his preface to the first edition of *The Sacred Harp*, White wrote: "While the churches may be supplied from this work, others have not been forgotten or neglected; a great variety will be found suited to singing-schools, private societies, and family circles; in fact, the Sacred Harp is designed for all classes who sing, or desire to sing."[18] As we shall see, this purpose has been fulfilled.

White included in his introduction to *The Sacred Harp,* two pages of "General Observations" that left no aspect of proper behavior untouched, from keeping time to avoiding affectation and observing strict decorum. Moreover, "too long singing at a time injures the lungs," and "an excessive use of ardent spirits will speedily ruin the best voice."[19] One is reminded of William Chappell's remark that "Primitive Methodists, or Ranters, . . . collect the airs which are sung at pot and public houses, and write their hymns to them."[20] The point is that one might take the tune but not the liquor.

An overview of this famous shape-note collection begins with part 1, "Consisting of Pieces Used by Worshipping Assemblies." This is by far the largest part, but by no means confined to formal church worship, for it included revival hymns that were popular at camp meetings, such as "The Hebrew Children" and "The Morning Trumpet," both attributed to B. F. White. Another hymn tune of this type, "The Promised Land," is ascribed to "Miss M. Durham." The selection is eclectic, as we encounter "Pleyel's Hymn Second," followed by Ingalls's "Northfield," the anonymous "Wondrous Love," and "Sweet Home," a paraphrase of the perennial song by Henry Bishop, taken from *Baptist Harmony.*

Part 2 is described as "Consisting Principally of Pieces in Singing Schools and Societies." Again variety is the keynote, with a number of fuging tunes by the New England pioneers, such as Read's "Sherburne," Shumway's "Schenectady," and that durable revival rouser "The Good Old Way." Part 3, "Consisting of Odes and Anthems," is notable especially for its inclusion of several anthems by Billings, among them the "Easter Anthem" and "Rose of Sharon." This is the shortest section in the book, and it is dominated by Billings.

The Sacred Harp has survived and prospered in many editions by various hands, with sundry supplements and revisions. Thanks largely to the influence of this tunebook, Sacred Harp singing has enjoyed a remarkable revival in the twentieth century.

As we have noted, the shape-note leaders came from varied backgrounds, and a conspicuous example is the Reverend William Hauser, M.D. (1812–80)—doctor, preacher, editor, composer, singer—whose *Hesperian Harp* (Philadelphia, 1848), if it did not have a thousand strings, was nevertheless impressive, with more than 550 pages of music. A native of North Carolina, Hauser was educated in Virginia and settled in Georgia. His big collection contains thirty-six of his own tunes, including "Hope Hull," set to a pentatonic melody.

In contrast we have John Gordon McCurry (1821–86), of Hart

County, Georgia, who was a tailor and a farmer, as well as a singing-school master. (He was also a Missionary Baptist and a Royal Arch Mason.) McCurry was well regarded in his community, but when it came to finding a publisher for his collection *The Social Harp,* he encountered (so he later said) a "thousand and one obstacles thrown in his pathway by those who looked on his efforts as visionary and vain."[21] Nevertheless, he did find a publisher in Philadelphia, and the book appeared in 1855, with reprints in 1859 and 1868.

McCurry was partial to lively tunes in the camp-meeting spirit. Typical of this preference is a song called "Few Days," with its syncopations that savor more of minstrelsy than of hymnody. Actually, a song embodying the same idea ("I am going home") and the identical refrain appeared in *The Negro Singer's Own Book* (Philadelphia, 1846), although without any tune. McCurry's version is reproduced on p. 178.

A variant of McCurry's tune and text, with the interpolation of two lines about Jonah and the whale, was recorded among the mountain folk of Tennessee in the 1920s. It is evident that this tune, like many others of its kind, has had a long life in America's music. Whatever the prototype may have been, the inclusion of such a song in *The Social Harp* confirms the immense contribution of the shape-note fasola tradition to diffusing and preserving the demotic music of America. As George Pullen Jackson wrote: "If ever a book grew out of its native soil, that book was McCurry's *Social Harp.*"[22]

In his introductory "Rudiments of Music," McCurry included a section on "Harmony and Composition" that is of particular interest for the remarks on part writing: "Be careful not to let the treble have the same turn with the bass, for it is very injurious, if not ruinous, to any piece of music. *Variety and turn is the chief thing in making good music.* If the tenor runs high, let the treble take a medium position; if the tenor runs on a medium line, let the treble run above or below" (italics added).[23] The important point here is that the fasola composers and arrangers had a genuine appreciation for what in the seventeenth century was called "The Art of Descant, or Composing Musick in Parts." In contrast, the "better music" advocates merely succeed in reducing most hymn settings to a melody with chordal accompaniment.

It should also be observed that in most of the fasola tunebooks, the vocal settings were for three parts rather than the customary four. (As we noted, *Kentucky Harmony* was an exception.) As Charles Seeger remarked in a path-breaking analysis of the shape-note tunebooks:

"Few Days," from *The Social Harp*

These collections present a distinctive style of choral composition. It is not, in any orthodox sense, a harmonic style. The tones sung by the various voices upon any given beat are not conceived of as being fundamentally a unit—a chord. Instead, each voice added to the tune is related to it independently of the relation between the tune and the other added voice. Thus these pieces may be said to show a definitely contrapuntal style.

The melody is given to the tenor or middle voice, and the relation between each of the two added voices is separately considered.[24]

The style was technically archaic but vitally expressive. Seeger found that it violated most of the established rules for "correct" composition, such as those forbidding parallel fifths, octaves, and unisons; parallel fourths between outer voices or between upper voices without a third in the bass; unprepared and unresolved dissonances; and crossing of voices. I readily echo Seeger's exclamation: "Here is true style!" He goes on to say: "I would as soon change the tunes as change the settings. . . . There is a rigorous, spare, disciplined beauty in the choral writing that is all the more to be prized for having been conceived in the 'backwoods' for which many professional musicians have such scorn, and in the face of the determined opposition of sophisticated zealots in no small number. . . ."[25] That was written in the 1930s; it is pleasing to note that since then any surviving "sophisticated zealots" are spending their energy in other directions.

An example of this early American, three-part contrapuntal style can be seen on p. 180, where a setting of "Wondrous Love" as it appears in *The Harp of Columbia* (Knoxville, 1848) is presented. "Wondrous Love" belongs to the category of folk hymn, defined by Irving Lowens as "basically a secular folk-tune which happens to be sung to a religious text."[26] Dorothy Horn expanded the concept by stating: "A folk hymn would seem . . . to be (a) a contrafactum of a secular folk tune, (b) an original tune composed in the idiom of secular folk music, or (c) a tune patched together, either wholly or in part, from pre-existent melodic fragments, a process known . . . as centonization."[27] In her book *Sing to Me of Heaven* (the title of a folk hymn from the Sacred Harp repertory), Horn analyzes and illustrates the foregoing categories, including familiar examples such as "Wayfaring Stranger," "Greenfields," and "Amazing Grace." The result is a more complex and fluid situation than can be contained in a single restrictive definition.

Jackson observed that the tune and stanzaic structure of "Wondrous Love" "is that of the 'Captain Kidd' ballad which has been widely sung and

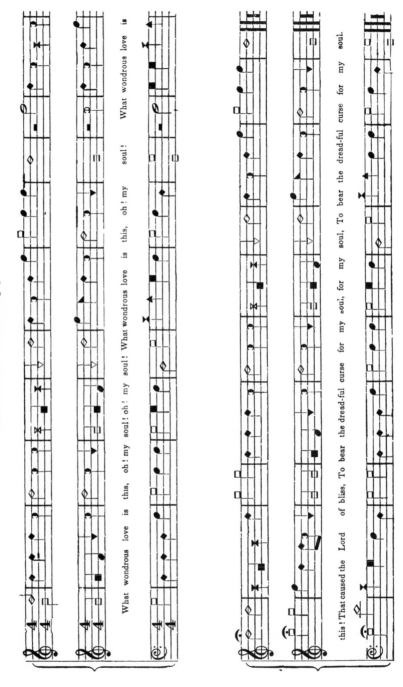

"Wondrous Love" from *The Harp of Columbia*

parodied since the beginning of the eighteenth century."[28] In William Moore's *Columbian Harmony* (1825) it was used with a hymn text beginning,

> Through all the world below,
> God is seen all around,
> Search hills and valleys through,
> There He's found.

Without doubt the most famous of all the folk hymns is "Amazing Grace," with its pentatonic melody and its text by the English evangelist John Newton, a repentant sinner. The tune, under various names, is found in many of the shape-note books, without attribution to any composer. In *The Southern Harmony* it appears in a three-part setting under the title "New Britain" (see p. 183).

In 1936 Jackson recorded an ornamented version of "Amazing Grace," which he characterized as "an excellent illustration of the widespread southern folk-manner in the singing of hymns of this sort."[29] This is but one example among many that confirm the persistence of an ornamental style in the oral tradition of American demotic hymnody:

Ornamented version of "Amazing Grace," as collected by George Pullen Jackson

An appendix to *The Southern Harmony,* "Containing Several Tunes Entirely New," includes an anonymous hymn tune titled "Long Time Ago," which has an exceptionally curious history. According to the editors of *Slave Songs of the United States,* the melody was used by the blacks in a song that began with "Way down in Raccoon Hollow." We have also noted in a different context versions by William Clifton and by Charles Horn, both with identical refrains. It was evidently contagious. The religious version is as follows:[30]

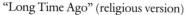

Je - sus died on   Cal - vary's moun-tain,   Long   time   a - go,

And   sal - va - tion's   roll - ing foun-tain,   Now   free - ly   flows!

Having previously mentioned *The Harp of Columbia* in connection with "Wondrous Love," we should note the importance and continuous use of this remarkable shape-note book. First published in 1848 in Knox-ville, Tennessee, a second and larger edition appeared there in 1867. Its de-scriptive title page (see p. 185) includes the initials "M. L.," which stand for the compiler's name, the impressive "Marcus Lafayette." We might indeed say that he was a conquering hero of the shape-note era, at least in Tennes-see, where his book has enjoyed a continuous popularity to the present day. Furthermore, he was among those "advanced" tunebook compilers who decided to adopt the seven-shape system instead of the four that had been used generally.

The four shape-note practice had begun to be challenged as early as the 1830s, and the more modern European system using seven different syl-lables (which the shape notes represented) was rapidly gaining ground. Among those tunesmiths who ventured into this area, the most influential was Jesse B. Aikin, who introduced his seven-shape system in *The Chris-tian Minstrel* (Philadelphia, 1846). This was an immediate success and went into many editions between 1846 and 1873. Although at least six other seven-shape sequences were introduced by 1866, none competed effectively with Aikin, whose system became standard practice for the many seven-shape tunebooks of the period. His procedure was simply to add three more shapes to complete the scale:

△ ▽ ◇ ◁ ▷ ▢ ◯

In his introduction to *The Southern Harmony*, William Walker dis-cussed "The Different Plans of Notation," including what he calls the Ital-ian "do, rae, me" sequence:

> Some contend that no one can learn to sing correctly without using the seven
> syllables. Although I have no objections to the seven syllable plan, I differ a lit-
> tle with such in opinion, for I have taught the four syllables patent notes, the
> Italian seven syllables, and the numerals also, and in twenty-five years' experi-

"New Britain," from *The Southern Harmony*

1 Amazing grace! (how sweet the sound) That saved a wretch like me! I once was lost, but now am found, Was blind, but now I see

2 'Twas grace that taught my heart to fear, And grace my fears relieved: How precious did that grace ap - pear, The hour I first believed!

3 Through many dangers, toils, and snares,
I have already come;
'Tis grace has brought me safe thus far,
And grace will lead me home.

4 The Lord has promised good to me,
His word my hope secures;
He will my shield and portion be,
As long as life endures.

5 Yes, when this flesh and heart shall fail,
And mortal life shall cease,
I shall possess, within the veil,
A life of joy and peace.

6 The earth shall soon dissolve like snow,
The sun forbear to shine;
But God, who call'd me here below,
Will be for ever mine.

ence, have always found my patent note pupils to learn as fast, and sing as correct as any.[31]

But ten years later, "Singin' Billy" Walker was wavering. The seven-
syllable promoters appeared to be aligned with progress. By the 1860s he
was asking rhetorically: "Would any parents having seven children, ever
think of calling them by only four names?"[32] When he published *The Christian Harmony* in Philadelphia in 1866, it appeared with a seven-shape system that he devised, and he proclaimed that the "seven-syllable character-
note singing [was] the quickest and most desirable method known." But if
Walker's tunebooks did not enjoy the lasting success that came to the various editions of *The Sacred Harp,* this may have been caused by his defection to the Italianate *do-re-mi* system.

The seven-shape trend was geared to the idea of "progressive improvement," as indicated by Walker's prefatory statement that in *The Christian
Harmony* he had endeavored to include "more music suitable for church
use"; and in the 1873 edition he boasted of presenting "the most beautiful
and desirable of modern tunes." The editors of *The New Harp of Columbia*
(1867), using seven shapes, stated in the preface that many tunes originally
published in the first edition (1848) had been discarded "and their places
filled by others of superior merit." It is odd to think of Billy Walker and his
quondam cohorts riding on the coattails of Lowell Mason.

A transition from four to seven shapes can also be observed in the
widely used and influential publications of Joseph Funk (1777–1862), who
was active in the Shenandoah Valley of Virginia. He was of German origin, and his first collection, *Die allgemein nützliche Choral-Music* (Harrisonburg, 1816), used German texts. Sixteen years later he brought out his first
English collection, *A Compilation of Genuine Church Music* (Winchester,
Va., 1832), which continued to use the four shapes in its next three editions
(1835, 1842, 1847). The title page announced that it included "a copious elu-
cidation of the science of vocal music." The doctrine of scientific improvement was obviously in the air, and Funk was setting the tune for the
South.[33]

Thus, in 1851 Funk shifted to the seven-shape notation and at the same
time changed the title of his collection to *Harmonia Sacra.* By 1860 this im-
pressive book achieved six editions, easily outrunning its rivals such as
John W. Steffy's *The Valley Harmonist* (Winchester, Va., 1836), George
Henrickson's *The Union Harmony* (Mountain Valley, Va., 1848), and Levi
C. Myer's *Manual of Sacred Music* (1853). Funk's work was continued by his

THE

New Harp of Columbia:

A SYSTEM OF MUSICAL NOTATION,

WITH A NOTE FOR EACH SOUND, AND A SHAPE FOR EACH NOTE;

CONTAINING A VARIETY OF MOST EXCELLENT

PSALM AND HYMN TUNES, ODES AND ANTHEMS,

HAPPILY ADAPTED TO

CHURCH SERVICE, SINGING-SCHOOLS AND SOCIETIES.

ORIGINAL AND SELECTED.

By M. L. SWAN.

The New Harp of Columbia (1867), title page.

sons, with whom he published a periodical, *The Musical Advocate and Singer's Friend* (4 vols., 1859–68). The long and continuous history of Funk's major compilation is attested by the republication in 1959 of *The New Harmonia Sacra: A Companion of Genuine Church Music* (Harrisonburg, Va.: H. A. Brunk).

Titles such as Walker's *The Southern Harmony and Musical Companion* and McCurry's *The Social Harp* indicate the social and recreational aspect of the fasola singing movement. Of course, many of the hymns, with their generous portions of folk tunes and popular melodies, could be fun to sing, and the revival hymns, in particular, were lively and contagious. The same could not always be said for the scattering of secular songs found in the shape-note books.[34] Some of them were doleful reminders of misspent lives, such as the traditional ballads "Musgrove" and "John Adkin's Farewell." The former addresses the issues of deceit caused by greed and the pride of wealth and property, while the latter tells of a drunkard who killed his wife and was hanged for his crime, even though he repented and humbly pleaded for God's mercy. In contrast to "Musgrove" is the story of "The Beggar," who says:

> I'd rather live a beggar while here on earth I stay,
> Then to possess the riches of all America.

But in the next three stanzas he is off "For China's distant shore," presumably to help convert the heathen Chinese, thus combining adventure with edification.

A considerable number of patriotic songs are found in the tunebooks. For example, "Jolly Soldier" harks back to the Revolution and the apotheosis of George Washington as our national hero. "The American Star" smacks of early republican euphoria:

> To us the high boon by the gods have been granted,
> To spread the glad tidings of liberty far.
> Let millions invade us, we'll meet them undaunted,
> And conquer or die by the American star.

The most popular patriotic tune was "Hail Columbia," but several collections also include "Star of Columbia," with words by the New England poet Timothy Dwight (b. 1752), here set to music by "Miss M. T. Durham," whose identity has not been further determined. The opening couplet is:

> Columbia! Columbia! to glory arise,
> The queen of the world and the child of the skies.

There are six eight-line stanzas, and the tunebooks print them all. In *The Sacred Harp* there is also the curiosity of a "wandering stanza," printed under the title "Murillo's Lesson," with attribution (for both words and music) "unknown." The text, however, is the sixth stanza of Dwight's "Star of Columbia":

> As down a lone valley with cedars o'er spread,
> From war's dread confusion I pensively stray'd,
> The gloom from the face of fair heaven retired,
> The winds hush'd their murmurs, the thunders expir'd;
> Perfumes as of Eden flow'd sweetly along,
> A voice as of angels enchantingly sung,
> Columbia, Columbia, to glory arise,
> The queen of the world and the child of the skies.

The tune used is different from the setting by Miss M. T. Durham found in most tunebooks. Perhaps the "unknown" who produced the strangely titled "Murillo's Lesson" was attracted by the pastoral/elegiac quality of this last stanza. Whatever the circumstances, the settings of poetry by Dwight in the shape-note tunebooks give evidence of a considerable cultural scope.

The fasola collections were indeed spiced with variety, from fuging tunes to minstrel melodies, from old-time ballads to sentimental tearjerkers. In *The Social Harp* there is an example of the latter, titled simply "Good-By," which is a reminder of the Mexican War. It tells of a dying soldier "On Buena Vista's bloody field," who asks his comrades to convey "a few brief words" (seven stanzas!) to his family and sweetheart "some thousand miles away." A headnote informs us that McCurry (who was partial to instrumental music) transcribed the tune "As played on the Accordeon by Mrs. Martha J. Hodges, of Hartwell." That was about 1855, and it makes us wonder how many housewives were playing the accordion in the rural areas of the South during the mid-nineteenth century. Surely Martha Hodges was not unique.

I must quote one more song before passing on to the peroration, because it again illustrates the varied charm of the fasola tradition. This is "Soft Music" (see p. 188), to which B. F. White appended his name in *The Sacred Harp*.

George Pullen Jackson (1874–1953), the "discoverer" of Sacred Harp music and founder of the Tennessee Sacred Harp Singing Association, rightly remarked that "*Sacred Harp* type of music is to be sung and not listened to."[35] It is essentially a *social* music. It was originally disseminated by

"Soft Music," from *The Sacred Harp*

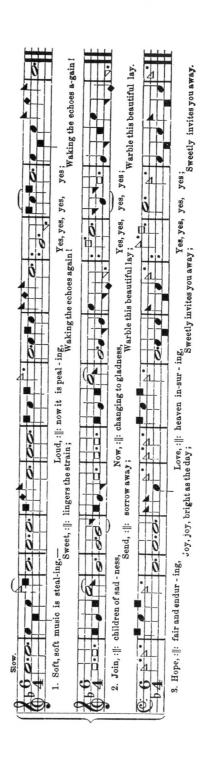

singing conventions and other social groups, and so it has continued to the present day. As described by Harry Eskew:

> A Sacred Harp singing is a musical, religious, and social event. The singings take place mostly in churches, but also in country courthouses, school buildings and community centers. The singers usually sit informally in sections according to their voice parts. Each singing session opens and closes with prayer. In democratic fashion each singer who wishes is given the opportunity to lead the group in a selection. Each piece is first rehearsed once in the fasola syllables and then sung with words. . . . Although the majority of the singings are of one day's duration, there are also numerous night singings and some two- and three-day singings. In most singings the majority of singers are of the older generation, having learned this musical tradition from their childhood. There is a certain emotional fervor and vitality in this country singing that is reflected in the faces of the singers themselves. The purpose of these singings is not public performance for an audience but rather whole-hearted participation. Thus the vocal quality is that of the country singer and not the fine-art oriented singing of urban culture.[36]

While Sacred Harp singing has become to a certain extent "listener's music" through recordings issued since the 1940s,[37] its basic function as "singer's music" has been greatly widened through its acceptance by an ever-increasing number of people who have not grown up with the fasola tradition but nevertheless immediately respond to its appeal. Many people, especially students, have enthusiastically participated in this trend. One of its leading proponents, Neely Bruce, brought the fasola singing to many campuses with his American Music Group. He then took the initiative in founding the Annual New England Sacred Harp Singings, which began in 1976 in Montpelier, Vermont. The second was held in Lexington, Massachusetts, and the third in Middletown, Connecticut, which thereafter became the main locus. Participating groups have included the Wesleyan Singers, the Word of Mouth Chorus, and Sacred Harp singers from Alabama and Georgia. We should also note that in Bremen, Alabama, the original *Sacred Harp* was still being published, with Hugh McGraw taking the initiative in its wide dissemination throughout the South. Clearly, the spirit of the fasola folk and the heritage of the tunebook compilers are flourishing throughout the land.

Notes

1. See Irving Lowens, "John Wyeth's *Repository of Sacred Music, Part Second* (1813): A Northern Precursor of Southern Folk-Hymnody," in Lowens, *Music and Musicians in Early America,* pp. 138–55.

2. Ibid., p. 147.

3. Ananias Davisson, *Kentucky Harmony; or, A Choice Collection of Psalm Tunes, Hymns, and Anthems*, 4th ed. (Harrisonburg, Va.: Author, 1821), p. 13; as quoted in George Pullen Jackson, *White Spirituals in the Southern Uplands*, p. 28

4. Dorothy D. Horn, *Sing to Me of Heaven*, p. 7.

5. Ibid., pp. 7–8.

6. James P. Carrell and David L. Clayton, comps., *The Virginia Harmony: A New and Choice Selection of Psalm & Hymn Tunes, Anthems, & Set Pieces* (1831; 2d rev. ed., Winchester, Va.: Robinson and Hollis, 1836), p. [3].

7. Ibid., p. 9.

8. Richard J. Stanislaw, *A Checklist of Four-Shape Shape-Note Tunebooks*, p. 27, no. 183.

9. Quoted in Jackson, *White Spirituals in the Southern Uplands*, pp. 17–18. Jackson drew his quote from an edition published in Cincinnati by Truman and Smith in 1840.

10. Ibid., p. 18.

11. William Moore, "General Observations," *Columbian Harmony; or, A Choice Collection of Psalm Tunes, Hymns, and Anthems* (Cincinnati: Morgan, Lodge, and Fisher, 1825), p. xii; quoted in ibid., p. 45.

12. Quoted in Jackson, *White Spirituals in the Southern Uplands*, p. 51.

13. *The Virginia Sacred Minstrel*, comp. Wheeler Gillet (Winchester, Va.: J. Foster, 1817), p. 4; quoted in Stanislaw, *A Checklist of Four-Shape Shape-Note Tunebooks*, p. 12, no. 74.

14. J. B. O. Landrum, *History of Spartanburg County* (Atlanta: Franklin Printing and Publication, 1900), pp. 491–95; quoted in Jackson, *White Spirituals in the Southern Uplands*, pp. 56–59, especially p. 57.

15. William Walker, preface to *The Southern Harmony, and Musical Companion* (Philadelphia: E. W. Miller, 1835), p. iii. See the facsimile of the 1854 edition, ed. Glenn C. Wilcox (Los Angeles: Pro Musicamericana, 1966).

16. Walker, *The Southern Harmony*, ed. Wilcox, p. 265.

17. Joseph Summerlin James, *A Brief History of the Sacred Harp, and Its Author, B. F. White, Sr., and Contributors* (Douglasville, Ga.: New South Book and Job Print, 1904), pp. 27–35; quoted in Jackson, *White Spirituals in the Southern Uplands*, pp. 81–93, especially p. 84.

18. Benjamin Franklin White, preface to *The Sacred Harp: A Collection of Psalms and Hymn Tunes, Odes, and Anthems* (Philadelphia: T. K. and P. G. Collins, 1844), p. 3. See the facsimile of the third edition (Philadelphia: S. C. Collins, 1859), including a historical introduction ("The Story of the Sacred Harp") by George Pullen Jackson (Nashville: Broadman Press, 1968).

19. Ibid., p. 23.

20. William Chappell, *The Ballad Literature and Popular Music of the Olden Time* 2:748.

21. Aldine S. Kieffer, "A Visit to the Home of a Southern Musician," *Musical Million* 14 (May 1883): 72; quoted by Daniel W. Patterson in his introduction to John G. McCurry, *The Social Harp*, ed. Daniel W. Patterson and John F. Garst (Athens: University of Georgia Press, 1973), p. xiii.

22. Jackson, *White Spirituals in the Southern Uplands*, p. 80.

23. McCurry, "Rudiments of Music," *The Social Harp*, ed. Patterson and Garst, p. 14.

24. Charles Seeger, "Contrapuntal Style in the Three-Voice Shape-Note Hymns," p. 483.

25. Ibid., pp. 484–85, 488.

26. Lowens, "John Wyeth's *Repository of Sacred Music, Part Second,*" p. 138.

27. Horn, *Sing to Me of Heaven*, p. 18.

28. George Pullen Jackson, comp., *Spiritual Folk-Songs of Early America*, p. 115.

29. Ibid., p. 153.

30. See Walker, *The Southern Harmony*, ed. Wilcox, p. 313.

31. Ibid., p. xxxi.

32. William Walker, comp., *The Christian Harmony, Containing a Choice Collection of Hymn and Psalm Tunes, Odes and Anthems from the Best Authors in Europe and America* (Philadelphia: Miller, 1866), p. iv.

33. See Harry Eskew, "Joseph Funk's 'Allgemein nutzliche Choral-Music' (1816)," in Society for the History of the Germans in Maryland, *Thirty-second Report*, ed. Klaus G. Wust (Baltimore, 1966), pp. 38–46.

34. The songs discussed below are found in McCurry, *The Social Harp*, ed. Patterson and Garst. They are: "Musgrove" (p. 87), "John Adkin's Farewell" (p. 200), "Jolly Soldier" (p. 194), "Star of Columbia" (p. 63), "Murillo's Lesson" (pp. 90–91), "Good-By" (pp. 253–54), and "Soft Music" (p. 76).

35. Jackson, *White Spirituals in the Southern Uplands*, p. 126.

36. Harry Eskew, "American Folk Hymnody," *Hymn Society of Great Britain and Ireland Bulletin* 7 (Nov. 1971): 151–52.

37. *Old Harp Singing*, liner notes by Sidney Robertson Cowell, Folkways Records FA 2356; *Fasola: 53 Shape-Note Folk Hymns Recorded at an All-Day Sacred Harp Singing, Stewart's Chapel, Houston, Mississippi, by Amelia and Frederic Ramsey, Jr.,* ASCH Mankind Series AHM 4151; and *White Spirituals from The Sacred Harp—The Alabama Sacred Harp Convention*, recorded and edited by Alan Lomax, New World Records NW 205.

Chapter 11
Revival Hymns and Spiritual Songs

Shout, shout, we're gaining ground,
  Halle, hallelujah!
Satan's kingdom is tumbling down,
  Glory hallelujah!
—*Revival Hymns* (Boston, 1842)

It has been said that "to the American frontier Methodism gave the circuit rider and to Methodism the frontier gave the camp meeting." The circuit rider was an itinerant preacher who traveled up and down the countryside, over the mountains and through the wilderness, bringing the gospel to widely scattered families in their farms and small communities. Francis Asbury, the first prominent circuit rider, is credited with having ridden over 275,000 miles. But no matter how many miles the preacher on horseback might travel, he could bring the gospel only to a few people at any given time and place. The solution for this problem soon became obvious: the people must be brought together at a particular time and place in order to receive the word of the Lord en masse.

Such was the origin and motivation of camp meetings, which gave a strong impetus to the grass-roots religious fervor that swept through America in the aftermath of eighteenth-century revivalism. The first frontier camp meeting that has been historically verified took place in Logan County, Kentucky, in July 1800. This was organized by a Presbyterian minister, James McGready, in an effort to stimulate religious fervor among his widely scattered congregation. The idea caught on and soon spread through the frontier territory like the proverbial wildfire.

An immediate result was the historic camp meeting held at Cane Ridge, Kentucky, in August 1801, when people assembled from all over that state, as well as from Tennessee and the territory north of the Ohio

River. The meeting went on for six days, and the attendance was variously estimated at from ten to twenty thousand. Again this was a Presbyterian initiative, but Methodist preachers also participated—and obviously it took a considerable number to handle such huge crowds. The backwoods preacher Peter Cartwright reported that "between one and two thousand souls were happily and powerfully converted to God during the meeting."[1] According to later accounts, such emotionally induced conversions were often more powerful than happy in their results.

Although Presbyterian ministers had taken the initiative, Methodists and Baptists soon gained the ascendancy in the camp-meeting movement, mainly because their preachers were less cultivated and dogmatic, hence closer to the common folk. Salvation was their message, conversion the means, and extirpation of sin the outward and visible effect. Direct communion with God through the intercession of Jesus Christ was the ultimate reward of conversion.

The Methodists had the advantage of possessing a large body of popular hymnody, mainly inherited from John Wesley and his followers. Speaking of the Methodist invasion of the early camp meetings, a historian writes: "They succeeded in introducing their own stirring hymns, familiarly, though incorrectly, entitled 'Wesley's Hymns;' and as books were scarce, the few that were attainable were cut up, and the leaves distributed, so that all in turn might learn them by heart."[2]

The book so roughly handled at these first camp meetings was probably *The Pocket Hymn Book* (Philadelphia, 1797), which was rapidly going through one edition after another in response to the demand for revival hymns. Like many other such books, it contained only the words, not the music. The tunes were either familiar ones that everybody knew or of such a simple and catchy nature that they could be picked up quickly. As Benson remarks, "Of the tunes to which the Camp Meeting Hymns were sung the leaders demanded nothing more than contagiousness and effectiveness."[3] The preachers were also the song leaders.

In a previous chapter, tracing the development of evangelical hymnody in England under the influence of the Wesleys and their followers, with particular reference to the intensely emotional and folksy hymns of Cennick and Newton, we described the background out of which came the popular religious songs of the American camp meetings. Here we should recall the use of the term *spiritual songs* in many collections of evangelical hymnody, including the *Hymns and Spiritual Songs* of Isaac Watts. This term was taken over in American collections such as Joshua Smith's *Divine Hymns or Spiritual Songs* (Norwich, 1794), Henry Alline's *Hymns and Spiritual Songs* (1802), David Mintz's *Spiritual Song Book* (n.p., 1805), and John C. Totten's *A Collection of the Most Admired Hymns and Spiritual Songs, with the Choruses Affixed As Usually Sung at Camp-Meetings* (New York, 1809). More than fifty such books were published prior to the Civil War. Totten's collection is particularly interesting for its specific mention of camp meetings and of the choruses that constituted the most striking feature of revival hymnody.

Before going on to describe and illustrate some of the camp-meeting hymns and spiritual songs, let us share the experiences and comments of that colorful character Lorenzo Dow (1777–1834), who was so fervently involved in the revivalism of the camp meetings. A native of Connecticut, he felt the call to preach early in life, and in spite of much opposition and many difficulties—caused in part by his eccentric and extravagant character—he succeeded in carrying the gospel throughout most of the United States and even brought the camp meetings to Great Britain, where he aroused large crowds with his fervor and enthusiasm. He married a person as enthusiastic and eccentric as himself, Peggy Dow, who in 1816 brought out *A Collection of Camp-Meeting Hymns* (words only). Lorenzo Dow left a voluminous journal of his travels, from which we shall freely quote.

According to a footnote in Dow's journal, "camp meetings began in Kentucky—next North Carolina—attended them in Georgia—introduced in the centre of Virginia, N. York, Connecticut, Massachusetts and Mississippi Territory—1803–4–5."[4] Thus within five years the camp meetings had spread widely from South to North. In 1804 Lorenzo attended a meeting in Liberty, Tennessee, of which he wrote:

> Friday 19th. Camp-meeting commenced at Liberty: here I saw the *jerks;* and some danced: a strange exercise indeed; however, it is involuntary, yet requires the consent of the will; i.e. the people are taken *jerking* irresistibly, and if they strive to resist it, it worries them much, yet is attended with no bodily pain, and those who are exercised to dance, (which in the pious seems an antidote to the jerks) if they resist, it brings deadness and barrenness over the mind; but when they yield to it they feel happy, although it is a great cross; there is a heavenly smile and solemnity on the countenance, which carries great conviction to the minds of the beholders; their eyes when dancing seem to be fixed upwards as if upon an invisible object, and they are lost to all below.[5]

The question of dancing, so closely related to the jerks, was evidently a matter of theological concern, for on Sunday, the twenty-first, Dow wrote: "I heard Doctor Tooley, a man of liberal education, who had been a noted Deist, preach on the subject of the *jerks* and the *Dancing exercise:* He brought ten passages of Scripture to prove that dancing was once a religious exercise, but corrupted at Aaron's calf, and from thence young people got it for amusement. I believe the congregation and preachers were generally satisfied with his remarks."[6]

Lorenzo Dow found that the jerks were not restricted to a particular denomination. In Tennessee he met some Quakers who said, "the Methodists and Presbyterians have the *jerks* because they *sing* and *pray* so much, but we are a still peaceable people wherefore we do not have them." But later, at a meeting, he found that about a dozen Quakers "had the jerks as keen and powerful as any I had seen, so as to have occasioned a kind of grunt or groan when they would jerk." Summing it up, he wrote: "I have seen Presbyterians, Methodists, Quakers, Baptists, Church of England, and Independents, exercised with the *jerks;* Gentleman and Lady, black and white, the aged and the youth, rich and poor, without exception. . . ."[7] So much for the universal democracy of the "jerks!"

Back in his native Connecticut, Lorenzo Dow gives us a brief picture of the typical camp-meeting scene: "About three thousand appeared on the ground, and the rejoicing of old saints, the shouts of young converts, and the cries of the distressed for mercy, caused the meeting to continue all night. . . ."[8]

It was at night that the revival frenzy reached its greatest intensity. As the campfires blazed, preachers went through crowds exhorting the sinners to repent and be saved from the fires of Hell. The volume of song rose to a mighty wave of sound; repentant singers jerked, leaped, rolled, or writhed on the ground until they swooned and had to be carried away. Emotions and frustrations found release in "the singing ecstasy" of a rousing hymn:

> Jesus, grant us all a blessing,
> Shouting, singing, send it down;
> Lord, above may we go praying,
> And rejoicing in Thy love.
> Shout, O Glory! sing glory, hallelujah!
> I'm going where pleasure never dies.

Of all the contemporary accounts of camp meetings, probably none has attracted more attention than that of the English writer Frances Trollope, included in her widely read book *Domestic Manners of the American People* (London, 1832). She lived for a time in Cincinnati and in the summer of 1829 attended a nearby camp meeting as a spectator (a common practice in those days). She prefaced her description as follows: "I had heard it said that being at a camp-meeting was like standing at the gate of heaven, and seeing it open before you; I had heard it said, that being at a camp-meeting was like finding yourself within the gates of hell. . . ."[9] Her experience evidently swayed her to the latter view.

Herewith are some excerpts from Mrs. Trollope's account:

> We reached the ground about an hour before midnight, and the approach to it was highly picturesque. The spot chosen was the verge of an unbroken forest, where a space of about twenty acres appeared to have been partially cleared for the purpose. Tents of different sizes were pitched very near together in a circle round the cleared space; behind them were ranged an exterior circle of carriages of every description, and at the back of each were fastened the horses which had drawn them thither. Through this triple circle of defence we distinguished numerous fires burning brightly within it; and still more numerous lights flickering from the trees that were left in the enclosure. . . .
>
> . . . . Four high frames, constructed in the form of altars, were placed at the four corners of the enclosure; on these were supported layers of earth and sod, on which burned immense fires of blazing pine-wood. On one side a rude platform was erected to accommodate the preachers, fifteen of whom attended this meeting, and with very short intervals for necessary refreshment and private devotion, preached in rotation, day and night, from Tuesday to Saturday.[10]

She later notes that there were about 2,000 persons assembled, and remarks that "great numbers of persons were walking about the ground, who appeared like ourselves to be present only as spectators. . . ."[11]

Trollope then describes the "private worship" that went on in tents, with men and women together, all kneeling on the floor. What she saw and heard reminded her of Bedlam. She was more attracted by a tent that "was occupied exclusively by Negroes," of whom she remarks: "They were all full-dressed, and looked exactly as if they were performing a scene on the stage."[12]

The hour was now at hand for the climax of the nocturnal proceedings:

> At midnight a horn sounded through the camp . . . to call the people from private to public worship; and we presently saw them flocking from all sides to the front of the preachers' stand.
>
> . . . . The preacher told them that "this night was the time fixed upon for

anxious sinners to wrestle with the Lord;" that he and his brethren "were at hand to help them," and that such as needed their help were to come forward into the "pen. . . ." "The pen" was the space immediately below the preachers' stand. . . .

The crowd fell back at the mention of the *pen*, and for some minutes there was a vacant space before us. The preachers came down from their stand, and placed themselves in the midst of it, beginning to sing a hymn, calling upon the penitents to come forth. As they sung they kept turning themselves round to every part of the crowd, and, by degrees, the voices of the whole multitude joined in chorus. This was the only moment at which I perceived any thing like the solemn and beautiful effect which I had heard ascribed to this woodland worship.[13]

Although Mrs. Trollope does not tell us what hymn or "spiritual song" was heard on this occasion, it might well have been something like this one, called "Satan's Kingdom":

> This night my soul has caught new fire,
>   Halle, hallelujah!
> I feel that heav'n is drawing nigh'r,
>   Glory hallelujah!
>
> Shout, shout, we are gaining ground,
>   Halle, hallelujah!
> Satan's kingdom is tumbling down,
>   Glory hallelujah!

This song has a long and significant history. When it appeared in *Revival Hymns* (Boston, 1842), the compiler of that collection, H. W. Day, stated in a headnote: "This hymn and the original melody, which have been so useful in revival seasons, for more than half a century, and which, it is believed, have never before been published together, were lately procured after considerable search, from the diary of an aged servant of Christ, bearing the date 1810." So it is more than likely that Mrs. Trollope may have heard this very popular and typical revival hymn in 1829.

It should also be noted that the text of "Satan's Kingdom" is pieced together by an accumulation of "wandering verses" and tag lines that formed the stock-in-trade of revivalism. By having an immense reserve of such material to draw on, which could be continually recombined according to the circumstances or the improvisational impulse, the revival hymns proliferated rapidly while always maintaining their typical features. Some examples will illustrate this development.

By inserting a familiar tag line after each verse, adding a chorus, and

singing the whole to a rollicking tune, any standard hymn could be transformed into a "spiritual song" for the camp-meeting revivals. This is what
happened to Charles Wesley's hymn "He comes, he comes, the Judge severe," as follows:

> He comes, he comes, the Judge severe,
> Roll, Jordan, roll;
> The seventh trumpet speaks him near,
> Roll, Jordan, roll.
>
> I want to go to heav'n, I do, Hallelujah, Lord;
> We'll praise the Lord in heav'n above, Roll, Jordan, roll.

The typical revivalist was pictured as a pilgrim traveling through the
wilderness, burdened with the sins of the world but rejoicing in a vision of
the Promised Land, which is just across the Jordan River. When he gets
there, he'll lay his burdens down and his troubles will be over.

This prospect is the theme of a widely popular hymn by the English
dissenting divine Samuel Stennett, which appears in many shape-note
tunebooks under various names and with a variety of camp-meeting choruses. In *The Southern Harmony* alone there are four versions, including
one titled "Jordan's Shore"(see p. 199), with the music attributed to J. T.
White. "Jordan's Shore" is particularly interesting because of the way in
which the chorus is syntactically tied to the verses.

The "happy" chorus was a favorite device for infusing a standard
hymn with the revival spirit. For example, John Cennick's popular hymn
"Jesus, my all, to heaven is gone" was sung with the following chorus:

> We'll cross the river of Jordan,
> Happy, O happy,
> We'll cross the river of Jordan,
> Happy, in the Lord.

Another of Cennick's hymns, "Children of the Heavenly King," appears in
The Social Harp with a favorite "happy" chorus tag line:

> I want to be as happy as I well can be,
> Lord, send salvation down.

The reader who wishes to find any of these hymns in the tunebooks
should bear in mind they appear under various names instead of being identified by their first lines as is customary in modern practice. For example,
"He comes, he comes, the Judge severe" appears under tune names such as
"Roll Jordan," "Welcome Souls," and "Hallelujah." Robert Robinson's fa-

"Jordan's Shore," from *The Southern Harmony*

1. On Jordan's storm-y banks I stand, And cast a wish-ful eye, On the oth - er side of Jor-dan, hal - le - lu - jah!
   To Ca-naan's fair and hap - py land, Where my pos - ses - sions lie, On the oth - er side of Jor-dan, hal - le - lu - jah!

2. Oh! the trans-port-ing, rapt'rous scene, That ri - ses to my sight! On the oth - er side of Jor-dan, hal - le - lu - jah!
   Sweet fields, ar - ray'd in liv - ing green, And ri - vers of de - light, On the oth - er side of Jor-dan, hal - le - lu - jah!

3. O'er all those wide-ex - tend-ed plains Shines one e - ter-nal day, On the oth - er side of Jor-dan, hal - le - lu - jah!
   There God the Son for - ev - er reigns, And scat-ters night a - way, On the oth - er side of Jor-dan, hal - le - lu - jah!

Chorus.

On the oth - er side of Jor-dan, hal - le - lu - jah, On the oth - er side of Jor-dan, hal - le - lu - jah!

4. No chilling winds, nor pois'nous breath
   Can reach that healthful shore;
   Sickness and sorrow, pain and death
   Are felt and fear'd no more.

5. When shall I reach that happy place,
   And be forever blest?
   When shall I see my Father's face,
   And in his bosom rest?

6. Fill'd with delight, my raptured soul
   Would here no longer stay;
   Though Jordan's waves should round me roll,
   I'd fearless launch away.

miliar hymn "Come, thou fount of ev'ry blessing" appears in four versions in *The Social Harp*, each with a different name: "Glorious News," "Hallelujah Third," "Palms of Victory," and "Olney." This follows the traditional practice of psalmody, in which each musical setting was identified by its tune name. For the uninitiated, finding a particular hymn in the index of a tunebook is very much like looking for a needle in the proverbial haystack.

Returning to our camp-meeting songs, we find in Hauser's *Hesperian Harp* (Philadelphia, 1848) an example of the river Jordan theme combined with the highly popular and widespread theme of the "Old Ship of Zion," which appears in the second stanza:

> What ship is this that will take us all home?
> O glory hallelujah!
> 'Tis the old ship of Zion,
> O glory hallelujah!

In the fifth stanza we find another familiar theme of the revival spirituals:

> If you get there before I do,
> You may tell them that I'm coming.

This is linked to the larger "traveling to Canaan" theme that recurs in so many spirituals. As the revivalist preacher passed through the crowds on the camp-meeting ground, clapping his hands, he would loudly sing out:

> O brethren, will you meet me,
> In Canaan's happy land?

And hundreds—or thousands—of voices would reply in a mighty burst of song:

> By the grace of God, we'll meet you,
> In Canaan's happy land.

Another time the preacher would sing out:

> I feel the work reviving,
> I feel the work reviving,
> Reviving in my soul.

Then the jubilant throng would respond:

> We'll shout and give him glory,
> We'll shout and give him glory,
> We'll shout and give him glory,
> For glory is his own.

Such redundancy was essential to the camp-meeting spirit both for emotional emphasis (repetition carried conviction) and as an aid to memory (very few sang from books). It was possible to keep a song going almost indefinitely, simply by changing one word in each stanza. For instance, in the line "O brothers will you meet me?" the word *brothers* could be replaced in subsequent repetitions by *sisters, mourners, sinners,* and so on. In the same manner, "We have fathers in the promised land" could be followed by "We have brothers (sisters, mothers, children, etc.)."

Then there were the "dialogue songs" in which one line was sung by men, with the women responding in the next line. Here is an example from *The Millennial Harp* (Boston, 1843), called "Mariner's Hymn":

"Mariner's Hymn," from the *Millennial Harp*

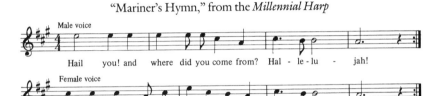

The dialogue continues:

> Hail you! and where are you bound for? Hallelujah!
> Oh, I'm bound for the land of Canaan, Hallelujah!
>
> Hail you! and what is your cargo? Hallelujah!
> Oh, religion is my cargo. Hallelujah!

(Guy B. Johnson believes that the pentatonic tune of this revival spiritual came from a sailor's song, and points to its similarity with the hoisting chantey "Blow, Boys, Blow.")[14]

The idea of "gaining ground against sin" is another basic theme of the revival spirituals. One example among many is a camp-meeting chorus affixed to the eighteenth-century hymn "I know that my Redeemer lives," which appears in *The Social Harp* under the tune name "Antioch":

> Shout on, pray on, we're gaining ground,
>   Glory hallelujah!
> The dead's alive and the lost is found,
>   Glory hallelujah!

The idea of gaining ground is often identified with the perpetual struggle against Satan, as in this revival spiritual, "The Good Old Way," which appeared with words only in *Zion's Songster* (New York, 1832) and with the music in *The Southern Harmony:*

> Though Satan may his power employ,
>   O halle, hallelujah!
> Our peace and comfort to destroy,
>   O halle, hallelujah!
> Yet never fear, we'll gain the day,
>   O halle, hallelujah!
> And triumph in the good old way,
>   O halle, hallelujah!

Revivalist fervor reached its peak in the 1830s and 1840s, owing largely to the preaching of a Vermont farmer by the name of William Miller (1782–1849), who predicted that the end of the world would come in the spring of 1843:

> In eighteen hundred forty-three
> Will be the Year of Jubilee.

Obtaining a Baptist license to preach, Miller traveled around the country carrying his message of the coming Day of Wrath, distributing tracts, hymnbooks, and printed propaganda of every kind. His message of impending doom was reinforced by the portents of Nature. In 1833 there was a meteoric shower of "falling stars"; in 1835 Halley's comet reappeared; and in 1843 the "Great Comet" appeared, seemingly in cooperation with Miller's schedule. The universe, however, did not fully cooperate. When the spring of 1843 had passed and the world had not come to an end, Miller announced that he had made a slight miscalculation. The Day of Judgment was definitely set for October 22, 1844.

"Miller Madness" seized large sections of the population, driving some to insanity or suicide, while others sought protection by becoming "Millerites." By 1843 Miller had become the leader of his own sect, known as the Millennialists and later as the Seventh-day Adventists. His chief lieutenant in the millennial movement was Joshua V. Himes, pastor of the First Christian Church in Boston, who in 1843 compiled and published a songbook called *The Millennial Harp*, containing over 200 songs, mostly in the style of revival spirituals, written or adapted for conveying the message of the Second Advent.

By some unaccountable obstinacy of Nature, the world survived the

fateful day of October 22, 1844. Miller himself survived this disappointment by five years, dying in 1849. His followers evidently did not lose faith,
for a few years later they were singing:

> O praise the Lord, we do not fear
> To tell the world he'll come next year,
> In eighteen hundred fifty-four
> The saints will shout their suff'rings o'er.
> [*Pilgrim's Songster*, 1853]

One of the most stirring songs in *The Millennial Harp* is "Old Churchyard," sung especially at meetings in cemeteries, for many Millerites
"sought the graveyards where friends were buried, so as to join them as
they arose from their earthly resting places and ascend with them." The
tune has been widely used in America's demotic music. As we observed in
an earlier chapter, it was the tune to which the Hutchinson Family sang
their famous theme song, "The Old Granite State." Here are the words
and melody of the first stanza and chorus (notice how the text of the
former leads directly into the latter):

"Old Churchyard," from the *Millennial Harp*

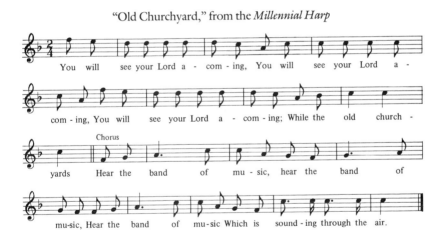

We have learned something about the revival spirit, the atmosphere of
the camp meetings, and various types of revival spirituals and camp-meeting hymns. The question remains—and it is an important one—how did
the singing sound? Unfortunately, those who witnessed the early camp
meetings have left us more detailed accounts of the sensational manifesta-

tions of religious hysteria than of the singing. The evidence indicates that singing was not valued per se, but rather as an incentive to conversion and the promise of salvation.

The southern revivalist preacher Lucius Bellinger has some references to revival singing strewn among his autobiographical *Stray Leaves from the Port-folio of a Methodist Local Preacher* (Macon, Ga., 1870), such as that of a preacher who led the singing: "He was a man with a sharp, strong, piercing voice. We now have old-time singing—clear, loud, and ringing."[15] All accounts agree that the singing was loud. For example, Samuel E. Asbury, a descendant of the Francis Asbury who was America's pioneer circuit rider, recalled the old-time revival singing of his youth: "The immediate din was tremendous; at a hundred yards it was beautiful; and at a distance of a half mile it was magnificent."[16]

No musical instruments were used—not even a tuning fork. Some brass-lung male pitched the tune, and many others took it up and carried it along. As in the time-honored tradition of the tunebooks, it was the men, not the women, who sang the "melody." But the women's voices were conspicuous as they sang their parts an octave higher—often, as Asbury remarks, "singing around high C with perfect unconcern because they didn't realize their feat." They no doubt enjoyed it, but they were not singing for art's sake: "What they were there for was to hammer on the sinner's heart and bring him [more often "her"] to the mourners' bench."[17] The great majority of converts were young women.

The tunes—drawn mostly from the demotic tradition of the British Isles—were often beautiful and stirring. To hear them sung at the height of the revival fervor must have been a thrilling experience. As an example, we present one of the best-known and most typical camp-meeting songs, "Morning Trumpet," based on a hymn text by John Leland:

"Morning Trumpet"

Shout_ O____ glo - ry, for I shall mount a - bove the

skies When I hear the trum - pet sound_ in that morn - ing.

History records a joint meeting of Millerites and Shakers at Enfield, Connecticut, in February 1847. According to a Shaker journal, "The Adventists [Millerites] and Believers [Shakers] took turns, one lectured an hour, then the other side an hour, sometimes the Believers would sing and sometimes they would sing; any shouted or said amen, who felt to." As summarized by Daniel Patterson in *The Shaker Spiritual:* "On this occasion there was little meeting of minds, but a number of disillusioned followers of William Miller did enter the various [Shaker] societies, bringing a few songs into the Shaker repertory."[18]

That repertory had been increasing with extraordinary rapidity since the time when Mother Ann came to America on the eve of the Revolution with a handful of followers from England. Patterson, who has worked with over 800 Shaker songbooks, estimates that "the entire body of surviving manuscripts must preserve 8,000 to 10,000 songs."[19] But there are few printed sources. The first Shaker hymnal to appear in print, *Millennial Praises* (Hancock, Mass., 1813), contained only the texts of 140 hymns and spiritual songs. Not until 1852 did a collection appear with tunes: *A Sacred Repository of Anthems and Hymns* (Canterbury, N.H.). The title is misleading in its implication of a standard repertory, whereas the most numerous and typical Shaker songs were functionally related to the peculiar rituals or "exercises" that they practiced, which were called "laboring." The "Solemn Songs" introduced by Mother Ann and other early leaders were often wordless or sung to meaningless syllables—probably because the emphasis was on the dancing rituals.

The "Gift Songs from Mother Ann's Work" were received by her American followers (mostly young women in this case) in visions and trances. They appeared with profusion during the decade 1837–47, and together with the "laboring" songs, they form the largest and most characteristic body of Shaker song. Both types could be used for ritual exercises. For example, the most enduring and widely known of all Shaker songs, "Simple Gifts," is identified as a "Quick Dance." Its exact origin and authorship are undetermined, but it probably dates from 1848. Not only was it a favorite of all Shaker communities, but it became nationally and internationally known as an American "folk-classic" through its use by Aaron Copland as a theme with variations in the score of his ballet *Appalachian Spring*. Here are the words and melody (the tempo is *allegro*):

"Simple Gifts"

'Tis the gift to be sim-ple, 'tis the gift to be free, 'Tis the gift to come down where we ought to be, And when we find our-selves in the place just right, 'Twill be in the val - ley of love and de - light. When true sim - pli - ci - ty is gain'd, To bow and to bend we shan't be a - sham'd, To turn, turn will be our de - light till by turn - ing, turn - ing we come round right.

The Shakers, like other schismatic revivalists, made no bones about plundering "carnal" tunes for the service of the Lord:

> Let justice seize old Adam's crew,
> And all the whore's production;
> We'll take the choicest of their songs,
> Which to the Church of God belongs,
> And recompense them for their wrongs,
> In singing their destruction.

Since they also believed that their religion brought them joy and holy mirth, the Shakers often expressed their joyful feelings not only in hymns and spiritual songs but also in ritual dances and many kinds of symbolic exercises. The joy of praise is expressed in this quatrain:

Two paintings of Shaker dances.

> We Love to sing and dance we will
> Because we surely, *surely* feel
> It does our thankful spirits fill
> With heavenly joy and pleasure.

A similar joyful spirit is expressed in a song called "The Happy Journey":

> O the happy journey that we are pursuing,
> Come brethren and sisters let's all strip to run.

The act of "stripping" was of course symbolic, but in many instances the Shakers interpreted literally and realistically the actions described in their song—as in this tribute to chastity:

> I love to see them *stamp* and *grin*,
> And curse the flesh, the seat of sin.

This theme is martially expressed in the following song, "Shake Off the Flesh":

> Come, let us all unite
> To purge out this filthy, fleshy, carnal sense,
> And labor for the power of God
> To mortify and stain our pride.
> We'll raise our glitt-'ring swords and fight,
> And war the flesh with all our might,
> All carnal ties we now will break
> And in the pow'r of God we'll shake.

In the autumn of 1837 the Shakers experienced a great revival that lasted for more than ten years and that produced a large number of songs. Many of these were "gift" or "vision" songs, revealed to the faithful in dreams or visions, sometimes by the spirit of Mother Ann, sometimes by angels, and other times by the spirits of famous persons whose relation to the Shakers remains mysterious, among them Alexander the Great, Queen Elizabeth I, George Washington, William Penn, Christopher Columbus, Thomas Jefferson, and Napoleon. "Native" songs were received from the spirits of American Indians, Eskimos, Chinese, Hottentots, and other heathen races—a truly ecumenical scope! When the Shakers were possessed by the spirits of American Indians, they behaved according to their concept of the "red man's" culture. An eyewitness described a "dancing night" at which "eight or nine of the Sisters became possessed of the Spirits of Indian Squaws and about six of the Brothers became Indians: then ensued a regular

'Pow Wow,' with whooping, yelling, and strange antics."[20] The Shakers were truly resourceful in compensating for the restrictions of celibacy.

The Shaker "laboring" songs, for ritualistic exercises, were often graphic in their description of the actions involved. For example, in a ritual song of mortification:

> Bow down low, bow down low,
> Wash, wash, clean, clean, clean.
> Scour and scrub, scour and scrub,
> From this floor the stains of sin.

The consubstantial concept of work and worship was evidently a basic tenet of the Shaker faith.

The symbolic drinking of wine was another Shaker ritual that had its appropriate songs. "The Gift of spiritual wine," wrote Isaac N. Youngs, "carried a great evidence of its reality, by the paroxysms of intoxication which it produced, causing those who drank it to stagger and reel like drunken people."[21] The following is a typical "drinking" song:

> Drink ye of Mother's wine / Drink, drink, drink ye freely,
> Drink ye of Mother's wine, / It will make you limber.
> If it makes you reel around, / If it makes you fall down,
> If it lays you on the floor, / Rise and drink a little more.

In contrast is the lovely simplicity of "Willow Tree," from the category of "bowing songs" (also known as "I Will Bow and Be Simple"):

> I will bow and be simple, / I will bow and be free,
> I will bow and be humble, / Yea bow like the willow tree.
> I will bow, this is a token, / I will wear the easy yoke,
> I will lie low and be broken, / I will fall upon the rock.

Highly formalized dances and marches were an essential part of Shaker rituals, which they cultivated methodically and with precision. Symbolic meanings meshed with the satisfaction of coordinated bodily movements and formations. Whether in dancing or marching, the religious message was embodied in the text as well as in the motion. Here, for example, are the words of an early "Quick Dance" song:

> For dancing is a sweet employ;
> It fills the soul with heav'nly joy;
> It makes our love & union flow,
> While round and round we go.

But going "round and round" had many modes, ranging from the moderate turn to the swift whirl—and it was obviously the latter that attracted the most attention, with results not always gratifying to the leaders of the Shaker communities. In the words of Harold Cook: "Shaker meetings became one of the greatest shows in America, and Americans from far and near and distinguished foreign visitors went to see this spectacle of song and dance. Even from the earliest days, visitors had come in great numbers to the Sunday meetings and the Shakers had realized the value of publicity if a group of celibates were to go on replenishing their ranks."²²

On the other hand, such a fascinating spectacle could also result in publicity that was far from pleasing to the faithful. In 1846, for example, a communication from the Ministry of Enfield, New Hampshire, expressed its concern: "The Apostates from Canterbury, have joined together, and are exhibiting themselves for money, in Shaker attire: in dances, songs, speaking in unknown tongues &c. &c. . . . We have seen their great *glaring* show Bills and enclose two slips from a Boston Paper to you."²³

As may be seen from the handbill, these public Shaker performances featured "The Celebrated and Far-Famed Chase Family," whose whirling star was Miss L. [Lydia] A. Chase, featured as "The Miraculous Shaker Tetotum."²⁴ The apostate troupe also appeared with great success in New York City and toured extensively—perhaps competing with Barnum.

Much of the music used by the Shakers was anonymous and strongly permeated by preexisting tunes drawn from the Anglo-American folk tradition. They also drew on the New England tunebooks and the shape-note repertory. At first there was little attempt to codify their musical practice, but gradually they developed their own system of notation (at first using letters) and provided musical instruction for their communities. One of their earliest composers was Issachar Bates (1758–1837), of Massachusetts, who had served as a fifer in the American army during the Revolutionary War and later became a singing master and choir leader. He joined the Shakers in 1801 and was one of the pioneers of their westward expansion.

Bates was said to have known "nearly every song that was going, whether civil, military, sacred, or profane"—and he put them to good use in his hymns and spiritual songs. In the hymn titled "Rights of Conscience," he refers to George Washington and appropriately uses the tune of "The President's March." Bates's best-known song—and one of the most popular in the Shaker repertory—is "Come Life, Shaker Life," written in 1835. It is a lively tune in the "Quick Dance" category. The text refers to the Bible passage: "And David danced before the Lord with all his might."[25]

"Come Life, Shaker Life"

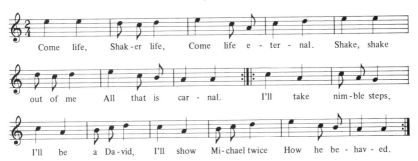

Since the dance, in all its myriad forms (except carnal contact), and in its symbolic, ritualistic, and realistic expressions, was the outward and visible manifestation of the Shaker creed and faith, it seems fitting to close this chapter with a tune that comes close to representing the essence of Shaker life.

Notes

1. *Autobiography of Peter Cartwright,* p. 31.
2. Robert Davidson, *History of the Presbyterian Church in the State of Kentucky,* p. 141.
3. Louis F. Benson, *The English Hymn,* pp. 293–94.
4. Lorenzo Dow, *History of Cosmopolite; or, The Four Volumes of Lorenzo's Journal,* 8th ed. (Cincinnati: H. S. and J. Applegate and Co., 1851), p. 235. All subsequent references to Dow's journal are to the 1814 edition cited in full in the Bibliography.
5. Lorenzo Dow, *History of Cosmopolite,* p. 229.
6. Ibid.
7. Ibid., p. 197.
8. Ibid., p. 201.
9. Frances Trollope, *Domestic Manners of the American People,* p. 139.
10. Ibid., pp. 139–40.
11. Ibid., p. 140.
12. Ibid., p. 141.
13. Ibid., pp. 142–43.
14. Guy B. Johnson, *Folk Culture on St. Helena Island,* p. 122 n. 90.

15. Lucius Bellinger, *Stray Leaves from the Port-folio of a Methodist Local Preacher*, p. 53.

16. Samuel E. Asbury and Henry E. Meyer, *Old-Time White Camp-Meeting Spirituals*, p. 2.

17. Ibid.

18. Daniel W. Patterson, *The Shaker Spiritual*, p. 351.

19. Ibid., p. xiii.

20. Quoted in Edward D. Andrews, *The Gift to Be Simple*, p. 29.

21. Quoted in ibid., p. 124.

22. Harold E. Cook, *Shaker Music*, p. 183.

23. Patterson, *The Shaker Spiritual*, p. 401.

24. Ibid.

25. Tune and text from ibid., p. 254 (punctuation added).

Chapter 12

The Negro Spirituals

Ole Satan is a busy ole man,
  He roll stones in my way.
Mass' Jesus is my bosom friend,
  He roll 'em out o' my way.
—Traditional Negro spiritual

The Negro "spirituals" are undoubtedly the most controversial body of music in the cultural history of America. The perspectives and interpretations have differed widely, particularly as to origins and formative influences. What has never been in doubt is their deep and lasting impact, not only in the United States but also throughout much of the world. As we shall note, this far-reaching impact covers a wide communicative spectrum, from ethnic values and folk traditions to continuous acculturation and artistic expression.

The verses quoted above express the struggle between good and evil forces that blacks have endured in slavery and in the aftermath of a limited freedom. Christian symbols have been adapted to special conditions that affect this mode of life. Jesus, as a "bosom friend," meaning "beloved, intimate," appears as the antithesis and antagonist of "Ole Satan," who makes life for the slaves a rough road strewn with rocks. Satan may also be identified with the overseer's harsh treatment.

About 1830 a visiting Scotsman who wrote about the religious songs of the blacks in Charleston, South Carolina, observed that "the downfall of the archfiend forms the principal topic of their anthems" (meaning their religious songs). He continued with "a few lines recollected at random [that] may serve as an example."[1] Here they are:

> Sturdy sinners, come along,
> Hip and thigh, we'll pull him down.
> Let us pull old Satan down,
> We shall get a heavenly crown, &c., &c.

As we observed in the previous chapter, many camp-meeting hymns harped on this theme, and the foregoing stanza consists of tag lines familiar to the whole body of revival hymnody, both black and white. However, our Scottish informant cites another camp-meeting verse that does indicate a Negro reworking:

> Old Satan, come before my face
> To pull my kingdom down.
> Jesus come before my face
> To put my kingdom up.
> > Well done, tankee, Massa Jesus.
> > Halleluja, &c.

This is a variant of the headnote quoted for this chapter, with its symmetrical antithesis of Satan as destroyer and Jesus as restorer. The colloquialism of the added line is of course highly characteristic: an expression of humble, heartfelt thanks to the master who saves as opposed to the master who enslaves.

By the 1840s we find increasing evidence of Negro colloquialisms and homespun images:

> Oh, Satan he came by my heart[h],
> Throw brickbats in de door,
> But *Master Jesus* come wid brush,
> Make cleaner dan before.[2]

Further evidence of a characteristic type of Negro religious song comes from various printed sources. A didactic work published in 1841 advocates that the black pupils in Sunday schools be taught "hymns and psalms, and how to sing them," as an inducement to "lay aside the extravagant and nonsensical chants, and catches and hallelujah songs of their own composing." Another writer states that when blacks attended the church of their masters they used the hymnbooks, but in their own meetings they often made up their own words and tunes: "They said their's had 'more religion than those in the books.' " It seems certain that whatever influences were brought to bear on the blacks, from whatever sources they gathered the ingredients, the end product was something different—something sui generis if we take into account not only tune or text in isolation, but the whole complex of words, music, timbre, style, form, improvisation, transformation, and kinetic projection. And the vital factor behind all this was the cultural heritage of Africa.

The English actress and writer Fanny Kemble, who spent the years 1838–39 on the Georgia plantations owned by her husband, Pierce Butler, was fascinated by the ambivalent character of the singing by blacks, which she perceived as fluctuating between the familiar and the strange. Describing a Negro funeral that she attended in the evening by torchlight, she writes: "Presently the whole congregation uplifted their voices in a hymn, the first high wailing notes of which—sung all in unison . . . sent a thrill through all my nerves."[3] Many were the "thrills" to come, for millions of listeners around the world, when Negro voices were uplifted in freedom.

Fanny Kemble also describes the singing of the blacks who rowed her to the various plantations belonging to her husband. Noting that "they all sing in unison," she adds that "the tune and time they keep, [is] something quite wonderful."[4] She observes that many of the tunes resembled Scotch or Irish airs, which they probably learned from the whistling of their overseers or masters. Certainly, the blacks were never immune to a pleasing or lively tune; eclecticism is inherent in both the sacred and secular songs that they developed in America.

Nevertheless, Mrs. Kemble confesses that in her daily voyages up and down the river she encountered a number of Negro songs that seemed to her "extraordinarily wild and unaccountable." Of these she writes: "The way in which the chorus strikes in with the burden, between each phrase of the melody chanted by a single voice, is very curious and effective. . . ."[5] What she describes is, of course, the characteristic pattern of African singing.

Kemble refers repeatedly to the "strangeness" of the words in the Negro songs, most of which made no sense to her (much of this may have been a kind of code language). She was struck by the oddness of one refrain: "God made man, and man makes money!"—but surely that reveals the Yankee influence!

Apparently no sharp distinction was made, either in the occasion or the manner, between the singing of secular songs and those having a religious import. Sir Charles Lyell, writing about his visit to a southern plantation in 1846, remarks of the Negro boatmen: "Occasionally they struck up a hymn, taught them by the Methodists, in which the most sacred subjects were handled with strange familiarity. . . ."[6] Just such a rowing song is included in the first published collection of Negro songs, *Slave Songs of the United States* (1867).[7] Its purport being obviously religious, it clearly belongs to the category of spirituals, as well as the subcategory of rowing songs. Each line of verse is followed by the refrain, "Hallelujah!":

Rowing song, from *Slave Songs of the United States*

1. Mi - chael   row   de boat a - shore,   Hal - le - lu   jah!

2. Mi - chael   boat   a gos - pel   boat, Hal - le - lu   jah!

Additional verses, with the interjection omitted, are as follows:

I wonder where my mudder deh.
See my mudder on de rock gwine home.
On de rock gwine home in Jesus' name.
Michael boat a music boat.
Gabriel blow de trumpet horn.
O you mind your boastin' talk.
Boastin' talk will sink your soul.
Brudder, lend a helpin' hand.
Sister, help for trim dat boat.
Jordan stream is wide and deep.
Jesus stand on t'oder side.
I wonder if my maussa deh.
My fader gone to unknown land.
O de Lord he plant his garden deh.
He raise de fruit for you to eat.
He dat eat shall neber die.

Besides incorporating basic tag lines of revival hymnody such as Gabriel's trumpet, crossing the river Jordan, and many other images derived from Holy Scripture, the song is extraordinary for how it adapts this imagery and vocabulary to concrete situations relating to a particular environment and a specific task that the singers must accomplish. In the last verse, for instance, the need to save one's soul is merged with the need to row as hard as possible in order to reach the shore. "Crossing over Jordan" is an image transposed into the reality of crossing a river to reach the next plantation. The line "Michael boat a music boat" is probably an improvised variant of "Michael boat a gospel boat" and takes us by surprise, yet it leads naturally to mention of Gabriel's trumpet (which is also identified with the more familiar plantation "horn"). This in turn suggests the Last Judgment and the need to care for one's soul:

O you mind your boastin' talk.
Boastin' talk will sink your soul.

Clearly, the soul, like the boat, is in possible danger of *sinking* (into Hell instead of rough water)—a bold and brilliant metaphor. The danger in-
curred by the sinner is assimilated into the peril that threatens the boat if
overtaken by darkness and rising waters:

> When de ribber overflow,
> O poor sinner, how you land?
> Ribber run and darkness comin',
> Sinner row to save your soul.

The more one lingers over this great Negro spiritual, the more one is
impressed by how beautifully its seemingly disparate elements are bound
together by an imaginative fusion of themes and images.

To demonstrate that in their original context as an oral tradition the
spirituals might have had any number of different verses referring to the
same title or topic, we quote the following lines for "Michael Row the
Boat Ashore," as heard at Hilton Head, South Carolina:

> Michael haul the boat ashore.
> Then you'll hear the horn they blow.
> Then you'll hear the trumpet sound.
> Trumpet sound the world around.
> Trumpet sound for rich and poor.
> Trumpet sound the jubilee.
> Trumpet sound for you and me.[8]

Indicating the musical or rhythmic functionalism of such rowing
songs, Charles Pickard Ware, who transcribed the tunes for *Slave Songs of
the United States,* remarked: "As I have written these tunes, two measures
are to be sung to each stroke, the first measure being accented by the beginning of the stroke, the second by the rattle of the oars in the rowlocks." He
adds: "Of the tunes I have heard, I should say that the most lively were
'Heaven bell a-ring,' 'Jine 'em,' 'Rain fall [and wet Becca Lawson],' 'No
man [can hinder me],' 'Bell da ring,' and 'Can't stay behind' "; adding that
" 'Lay this body down,' 'Religion so sweet,' and 'Michael Row,' were used
when the load was heavy or the tide was against us."[9] We are also told that
(with the exception of "Michael Row") "the same songs are used for rowing as for shouting"—the latter being a religious ceremony about which
more will be said later. The point is that Negro spirituals can seldom be regarded as having a single sociocultural context.

Of the related religious and rowing spirituals mentioned by Ware,
one of the most impressive and characteristic is "Heaven Bell A-Ring,"
which presents the plight of a sinner seeking salvation. It begins with "My

Lord, my Lord, what shall I do?" followed by the refrain: "And a heav'n bell a-ring and praise God." Another typical verse is:

> What shall I do for a hiding place?
> I run to de sea, but de sea run dry.
> I run to de gate, but de gate shut fast.
> No hiding place for sinner dere.

"Lay This Body Down" was to become one of the best-known Negro spirituals, often sung at funerals in the nighttime:

> O grave-yard, O grave-yard,
> I'm walkin' troo de grave-yard;
> Lay dis body down.
> I know moonlight, I know starlight,
> I'm walkin' troo de starlight;
> Lay dis body down.

This is the spiritual that the English journalist W. H. Russell describes in the diary of his American journey (1863) as being sung by the boatmen who rowed him from Pocotaligo to Barnwell Island in the middle of the night. After remarking that the black rowers kept up the singing "with unabated energy through the whole of the little voyage," Russell gives his impressions of the scene: "The stream, dark as Lethe, flowing between the silent, houseless, rugged banks, lighted up near the landing by the fire in the woods, which reddened the sky—the wild strain, and the unearthly adjurations to the singers' souls, *as though they were palpable,* put me in mind of the fancied voyage across the Styx" (italics added).[10]

The phrase I have italicized is a reminder that blacks regarded everything pertaining to the soul, the spirit, and the supernatural as "palpable"—and indeed from this conviction the Negro spirituals derive much of their power and their glory.

In an earlier chapter dealing with the African backgrounds of Afro-American music, we noted that, in spite of considerable opposition from slave owners, many blacks were exposed to Anglo-American psalmody and hymnody as early as the mid-eighteenth century, and the Reverend Samuel Davies wrote that "they have a kind of ecstatic delight" in psalmody and hymnody. Although the religious instruction of the blacks left much to be desired, they had ample opportunity to become acquainted with English hymnody, in both its more formal context and in the revival hymns and spiritual songs of the camp meetings in which they participated. There were also a number of didactic efforts, as in 1833, when the Reverend Samuel J. Bryan of Savannah published *A Plain and Easy Catechism: Designed for the Benefit of Colored Children, with Several Verses and Hymns.* And Charles C. Jones stated that the twenty years prior to the publication of his book *The Religious Instruction of the Negroes* (1842) marked "a period of revival of religion . . . throughout the Southern States. . . ."[11]

Most significant was the formation of independent Negro congregations, beginning in the late eighteenth century with the African Episcopal Church. Prominent in this development was the Reverend Richard Allen (1760–1831), who in 1801 published *A Collection of Spiritual Songs and Hymns Selected from Various Authors*—"the first hymnbook compiled by a black man for use by a black congregation."[12] It included only the words of standard English hymns, some with an added "Hallelujah" refrain. Whatever the sources or the circumstances, the point is that this entire body of English evangelical hymnody was simply a point of departure for the creative innovations of the Negro spiritual. There was a process of *transformation* that was noted by many observers. For example, the English musician Henry Russell, who was in the United States from circa 1834 to 1844, wrote about a Negro service that he attended in Mississippi:

> On my entering the chapel at Vicksburg . . . there was a restlessness about the little congregation—whether it emanated from one or two white people being present I cannot say. There was one peculiarity that struck me very forcibly. When the minister gave out his own version of the Psalm, the choir commenced singing so rapidly that the original tune absolutely ceased to exist—in fact, the fine old psalm tune became thoroughly transformed into a kind of negro melody; and so sudden was the transformation, by accelerating the time, that, for a moment, I fancied that not only the choir but the little congregation intended to get up a dance as part of the service.[13]

Russell was right about the impulse to dance, as we learn from the account of another white observer, Frederick Law Olmsted, who in the 1850s attended a Negro church service in New Orleans. (The reference to lining out is also interesting.) During the sermon "a small old woman, perfectly black . . . suddenly rose, and began dancing and clapping her hands; at first, with a slow and measured movement, and then with increasing rapidity, at the same time beginning to shout "*ha! ha!*"" Then "a voice in the congregation struck into a tune, and the whole congregation rose and joined in a roaring song."[14] Another preacher delivered a second sermon, and there was more singing:

The speaker at length returned to the hymn, repeated the number and page and the first two lines. These were sung, and he repeated the next, and so on, *as in the Scotch Presbyterian service.* The congregation sang; I think every one joined, even the children, and the collective sound was wonderful. The voices of one or two women rose above the rest, and one of these soon began to introduce variations, which consisted mainly of shouts of oh! oh! at a piercing height. Many of the singers kept time with their feet, balancing themselves on each alternately, and swinging their bodies accordingly. The reading of the lines would be accompanied also by shouts, as during the previous discourse.

When the preacher had concluded reading the last two lines, as the singing again proceeded, he raised his own voice above all, turned around, clapped his hands, and commenced to dance, and laughed aloud, first with his back, and then his face to the audience.[15] (Italics added)

Summarizing his impressions, Olmsted wrote: "I was once surprised to find my own muscles all stretched, as if ready for a struggle—my face glowing, and my feet stamping—having been infected unconsciously . . . with instinctive bodily sympathy with the excitement of the crowd."[16] This kinetic factor has given much of its emotional impact to the religious expression of the blacks, from spirituals to gospel. Nearly 100 years after Olmsted's account, an American folklorist wrote: "Anyone who has heard the spiritual properly sung has found it practically impossible to keep still while listening. The rhythm demands bodily movement. The feet insist on tapping, the body sways in time, or the hands pat. There is an almost uncontrollable desire to rise and throw the whole body into the rhythm."[17]

All this results from the "hot" rhythm of Afro-American musical expression, about which Richard Waterman writes: "The religious songs the Negroes learned from the missionaries were soon given the 'hot' treatment. Known today as 'Spirituals,' they are found, in their folk setting . . . to employ hand-clapping and foot-stamping in lieu of drumming, and to make consistent use of off-beat phrasing in a manner directly in line with African musical thought-patterns."[18]

The Civil War brought about the exciting and far-reaching "discovery" of the Negro spirituals. The first significant contact was at Fortress Monroe, Virginia, in May 1861, when refugee slaves, called "contrabands," sought protection under the Union army. Thus the first spirituals to attract wide attention were called "Contraband Songs." The one that had the most immediate and lasting impact was "Go Down, Moses" (also known as "Let My People Go").[19]

The principal area of contact and diffusion was in Port Royal, one of the many islands off the coast of South Carolina. Port Royal had been quickly occupied by the Union forces, and an educational mission was sent there in 1861 to care for the welfare of the blacks. As a member of the mission wrote: "The agents of this mission were not long in discovering the rich vein of music that existed in these half-barbarous people, and when visitors from the North were on the islands, there was nothing that seemed better worth their while than to see a 'shout' or hear the 'people' sing their 'sperichils.' "[20] (Why they should *see* a "shout" will soon be explained.)

Among these northern visitors was Lucy McKim of Philadelphia, then nineteen years of age, whose father, James Miller McKim, was closely associated with William Lloyd Garrison in the Anti-Slavery Society. (She later married Garrison's son Wendell, literary editor of the *Nation*.) Lucy McKim, who was trained in music, wrote the first account of the spirituals that attempted to describe some of their characteristic features:

> It is difficult to express the entire character of these negro ballads by mere musical notes and signs. The odd turns in the throat; and the curious rhythmic effect produced by single voices chiming in at different irregular intervals, seem almost as impossible to place on score, as the singing of birds, or the tones of an Aeolian Harp. The airs, however, can be reached. They are too decided not to be easily understood, and their striking originality would catch the ear of any musician. Besides this, they are valuable as an expression of the character and life of the race which is playing such a conspicuous part in our history. The wild, sad strains tell, as the sufferers themselves never could, of crushed hopes, keen sorrow, and a dull daily misery which covered them as hopelessly as the fog from the rice-swamps. On the other hand, the words breathe a trusting faith in rest in the future—in "Canaan's [f]air and happy land," to which their eyes seem constantly turned.[21]

Lucy McKim transcribed the words and melodies of several spirituals, two of which ("Poor Rosy, Poor Gal" and "Roll, Jordan, Roll") were published in arrangements for solo voice with piano—precursors of many more to come by other hands. But her chief contribution was as one of the compilers, with William Francis Allen and Charles Pickard Ware, of *Slave Songs of the United States*. It was, of course, no easy task to transcribe and notate this strange music; they were well aware of this and confessed that the best they could do would "convey but a faint shadow of the original." As Allen (who wrote the introduction) went on to explain: "The voices of the colored people have a peculiar quality that nothing can imitate; and the intonations and delicate variations of even one singer cannot be reproduced on paper. And I despair of conveying any notion of the effect of a number singing together. . . ." His description continues:

There is no singing in *parts,* as we understand it, and yet no two appear to be singing the same thing—the leading singer starts the words of each verse, often improvising, and the others, who "base" him, as it is called, strike in the refrain, or even join in the solo, when the words are familiar. . . . And the "basers" themselves seem to follow their own whims, beginning when they please and leaving off when they please, striking an octave above or below . . . or hitting some other note that chords, so as to produce the effect of a marvellous complication and variety, and yet with the most perfect time, and rarely with any discord.[22]

Here it will be pertinent to quote what J. H. Kwabena Nketia writes about the flexible forms and styles of African singing:

There is always room for extemporisation and for rearrangement of the order of verses, so that the actual shape of a song grows out of the situation in which it is sung.

In African musical practice, therefore, one has always to distinguish between basic forms, basic patterns, basic length on the one hand, and on the other resultant forms, resultant patterns and the duration of a particular performance at a particular time. The verses that are sung on a particular occasion may not be repeated in exactly the same form or in precisely the same order, except where other sanctions make this absolutely essential.[23]

(Let it be remarked that the foregoing applies also to other types of Afro-American music, including blues and jazz.)

Nketia's description recalls a rather jocose but perceptive definition by an American folklorist: "A spiritual is nothing but a tune—never twice the same—accompanied by not over two standard verses—not the same—followed by as many other verses from different songs as the singer happens at the time to remember."[24]

Unlike some later writers and editors, the compilers of *Slave Songs of the United States* were objective in their attitude toward the Negro spirituals—mainly because they had no axe to grind. To state it bluntly, they did not believe that everything had to be either black or white. Instead of the "either/or" view they took the "both/and" stance. To them it seemed that "the chief part of the negro music is *civilized* in its character—partly composed under the influence of association with the whites, partly actually imitated from their music." On the other hand, "in the main it appears to be original in the best sense of the word, and the more we examine the subject, the more genuine it appears to us to be."[25] The key word is *genuine*—which nobody can deny.

Referring to "O'er the Crossing," Allen describes it as "one of the most peculiar and wide-spread of the spirituals."[26] In addition to the usual meanings of unusual, strange, odd, the term *peculiar* also signifies belonging distinctively or especially to one person, group, or kind. The Negro spirituals come within that category. Origins are significant, but usage is decisive. A brick house can be of many shapes.

"O'er the Crossing" is indeed a genuine and "peculiar" Negro spiritual, and we quote herewith from the fourth stanza, which has some striking imagery:

"O see dat forked lightnin' A-jump from cloud to cloud,
A-pickin' up God's chil'n; Dey'll git home bime-bye.
Pray mourner, I do believe, etc."

We noted earlier the attraction of the "shout" (also called "ring shout") for Northerners who went to the South Carolina Sea Islands. Among these was Henry G. Spaulding, a Unitarian minister, who later published an article that included a description of this Negro ritual:

After the praise meeting is over, there usually follows the very singular and impressive performance of the *"Shout,"* or religious dance of the negroes. Three or four, standing still, clapping their hands and beating time with their feet, commence singing in unison one of the peculiar shout melodies, while the others walk round in a ring, in single file, joining also in the song. Soon those in the ring leave off their singing, the others keeping it up the while with increased vigor, and strike into the shout step, observing most accurate time with the music. This step is something halfway between a shuffle and a dance. . . . At the end of each stanza of the song the dancers stop short with a slight stamp on the last note, and then, putting the other foot forward, proceed through the next verse. They will often dance to the same song for twenty or thirty minutes, once or twice, perhaps, varying the monotony of their movement by walking for a little while and joining in the singing.[27]

Spaulding adds that "the words of the shout songs are a singular medley of things sacred and profane. . . . The tunes to which these songs are sung, are some of them weird and wild . . . while others are sweet and impressive melodies. . . . This music of the negro shout opens up a new and rich field of melody. . . ."[28] The "shout songs" that he printed in his article include well-known spirituals such as "I'd like to die as Jesus die," "Hold Your Light," "Lonesome Valley," and one of the earliest emancipation songs, "Done wid Driber's Dribin." There was actually no "dancing" in the usual sense, since "free foot movement" was prohibited; instead the participants moved single file in a circle, usually counterclockwise.[29]

The editors of *Slave Songs* acknowledged assistance and contributions from many individuals, particularly Colonel Thomas Wentworth Higginson, the versatile and cultivated New Englander who was one of the first to collect the texts of Negro spirituals that he heard and transcribed during the Civil War. In summarizing his impressions of these songs, he wrote: "There is no parallel instance of an oppressed race thus sustained by the religious sentiment alone. These songs are but the vocal expression of the simplicity of their faith and the sublimity of their long resignation."[30] As an example, he quotes "Blow Your Trumpet, Gabriel":

> O, I was lost in de wilderness,
> King Jesus hand me de candle down.
> So blow your trumpet, Gabriel,
> Blow your trumpet louder;
> And I want dat trumpet to blow me home
> To my new Jerusalem.

Before going on to further developments in the diffusion of the Negro spirituals during the postbellum period, it would be well to summarize the characteristic traits and antecedents that we have discussed.

1. There was much singing of standard hymns, especially Methodist and Baptist, among black congregations of the South.
2. At some Negro church services, psalms and long-meter hymns were sung according to the practice of lining out (which could be readily assimilated into the leader-and-group pattern).
3. The singing of the blacks was characterized by peculiar vocal effects, difficult, if not impossible, to indicate by standard notation.
4. The vocal lines were often profusely ornamented, and extramelodic interjections were frequent.
5. The spirituals were sung with a freedom, independence, and individuality of the vocal lines that conveyed the effect of "a marvelous complication and variety."
6. Some of the melodies resembled familiar European tunes or "Ethiopian melodies," while others were "extraordinarily wild and unaccountable."
7. There was a strong kinetic factor in the singing, emphasizing the rhythmic element and impelling to bodily motion, as in the "shout."
8. Spirituals were used as work songs, especially for field tasks and rowing.
9. The "form" of a spiritual (including the text) was not static but variable, depending on combinative, improvisational, and situational factors.

10. Continuous acculturation notwithstanding, the spirituals retained numerous African traits.

With regard to the last-mentioned factor, the musicologist Mieczyslaw Kolinski completed in 1938 a study that compared a large number of spirituals with African prototypes. He found that thirty-six spirituals were either identical or closely related in tonal structure (scale and mode) to West African songs. Certain features of melodic progressions, such as "pendular thirds," sequences of at least three intervals of a third moving in the same direction, and both linear and pendular combinations of fourths, are common in both African and Afro-American songs. Duple or ternary meters predominate in both groups. Syncopated and rubato figures, triplets, off-beat phrases, and sequences with several notes of equal time value appear in similar forms. The beginning rhythms of thirty-four spirituals are almost exactly like those of several songs from Benin (formerly Dahomey) and the Gold Coast. In many instances the overlapping of parts in leader-and-group singing produced identical polyphonic patterns. In this connection, fifty spirituals were discovered to have the identical formal structure of certain West African songs.

Kolinski concludes that, while many of the spirituals are evidently patterned after European tunes—some without apparent distortion—all of them are either altered so as to conform or selected because they already did conform to West African musical patterns. It is on this premise that he postulates a "common musical base" of European and West African music in the evolution of the Negro spirituals.[31]

The sociocultural trajectory of the Negro spirituals in the postbellum period was characterized by a bifurcation of the folk tradition and the artistic trend, with the latter rapidly achieving a worldwide impact. The publication of *Slave Songs of the United States* had a relatively slight influence. The title was unfortunate in an era of emancipation, and the music was not particularly well arranged for group singing. Moreover, it was entirely the enterprise of whites, whereas by the 1870s blacks were asserting their own identity and promoting their own cultural achievements—it was the beginning of a new epoch.

For the cultivation and diffusion of the spirituals, a prime factor was the founding of black institutions of higher learning and the manual arts, such as Fisk University in Tennessee, Hampton Institute in Virginia, and Talladega College in Alabama. Of these, Fisk and Hampton took the lead in bringing the spirituals to the outside world. They brought out their own collections of spirituals, notably *Jubilee Songs As Sung by the Jubilee Singers of Fisk University* (1872) and *Cabin and Plantation Songs As Sung by the Hampton Students* (1874).[32] The first edition of the former contained 28 spirituals, the second (in the same year) had 64, and the last (1892) had 139. By that time, according to the publishers, 130,000 copies had been sold.

Fisk University, located in Nashville, Tennessee, opened its doors in January 1866. Its treasurer, George L. White (a Northerner and the son of a village blacksmith), was musical and had taught singing school. At Fisk he trained a small mixed chorus of eleven students, which by 1870 was giving concerts in nearby cities. Because the university was in dire need of funds, White had the idea of an extensive concert tour to raise money. The group took to the road in October 1871 and immediately encountered the disaster of the great Chicago fire. The going was rough, and they hovered on the brink of failure. But in New York they acquired a powerful champion in the person of Henry Ward Beecher, famous preacher and lecturer, who helped them to raise funds and recommended them to other influential patrons. To a colleague in Boston he wrote: "They will charm any audience; they make their mark by giving the 'spirituals' and plantation hymns as only they can sing them who know how to keep time to a master's whip [!?]. Our people have been delighted."[33]

People everywhere continued to be delighted, and the Fisk Jubilee Singers went from one triumph to another, including a performance at the Second World's Peace Jubilee in Boston. There was no longer any sting in having been dubbed "Beecher's Negro Minstrels" by the *New York Herald*. They became most famous for their singing of spirituals, but an article in the *New York Evangelist* tells us that "they do not confine themselves to their own songs, but have a wide range of pieces, choruses from the operas, familiar English and Scotch ballads, and occasionally a Sunday-school hymn." But the writer adds: "Every thing becomes new under the charm of their un-English voices." According to another writer (in the *New York Tribune*), they sang "not only the well known slave songs 'Go down, Moses,' 'Roll, Jordan, Roll,' and 'Turn back Pharaoh's army,' but a fresh collection of the most weird and plaintive hymns sung in the plantation cabins in the dark days of bondage."[34] These black singers, after all, had been born and raised in slavery. Now they were born again in freedom, and they aspired not only to preserve their cultural heritage but to assert their dominion over the realm of cultivated artistry.

The first edition of Fisk *Jubilee Songs* was compiled by Theodore F. Seward, whose preface attempts to describe the musical traits of the Negro melodies, including the prevalence of a "gapped" scale, that is, "with the fourth and seventh tones omitted" (p. 3), as well as "the entire absence of triple time." Regarding the latter he writes: "The reason for this is doubtless to be found in the beating of the foot and the swaying of the body, which are such frequent accompaniments of the singing. These motions are in even measure, and in perfect time; and so it will be found that however broken and seemingly irregular the movement of the music, it is always capable of the most exact measurement. In other words, its irregularities invariably conform to the 'higher law' of the perfect rhythmic flow."[35]

In view of the increasingly "artistic" status that the spirituals were to assume in concert performance, Seward's comments on the charge that the musical presentation is "too refined" to be "a genuine representation of slave-music," are worth quoting:

> The manner and style of singing at the South depends entirely upon the degree of culture in the congregation. There is a very great difference between the lowest and the highest, in this respect. It cannot be thought strange that the musical feeling which is so prolific in original melodies should soon find its way to the enjoyment of harmony in the singing of various parts. The Jubilee Singers, no doubt, represent the highest average of culture among the colored people, but the singing of these songs is all their own, and the quickness with which they received impressions and adopted improvements from the cultivated music they have heard, only affords an additional illustration of the high capabilities of the race.[36]

The initial efforts of the Jubilee Singers brought $40,000 to the treasury of Fisk University and immense prestige to the artists—as we must now call them. The next step was to concertize in Europe: first in Great Britain, where they joined forces with the famous white gospel team of Moody and Sankey, and then in Germany, where the prestigious *Berliner Musik-Zeitung* set its authoritative seal on their performances: "What wealth of shading! What accuracy of declamation! Every musician felt then that the performances of these Singers are the result of high artistic talent, fine trained taste, and extraordinary diligence."[37]

The Jubilee Singers severed their connection with Fisk University in 1878 and were reorganized as a stock company. By the 1880s they had become big business, hence manifestly Americanized. In the spring of 1886 they sailed from England to the Antipodes and for three and a half years concertized widely throughout Australasia. They then proceeded to tour the Orient, performing spirituals in the Tāj Mahal of India and the principal cities of Japan. Their chronicler wrote that they had "made the circuit

of the globe in six years and two months"—thus, Negro spirituals had literally gone around the world.

Meanwhile, at home, the folk tradition of the Negro spiritual persisted, as did the related ritual of the "shout." But the enthusiasm of discovery that had permeated the immediate Civil War period had waned,
and fewer collectors were on the trail. The most dedicated investigator appears to have been a Congregational minister named William Eleazor Barton, who in 1899 published a collection titled *Old Plantation Hymns.* The
contents had previously appeared separately as three articles in the *New
England Magazine:* "Old Plantation Hymns," "Hymns of the Slave and
the Freedman," and "Recent Negro Melodies."[38] The material was gathered while he was living in the South from 1880 to 1887, and the songs he
transcribed are given with the words and melody only (with two or three
exceptions).

Barton evidently had a good knowledge of music, and many of his remarks on specific traits are perceptive. He observes, for example, that in
the diatonic scale the Negro "rarely sings the seventh note true, to a musical instrument, but generally flats it more or less as in the minor scales.
Fondness for these slightly variable tones suggests a reason for the negro's
love of a banjo or violin."[39] One of the most characteristic "plantation
hymns" that he quotes is "Tell Bruddah 'Lijah":

"Tell Bruddah 'Lijah"

Barton attended the praise meetings frequently and got to know individually the singers who participated. He tells us, for instance, of Sister

Fisk Jubilee Singers (Fisk University Library).

Bemaugh, who usually led the singing: "I can see her now, as in the dimly lighted tobacco barn where the meeting was held she stood holding her lantern and singing. She was slender and had high cheek bones, but her face was pleasant, and her voice had a certain soul-quality, with a ring of satisfaction."[40]

With his perception of the "soul quality" of black religious singing, Barton had touched the heart of the spirituals and their undying power to communicate and convince, whether sung in a dimly lit tobacco barn or in the gorgeous splendor of the Tāj Mahal.

Notes

1. Peter Neilson, *Recollections of a Six Years' Residence in the United States . . .* (Glasgow: D. Robertson, 1830), pp. 258–59; quoted in Dena J. Epstein, *Sinful Tunes and Spirituals,* p. 220.

2. *Musical Gazette* (Boston) 1 (July 6, 1846): 91; quoted in Epstein, *Sinful Tunes and Spirituals,* p. 222.

3. Frances Anne Kemble, *Journal of a Residence on a Georgian Plantation in 1838–39,* p. 147.

4. Ibid., p. 163.

5. Ibid., p. 259.

6. Charles Lyell, *A Second Visit to the United States of North America* 1:244–45.

7. William Francis Allen, Charles Pickard Ware, and Lucy McKim Garrison, comps., *Slave Songs of the United States.* The song cited, "Michael Row the Boat Ashore," appears on p. 23.

8. Ibid., p. 24.

9. Ibid., p. xvi.

10. William Howard Russell, *My Diary, North and South,* p. 140.

11. Charles C. Jones, *The Religious Instruction of the Negroes,* pp. 96–97.

12. Eileen Southern, ed., *Readings in Black American Music,* p. 52.

13. Henry Russell, *Cheer! Boys, Cheer!* p. 85.

14. Frederick Law Olmsted, *A Journey in the Back Country* 1:212–13.

15. Ibid., pp. 216–17.

16. Ibid., p. 210.

17. Robert W. Gordon, "The Negro Spiritual," in Society for the Preservation of Spirituals, *The Carolina Low-Country,* pp. 191–92.

18. Richard A. Waterman, " 'Hot' Rhythm in Negro Music," p. 30.

19. See Epstein, *Sinful Tunes and Spirituals,* pp. 243–50.

20. Allen, Ware, and Garrison, comps., *Slave Songs of the United States,* pp. i–ii.

21. Lucy McKim Garrison, "Songs of the Port Royal 'Contrabands,' " p. 255.

22. Allen, Ware, and Garrison, comps., *Slave Songs of the United States,* pp. iv–v.

23. J. H. Kwabena Nketia, *African Music in Ghana,* p. 27.

24. Gordon, "The Negro Spiritual," p. 198.

25. Allen, Ware, and Garrison, comps., *Slave Songs of the United States*, p. vi.

26. Ibid., p. 72.

27. Henry G. Spaulding, "Under the Palmetto," pp. 196–97.

28. Ibid., pp. 197–98.

29. For an excellent discussion of the "shout," see Harold Courlander, *Negro Folk Music, U.S.A.*, pp. 194–200.

30. Thomas W. Higginson, "Negro Spirituals," p. 694.

31. This data was kindly provided by M. Kolinski from his then unpublished study, "Die Musik Westafrikas." The introductory chapter, "Europaische und nichteuropaische Musik," appeared (translated into Spanish) in *Revista de estudios musicales* I (1949): 191–215. (Letter to author, July 24, 1975.)

32. In the preface to *Cabin and Plantation Songs As Sung by the Hampton Students*, the compiler, Thomas Putnam Fenner, remarked that "one reason for publishing this slave music is, that it is rapidly passing away. . . . At present . . . the freedmen have an unfortunate inclination to despise it, as a vestige of slavery."

33. J. B. T. Marsh, *The Story of the Jubilee Singers*, p. 30.

34. Quoted under "Notices from the Press," in *Jubilee Songs As Sung by the Jubilee Singers of Fisk University*, ed. Theodore F. Seward.

35. *Jubilee Songs As Sung by the Jubilee Singers of Fisk University*, ed. Seward, p. 2.

36. Ibid., p. 3.

37. Quoted in Marsh, *The Story of the Jubilee Singers*, p. 95.

38. The three articles are reprinted in Bernard Katz, ed., *The Social Implications of Early Negro Music*, pp. 75–118.

39. Ibid., p. 78.

40. Ibid., p. 80.

Chapter 13

The Ethiopian Business

The story of minstrelsy is the story of the increasing
influence of the Afro-American style of song and dance
in American life.
—Marshall W. Stearns and Jean Stearns, *Jazz Dance* (New York, 1968)

One evening in February 1843, four white men with faces blackened by
burnt cork appeared on the stage of the Bowery Amphitheatre in New
York City, wearing white trousers, striped calico shirts, and blue calico
coats with long swallowtails. They proceeded to entertain the audience
with a combination of singing, dancing, and instrumental music on the
banjo, violin, bone castanets, and tambourine—interspersed with jokes, anecdotes, and repartee in pseudo-Negro dialect.

This was the historic debut of "the novel, grotesque, original and surprisingly melodious Ethiopian band, entitled the *Virginia Minstrels,*" as advertised in the *New York Herald* (February 6–11, 1843). The group consisted of Dan Emmett (violin), Billy Whitlock (banjo), Frank Brower
("bones"), and Dick Pelham (tambourine), all of whom had previous experience as independent blackface entertainers, mostly with circuses. According to their account, the idea of appearing on stage as a foursome occurred
to them by chance when all happened to be together at the boardinghouse
in Manhattan where Emmett lived. None was from Virginia, but that
seemed a good name to use. Whatever the circumstances, this marked the
beginning of an era in American popular entertainment, which in its time
was often called "the Ethiopian business." With many transformations and
vicissitudes, it would continue to have a tremendous impact, both nationally and internationally, throughout the rest of the nineteenth century.

The novelty represented by the Virginia Minstrels was that of a *group*
performance, previous blackface entertainers having appeared as soloists.
Songs, dances, and theatrical sketches imitating Negroes (mostly in the
style of parody) were popular in England during the late eighteenth and

early nineteenth centuries, and these also circulated in America. An English comedian, Charles Mathews, came to the United States in 1822 and was immediately attracted by the broken English of the blacks and what he called their "scraps of songs and malaprops."¹ He attended a Negro theater in New York and heard a song, "Possum up a Gum Tree," that fascinated him and that he included in his American concert tours. (It eventually became widely known as a frontier folksong.) Mathews's use of this song in his theatrical sketch *A Trip to America* is said to be "the first certain example of a white man borrowing Negro material for a blackfaced act."²

Among the early American blackface entertainers who performed individually, George Washington Dixon (1808–61) and Thomas Dartmouth Rice (1808–60)—better known as "Daddy"—are outstandingly representative. Dixon made his debut in Albany in 1827 and two years later appeared at the Bowery Theatre in New York, where he introduced a song that became widely popular, "Coal Black Rose," and that has been called "the first burnt-cork song of comic love."³ Dixon also claimed authorship of another widely successful song, "Long Tail Blue," in which the character portrayed—or rather, caricatured—is that of a black dandy, strolling on a Sunday and dressed in a blue swallow-tailed coat. This was one of many comic songs that featured the Negro dandy as an urban strutter, in contrast to the tattered plantation "darkey." A later example, from the mid-1840s, is "Dandy Jim from Caroline."

The man who has been called "the father of American minstrelsy," known to his contemporaries as "Daddy" or "Jim Crow" Rice, was born of poor parents in New York City and was trained as a woodcarver. Lured by the stage, he got occasional jobs as a supernumerary at the Park Theatre in Manhattan, then took to the road as an itinerant player, heading for the frontier settlements of the Ohio Valley. In 1828 he joined a stock company in Louisville, Kentucky. It was then customary for blackface entertainers to interpolate songs, dances, and comic sketches between the acts of a play, whether it was a serious drama or a comedy. For this kind of entertainment, Rice concocted a number called "Jim Crow," which had a sensational success and became the first big international song hit of American popular music.

Tradition has it that Rice saw an old "darkey" who, while working in a nearby stable, was singing an odd tune and doing a curious sort of shuffling dance. Every time he reached the chorus of his song he gave a little jump that set his "heel a-ricken." His right shoulder was drawn up high, and his left leg was crooked at the knee and stiff with rheumatism, so that he walked with a limp. Rice decided to do an imitation, making up new words for the song. His impersonation, with a fantastically patched-up costume, grotesque gestures, and an oddly effective dance with a shuffling step and jump, caught the fancy of the public from Cincinnati to New York, and thence to London, where in 1836 "Jim Crow" Rice enjoyed a sensational success.

In Pittsburgh, Rice got his friend W. C. Peters to write down the tune of "Jim Crow," and within a short time many editions of the song appeared, with much variation in both words and music. (Some of these editions made no mention of Rice.) In the innumerable verses that "Jim Crow" accumulated as it went through the minstrelsy mill, there are topical allusions ranging from politics ("I put de veto on de boot/An nullify de shoe") to the sensational violin virtuoso Paganini:

> I'm a rorer on de fiddle,
> An down in ole Virginny
> Day say I play de skientific
> Like massa Pagganinny.

Unfortunately, the term *Jim Crow* would later acquire an obnoxious connotation—but old "Daddy" Rice was certainly not to blame! In addition to his "Negro" songs and impersonations, he achieved great success with his so-called Ethiopian operas—actually, theatrical farces in blackface—such as *Long Island Juba, The Black Cupid,* and (most conspicuously) *Bone Squash Diavolo.* But from the 1850s his popularity declined, and he died in poverty and neglect.

One of Rice's songs is said to have contained "the idiotic line, 'Kitty-co-dink-a-ho-dink! oh, oh, roley-boley-Good morning, ladies all!' "[4] But the use of nonsense syllables was not necessarily "idiotic": it could serve as droll patter or as rhythmic accompaniment to a jig or clog dance. Moreover, the use of such syllables is quite common in many kinds of traditional songs.

As for the tag line, "Good morning, ladies all," it occurs in what was described as "a genuine Negro song," submitted by a southern plantation owner and printed in *Putnam's Monthly Magazine* (January 1855):

> De ladies in de parlor,
> Hey, come a rollin' down—
> A drinking tea and coffee;
> Good morning, ladies all!
>
> De gemman in de kitchen,
> Hey, come a rollin' down—
> A drinking brandy toddy;
> Good morning, ladies all.

Sheet-music cover to "Jim Crow" (ca. 1835), as popularized by Thomas Dartmouth "Daddy" Rice.

This is evidently the same song that Fanny Kemble mentions as having been sung by blacks on her husband's plantation in 1839. But where, when, or how it originated is anybody's guess.

Among the songs of this period, "Long Time Ago" is of special interest because of its many versions and wide popularity, both in and out of blackface minstrelsy. The editors of *Slave Songs of the United States* (New York, 1867) state that it was "borrowed from the negroes, by whom it was sung to words beginning, 'Way down in Raccoon Hollow.' "[5] (From "raccoon" came the "coon" songs of a later period.) A version by minstrel entertainer William Clifton, published in 1836, strikes the theme of manumission:

"Long Time Ago" (version by minstrel entertainer William Clifton)

As we noted at the outset of this chapter, the 1840s saw the transition from blackface entertainment by a single performer to four-man presentations. Of the four standard instruments mentioned—banjo, violin, bone castanets, tambourine—the first was the most important because of its relative novelty and its derivation from African cultures. As mentioned in a previous chapter ("The African Presence"), the banjo was also known by various other names such as *banjar* and *bonja*. Thus we note that a minstrel "Bonja Song" appeared in the 1820s, and in the same decade an early sheet music cover depicts "Lubly Rosa" and "Sambo," each playing the primitive Negro gourd banjo, with four strings. Our question now is: When, where, and how did the standard five-string banjo make its appearance?

The man generally credited with this development is Joel Walker Sweeney (ca. 1810–60), one of the few celebrated blackface entertainers to be born and raised in Virginia. According to an apocryphal tradition: "Dissatisfied with the four-stringed gourd, he cut an old cheese-box in half, covered it with skin, and strung it with five strings, thus inventing the modern banjo."⁶ We may accept the dissatisfaction with the primitive gourd, but one smells a rat in the old cheese box. Hence the olfactory sense of modern scholars denies to Sweeney his presumed invention of the five-string banjo.

We should, however, give credit to Sweeney as the "first well-known and widely travelled white banjoist [who] played a role in bringing the banjo to the attention of urban audiences in the USA and England and presumably in popularizing the type of banjo that he played."⁷

Minstrel music for banjo is an extremely interesting phase of early American popular music. As Hans Nathan writes: "In early minstrel music there are a sizable number of banjo tunes which quite undeservedly have fallen into oblivion. They made their first appearance at the beginning of the forties when the blackface banjoist, playing as a soloist, and often singing as well, or accompanying a dancer, established himself in the popular theater. The tunes continued to be written for about fifty years without essentially deviating from their original style."⁸

In his pioneer chapter "Early Banjo Tunes and American Syncopation," Nathan includes copious examples of various types and origins (including the British Isles). From these sources "banjo music proceeded to an idiom infinitely more complex in rhythm than could have originated within a predominantly white cultural milieu and its nineteenth-century concepts."⁹

We have seen how Dan Emmett and his associates of the Virginia Minstrels launched what is regarded as the first organized minstrel troupe in New York in 1843. There is, however, some controversy as to whether this was really the first minstrel group to appear in America. It has been claimed that E. P. Christy presented his four-man show at Buffalo in 1842, but we need not concern ourselves overmuch with such claims and rivalries. In any case, it appears that Christy was influential in organizing the various routines of the minstrel show into a coordinated two-part sequence.

After presenting his troupe in Buffalo, E. P. Christy (1815–62) toured through the West and the South with great success. An appearance in 1846 at Palmo's Opera House, New York City, was so well received that Christy soon afterward leased Mechanic's Hall on Broadway, where his troupe continued to perform for almost ten years. They featured many songs by Stephen Foster—not always to the latter's entire satisfaction, as we shall learn in chapter 14. In 1855 Christy retired with a fortune, and the company was taken over by his brother George. Subject to attacks of depression, E. P. Christy died as a result of jumping from a second-story window of his house in New York.

Once the pattern had been set and its success assured, blackface minstrelsy proliferated in the United States. Some troupes were named after states (Alabama Minstrels, Georgia Champions, Virginia Serenaders); others took names that sounded "African" (Congo Minstrels, Ethiopian Serenaders) or that conveyed the idea of blackness (Sable Harmonists); some simply took the name of the leader. Often the names were flamboyantly "padded," for publicity, as when a "Music Saloon" in New York announced in 1848 that it was booking the "Great Southern Original Sable Harmonists, the Best Band of Singers in the United States."

One of the members of this troupe was the performer and composer Nelson Kneass, who wrote popular minstrel songs such as "Mary Blane" and "Julia Am a Beauty." He also organized the Kneass Opera Troupe, which—in spite of its name—performed in the style of blackface minstrelsy. The troupe specialized in parodies or burlesques of well-known operas—a very popular kind of entertainment during much of the nineteenth century. Kneass and his Ethiopian Troupe of Burlesquers thus parodied standard operas such as Balfe's *The Bohemian Girl,* Rossini's *La cenerentola,* Auber's *Fra diavolo,* and Bellini's *La sonnambula.* The burlesque titles perpetrated outrageous puns (a feature of minstrelsy as a whole) such as "Son-Am-Bull-Ole" on the name of Bellini's opera, with its contrived allusion to the famous violinist Ole Bull, then touring in the United States.[10] In general, most of the big minstrel troupes, the New Orleans Serenaders being a notable example, engaged in operatic parodies. This was especially true in the eastern cities.

Blackface minstrelsy was also a big success in Great Britain, where both American and English troupes were active. The Virginia Minstrels, for example, were enthusiastically received in London, soon after their opening in New York. It has been estimated that by 1846 there were ten minstrel troupes performing in London. The vogue continued until the 1880s, by which time "one American troupe, Moore and Burgess Minstrels, established a London record of 7,805 consecutive performances, moving one newspaper in 1881 to comment: 'Dynasties have fallen, whole empires have been upset, but the Moore and Burgess Minstrels go on forever.' "[11]

After attending a minstrel show, the English novelist Thackeray wrote: "A vagabond with a corked face and a banjo sings a little song, strikes a wild note, which sets the heart thrilling with a happy pity." There was more than slapstick and "darkey" jokes in blackface minstrelsy. Somehow, the "wild note" on the banjo and the touch of pity in the heart may have been subconsciously rooted in the memory of an oppressed people.

The two outstanding composers of minstrel songs, Stephen Foster and Daniel Decatur Emmett, had contrasting backgrounds and careers. The former came from a well-to-do family and was raised in an atmosphere of genteel respectability that excluded the possibility of becoming a blackface entertainer on the stage. The latter was the offspring of an Irish-American family that had followed the path of westward migration from Virginia to the frontier country of Ohio. Born in 1815, Dan Emmett had little schooling but learned to read and write while helping in his father's blacksmith shop. Musically gifted, with a good singing voice, he learned to play the flute and the violin in his spare time. At seventeen he joined the army as a fifer (even though he was underage), and in 1835 he was discharged "by reason of minority."[12] He then got into show business via the circus, traveling throughout the West and South before going on to New York City and eventually joining the Virginia Minstrels.

Unlike Foster, who made only one brief excursion to the South, Emmett knew that region well, including the lore of the Mississippi boatmen. This is reflected in one of his best-known songs, "De Boatman's Dance" (1843), with such typical stanzas as the following:

> When you go to de boatman's ball,
> Dance wid my wife, or don't dance at all.
> Sky blue jacket and tarpaulin hat,
> Look out my boys for de nine-tail cat.

Referring to another very popular song, Emmett in his old age reminisced: "I composed *Old Dan Tucker* in 1830 or 1831, when I was fifteen or sixteen years old."[13] But according to Hans Nathan, "Emmett said all kinds of things when he was old. The *tune* of 'Old Dan Tucker' is definitely *not* by him." An 1843 edition of the song, published by Miller's Music Salon in New York City, describes it as "A Favorite Original Negro Melody . . . By Dan. Tucker, Jr."—obviously either a put-on or a cover-up.

A prominent feature of minstrel shows was the "walk-around," a lively song-and-dance routine that usually came as the grand finale. Emmett was evidently convinced that his walk-around numbers faithfully reflected the traditional character of Negro life on the plantations. He wrote in some preliminary remarks for a manuscript collection of his walk-arounds: "In the composition of a 'Walk 'Round' (by this I mean the style of music and character of the words), I have always strictly confined myself to the habits and crude ideas of the slaves of the South. Their knowledge of the world at large was very limited, often not extending beyond the bounds of the next plantation; they could sing of nothing but everyday life or occurrences, and the scenes by which they were surrounded. This being the undeniable fact, to be true to the negro peculiarities of song, I have written in accordance."[14]

Although Emmett may have been sincere in his statement and intentions, the idea that every aspect of Negro culture was "crude" and mentally confined reflected a general attitude of condescension and assumed superiority. A recent historian of minstrelsy summarizes this attitude: "Like every other aspect of the show, minstrelsy's racial content grew out of the intimate interaction between the performers and their vocal patrons. When public opinion shifted, the content of minstrelsy shifted. Thus, minstrelsy's portrayals of slavery and blacks reveal the evolution and functioning of American racial stereotypes better than any other source."[15]

The most important and influential phase of Emmett's career began when he joined Bryant's Minstrels in 1858. Tension over the slavery issue was rapidly increasing, and enforcement of the fugitive slave law in the North was one of the main issues. Yet it is curious, and significant of one aspect of the minstrel stereotype, that even under these circumstances the image of the "homesick darkey," longing to be back on the plantation, continued to be projected on the stage.

Emmett's song "Johnny Roach," performed in March 1859 and published in New York the following year, tells of a slave who is bound for Canada by "de railroad underground," but wishes "he was back agin."

> Gib me de place called Dixie's Land,
> Wid hoe an shubble in my hand;
> Whar fiddles ring an banjos play,
> I'de dance all night an work all day.

Of course, there could be a modicum of nostalgia in such a view, for slaves who escaped to the North did not always find a congenial environment. Doubtless they did not miss the backbreaking field work or the overseer's lash, but they could have recalled the gaiety of the fiddles and banjos and the fun of dancing. Regardless, it was certainly no Paradise Lost.

The use of *Dixie* in "Johnny Roach" is believed to be the first appearance in print of that term as a designation of the South. The evidence indicates that the term was of northern origin, and its earliest use is believed to

Daniel Decatur Emmett (center) and cohorts pictured in various minstrel poses, on sheet-music cover to "Dandy Jim from Caroline" (1844).

have occurred in 1850, in a minstrel skit titled *United States Mail and Dixie in Difficulties*. Here the name is given to a stupid black postboy. Hans Nathan is probably right when he surmises that the name *Dixie* was used by white showmen to designate a Negro character by phonetic analogy with common stage names such as "Pompey" and "Cuffee."[16]

But it was Emmett who popularized the term *Dixie* as a designation for the South. More specifically, it was originally presented as such when billed as "Dixie's Land"—a song that Emmett wrote for Bryant's Minstrels and that they performed at Mechanic's Hall, New York City, on April 4, 1859. It was described as a "Plantation Song and Dance" and was presented as a walk-around, next to the last number. The first part of the song (it is divided into two sections of sixteen measures each) was sung alternately by a soloist and by a small chorus in unison, which came in after every other line with the refrain "Look away! Look away! Dixie Land." As performed on the minstrel stage, it also had, like other walk-arounds, an instrumental section of eight measures, during which members of the troupe would do a "grotesque" dance.

"Dixie" (as it came to be generally called) became an instant success, with several publishers clashing over the copyright. Emmett gave it to Firth, Pond and Company of New York, which brought it out in June 1860. Several other editions appeared in that year, without giving credit to Emmett, including one published in New Orleans by P. P. Werlein—with the song credited to J. C. Viereck! (In subsequent editions Viereck's name appeared as "arranger.") But when the Civil War broke out, Werlein took advantage of the hostilities to restore Viereck's name as author and omit Emmett's—a minor skirmish of the war.

The writs of northern publishers did not run in the Confederacy, and soon there were many pirated editions of "Dixie" in the South. According to a contemporary account it swept through the South like a blaze: "It is marvellous with what wild-fire rapidity this tune 'Dixie' has spread over the whole South. Considered as an intolerable nuisance when first the streets re-echoed it from the repertoire of [blackface] wandering minstrels, it now bids fair to become the musical symbol of a new nationality, and we shall be fortunate if it does not impose its very name on our country."[17]

A Confederate band played "Dixie" at the inauguration of President Jefferson Davis, and many Southern regiments marched in quickstep to its enlivening rhythm. The North was no less bent on claiming "Dixie" for the Union, and various patriotic texts were concocted, including a "Unionized" version published in *John Brown and the Union Right or Wrong Song-ster* (San Francisco, 1863).

At the end of the war—in fact, the day after the surrender of General Lee's army at Appomattox—President Lincoln took steps to reclaim "Dixie" for the Union. As he told a crowd that appeared to serenade him with a band at the White House: "I had heard that our adversaries over the way had attempted to appropriate it. I insisted yesterday that we had fairly captured it. . . . I ask the band to give us a good turn on it."[18]

Thus, with Lincoln's touch of dry humor, "Dixie" was "officially" re-stored to the Union; but since the South never relinquished its hold on the song, it has remained a truly "national" tune of the United States—in the sense of being widely familiar and frequently quoted by composers of all the States. What everybody seems to have forgotten is that Emmett's im-mortal song was originally titled "I Wish I Was in Dixie's Land," and that it was one of some thirty-five walk-arounds for which he wrote both the words and music between 1859 and 1868.

In 1888 "Old Dan" Emmett retired to a country home near Mt. Ver-non, Ohio; but in 1895 he was persuaded to take the road again with Field's Minstrels, including a tour of the South, where he was enthusiastically re-ceived as the composer of "Dixie." He died on June 18, 1904, at the age of eighty-eight.

The songs of minstrelsy, as we have observed, covered a wide range of topics and types, from the sentimental to the grotesque and from the hu-morous to the pathetic. Many of its greatest hits came from the pen of Ste-phen Foster, such as "Camptown Races" and "Old Folks at Home," which will be discussed in the next chapter. Here we shall take a retrospective glance at some earlier minstrel songs that give us a sampling of the scope and variety of blackface tunes and themes.

Recalling that Jefferson had proposed the establishment of a "haven" for American blacks outside of the United States, and noting that in the 1830s the Negro Republic of Haiti appeared to offer such a haven, we turn to a blackface minstrel song published in Boston in 1833, titled "Sambo's Address to He' Bred'rin" (more popularly known as "Ching a Ring Chaw"). The "bred'rin" are urged to emigrate to "Hettee," depicted as a utopia where each will be received "gran' as Lafayette"; where all will "lib so fine wid our coach and horse"; where "our wibes be gran'", and in dimons shine"; and "dar dance at nite jig, what white man call cotillion, in hall so mity big it hole half a million." In contrast to this life of ease and luxury, the song depicts the hard lot of blacks in the United States, forced to perform all the menial and unpleasant tasks. Obviously a white man's concoction, it anticipates the "social significance" satire of some later musical shows such as *Pins and Needles* and *The Cradle Will Rock* (in its burlesque numbers). One of the most widely popular of the early blackface songs was "Jim Along Josey," written and introduced on the stage by Edward Harper about 1838. The song was followed by a lively dance in which the comic actor had a chance to "do his stuff"—reminding us of the great importance that dancing had in blackface minstrelsy. Its popularity doubtless owed much to the song's chorus, with its catchy tune using only the five tones of the pentatonic scale.

Apart from its popularity on the minstrel stage, "Jim Along Josey" became widely used as a white "play party song" in the Midwest. As Foster Damon observed, it was admitted as a game tune even among those stricter sects that prohibited dancing, "although to uncritical eyes the players seemed to be doing something easily mistaken for a Virginia Reel."[19] There are many other examples of minstrel tunes passing into the realm of folklore.

To complete the cycle of borrowings and transformations, we should also note that many minstrel melodies had their origin in anonymous folk tunes, as they passed from folklore to theater—and then reversed the process. A case in point is "Zip Coon," one of the best-known early minstrel tunes, which has persisted in American folklore with several versions. As "Turkey in the Straw," for example, it became a favorite fiddle tune for country dances. Bob Farrell, who sang "Zip Coon" in a New York show in 1834, claimed its authorship, but this was disputed by G. W. Dixon. If we are talking about the *words,* either entertainer may have written them; but when it comes to the *music,* there is evidence that this was one of the many blackface minstrel tunes of Scotch-Irish origin. Hans Nathan has found a Scotch reel that is very similar to parts of "Zip Coon," and Francis O'Neill states that there is "convincing evidence of its Irish antecedents."[20] Of course, antecedents alone do not necessarily make a tune per se, but they shape its essential contours.

We have observed some of the racial stereotypes depicted by white minstrel performers in blackface, such as the banjo-picking plantation "darkey," the flamboyant Negro "wench," and the strutting "dandy" of the cities. But black minstrel performers soon got into the picture, generating a highly successful impact both in the United States and abroad. Even prior to the Civil War and emancipation, some blacks had begun to form their own minstrel troupes. Musically gifted as they were, talented as dancers, singers, fiddlers, and banjo players—as well as virtuosi of the ubiquitous "tambo" and "bones"—the minstrel stage offered for blacks one of the few opportunities for getting ahead in the white man's world. But the interesting question arises: To what extent, and in what ways, were the Negro stereotypes maintained or modified by black minstrel performers?

When the first black minstrel troupes appeared in the 1850s, critical opinion tended to stress that they offered "the genuine article." This aura of authenticity, however, proved to be a handicap as well as an asset for black performers. It was an asset because only they could rightfully claim to be "genuine" black entertainers. But, as Robert Toll writes, "since they inherited the white-created stereotypes and could make only minor modifications in them, black minstrels in effect added credibility to these images by making it seem that Negroes actually behaved like minstrelsy's black caricatures."[21]

From the 1870s on, white blackface minstrel troupes not only became much larger, numbering as many as 100 performers, but also offered more varied types of entertainment, including highly fashionable and elegant female impersonators (such as the famous Francis Leon, who set the trend for women's fashions) and novelty numbers of every kind that prefigured vaudeville and the variety shows that came into vogue at the turn of the century. White entertainers were regarded as professionals with full scope to display their talents in any direction they chose. Blacks, on the contrary, were given credit mainly for "authenticity" in a subcultural context. Thus they could appeal to white audiences only by portraying the plantation "darkey" as he "really was"—i.e., by imitating and if possible enhancing the preconceived white stereotype.

The first successful black troupe, Brooker and Clayton's Georgia Minstrels, was billed as "The Only Simon Pure Negro Troupe in the World."[22] In 1865–66 they toured widely and with great acclaim in the Northeast, thereby stimulating the formation of other black minstrel troupes. The success of the Georgia Minstrels also caught the attention of white entrepreneurs, who were quick to realize the commercial possibilities of "the genuine article." One of them, Sam Hague, took a "Slave Troupe" to England in 1886, thereby launching the vogue for "genuine" black minstrelsy.

Color, however, created an anomalous situation. White minstrels looked black because they blackened their faces with burnt cork. But the Afro-Americans were not all "black"—their complexions displayed many "hues and complexions from light cream" to coal-black (as an American reporter wrote). This could prove disconcerting to white audiences, hence the early Negro troupes made a "concession" by having the two end men blacken their faces.

Whatever the degree of coloring might be, a presumed genuineness was the main attraction; the white performer in blackface was obviously a mere imitator. An extreme statement of this point of view appeared in the *New York Clipper* (1880), a popular periodical, which declared that Haverly's Colored Minstrels depicted plantation life "with greater fidelity than any 'poor white trash' with corked faces can ever do."[23]

When a white entrepreneur, Charles Callender, took over Hague's troupe in 1872, the vogue of "genuine" black minstrelsy reached its peak. Actually, some thirty black minstrel troupes were active during this decade, and black performers such as the comedian Billy Kersands and the banjoist Horace Weston became famous. These two performed with Haverly's Colored Minstrels, the most lavish and enterprising of the black troupes—which was owned and managed by whites! They undertook to represent "The Darky as he is at Home, Darky Life in the Cornfield, Canebrake, Barnyard, and on the Levee and Flatboat."[24] The troupe numbered more than 100 performers, all ostensibly bent on portraying the carefree, frolicking life of blacks in the Old South with "wholesome and hearty simplicity."

But Toll invites us to take a close look at some of the posters used by Callender and Haverly to advertise their shows. In one of these, some children are dancing and playing various crude instruments to the accompaniment of grandpa's banjo. Yet all is caricature—deliberately grotesque and even somewhat sinister.[25]

It would take some time before blacks would be accepted as talented entertainers in their own right, free to display their skills and gifts without racial stereotypes and creative restrictions. Nevertheless, the international success of black minstrel shows paved the way. Minstrelsy was America's first greatly successful and influential form of mass entertainment, both at home and abroad, and it could not have been conceived without the presence and impulse of an Afro-American heritage in the land.

Notes

1. Mrs. Mathews, *Memoirs of Charles Mathews, Comedian* (London, 1839), 3:391; quoted in Hans Nathan, *Dan Emmett and the Rise of Early Negro Minstrelsy*, p. 46.
2. Robert C. Toll, *Blacking Up*, p. 27.

3. S. Foster Damon, ed., *Series of Old American Songs,* no. 13.

4. Carl Wittke, *Tambo and Bones,* p. 29.

5. William Francis Allen, Charles Pickard Ware, and Lucy McKim Garrison, comps., *Slave Songs of the United States,* p. i.

6. Damon, ed., *Series of Old American Songs,* no. 27.

7. Jay Scott Odell, "Banjo," *The New Grove Dictionary of Music and Musicians* 2:120.

8. Nathan, *Dan Emmett and the Rise of Early Negro Minstrelsy,* p. 189.

9. Ibid., pp. 205–7.

10. Ernest C. Krohn, "Nelson Kneass," pp. 21–29.

11. John W. Brokaw, "The Minstrel Show in the Hoblitzelle Theatre Arts Library," p. 23.

12. Nathan, *Dan Emmett and the Rise of Early Negro Minstrelsy,* p. 108.

13. Quoted in Charles Burleigh Galbraith, *Daniel Decatur Emmett,* p. 9.

14. Quoted in ibid., p. 47.

15. Toll, *Blacking Up,* pp. 65–66.

16. Nathan, *Dan Emmett and the Rise of Early Negro Minstrelsy,* p. 265.

17. Ibid., pp. 271–72.

18. Carl Sandburg, *Abraham Lincoln: The War Years,* vol. 4 (New York: Harcourt, Brace and Co., 1939), pp. 207–8; quoted in ibid., p. 275.

19. Damon, ed., *Series of Old American Songs,* no. 24.

20. Francis O'Neill, ed. and comp., *Dance Music of Ireland,* p. 5.

21. Toll, *Blacking Up,* p. 196.

22. Ibid., p. 199.

23. Quoted in ibid., p. 202.

24. Quoted in ibid., p. 205.

25. Ibid., pp. 207–8.

Chapter 14

America's Minstrel

I find I cannot write at all unless I write for public
approbation and get credit for what I write.
—Stephen Foster, letter to E. P. Christy, May 25, 1852

In the spring of 1853 the pious, respectable Dr. Thomas Hastings took pen
in hand to indite an indignant epistle to the editor of the *Musical Review
and Choral Advocate*. The editor of that chaste periodical had recently commented on the deplorable fact that certain "Ethiopian melodies" were being adapted for use in Sunday schools. Dr. Hastings, while careful to pro-
tect his respectability by stating that he was not "very conversant with
Ethiopian minstrelsy," reported that he had discovered a Sunday-school superintendent endeavoring to foist the melody of "Old Folks at Home" on a
large class of innocent "infant scholars." He evidently thought the children
would not recognize the tune. So the teacher sang a line or two—with suitably pious words, of course—and then asked: " 'Children, have you ever
heard anything like that before?' *'Old folks at Home! Old folks at Home!'*
shouted the little urchins with such merry glances and gesticulations as
showed them upon the very point of 'Cutting up,' when the experiment
ended and the piece was abandoned."[1]

Dr. Hastings, in his letter, went on to castigate those responsible for
perverting the taste of children by "fishing up something from the lowest
dregs of music" by which their minds "are filled with poisonous trash, to
forget which in after life would be to them a blessing." The practice he describes, he says, is nothing new: "It is an old trick, which many seem determined to 'play off' every time they have an opportunity." He fears these
abuses would not be abandoned, although there were plenty of good
hymn tunes in circulation (including, no doubt, many of his own). But
"Christy has more melodies; and then 'Yankee Doodle,' 'Frog and Mouse,'
and 'Jim Crow,' I believe, have not yet been appropriated."[2]

Perhaps the perpetrator of "Old Folks at Home," before his tragic death at the age of thirty-seven, in poverty and neglect, had an opportunity to redeem himself in the eyes—and ears—of Dr. Hastings and other advocates of the "better music" crusade. Toward the end of his life, in 1863, Stephen Foster turned out what his niece described as "about a dozen uninspired expressions of religious hack-writing" that surely were sufficiently saccharine to satisfy the taste of Dr. Hastings. The latter lived to be eighty-eight; when he went to his final reward, he had perhaps been made happy by such masterpieces of bathos as Foster's "Little Ella's an Angel in the Skies" or "Willie's Gone to Heaven, Praise the Lord."

Nevertheless, in spite of personal problems and the painful vicissitudes of his last years, Foster succeeded remarkably well in producing the kind of songs that irritated the pundits while delighting millions of people throughout the world. The pontifical John Sullivan Dwight, in his highbrow *Journal of Music* (1853), had to admit that tunes such as "Old Folks at Home" were sung and whistled by everybody. But he asserted that their charm was only "skin-deep," and that melodies of this type "are not popular in the sense of musically inspiring, but that such and such a melody *breaks out* every now and then, like a morbid irritation of the skin."[3] With hindsight we can say that when Stephen Foster's melodies "broke out" the effect was more like a great river overflowing its banks and spreading far and wide over the fertile fields.

But we can also speak of the struggle in Foster's mind between the pressures of the genteel tradition that prevailed in his family circle and the strong appeal of blackface minstrelsy that was sweeping over the land as he reached maturity. Unlike Dan Emmett, he could not gravitate naturally into show business and the world of popular entertainment. In fact, he never became an entertainer, in the sense of performing publicly, like Henry Russell or Nelson Kneass. As we shall see, his exclusively offstage role as a songwriter proved to be a financial handicap.

Stephen Collins Foster was born on July 4, 1826, on his father's farm overlooking the village of Lawrenceville, near Pittsburgh. He was next to the youngest in the family and grew up with three sisters and five brothers. His father had moved from eastern Pennsylvania to Pittsburgh when the latter was little more than a frontier trading post. While on a business trip to Philadelphia, he met Eliza Tomlinson, from a substantial eastern family, whom he married in 1807. He became associated with a firm of local merchants and took charge of their river traffic, which obliged him to journey down the Ohio and Mississippi rivers about twice a year. He became wealthy but later suffered financial reverses that led to the loss of his property by foreclosure. The family lived for a while in the village of Harmony, and in the fall of 1832 moved to the town of Allegheny. Thus Stephen grew up in an atmosphere of genteel aspirations but reduced financial circumstances.

Mrs. Foster, who brought her ingrained ideas of gentility to the frontier, was eager to have her daughters receive the social benefits of a "polite education," including the accomplishment of playing the piano and singing sentimental ballads. Opportunities for acquiring the "polite arts" were not lacking. For example, sister Charlotte's music teacher was William Evens, who in 1826 issued the following advertisement:[4]

> Wm. Evens, teacher of the French Horn,
> Trumpet, Bugle, Serpent, Bassoon, Clarionet,
> German Flute, Hautboy, Violin,
> Violoncello, and Tenor Viol—
> at Six Dollars per quarter.
> W. E. professes the Andante stile. Those
> who wish to play Concerto's or become
> Prestissimo Players need not apply.
> Tempo Gusto.

Here, indeed, was every guarantee of sedate respectability, even to the exclusion of *tempo rubato!*

It is not true, as has been stated, that Stephen Foster grew up in a musical wilderness. Pianos were certainly not unknown in Pittsburgh. Some were transported from the East; some were made to order, locally, as early as 1815. By 1818 the Fosters had a piano, although they had to give it up in 1821. But brother William, hardworking and prosperous, presented the family with a new piano in 1828. Thus, as Stephen's niece, Evelyn Foster Morneweck writes: "From early childhood, Stephen Foster always was accustomed to music in the home of his parents and their friends. . . ." In her *Chronicles of Stephen Foster's Family,* Morneweck evokes a picture of little Stephen leaning against the parlor piano "whilst his sisters charmed their admiring family circle with 'Come Rest in This Bosom,' 'Go, My Love,' 'Like the Gloom of Night Retiring,' 'Flow on, Thou Shining River,' 'I Have Loved Thee, Mary,' 'Home, Sweet Home,' 'I'd Be a Butterfly,' and 'Susan in the Valley.' "[5]

Among the more than 200 songs that Foster wrote, there are many of this type, such as "Come with Thy Sweet Voice Again," "The Hour for Thee and Me," "I Would Not Die in Summer Time," and "My Hopes Have Departed Forever." These, and many others like them, remain generally as obscure as most of the songs mentioned by Morneweck. The point to be made here is that the supersentimentality of the genteel tradition in which Stephen Foster was raised left its indelible imprint on a large number of his songs, which, until recently, have been almost entirely neglected. But viewed in a sociocultural context these songs are a mirror of the times in which he lived, like the architecture, paintings, furniture, and fashions of that period. They are musical museum pieces, if you like; but everyone knows that a museum also has its attractions.

Stephen showed musical aptitude from infancy and was allowed to amuse himself with various instruments—guitar, flageolet, clarinet, later the piano—but there was no question of preparing him for a professional career in music. That was not regarded as a serious occupation for boys or men in the Foster household. At best it could be a pastime or a social accomplishment (Stephen's father enjoyed "drawing a few notes on his violin"). But with Stephen music appears to have taken precedence over more "serious" studies from an early age. While at school, according to his father, "his leisure hours are all devoted to musick, for which he possesses a strange talent."[6] His first known composition was the "Tioga Waltz," written for a school exhibition when he was fourteen and arranged for three flutes.

More significant for his future career was the publication of his first song, "Open Thy Lattice, Love," brought out by George Willig of Philadelphia in 1844. The words were by George Pope Morris and had previously been set to music by the celebrated English songwriter Joseph Philip Knight, composer of "Rocked in the Cradle of the Deep," who had spent the years 1839–41 in the United States. We do not know if Foster was aware of that connection; but the interesting point, as John Tasker Howard observed, is that "Stephen's song is far more spontaneous, and is often sung to-day, while Knight's is forgotten."[7]

Stephen's above-mentioned song was probably composed in 1843, and for his dual role as songwriter, it is symbolically significant that this was the year in which the first blackface minstrel troupes made their appearance. Of course, blackface entertainment had been around for some time, and Stephen and his brothers were fascinated by it. In his earliest extant letter, written to his father when he was ten, Stephen wrote: "I wish you to send me a commic songster for you promised to."[8] So even at this early age he was already attracted to the comic songs that were to be so conspicuous in his production. He had a talent for comedy and a keen feeling for lively, zestful songs. He and his brothers, together with neighborhood youngsters, formed a "Thespian Company" for performing popular "Ethiopian" melodies such as "Long Tail Blue" and "Zip Coon." Stephen, according to his brother Morrison, was the star performer of the group.

A later phase in this development is described in Morrison Foster's biography of his brother: "In 1845 a club of young men, friends of his, met twice a week at our house to practice songs in harmony under his leadership. . . . At that time negro melodies were very popular. After we had sung over and over again all the songs then in favor, he proposed that he would try and make some for us himself. His first effort was called 'The Louisiana Belle.' A week after this he produced the famous song of 'Old Uncle Ned.' "[9]

There is evidence that about this time Stephen met the famous blackface performer Thomas D. Rice when the latter appeared in Pittsburgh, and supposedly submitted these early "Negro" songs to him. A friendship was formed, and some years later Stephen sold two of his songs, "Long Ago Day" and "This Rose Will Remind You," to Rice.

Either late in 1846 or early the following year, Stephen went to Cincinnati to work as a bookkeeper in the office of his brother Dunning. There he met and became friendly with William Roark of the Sable Harmonists, to whom he offered the as yet unpublished "Uncle Ned," which was accepted and performed with success. This was evidently Stephen's first professional contact with the "Ethiopian business," soon to loom so large in his career.

Cincinnati remained Stephen's home base until January 1850, when he returned to Allegheny, and it was during these years that he sprang into sudden fame as a songwriter—particularly of "Ethiopian" melodies, and especially with the immense success of "Oh! Susanna," first performed publicly in September 1847. For this crucial event our scene shifts to Pittsburgh, specifically to "Andrews' Eagle Ice Cream Saloon," whose musical director at the time was Nelson Kneass, the celebrated minstrel performer and songwriter. On September 11, 1847, the Eagle Saloon advertised a Grand Gala Concert that featured "SUSANNA—A new song, never before given to the public." Its success was immediate and soon became worldwide. To Stephen Foster it brought fame, but not fortune in the monetary sense. According to his brother Morrison, "he made a present of 'Old Uncle Ned' and 'Oh, Susanna' " to the publisher W. C. Peters of Cincinnati, and the latter "made ten thousand dollars out of them."[10] On the other hand, a contemporary of Foster tells us that Stephen was delighted "in receiving one hundred dollars in cash" for "Oh! Susanna," and has him saying that "the two fifty-dollar bills I received for it had the effect of starting me on my present vocation of song-writer."[11]

Contemporary accounts of what Stephen Foster said and did are often contradictory or inconsistent. But the fact remains that early songs such as "Lou'siana Belle," "Oh! Susanna," "Old Uncle Ned," and "Nelly Was a Lady" were quickly snapped up by both publishers and performers and inevitably launched him as a leading writer of "Ethiopian" melodies as well as of sentimental parlor songs. Yet Stephen's attitude toward these "Negro" songs was at first ambivalent and inconsistent. He appears to have been ashamed of "Nelly Was a Lady," calling it a "miserable song," telling his brother to take "10$, 5$ or even 1$ for it," and finally giving all the rights to Firth, Pond and Company, in return for fifty copies of the printed song. He did the same with "My Brudder Gum," but this at least led to the signing of a contract with that prestigious firm of music publishers in New York (December 3, 1849).[12]

The copyright law at that time lent itself to many abuses, as the author's rights per se were not protected. "First come, first served" appears to have been the current practice. For example, when Stephen's song "Away Down South" was performed at the Eagle Saloon in Pittsburgh, Nelson Kneass wrote down the words and the music and took it to the copyright office the next day! He was, however, thwarted by Morrison Foster, who was there on Stephen's behalf and headed him off.

Thanks to the researches of R. W. Gordon, we have a list of twenty editions of "Oh! Susanna" (including various instrumental arrangements) published between February 1848 and February 1851, and copyrighted by eleven different publishers or their agents. The list is revealing not only for the copyright situation but also for the light it sheds on the various contexts and transformations in which the song appears. The association with minstrelsy is prominent but not predominant. It is included in *The Ethiopian Glee Book* (Boston, 1848–50), *The Gems of the Christy's* ([New York?] 1848), and *Songs of the Sable Harmonists* ([Cincinnati,] 1848). Individually, it appears as "Sung by G. N. Christy of the Christy Minstrels" and as "Re-Written and Arranged by William Clifton." The only other vocal presentation is titled simply "Susanna," with no indication of context. Arrangements for piano constitute the large majority, with a variety of types, ranging from "Easy Variations" to quadrilles, quicksteps, and polkas. An aura of elegance and glamor certainly emanated from the arrangement "with introduction & brilliant variations" by the famous Austrian piano virtuoso Henri Herz, who was touring in America at the time. There are also two arrangements for guitar—a favorite parlor instrument.

The three arrangements of "Oh! Susanna" as a polka that Gordon cites are of special interest because, as William Austin has pointed out, the musical rhythm of Foster's song "was that of the polka, the latest fashionable dance from Paris, London, and New York."[13] It may have been fashionable, but it was also extremely popular and was considered great fun to dance, especially by young people, and among both blacks and whites. Foster was well aware of this, and in his song "Away Down South" he has the following chorus:

> No use talkin' when de darky wants to go
> Whar de corntop blossom and de canebrake grow;
> Den come along to Cuba, and we'll dance de polka-juba,
> Way down souf, whar de corn grow.

Encouraged by the wide popularity of his songs, and having signed a contract with Firth, Pond and Company, Stephen felt that he not only could risk giving up his job as accountant but also could venture into matrimony. Early in 1850 he returned to the family home in Allegheny, and in June of that year he married Jane McDowell. He was aware that his situation called for financial independence, and this meant going in the direction of popular entertainment. Having rejected the possibility of being a public entertainer himself, he had to rely on publishers' royalties and whatever dubious deals he could make with professional performers. Although he did fairly well with royalties, there were disconcerting exceptions: "Camptown Races" brought him $101.25 over a seven-year period, during which "Angelina Baker" earned only $16.87!

Ever since he began his songwriting career, Stephen had alternated between the genteel tradition of parlor songs and the popular appeal of "Ethiopian" melodies. In 1847, for example, "Lou'siana Belle" and "What Must a Fairy's Dream Be?" were copyrighted on the same date, as were "Away Down South" and "Stay Summer Breath" in the following year. In 1850 (a very productive year) parlor songs outnumbered minstrel tunes for the first time, with genteel gems such as "Ah! May the Red Rose Live Alway," "Molly! Do You Love Me?" and "I Would Not Die in Spring Time." This last song was published under the pseudonym of Milton Moore (said to be derived from the names of John Milton and Thomas Moore), and it appears that Stephen wrote only the music, not the words. He was evidently attracted by the cycle of death and the seasons, for in the

Stephen Foster (ca. 1859). Photo courtesy of the Foster Hall Collection, Stephen C. Foster Memorial, University of Pittsburgh.

following year appeared "I Would Not Die in Summer Time," presented as "Written and Composed by Stephen C. Foster," and described as "an answer" to its forerunner. The last two lines evoke another season:

> Then die when Autumn winds complain
> Among the blighted leaves.

It is tempting to speculate that Stephen may have been the author of another elegiac song that appeared in the same year, "I Would Not Die in Winter," with "music by J. H. Milton." In any case, John Hill Hewitt, with tongue in cheek, put a quietus on the seasonal mortality with his "I Would Not Die at All"!

Having decided to become a professional songwriter (he now had an "office" in Pittsburgh), Stephen was bent on playing both sides of the fence, and in February 1850 he wrote to E. P. Christy, enclosing copies of "Camptown Races" and "Dolly Day," and stating: "I wish to unite with you in every effort to encourage a taste for this style of music so cried down by opera mongers."[4] But his attitude toward blackface entertainment was ambivalent, as we gather from a letter that he wrote to Christy on May 25, 1852:

> Dear Sir:
>   As I once intimated to you, I had the intention of omitting my name on my Ethiopian songs, owing to the prejudice against them by some, which might injure my reputation as a writer of another style of music, but I find that by my efforts I have done a great deal to build up a taste for the Ethiopian songs among refined people by making the words suitable to their taste, instead of the trashy and really offensive words which belong to some songs of that order. Therefore I have concluded to reinstate my name on my songs and to pursue the Ethiopian business without fear or shame and lend all my energies to making the business *live*, at the same time that I will wish to establish my name as the best Ethiopian song-writer.[5]

All this sounds very self-confident and high-toned, but beneath it was a troublesome ostinato. In the summer of 1851 Stephen wrote what was to be the most famous of all his songs, "Old Folks at Home" ("Way Down upon the Swanee River"). He then made a deal whereby Christy would have first performance rights on his new songs, in advance of publication, in return for a payment of $10 for each song. For "Old Folks at Home" this was increased to $15, whereby Christy was allowed to put his name on the title page as author! It was published by Firth, Pond and Company, and the royalties were paid to Foster and his heirs. Nevertheless, it was not good for his reputation as a songwriter, and he soon repented of his folly. Hence the above-quoted letter to Christy, in which he goes on to say that he is not encouraged in his proposed undertaking "so long as 'The Old Folks at Home' stares me in the face with another's name on it." Then he makes an astonishing statement: *"As it was at my own solicitation that you allowed your name to be placed on the song,* I hope that the above reasons will be sufficient explanation for my desire to place my own name on it as author and composer, while at the same time I wish to leave the name of your band on the title page. This is a little matter of pride in myself which it will certainly be to your interest to encourage" (italics added).

Stephen's argument was neither logical nor convincing, especially in view of the italicized passage, and Christy certainly had no interest in fostering the "little matter of pride." He not only refused the request but also wrote on the back of the letter that Foster was "a vacillating skunk." Not until the copyright was renewed in 1879 did Stephen C. Foster's name appear on the title page of "Old Folks at Home." Yet it soon became widely known that he was the author of the greatest song hit written and composed by an American until that time.

What it meant for such a song to be really popular in mid-nineteenth-century America is humorously revealed in the following item from the *Albany State Register* of September 1852:

> "OLD FOLKS AT HOME" . . . is on everybody's tongue, and consequently in everybody's mouth. Pianos and guitars groan with it, night and day; sentimental young ladies sing it; sentimental young gentlemen warble it in midnight serenades; volatile young "bucks" hum it in the midst of their business and pleasures; boatmen roar it out stentorially at all times; all the bands play it; amateur flute blowers agonize over it at every spare moment; the street organs grind it out at every hour; the "singing stars" carol it on the theatrical boards, and at concerts; the chamber maid sweeps and dusts to the measured cadence of *Old Folks at Home;* the butcher's boy treats you to a strain or two of it as he hands in the steaks for dinner; the milk-man mixes it up strangely with the harsh ding-dong accompaniment of his tireless bell; there is not a "live darkey," young or old, but can whistle, sing, dance, and play it. . . .[16]

In spite of the contretemps with Christy, 1852 was a turning point in Stephen Foster's career. In September his publishers announced that "nearly *Forty Thousand Copies*" of "Old Folks at Home" had been sold and that the 100,000 mark would soon be reached. An item in the *Musical World* of New York (September 11) stressed the unprecedented significance of these figures: "When the reader takes into consideration the fact, that, fully one half of all the sheet music published proves to be a total failure—that three thousand copies of an instrumental piece, and five thousand copies of a song, is considered a *great sale,* he can form some idea of the surpassing popularity of 'Old Folks at Home.' "[17]

In January 1853 Firth, Pond and Company blundered by announcing that they had just published "My Old Kentucky Home, Good Night," with "Music and words by the author of "Old Folks at Home"—forgetting or overlooking Foster's commitment to Christy. But the "mistake" was soon rectified. The really significant fact was that "My Old Kentucky Home," together with "Massa's in de Cold Ground," both written in 1852, contributed immensely to Stephen's immediate prestige and lasting fame as a composer of "Plantation Melodies" (so designated by his publishers).

By this time Stephen's marriage was not running smoothly, and in May 1853 Jane left him. Soon afterward he went to New York, where he brought out such favorite songs as "Old Dog Tray," "Ellen Bayne," and "Jeanie with the Light Brown Hair," as well as an instrumental collection called *The Social Orchestra.* Jane rejoined him, yet difficulties remained and could not be easily dispelled. Stephen was in debt and overdrawn at his publishers. In 1857 he sold out all his future rights in the songs published by Firth, Pond and Company for the sum of $1,872.28. He also sold the complete rights to sixteen other songs (including "Camptown Races") to F. D. Benteen for $200. He thus raised immediate cash but forfeited the future income from royalties, upon which his family depended for a livelihood.

With the possible exception of "The Glendy Burk," no truly memorable songs were produced during this period until "Old Black Joe," the last of his great plantation melodies, appeared in November 1860. By the following spring the North and the South were at war, and Stephen was responding with appropriate songs such as the sentimental ballad "Oh! Tell Me of My Mother" and the stirring "We Are Coming, Father Abraham" (words by James Sloane Gibbons).

Stephen's songs were now being brought out by various publishers, but his affairs were far from flourishing. When "Our Bright Summer Days Are Gone" was rejected by Firth, Pond and Company, he gave it to a friend and asked him to submit it to another publisher and to "take what he will give you."[18] Stephen was composing industriously but was under much stress and financial pressure. He made a connection with a publishing firm specializing in hymns and Sunday-school songs and wrote ten of these for a collection called *The Golden Harp* (New York, 1863).[19] He was,

Sheet-music cover to Stephen Foster's "Ellen Bayne" (1854). Photo courtesy of the Foster Hall Collection, Stephen C. Foster Memorial, University of Pittsburgh.

in short, a penurious hack at this time, living from hand to mouth in New York, separated from his wife and child, and according to accounts that have not been convincingly refuted, drinking heavily.

The one bright spot in Stephen's last, sad years in New York was his friendship with a young versifier named George Cooper (1840–1927), whom he met in the back room of a grocery store where—according to the custom of the time—rum was the specialty of the house. That was in 1862, shortly before Cooper enlisted in the Union army, with which he served until July 1863. During this time he provided Foster with the words for a number of songs, including "Willie Has Gone to the War." Their collaboration continued until Foster's death, and to Cooper we owe the only first-hand account of the circumstances in which Stephen died.

Although Cooper wrote his share of sentimental lyrics and saccharine hymn texts, he also provided Stephen Foster with delightfully humorous topical lyrics such as "If You've Only Got a Moustache" and "Mr. and Mrs. Brown," the latter a dialogue between an errant husband and a neglected wife who nevertheless proves that Cupid has more arrows than one. "There Are Plenty of Fish in the Sea" tells of a young woman, too confident and coy, who finally learns that

> There are plenty of fish in the sea,
> But oh! they're hard to be caught.

"Katy Bell" is more in the style of Foster's own lyrics, except that instead of leaving his sweetheart asleep in the dell, the swain woos and wins her.[20]

Of the Civil War songs on which Cooper and Foster collaborated, the best known are "When This Dreadful War Is Over" and "Willie Has Gone to the War," both dating from 1862. Among those for which Foster wrote both the words and music are "We've a Million in the Field" and "Was My Brother in the Battle?" (both 1862), along with "Nothing but a Plain Old Soldier" (1863), described as a "Patriotic Ballad," and distinctive for its evocation of an old Revolutionary War veteran who recalls George Washington as a leader whom the Union forces cannot emulate:

> You've had many Generals over the land,
> You've tried one by one and you're still at a stand,
> But when *I* took the field we had *one* in command.

Obviously, this song was more didactic than inspiring. One other song that Foster wrote in collaboration with Cooper, "A Soldier in de Colored

Brigade" (1863), remains in obscurity—whether deservedly or not remains to be determined.

These last painful years in New York were also those of Foster's most prolific output, as the song "factory" was fueled by pecuniary pressures. But at least two songs stand out during this struggle for existence: "Gentle Lena Clare" (1862) and "Beautiful Dreamer" (1864). Both evoke those elusive, ideal maidens who exist only in the realm of poesy and melody. The first was written while Jane was in New York with Stephen and their daughter Marion, still hoping for reconciliation and a modus vivendi. They left in June 1862, returning to Lewiston, Pennsylvania; but Jane continued to be solicitous for Stephen's health and welfare, and in October 1863 she wrote to brother Morrison, saying that "all will soon be well with him again,"[21] if he could be persuaded to return to Cleveland (where Morrison was then living). Obviously, she felt that New York was the cause of Stephen's downfall.

Whatever the cause, there was evidently no remedy. During his last days in New York, Stephen was living at the New England Hotel, on the corner of Bayard Street and the Bowery. There, on January 9, 1864, he went to bed ill and weak with fever. The next morning, when he tried to get a drink of water, he fell against the washbowl and cut a severe gash in his face and neck. When George Cooper arrived in response to an emergency call, Stephen gasped, "I'm done for." Cooper took him to Bellevue Hospital and sent a telegram to Henry Foster telling him that his brother Stephen was very sick and wished to see him. He also wrote to Morrison Foster with the same message, adding, "He desires me to ask you to send him some pecuniary assistance as his means are very low."[22]

For a while Stephen seemed to rally, but on Wednesday afternoon he fainted and did not regain consciousness. He died at half past two o'clock on the afternoon of January 13, with no friend or relative at his bedside. The next day Cooper telegraphed to Henry and Morrison: "Stephen is dead. Come on."

On January 21, 1864, while the Citizen's Brass Band played "Come Where My Love Lies Dreaming" and "Old Folks at Home," the remains of Stephen Collins Foster were interred in Allegheny Cemetery, Pittsburgh, and the grave was marked by a simple marble tombstone. In 1900 a monument was erected at Pittsburgh's Highland Park, with a statue of Foster, seated and writing a song, while "Uncle Ned," below, plays the banjo.

There has been considerable diversity of opinion—and some controversy—concerning the sources of Foster's melodies. A contemporary writer in *Putnam's Monthly Magazine* (November 1853) stated that "the substance of the melody, which is very much the same thing in each of these songs, is purely Italian. . . ." This is, of course, a gross exaggeration, but not entirely wide of the mark, since Italian melodies, mostly from the popular operas of Bellini, Donizetti, and Rossini, permeated large sectors of American society.[23] The view that identifies the songs with "Negro" melodies is confused and misleading, because in Foster's time this was simply a term for the "darkey" songs of blackface minstrelsy. Charles Hamm makes a strong case for Irish sources, while William Austin suggests the influence of the Irish poet-musician Thomas Moore (1779–1852), who was likewise a master of nostalgia, sentimentality, and humor.[24]

My own view is based on a composite concept, in accordance with the dictum of Marius Schneider that the popularity of a melody depends partly on its degree of simplicity and partly on its conformity "to the melodic type current in a given culture." The melodies of Stephen Foster fulfill these conditions to the highest degree, for they conform to melodic types widely current in the popular music of America. These melodic types and their basic harmonic patterns, in turn, are deeply rooted in the folk-music traditions of Anglo-Celtic culture transplanted to America, with an overlay of nineteenth-century European operatic melodies. Whatever the sources or influences, it was by the inspiration of his great gifts that Stephen Foster became America's best-loved songwriter, admired and cherished by most of the world.

Like the Ohio and the Missouri flowing into the great Mississippi, two main currents converged in the broad stream of Stephen Foster's songs: the popular and the cultivated—in combining the two he particularly excelled. To fully appreciate his musical output in relation to the cultural context in which it was produced and disseminated, one should go through all of his songs in their original sheet-music editions and in nineteenth-century songbooks such as *The Love and Sentimental Songster* (New York, ca. 1862) and *The American Dime Song Book* (Philadelphia, n.d.), observing the illustrated covers, ranging from sentimental maidens and their swains in stilted attitudes to blackface minstrel entertainers and plantation "darkeys." Visual images were important for full enjoyment of these songs, either in the parlor or on the minstrel stage, for they set the mood and the scene that were to be enjoyed, or lamented, as the case might be.

One of Foster's biographers has remarked that "the repetitiousness of Foster's melodies is such that one cannot fail to wonder that they exert such an influence upon the listener as they do."[25] But, being such good tunes to begin with, it is precisely through this repetition that they make their unfailing effect. One should consider, however, that the chorus often presents a contrast, or at least a touch of variety, which is lost when it is omitted or sung as a solo. There are also slight rhythmic variations in many of Foster's melodies, which in the original editions were often introduced for different stanzas, as in the original edition of "Old Folks at Home," where the following variants occur in the second and third stanzas:

In his treatment of harmony, Foster stays close to the tonic, dominant, and subdominant. A rare example of secondary chords is to be found in the artistically conceived song "Ah! May the Red Rose Live Alway." Modulations are scarce and confined chiefly to the dominant key, as in "My Old Kentucky Home" and "Old Black Joe."

Next to the piano, the guitar was the most fashionable instrument of the period, and Foster wrote guitar accompaniments for many of his songs. In 1854 his publishers brought out *The Social Orchestra*, which was advertised as "a collection of the most popular operatic and other melodies, arranged as SOLOS, DUETS, TRIOS, and QUARTETTES for Flutes, Violins, and Violoncello (or pianoforte) and particularly adapted to Evenings at Home, Serenades, &c."[26] This included arrangements of music by celebrated European composers such as Bellini, Donizetti, Boieldieu, Mozart, Weber, Schubert, Lanner, and Johann Strauss—mainly a mixture of operatic arias and waltzes. He also included several pieces by his friend Henry Kleber of Pittsburgh, notably the "Rainbow Schottische" and "Coral Schottische," both highly popular.[27]

There are, of course, many pieces by Foster in *The Social Orchestra*, notably the "Old Folks Quadrilles," which includes arrangements of "Old Folks at Home," "Oh, Boys, Carry Me 'Long," "Nelly Bly," "Farewell My Lucy Dear," and "Plantation Jig." (The last piece was originally published as "Cane Brake Jig," for piano.) There is also "Jennie's Own Schottisch," arranged for trio, and a remarkably original piece for violin (or flute) titled "Anadolia." The collection adds another dimension to Foster's wide impact on the musical culture of his time.

In our culture, as in the mythology of ancient Greece, transformations are a symbol of immortality. From his time to ours the melodies of Stephen C. Foster have been "transformed" countless times and in far-ranging contexts, from the hurdy-gurdy barrel organ to the brass band, from the fiddle to the electronic synthesizer, from classical to "pop," and from jazz to "rock." I personally cherish Ray Charles's "Swanee River Rock" (1957), which was also a favorite of my students. The choice is vast, the options are open, and the melodies (in whatever guise) are immortal.

Notes

1. Quoted in Evelyn Foster Morneweck, *Chronicles of Stephen Foster's Family* 2:467.
2. Ibid., p. 468.
3. *Dwight's Journal of Music* 4 (Nov. 19, 1853): 54; quoted in John Tasker Howard, *Stephen Foster, America's Troubadour*, p. 215.
4. Morneweck, *Chronicles of Stephen Foster's Family* 1:30.
5. Ibid., pp. 39, 41.
6. Howard, *Stephen Foster, America's Troubadour*, p. 81.
7. Ibid., p. 116.
8. Morneweck, *Chronicles of Stephen Foster's Family* 1:121.
9. Morrison Foster, *My Brother Stephen*, p. 34.
10. Ibid., p. 35.
11. Robert Peebles Nevin, "Stephen C. Foster and Negro Minstrelsy," *Atlantic Monthly* (Nov. 1867); quoted in Howard, *Stephen Foster, America's Troubadour*, p. 138.
12. See Howard, *Stephen Foster, America's Troubadour*, pp. 152–54.
13. William W. Austin, *"Susanna," "Jeanie," and "The Old Folks at Home,"* p. 8.
14. Quoted in Morneweck, *Chronicles of Stephen Foster's Family* 2:377.
15. Ibid., p. 398. This and other letters from Foster to Christy are reprinted in *The American Composer Speaks*, ed. Chase, pp. 54–57.
16. Reprinted in *Dwight's Journal of Music* 1 (Oct. 2, 1952): 202; quoted in Howard, *Stephen Foster, America's Troubadour*, pp. 214–15.
17. Quoted in Howard, *Stephen Foster, America's Troubadour*, p. 202.
18. Quoted in ibid., p. 321.
19. *The Golden Harp* was copyrighted by Horace Waters and Co., who published forty-seven songs by Foster.
20. For a representative selection of Foster's songs reproduced from the original sheet-music editions, see the *Stephen Foster Song Book*, ed. Richard Jackson.

21. Quoted in Howard, *Stephen Foster, America's Troubadour*, p. 309.

22. Quoted in ibid., p. 341.

23. See the recording *Stephen Foster's Social Orchestra*, Columbia M 32577, which includes "Gems from *Lucia*" (Donizetti).

24. Charles Hamm, *Yesterdays*, pp. 42–61, 215–19; Austin, *"Susanna," "Jeanie,"* and "The Old Folks at Home," pp. 131–36 and passim.

25. Harold Vincent Milligan, *Stephen Collins Foster*, p. 113.

26. Published in New York in 1854, *The Social Orchestra* was advertised well in advance of publication in order to attract attention, as in the advance notice quoted above from the *Musical World* of Nov. 12, 1853. See Austin, *"Susanna," "Jeanie,"* and "The Old Folks at Home," p. 207.

27. See the facsimile edition of *The Social Orchestra*, with an introduction by H. Wiley Hitchcock.

Chapter 15

Romantic Americanism

Should he be able . . . to create but one single *Star* in the *West*,
no one would ever be more proud than himself, to be called
an *American Musician*
—Anthony Philip Heinrich, *The Dawning of Music in Kentucky* (1820)

In 1833 the geologist Edward Hitchcock completed his catalogue of the natural resources of Massachusetts, intended primarily for the benefit of businessmen, farmers, and scientists. Nevertheless, he included a guide for the curious traveler so that "the man of taste" would know "where he will find natural objects calculated to gratify his love of novelty, beauty, and sublimity."[1]

Hitchcock's catalogue-guide exemplifies three main themes in American culture of the pre–Civil War period: concern for the development of natural resources, recognition of the central importance of science, and emphasis on the "novelty, beauty, and sublimity" of the American landscape. The last had strong nationalistic overtones, stressing the grandeur and uniqueness of the vast American wilderness, surpassing (it was said) anything Europe could offer. The cult of the wilderness was stimulated by the rise of Romanticism, and it attracted Europeans as much as it did Americans—sometimes even more.

In the first half of the nineteenth century, the trans–Mississippi West was explored, mapped, fought over, exploited, settled, claimed, and—simultaneously—scientifically studied. It was a bonanza for archaeology, ethnology, and geology, described in prose and poetry, and depicted in the visual arts. For most Americans the incentives were practical and mundane: profitable trade, natural resources, free land, and national expansion to the Pacific. In the process, arduous adventure, ambitious aims, heroic exploits, savage warfare, scientific investigation, and aesthetic satisfaction blended in a uniquely American experience that also fascinated foreigners. In the words of cultural historian William Goetzmann: "To the artist and the scientist, European and American alike, the West was important not as a place for settlers and civilization; it was important as a source of new experiences, new data, new sensations, and new questions. . . . Both the scientist and the artist in the West dedicated themselves to the concrete and the particular, with the result that they suddenly found themselves romantics, breathing the life of exoticism into the remote extremities of the body of nature."[2]

The Romantic image of the "noble savage" was popularized in Europe by Chateaubriand, who visited North America in 1791 and later (in his short novel *Atala*) rhapsodized on how "the soul delights to bury and lose itself amidst boundless forests . . . to mix and confound . . . with the wild sublimities of Nature." Thus he "spread a Romantic glow over Indian life in 'the magnificent wilds of Kentucky' "—where he had actually never been.[3] Yet so emotionally convincing and spiritually persuasive was his vicarious identification with the American wilderness that his writings exerted a deep and enduring impression both in Europe and America.

Goetzmann, for example, finds echoes of Chateaubriand in what he calls the "romantic ethnology" of George Catlin (1796–1872), the American artist and ethnologist who first systematically studied and depicted the tribal lore and customs of American Indians. Goetzmann also postulates that this "romantic ethnology" and especially Catlin's view that Nature is exotic and primitive, hence more interesting and attractive than "civilization," appealed more to Europeans than to Americans, "who were preoccupied with the march of empire."[4]

It is not surprising, then, that the first—and for a long time the only—American composer to be strongly attracted by the lure and the lore of the wilderness was of European origin: Anthony Philip Heinrich (1781–1861). Also significant is the remark of a contemporary writer who characterized him as "a species of musical Catlin." The passage is worth quoting in full: "Heinrich passed several years of his life among the Indians that once inhabited Kentucky, and many of his compositions refer to these aboriginal companions. He is a species of musical Catlin, painting his dusky friends on the music-staff instead of the canvas, and composing laments, symphonies, dirges, and war-songs, on the most intensely Indian subjects. He would be the very one to set Hiawatha to music."[5] (Let it be remarked, parenthetically, that Heinrich would be loath to set Longfellow's *Hiawatha* to music, for he was only interested in *genuine* Indian lore.)

While we may be skeptical about Heinrich's consorting with "aboriginal companions" or having them as "dusky friends," we can assume that he saw some Indians during his sojourn in Kentucky from 1817 to 1823. We do know that he was strongly attracted by Indian lore and that he was familiar with John McIntosh's standard work, *The Origin of the American Indians* (New York, 1843). He may also have known Catlin's *Letters and Notes on the Manners, Customs, and Condition of the North American Indians* (New York, 1841) and Henry R. Schoolcraft's *The Indian in His Wigwam; or, Characteristics of the Red Race of America* (New York, 1848). His interest in the American Indians was not confined to their ceremonies and customs but embraced their tragic plight as victims of the march of civilization under the banners of material progress, national expansion, and white supremacy. He was composing at the time (the 1830s and 1840s) when the government's policy of moving the eastern tribes to lands west of the Mississippi was being harshly pursued—particularly during President Jackson's administration—and these events are also reflected in his music.

The beginnings of the "Indianist" movement in American musical composition have generally been placed near the end of the nineteenth century, and it is true that many composers began to take an interest in tribal lore and Indian melodies about that time. But Heinrich was the precursor, and no composer after him has surpassed the magnitude of his Indianist works, particularly in symphonic music. (We can be thankful that he wrote no "Indian" operas!) He wrote eight large works for orchestra on Indian subjects and a number of other instrumental and vocal pieces. Yet this was only one aspect of his many-sided musical Americanism, covering an impressive range of history, social life, political events, places and people, patriotic and popular music, and the wildlife of the wilderness—notably in his extraordinary "Characteristic Symphony," *The Columbiad; or, Migration of American Wild Passenger Pigeons.*

How, then, did it happen that the music of this remarkable Americanist, this exuberant and original Romantic composer, fell into oblivion after his death, and that until recently he appeared in the histories as an eccentric whose hour of triumph left no lasting traces? Before attempting to answer these difficult and perhaps embarrassing questions, let us review the circumstances of his rise and fall.

Heinrich, who was fond of autobiographical references expressed in musical metaphors, tells us that "at Schönbüchel in the Kingdom of Bohemia" he entered the Gamut of Life; and "at Schönlinde and Georgswalde . . . commenced his Chromatic Variations, in the Counterpoint of human affairs." Bohemia was then part of the Austrian Empire, to whose sovereigns he later paid homage in flowery dedications; but his fondest memories were of the three towns associated with his birthplace, their charming names evoking beech groves and pleasant woodlands. Adopted by a wealthy uncle whose mercantile-banking business he inherited, he traveled widely, enjoyed himself, and took up the violin as an avocation. In 1805 he made a brief visit to America, "actuated by curiosity to take a peep at the New World."[6]

On his return to Europe he found his business in bad shape, a result of mismanagement aggravated by financial depression caused by the Napoleonic Wars. In 1810, with a cargo of Bohemian glassware as merchandise, he again sailed for America, hoping to improve his situation. But a year later the financial crash in Austria wrote *finis* to his hopes. He decided to remain in America and to devote himself to music, for better or for worse.

As we have previously noted, European musicians who established themselves in America were highly trained and experienced professionals. But Heinrich was an amateur violinist who had not undergone any such rigorous training, and at thirty he was beyond the age when one normally began a musical career. Yet he was musically gifted, resourceful, energetic, enthusiastic, and industrious. He took the chances and made the most of them. But he also went his own way, refusing to compromise for the sake of success. Thus his path as a composer included both fame and frustration, both satisfaction and disappointment—and a considerable share of hardship.

Sometime between 1810 and 1813, Heinrich married a young lady from Boston. In 1813 they traveled to Europe to visit his homeland, and their daughter, Antonia, was born at Schönlinde. His wife being unwell, Heinrich brought her back to America, leaving the infant in care of a relative. Soon afterward, Mrs. Heinrich died. (Contrary to statements in some biographical dictionaries, Heinrich never remarried.) Many years later Antonia rejoined her father in America and was a consolation to him in his old age.

In Philadelphia Heinrich achieved some success as a violinist and was also appointed music director of the Southwark Theatre—without salary! As he could not live on prestige, he accepted an offer to be music director of a theater in Pittsburgh—with salary. But his luck was deceptive. After walking all the way from Philadelphia to Pittsburgh—some 300 miles—he found the theater in the throes of bankruptcy. Out of a job, he decided to go West—even though he was no longer a young man. He made his way down the Ohio River, probably by flatboat, disembarked at Limestone (now Maysville), Kentucky, and walked the sixty miles or so to Lexington, where he arrived in October or November 1817.

Lexington, then a town of some 5,000 inhabitants (including 1,500 blacks), was far from crude culturally, as Heinrich's reception will show. On November 12 he conducted a "Grand Concert of Vocal and Instrumental Music," which opened with Beethoven's First Symphony and included works by Haydn, Mozart, and Viotti. Heinrich had evidently been accepted as a "professor" rather than an amateur, and music was henceforth to be his sole life's work, with composition as his main ambition.

Working strenuously to maintain his professional status as conductor, performer, and teacher, Heinrich became seriously ill. Seeking a rural retreat where he could recuperate, he was offered the use of a log cabin in the woods near Bardstown, and it was there that he began to compose. This sylvan retreat also provided the background for the Romantic-American persona that he was to adopt as "The Log-Cabin Composer of Kentucky."

By January 1819 Heinrich had moved to "Farmington," the estate of Judge John Speed, near Louisville. While the log-cabin image remained, it was expanded to include not only the backwoods setting of the frontier but also the no less Romantic image of a cultivated pastoral setting. In the two years that he spent at Farmington, encouraged by the sympathetic patronage of Judge Speed and the friendly esteem of the family, including two gifted daughters, Heinrich composed assiduously. He soon had enough pieces to form a collection, which was published in Philadelphia in May 1820. Titled *The Dawning of Music in Kentucky; or, The Pleasures of Harmony in the Solitudes of Nature*, it contained forty-six compositions (vocal and instrumental) with a total of 269 pages. Nothing like it had ever appeared, either in Europe or America, and I agree with Wiley Hitchcock that it "certainly must be the most extraordinary Opus 1 in the history of music."[7]

In his preface Heinrich included a historic manifesto of musical Americanism: "The many and severe animadversions, so long and repeatedly cast on the talent for Music in this Country, has been one of the chief motives of the Author, in the exercise of his abilities; and should he be able, by this effort, to create but one single *Star* in the *West*, no one would ever be more proud than himself, to be called an *American Musician*." In a "Proposal" that he issued for the publication of the book by subscription, Heinrich described it as comprising "a variety of original *Songs* and *Airs* for the *Voice* and *Pianoforte, Waltzes, Cotillions, Minuets, Polonaises, Marches, Variations* with some pieces of a national character adapted for the Piano Forte and also calculated for the lovers of the Violin."[8] In the last-mentioned category the most extraordinary piece is "The Yankee Doodleiad," subtitled "A National Divertimento," for strings and piano. While it also brings in

"Hail Columbia" ("The President's March"), the tour de force consists of fourteen virtuoso variations for violin on "Yankee Doodle," with an interlude that features an incredible "Yankee Doodle Shake," prefaced by an appropriate jingle:

> Yankee Doodle—what a shake!!!
> Sure such a shake's the dandy,
> A shake of shakes, a mighty shake!
> O shake it! shake it handy!!!!

A postscript in verse indicates that Heinrich had anticipated the vogue of multimedia performance:

> Now take your stand, ye mighty Band,
> With Fiddle, Drum, and Trumpet,
> Da Capo Yankee Doodle doo,
> As loud as ye can thump it.

One trait that Heinrich had in common with Billings was his love for picturesque and exuberant verbal expression, often expressed in his titles and interpolations. In his most brilliant and characteristic piece for piano, "A Chromatic Ramble of the Peregrine Harmonist," he actually directs that the interlinear text be *sung*—presumably by the pianist. The words describe what is going on in the music as the "peregrine harmonist" (a musical wanderer) takes a ramble "among the flats and sharps," loses himself "in knots of Chords, of Chords," then reaches "the half tones," for "a touch of the chromatic"—which for Heinrich meant the realm of musical bliss. He was as partial to chromatic intervals as Billings was to fuging tunes, and he once lamented that "chromatic ears are as rare as diamonds." So are pianists who can both play and sing "A Chromatic Ramble" at the same time! (Neely Bruce was evidently the first to do so, in 1978.)

Another highly characteristic piano piece is the sonata titled "La buona mattina," which also has an interlinear text (but only as introduction and coda). Ignoring "the grammar of composition," he allows a succession of fifths; but the point is that "he used them with true twentieth-century effect—he was merely a hundred years ahead of his time!"[9] That remark (by his best biographer) sums up Heinrich's historical predicament.

A supplement to *The Dawning of Music in Kentucky,* titled *The Western Minstrel,* was published in the same year in Philadelphia "for the Author"—which meant that Heinrich had to pay the cost of printing. This was usually done by soliciting subscriptions from friendly individuals; but on this occasion Heinrich evidently had some difficulties with his creditors, with the result that he spent several days in jail. In his own picturesque language: "Dame *Capriccio* so frowned on the ill-fated Author, as to *transpose* him, *sforzando,* to the diatonic, chromatic, en-harmonic, *Turnkey* of one of those hospitable public mansions, where the unfortunate finds an Asylum, *free* and *safe;* Bread and Water to prolong starvation, and a Brick, cold as the heart of the extortionate, for a Pillow. . . ."[10] Nevertheless, the book is "Respectfully Dedicated to the Citizens of Philadelphia"—perhaps an indication that Heinrich, having established his "wild wood" persona, was now looking toward the seaboard cities as a more propitious milieu for his musical ambitions.

The Western Minstrel contains songs and piano pieces, the latter less elaborate than those contained in the preceding collection. The most characteristic piece for piano is "The Minstrel's March; or, The Road to Kentucky," which ingeniously and amusingly depicts Heinrich's journey from Philadelphia to Louisville, with verbal interpolations: "Turnpike," "Alleghanies," "Passage on the Ohio," and so on. Among the songs, the most impressive is "Irradiate Cause!" to a text by W. B. Tappan from *Songs of Judah.*

Disappointed in his hopes for recuperating his printing costs by subscriptions (although he expressed heartfelt gratitude to the handful of patrons in Kentucky), Heinrich reveals some disenchantment with the frontier. He laments that his artistic efforts have not been fully appreciated "in Regions, particularly, where, since the yell of the war-whoop has become *tacet* . . . the whistling of the tomahawk and other *Furiosos* of the ruthless savage ceased to vibrate, scarcely any other strains are heard than the *music of the axe, the hammer's din, or the cadences of the Banjo.*"[11]

Many other European-born musicians (and not a few American-born culture-snobs) were to deplore the ubiquity of the banjo. In contrast, Heinrich was the first to recognize its artistic potential and to seize upon it as the inspiration for a piano piece titled "The Banjo"—some thirty years before Gottschalk wrote his celebrated piece with the same title! Heinrich's piece is the most substantial part of a composite work for piano titled "Barbecue Divertimento," which appeared in his collection *The Sylviad* (vol. 2). It forms a part of what he calls "A Sylvan Scene in Kentucky," and the full title is "The Banjo; or, The Negro's Banjo Quickstep." Neely Bruce, the first pianist to make Heinrich's music widely known in the twentieth century, considers this a work "virtually unique in the entire 19th century" and "one of Heinrich's most amazing compositional achievements."[12] Because of its nonrepetitive free form and its numerous (but unobtrusive) quotations (including self-quotation), he compares it to the "stream-of-consciousness" process that we also find in the music of Charles Ives.

After a sojourn in Philadelphia, where several of his orchestral works were performed by the newly established Musical Fund Society, Heinrich returned to his friends in Kentucky. But soon an authoritative voice from Boston struck a note that changed the course of his career.

On April 13, 1822, the *Euterpeiad; or, Musical Intelligencer*, a prestigious periodical edited by John R. Parker, published a lengthy and laudatory review of *The Dawning of Music in Kentucky*, including the following excerpts:

> The vigour of thought, variety of ideas, originality of conception, classical correctness, boldness and luxuriance of imagination, displayed throughout this voluminous work, are the more extraordinary, as the author but a few years since, was merely an amateur and a prosperous merchant whom sudden misfortune transformed into a professor. . . . His genius however triumphs over every thing.—There is enough in his well-stored pages to gratify every taste and fancy. There is versatility for the capricious, pomp for the pedant, playfulness for the amateur, learning for the scholar, business for the performer, pleasure for the vocalist, ingenuity for the curious, and puzzle for the academician [here Parker hit the bull's eye!]. He seems at once to have possessed himself of the key which unlocks to him the temple of science and enables him to explore with fearless security the mysterious labyrinth of harmony. He may, therefore, be styled *the Beethoven* of America. . . .[13]

In February 1823 the *Euterpeiad* published an article claiming for Boston the merit of having discovered this "neglected genius," "perhaps the most profound and scientific composer of the new world [whose] voluminous works [are] disdained by Professors for their very originality, breaking forth in all the wildness of native grandeur. . . ." Hence this original genius "has been invited to come to Boston, with a view to permanent residence"—to transplant himself "from the wilderness where he now languishes" to an "atmosphere more congenial to the exertion and expansion of musical talent."[14]

Thus, in the spring of 1823 Heinrich was in Boston, ready to participate in a concert for his benefit on May 29. The concert was more of an artistic than a financial success, contributing to his prestige rather than his purse. In his card of thanks to the musicians and the public, Heinrich clung to his image as "the humble Minstrel of the Western Wilds." He sensed that it was both distinctive and Romantic, as well as exotic in an urban setting.

When *The Sylviad* appeared, it was favorably reviewed in the *Euterpeiad*, with praise for "the compositions of this great, original genius," which are "filled with difficulties and beauties of every sort." The writer perceptively conveys the peculiar character of the music. "His style is almost always chromatic, the harmony abstruse, and the subject chosen apparently more to please himself than others. In all his compositions a rich and visionary fragrance breathes through them, uncommon and delightful, and no one need to make anything of them in performance, if they cannot enjoy the luxury of 'wand'ring thoughts and visionary fears.' "[15]

These remarks are especially pertinent to one of Heinrich's most characteristic works, "The Log House, A Sylvan Bravura" (no. 19 of *The Sylviad*), also described as "A Song presented to the Western Minstrel by John Mills Brown" (who wrote the words). The cover illustration depicts the composer seated on the rung of a ladder outside his log cabin, playing the violin, while around the corner comes a Negro with his banjo. The author of the text must have had complete empathy with Heinrich, as well as with the spirit of Romanticism, as indicated by the opening stanza:

> Far to the West an endless Wood,
> Sighs to the rushing Cataract's flood;
> 'Twas there an humble Log-House stood
>   To fame unknown;
> There first-loved Minstrelsy I woo'd,
>   And woo'd alone.

This "Sylvan Bravura" is truly a bravura piece, both vocally and pianistically, containing some of Heinrich's most brilliant keyboard writing, culminating in a brief but fantastically effective *Cadenza volante*. It is an extended composition of twenty pages and might be thought of as the "Minstrel's Progress" from a bucolic to an urban milieu, assuming in the process several Romantic personae: "Il malinconico," "L'entusiasta," and, most decisively, "Il romantico."

According to cultural historian Russel B. Nye, "The heart of American Romanticism lay in three major precepts: that literature was expression; that it was organic; that it was imaginative."[16] Thus, the Romantics viewed literature primarily as "an experience of self and a projection of the writer's interpretations of experience." It follows that Romanticism "became autobiographical and confessional; what the writer felt became of paramount importance." Instead of imposing a predetermined form on the

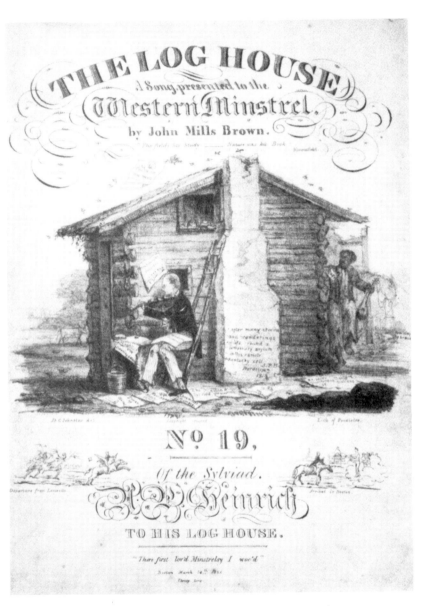

Title page to Anthony Philip Heinrich, "The Log House," *Sylviad*, no. 19.

material of experience, Romanticism adopted Coleridge's concept of *organic form*, which is "innate, it shapes as it develops itself from within." In the words of Nye: "As opposed to the neoclassic writer, who conceived of literature as essentially static, fixed, controlled, the Romantic saw it as responsive, fluid, changing, shaped from within by its own laws, each artifact possessed of its own form and unity."[17]

Substituting *music* for *literature* in the foregoing, we have a comprehensive explanation of Heinrich's essential role as a composer in the pristine Romantic period of America's music, from 1820 to 1860. He alone embodied in music Coleridge's concept of organic form.

In spite of his commitment to the New World, Heinrich could not entirely sever himself from Europe, where he also aspired to be recognized and lauded. It was in London, during 1826–31 and 1833–35, that he began to compose his symphonies and other large orchestral works, and in 1835–37 he was on the Continent, visiting Prague, Vienna, and Graz, where his music was performed with considerable success. But it was in America that he achieved his greatest triumphs, while also experiencing more than his share of frustration and disappointment.

Returning to America in the fall of 1837, Heinrich settled in New York, which had been competing with Boston for the honor of his presence. What ensued was a competition between the two cities for performing Heinrich's larger compositions with as much éclat and fanfare as possible. New York presented "Heinrich's Grand Musical Festival" at the Broadway Tabernacle on June 16, 1842, followed by a benefit concert on May 6, 1846, and a "Grand Valedictory Concert" on April 21, 1853, in Metropolitan Hall. Boston responded with a "Grand Festival and Complimentary Concert" in Fremont Temple on June 13, 1846. (Of the ten works on the program, seven were by Heinrich.)

In spite of such efforts, all was not glory and triumph. A public announcement might state that "the ORCHESTRA will be *numerous* and *powerful*"—but all is relative, and Heinrich's music often demanded a more numerous and powerful orchestra than either Boston or New York could command. Thus the result was a mixture of satisfaction and frustration, with probably more of the latter. Many of his larger symphonic and choral works were never performed in his lifetime. He was a prophet not without honor in his adopted land, but his vision exceeded the capacities of a republic bent on developing its industrial capacity and commercial scope.

Some of Heinrich's grandest and most characteristic efforts were directed toward celebrating American national themes. In 1837 he composed *The Columbiad: Grand American National Chivalrous Symphony*, featuring "Hail Columbia" and "Yankee Doodle." He treated American national airs not merely as patriotic signals but as an integral and artistically controlled element of his musical thought. No other composer achieved a comparable effect until Charles Ives.

Heinrich's persistent ambition was to compose a "grand national song of triumph" or "historical oratorio" on the origins of the United States of America. This he undertook in 1840 with *The Jubilee,* for orchestra and chorus, "commemorative of events from the landing of the Pilgrim Fathers, to the consummation of American liberty," ending with a "Prophetic Vision of the Future Glory of the Nation." A section on "The Celebration of the Feast of Shells" refers to the New England clambake.[18]

All this was but a prelude to a much larger work in four parts, for which he issued proposals in December 1842, to be titled *The Wild Wood Spirits' Chant: Grand National Song of Triumph,* "embracing from five to six hundred pages. All of which are to be presented as a legacy to his adopted country: The land of Washington."[19] Although it was never actually completed in this form, it not only reveals Heinrich's grandiose patriotic vision but also involves his stubborn delusion that the "statesmen, legislators and other distinguished citizens" from whom he solicited subscriptions for at least a partial publication of his magnum opus would respond in the name of America's national glory and cultural prestige. This delusion caused him not a little anguish, frustration, and humiliation, as he persistently sought the patronage of persons in power, from the mayor of Washington to the president of the United States.

In spite of disappointments he kept his sense of humor and covered his frustration with a jocose style, as in his letter to "Mr. Seaton, Mayor of Washington, D.C.," dated Georgetown, March 2, 1843:

During 2 weeks, I have at least been trotting about 140 miles, by day and night, to and fro, from the *Tiber* to the *Capitol,* inclusive of many Zig Zags, taken with heavy letters of introduction, Pitts, Patts, Puffs and Packages of music to the Colossuses of learning and patriotism of the Commonwealth . . . in quest of Patronage for my Grand National Musically historical work. One night, as an utter stranger, I was actually lost in the swamps of Washington City and the Quagmires of Georgetown, thus sustaining many rough Counterpoints but not one cheering subscription corresponding to my harmonious enterprise.[20]

Nevertheless, Heinrich was not easily discouraged, and he never completely dampened in his enthusiasms. In the same letter to Mayor Seaton, he went on to say: "If the venerable Patriarch J. Q. Adams, so exalted as Statesman and Poet, would furnish me a Poem on the Emancipation of the Slaves . . . I will compose and arrange a Score or an Oratorio, whose gigantic effects may possibly reverberate more stentorian through the welkin and impressive through the World, than all the ponderous dissonant speeches of his opponents, or the Thunders of Niagara. . . . If you please, mention this . . . to the enthusiastic and philanthropic John Quincy Adams as coming from the ardent Loghouse Composer of Kentucky."

Nothing came of this scheme. Former President Adams, now a member of Congress, was evidently more interested in emancipation than in extending his philanthropy to an eccentric composer with delusions of grandeur. And there was no National Endowment for the Arts and Humanities. Heinrich, as always, was ahead of his time.

Two Romantic themes predominant in Heinrich's symphonic oeuvre were the grandeur of Nature and the fate of the American Indians. Typical of the former is *The Ornithological Combat of Kings; or, The Condor of the Andes and the Eagle of the Cordilleras*—"A grand symphony" in four movements. He regarded this as his greatest work and in 1846 wrote that he had "worked it over *six times* and it is now the *seventh time* that I recast and recopy this stupendous production. . . ."[21] Curiously, it is the condor, not the eagle, that proves to be the protagonist of the score, emerging victorious in the *Finale: Vivace brillante*—which is also the triumph of this amazing symphony.[22]

Another extraordinary work depicting a phenomenon of Nature is *The Columbiad; or, Migration of American Wild Passenger Pigeons* (1857), described as "A Characteristic Symphony in two parts."[23] Appended to the score are some passages paraphrased from Alexander Wilson's *American Ornithology* (Philadelphia, 1808–14), of which the following are most pertinent:

> The fertile regions of Ohio, Kentucky and Indiana abound with beech nuts, which are the principal food of the wild Pigeon; when these nuts are consumed in one place, they discover another supply, often at a distance of seventy or eighty miles from the place which they appear to have agreed on among themselves to spend the night. These places are always in the woods and sometimes occupy a large extent of forest. . . . The top of every tree presented a tumult of Pigeons, crowding about their young, and fluttering with their wings, so as to produce a perpetual roar like that of thunder. Mingled with this was the frequent crash of falling trees. . . .

Heinrich goes on to quote some statistics from Wilson that evidently impressed him. The pigeons were flying in such vast numbers that if "each square yard of this moving body comprehended three Pigeons, the square yards in the whole space multiplied by three, would give 2,230,272,000 pigeons in a column, one mile broad, moving at the rate of one mile in a minute for four hours." At this point even the most Romantic of composers might have preferred to invoke the lark or the nightingale; but Heinrich saw this incredible mass of sound and motion zooming over the American wilderness as a terrific challenge for the musical tone painter, to which he responded with all the resources at his command. With a characteristic quirk, Heinrich concludes this ornithological epic with an *Andante maestoso e quasi presto* that introduces "Hail Columbia" and "Yankee Doodle"!

While living in Kentucky, Heinrich formed a lasting friendship with the ornithologist, naturalist, and artist John James Audubon, who probably stimulated Heinrich's interest in the flora and fauna of North America.

As we noted earlier, Heinrich was deeply interested in American Indian lore and had read widely on the subject. It is not surprising, then, that he wrote eight large orchestral works and a number of smaller pieces dealing with Indian themes. His first composition for large orchestra was *Pushmataha, a Venerable Chief of a Western Tribe of Indians* (1831). According to his biographer, this was "probably the first attempt in all history to treat in music, in any adequate manner, the idea of the American Indian."[24] The key word here is *idea*. Unlike the later Indianist composers, Heinrich did not use (or misuse) Indian melodies but relied on all the evocative and associative elements that his musical resources could command. He also drew on literary sources, from which he extracted descriptive data appended to his scores. In *Pushmataha,* for example, he quoted from John McIntosh's *Origin of the North American Indians:*

No less felicitous was the close of a speech made by *Pushmataha* . . . at a Council held, we believe, in Washington, many years ago. In alluding to his extreme age, and to the probability that he might not even survive the journey back to his tribe, he said: "My children will walk through the forests, and the *Great Spirit* will whistle in the treetops, and the flowers will spring up in the trails— but *Pushmataha* will hear not—he will see the flowers no more. He will be gone, his people will know, that he is dead. The news will come to their ears, *as the Sound of the fall of a mighty oak in the stillness of the woods."*

As far as is known, this work was never performed in Heinrich's lifetime; hence a performance in New York on December 9, 1961, conducted by Howard Shanet with the Columbia University Symphony Orchestra, is believed to be the first. (The second half of the twentieth century is full of Heinrich "firsts.") On December 6, 1958, Shanet conducted what was evidently the first performance of *Manitou Mysteries; or, The Voice of the Great Spirit* (ca. 1845), subtitled *Gran sinfonia misteriosa-indiana*, in four movements. As Shanet was the first to conduct major symphonic works by Heinrich in our time, his remarks on the music are worth quoting:

> Heinrich's method of composition is usually to start each movement with simple and even old-fashioned material and then to give his fantasy free rein in expanding and developing it. Daring modulations, ingenious instrumental devices, and a very distinctive kind of chromatic decoration that is peculiarly his own, are characteristic of this unjustly neglected composer. When one adds to this Heinrich's ability to take the long view—the first movement of the *Manitou Mysteries* is twelve minutes long, yet it is a truly and beautifully unified piece—it does not seem so far-fetched that some of his contemporaries called this forceful musician the "Beethoven of America."

Although not present at these concerts, I was privileged to hear tapes of both performances and found them uniquely fascinating. I was particularly attracted by the "Minuetto" in *Manitou Mysteries*—a perfect example of calculated incongruity that somehow manages to sound both stately and "savage."

Another Indianist work of large dimensions (189 pages in the autograph score!) is *The Mastodon*, undated but certainly written before 1845. It is described as "Containing Musical Portraitures on the Following Subjects: (1) Black Thunder, the Patriarch of the Fox Tribe; (2) The Elkhorn Pyramid, or, The Indians' Offering to the Spirit of the Prairies; (3) Shenandoah, a Celebrated Oneida Chief."[25]

The first part relates to a speech by Chief Black Thunder at a council in 1815 held with the American commissioners, whose charges of a breach of treaties he eloquently refuted. His final message "to my Great Father, the President of your nation," was this: "I will not surrender my country, but with my life." Wilbur Maust surmises that this reference to the president of the United States may explain why Heinrich introduced his own "Tyler's Grand Veto Quick Step" march into this movement. (John Tyler was president in 1841–45.)

"The Elkhorn Pyramid" refers to a ceremony of the Blackfeet tribe for assuring success in the hunt, as described in *Travels in the Interior of North America, 1832–34*, by Maximilian, prince of Wied (London, 1843), which

Heinrich cites at the head of this movement—another instance of his wide reading on Indian lore.

After his frustrations in the nation's capital—or, as he put it, his "haps in Washington City"—Heinrich had to reconcile himself to adverse fortune. He wrote, "I shall forwith return very independent, nay stoically to my loft garret in New York."[26] There he endured poverty and illness in the loneliness of old age. "When I compose now," he said, "it is always with the image of death before my eyes: my sun is setting: I am an old minstrel, *diminuendo e morendo.*" Whereupon a devoted feminine admirer who signed herself "Estelle" wrote a poem (printed in the *Evening Post*) proclaiming, among other eulogies:

> *Genius* outlives the transient days,
> To man allotted here:
> The "Spirit of Beethoven" smiles,
> Thy setting sun to cheer.

Yet all was not sentimental incense in the Heinrich cult. In 1842 a judicious critic appraised his achievement with perceptive and prophetic insight: "His musical ideas [are] very profound, his harmonies and resolutions are complex, but wrought out in masterly style, he grapples with every sort of musical expression, he calls into action and combination every species of musical instrument, his ideas are exceedingly grand at proper times,—and yet, his music will not be popular in his own day. . . . He is in advance of his age, the learned will study him, and another generation will cultivate him." There are signs that such a generation has arrived.

But what happened in between the eclipse and the revival? Why the swift oblivion, the long neglect, the later deprecation? The answers are complex, involving a spectrum of aesthetic attitudes and cultural values. Heinrich died on the eve of the Civil War, and when that was over, American musical composition became increasingly dominated by conformity to and emulation of European (mainly German) academic standards, as represented by composers such as J. K. Paine and Dudley Buck. Symphony orchestras catered to the standard classics and the neoconformists. Music, according to J. S. Dwight, was to be regarded as a "beautiful corrective of our crudities." Heinrich's music was neither "polite" nor polished, neither academic nor conformist. It was like Niagara Falls compared to the fountains of Versailles. Much of it was also very difficult to perform, and very little of it was published (especially the larger works). Much of his orchestral music might have disappeared entirely had the manuscripts not been acquired by the Library of Congress. This was the primary source for the twentieth-century revival of his music.

A lone precursor to later Heinrich "revivalists" was Robert Whitney, who in the fall of 1951 conducted three performances of Heinrich's overture *The Wildwood Troubadour* with the Louisville Orchestra. He was followed, as already mentioned, by Howard Shanet, with two large Indianist works for orchestra. But the big turning point came in the 1970s, with the generation born between 1934 and 1944. Its leaders had doubtless been alerted by William Treat Upton's excellent biography of Heinrich, originally published in 1939 and reprinted in 1967. Two of the leading "revivalists," David Barron and Neely Bruce, wrote important dissertations on Heinrich's music, the former dealing with the songs, the latter with the piano music.[27] Both also brought his music before the public, Barron as a concert singer, Bruce as pianist and choral director. The latter was responsible for the first recording devoted entirely to the music of Heinrich, issued in 1973.[28] As leader of the American Music Group, he performed a quantity of Heinrich's vocal music, including that extraordinary opus *La Toilette de la cour*, described as a "concerto for voice and piano," which evokes with amazing virtuosity the emotions of the young Queen Victoria when she parted from her beloved Albert. More than any other work, this piece confirms Bruce's statement that insistence "upon extravagance as a positive value is the very essence of Heinrich's music."[29]

Here we should recall that it was Charles Ives who said: "Perhaps music is the art of speaking extravagantly." And it can be maintained that the timing of the Heinrich revival had something to do with our belated recognition of Ives and his highly idiosyncratic concept of musical "extravagance." Bruce also points out that "Heinrich's use of pre-composed materials is strikingly similar to Ives' use of such tunes."[30] There is also the nonfunctional character of Heinrich's harmonies, for which he compensates by making "non-harmonic parameters, notably texture and rhythm, but occasionally form and register, so significant and interesting that they amply compensate for lack of harmonic foundation."[31]

In contrast to the approved nineteenth-century norm of thematic development and formalized structure, Heinrich's music is largely ornamental and nonrepetitive. As David Barron writes: "In Heinrich's vocal works, not only are themes embellished, but the formal structure is embellished with preludes, interludes, and postludes. Heinrich's approach . . . was not evolutionary or developmental, but one of ornamenting a basic, melodic-harmonic structure."[32] Wilbur Maust writes of the orchestral music that

> the prevailing texture in Heinrich's symphonies is melody with accompaniment. Embellishing counter-melodies or counter-motifs and the imitative treatment of the themes, along with a wide variety of accompanimental patterns enliven the basically homophonic texture. Several works have sections which use two-part invertible counterpoint. . . . Tonal ambiguity is created by brief modulations which often avoid the tonic chord of the new key. Surprising harmonic progressions are the result of augmented sixth chords built on almost any scale degree, of deceptive resolutions of dominant or secondary dominant sevenths, and of chromatic transitions which lead to an unexpected key or back to the one just abandoned.[33]

Whatever the pattern or procedure, Heinrich's beloved chromaticism is always present as the mark of consistency.

Heinrich wrote about fifty works for orchestra (some with vocal parts), nearly 400 songs and other vocal works, a quantity of piano pieces, and some chamber music. Approximately 300 compositions, mostly songs and piano pieces, were printed during his lifetime. (*The Dawning of Music in Kentucky* and *The Western Minstrel* were reprinted in 1972.) His orchestral works remained in manuscript as of 1980. At that time about twenty pieces, small and large, had been recorded.

Indirectly, by opening up new vistas and values, the music and the writings of articulate and opinionated composers such as Ives, Cowell, Partch, and Cage prepared the way for an appreciation of Anthony Philip Heinrich, who—in spite of being hailed as "the Beethoven of America"—was always his own *eccentric* self (i.e., as commonly defined, deviating from a conventional or established pattern), hence uniquely articulate and quintessentially Romantic.

Notes

1. Cited in Russel Blaine Nye, *Society and Culture in America, 1830–1860*, p. 245.
2. William H. Goetzmann, *Exploration and Empire*, p. 181.
3. Roderick Nash, *Wilderness and the American Mind*, pp. 49–50.
4. Goetzmann, *Exploration and Empire*, p. 191.
5. *Criterion: Literary and Critical Journal* 2 (May 24, 1856): 58.
6. Anthony Philip Heinrich, "Scrapbook," Library of Congress, Washington, D.C., p. 1027; quoted in William Treat Upton, *Anthony Philip Heinrich*, p. 4.

7. Introduction to Anthony Philip Heinrich, *The Dawning of Music in Kentucky . . . /The Western Minstrel.*

8. *Philadelphia Literary & Musical Magazine* 4 (Apr. 26, 1819); quoted in Upton, *Anthony Philip Heinrich*, p. 260.

9. Upton, *Anthony Philip Heinrich*, p. 47.

10. Heinrich, notice to the public (Philadelphia, 1820), opposite title page of *The Western Minstrel.* See Heinrich, *The Dawning of Music in Kentucky . . . /The Western Minstrel.*

11. Ibid.

12. Frank Neely Bruce, liner notes to *The Dawning of Music in Kentucky*, Vanguard VSD 71178(stereo) and VSQ 30023(quad).

13. Quoted in Upton, *Anthony Philip Heinrich*, pp. 66–67.

14. Quoted in ibid., p. 68.

15. *Euterpeiad* (Sept. 1823); quoted in ibid., pp. 78–79.

16. Nye, *Society and Culture in America, 1830–1860*, p. 73.

17. Ibid., pp. 73–74.

18. See Upton, *Anthony Philip Heinrich*, p. 280.

19. See ibid., p. 281.

20. Heinrich, "Scrapbook," p. 39; quoted in ibid., pp. 175–76.

21. From an extremely interesting letter by Heinrich to a friend in Boston (July 11, 1846), in which he takes potshots at J. S. Dwight and laments the "instrumental bankruptcy with which I was so cruelly served by many delinquint performers in Boston." See Heinrich, "Scrapbook," p. 517; quoted in Upton, *Anthony Philip Heinrich*, pp. 203–4.

22. Recorded on New World Records NW 208, with extensive commentary by David Barron.

23. To avoid confusion, it should be noted that Heinrich gave the title "Columbiad" to at least four different compositions, otherwise identifiable only by their subtitles.

24. Upton, *Anthony Philip Heinrich*, pp. 114–15.

25. See ibid., p. 282.

26. Letter to Mr. Seaton, mayor of Washington, D.C., Mar. 2, 1843, in Heinrich, "Scrapbook," p. 39; quoted in ibid., p. 176.

27. David Milton Barron, "The Early Vocal Works of Anthony Philip Heinrich Based on American Themes"; Frank Neely Bruce, "The Piano Pieces of Anthony Philip Heinrich Contained in *The Dawning of Music in Kentucky* and *The Western Minstrel.*"

28. *The Dawning of Music in Kentucky;* performed by the American Music Group; Frank Neely Bruce, director and piano solo. See n. 12 above.

29. Bruce, "The Piano Pieces of Anthony Philip Heinrich," p. 367.

30. Ibid., p. 353.

31. Ibid., p. 361.

32. Barron, "The Early Vocal Works of Anthony Philip Heinrich," p. 71.

33. Wilbur Richard Maust, "The Symphonies of Anthony Philip Heinrich Based on American Themes," pp. 208–9.

Chapter 16
Exotic Romanticism

ex-ot-ic (ĕg-zŏt´ ĭk), *adj*. 1. From another part of the world; not indigenous; foreign. 2. Having the charm of the unfamiliar; strikingly and intriguingly unusual or beautiful.
—*The American Heritage Dictionary of the English Language*

The cult of the exotic was an important aspect of Romanticism, and we have noted how the wilderness of the American West enticed not only explorers and pioneers but also artists and writers. In contrast to the formidable cordilleras and canyons of the Far West, the eastern mountain ranges such as the Catskills and the Adirondacks provided picturesque grandeur on a scale compatible with the aesthetic and ethical sensibilities of high-minded but unadventurous individuals who sought to elevate their souls through communion with Nature.

The paradigm of this edifying approach to an impressive natural environment is the painting by Asher B. Durand, *Kindred Spirits* (1849), that depicts the poet William Cullen Bryant and the painter Thomas Cole conversing on a rocky ledge overlooking a deep gorge of the Catskills. They appear, however, to be less rapt in contemplating the grandeur of the scene than in studying some geological formation on the opposite side of the gorge. But Heaven only knows what mystical message they may have found in those cliffs, for as Durand wrote, Nature, "in its wondrous structure and functions that minister to our well-being is fraught with high and holy meaning, only surpassed by the light of Revelation."[1]

We may well believe that Nature could be "fraught with high and holy meaning" for the New England poet who wrote *Thanatopsis* or the high-minded painter of *The Voyage of Life* (Cole), who firmly believed that "Man is in need of a Redeemer."[2] Yet for another American artist—a musician—who was their contemporary (and doubtless badly in need of a Redeemer), the effect of contemplating Nature was not so much edifying as nepenthean, an invitation to self-indulgent reverie, a release from social pressures and the demands of civilization. He, too, had his wilderness, his mountains and immensities; but they were of the tropics, of those once-fabled "Indies," about which he wrote in his memoirs: "The islands of the Antilles impart a voluptuous languor that is contagious; it is a poison that slowly infiltrates all the senses and benumbs the soul with a kind of ecstatic torpor."³

This nepenthean "poison" of the senses was an irresistible magnet for Louis Moreau Gottschalk, born and nurtured in the semitropical lushness of Louisiana, pampered and applauded in the salons of Paris and the courts of Europe, acclaimed in the Old and New World as a precocious composer and a brilliant virtuoso of the piano. Yet from this acclaim and its inevitable exigencies he suddenly fled, to enjoy five years of wanderlust in the tropics—"years foolishly spent, thrown to the wind, as if life were infinite, and youth eternal." He later recalled these years of vagabondage,

> during which I have roamed at random under the blue skies of the tropics, indolently permitting myself to be carried away by chance, giving a concert wherever I found a piano, sleeping wherever the night overtook me—on the grass of the savanna, or under the palm-leaf roof of a *veguero* [tobacco-grower] with whom I partook of a tortilla, coffee, and a banana. . . .
>
> When I became tired of the same horizon, I crossed an arm of the sea and landed on a neighboring island or on the Spanish Main. . . . Sometimes the idol of an ignorant *"pueblo,"* to whom I have played some of their simple ballads, I have stopped for five, six, or eight months among them . . . or, detained in a village where the piano was still unknown, by the ties of an affection with which my fingers had nothing to do (O rare and blessed affections!), I forgot the world, and lived only for two large black eyes, which veiled themselves with tears whenever I spoke of beginning my vagabond course again, again living as the bird sings, as the flower opens, as the brook flows, forgetful of the past, careless of the future.⁴

Then, with heart and purse exhausted, came a revulsion: "Seized with a profound disgust of the world and of myself . . . I hastened to hide in the wilds on the extinguished volcano of N——[on the island of Guadaloupe], where I lived for many months like a cenobite. . . ."⁵ This interlude of austerity brought him into closer communion with the grandeur of Nature:

> Perched upon the edge of the crater, on the very top of the mountain, my cabin overlooked the whole country. The rock on which it was built hung over a precipice whose depths were concealed by cacti, convolvuluses, and bamboos. . . . Every evening I moved my piano out upon the terrace, and there, in view of the most beautiful scenery in the world, which was bathed by the serene and limpid atmosphere of the tropics, I played, *for myself alone,* everything

that the scene opened before me inspired—and what a scene! Imagine a gigantic amphitheater, such as an army of Titans might have carved out in the mountains; to the right and left virgin forests filled with wild and distant harmonies that are like the voice of silence; before me sixty miles of country whose magic perspective is rendered more marvelous by the transparency of the atmosphere; over my head the azure of the sky; below the declivities, surmounted by the mountain, descending gradually toward the plain; farther on, the green savannas, then, lower, a gray point—it is the town; and farther on again the immensity of the ocean, whose line of deep blue forms the horizon.

Behind me was a rock on which broke a torrent of melted snow that turned from its course, leaped with a desperate bound, and engulfed itself in the depths of the precipice that gaped under my window.[6]

Gottschalk himself had "leaped with a desperate bound" into the lush sensuality of the tropics, preferring to be engulfed in their precipitous depths rather than to cope with the constraints and hypocrisies of Anglo-American society and the neo-puritanical idealism of the New England transcendentalists such as Ralph Waldo Emerson and John Sullivan Dwight—the latter his particular bête noire. Nor did he regard with less antipathy the North American cult of material progress via industry and technology. Speaking of "the demisavages of the savannas," he finds that they have reason to "prefer their poetic barbarism to our barbarous progress."[7]

It has been said that "all Romantics regarded Nature as the temple of God." But surely this is too sweeping a statement. It may be true of Wordsworth but not of Byron, of Whittier but not of Poe, of Victor Hugo but not of Baudelaire—and it is certainly not true of Gottschalk, the quintessentially Romantic musician of the New World. For him, Nature signified an escape from the industrialized society of the United States and its materialistic pressures. It was both balm and stimulus. In one of his tours in the Far West, after a grueling schedule, he reached the town of Grass Valley and his spirit immediately revived: "Here the roses climb to the roof tops . . . the brooks gayly roll their crystal waters, wantoning amid rocks in their way. . . . I breathe, I live again."[8]

The roses climbing to the rooftops are a symbol of extravagance and excess, in contrast to the trim and orderly gardens of New England. The "gayly" wantoning brooks are the antithesis of the "high and holy meaning" that Durand attributed to Nature. For Gottschalk, no earthly paradise would be complete without an Eve as temptress. Writing of his sojourn at Caimito, in the interior of Cuba, he said: "Théophile Gautier would have gone mad in contemplating this paradise, in which only an Eve was wanting."[9] His temperamental kinship was with such Romantic poets as Byron,

Baudelaire, and Gautier. There was in his character a streak of Byronic cyni-
cism and self-destructiveness. He burned himself out at the age of forty, as
Byron had done at thirty-six. Both died far from their homelands, the poet
attempting to be heroic in Greece, the musician in an apotheosis of glory
and grandeur in Brazil. Both achieved a disreputable notoriety, both defied the proprieties and pieties of "respectable" society, and both attained
the pinnacle of Romanticism in art and life.

The American critic William F. Apthorp, reviewing a posthumous
Chant de guerre (1859) by Gottschalk, wrote: "As Chopin was the most perfect exponent of the Polish element in music, so was Gottschalk the great
interpreter of the Hispano-Ethiopian element, and by as much as the Polish esthetic spirit is higher and more developed than the Negro, by so
much was Chopin higher than Gottschalk."[10] To this fascinating example
of ethnocentric aesthetics, we may add the epithet "a Chopin for Creoles,"
applied to Gottschalk by John Sullivan Dwight. Both critics pay tribute to
Gottschalk by comparing him with Chopin, but what the left hand gives,
the right hand takes away. How could an artist identified with Hispano-
Ethiopian-Creole culture be placed on a par with an artist who, while not
blessed with the benefits of Anglo-Saxon-Germanic supremacy, was nevertheless untainted by contact with inferior breeds?

A glance at our hero's background may help to elucidate these para-
doxes. The region of Louisiana and the city of New Orleans, where Louis
Moreau Gottschalk was born on May 8, 1829, were certainly an exotic milieu compared with the rest of the United States. Founded by the French in
1718, New Orleans became a city of strong contrasts, from refined elegance
to unbridled depravity. Large numbers of Negro slaves were brought from
Africa and later from the West Indies. In 1762 France ceded Louisiana to
Spain, and New Orleans became a Spanish colonial city, although much of
the French culture remained. In 1800 Spain retroceded Louisiana to
France, but before the French authorities could take possession, the territory was purchased by the United States, and in 1803 New Orleans became
officially an American city. Yet culturally and racially it remained a mixture
of French, Spanish, African, and Anglo-American elements. In the first decade of the nineteenth century it received a large influx of French families
and other refugees from the West Indies, as an aftermath of the slave uprisings and revolutions. The refugees included many blacks and "free persons
of color," who took an active part in the musical life of the city. The term
Creole was originally applied to persons of European ancestry born and

raised in the New World; later it was also applied to blacks and "free persons of color," as well as to the *patois,* or dialect, that they spoke.[11]

Gottschalk, like the city of his birth, had a mixed cultural heritage. His father, born in London, was of Jewish extraction and had been educated in Germany.[12] After migrating to New Orleans, where he established a brokerage business, he married Aimée de Bruslé, of a prominent French Creole family. Of their several children, Moreau (as he was always called) proved to be precociously gifted musically. He studied both violin and piano but chose the latter for his professional career. Shortly after his thirteenth birthday, in May 1842, he was sent to France to complete his education and to pursue his musical training with the best teachers available in Paris. Through a family connection on his mother's side, he was received in the social circles of the elite and indeed was quickly "lionized" both as pianist and composer—as well as for his charming manners and good looks. He had, of course, spoken French almost from the cradle, and it remained his primary language throughout his life, although he also spoke Spanish and English— the latter with an accent. At his first public concert in Paris, just before his sixteenth birthday, he was warmly praised by Chopin, whose Concerto in E Minor he had brilliantly performed. Thereafter his rise was rapid, with triumphant tours in France, in Switzerland, and especially in Spain, where he remained for nearly two years, a favorite of the court as well as of the people. (His Spanish pieces rank with the best written by any foreigner.)

It was above all the fascination of the exotic—the strange and unfamiliar—that accounted for the immediate impact of Gottschalk's music in Europe. Hector Berlioz, who admired and befriended the precocious youth from Louisiana, was perceptive in his praise: "Gottschalk was born in America, whence he has brought a host of curious chants from the Creoles and the Negroes; he has made from them the themes of his most delicious compositions. Everybody in Europe now knows *Bamboula, Le Bananier, Le Mancenillier, La Savane,* and twenty other ingenious fantasies in which the nonchalant graces of tropical melody assuage so agreeably our restless and insatiable passion for novelty."[13] Théophile Gautier also struck the note of exotic Romanticism: "If Mr. Gottschalk has been able, although still young, to acquire this individuality that escapes so many others, it is perhaps owing to the fact that, after having formed his talent by solid studies, he has left it to wander carelessly in the fragrant savannas of his country, from which he had brought back to us its colors and perfumes."[14]

At this time, of course, Gottschalk had not yet actually "wandered carelessly" through any "fragrant savannas," in Louisiana or elsewhere. But during his boyhood he had absorbed many of the familiar Creole melodies (most of them based on familiar French tunes) that could be heard almost anywhere in the older section of New Orleans, especially in the so-called *Vieux Carré* or French Quarter, where the Gottschalks lived. Thus, for example, writing to his father from Paris in 1851, he tells him that he has written a piece based on "a Creole air, that you in New Orleans must have often heard." The piece was *Le Bananier* (The banana tree), and the tune to which he refers was that of "En avant, grenadié" (a colloquial contraction of *grenadiers*), a well-known French popular song. Curiously, Gottschalk's piece was published with the subtitle *Chanson nègre*—very likely to emphasize its exotic appeal (anticipating the craze for "la musique des noirs" in Paris of the 1920s).

Le Bananier was one of three pieces based on Creole tunes that had a tremendous success in Europe and that I have called the "Louisiana Trilogy." Its companion pieces are *La Savane: Ballade créole* and *Bamboula: Danse des nègres*. All three were composed between 1844 and 1846, when Gottschalk was still a teenager. In *La Savane* he used a melody from the Creole song "Lolotte." Poor Lolotte, says the song, has only a heartache, while Calalou, her rival in love, has an embroidered petticoat and a Madras kerchief. It is interesting to note that the melody is similar to that of the American play-party song "Skip to My Lou."

The piece that created the greatest sensation was *Bamboula*, incongruously dedicated "à sa Majesté Isabelle II, Reine des Espagnes." Its subtitle, *Danse des nègres*, is justified by the fact that the *bamboula* was widely popular among blacks, especially in the West Indies and Louisiana. But in New Orleans, if we are to believe the words of a Creole song, "black and white both danced the bamboula." Gottschalk treats it both as a dance, with a strongly marked syncopated rhythm, and as a melody (*"il canto ben marcato"*). He evidently used two well-known, syncopated Creole tunes, "Musieu banjo" (see example below) and "Quand patate la cuite."

"Musieu Banjo"

Although the "Louisiana Trilogy" represents Gottschalk's most brilliant and original achievement as a composer during his ten-year stay in Europe, he also participated fully in the Romantic trend of the moment, emulating Chopin and Liszt in writing études, ballades, mazurkas, waltzes, marches, variations, descriptive pieces, works for bravura display, and operatic transcriptions.[15] In all, he wrote more than fifty pieces in this period. His achievement was twofold: to Europe he brought American exoticism, and to America he brought the full tide of European Romanticism.

In January 1853, at the age of twenty-three, already famous and triumphant, Gottschalk returned to America—but not to his native Louisiana. He did eventually visit New Orleans, but now his immediate aims were to conquer New York as a renowned virtuoso of the piano and to organize concert tours that would presumably be profitable. His father was in debt and in ailing health, and Gottschalk felt financially responsible for his mother and his younger brothers and sisters.

To dazzle the city he presented the following come-on: "L. M. Gottschalk respectfully announces to the musical public of New York that he will give a grand concert on FRIDAY EVENING, FEBRUARY 11, at Niblo's Salon." His entrepreneur stated below that "Tickets One and Two Dollars, according to location," would be available and the "Doors open at 6 1/2 o'clock."[16]

Although Gottschalk was the kingpin, he was "assisted" by four other well-known performers, three men and a woman, of whom the latter, Mme Rose de Vries, went for Verdi and Meyerbeer. Gottschalk also went in for Verdi, as together with Mr. Richard Hoffman he presented " 'Jerusalem,' Grand Triumphal," a "Fantasia for two Pianos," taken from the French version of Verdi's *I Lombardi*. Only one Creole piece, "The Bananier, Negro Dance," was presented. Gottschalk then finished with the "Carnival of Venice, composed and executed by" himself (although it has been suggested that it was taken from the famous Niccolò Paganini, who did write *Il carnevale di Venezia*). The public response was gratifying, the press generally favorable—and the receipts disappointing. But his next concert was a great success, and by the season of 1855–56, when he gave eighty concerts in New York, his admirers far outnumbered his detractors.

In Boston, however, he was confronted by his nemesis, the redoubtable John Sullivan Dwight, who chastised him for not playing more "classical" music. The name of Dwight continually reappears in Gottschalk's diary as a symbol of whatever he found distressing or depressing in American culture. Stung by continuous sniping from the *Journal of Music,* he described "Dwight's paper" as "the reservoir of every little bilious envy, of every irritating impertinence, of all sickly spleen. . . ."[17]

Yet, resisting the further lures of Europe, Gottschalk pursued his concert career in America with extraordinary perseverance and fortitude. I like to see a symbolic coincidence in the fact that the first American railroad was begun in 1829—the year of his birth! He claimed to have traveled 80,000 miles by train through the United States and Canada—and surely that is no exaggeration, considering that he covered not only the big cities but also the smaller towns, from Canandaigua to Kalamazoo, from Oswego to Sandusky, from Peoria to Carson City. Wherever he went he talked to people in every walk of life, made copious observations in his diary, and endured the vicissitudes of a traveling salesman while holding his head high as an artist—but never too proud to play what he knew the public liked best: his own music.

Two of his most popular pieces, *The Banjo* (1854–55) and *The Last Hope* (1853–54), which are poles apart in style and character, vividly illustrate the wide scope of Gottschalk's appeal, from the grotesque to the saccharine. *The Banjo* is actually labeled *Grotesque fantasie,* and further described as "An American Sketch." The term *grotesque* is sufficient to identify it with blackface minstrelsy, although this is merely a point of departure for a brilliant paraphrase and a virtuosic extension of the syncopated banjo style.

With *The Last Hope,* subtitled *Religious Meditation,* we enter the realm of pious sentimentality that so widely prevailed in nineteenth-century America. While the genre certainly abounded in America, as a staple of the parlor piano, none of its products had such a wide and enduring success as the perennial *Last Hope.* It forms, indeed, an indestructible triptych, together with two other lachrymose gems by Gottschalk: *The Dying Poet* and *Morte!!* (*She Is Dead*)—both dating from the 1860s and probably immortal in spite of their titles.

In the summer of 1857 a Cuban newspaper published a poetic eulogy, illustrated with a superb colored engraving, titled "Funeral Homage to the Bard of the Tropics." The allegedly deceased "bard" was Gottschalk, who had in fact been recently ill in Santiago de Cuba but by this time was alive and active in the tropics. The premature obituaries and eulogies that appeared in many local periodicals at least gave evidence of the esteem and affection that the Spanish- and French-speaking people of the Antilles had for the gifted and generous musician from Louisiana who spoke their languages fluently, made love to their women, and did not behave at all like a "Yanqui."

We have already shared some of his experiences, perceptions, and emotions during the five years (1857–62) that he spent in the West Indies and the Spanish Main. But these were also years of creative activity and remarkable accomplishments, to which we should now give our attention.

Gottschalk had previously spent a year in Cuba (1854–55), so it was now like a second home to him. Although he traveled and concertized widely during his second stay in the Caribbean area, Cuba—and especially Havana—remained his principal base. Although he was glad to write piano pieces that sold well and provided the bulk of his concert repertory, Gottschalk was also ambitious to compose in the larger orchestral and vocal forms, and to have them performed on the grand scale that befitted a disciple of Berlioz. In Cuba he was indeed regarded as a composer of the first rank, and no effort was spared to provide the opportunities and resources that he needed.

Stimulated by the prospect of a "grand festival" in Havana, Gottschalk set to work and quickly composed a one-act opera evoking the rural scenes of Cuba, *Escenas campestres* (also known by its French title, *Fête champêtre cubaine*), as well as a *Triumphal Hymn* and a *Grand March*. The event took place on February 17, 1860, with an orchestra consisting of 650 performers (including all the military bands of the capital), 87 choristers, 15 solo singers, 50 drums, and 80 trumpets. It was a BIG success!

According to some accounts, this "mammoth festival" also included a symphony in two movements, *La Nuit des tropiques* (The night of the tropics), which Gottschalk had composed in 1858–59. In any case, we know that it was performed at another big concert in Havana, on April 17, 1861. The first movement, titled "Nuit dans les tropiques" and marked *Andante,* is sectional in structure and lyrical in mood. It fully justifies the subtitle of the work, *Symphonie romantique.* Its 6/8 time signature is typical of Hispanic-Cuban folk music, as contrasted with the 2/4 time of Afro-Caribbean music, which forms the rhythmic basis (with many variants) of the second movement. The latter, titled "Une Fête sous les tropiques" (A festival in the tropics), is marked *Allegro moderato,* and the instrumentation calls for a large array of African-type percussion, including a battery of bamboula drums. Historically, it marks the first appearance of Afro-Caribbean instruments in a symphonic composition.[18]

It is interesting to note that in spite of its "primitive" character (or the use of non-European elements), the second movement of the Symphony no. 1 includes considerable counterpoint, culminating in a fugato section. Apropos of this, Robert Offergeld makes an interesting comment on the symphony: "It isn't a German academic symphony but it is a beautifully realized symphonic concept, not a piano piece blown up. As written by an American in 1860 [*sic*] it is a historic treasure—as is, for other reasons, the fugato section of the second movement, which is I'm certain Gottschalk's considered and ironic reply to Dwight and the other Teutonic snobs."[19]

The *Escenas campestres,* ostensibly a one-act opera, is more aptly described as a "bucolic cantata," or perhaps comparable to the Spanish *tonadilla,* with dancing. Some of the music is taken from a lively and graceful *Danza* (op. 33), which Gottschalk wrote in Puerto Rico (1857). This is one of numerous dances for piano that he composed during his long sojourn in the Antilles, and which many of his admirers (myself among them) consider to be his most artistically satisfying and sensuously gratifying compositions.

At the time when Gottschalk was active in Cuba, he enjoyed the friendship and esteem of two Cuban composers who where also pianists and who were writing various types of *danzas cubanas* such as the *danzón,* the *contradanza,* the *habanera,* and the *guajira.* They were Manuel Saumell (1817–70) and Nicolas Ruiz Espadero (1832–90). The former paid tribute to Gottschalk by dedicating to him a piece titled *La Luisiana.* Espadero, with whom Gottschalk formed a close friendship, had an important role in editing and preserving some of the latter's musical manuscripts, which might otherwise have been lost to posterity. These include the *Grand tarantelle* for piano and orchestra, of which Espadero made a transcription for two pianos that was published posthumously.

While we can scarcely avoid the assumption that Gottschalk took as his models the Cuban pieces of Saumell and Espadero, it is nevertheless evident that his Louisiana-Creole background and his extraordinary assimilative capacity, nourished by his long sojourn in the Antilles, resulted in a body of music that is both authentic and distinctive. In a headnote to one of his Cuban dances we read: "The Author . . . has endeavored to convey an idea of the singular rythm [*sic*] and charming character, of the music which exists among the Creoles of the Spanish Antilles."[20] He also wrote of "the singing sonorousness and passionate languor which are the peculiar traits of Creole music."[21] But there are vigor and vivacity too, as manifested in the rhythmic verve and vivacity of *La gallina* (The hen). In *Ojos criollos*

Louis Moreau Gottschalk. Photo courtesy of the Music Division, The New York Public Library at Lincoln Center, Astor, Lenox and Tilden Foundations.

(Creole eyes) there is a fascinating combination of the swaying *habanera* rhythm in the bass and the so-called cakewalk figure in the treble.

In January 1862 Gottschalk received a letter from the impresario Max Strakosch offering him an engagement for a round of concerts in the United States. In his own words, he "hesitated an instant, cast a last glance at the past, gave a sigh, and signed. The dream was finished—I was saved, but who shall say if, in this salvage, youth and poesy had not been wrecked?"[22] He was going to a land where "poesy" was overshadowed by conflict, where many hopes had been wrecked, and the flower of youth was perishing in the carnage of battle. After going to the American Consulate and swearing allegiance to the Union, he sailed on January 18 from Havana, which he was never to see again.

His New York concert on February 11 marked the beginning of strenuous concertizing and persistent composing—the latter bringing his total output to nearly 300 pieces. In spite of the war, concerts (at least in the North) went on, although not without some danger and difficulty, as when Gottschalk's two oversize grand pianos went astray in the aftermath of Gettysburg. As Gottschalk never did anything halfway, he threw himself with energy and enthusiasm into uplifting the spirit of the Union cause. In the spring of 1862 he published a rousing patriotic concert piece for piano titled *Union,* paraphrasing and combining the three most popular "national" airs: "Star-Spangled Banner," "Yankee Doodle," and "Hail Columbia." (Unfortunately, it was dedicated to General McClellan, whose star would soon set.)

The following year he composed another "grand concert paraphrase" for piano, on George F. Root's "The Battle Cry of Freedom," which he greatly admired. He wrote in his diary: "[It] ought to become our national air; it has animation, its harmonies are distinguished, it has tune, rhythm, and I discover in it a kind of epic coloring, something sadly heroic, which a battle song should have."[23] Root's patriotic tune was also known as "We'll Rally round the Flag," and a contemporary writer tells us that during a patriotic rally Gottschalk "sprang to the piano again, and gave such an astounding rhapsody on George F. Root's well-known 'We'll Rally Round the Flag' as is entirely beyond description."[24] Gottschalk in action was always spectacular.

In February 1865 Gottschalk signed a contract to concertize in California. Preparing to depart by sea on April 3, he wrote: "It was not until then that I discovered, by feeling them break one by one, by how many invisible threads I was attached to the United States."[25] Four days earlier, at a farewell concert in his honor, he had taken part in a performance of "The Battle Cry of Freedom," arranged for six pianos, after which he was presented with a silver wreath studded with amethysts and rubies. The accompanying verbal tribute stated that Americans would cherish the memory of Gottschalk as Europeans do that of Mozart, Mendelssohn, and Beethoven. Prior to his departure Gottschalk distributed a farewell card that betrays both his emotion and his foreboding:

> ### To My Friends and the Public
>
> On the eve of my departure from this country—my native land—the land of my earliest affections—I feel that I must express my heartfelt regret on parting with the public, whose kindness has sustained me throughout my public career. To all my friends, who have given me so many proofs of warm interest, I bid you a warm farewell. The clouds that conceal the future are transparent and bright only in the morning of life. I have already come to the age when they show more deception than joys. Even as I say to all farewell, methinks a distant echo faintly answers "adieu"! A last, a long farewell![26]

The voyage to California involved crossing the Isthmus of Panama by railroad, amid "thick jungles of mangroves, bindweed, bamboos, and palms." Then aboard the steamer *Constitution*, while "the dull monotony of the life on board continues to unfold slowly and heavily day by day under the heat of an atmosphere like a lead foundry, like a benumbed boa slowly unfolding his rings to the perpendicular rays of an African sun." Acapulco was "an agreeable diversion to the monotony of the ship." Finally, on the morning of April 27: "The sky is blue and the air is pure. We shall be in San Francisco today. We see the mountains and the whole coast distinctly. The steamer slowly advances. The mountains unfold themselves majestically to our astonished sight. We are entering into the bay. The pen and the imagination are powerless to portray the splendor of the spectacle that is opened to our eyes."[27]

In San Francisco he found that both his fame and his music had preceded him. In the ladies' parlor of the Cosmopolitan Hotel, he saw on the piano a copy of *The Maiden's Prayer*—at which he exclaims, "et tu quoque, O California!"[28] Everything pleased him, but he had great difficulty rounding up thirteen pianists to join him in performing his own arrangement of the March from *Tannhäuser* for fourteen pianos! He had a truly extravagant passion for the multiple piano ensemble, which he endeavored to propagate throughout the Americas. On September 16 the *Daily Alta California* announced that "Gottschalk, who seems to be indefatigable, is composing a piece for THIRTY pianos with orchestra accompaniment."²⁹ Was this genuine megalomania, or merely California hyperbole?

At all events Gottschalk was feted and dined and wined; applauded, acclaimed, and adulated. At a gala banquet on August 25, he was presented with a gold medal nine inches in circumference. On one side his initials were affixed in diamonds, surrounded with a wreath of laurels in diamonds and rubies, and on the reverse the arms of California were encircled with diamonds. A local newspaper reported: "This present is worthy of a monarch, and it appertained to the Queen City of the Pacific to present to the first musician of America a testimony which was at the same time worthy of the artist and in harmony with the magnificent generosity and the marvelous development of the modern El Dorado."³⁰

We do not know what effect these lavish tributes may have had on Gottschalk's privately expressed opinion that "California is a humbug." Moreover, he declared, "the women are not pretty."³¹ Nevertheless, the fair sex was his undoing. On a Sunday afternoon in September, he and a friend took two young ladies from the Oakland Female Seminary out for a long drive. Returning at a late hour, the girls were apprehended, and the next day the scandal broke out. Anyone as successful as Gottschalk makes enemies, and one of them fed the press with scandal fodder in the name of morality. "Villains Who Should Suffer Death" was a typical headline. "Tar and feathers" and "horsewhipping" were recommended for "bawdy miscreants who should be shot like rabid dogs."³²

Inevitably the scandal and the slander spread like the proverbial wildfire. Urged by his friends to vindicate himself, Gottschalk replied, "It is beneath my dignity as a man of honor to notice such slanders."³³ But it was imperative for him to leave San Francisco, where he faced not only disgrace and vituperation but also physical violence. Aided by the French consul, he clandestinely boarded a ship and made his escape, heading for South America. From Panama he continued down the Pacific coast to Peru and Chile; then around Cape Horn to Argentina and Uruguay; finally, Brazil: four years of glory and adulation before the final curtain.

Although Gottschalk's last years in South America were everywhere filled with enthusiastic acclaim, it was along the Atlantic coast that he achieved his greatest and most enduring triumphs, both as performer and as composer. Nor should we overlook the impression he made as an ambassador of goodwill from the United States and a pioneer proponent of Pan-Americanism. That he could fully rise to the occasion is confirmed by the following statement that he published in *La tribuna* of Buenos Aires (October 19, 1867):

> Son of the great republic to the north, I became accustomed from earliest youth to considering the entire Western Hemisphere, irrespective of language or latitude, as the common fatherland of all who desire progress and liberty. As a citizen of the United States, I find myself profoundly grateful for your divination of the basic Americanist urge that drives me forward. Were only my limited abilities the equal of my boundless desires and my limitless patriotic impulse, New World art would soar to new zeniths.[34]

In addition to such staples as *The Banjo,* and *Ojos criollos,* he included in his Buenos Aires programs the *Grand tarantelle* for piano with orchestra, and *Grand Caprice on the Argentine National Anthem.* During his stay in Uruguay he composed the Symphony no. 2, named in honor of that nation's capital, "To Montevideo," and subtitled *Symphonie romantique pour grand orchestre* (1868). This is in one movement with seven sections, the third being an arrangement of the Uruguayan national anthem. In section five there is the familiar combination of "Hail Columbia" and "Yankee Doodle"—so that we have here the first inter-American symphony of the New World.

It was in Brazil that Gottschalk, the conquering hero of Pan-American Romanticism, achieved the ultimate triumph of his career. To a friend in Boston, Gottschalk wrote: "My concerts here are a perfect *furore*. All my houses are sold eight days in advance. . . . The emperor, imperial family, and court never missed yet one of my entertainments."[35] The liberal Emperor Dom Pedro II was both an enthusiastic admirer and a generous patron. And to his publishers in New York, Gottschalk wrote: "Herewith I send you a new piece ('Morte,'—'She is Dead'),—a lamentation. . . . Ever since I have played it, it has been encored; and a great many women have hysterics and weep over it—maybe owing to the romantic title."[36] Here Gottschalk was too modest: *he* was always the emotional catalyst for the fair sex.

In August 1869 Gottschalk was stricken with yellow fever. But by September he had miraculously recovered and was planning "three grand festivals, with 800 performers, at which I will produce my symphonies, and the grand 'Marche Triumphale' I dedicated to the emperor."[37] As had been done in Havana, all the military bands in the district were placed at his disposal. In all there were some 650 performers. The concerts were scheduled for November 24 and 26, with a piano recital for the Philharmonic Society in between. Although the first program was a huge success, Gottschalk was too weak to conduct the second festival concert, which had to be canceled.

Gottschalk was indeed fatally stricken, although the exact causes remain a matter of controversy. He was removed to the suburb of Tijuca, where, after much suffering, he died at four o'clock on the morning of December 18. The next day his embalmed body was exposed in the state hall of the Philharmonic Society of Rio de Janeiro before burial at a cemetery outside the capital. The newspapers printed glowing eulogies of the dead musician whom they had both praised and caricatured. (Unfortunately, his personal effects were confiscated and dispersed.)

The following year Gottschalk's remains were taken to New York City and, after a funeral service in St. Stephen's Church, were reinterred in Brooklyn's Greenwood Cemetery on October 3, 1870. He was far from his natal soil of *la Louisianne;* but he had always been the adventurous virtuoso of the Western world and the volatile lover of exotic lands: the grave was his only home.

Notes

1. Quoted in James Thomas Flexner, *That Wilder Image,* pp. 72–73.
2. Ibid., p. 40.
3. Louis Moreau Gottschalk, *Notes of a Pianist,* p. 34.
4. Ibid., pp. 39–40.
5. Ibid., p. 40.
6. Ibid., pp. 41–42.
7. Ibid., p. 43.
8. Ibid., p. 313.
9. Ibid., p. 35.
10. William F. Apthorp, "Music," p. 256.
11. For a discussion of the black Creole *patois,* see Henry Edward Krehbiel, *Afro-American Folksongs,* pp. 127–39.
12. See Bertram W. Korn, "A Note on the Jewish Ancestry of Louis Moreau Gottschalk, American Pianist and Composer," pp. 117–19.
13. Hector Berlioz, "Mr. Gottschalk's Concert," *Journal des débats,* Apr. 13, 1851; quoted and translated by Jeanne Behrend, in Gottschalk, *Notes of a Pianist,* p. xxii.
14. *Feuilleton de la presse,* Mar. 31, 1851; quoted and translated by Behrend, in Gottschalk, *Notes of a Pianist,* p. xxii.
15. For the most comprehensive edition of his music, see *The Piano Works of Louis Moreau Gottschalk,* ed. Vera Brodsky Lawrence; see also the Desto recording

Forty Works for Piano, DC 6470–73; performed by Alan Mandel; and the Angel recording *Battle Cry of Freedom,* S-36090; performed by Leonard Pennario, piano.

16. Quoted in Gottschalk, *Notes of a Pianist,* p. xxvi.

17. Ibid., p. 168.

18. For a recording of *La Nuit des tropiques* and other orchestral works, see *A Gottschalk Festival,* Turnabout-Vox TV-S 34440–42; featuring pianist Eugene List.

19. Letter of Aug. 6, 1969 (New York); quoted in William E. Korf, *The Orchestral Music of Louis Moreau Gottschalk,* p. 86.

20. In the *Piano Music of Louis Moreau Gottschalk,* comp. Richard Jackson, p. 189.

21. Ibid., p. 146.

22. Gottschalk, *Notes of a Pianist,* p. 43.

23. Ibid., pp. 181–82.

24. Octavia Hensel [Mrs. Mary Alice Ives Seymour], *Life and Letters of Louis Moreau Gottschalk,* p. 209.

25. Gottschalk, *Notes of a Pianist,* p. 269.

26. Ibid.

27. Ibid., pp. 273, 276, 282, and 285.

28. Ibid., p. 290.

29. Quoted in ibid., p. 316.

30. Ibid., p. 319.

31. Ibid., pp. 314, 315.

32. Ibid., p. 320.

33. Quoted in Hensel, *Life and Letters of Louis Moreau Gottschalk,* p. 162.

34. *Daily American Flag,* Sept. 18, 1865; quoted in Robert Stevenson, "Gottschalk in Buenos Aires," p. 1.

35. Quoted in Hensel, *Life and Letters of Louis Moreau Gottschalk,* pp. 170–71; and in Gottschalk, *Notes of a Pianist,* p. 320.

36. Quoted in Hensel, *Life and Letters of Louis Moreau Gottschalk,* p. 175.

37. Quoted in ibid., p. 173.

Chapter 17

Europe versus America

The applause of Philadelphia is quite as good as that
of Vienna—each for its "native Art," and of the two I prefer
that of Philadelphia.
—William Henry Fry, in *Dwight's Journal of Music*

During the eighteenth century, many who lived in the British colonies of
North America began to think of themselves as Americans. The glorifica-
tion of America—poetically apotheosized as "Columbia"—did not await
the winning of political independence. In 1777, when victory for the American "rebels" was a hazardous prediction, the poet Timothy Dwight exulted
in the glory of his native land:

> Columbia, Columbia, to glory arise,
> The queen of the world, and the child of the skies!
> Thy genius commands thee; with rapture behold,
> While ages on ages thy splendors unfold.[1]

It was Dwight who, after the United States of America had become a
reality, exhorted his countrymen to "shun the lures of Europe" (*Greenfield
Hill,* 1794). But few Americans, then or later, were willing to follow his advice—especially those with an artistic bent or a yearning for "high culture."
Yet the opinion that being American was essentially different from being
European had been memorably expressed by Crèvecoeur, a French émigré
who became an American farmer: "The American is a new man, who acts
upon new principles; he must therefore entertain new ideas and form new
opinions."[2]

With the achievement of independence, American nationalism became a matter of policy as well as poetic expression. Alexander Hamilton
wrote to Rufus King: "We are laboring hard to establish in this country
principles more and more *national*." Noah Webster, the famous educator
and lexicographer, declared: "Every engine [i.e., mechanism] should be
employed to render the people of this country *national* . . . and to inspire

them with the pride of national character."³ As summarized by Nye: "For this reason the postwar years rang with demands for a national literature, a national culture, a national system of education, a national history, even a national language . . . to help create a nation where none had before existed."⁴

In spite of this surge of enthusiasm and zeal, the results—at least in the realm of the fine arts—fell short of the aspiration and the vision. Or so it seemed to Ralph Waldo Emerson, who in 1838 publicly expressed his disappointment: "This country has not fulfilled what seemed the reasonable expectation of mankind." In his address at Dartmouth College he went on to say: "Men looked, when all feudal straps and bandages were snapped asunder, that nature, too long the mother of dwarfs, should reimburse itself by a brood of Titans, who should laugh and leap in the continent, and run up the mountains of the West with the errand of genius and of love. But the mark of American merit in painting, in sculpture, in poetry, in fiction, in eloquence, seems to be a certain grace without grandeur, and itself not new but derivative; a vase of fair outline, but empty. . . ."⁵

Emerson did not even bother to mention the art of music; his interest in it was minimal. As for literature, at least two titans—Herman Melville and Walt Whitman—would soon appear on the scene. Ironically, in the 1830s the only composer in America who personified "the errand of genius and of love" from the West was the Austrian-born Anthony Philip Heinrich, who first expressed in music the Romantic vision of America's grandeur and variety. His native predecessor was William Billings, whom only future generations would acclaim as the great American "primitive" in musical and verbal expression.

In the very year that Emerson delivered his Dartmouth oration, a young composer named William Henry Fry (1813–64) had his *Pastoral* Overture performed in the concert hall of the Musical Fund Society of Philadelphia. The twenty-three-year-old composer belonged to one of the most prominent, influential, and cultivated families of that city.⁶ His grandfather, Joseph Fry, was an officer in the Revolutionary War, had endured the winter at Valley Forge, and afterward was the singer who "set the tune" in Christ Church—"a small man with a great voice, who standing in the organ gallery was wont to make the whole church resound with his strong, deep and grave tones."⁷ (His grandson was said to have had a pretty good voice too.) Our composer's father, William Fry, became in 1820 the publisher and proprietor of the newly founded *National Gazette,* a newspaper that gave much importance to literature and the arts, including music. He had five sons, of whom the eldest, Joseph, was to be closely associated with the operatic ventures of William Henry. All received an excellent education and were much devoted to the arts, while maintaining a lively interest in national and international affairs—none more so than William Henry Fry, who took up journalism as his profession. Music was his first and lasting love, but it was no way to make a competent living (as Heinrich found to his sorrow).

As a journalist, Fry covered musical events for the *National Gazette* from 1836 to 1841. One of his notices is of special interest both because of the individual involved and of a possible connection with Fry's own music. The article refers to "Francis Johnson, the well known leader of a band of colored musicians, [who] is about to visit England. . . . Few individuals have been better known and more in demand here for many years than he has."[8] Frank (Francis) Johnson (1792–1844) was a black composer, orchestra leader, and bandmaster who did indeed enjoy a great vogue in America and Europe.[9] According to a writer in the *Detroit Free Press* (September 23, 1839), "It may be said without fear of contradiction, that as a composer or musician, he stands without rival in the United States."

In January 1839 Fry attended a concert by Frank Johnson and his band that included as part 1: "Sleigh Waltzes: No. 1, an Introduction; No. 2, Bell Solo; No. 3, Blacksmith making nails to shoe his horses; No. 4, Clock striking twelve and Watchman springing his rattle; No. 5, *Sleighing party in an uproar, the horses supposed to be running away, with cracking of whips, jingling of bells, sound of post horns, etc*" (italics added). Part 2 included "The Philadelphia Firemans Quadrille—showing the manner in which they communicate the alarm, composed and respectfully dedicated to the Fireman's Association by F. Johnson."[10]

The connection to bear in mind here is with Fry's most controversial composition, the *Santa Claus* Symphony (1853), in which the realistic sound effects are similar to those described in Frank Johnson's program. Surely it is not amiss to suppose that this concert may have left a lasting impression.

However, the great formative experience for Fry at this time was his frequent opportunity to hear French and Italian opera. From 1827 to 1833, John Davis's French Opera Company from New Orleans appeared for short seasons in Philadelphia, where they gave a total of 109 performances. In 1833 the first season of Italian opera was given by the Montressor Company, including Bellini's *Il pirata* and three operas by Rossini. In a postseason concert by this company, the program included "an Overture by an Amateur of this city, pupil of Mr. Meignen."[11] We can assume that this was Fry.

The Fry brothers were directly responsible for one of the most impressive operatic events in Philadelphia: the first American production of Bellini's *Norma*. Joseph adapted and translated the libretto into English, Edward served as general manager, and William Henry was the musical director. Following the premiere at the Chestnut Street Theatre on January 11, 1841, the *Evening Bulletin*, with evident local pride, proclaimed that "its success is among the traditional glories of the opera in Philadelphia."[12]

Fry had already begun to try his hand at opera, beginning in 1838 with *Cristiani e pagani* (the libretto in Italian), which he left unfinished. His aim was evidently to write an opera with a libretto in English, and this he did with *Aurelia the Vestal* (1841), described as "A Lyrical Tragedy in Three Acts," the libretto by Joseph Fry. He tried to get it performed in London, but without success. (In fact, it was never performed anywhere.)

Nevertheless, Fry was encouraged by the success of his next opera, *Leonora*, again with a libretto by his brother Joseph. This was adapted from a play by Bulwer-Lytton, *The Lady of Lyons*, with the action shifted to Spain in the early sixteenth century. First produced at the Chestnut Street Theatre on June 4, 1845, it was enthusiastically received and had a run of twelve performances. The following year its success was repeated at the Walnut Street Theatre.

Fry's success was all the more remarkable because of the current vogue for opera sung in Italian or French. The use of English was paramount for Fry, because on it he based his claim as an absolute innovator in the lyrical drama. He emphasized that this was an *American* achievement: "As England denies the possibility of having a grand opera written originally in our tongue, it was the business of America to prove the possibility— and I did so. . . . [Hence] the first successful grand opera in the English language was produced in this country."[13] Fry also made a point of having rejected "the wretched, vulgar plan of speaking and singing by turns" and of having, instead, made "the English language the medium for the grand, serious, or tragic opera." This view was certainly radical for its time. Musically it adhered to the patterns of the leading Italian opera composers such as Bellini and Donizetti, including florid cadenzas and coloratura passages.[14]

Fry was aware of the flaws in *Leonora,* and he completed a much-revised definitive version, which was produced at the Academy of Music in New York on March 29, 1858. Ironically, because the performing company was Italian, it was presented in that language. For Fry, who had matured as a composer in the intervening thirteen years, the chief satisfaction of the New York revival was to hear his opera performed in its revised version— in four acts, with many cuts, some interpolations, and, above all, many changes in the music. The final irony is that, to the extent *Leonora* is known at all to later generations, such knowledge—and consequent judgments—are based on the earlier published version rather than on the later revision that reveals Fry's capacity for self-criticism and persistent attention to detail.

In 1840, while still in his twenties, Fry optimistically expressed his conviction regarding the promise of America's achievement in the arts: "We are among those who believe that this country must produce genius in every department of art and science, the peer of the greatest in ancient or modern times. Already in mechanical inventions and scientific discoveries Americans are in the front rank, and in brief time the world will witness achievements of imagination worthy a place among the mightiest extant. Our origin, climate and institutions alike favor mental advancement; and all, taken in one view, are the basis of expectations which, lofty as they may be, are most amply sustained."[15]

In later years Fry's faith in America was to suffer severe trials, and what he has to say about rampant materialism and indifference to the arts is often excoriating. He was no chauvinist of the my-country-right-or-wrong school. Again and again he deplored the lack of support for native art, especially music. Yet his basic confidence persisted; even though he might complain that musical composition in America "is pursued in a desert of trade and politics," he believed such conditions could be overcome: "It needs however a little time in this country to arrive at the belief . . . that Romance, Religion, the Elements, Nature—all offer new fields for genius in music—*but it must be genius and not conformity*" (italics added).[16]

This is very close to the thought and vision of Emerson. It is also an all-out manifesto of Romanticism. A Romantic perspective is likewise evident in Fry's partiality for the symphonic poem—the quintessential Romantic expression in music—as reflected in titles such as *The Breaking Heart* (1852), *The Dying Soldier* (n.d.), *Hagar in the Wilderness* (1854), *A Day in the Country* (ca. 1853), *Niagara* (performed 1854), and, above all, *Childe Harold* (performed 1854), after Byron's poem. We shall soon take note of Fry's spirited defense of Romanticism in an encounter with his conservative critics; but first we accompany him to Europe, where he was both critical and observant.

Pursuing his professional career as a journalist, Fry in 1846 sailed for Europe, where he remained for six years, traveling widely but making his headquarters in Paris. As correspondent for the *New York Tribune* and the Philadelphia *Public Ledger,* he wrote on many topics, from politics to fashions. He was independent, indefatigable, and outspoken in expressing his opinions, describing his impressions, attacking imperial pomp, and praising French wines. He was both a man of the world and an incorrigible moralist. After an impressive ceremonial occasion he burst out: "Oh! My countrymen: from California to the Bowery, do study how the French manage these things." But he also complained that "the French Opera House might as well not exist, so far as it diffuses spiritual culture among the people." He was strongly attracted by the cathedrals of France, yet deplored "the dreamy learned scholars who see light through painted church windows and take refuge from the roar of democratic change in the aisles and cloisters of Gothic architecture. . . ."[17]

Fry had no use for the limited view of a cloistered life. Returning to New York in November 1851, he joined the editorial staff of the *Tribune.* No sooner had he arrived, moreover, than he began the ambitious and controversial series of ten public lectures on the "History and Esthetics of Music" that he had been planning for several years. Musical illustrations on a lavish scale were provided by soloists from two visiting opera companies, the orchestra of the Philharmonic Society, and the chorus of the Harmonic Society, all under the direction of George F. Bristow. The plan was to present the "history of the rise, progress and present state of all departments of instrumental and vocal music—whether sacred, dramatic, symphonic, classic, romantic, or national. . . ." The lectures were well attended, received much notice in the press—and put Fry $4,000 out of pocket![18]

The prestigious journalist Richard Storrs Willis provides the following impression of Fry as lecturer:

Decidedly the boldest lecturer of our day is Mr. Fry. He is the most free-thoughted man we ever heard address an audience. Riding over prejudices, convictions, creeds—now electrifying an audience with splendid bursts of genuine American democracy (somewhat red-republican, perhaps, at times) and then fairly shocking them with his onslaught upon things of revered and hallowed association—we cannot, after all, but admire the "youth and juice" of this nervous and bold "young American" however we may feel aroused to an equally fierce opposition upon certain principles intimated and actually advanced. Mr. Fry keeps an audience alive and warm at all events.[19]

We do not have the text of the lectures, so we do not know what he actually said on the final topic announced in the printed syllabus, "American Music." He is reported to have called for a declaration of independence by American composers, most of whom were subservient to European styles and standards. There is no evidence in any of his writings that he ever advocated a complete break with the cultural heritage of Europe. His cult for grand opera alone would have belied such an attitude. What he advocated was more independence and self-determination on the part of American composers, as well as more encouragement and support from the American cultural establishment.

On the practical side, Fry, like his friend and colleague Bristow, was much concerned with the basic question, How does an American composer get his music—especially his orchestral works—performed? On this question Fry and Bristow quarreled with the New York Philharmonic Society (founded in 1842), which was largely controlled by musicians of German extraction. In January 1854 Fry complained in the press that "the Philharmonic Society of this city, consecrated to foreign music, is an incubus on Art, never having asked for or performed a single American instrumental composition during the eleven years of its existence. . . ."[20]

This proved to be a slight exaggeration. Nevertheless, Bristow jumped to the defense of his colleague with a letter to Willis: "As it is possible to miss a needle in a hay-stack, I am not surprised that Mr. Fry has missed the fact, that during the eleven years the Philharmonic Society has been in operation in this city, it played once, either by mistake or accident, one single American composition, an overture of mine. . . . This single stray fact shows that the Philharmonic Society has been as anti-American as if it had been located in London during the revolutionary war, and composed of native born English Tories."[21]

The dispute grew more acrimonious. Bristow accused the Philharmonic of a "systematized effort . . . for the extinction of American music" and announced his intention to form an "American Philharmonic" that would play mainly music by Americans. In righteous indignation he asked: "Who are the men who told you that Americans cannot 'write up' to the standard of the New York Philharmonic Society? The same style of *illuminati* that in the London Philharmonic, after attempting to rehearse it, kicked Beethoven's C minor Symphony under their desks and pronounced the composer a fool or a madman."[22]

Infuriated by ridicule from *Dwight's Journal,* Bristow intemperately pressed the attack:

What is the Philharmonic Society—or Harmony-lovers' Society—in this country? Is it to play exclusively the works of German masters, especially if they be dead. . . . Or is it to stimulate original Art on the spot?

From the commencement there has been on the part of the performing members or the direction of the Philharmonic Society little short of a conspiracy against the Art of a country to which they have come for a living; and, it is very bad taste, to say the least, for men to bite the hand that feeds them. If all their artistic affections are unalterably German, let them pack and go back to Germany. . . .[23]

The sense of injury might have been easier to bear if the Philharmonic *had* concentrated on the works of the great German masters. But how was an American composer to react when ousted by such nonentities as Gumbert, Heinemyer, and Schindlemeisser?

Nevertheless, Bristow eventually made his peace with the Philharmonic, which in due course performed his four symphonies and other orchestral works such as the *Columbus* Overture. George Frederick Bristow (1825–98) was the son of an English professional violinist who settled in New York, where he played in the orchestra of the Olympic Theatre, which specialized in comic operas and musical burlesques. It was there that George began his professional career at the age of twelve, playing violin with his father in the orchestra pit. In 1843 he graduated to the first violin section of the New York Philharmonic Society, with which he remained until 1879—except for the brief period of his withdrawal in protest (1853–54 season).

Bristow's professional activities were widespread, as he moved energetically in various directions. He directed several choral groups, including the New York Harmonic Society (1851–63) and the Mendelssohn Union. He was one of the organizers of the American Music Association (1856), its aim being "to further the interest of musical composers residing among us, by having their works effectively presented to the public, in order that they may be fairly criticized and impartially judged."[24] There was much wishful thinking in the enterprise: the public was not receptive, and within two years the association was dissolved. From 1854 Bristow was active as a music teacher in the public schools of New York City, while continuing to compose in both large and small forms, with about 135 titles in all.[25]

Among his major works are four symphonies (1848–72), culminating with the *Arcadian* (op. 50). Years later he wrote a large work for solos, chorus, and orchestra titled *Niagara* Symphony (1893). Other choral works with orchestra also have American associations, notably *The Pioneer: A*

Grand Cantata (1872) and *The Great Republic* (1880). He wrote a quantity of religious music, two string quartets, and many songs and piano pieces. These last included the Chopinesque *Andante et Polonaise pour piano*—a typical example of his adherence to the European Romantic tradition.

Bristow was also the first to compose an opera on an American subject that had an impressive success. As Richard Storrs Willis proclaimed in the *Musical World:* "Sebastopol has fallen, and a new American opera has succeeded in New York!" The opera was *Rip Van Winkle,* based on the story by Washington Irving, and its premiere took place at Niblo's Garden on September 27, 1855. It ran for four weeks, and the box-office receipts compared favorably with those of current attractions—including those of the Italian opera at the Academy of Music.

In spite of its billing as a "Grand Romantic Opera," it was "Romantic" but not "Grand," as it fluctuated between light opera and what the French call *opéra-comique,* with spoken dialogue interspersed. In style and subject it most resembles Donizetti's *The Daughter of the Regiment*—thanks to an interpolation in the plot not found in Irving's story. Rip's daughter, Alice, falls in love with a captain in the Continental army, and to be with him she goes to the war as a *vivandière.* This subplot not only provides for the indispensable tenor and soprano duets but also gives the leading lady a chance to stop the show with her vivacious and defiantly patriotic "Vivandière Song." To fill the time while Rip is offstage during his twenty-year sleep, a nasty villain schemes to marry Alice for the money she has inherited from an aunt. Needless to say, he is foiled when Rip reappears after his long nap, and the curtain comes down amid general rejoicing.

A critic for the *New York Times* wrote: "In the treatment of his subject Mr. Bristow has evidently consulted the popular appetite for light and cheerful music, with a leaning at times towards the sentimental and martial school. . . . The writing throughout is fluent, and usually well-proportioned, although sometimes exuberant. . . . One or two of the melodies will get on the street organs."[26] If this last did happen, it would put Bristow in a class with Verdi and Sousa.

In 1870 the libretto of *Rip Van Winkle*—originally written by J. W. Wainwright, a military man turned author—was revised by J. W. Shanon, with most of the spoken dialogue deleted. This version was evidently used for its revival in that year at Niblo's Garden in New York, on November 9, 10, and 11.[27] On February 2 and 3, 1974, it was revived by the American Music Group of the University of Illinois at Urbana-Champaign, under the direction of Neely Bruce. The critical reception was generally favorable, with

Richard Jackson observing that Bristow's music, in spite of the Italian influence, "is also very much of its place, i.e. mid-century America. The Bristow style here seems to be a natural extension of the parlor ballad, the patriotic song, and the Protestant hymn"—for example, the chorus and solo "Great God of Battles, Hear Our Prayer." Jackson adds: "The choral writing (occasionally in eight parts) is superb throughout; the orchestration is also sure and strong and reflects Bristow's long experience as a professional orchestral musician. . . ."[28] Surely the time has come for Bristow's *Rip Van Winkle* to assume its enduring place in the operatic and patriotic context of America's musical heritage.

Returning now to William Henry Fry, we note that he was a complete contrast to Bristow, both in his career and his character. He defied the established order, thereby enduring ridicule and neglect (the Philharmonic Society never played any of his music). The scheduled performance of his grand oratorio, *Stabat Mater; or, The Crucifixion of Christ,* at the New York Academy of Music (April 1855), was canceled at the last moment through the machinations of his enemies.[29] Through all his disappointments and frustrations, he never wavered in his conviction that freedom of expression was to be valued above conformity.

When Fry's orchestral works came (for a time) to be widely performed and publicly acclaimed in the United States, it was as a result of the European-American cultural counterpoint that shaped much of the arts and letters of America throughout the nineteenth century. Also involved was the meshing of musical forms in the classical tradition and their presentation as popular entertainment. This pattern was embodied in the person of a celebrated French conductor, Louis Antoine Jullien, who in 1853 brought members of his orchestra to America for an immensely successful series of concerts in New York and other cities. In his programs he catered to the public's taste for international quadrilles, national airs, and sensational descriptive pieces such as a firemen's drill. He claimed to have a repertory of 1,200 numbers and to have given 300 concerts during his tour in the United States.[30]

Although he was accused of being a mountebank, Jullien, in fact, had an excellent orchestra, and many of his first-desk players were virtuosi of the highest rank. He mixed popular attractions with a selection of the classics (including Beethoven) as well as contemporary works. As a bow to America, he included among the latter some compositions by Bristow and Fry. The latter's controversial but highly successful *Santa Claus (Christmas)* Symphony was written especially for Jullien's orchestra, which performed it for the first time in New York on Christmas Eve 1853. Thereafter it was played some forty times during the American tour.

The *Santa Claus* Symphony has been called "program music with a vengeance." The detailed synopsis, prepared by Fry at Jullien's request, fills four printed pages, ranging from Heaven to Earth, with a glimpse of Hell as "a few loud chords of a fierce character portray the rage of fallen angels." The central event depicts "the Festivities of a Christmas Eve party." This is followed by a violent snowstorm that threatens a "Perishing Traveler" in the night, hence the music imitates "the howling and whistling of the winds and other winter signs." Meanwhile, Santa Claus is making his way to the happy home where his gifts are eagerly expected, accompanied by the sound of sleigh bells and the cracking of a whip. Then the Christmas hymn "Adeste Fideles," played by the full orchestra, announces the break of day. Soon the children are up and rush with joy to seize their toys, while the orchestra plays "Little Bo-peep" on toy trumpets and drums. For the joyous finale, "Adeste Fideles" ("Come, All Ye Faithful") returns, "with grand chorus and orchestra."[31]

What is really significant in Fry's synopsis is the continuous reference to specific instrumental effects and to the virtuoso performers who would produce them. He refers, for example, to "the genius of M. Bottesini having elevated the Double Violoncello or Double Bass to the rank of a solo instrument," so that a "sombre pathos yet unachieved in the history of instrumental art can be depicted by this great master of expression." (Bottesini was the Charles Mingus of the classical string bass.) Fry also refers to "the marvellously human-like saxophone (as just perfected by M. Sax of Paris)"—an instrument whose possibilities he was one of the first to exploit.

The American conductor Howard Shanet, who in 1958 was the first to revive the *Santa Claus* Symphony (with the Columbia University Orchestra), commented on Fry's instrumental innovations: "In orchestration Fry is an experimenter. *Santa Claus* is probably the first American composition to employ a saxophone (only a few years after the invention of the instrument). It also requires such special instruments as a whip, sleigh bells, and a toy trumpet, and imitates the dying of a traveler by a double-bass solo, and the howling and whistling of the winds by having the players slide their fingers up and down the fingerboard. . . ."[32]

Conservative critics who defended classical values, such as John Sullivan Dwight and Richard Storrs Willis, took a dim view of the *Santa Claus* Symphony. As Willis condescendingly wrote: "Mr. Fry's 'Santa Claus' we consider a good Christmas piece but hardly a composition to be gravely criticized like an earnest work of Art. It is a kind of *extravaganza* which moves the audience to laughter, entertaining them seasonably with imitated snow-storms, trotting horses, sleigh-bells, cracking whips, etc."[33]

This was the fuse that set off a series of explosive letters from Fry that were printed in the musical press, with more circumspect but unyielding replies from Willis and pontifical *obiter dicta* by Dwight. Bristow's involvement in this heated exchange has already been discussed, and the whole forms one of the most extraordinary public correspondences in the annals of American music, far transcending the faults or merits of Fry's *Christmas Symphony*. (It seems to me that this title is preferable; *Santa Claus* invites a snicker.) Fry seized the occasion to air his views and convictions on musical composition and struck hard (if sometimes rather wildly) at the conservative defenders of the Sublime and the Beautiful in classical garb. From the vast verbiage we can extract the first fighting manifesto by an American composer in the larger forms (this excludes Billings, a master of verbal attack and defense "in his own write"). It is only fair to let his voice be heard today, for later generations and other minds may be more responsive to his essentially Romantic message of creative freedom.

Fry's first point is that he had written a symphony "in the school of romantic and not formalistic Art"—a statement crucial for understanding his historical position in America's music. He further describes the work as "novel in design, novel in treatment, novel in effects, novel in instrumentation . . . written so as to double the resources and sonority of the orchestra compared with classic models. . . ."[34] Then he rises to the attack:

> I do not know what the meaning of serious Art is—you saying my symphony is not serious. [Charles] Lamb said once to a knot of wits around him—"Let's be serious, the fools are coming." And this grandiose swindle of seriousness is made the touchstone of Art, though the great writer of humanity, SHAKSPEARE, owes his greatness to his equal power over mirth and wit, with passion and grief. . . . As for myself, I utterly and absolutely contemn such a view of serious Art. It is for the want of this whole genius, that Europe has given us no Shakspeare in music. . . .
>
> I have heard [Beethoven] called the Shakspeare of music a hundred times: to which I reply, also, "Fudge!"

Fry then goes on to a general exposition of what he thinks music is:

> What is music, let me ask, in defining my position as a composer? Is it learning, or mathematical intricacies? No: if it be only these, I would leave off writing and take up mathematics where I left, and learn to calculate an eclipse. Is it

imitating classical models? No. Is it "linked sweetness long drawn out?" No, it is the original mode of expressing an original idea. In the dreary ignorance of what is music, *"imitative* music" is called "the lowest kind." But all music is imitative, or it is good for nothing. If it be music painting passion or emotion, it but imitates artistically the tones of the voice which in speaking symbolize the thoughts and feelings. If it be descriptive music, it imitates either the language of nature as expressed in the elements or in vocal creation.

Fry by no means repudiated the concept of "High Art": he simply objected to having it identified with what pundits such as Dwight and Willis called "Serious Art." (In this, his position was akin to that of Charles Ives with regard to critics such as Philip Hale and W. J. Henderson.) In reply to a disparaging remark by Willis on his symphonic poem *A Day in the Country,* Fry hit back straight from the shoulder:

> I am aware that it is not classical; but remember, Mr. Willis, if I thought the classic models perfect and unalterable, I would not write at all, or be their obedient ourang-outang; and as there are but two things in this world—substance and shadow—and a man is either the one or the other, I would not play shadow. If I did not think I could make a school for myself, I would not write at all; for so has done every man who has made any name. But every such composer has considered it beneath the dignity of his mission, servilely to copy pre-existing forms, and follow in the steps of "illustrious predecessors," as the critics always and invariably would have him do, ramming authorities down his throat, when he feels that he could teach those authorities. If he has not studied and made himself master of the art of writing fugues and sonatas, he is an ignoramus, a quack and pretender, who does not know the rules of the trade; but if he publish fugues and sonatas for the purpose of showing that he can do so, it is about as much to his credit, as to publish the multiplication table to show that he has committed it to memory, and was able to write it down.

Stung by the criticism that his symphonies (i.e., symphonic "tone poems") lacked "classical unity," Fry retorted that *The Breaking Heart* "has a great deal of *classical* unity." Moreover, "the classical modulations are followed, besides some that they did not use, *but which I intend to render classical*" (italics added). Fry's position appears to be that he respected the principle of "classical unity" but would not be subservient to it. He evidently rejected a dictionary definition of *classical* as signifying "standard and authoritative rather than new or experimental." In the clause italicized above, the meaning Fry probably had in mind was "having lasting significance or recognized worth." It is in this sense that the music of innovative composers such as Debussy, Stravinsky, or Schoenberg has become "classical."

Fry's ambitions probably exceeded his powers, given the conditions of his career and his environment. Journalism demanded much of his time and energy, and he often composed under the pressure of time and circumstance. He tells us that two of his symphonic poems, *A Day in the Country* and *The Breaking Heart*, "were both written in the same week, previous to the Lectures which I delivered at Metropolitan Hall. . . ."[35] (They were, in fact, performed on that occasion.) Neither of these works is extant; at least, they have not been located.

The difficulty that Fry had in completing his compositions is indicated by the fragmentary condition of his chamber music. There are two completed string quartets, each in four movements, numbered respectively "Tenth" and "Eleventh," as well as three unfinished quartets and fragments of two others, besides sketches for a sextet and a piano trio.

Fry expended a great deal of energy in his multiple activities as journalist, lecturer, and composer. Never robust, his health failed rapidly in the 1860s, just when he was about to receive a diplomatic appointment that would have given him more leisure to compose (thus it was in those days!). At this time he was working on his opera *Notre Dame of Paris* (based on Victor Hugo's *The Hunchback of Notre Dame*), which according to his brother Edward "was composed in 30 days."[36] This opera (also known as *Esmeralda*) was first performed, with considerable acclaim, "by 350 executants at the Grand Music Festival inaugurating the National Fair for the benefit of wounded and ill Soldiers and Sailors of the United States Army and Navy, held in Philadelphia at the great Academy of Music, May 4, 1864."[37]

But Fry himself was very ill and desperately in need of succor. In November 1864 he went to the West Indies, hoping that the mild climate might be beneficial (his malady was consumption). On the island of Santa Cruz (St. Croix), he worked on a Mass, including two versions of "Dona Nobis Pacem," which remained unfinished at his death on December 21, 1864.

An obituary in the *Independent* of New York (January 26, 1865) gave this sketch of his personality: "Not a more eccentric, brilliant, nondescript, unaccountable man have we ever known than William Henry Fry. And to all others who knew him, he was the same delightful enigma. Chiefly a musician, his genius nevertheless was universal—running like a gadding vine over almost every subject. An orator, a writer, a politician, a conversationist, he was one of the most versatile of men. . . . Frailties, virtues, and genius all had equal part in this strange and fascinating man."[38] The last sentence could well be applied to his music also.

A cultural historian has remarked that during the period from 1830 to 1860, "technology made the American economy genuinely independent of Europe." Moreover, "the majority of Americans believed that the American technology, which put machines to man's service, was the crowning glory of American society."[39] The spirit of Franklin and Fulton prevailed over the spirit of Emerson and Thoreau.

What technology accomplished for the American economy was not achieved in the fine arts, where imitation and replication prevailed. As the editor of *Harper's Magazine* cynically remarked in 1859: "What is fine in the buildings of old countries we can borrow; their statues and their pictures we will be able in good time to buy. . . ."[40] This was the pragmatic, dollars-and-common-sense point of view, which had a stronger appeal than Emerson's idealistic vision: "It is in vain that we look for genius to reiterate its miracles in the old arts; it is its instinct to find beauty and holiness in new and necessary facts."

But the "new and necessary facts" in American society, which aroused pride and admiration, were machines and inventions: the whole apparatus of technology and industry that could impress the world and bring progress and prosperity to the nation. This was the keynote of the Centennial Exhibition of 1876, authorized by an act of Congress as "an International Exhibition of Arts, Manufactures and Products of the Soil and Mine. . . ." The exhibition opened on May 10, 1876, in Fairmount Park, Philadelphia, with ceremonies that included a concert by a symphony orchestra and chorus of mixed voices under the direction of Theodore Thomas, a musician of German origin who had been brought to America at the age of ten in 1845. From 1862, when he organized his own orchestra and began to tour throughout the United States, he had a major role in bringing symphonic music to the American people. (For fourteen years, 1877–91, he was director of the New York Philharmonic.) Thomas was put in charge of the musical programs for the Centennial Exhibition, but without any subsidy. As far as the Congress was concerned, music could shift for itself. More people were attracted by the machinery than by the music, and the result was a financial disaster for Thomas.

But now we return to the pomp and glory of the inaugural concert, attended by 4,000 invited guests and a general audience estimated at 200,000. The program included the twelve national anthems of countries represented in the exhibition, together with three commissioned works:

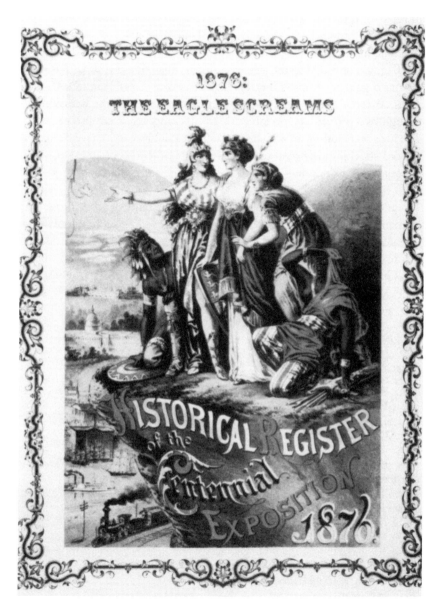

1876: The Eagle Screams, a "Historical Register of the Centennial Exposition of 1876."

Richard Wagner's *Grand Inaugural Centennial March* (an expensive pot-boiler); *The Centennial Hymn,* with text by John Greenleaf Whittier and music by John Knowles Paine; and *The Centennial Meditation of Columbia,* with text by Sidney Lanier and music by Dudley Buck.[41]

The high moment of the inaugural ceremony came when the American flag was unfurled to the accompaniment of a huge chorus with orchestra and organ, performing the "Hallelujah Chorus" from Handel's *Messiah.* Thus, Wagner and Handel were the musical heroes of the occasion, although two properly respectable American composers were also included. The idea of including an anthem by William Billings would have been considered shocking; that had to wait for the bicentennial celebration, when America was at long last ready to recognize its early musical heroes—"Be Glad, Then, America!"

If we take five sample concert programs at random from those performed at the Centennial Exhibition, we find the following composers represented: Adam, Beethoven, Flotow, Gounod, Gugl, Hartmann, Heinemann, Lanner, Lecocq, Liszt, Mozart, Nicolai, Mercadante, Offenbach, Rossini, Schubert, Schneider, Strauss, Saint-Saëns, Verdi, Wagner, and Weber. Europe versus America? At the Centennial Exhibition it was not even a contest—simply a knockout in the second round.

Notes

1. Written in 1777 and first published in *American Museum* 3 (June 1787); reprinted in Vernon Louis Parrington, ed., *The Connecticut Wits,* pp. 273–74.
2. J. Hector John de Crèvecoeur, *Letters from an American Farmer,* p. 64.
3. Quoted in Russel Blaine Nye, *This Almost Chosen People,* pp. 63–64.
4. Ibid., p. 64.
5. Ralph Waldo Emerson, *An Oration Delivered before the Literary Societies of Dartmouth College, July 24, 1838,* pp. 4–5.
6. There is some doubt as to whether Fry was born in 1813 or 1815. See William Treat Upton, *William Henry Fry,* pp. vii–x.
7. Ibid., p. 9.
8. Ibid., p. 35.
9. For biographical and bibliographic data on Johnson, see Richard J. Wolfe, *Secular Music in America, 1801–1825* 2:451–55.
10. Upton, *William Henry Fry,* pp. 39–40.
11. Ibid., p. 16.
12. Ibid., p. 26.
13. Ibid., p. 128.
14. The original version of *Leonora* was published in 1846, with important "Pref-

atory Remarks" by Fry. These are reprinted in ibid., pp. 327–31; and in Gilbert Chase, ed., *The American Composer Speaks,* pp. 47–52.

15. *Philadelphia National Gazette,* Dec. 30, 1840; quoted in Upton, *William Henry Fry,* p. 45.

16. From Fry's letter to Richard Storrs Willis, Jan. 10, 1854; printed in *Musical World and New York Musical Times* (hereafter *Musical World*), Jan. 21, 1854; reprinted in *Dwight's Journal of Music* 4 (Feb. 4, 1854): 140; and quoted in Upton, *William Henry Fry,* p. 137.

17. Upton, *William Henry Fry,* pp. 103, 111, 110.

18. The synopsis or "Syllabus" of Fry's lectures was printed in *Dwight's Journal of Music* 1 (July 24, 1852): 126; also quoted in Upton, *William Henry Fry,* p. 123.

19. Upton, *William Henry Fry,* pp. 125–26.

20. Letter of Jan. 10, 1854; printed in *Musical World,* Jan. 21, 1854; reprinted in *Dwight's Journal of Music* 4 (Feb. 4, 1854): 138.

21. *Musical World,* Mar. 4, 1854; quoted in *Dwight's Journal of Music* 4 (Mar. 11, 1854): 182.

22. *Musical World,* Mar. 4, 1854, p. 100.

23. Ibid.

24. *Dwight's Journal of Music* 10 (Dec. 20, 1856): 93; quoted in Delmer D. Rogers, "Nineteenth-Century Music in New York City," p. 87.

25. See Rogers, "Nineteenth-Century Music in New York City."

26. *New York Times,* Sept. 29, 1855; quoted in ibid., p. 110.

27. George C. D. Odell, *Annals of the New York Stage,* vol. 9, *1870–1875,* p. 25.

28. MLA *Newsletter* 16 (Mar.–Apr. 1974): 3.

29. James Gordon Bennett, publisher of the *New York Herald,* not only was feuding with the *Tribune* but also had declared a vendetta against Fry and Fry's brother Edward, who was an opera impresario. It was Bennett's influence that caused the Academy of Music to cancel the performance of Fry's oratorio. See Upton, *William Henry Fry,* pp. 150–55.

30. Adam Carse, *The Life of Jullien,* p. 83.

31. Fry's detailed synopsis of the *Santa Claus* Symphony is reproduced in Upton, *William Henry Fry,* pp. 335–38.

32. Howard Shanet, program notes, Columbia University Orchestra, Dec. 6, 1958.

33. *Musical World,* Jan. 7, 1854.

34. Letter of Jan. 10, 1854; printed in *Musical World,* Jan. 21, 1854; reprinted in *Dwight's Journal of Music* 4 (Feb. 4, 1854): 138. The quotations that follow are from the reprinted version in *Dwight's Journal,* pp. 138–39.

35. *Dwight's Journal of Music* 4 (Feb. 4, 1854): 139.

36. Upton, *William Henry Fry,* p. 165.

37. Ibid., p. 310.

38. Quoted in ibid., pp. 172–73.

39. Russel Blaine Nye, *Society and Culture in America, 1830–1860,* pp. 282, 278.

40. *Harper's New Monthly Magazine* 19 (Aug. 1859): 406.

41. The poet Sidney Lanier (1842–81), from Macon, Ga., was also a musician: an excellent flutist who played with the Peabody Symphony in Baltimore and a composer who wrote many pieces for flute, as well as several songs for voice and piano.

PART THREE

Toward a Composite Culture

Chapter 18

Music for the Millions

Probably there is no term more abused and more often
mistaken in its real meaning than "popular music."
—John Philip Sousa, *Marching Along* (1928)

On a pleasant day, when the twentieth century was still to come, John
Philip Sousa took a stroll along Broad Street in Philadelphia. As he ap-
proached a corner where a man with a hand organ was grinding out a tune,
he paused, listened intently, and recognized the strains of his own march
"The Gladiator." (The organ-grinder, like most of his kind, was an Italian-
American.) Rushing up to him, Sousa exclaimed, "My friend! My friend!
Let me thank you! Please take this as a little token of my appreciation!"
The immediate response was an amazed stare; but a close look at the coins
thrust into his hand changed this to bewildered pleasure, and he probably
said to himself, "Quello è pazzo!" (That guy's crazy!).

Sousa was simply overcome by emotional excitement. Recalling the incident many years later, he commented: "I was exultant. My music had
made enough of a hit to be played on a street organ. At last I felt it had
struck a popular chord."[1] This is the keynote of Sousa's career and the guiding impulse of his tremendously varied output. When asked by an interviewer, "What makes a composition popular?" he replied: "Its measure of
inspiration."[2] And in his autobiography he remarked: "Artistic snobbery is
so ridiculous!"[3]

Finding what he regarded as conclusive evidence that one of his
marches was truly reaching the people, then, was the cause of his excitement, his intense gratification. He had written "The Gladiator" in 1886,
when he was thirty-one and already had a long list of works to his credit;
but this was the first to sell over a million copies—hence a turning point in
his career.

Sousa's choice of a title for this march has hitherto been regarded as a
mystery. But there is a clue to be followed when we learn that his daughter

Helen "conjectured that her father might have been inspired by a literary account of some particular gladiator."[4] It appears highly probable that the gladiator was Spartacus, the Thracian leader of a slave revolt against the Romans (73–71 B.C.) and that the literary source was a very successful play by Robert M. Bird, titled *The Gladiator,* first performed in 1831 with Edwin Forrest in the title role. Forrest continued to appear in it until 1865 and thereafter gave some public readings, so the play continued to be well known. It was also widely read in book form. Americans identified the story with the struggle against tyranny and oppression—a theme to which Sousa was surely sympathetic. The play, moreover, came to be identified with a class struggle between the cultivated elite and the common people who represented true democracy—which is in line with Sousa's disapproval of "artistic snobbery."

Although Sousa rose to be a man of wealth and a worldwide celebrity, he came from a lower middle-class milieu of immigrant parents—his father Portuguese, his mother Bavarian. From Brooklyn they moved to Washington, D.C., where John Philip was born in 1854. His father joined the U.S. Marine Band as a trombonist—a connection that was to prove decisive for the son, whose remarkable musical talent was soon discovered and encouraged. He received four years of intensive training at a local conservatory and at age eleven showed his enterprising spirit by forming a quadrille orchestra to play for dances. Eager for adventure, he almost joined a circus band, but his father thwarted the scheme and enrolled him as an apprentice in the U.S. Marine Band. He also continued his formal training in harmony, composition, and violin. He left the Marines in 1875 and thereafter took whatever musical jobs he could get, while continuing to compose industriously—marches, songs, dances, fantasies, operettas.

The turning point came in 1880, when Sousa was appointed leader of the U.S. Marine Band—to which he gave unprecedented prestige during his twelve-year stint. In 1889 he wrote the march that brought him international fame, "The Washington Post," and by 1891 he was acclaimed as the "March King." He was delighted when an association of dance instructors officially adopted "The Washington Post" as especially suitable for a fashionable new dance called the two-step. As we shall see, the march, the two-step, and ragtime were closely intertwined.

By 1892 Sousa was ready to leave the Marine Corps for an independent career in music. By this time his compositional output was very large, including not only marches but also several operettas, among them *The Smugglers* (1882) and *Desiree* (1883). He was to continue in this theatrical

John Philip Sousa (center) and the United States Marine Band (1882). Photo courtesy of the John Philip Sousa Archive, University of Illinois Bands.

vein, most notably with *El Capitan* (1895), *The Bride Elect* (1897), and *The Charlatan* (1898). As we shall see, he became a prolific composer in many genres, but his immediate aim was to establish himself as a leader in the "business-band" boom that was sweeping the nation. In his methodical manner he reviewed the alternatives: "First, the purely brass band. Second, the so-called military band. . . . Thirdly, the beer hall or casino string band . . . and fourthly, the symphony orchestra. . . ." Having concluded that each was "hemmed in by hide-bound tradition," he decided to "form a fresh combination" in which he would be "untrammeled by tradition," hence in a position "to cater for the millions rather than the few."[5]

As Paul Bierley observes, the new Sousa Band "was in actuality a compromise between a band and a symphony orchestra."[6] Hence the range of its repertory and the scope of its appeal were correspondingly wider. Although Sousa's own marches such as "Semper Fidelis" (1888), "The Thunderer" (1889), "The High School Cadets" (1890), "Manhattan Beach" (1893), and "The Stars and Stripes Forever" (1896) formed the solid core of his concerts, the programs offered a wide variety. The band might begin with Rossini's *William Tell* Overture and continue with favorite selections from standard operas. An attractive female vocalist would sing popular songs as well as operatic arias. Marches were usually interpolated by popular demand and as encores. A distinctive feature was the instrumental solo, in which a high degree of artistry and virtuosity was displayed by fabulous performers such as Herbert L. Clarke on cornet, Arthur Pryor on trombone, and E. A. Lefebre on saxophone.

Pryor's role was especially important, not only as soloist but also as arranger and assistant conductor. To be true to his policy of music for the millions, Sousa had to include some ragtime or "cakewalk" numbers in his programs, for these were the latest sensation both at home and abroad. Arthur Pryor (1870–1942) was born in Missouri, the home of ragtime, and he had more of a feeling for syncopation than Sousa, so he undertook the ragtime arrangements. When Sousa took his band on its first European tour in 1900—including an official appearance at the Paris World Exposition—the programs featured such current ragtime hits as Abe Holzmann's "Smoky Mokes" and Kerry Mills's "Whistling Rufus." The response of the French public was particularly enthusiastic.

Sousa was a great showman, but he was also more than that. From the time he became leader of the U.S. Marine Band until after World War I, he was *the* national musician of the United States, both officially and by popular acclamation. Not only did he serve under five presidents, but he identified himself and his music with every national, regional, or local event that took place in his lifetime, from the Chicago World's Columbian Exposition of 1893 to the Liberty Loan Drive of 1917; from the resumption of the use of gold and silver coins in 1879 ("Resumption March") to the annual exposition of the Boston Retail Grocer's Association ("The Fairest of the Fair"). "I've always been inspired by an occasion," said Sousa. While real inspiration did not come with every occasion—of the 136 marches that he wrote, scarcely three dozen have survived—it is nevertheless true that the pageant of American life and history from 1879 to 1931 could be presented with an unfailing accompaniment of Sousa's music.

For a historical extravaganza produced at the New York Hippodrome in 1917, titled *Cheer Up,* Sousa wrote the music for a presentation called "Land of Liberty," an allegory of American immigration. (It was originally titled "The Making of a Nation.") The countries represented were Denmark, England, Finland, France, Germany, Holland, Hungary, Ireland, Italy, Russia, Scotland, Spain, and Sweden. Although the Irish had emigrated to America early, in large numbers, it was during the decades from 1870 to 1910 that more than nine million immigrants "of racial stocks not allied to our own" entered the United States (they were thus characterized by historian James Truslow Adams, who probably meant they were not related to the Adamses of Massachusetts).[7] As the son of a Portuguese immigrant who had reached the United States via Spain, Sousa symbolizes the trend toward American leadership in music by "non-Nordic" individuals.

My favorite writer on American music, Rupert Hughes, included a rousing tribute to Sousa in his book *Famous American Composers* (1900): "The music is conceived in a spirit of high martial zest. It is proud and gay and fierce, thrilled and thrilling with triumph. Like all great music it is made up of simple elements, woven together by a strong personality. . . . The glory of Sousa is that he was the first to write in this style; that he has made himself a style; that he has so stirred the musical world that countless imitations have sprung up after him. . . . When all's said and done, Sousa is the pulse of the nation. . . ."[8]

Whatever the previous accomplishments of American musical composition, it had not induced worldwide emulation. Sousa's great achievement was to create a kind of American composition that was universally admired and imitated. True, he did not invent the military march, any more than Beethoven invented the symphony; it is not a question of form but of style, of individuality. A march by Sousa is as distinctive as a symphony by Beethoven.

Most of us know Sousa's marches only in their original settings for band. To appreciate their full impact in the social context of America's music, we should not only remember the ubiquitous hand organ-grinder but also take a look at the great variety of arrangements that were made for individual or group entertainment, from the parlor to the club and from variety shows to vaudeville. At least fifteen of Sousa's marches, for example, appeared in arrangements for banjo, an instrument very popular with both amateurs and professional entertainers. Some were also arranged for banjo duet or for banjo and piano. Arrangements for piano were, of course, common. To take one example, "El Capitan" (a march from the operetta of that title) appeared in the following arrangements (all from the same year, 1896): piano, piano duet, piano six hands; banjo, banjo duet, banjo and piano; guitar, guitar duet; mandolin, mandolin and piano, two mandolins and piano, two mandolins and guitar; zither and zither duet.

A list of gramophone plates issued by the United States Gramophone Company in 1895 includes twenty-one numbers under "Band Music," of which six are marches by Sousa. Although he objected to recordings as "canned music" (he is said to have coined the term), Sousa recorded some sides for Victor, mostly of classical music.[9] It should be noted, however, that many recordings labeled "By Sousa's Band" were actually made by a mixed personnel under the direction of Arthur Pryor. After forming his own band in 1903, Pryor made many recordings under his own name, including not only marches but rags, pop tunes, and operatic selections. Some celebrated arias, including "Celeste Aida," he performed as trombone solos. From 1910 Pryor recorded for Victor and became the most famous and prolific conductor in this field. It was truly a democratic period in America's music, and the bands did much to make it so.

According to a writer in *Harper's Weekly,* there were over 10,000 military bands in the United States in 1889. In 1900 Rupert Hughes stated that Sousa's music "has been sold to eighteen thousand bands in the United States alone."[10] Whether or not these figures are accurate, there were certainly a great many bands throughout the country at the turn of the century. Each city and town took pride in having its own band, with concerts in the public bandstand a regular feature of social life. In smaller cities the usual number of players was about twenty-five, while in country towns there would be twelve to eighteen. The author of the article in *Harper's Weekly* commented on "the larger musical field which military bands have entered, and which was formerly monopolized by the stringed orchestras. . . . The gavot, the waltz, the polka, and compositions reaching into the classics are now the common property of military bands."[11]

That this trend continued well into the twentieth century may be seen by the large amount of music that Sousa wrote, other than marches, operettas, and songs: eleven suites, eleven waltzes, thirteen other dances, fourteen humoresques, twenty-seven fantasies, four overtures, and 322 arrangements and transcriptions. Among the "classical" works are selections from Bizet, Smetana, Mascagni, Gounod, Mendelssohn, Haydn, Verdi, Richard Strauss, Wagner, Dvořák, Brahms, Liszt, Saint-Saëns, Bach, Donizetti, Delibes, Massenet, Grieg, and Debussy. A typical Sousa program might include anything from an overture by Wagner to a Brazilian polka ("Boa noite"); from "A Collection of Hymn Tunes of the American Churches" to *The Coon Band Contest;* from Liszt's second Hungarian Rhapsody to the sextet from *Lucia de Lammermoor*—this last played by six cornetists! It was all "popular" music because the bands made it so.

The big touring bands, independent of any municipality or military establishment, were called "business bands." They had professional managers and were very much a part of the entertainment business. From 1890 to 1910, which was their peak, business bands proliferated, and competition was keen. With the influx of immigrants from Italy, the Italian bands had a large following. That their appeal went far beyond ethnic boundaries was, above all, due to the flamboyant personalities of such Italian conductors as Stanislao Gallo, Alfredo Tommasino, Francesco Fanciulli (who succeeded Sousa as director of the U.S. Marine Band), and the sensational Giuseppe Creatore, a Neapolitan firebrand. Arriving with his Italian band in 1899, he made headlines and turned heads wherever he appeared. A New York newspaper headline is typical: "WOMEN ON TABLES IN HYPNOTIC FRENZY. Broadway Pleased by Exhibition of Athletic Leadership."[12]

The music critic of the *Kansas City Journal* was inspired to vivid description beyond the call of duty:

Now he leans over the row of music stands, he smiles the smile of a lover—pleading, supplicating, entreating, caressing—with outstretched hand, piercing the air with his baton, like a fencing master. Almost on his knees, he begs, he demands, he whirls around with waving arms. He laughs, he cries, he sings, he hisses through his clenched teeth.

He feels the music with every fibre. Now it is the rushing winds; now the mad plunging of galloping horses; now the booming of the surf on bleak rocks; and now the birds singing in the treetops, the sound of angels' wings.[13]

Anyone who could create such an impression in Kansas City deserves his share of immortality. What a pity that we do not have a recording of what he did to the *Tannhäuser* Overture at Chicago's Sans Souci Park in 1904! But, of course, he would have to be seen to be believed. Making a business of flamboyance, he overstepped the mark: the Italian vogue that he had started became a tidal wave of competition that overwhelmed him.

America's cultural pluralism was emphasized during this period not only by Italian bands and the influx of ethnic minorities but also by the rise of black musicians and their increasing prominence in the world of entertainment and popular music. The careers of James Bland and James Reese Europe are typical—although each came to a tragic end.

We have previously traced the rise of black performers in American minstrel shows, and this is how James Bland (1854–1911) got his start as an entertainer and songwriter, when he joined Haverly's Colored Minstrels. He went to England with this troupe in 1881, but his personal popularity was so great that he was encouraged to leave the company and make his own career abroad. He toured in Great Britain and on the Continent, where he was especially admired in Germany. His European reputation at that time was comparable to that of Stephen Foster or Sousa.

Songwriting—both words and music—must have come easily to Bland, for he is said to have written nearly 700 songs, some of which became popular classics. Among these are "Carry Me Back to Old Virginny," "Oh, Dem Golden Slippers," "In the Evening by the Moonlight," and "In the Morning by the Bright Light." This last was advertised as "the immensely popular End Song as Performed by Harrigan and Hart"—a celebrated team of white variety entertainers. Another very popular number was "Dandy Black Brigade—March Song and Chorus," published in 1881 "As Performed by Haverly's Colored Minstrels."

Bland's songs were equally popular with black and white entertainers and audiences, but his personal impact on the American scene was cut short by his long career in Europe. Astonishingly successful as that was, it came to an end after twenty years, when the vogue of "darkey" songs declined, and in 1901 Bland returned to the United States. By then the competition was keen, and other black entertainers and songwriters had risen to stardom. After an unsuccessful attempt to make a comeback with a musical show, *The Sporting Girl,* he died destitute, in Philadelphia. While his songs lived on, he was forgotten.

In 1940 the Virginia legislature adopted "Carry Me Back to Old

Virginny" as the official state song. But of the millions who have heard or sung it, how many are aware of the author? It might be said that James Bland achieved an enduring anonymity. But surely the composer of such lasting favorites as "In the Evening by the Moonlight" and "Oh, Dem Golden Slippers," as well as hundreds of plantation melodies, jubilee songs, sentimental ballads, and comic ditties, deserves a greater share of personal fame and a larger place in the history of America's music.

Unlike Bland, who outlived his heyday, James Reese Europe (1881– 1919) was cut down in the prime of life and at the moment of his greatest glory. He, too, wrote songs, but he was best known as a bandleader and a composer of dance music and marches. Concerning the latter, a critic for the *New York Tribune* wrote that they were "worthy of the pen of John Philip Sousa."[14] Born in Mobile, Alabama, and raised in Washington, D.C., Europe was active in New York City from 1904. There he joined a group of black instrumental performers who called themselves the Nashville Students—even though they were neither students nor from Nashville. In the spring of 1905 they gave a concert of music written and orchestrated by the black composer and performer Joe Jordan (1882– 1971), especially known for his ragtime songs and piano rags.

A novel feature of the instrumentation of this concert was the preponderance of banjos, mandolins, and guitars. In typical Afro-American style was the role of the "dancing conductor," Will Dixon. As described by an observer: "All through a number he would keep his men together by dancing out the rhythm, generally in graceful, sometimes grotesque, steps. Often an easy shuffle would take him across the whole front of the band. This style of directing not only got the fullest possible response from the men, but kept them in just the right humour for the sort of music they were playing."[15] Another novelty was that the musicians who played stringed instruments also sang in four-part harmony. Their performance was so successful that the group was booked as a daily and nightly show in New York and later appeared with acclaim in London, Paris, and Berlin.

This experience gave Jim Europe the idea of organizing, in 1910, the Clef Club Symphony Orchestra. The Clef Club was actually a musicians' union, founded to provide employment for black performers, mainly in dance orchestras. It did a thriving business, but Europe had higher ambitions. His aim was to create a "Negro Symphony Orchestra" that would embody the characteristic traits of Afro-American music in its instrumentation. Thus, at a gala concert given by the Clef Club Symphony Orchestra at the Manhattan Casino on November 9, 1911, the instrumentation consisted of fifty mandolins, twenty violins, thirty harp-guitars, ten cellos, one saxophone, ten banjos, ten pianos, two organs, five flutes, five clarinets, five double basses, timpani, and drums.

As may be seen from the printed program, this occasion was more of an entertainment than a formal concert.[16] But in May of the following year, Europe brought his symphony orchestra to Carnegie Hall, with very much the same type of instruments, including forty-seven mandolins and bandores, twenty-seven harp-guitars, eleven banjos, five trap drums, and ten pianos. The program opened with a ragtime march and included three songs by the black composer Will Marion Cook—famous for his show tunes—as well as various dances such as the tango and the waltz.

A critic for the *New York Evening Post* called this "one of the most remarkable orchestras in the world"[17]—which was literally true if we accept the meanings "extraordinary" and "uncommon." But there were objections from both whites and blacks. A writer for *Musical America* urged the orchestra to give its attention to a Haydn symphony, and the black composers to base their pieces on "classic models." A black musician agreed with this view, arguing that "all races try to develop their art from examples set by masters of other periods; and if we expect to do anything that is lasting from an artistic standpoint, we, too, must study the classics as a foundation for our work."[18]

In an interview for the *New York Evening Post* (March 13, 1914), Europe expressed his opinion, which rested on the principle that the Negro should stick to his own specialties and not try to imitate the white man's work:

> You see, we colored people have our own music that is part of us. It's us; it's the product of our souls. . . . Some of the old melodies we played . . . were made up by slaves of the old days, and others were handed down from the days before we left Africa. Our symphony orchestra never tries to play white folks' music. We should be foolish to attempt such a thing. We are no more fitted for that than a white orchestra is fitted to play our music. Whatever success I have had has come from a realization of the advantages of sticking to the music of my own people.[19]

Seldom, if ever, has a more challenging and controversial statement been made by a black musician. In the full context of the interview it appears that Europe was arguing for an ethnic identity versus subservience to a consecrated aesthetic code: "Music breathes the spirit of a race, and, strictly speaking, it is a part only of the race which creates it." But there was also a defensive factor involved, as he pointed to the practical difficulties, the technical shortcomings, that would have prevented an all-Negro symphony orchestra from competing on equal ground with a professional white orchestra. To cite an example, he used two clarinets instead of an oboe, because "we have not been able to develop a good oboe player."[20] This may seem like quibbling, because such deficiencies could be remedied with time and training. Nevertheless, Jim Europe may be regarded as a precursor of "black nationalism" in music, for it was he who said, "If we are to develop in America, we must develop along our own lines. . . ."[21]

Leaving aside such speculative issues, let us turn now to Jim Europe's activities as dance-orchestra leader, bandmaster, and popular composer. In 1914 his Tempo Club Society Orchestra became the "house orchestra" of the famous dancing partners Irene and Vernon Castle, who promoted all the fashionable dances of the time, such as the turkey trot, one-step, fox-trot, tango, maxixe (from Brazil), and others, like the Castle walk, of their own invention. They gave, however, full credit to Europe's input. According to Irene Castle, "It was Jim Europe who suggested the fox trot to us, and for all I know he may have invented it." But W. C. Handy claimed a share in the "invention," while acknowledging assistance from Europe. This is his version: "The Castle Walk and One-step were fast numbers. During breath-catching intermissions [at the Castle House dance studio], Jim would sit at the piano and play slowly the *Memphis Blues*. He did this so often that the Castles became intrigued by its rhythm, and Jim asked why they didn't originate a slow dance adaptable to it. The Castles liked the idea and the new dance was introduced. . . ."[22]

Musicologists may question this evidence for the origin of the fox-trot and insist on further documentation. But Jim Europe confirmed that credit for the fox-trot, at least musically, belongs to Handy and his "Memphis Blues." Nevertheless, without Jim Europe and the Castles it would not have become the most popular of all social dances from this period. Among the many dance numbers that he composed for them are "The Castle Lame Duck" and "The Castle House Rag."

In 1913 Jim Europe and his Society Orchestra signed a recording contract with Victor, which announced the event with pride: "The success of this organization [Europe's Society Orchestra] is due to the admirable rhythm sustained throughout every number, whether waltz, turkey trot, or tango; to the original interpretation of each number; and to the unique instrumentation, which consists of banjos, mandolins, violins, clarinet, cornet, traps and drums."[23]

Eight sides were recorded, but the last two were not released. The numbers that were issued included "Down Home Rag" by Wilbur Sweatman (a black composer), Europe's "Castle Walk," an Argentine tango, a Brazilian maxixe, and Jerome Kern's "You're Here and I'm Here"—a cross section of the current pop scene.

In 1916 the gifted black vocalist Noble Sissle (1889–1975) joined Europe's orchestra. When the United States entered World War I on the side of the Allies, Sissle and Europe enlisted together as members of a regimental band that soon became famous as the 369th U.S. Infantry ("Hell-Fighters") Band. Sissle, who was the drum major, sent correspondence about the band to American newspapers, thereby attracting a lot of attention. A typical headline was: "Ragtime by U.S. Army Band Gets Everyone 'Over There.' "[24] Sissle wrote of his eagerness "to see what would be the effect of a 'real American tune,' as Victor Herbert calls our Southern syncopated tunes, as played by a real American band." He found out, to his satisfaction, in a village of northern France, where the band's program included a favorite ragtime number, "The Army Blues." As told by Sissle: "Among the crowd listening to that band was an old woman about 60 years of age. To everyone's surprise, all of a sudden she started doing a dance that resembled 'Walking the Dog.' Then I was cured, and satisfied that American music would some day be the world's music."[25]

Sissle found many other instances that confirmed his faith in the appeal of syncopation. He wrote in the same article: "All through France the same thing happened. Troop trains carrying allied soldiers from everywhere passed us en route, and every head came out of the window when we struck up a good old Dixie tune. Even German prisoners forgot they were prisoners, dropped their work to listen and pat their feet to the stirring American tunes."[26] Juba *redivivus* in the midst of war—or, Old Dixie never dies!

In October 1918 Sissle wrote to his buddy Eubie Blake, telling him that their song "Camp Meeting Day" was "the big hit that runs thru the Paris Follies of 1918 at Marejin [Marigny] Theatre."[27] Sissle, Blake, and Europe collaborated on several songs, such as "Good Night Angeline" and "On Patrol in No Man's Land," that became hit numbers, especially as performed with Jim's band.

Back in the United States, Sissle and Blake, billed as "The Dixie Duo," did much to enhance the prestige of black musicians in the world of entertainment, continuing the tradition established by such forerunners as James Bland and the duo of Robert Cole and J. Rosamond Johnson. When they went on tour for the Keith vaudeville circuit, they appeared as accomplished musicians dressed in tuxedos, presenting their songs as entertainers *and* artists. One of their big hits was "I Wish I Had Someone to Rock Me in the Cradle of Love." (The story of their big breakthrough with musical comedy is told in chapter 20.)

As fate would have it, the triple alliance of Sissle and Blake with Europe was soon to be shattered. After the armistice Jim returned to the United States with the band that his publicity described as "the Greatest Bunch of Musicians and Jazz Artists in the World"[28] (publicity and hyperbole are Siamese twins). The term *jazz* was now in vogue, and Europe's outfit was billed as the 189th Infantry Jazz Band; officially, however, it had marched as a military band in the victory parade along New York's Fifth Avenue. For the band's projected American tour, which promised to be a national sensation, the following features were announced:

> The Famous Singing Serenaders
> The World's Greatest Saxophone Septetts
> The Soul Stirring Negro Spirituals
> The Moaning Trombone—in the "Blues"
> The Bombardment of the Percussion Twins.

James Reese Europe was well on the way to becoming the John Philip Sousa of black America and the twentieth-century successor of Frank Johnson when tragedy intervened. On the night of May 9, 1919, he was leading his band in a concert at Mechanic's Hall, Boston. An altercation resulted when one of the musicians was reprimanded for crossing the stage during a performance. Resentment flared, and Europe was stabbed in the neck. He was rushed to a hospital, but by morning he had bled to death. His best eulogy was spoken many years later by Eubie Blake: "He was our benefactor and inspiration. Even more, he was the Martin Luther King of music."[29]

It was in the 1890s that American popular music really became big business. Songs were commercial products designed for a mass market based on accelerated population growth. The older established publishers were replaced by aggressive and highly competitive newcomers. Promotion and publicity were the means, profit the aim. Some of the most successful songwriters doubled as publishers, hence as marketers of their own products. The hired song-plugger appeared on the scene, to play and sing the latest tunes for professional entertainers who might transform them into instant hits. The goal was to sell at least a million copies, and a really big hit could go into several millions. Sheet-music sales were the barometer of profits, soon to be augmented by the rising phonograph industry. The age of mass media was beginning.

In the sphere of popular songs, sentimental "tearjerkers" vied with light humor (sometimes rather "heavy"!), while topicality was always on tap, at first with the telegraph and the telephone, later with the automobile. Of the thousands of songs that appeared from the 1880s through World War I, perhaps a hundred survive as classics of American popular culture, while an increasing number have been rediscovered and revived with remarkable success, notably by the vocal-and-piano duo of Joan Morris and William Bolcom.

Of the hundreds of songwriters who straddled the turn of the century, three stand out as embodiments of the burgeoning music industry that came to be symbolized by a mythical Tin Pan Alley. They are Paul Dresser, Charles K. Harris, and Harry Von Tilzer. All three were also important as publishers.

Paul Dresser (1857–1906) was born in Terre Haute, Indiana, and was the brother of Theodore Dreiser, the famous novelist. For reasons of his own, he decided to adopt the surname of Dresser. Leaving home at an early age, he appeared in minstrel shows and eventually settled in New York. As described by Sigmund Spaeth, he was "a huge mountain of a man, with a heart as big as his body, [and] his generosity was notorious. Whatever he had he shared with others, and most of his debtors never paid him back."[30] No wonder that he failed in the publishing business and died in obscurity and poverty, deprived of "the petty pettings and flattery of that little world of which he had been part, but which now was no more for him" (as Theodore Dreiser wrote).[31] Actually, his song "My Gal Sal," published in 1905, was a big hit, but its success came too late for him to enjoy.

According to Dreiser, his brother never wrote with tongue in cheek but was really moved to tears by some of his own "tearjerkers" such as "The Letter That Never Came" and "Just Tell Them That You Saw Me." The latter was a great success, and Dreiser tells us that it resulted from "an actual encounter with a girl whose life had seemingly if not actually gone to wreck on the shore of love."[32] Her former schoolmate encounters her on the streets of a big city and asks what message he should take to her family "in a village far away." The answer is in the chorus that became notorious:

"Just tell them that you saw me/She said, they'll know the rest." Others will simply have to guess.

Although Paul Dresser's large output included topical, patriotic, and humorous songs (for which he wrote both words and music), his wide appeal depended primarily on the sentiments that he expressed with such apparently genuine feeling, coupled with a limited but spontaneous melodic gift. Dreiser maintained that his brother's songs "set forth the moods, the reactions and the aspirations of the exceedingly humble, intellectually and emotionally. . . . What other than an innocent-minded and deeply illusioned and unsophisticated democracy could this indicate?"[33]

This statement may well account for the decline of Dresser's communicative rapport since the turn of the century. The mass media have put a quietus on innocence, illusion, and humble aspirations. We now have a deeply disillusioned and relatively sophisticated democracy whose reactions and aspirations are determined by what appears on television screens, backed up by Hollywood hype.

But nostalgia never dies, and popular culture often preserves relics of the past. A case in point is Dresser's "On the Banks of the Wabash, Far Away," which he wrote in 1897 (it was later adopted as the state song of Indiana). The verses evoke nostalgic images: scenes of childhood, the old mother in the doorway, the vanished sweetheart of one's youth. The survival kit is in the chorus, with its lilting melody still as fresh as "the breath of new-mown hay." As long as there are barbershop quartets (may their tribe increase!) to cherish the art and joy of pseudonostalgia, the memory of Paul Dresser will live in at least one song.

That indefatigable chronicler of Tin Pan Alley, Isaac Goldberg, once proposed that the period we are discussing should be called "the Harrisian age of our popular song."[34] Certainly no career epitomizes it more completely than that of Charles K. Harris (1867–1930), composer of the greatest hit of the century with "After the Ball," which sold over five million copies. Born in Poughkeepsie, New York, he grew up in Milwaukee, where he taught himself to play the banjo, acquired a rudimentary knowledge of harmony, and set himself up as a songwriter in his early teens. At age eighteen he opened an office in Milwaukee with a sign that said: "Songs Written to Order." He was in business. He wanted his supply to meet the demand.

In 1892, at age twenty-five, Harris hit the jackpot with that phenomenal best-seller "After the Ball." Bungled at first by a local singer, it was catapulted to fame when Harris persuaded a well-known baritone to include it in a highly successful musical show called *A Trip to Chinatown*. On top of that, Sousa took a liking to the tune and included it in his daily band concerts at the Chicago World's Columbian Exposition. The tune, with its catchy *Tempo di valse,* also profited by the current vogue of the waltz. The text was a deliberate heartbreaker, as an old man recounts the sad story of his lost love to his little niece (she asked for it!). "I had a sweetheart, years ago," he tells her; but at the ball he saw another man kissing her—she was unfaithful! More in sorrow than in anger he left the ballroom and never saw his beloved again. Only many years later, after she was dead, did he learn that "the other man" was her brother.

This immortal ballad was of course published by Harris's own firm, of New York and Chicago, and brought him a large fortune. He wrote many other songs as well and was advertised as "Author of 'Break the News to Mother,' 'Mid the Green Fields of Virginia,' 'Hello Central, Give Me Heaven' [a little girl tries to call her departed mother], 'I've a Longing in My Heart for You, Louise,' 'For Old Times' Sake,' etc., etc."—a typical cross section of "the Harrisian age."

Most of the popular songwriters of this period began their careers early and were trained in the school of experience and hard knocks. Harry Von Tilzer (1872–1946) ran away from home to join a circus, became a vaudeville entertainer in Chicago, and in 1891 dauntlessly made it to New York City on a shoestring. He had learned to play the piano as a boy and had done some singing in his vaudeville act, so it seemed that the next step toward fame and fortune would be to get into the songwriting business. When he made his first big hit with "My Old New Hampshire Home" in 1898, he was invited to become a partner in the publishing firm of Shapiro and Bernstein. In 1900 they brought out his most famous and enduring song, "A Bird in a Gilded Cage," for which he wrote only the catchy melody (the text was by Arthur J. Lamb, a past master of gilded lyrics).

Again the seductive waltz tempo is combined with bathos in this sad tale of a "wasted life" that tells of a young woman whose "beauty was sold/ for an old man's gold." Although "there's riches at her command," she "married for wealth, not for love." The second stanza brings her to the grave, where "she is happier here at rest" than when she was "only a bird in a gilded cage"—beautiful and wealthy, but inevitably unhappy according to the code of sentimentality that proved so profitable to songwriters and music publishers.

Von Tilzer's versatility is revealed in titles such as "Down Where the Wurzburger Flows" (1902), referring not to a river but to a brand of beer; "On a Sunday Afternoon" (same year), depicting the holiday pleasures of

New York (waltz-time again!); "Good-bye, Eliza Jane" (1903), one of several songs in pseudoragtime style; "Wait till the Sun Shines, Nellie" (1905), a big money-maker and perennial favorite of barbershop quartets; "The Cubanola Glide" (1909), which rode the crest of the first Latin American wave to reach the United States; "Under the Yum Yum Tree" (1910), a contribution to the comic exotica of the period; and "I Want a Girl Just Like the Girl That Married Dear Old Dad," which became a staple of the convivial-nostalgic and impromptu songfest.

Dubbed "The Man Who Launched a Thousand Hits," Harry Von Tilzer personifies the hustling spirit of Tin Pan Alley in its palmiest days.

Notes

1. Interview in the *American Boy*, Apr. 1907; quoted in Paul E. Bierley, *John Philip Sousa: A Descriptive Catalog of His Works*, p. 47.
2. John Philip Sousa, *Marching Along*, p. 296.
3. Ibid., p. 341.
4. Interview with Helen Sousa (Mrs. Hamilton Abert), Sept. 1963, in Bierley, *John Philip Sousa: A Descriptive Catalog of His Works*, p. 47.
5. "Why Is Sousa?" *Adelaide Advertiser* (Australia); quoted in the *Musical Courier* 63 (Aug. 9, 1911): 31; and in Paul E. Bierley, *John Philip Sousa: American Phenomenon*, p. 12.
6. Bierley, *John Philip Sousa: American Phenomenon*, p. 13.
7. James Truslow Adams, *The March of Democracy* 4:23.
8. Rupert Hughes, *Famous American Composers*, pp. 116, 118–19.
9. According to Harry Wayne Schwartz, *Bands of America*, p. 241, "By 1912, Sousa had made fifteen or twenty sides for Victor." Most of these were of classical music by Berlioz, Weber, Verdi, Wagner, and others.
10. Hughes, *Famous American Composers*, p. 115.
11. Leon Mead, "Military Bands in the United States," *Harper's Weekly* 33 (Sept. 28, 1889): 785; quoted in Schwartz, *Bands of America*, p. 129.
12. Quoted in Schwartz, *Bands of America*, p. 216.
13. Quoted in ibid., p. 218.
14. Quoted in Robert Kimball and William Bolcom, *Reminiscing with Sissle and Blake*, p. 59.
15. James Weldon Johnson, *Black Manhattan*, p. 122.
16. See Kimball and Bolcom, *Reminiscing with Sissle and Blake*, p. 57.
17. Quoted in ibid., p. 59.
18. Adolphus Lewis in the *Philadelphia Tribune*, Nov. 21, 1914; quoted in Eileen Southern, *The Music of Black Americans*, 2d ed., p. 288.
19. Quoted in Kimball and Bolcom, *Reminiscing with Sissle and Blake*, p. 61.
20. Quoted in ibid.

21. *Literary Digest,* Apr. 26, 1919; quoted in Southern, *The Music of Black Americans,* 2d ed., p. 289.
22. W. C. Handy, *Father of the Blues,* p. 226.
23. Quoted in Kimball and Bolcom, *Reminiscing with Sissle and Blake,* p. 60.
24. *St. Louis Post Dispatch,* June 10, 1918; quoted in ibid., p. 67.
25. Kimball and Bolcom, *Reminiscing with Sissle and Blake,* p. 68.
26. Ibid.
27. Quoted in ibid., p. 69.
28. See ibid., p. 76.
29. Quoted in ibid., p. 72.
30. Sigmund Spaeth, *A History of Popular Music in America,* p. 276.
31. Theodore Dreiser, "Concerning the Author of These Songs," p. x.
32. Ibid., p. vii.
33. Ibid., p. ix.
34. Isaac Goldberg, *Tin Pan Alley,* p. 94.

Chapter 19
Decorum and Diversity

Since not only political and religious, but artistic freedom
as well, must be predicated of America . . . we must expect
artistic types and styles of the utmost diversity.
—Arthur Farwell, *Wa-Wan Press* (1906)

In his *Memories of a Musical Life* (1901), the venerable pianist, composer,
and pedagogue William Mason remarked on the "enormous progress in
the art and science of music" that has been achieved in America during his
long lifetime. Not only had we produced accomplished teachers who were
doing much to further "the cultivation of a refined musical taste in America," but "our country has also produced composers of the first rank, and
the names MacDowell, Parker, Kelley, Whiting, Paine, Buck, Shelley,
Chadwick, Brockway, and Foote occur at once to the mind."[1]

These names would naturally occur to Mason's mind because their
possessors all had in common a proper respect for "the cultivation of a refined musical taste in America." Most of them had studied with recommended teachers in Germany, and all were imbued with the spirit of emulation. When the critic Henry T. Finck wrote that MacDowell "has placed
American music, so far as the *Lied* and the pianoforte are concerned, on a
level with the best that is done in Europe,"[2] he acknowledged the achievement of a goal sought by several generations of American composers who
adhered to the definition of *decorum* as that which is proper, suitable, and
seemly. For many of them, musical composition could be described by another definition of the same term: an act of polite behavior. This, indeed,
might be particularly important, for most of their "fans" were ladies—the
designated guardians of polite behavior and genteel culture.

Of the composers mentioned by Mason, the oldest was John Knowles
Paine (1839–1906), who became a prototype of the academic composer in
America. Appointed to the Harvard faculty in 1862 as instructor, he at-
tained a full professorship in 1875—the first musician to hold that rank in

the United States. He was born in Portland, Maine, of a musical family. His grandfather had built the first organ in Maine, and his father was conductor of the town band. His first teacher was Hermann Kotzschmar, a German musician who came to America as a member of the Saxonian Orchestra in 1848 and a year later settled in Portland, which he helped to make a thriving music center. From him Paine gained a thorough grounding in organ and theory, and the next step was to study counterpoint and instrumentation in Germany. He chose Berlin (1858–61), where he quickly established his reputation as an accomplished organist. In 1867 he revisited Germany, and his admirable Mass in D was performed with acclaim under his direction at the Berlin Singakademie.[3] Thus he achieved the German stamp of approval that was necessary for recognition as a "serious" composer in the United States.

Such recognition came rapidly to Paine. On June 3, 1873, the Haydn Society of Portland gave the first performance of his oratorio, *St. Peter*, with the celebrated English contralto Adelaide Phillipps as principal soloist. In 1876 his setting of Whittier's *Centennial Hymn*, for chorus and orchestra, was performed in Philadelphia, and Theodore Thomas conducted the premiere of his First Symphony in Boston. The first performance of his Second Symphony, subtitled *Im Frühling* (In the spring), also took place in Boston, in 1880, and was received with unprecedented enthusiasm. Ladies waved handkerchiefs, men shouted their approval, and the dignified Mr. Dwight, arbiter of musical taste in Boston, "stood in his seat, frantically opening and shutting his umbrella as an expression of uncontrollable enthusiasm."[4]

Contrasting the First and Second symphonies, the historian Louis Elson wrote: "In the earlier works, Paine allowed the rules of music to master him, becoming somewhat pedantic and *Kapellmeisterish;* now he became master of the rules, and his poetry began to assert itself. The final movement of the 'Spring' symphony (Op. 34) is a glorious outburst of thanksgiving almost comparable with the finale of that other tribute to spring, the great B flat symphony by Schumann."[5] The adverb *almost* signifies the prevailing attitude toward American composers: they were making progress on the straight and narrow path of emulation and with perseverance and good fortune might eventually catch up with the masterpieces of the past.

Paine wrote some of his most impressive music for a performance of Sophocles's *Oedipus Tyrannus* in Cambridge in 1881, consisting of a prelude, six choruses, and a postlude. Rupert Hughes, commenting on the opening chorus as suitably classic, ironically remarked that it "soon falls back into what is impudent enough to be actually catchy!"[6] Fortunately for his reputation as an eminent academic composer, Paine seldom succumbed to the temptation of writing a catchy tune.

With his orchestral tone poems *The Tempest* (ca. 1876; after Shakespeare) and *An Island Fantasy* (ca. 1888; referring to the Isles of Shoals, off the New England coast; later published under the title *Poseidon and Amphitrite*, 1907), Paine gave impetus to a genre that would be assiduously cultivated by many of his contemporaries and successors.

Paine's contemporary Dudley Buck (1839–1909) was likewise a New Englander, an organist, and a product of the German conservatories. His background delineates the transition from mercantile to artistic interests in an American family of the upper middle class. His father was a shipping merchant of Hartford, Connecticut, and the son was intended for a commercial career. Not until he was sixteen did he begin to receive music lessons. His progress was so impressive that his father consented to a musical career. Looking for the best that money could buy, he of course packed his son off to Germany, for study at Leipzig and Dresden. Young Dudley, however, also spent a year in Paris—with what results it is difficult to tell.

Unlike the professorial Paine, Dudley Buck earned his living mainly as a church organist and private teacher, supplemented by a quantity of church music that sold well.[7] He composed for the taste of the day and found a ready market by supplying the demand for music that was mellifluous and not difficult to perform. On a larger scale, he cultivated the dramatic cantata, notably with *The Voyage of Columbus* (1885; text adapted from Washington Irving's *Life of Columbus*), and set several of Longfellow's narrative poems to music, including *Scenes from the Golden Legend* (1880) and *King Olaf's Christmas* (1881).

From the demotic point of view, Buck was a more representative composer than Paine. He probably would not have been annoyed by Elson's comment that many of his songs were "too saccharine for the purest taste."[8] He preferred popularity to purity. He was versatile, resourceful, and prolific. If some critics considered him "too suave and too popular to rank with the best American composers" (as Elson notes),[9] we might ask whether the "best" should always be equated with the unpopular. Dudley Buck's music fulfilled its multiple function in American society.

No account of America's music would be complete without an example of that typical American product the self-made man. Such was Silas Gamaliel Pratt (1846–1916), a native of Vermont whose family moved to Il-

linois when he was a boy. His father's business failed, and he was obliged
to start working at the age of twelve. His liking for music induced him to
get employment as a clerk in several Chicago music stores. Determined to
make a career in music, he saved enough money (no foundation grants
then!) to go to Germany in 1868 for three years of study in piano and composition. An injury to his wrist from overstrenuous practice thwarted his
ambition to be a concert virtuoso. So he concentrated on composition and
became a figure of national and international stature, notably with his *Centennial* Overture for the American Centennial Exposition in Philadelphia
in 1876. His magnum opus of historical Americana was the scenic cantata
America: Four Centuries of Music, Picture, and Song (1894), performed with
stereopticon projections.

Some remarks by Pratt's biographer merit quotation not only as a
comment on his career but also as advice for all aspiring composers:
"Throughout his life he had been industrious and persevering and had succeeded in bringing his name before the public as a composer of rank. In
this he was greatly aided by his exaggerated opinion of the worth of his
own compositions."[10]

By the turn of the century, Pratt and other ambitious aspirants to
fame were overshadowed by a composer whose German credentials were
of the highest. This was Edward MacDowell (1860–1908),[11] of whom Rupert Hughes wrote in 1900 that "an almost unanimous vote would grant
him rank as the greatest of American composers. . . ."[12] One wonders what
voters he had in mind. Surely not a random sampling of *homo americanus,*
who no doubt would have voted for John Philip Sousa. He appears to
have tacitly assumed an electorate of the elite—the culturally enlightened
minority—perhaps typically represented by those earnest ladies and oblig-
ing gentlemen who every summer gathered daily in the reception room of
Mrs. Celia Baxter's cottage at Appledore, in the Isles of Shoals, to hear Professor Paine or Dr. Mason perform the music of Beethoven, Chopin, and
Schumann.

About these uplifting musicales, Mason tells us in his *Memories of a
Musical Life:* "After a while I enlarged the repertoire by introducing several
of Edward MacDowell's smaller works."[13] These might have included deli-
cately wrought and sentimentally evocative pieces such as "To a Wild
Rose," "At an Old Trysting-Place," "To a Water Lily," "Told at Sunset,"
and "An Old Garden; or, With Sweet Lavender." For a livelier mood, yet
still decorous, there were "Will o' the Wisp," "By a Meadow Brook," and

"The Joy of Autumn." For contrasting moods of lyrical tenderness and emotional emphasis, he could have played pieces such as "In Deep Woods," "To an Old White Pine," "From a Log Cabin," or "To the Sea." A sterner message was conveyed in "From Puritan Days," underlined by such directions as "pleadingly" and "despairingly."

Observing that these pieces "found immediate favor," Dr. Mason was emboldened to try the effect of larger and more ambitious works, beginning with MacDowell's First Piano Sonata, the *Tragica*, composed in 1891–92. With the zeal of a missionary, he decided to play the sonata "once a day during the season," evidently hoping that familiarity would breed admiration. In this he was not disappointed, "for the 'Sonata Tragica' became eventually the favorite of the majority, and it was constantly called for."[14] Mason, like a revivalist preacher, even made converts out of unbelievers, for he tells us that "one or two ladies who found it tedious at the outset became thorough converts, and finally experienced genuine musical enjoyment from it."[15] Cultivated American women of wealth or social status or both did indeed become the principal supporters and consumers of high-art music during the next half-century.

There is no doubt that in this kind of select milieu MacDowell was admitted to the company of the immortals—and critical opinion concurred. For Rupert Hughes, the piano sonatas were "far the best since Beethoven."[16] For Lawrence Gilman, MacDowell's music was "not unworthy of the golden ages of the world."[17] When MacDowell was offered the first professorship of music at Columbia University in 1896, the nominating committee cited him as "the greatest musical genius America has produced."[18] Hughes offered what he no doubt regarded as the pinnacle of international prestige when he pointed out that "practically all of his orchestral works are published in Germany."[19] Germany, in fact, was the matrix of MacDowell's career as well as the lodestone of his inspiration. There he lived and worked during his formative years from adolescence to maturity; its imprint never left him.

MacDowell felt thoroughly at home in Germany. "His keen and very blue eyes, his pink and white skin, reddish mustache and imperial and jet black hair, brushed straight up in the prevalent German fashion, caused him to be known as 'the handsome American.' "[20] In 1882 he was at Weimar with Liszt, who praised his First Piano Concerto and recommended him to the prestigious publishing firm of Breitkopf & Härtel in Leipzig. Two years later he married his former American pupil, Marian Nevins, and they made their home in a small cottage in the woods near Wiesbaden. MacDowell was captivated by this environment. As John Erskine wrote: "The Europe he loved was a dream country, suggested by the great poets and artists and by ancient monuments, by folk-lore, by enchanting forests."[21]

By the time MacDowell and his wife returned to America in 1888, he had been living in Europe for twelve years. To quote Erskine again: "The deep emotions of his early manhood were bound up with Europe, with a tradition and an atmosphere not to be found on this side of the ocean. Perhaps he was always looking for it here, wistfully and tragically. He gave the impression, against his will, of being a visitant in his own land, trying to establish himself in alien conditions."[22]

After their return the MacDowells lived for eight years in Boston, which had the advantage of being musically a German province. His symphonic poems such as *Lancelot und Elaine* (1886), *Hamlet* and *Ophelia* (1884–85), and *Lamia* (1887–88) were compatible with the cultural climate of Boston, and his two piano concertos, in which he performed as soloist with brilliant effect, were enthusiastically received.

MacDowell's four piano sonatas represent the most characteristic expression of his late Romantic aesthetics, including programmatic content. For example, the First Sonata, *Tragica*, attempts "to heighten the darkness of tragedy by making it follow closely on the heels of triumph." The Second Sonata, *Eroica*, was described by Gilman as "the noblest musical incarnation of the Arthurian legend which we have." The Third Sonata, *Norse*, evokes the Scandinavian legend of Gudrun and Sigurd, while the Fourth, *Keltic*, deals with "Keltic tales of yore, Dark Druid rhymes that thrall." This theme was close to MacDowell's heart, as evidenced by his statement: "I have made use of all the suggestion of tone-painting in my power."[23]

This last statement holds the key to MacDowell's concept of Romanticism: he was, in most of his music, a "tone-painter." This applies, for example, to his *Indian Suite* for orchestra, op. 48 (1891–95), first performed in 1896, which consists of five movements: "Legend," "Love Song," "In Wartime," "Dirge," and "Village Festival."

For MacDowell the definitive American landscape consisted almost exclusively of New England scenes, with piano pieces such as "By a Meadow Brook" and "The Joy of Autumn." Many others were included in the series known as *Woodland Sketches* (1896) and *New England Idyls* (1901–2). As noted above, however, there was another category in which the descriptive or emotional content goes toward the "dramatic" (see, for example, "In Deep Woods," "To an Old White Pine," and "From a Log Cabin").

Another prototype in this context is "From Puritan Days," in which the musical message is underlined by such directions as "pleadingly" and "despairingly." Thereafter, we have a set of *Sea Pieces* (1898), including "To the Sea," which is directed to be played throughout "with dignity and breadth."

Speaking of the type of music that "suggests" as contrasted with music that "paints," MacDowell writes: "The successful recognition of this depends not only upon the susceptibility of the hearer to delicate shades of sensation, but also upon the receptivity of the hearer and his power to accept freely and unrestrictedly the mood shadowed forth by the composer. . . . To those who would analyze it in such a manner it must remain an unknown language; its potency depends entirely upon a state of willing subjectivity on the part of the hearer."[24]

We come now to the artistic career and personal vicissitudes of Charles Tomlinson Griffes (1884–1920), whose tendency toward poetic refinement was counterbalanced by an adventurous eclecticism. In his home town of Elmira, New York, he studied piano with a woman teacher who not only encouraged him but also provided funds for him to continue his studies in Berlin (1903–7). He had planned to be a concert pianist but was soon more attracted toward composition. Rebelling against what he called the "terribly ordinary and common" modulations prescribed by a pedantic professor, he was happier when the gifted composer Humperdinck agreed to give him lessons.

He began by emulating the later German songwriters, then veered successively toward the impressionism of Debussy, the chromaticism of Scriabin, and the primitivism of Stravinsky. Obviously, he was not fettered by the single consecrated code of the German conservatories. He was also influenced by the arch-eclectic Busoni, as well as by the "Russian Five," especially Mussorgsky.

When Griffes returned to the United States, the only immediate solution he could find for the problem of earning a living was to accept, in 1908, a position as music teacher at the Hackley School for Boys in Tarrytown, New York. For him it was not a congenial or productive situation, and he vented his irritation when he exclaimed about his pupils: "Oh! how they bore me and weary me!" Nevertheless, he was destined to remain at this school for the rest of his life. His only physical escape was to a studio apartment in Manhattan, where he went as often as he could; but in his imagination—and hence in his music—he roamed far.

John Knowles Paine

Edward MacDowell

Griffes was among the many younger American composers befriended and encouraged by Arthur Farwell, on whose critical judgment he
greatly relied. When Griffes, in 1912, was at work on his tone poem *The
Pleasure-Dome of Kubla Khan,* he noted in his diary: "I think I shall play it
to Farwell soon. . . . I am curious to see what Farwell says to the piece." In
April of the same year, when it appeared that his publisher, G. Schirmer,
was not interested in bringing out his three piano pieces ("The Lake at Evening," "The Vale of Dreams," and "The Night Winds"), Griffes confided
to his diary: "Is it Schirmer's mercenary spirit or was Farwell mistaken in
thinking so highly of the pieces? It takes away one's confidence. Am I on
the right track or not?"[25]

In spite of doubts and frustrations, Griffes continued to compose assiduously. Schirmer relented, accepted five songs and six piano pieces, and
thereafter published most of what Griffes wrote. The three pieces mentioned above, composed in 1911–12, appeared in 1915 as *Three Tone-Pictures,*
op. 5. The first refers to Yeats's poem *The Lake Isle at Innisfree,* the second
and third to poems by Edgar Allan Poe. In 1917 the *Roman Sketches* were
published, including two of Griffes's most famous pieces for piano—*The
White Peacock* (1915) and *The Fountain of the Acqua Paola* (1916)—along
with *Nightfall* (1917) and *Clouds* (1916).[26] All four refer to poems by William
Sharp, who generally published under the pseudonym of Fiona MacCleod,
and are taken from a collection titled *Sospiri di Roma* (1891). These lines
from *The White Peacock* are typical:

> Here where the sunlight
> Floodeth the garden,
> Where the pomegranate
> Reareth its glory
> Of gorgeous blossom;
> Where the oleanders
> Dream through the noontides.

Although Griffes was sensitive to word painting, as he was to every aspect of color (he tended to associate colors with corresponding musical tonalities), it should not be assumed that his descriptive pieces were necessarily inspired by the poems to which he refers. Often the titles and the quotations were added after he had composed the music. While his literary allusions certainly indicated aesthetic affinities, when composing he thought
primarily in musical terms, and tone color was his principal concern.

Griffes soon developed an interest in the Orient, and from about 1912
he was reading widely in that field. As a result he wrote the *Five Poems of An-*

cient China and Japan, for voice and piano (1917), which he characterized as based on "the 5-tone and 6-tone scale." These were followed in the same year by "A Japanese Pantomime" titled *Sho-Jo,* concerning which Griffes wrote: "There is a striving for harmonies which suggest the quarter-tones of Oriental music, and the frequent employ of the characteristic augmented second; as well as the organ point common to both systems. . . . My harmonization is all in octaves, fifths, fourths and seconds—consonant major thirds and sixths are omitted. The orchestration is as delicate as possible: thin and delicate, and the muted strings *points d'orgue* serve as a neutral-tinted background, like the empty spaces in a Japanese print."[27]

More impressionistic and attenuated in its musical orientalism is the Poem for Flute and Orchestra (1918), of which there is a fine arrangement for flute and piano by the famous flutist Georges Barrère.

Early in 1912 Griffes began to write a piece for piano based on Coleridge's poem *Kubla Khan.* After frequent revisions over several years, he was persuaded that it would be more effective for orchestra. In this form it was completed in 1917 and titled *The Pleasure-Dome of Kubla Khan.* Its first performance was by the Boston Symphony Orchestra under the direction of Pierre Monteux, on November 28, 1919, and since then it has been widely performed and admired.

Although Griffes lived before the era of foundation and federal grants for the arts, he had the patronage of two wealthy ladies, the sisters Irene and Alice Lewisohn, who in 1916 commissioned him to write a piece for chamber ensemble on "a fine old druid legend." The result was a "Dance-Drama" in two scenes, *The Kairn of Koridwen,* scored for eight solo instruments. In his diary for July 25, 1916, Griffes noted that the Lewisohns "gave me carte blanche to be modern and anything else I chose."[28] These enlightened ladies were obviously not afraid of diversity.

After its first performance in 1917, the critic Paul Rosenfeld wrote about the "unusual conjunction of timbres, split horn and piano, chromatic harp, chromatic flute and celesta, the happy superposition of conflicting tonalities, the knitting of strongly contrary rhythms that abound throughout the work. . . ."[29]

In December-January 1917–18 Griffes wrote his Sonata for Piano, which on the whole is his most original as well as his most complex and ambitious work. Although presented as a "Sonata in one movement," it is usually regarded as consisting of three connected movements: (1) *Feroce-allegretto con moto,* (2) *Molto tranquillo,* (3) *Allegro vivace.* As observed by Donna K. Anderson: "It is obvious from the many sketches of the *Sonata* that Griffes worked a great deal on the composition before he arrived at the version published in 1921 after his death."[30]

While the influence of Scriabin may be perceived in its harmonic idioms, and probably that of Stravinsky in the rather savage cross rhythms, the essential impact of the sonata is that of a powerfully creative and consistently conceived work that will stand as a peak of neo-Romantic expression in American music for piano.

While Griffes was studying in Germany, a New England composer with the impressive name of Henry Franklin Belknap Gilbert (1868–1928) was writing songs with titles such as "The Lament of Deirdre" (ca. 1897), "Faery Song" (1905), "Orlamonde" (1907), "Zephyrus" (1903), and "Salammbô's Invocation to Tänith" (1902), as well as piano pieces, including *The Island of the Fay* (1904) and *Two Verlaine Moods* (1903). At first sight, these might appear to indicate an affinity with the decorum of MacDowell and the poetic eclecticism of Griffes. But, as we shall soon see, Gilbert's eclecticism was less discriminating than that of Griffes, and in spite of his *Celtic Studies* (Four Songs; 1905), he was far removed from the Celtic-Nordic predilections of MacDowell. His penchant for diversity is adumbrated in such early pieces as the *Negro Episode* for piano (1902), with its syncopated rhythm; the song titled "Fish Wharf Rhapsody" (1909); and *Two South American Gypsy Songs,* with piano and violin obbligato (1906).

Gilbert demonstrated both in his life-style and in the bulk of his compositions that any incipient decorum in his personality was scarcely skindeep. He was born in Somerville, Massachusetts, and died in Cambridge, virtually on the doorstep of Harvard. Yet, so great was his thirst for diversity that he is best characterized as a New England maverick. True, he took the decorous path when he enrolled at the New England Conservatory of Music, specializing in the violin, and followed by studying composition with MacDowell. But instead of applying for a position as violinist with the Boston Symphony Orchestra, he used his instrumental skill and training to achieve an independent livelihood, playing in theaters and resort hotels from the White Mountains to Florida. He then took up various odd jobs, from factory foreman to silkworm grower, and in 1893 was employed as a pie cutter in a restaurant at the World's Columbian Exposition. There he not only heard exotic music from various parts of the world but also met a Russian who told him about the music of Rimsky-Korsakov and other members of the "Russian Five," who were using native folk tunes to establish a national identity in their compositions.

In 1894, together with a music-loving professor at Harvard, he presented concerts of Slavic music in Cambridge by composers such as Smetana, Dvořák, Mussorgsky, and Rimsky-Korsakov. (Dvořák was then in America, where he spent the years 1892–95 as director of the National Conservatory in New York and composed his Symphony "From the New World.") Thus Gilbert was among the first to repudiate the German hegemony and to seek refreshing currents from eastern Europe.

But beyond that, he cherished the universal spirit of folk music. "More than the music of any individual composer; more than the music of any particular school," he wrote, "the folk-tunes of the world, of all nationalities, races, and peoples, have been to me a never-failing source of delight, wonder, and inspiration."[31] Thus it appears that he envisioned America's music as part of the universal chorus of mankind.

Although he composed *Indian Scenes* for piano (1912), Gilbert was more attracted to the Afro-American scene. His most successful work, *Comedy Overture on Negro Themes* (ca. 1906), draws on tunes from the Bahamas, a Mississippi River steamboat song ("I's Gwine to Alabammy, Oh!"), and the spiritual "Old Ship of Zion." In *Humoresque on Negro Minstrel Tunes* (publ. 1913; originally titled *Americanesque* [ca. 1902–8]), he used the familiar minstrel songs "Zip Coon," "Rosa Lee," and "Dearest Mae." The *Negro Rhapsody* (1912), drew on *Slave Songs of the United States* (1867) for the two spirituals "Listen to the Angels Shouting" and "I'll Hear the Trumpet Sound," which provide the main themes. The piece was originally titled *Shout*, referring to the kind of religious ceremony with shuffling steps that was described in chapter 12.

Gilbert's most ambitious "Negro" work, *The Dance in Place Congo* (ca. 1908; revised 1916), draws its subject matter from George W. Cable's notorious article of the same title.[32] He saw in this material "a strong and romantic picture . . . full of dramatic and colorful suggestion." He also stated that he had used "these melodic fragments much after the manner of Grieg or Tchaikovsky."[33] At least he was getting away from Mendelssohn and Brahms! The subject struck him as "so picturesque and so full of dramatic possibility" that he wrote a scenario for it and thus transformed it into a ballet-pantomime, produced at the Metropolitan Opera House in New York on March 23, 1918.

Arthur Farwell, in a tribute to his friend and colleague, wrote: "Often rough in technique, though greatly resourceful, and rich in orchestral imagination, it is to the spirit of the time and nation that Gilbert makes his contribution and appeal."[34] Elliott Carter has written sympathetically of

Gilbert's "struggle to cast off the erudite tradition and yet to surmount a crudeness and amateurishness that sometimes helped to stamp his music with personality and sometimes prevented him from realizing his intentions. . . ."[35] He also remarks that Gilbert "resembles Moussorgsky and Chabrier, [who] seem to have impressed him with their vitality and unconventionality." These are indeed qualities that make Henry F. B. Gilbert distinctive in a climate of conformity.

Arthur Farwell (1872–1952) was born in St. Paul, Minnesota, of parents with a New England background, and displayed musical aptitude from an early age. He soon learned to play the violin, but his parents thought he should take up a "practical" career, so he was sent to study electrical engineering at the Massachusetts Institute of Technology. While pursuing his studies as a filial duty, he was strongly attracted by the musical activity of nearby Boston, where he heard a symphony orchestra for the first time. Although this greatly stimulated his musical interests, he nevertheless completed the four-year curriculum at M.I.T. and graduated with a professional diploma. Having thus pleased his parents, he went his own way.

His lifelong penchant for diversity was strongly aroused in January 1892, when he met an eccentric German-American pianist and composer named Rudolph Gott (1872–1911), who was of the same age but had already led an exciting bohemian life. Recalling their first meeting later, Farwell wrote: "Neither before nor since . . . have I ever approached so near to the deep, the spontaneous and torrential fountain-source of natural creative force in music. . . ."[36] He quotes Gott as saying that "Madness with method is better than method and no madness."[37] Farwell never forgot the impact of that extraordinary and visionary personality, and many years later (1932–34) he composed the *Rudolph Gott* Symphony, based on themes and unfinished sketches found among Gott's papers. As such, it is a unique landmark of musical Romanticism in America.

After graduating from M.I.T., Farwell studied theory and composition with Homer A. Norris, an organist and theorist who had received his training in Paris, and who in 1896 published *Practical Harmony on a French Basis*—a precursor of the trend away from Germany and toward France in American composition. Farwell also sought advice from MacDowell, who gave him a critical drubbing and then found a publisher for some of his early piano pieces. In 1897–99 he pursued his musical studies in Germany and France, then returned to the United States and looked for a job. Less bohemian than Gilbert, he accepted a lectureship at Cornell University but soon decided that the groves of academe were too confining. He was a man with a vision: an ideal to pursue and a mission to accomplish—not only for himself but for America and its people. Diversity for him was not only an ideal but a way of life: he was a teacher, a prolific composer, a community choral director, a creator of musical pageants as well as song and light festivals, a student of Indian lore, lecturer, author, journalist, editor, publisher, and artistic lithographer. He brought the message of America's music from the Atlantic to the Pacific and insisted on diversity as its essence, including "notably, ragtime, Negro songs, Indian songs, Cowboy songs, and, of the utmost importance, new and daring expressions of our own composers, sound-speech previously unheard."[38]

In reply to a colleague who asked his advice on whether to settle in Chicago or Boston, Farwell wrote: "I cannot uphold you in sympathizing with *all* that is being done in Boston, for despite much that is truly worthy in its achievement, I believe that much that is being done here is in direct opposition to what America must eventually affirm and maintain. Modern European culture can be gained here, as in New York . . . but not so easily a sense of the great awakening spirit of this nation, which must sooner or later infuse all art which is to strike root and live in this soil."[39]

Because of his strong feeling for symbolic values and what he called the "art-spirit," which he regarded as closer to religion than to what "is commonly regarded as Art" in Western civilization, Farwell was deeply attracted to American Indian lore. He went among the Indian tribes, especially the Omahas, and learned of their ceremonies, dances, and melodies. Much of his Indianist music was composed from 1897 to 1937, mostly for piano, or for voice with piano. *The Domain of Hurakan* (1902) and *Navajo War Dance* no. 1 (1905) were orchestrated (1910 and 1944 respectively), and there is a version for piano and small orchestra of *Dawn: Fantasy on Two Indian Themes* (1904), while *The Hako* (1922) was written for string quartet. The *Navajo War Dance* no. 2, for piano (1904), became one of his best-known pieces. There are versions of both Navajo dances for chorus a cappella, no. 1 included in *Four Indian Songs* (1937) and no. 2 arranged by Farwell in 1947 for the Westminster Choir directed by John Finlay Williamson. This version is remarkable for its unique combination of tribal authenticity and concert effectiveness.

American Indian Melodies, harmonized for piano, appeared in 1900, followed in 1905 by *From Mesa and Plain* and *Impressions of the Wa-Wan Ceremony of the Omahas,* also for piano. *Three Indian Songs* (1908), for medium voice (also arranged for mixed voices or chorus), are deeply effective:

"Song of the Deathless Voice," "Inketunga's Thunder Song," and "The Old Man's Love Song."

Farwell took an interest in all aspects of American folk-ethnic music within his reach. In 1905 he published in his Wa-Wan Press edition *Folk-Songs of the West and South,* consisting of six numbers with only one from Indian lore: "Bird Dance Song" of the Cahuilla tribe. Two were Negro spirituals, two Spanish-Californian songs, and one a cowboy song, "The Lone Prairee"—of which Farwell commented that it was "perhaps the first cowboy folk-song to be printed, both words and music."[40] The spirituals are "De Rocks a-Renderin' " and "Moanin' Dove," both collected by Alice Haskell in the South Carolina Sea Islands.

These songs, together with many other pieces by Farwell and other American composers who had difficulty finding publishers, appeared in the Wa-Wan Press editions, an enterprise founded by Farwell in 1901, which continued until 1912, having published music by thirty-seven composers, including ten women. Among the latter was Gena Branscombe (1881–1977), who later achieved prominence with several large symphonic and choral works such as *Pilgrims of Destiny* (1929) and *Youth of the World* (1933), as well as many songs. Also well represented were Edgar Stillman Kelley (1857–1944) and Harvey Worthington Loomis (1865–1930), both of whom await a revival.

Farwell himself had to wait until the 1970s for a revival—and even a revelation—of his copious and varied output, much of which remained unpublished. Moreover, after his death his manuscripts were dispersed and eventually turned up at a warehouse sale, where they were acquired by a devoted admirer of his music, Evelyn Davis Culbertson. In 1970 a complete reprint of the Wa-Wan Press was published in five volumes, edited by Vera Brodsky Lawrence, and two years later *A Guide to the Music of Arthur Farwell* appeared, edited by his son Brice Farwell. Many performances of the music followed thereafter, most notably the first public presentation of the great Sonata for Piano, op. 113 (1949), played by Neely Bruce in 1974. Also revealed were the innovative *Polytonal Studies* for piano (1940–52), of which forty-six were "conceived" but only twenty-three completed.

Farwell was both a man of practical action and a mystic who thought in terms of symbolism and visionary values. These views are reflected in the various *Symbolistic Studies* that he wrote, such as "Perhelion" (no. 2, 1904)—signifying "the point nearest the sun in the orbit of a planet"—and "Mountain Vision" (no. 6, 1912). Both were originally written for piano, but the latter was rewritten for piano solo with orchestra (1938).

Other belated revelations are the chamber-music works such as the impressive Piano Quintet, op. 103 (1937), the Sonata for Flute and Piano (1949), and the Sonata for Cello and Piano, op. 116 (1950). Many of the songs have also been rediscovered, most notably those to poems by Emily Dickinson, of which he wrote thirty-nine, beginning with "The Sea of Sunset" in 1907 and ending with "I Had No Time to Hate" in 1949—but only six were published in his lifetime. The creative surge began with settings of twelve poems in 1938–41, followed by a group of ten in 1944. He was evidently experiencing and expressing an ever-deeper identification with the mystical-symbolic message of poems such as "Wild Nights! Wild Nights!" "The Grass So Little Has to Do," and "An Awful Tempest Mashed the Air," which constitute the *Three Emily Dickinson Songs* of 1949. An impressive recognition of the songs was signaled by the selection of twelve to be included in the vocal competition sponsored by the John F. Kennedy Center for the Performing Arts and the Rockefeller Foundation in 1979.

Meanwhile, a number of black American composers were coming to the fore, notably Harry Thacker Burleigh (1866–1949), Clarence Cameron White (1880–1960), R. Nathaniel Dett (1882–1943), and William Grant Still (1895–1978), all of whom cultivated the Afro-American heritage.[41]

In the context of compositional diversity, Still stands out as a leading figure. To begin with, he had a mixed heritage, for his maternal grandfather was a Spaniard who settled in Florida. Then he was exposed to various types of American popular music, from Mississippi, where he was born, to Arkansas, where he was raised. Moving to the East, he played in the pit orchestra for performances of *Shuffle Along* in New York and Boston. But he was determined to become a full-fledged composer, and for this he sought—and received—lessons from Chadwick in Boston, followed by two years of study with Varèse in New York (1923–25). Thereafter he combined "serious" composition with popular arrangements for leading jazz bands.

Among the numerous works that made him famous, the *Afro-American* Symphony (1930) was conspicuous for its first performances by the Rochester Philharmonic Orchestra in 1931 and 1932, followed by three performances in Germany, directed by Howard Hanson in 1933. In his later years Still wrote as follows about the symphony:

Twenty-two years ago when I wrote the *Afro-American Symphony*, I did so in the hope that I would achieve one principal objective: to present in symphonic form a typically American idiom. To that end, I devised an original theme in the manner of the Blues and around it constructed the symphony. Because this principal theme appears so prominently in each of the four movements in various forms, it may well be considered the basic unifying factor in the work as a whole. After the symphony was composed as an abstract work, it seemed advisable to invent a program for it, so that audiences might be able to understand the music better. I there prefaced each movement with excerpts from the poems of Paul Laurence Dunbar, explaining that the symphony was intended to portray Colored Americans of the period following the Civil War, the "Sons of the Soil."[42]

The following presents one of the poems to which he refers:

IV. Lento, con resoluzione
Be proud, my Race, in mind and soul.
Thy name is writ on Glory's scroll
In characters of fire.
High mid the clouds of Pam's bright sky
And truth shall lift them higher.[43]

Still's concept of the "Americas" went beyond the United States, and he was particularly drawn to the Afro-Hispanic cultures of Latin America, especially in the Caribbean area. In the *Danzas de Panama* (1948) he draws on authentic Panamanian folk dances: "Tamborito," "Mejorana y socavón," "Punto," and "Cumbia y Congo." The suite is written for string quartet (or orchestra) but makes use of percussive effects as the musicians simulate the sound of native drums.

Thus we have delineated the triumph of diversity that Arthur Farwell predicted when he wrote: "America is too diverse in its sympathies and ideals to acknowledge any one national or racial influence as paramount in its musical art, but absolute creative freedom is essential to its national character."[44]

Notes

1. William Mason, *Memories of a Musical Life,* p. 261.
2. Henry T. Finck, *Songs and Song Writers,* p. 246.
3. See John Knowles Paine, *Mass in D,* with copious documentation by Peter Eliot Stone, Andrew Raeburn, and Gunther Schuller, New World Records NW 262/263.
4. Richard Aldrich, "Paine, John Knowles," *Dictionary of American Biography* 14:152.

5. Louis C. Elson, *The History of American Music*, p. 166.
6. Rupert Hughes, *Famous American Composers*, p. 157.
7. See William K. Gallo, "The Life and Church Music of Dudley Buck."
8. Elson, *The History of American Music*, p. 232.
9. Ibid., p. 233.
10. Fannie L. Gwinner Cole, "Pratt, Silas Gamaliel," *Dictionary of American Biography* 15:178.
11. See Arnold T. Schwab, "Edward MacDowell's Birthdate," pp. 233–39. (Previously it had been assumed that he was born in 1861.)
12. Hughes, *Famous American Composers*, p. 34.
13. Mason, *Memories of a Musical Life*, p. 255.
14. Ibid., pp. 255, 256.
15. Ibid., p. 256.
16. Hughes, *Famous American Composers*, p. 52.
17. Lawrence Gilman, *Edward MacDowell*, p. 176.
18. Quoted in ibid., p. 39.
19. Hughes, *Famous American Composers*, p. 49.
20. Gilman, *Edward MacDowell*, p. 12.
21. John Erskine, "MacDowell, Edward Alexander," *Dictionary of American Biography* 12:26.
22. Ibid.
23. Gilman, *Edward MacDowell*, pp. 149, 152, 156, 158.
24. Edward MacDowell, *Critical and Historical Essays*, ed. W. J. Baltzell, p. 259.
25. Quoted in Donna K. Anderson, *The Works of Charles T. Griffes*, pp. 247, 232.
26. Griffes made an orchestral version of *The White Peacock*, which in June 1919 was used to accompany a dance presentation by Adolf Bohm and his Ballet-Intime.
27. Anderson, *The Works of Charles T. Griffes*, p. 363.
28. Quoted in ibid., p. 341.
29. Paul Rosenfeld, "Mr. Griffes en Route," *Seven Arts*, Apr. 1916; quoted in Edward M. Maisel, *Charles T. Griffes*, p. 340. For a reprint of this entire review, see Anderson, *The Works of Charles T. Griffes*, pp. 339–43.
30. Anderson, *The Works of Charles T. Griffes*, p. 307.
31. Quoted in Arthur Farwell and W. Dermot Darby, eds., *Music in America*, vol. 4 of *The Art of Music*, ed. Daniel Gregory Mason et al., p. 409.
32. See George Washington Cable, "Creole Slave Dances: The Dance in Place Congo," in Bernard Katz, ed., *The Social Implications of Early Negro Music*, pp. 31–68.
33. Henry F. Gilbert, "Program Notes," *Boston Symphony Orchestra Programs, 1919-20*, Feb. 20, 1920, pp. 1087–88; quoted in Katherine Marie Eide Longyear, "Henry F. Gilbert, His Life and Works," p. 230.
34. Farwell and Darby, eds., *Music in America*, p. 410.
35. Elliott Carter, "American Figure, with Landscape," p. 223.
36. Arthur Farwell, "Story of Rudolph Gott," *Musical America* 22 (Aug. 14, 1915): 9.
37. Ibid. (Aug. 21, 1915): 10.

38. Arthur Farwell, *Wa-Wan Press Monthly* 2 (Sept. 1903); quoted in Gilbert Chase, "The Wa-Wan Press: A Chapter in American Enterprise," introductory essay to *The Wa-Wan Press, 1901–1911,* ed. Vera Brodsky Lawrence, vol. 1, p. ix.

39. Farwell, *Wa-Wan Press Monthly* 6 (Sept. 1907); quoted in Chase, "The Wa-Wan Press," pp. x–xi.

40. Arthur Farwell, introduction to "Folk-Songs of the West and South: Negro, Cowboy, and Spanish-Californian," *Wa-Wan Press* 4 (1905); reprinted in *The Wa-Wan Press, 1901–1911,* ed. Lawrence, vol. 3, p. 44.

41. Eileen Southern, *The Music of Black Americans,* 2d ed., pp. 266–68, 272–75, 423–27, and passim.

42. Quoted in Ralph Ricardo Simpson, "William Grant Still," pp. 44–45.

43. Ibid., p. 46.

44. Arthur Farwell, introduction to Farwell and Darby, eds., *Music in America,* p. xvii.

Chapter 20

On with the Show

My dream was all about New York theaters, music-publishing
houses, and famous actors and actresses with whom I was
hobnobbing along Broadway.
—George M. Cohan, *Twenty Years on Broadway*

In the 1860s, while blackface minstrelsy was still flourishing and melodrama was the prevailing type of theatrical fare, two events occurred that
heralded a new era in American musical entertainment: an extravaganza
called *The Black Crook* had its premiere at Niblo's Garden, and Tony Pastor
opened his "Music Hall" in the Bowery. Both events had their locus in
New York City.

The Black Crook, billed as an "Original and Grand Magical Spectacular
Drama," opened on September 12, 1866, and had a run of sixteen months.
Its production was the result of fortuitous circumstances. An American
impresario had brought to New York a French ballet troupe for a presentation at the Academy of Music, which burned down while their show
was in rehearsal. Meanwhile, the manager of Niblo's Garden had con-
tracted to produce a melodrama titled *The Black Crook,* based on the familiar legend of a man who makes a pact with the devil by agreeing "to win
over to the Devil's cause one human soul for each year of life vouchsafed
to him."[1]

The bright idea then occurred of combining the fanciful melodrama
with the stranded French ballet troupe. The result was an unprecedented
triumph, with an extraordinary blending of elegance and allurement, elaborate sets, dazzling stage effects, romantic mystification—and, of course, the
imported ballet corps of 100 female dancers. The daring display of female
figures clad in tights was sensational—that is, in a respectable theater. The
most effective publicity came from clergymen and other guardians of morality who denounced it from the pulpit and press, often with the titillating
detail of an eyewitness. For example, "*ladies* dancing so as to make their un-

dergarments spring up, exposing the figure beneath from the waist to the toe. . . ."[22]

Although the music for the original production of *The Black Crook* was credited to Thomas Baker (who wrote the "Transformation Polka"), it actually consisted of borrowings and interpolations by various hands. One of its most successful and catchy songs was "You Naughty, Naughty Men"—but this was dropped when the performer who sang it left the show the following year. Regardless of this or that omission or alteration, *The Black Crook* continued to fascinate American audiences for most of what remained of the nineteenth century.[3] Indeed, the interpolations and innovations contributed largely to its enduring success, as "successive revivals increasingly replaced the formal French ballets with popular dancing and topical variety entertainment."[4]

The mixture of extravaganza and variety was to flourish in the early decades of the new century, notably in the grandiose productions of the New York Hippodrome and such spectacular revues as the *Ziegfeld Follies*. Meanwhile, the late decades of the nineteenth century saw the rise of comic opera and operetta, as well as plays with music, singing, and dancing that prefigured the rise of musical comedy. Many of these shows were imported from Europe or were written by Europeans who came to America, so that the native product faced strong competition—and there was no protective tariff for musical entertainment. While many American composers and librettists reached for success by imitation—often under the overwhelming impact of Gilbert and Sullivan—the indigenous musical theater was increasingly marked by national or local traits, notably in the modes of popular music, dance, speech, and manners. Social patterns and characteristic themes were also derived from a rapid and varied increase in immigration. With the burgeoning of variety, vaudeville, farce-comedy, extravaganza, revue, comic opera, and operetta—as well as updated versions of the old burlesque shows—the American musical theater was emerging and taking shape.

In the realm of extravaganza, an immediate follow-up to *The Black Crook* was *Humpty-Dumpty*, which opened in New York on March 10, 1868, and had a longer run than its sensational predecessor. Although its special effects were lavish and even startling (such as a steamboat explosion and fire), its appeal relied less on sexy displays than on the unique talent of America's greatest pantomime artist, George L. Fox, who starred in the role of the Clown, giving 1,128 performances as the show went on tour and had several revivals.

The next sensational success was *Evangeline,* which opened at Niblo's Garden in 1874 and had a more distinctive American quality. To begin with, the music was by an American, Edward E. Rice, and he and his librettist, John Cheever Goodwin, were prompted by their negative reaction to British burlesque. Their motto appears to have been: "Anything they can do, we can do better." (Often, *better* meant *different.*)

Evangeline had elements of both burlesque (in its primary meaning of comic parody) and extravaganza, for it was a wildly fantastic parody of Longfellow's famous narrative poem. America's favorite household poet receives an accolade in the opening number (obviously aimed at the masses rather than the classes):

> There's a man you all have heard about,
> Who poetry has written,
> That all of you have read,
> And on it have been smitten.

The public was more immediately "smitten" by the quirks and eccentricities and surprises of the plot, which Rice refers to as "audacious contingencies"—such as the spouting of a predatory whale on stage and the dancing of a trick cow, activated by two men operating fore and aft. The most original and enigmatic figure is that of "The Lone Fisherman," a silent character who appears in various marginal routines, as though meditating on the follies and foibles of humanity. In a way difficult to define, he seems a typical American character—perhaps a figure of folklore, or on the way to becoming one.

Although *Evangeline* was labeled an "opera bouffe" in the published edition with words and music, it was billed in performance as a "musical comedy"—presumably the first American show to be thus designated. The tremendous success of *Evangeline* was unprecedented, and it is much more significant in the development of American musical comedy than the much-touted *Black Crook,* which was essentially European in context and character. The chances for a revival of *Evangeline* are unpredictable—at least in these pages. But a revival might be envisaged, on stage or screen, as an updated imitation of an outmoded parody of a familiar American poem.[5]

Contemporaneous with the vogue of musical extravaganzas was the transition from variety to vaudeville, personified in the remarkable career of Tony Pastor (1837–1908), who brought variety entertainment out of the

Grotto of Talacta scene from *The Black Crook,* as depicted on sheet-music cover to
the "Black Crook Waltzes" (1867). Photo courtesy of the Billy Rose Theatre Collection, The New York Public Library at Lincoln Center, Astor, Lenox and Tilden
Foundations.

disreputable saloons, where singing waitresses were the chief attraction for male customers, and transformed it into decent entertainment that respectable women could enjoy.

Pastor's father, a violinist in the orchestra of the Park Theatre in New York, disapproved of Tony's boyhood penchant for minstrel shows and circuses. But there was no restraining the talented and ambitious youngster, who at fourteen was already into show business. He soon became "chief clown" and later ringmaster in a traveling circus. The Civil War interrupted his circus career; but he soon hit upon the idea that was to transform the entire social situation of American popular entertainment, when "he made the first bid in history for women customers in the variety theater."[6]

In 1875 Tony Pastor moved his theater from the Bowery to Broadway, and by 1881 he was established in his highly respectable "New Fourteenth Street Theater." There he lured the ladies not only with excellent entertainment but with additional inducements such as door prizes, ranging from sewing machines and new hats to dress patterns and sewing kits.

Although versatile in many roles, Tony Pastor's forte was the comic song, most often with topical allusions, so that his repertory became a musical mirror of the times—and as such deserves to be revived, if only for its historical interest. If effectively performed, it also might have more rewarding qualities. Among the topical songs are "Root, Hog, or Die," "Down in the Coal Mines," and "The Girl All Dressed in Blue." One of the most popular numbers that Pastor introduced was "Hunkey Dorey"—a title that soon became a part of American slang as the equivalent of *okay*.

Tony Pastor's tactics enticed not only women but whole families, from children to grandparents. This made variety not only respectable but highly profitable. The result was the type of family entertainment called vaudeville, which did not shun sexiness (vide Eva Tanguay!) but never tolerated indecency or vulgarity. Under the expert management of two theatrical producers, B. F. Keith and E. F. Albee, vaudeville soon became big business, with a chain of lavishly ornate theaters in the principal cities and a national network of booking offices.

Vaudeville was entertainment for the people, providing amusement from morning till night at prices that everyone could afford. But surely the typical American touch was that for a quarter you could also bask in the splendor of a gorgeous "palace"! The shows drew on every type of popular entertainment, incorporating much from the circus—especially the acrobats and trained animals, as well as jugglers and clowns—but also featuring magicians, comedians, impersonators, instrumentalists, singers, and whatnot. Famous artists also performed (I remember hearing—and seeing!— Paderewski playing the piano at Keith's in my youth). Current types of popular music such as ragtime were widely featured, including performances on a variety of instruments, from mandolins to drums and banjos to saxophones. Tom Brown and his Six Brown Brothers were a big hit as they played arrangements of catchy tunes with their "combo," comprising the entire saxophone family, from soprano to bass. Music was also used as background for acrobats and jugglers and, of course, for dancers, as well as for walk-on and exit cues.

By the end of the 1920s, vaudeville was being eclipsed by the movies, and soon its golden harvest would turn into dross as Hollywood's output swept the nation. Yet, when sound was added to the silver screen, motion pictures continued to provide music for the millions on an unprecedented scale.

Until now our focal point has been Manhattan, from the Bowery to Broadway. New York City had become the symbol of success in show business, with "Broadway" as a metaphor of the American theater. Hence we must inevitably return to that metropolis of entertainment; but we shall do so by a roundabout route that will take us from the Atlantic to the Pacific, and from the Mississippi to the Great Lakes. The protagonist of this odyssey will be Ned Harrigan (1844–1911).

His father had been first mate on a windjammer before settling in Manhattan, where Ned was born and raised. Adventure and the sea were in his blood, with an undercurrent of music as he picked on the banjo or sang the songs that his mother had learned in the South. At sixteen he was apprenticed to a shipyard but preferred to appear with a minstrel show in the Bowery. His mother's death, followed by family dissension, prompted him to ship for New Orleans as an able seaman. Then he went to sea again, this time sailing for California, which he eventually reached after being rescued from a shipwreck. His career as a professional entertainer began in San Francisco, where for two years (1867–69) he polished his impersonation of ethnic types and featured topical songs in his repertory. There he also acquired a stage partner, Sam Rickey, with whom he went on the road throughout the West, heading for Chicago, where their show was a big success. Thus they were encouraged to go on to New York, where they made an immediate hit with two comic sketches, *The Little Fraud* and *The Mulcahey Twins*. But the partnership broke up, and Ned was on the road again, doing blackface with a minstrel troupe.

Soon Harrigan was in Chicago again, and there he met a youngster called Tony Hart (1855–91), who was also appearing in a minstrel show. Hart's speciality was female impersonation, but he was a versatile actor and entertainer. A partnership was formed, and they revived *A Little Fraud* with great success in Chicago and Boston. In October 1871 they reached New York. Harrigan's career had gone full circle, and soon he and Hart were to make theater history in the city of his birth.

They played at several Manhattan theaters and toured with Tony Pastor; then, in December 1872 they began a two-year run at the Theatre Comique (formerly the Globe), which marked their big breakthrough in New York. Greatly contributing to their success was an association with the English composer David Braham, who had come to the United States at the age of eighteen and soon made a name and a career as theater conductor and songwriter. He wrote the music for the song that made Harrigan and Hart famous, "The Mulligan Guards," which swept the country with its grotesque satire of pseudomilitary exhibitionism.

During the 1870s Harrigan and Hart continued to present topical sketches at various New York theaters, with Braham providing the music, and with additional actors as needed. Typical titles were *The Italian Ballet Master* (1876), *Walking for dat Cake* (1876), *The Maloney Family* (1876), and *Our Irish Cousins* (1877)—all indicative of the ethnic emphasis that came to be the cultural trademark of their shows.

With the presentation of *The Mulligan Guard Ball* at the Theatre Comique on January 13, 1879, Harrigan and Hart made the transition from variety to musical play, interspersing songs and dances with spoken dialogue and involving a larger cast of characters. At first the plays centered on Irish-Americans and black Americans, but soon brought in Italians, Germans, Chinese, and other ethnic groups. We can agree with Robert Toll that "Harrigan established urban ethnic groups as major characters on the American stage."[7] While Hart was indispensable as a versatile actor, including blackface roles and female impersonations, it was Harrigan who wrote the dialogue and the words of the songs. These ranged from the topical to the farcical, and from the nostalgic to the satirical. Although the songs now seem very dated, it is precisely this quality that makes them so representative of the American urban-ethnic scene in the last decades of the nineteenth century.

Typical Harrigan songs are "The Babies on Our Block," a spirited picture, both humorous and sympathetic, of family life and social recreation, interspersed with references to familiar Irish tunes; "The Skidmore Fancy Ball," referring to the black Belvidere Militia's fund-raising entertainment; and "Paddy Duffy's Cart," evoking memories of boyhood pals. Sigmund Spaeth has summarized the achievement of Harrigan and Hart as follows: "The team of Harrigan and Hart had made a permanent place for itself in the history of the American stage and of our popular music. They had created a distinctive type of entertainment and summed up the manners of their time in a fashion that must be considered unique."[8]

Playwright-lyricist Charles H. Hoyt (1860–1900) and director-composer Percy Gaunt (1852–96) next appeared on the scene with their musical farces presenting everyday local characters instead of the mythical, exotic, fantastic, or fashionable personages favored in most extravaganzas and many operettas. Of course, the characters represented farcical stereotypes but were nonetheless recognizable as specimens of common humanity. Hoyt and Gaunt hit the jackpot with their musical farce-comedy *A Trip to Chinatown* (1890), the first Broadway show to achieve 657 performances. (We have previously mentioned the interpolation of "After the Ball" as one of its unexpected hit songs.)

A Trip to Chinatown was not only extraordinarily successful but also highly typical of the musical farce-comedy that flourished at the turn of the century. A wealthy bachelor, Mr. Ben Gay, refuses to allow his niece and nephew to visit San Francisco's Chinatown with a group of their friends. The young people, however, are only using Chinatown as a pretext; their real intention is to attend a masked ball at a fashionable restaurant. A note from Widow Guyer intended for the nephew, saying she will meet him at the restaurant, is delivered by mistake to Uncle Ben. Delighted at the prospect of a rendezvous with the widow, he tells the young people that he has changed his mind and they may go to Chinatown. Act 2 is built around the resulting imbroglio at the restaurant, as both Uncle Ben and the younger set try to avoid being "discovered" while dining in adjacent rooms.

Besides "After the Ball," two other songs from this production became best-sellers and have endured as popular staples: "Reuben and Cynthia" ("Reuben, Reuben, I've Been Thinking") and "The Bowery." The latter, combining a contagious *Tempo di valse* with a humorous account of misadventure in Manhattan's tough Bowery district, is a classic of its kind. The fourth stanza is both typical and topical:

I went into a concert hall,
I didn't have a good time at all;
Just the minute that I sat down
Girls began singing, "New Coon in Town,"
I got up mad and spoke out free,
"Somebody put that man out," said she;
A man called a bouncer attended to me,
I'll never go there any more!

The song "New Coon in Town," written by Paul Allen and referred to in the above stanza, had been a hit song in 1883—one of the many "coon" songs by both whites and blacks that appeared at this time. Along this line, and in the wake of the immense success of *A Trip to Chinatown*, an all-Negro musical show titled *A Trip to Coontown* was successfully produced in New York in 1898. It will be appropriate now to discuss both the antecedents and the further development of Negro musicals.

Early attempts to launch Negro musicals, such as *The Creole Show* (1889) and *Black America* (1895), were linked to minstrelsy. *The Creole Show*, however, in featuring a chorus line with sixteen girls, also offered what came to be a staple of musical comedy. Eileen Southern has noted that *A Trip to Coontown* was "the first full-length musical play written and produced by blacks on Broadway."[9] The leading spirit behind this enterprise was the celebrated entertainer and playwright Robert ("Bob") Cole (1863–1911), who had achieved success in vaudeville with his partner J. Rosamond Johnson. *A Trip to Coontown* appears to have fluctuated between musical comedy and operetta, as happened with *The Shoo-Fly Regiment* (1906) and *The Red Moon* (1909). These were written in collaboration with J. Rosamond Johnson and his brother James Weldon Johnson (well known as a poet).

The year 1898 was also notable for the production of an all-Negro musical show (or comedy-revue) that had a big success on Broadway. This was *Clorindy; or, The Origin of the Cake-walk*, with music by the highly gifted and well-trained black composer Will Marion Cook (1869–1944) and lyrics by the poet Paul Laurence Dunbar. Cook had studied violin at the Oberlin Conservatory and with Joseph Joachim at the Berlin Hochschule, and composition with Dvořák at the National Conservatory in New York. But he still kept the popular touch.

Reminiscing about the memorable opening of *Clorindy* at New York's fashionable Casino Roof Garden in the summer of 1898, Cook wrote:

When I entered the orchestra pit, there were only about fifty people on the Roof [Garden]. When we finished the opening chorus, the house was packed to suffocation. . . . The show downstairs in the Casino Theatre was just letting out. The big audience heard those heavenly Negro voices and took to the elevators. . . .
. . . . My chorus sang like Russians, dancing meanwhile like Negroes, and cakewalking like angels, black angels! When the last note was sounded, the audience stood and cheered for at least ten minutes.[10]

Clorindy owed much of its success to its star performer, Ernest Hogan—dancer, actor, comedian, songwriter—who had come up from minstrelsy. In 1896 he wrote the hit song "All Coons Look Alike to Me," which aroused resentment among many blacks who objected to the term *coon*— and especially to its connotation in the title. Later in life (he died in 1909), Hogan tried to justify himself by saying: "The coon [raccoon] is a very smart animal." While admitting that the song "caused a lot of fights," he asserted that "it gave the big lift to the show business."[11]

In his subsequent shows, Cook relied strongly on the team of George Walker and Bert Williams, stars of the vaudeville circuit, who also had their own theatrical company. His next three shows flopped; but with *In Dahomey* (1902) he had better luck, and after a run in New York, it played in London for seven months. It had a topical theme, satirizing the "back to Africa" movement promoted by the American Colonization Society. Two other successful productions followed: *In Abyssinia* (1906) and *In Bandana Land* (1907).

With Walker's retirement in 1907 the production partnership came to an end. Will Marion Cook was too optimistic when he said, after *Clorindy,* "Negroes were at last on Broadway, and there to stay."[12] In the words of James Weldon Johnson, the years from 1910 to 1917 were "the term of exile of the Negro from the downtown theatres of New York."[13]

These were crucial decades in the development of the American musical theater, and one of the main problems was to emulate the high standard set by Gilbert and Sullivan without entirely succumbing to their overwhelming influence. When the first American production of *H.M.S. Pinafore* took place in 1878, its impact was tremendous. It launched the vogue of light opera (also called comic opera or operetta) that swept the United States over the next several decades. Among the native-born Americans to achieve success in this field was the versatile and dynamic John Philip Sousa. From 1882 to 1915 he completed twelve operettas, of which only a few have withstood the difficult test of time. One problem that no American composer could really solve during this period was the lack of a brilliant librettist, such as Gilbert was for Sullivan. Nevertheless, even if enduring masterpieces were relatively few, many a lasting tune and lilting lyric have become a viable contribution to America's musical heritage.

Sousa's early operettas from the 1880s, such as *Desiree* and *The Queen of Hearts,* were failures. But in the next decade he reached his peak with *El Capitan* (1895), *The Bride Elect* (1897), and *The Charlatan* (1898). The first of these, produced in Boston on April 13, 1896, had the greatest success and has been the most frequently revived. With the celebrated singing comedian De Wolf Hopper in the title role, *El Capitan* was performed almost continuously for four years in the United States and Canada, with a run of six months in England. The libretto was by Charles Klein, with lyrics by Tom Frost and Sousa.

Except for a secondary love interest, the plot is broadly farcical. Don Errico Medigua, newly appointed viceroy of Peru, finds that his predecessor is attempting to regain power, presumably with the help of a fierce rebel leader called "El Capitan." Although it is Medigua's duty to confront the rebels, he has no stomach for fighting. As he later confesses to his *innamorata:*

> I'm an animated bluffer,
> And at fighting I'm a duffer.
> My adventures grim and gory
> Are a highly seasoned story;
> I'm as hollow and as noisy as a double-bass bassoon,
> Why, the very smell of powder makes me tremble like a leaf.

El Capitan is ostensibly a spoof of militarism. Medigua is a fake hero; his saving grace is that he admits it. Yet he must thwart the rebels or lose his job. Learning by chance that "El Capitan" has been killed in a brawl (unknown to the ex-viceroy), Medigua disguises himself as the ferocious chieftain and leads the rebel soldiers in forced marches until they are overcome by fatigue and demoralized by drink. Meanwhile, he is hailed as a hero, and the daughter of the deposed viceroy falls in love with him. This thickens the plot because Medigua is married to a domineering and possessive wife. Eventually all the strings are unraveled, the mistaken identities are revealed, the appropriate couples are united, and the curtain comes down with all principals and chorus singing "We beg your kind consideration for El Capitan," to the rousing strains of the title march. Not even Gilbert and Sullivan could match that glorious sound!

When Gilbert and Sullivan came to the United States in 1879 to direct the first authorized performance of their most popular light opera, *H.M.S. Pinafore* (previous American performances were pirated), they set a standard that challenged the best efforts of American librettists and composers. French and Viennese operettas—products of a long tradition—also flooded the market. Soon European composers began coming to America and presenting their products in person. A very special case was that of Victor Herbert (1859–1924).

Born in Dublin, Ireland, Herbert was musically trained in Germany and became an accomplished cellist. In 1886 he married the Viennese singer Therese Förster, whose engagement at the Metropolitan Opera of New York motivated his coming to America. For the next ten years he was active as a cello performer, orchestra leader, bandmaster, and composer mainly of "standard" works. A turning point came in 1894, when he was persuaded to write an operetta titled *Prince Ananias*. Although it was not a success, it gave him an incentive to continue and to persevere in this direction—with results unprecedented in the history of America's music.

Beginning with *The Wizard of the Nile* in 1895 and ending with *The Dream Girl* in 1924, he wrote forty operettas, of which several have remained enduring landmarks of the American musical theater—also sustained in motion-picture versions. Among the best known are *The Fortune Teller* (1898), *Babes in Toyland* (1903), *Mlle Modiste* (1905), *The Red Mill* (1906), *Little Nemo* (1908), *Naughty Marietta* (1910), *Sweethearts* (1913), and *The Princess Pat* (1915).

Apart from their stage presentations, the operettas of Victor Herbert have yielded a lasting heritage of popular songs. From *Mlle Modiste*—originally a great success with the vivacious Fritzi Scheff in the title role—we have "The Time and the Place and the Girl," "I Want What I Want When I Want It," and, above all, "Kiss Me Again." *Naughty Marietta* brings us "Italian Street Song," " 'Neath the Southern Moon," "I'm Falling in Love with Someone," and "Ah, Sweet Mystery of Life." The ever-popular *Babes in Toyland* has "Toyland" and "March of the Toys," while the much-revived *The Red Mill* had a big hit with "Streets of New York," along with such perennial favorites as "The Isle of Our Dreams" and "Because You're You."

Sigmund Spaeth lauds Herbert for having achieved "the conscious and studied creation of a well-made piece of music that deliberately aims at popular appeal and miraculously attains it"[14]—no mean achievement for a musician who studied composition at a German conservatory! But his indoctrination was brief, whereas his American-born contemporary Reginald de Koven (1859–1920) spent many years in Europe, studying harmony and composition in Stuttgart, Frankfurt, Vienna, and Paris. As it happened, this did not prove to be a handicap for his success as a writer of operettas: he wrote seventeen that were produced and were well received. But in the severe test of time, he lags far behind Herbert. Beginning with *The Begum* in 1887, he ended with *Her Little Highness* in 1913; his most enduring work is *Robin Hood* (1890)—although its best-remembered number, "Oh! Promise Me," survives mainly as an adjunct to weddings.

Readers interested in tracing the rise of our popular musical theater from the turn of the century to World War I may find some precursory significance in two productions from the year 1894 that serve as prototypes for what came to be known respectively as revue and musical comedy. The former is represented by *The Passing Show,* with music by the Viennese-born Ludwig Englander (1859–1914); the latter by *A Gaiety Girl,* an import from London. Both immediately led to a string of imitations. The foreign antecedents of these shows might chagrin a confirmed Americanist, but the essence of a trend is not its origins but its transformations. The growth of our musical theater is analogous to the development of American society as a whole: vastly heterogeneous yet unmistakably distinctive.

Discussing *A Gaiety Girl,* Cecil Smith discerns a product of mixed parentage, with American farce-comedy taking "a trip to England, where it entered into a liaison with British comic opera and burlesque. A *Gaiety Girl* was the result of that union; she was part English and part American. . . ."[15] Well and good; but beyond that liaison were multiple strands and ethnic entanglements, ranging from Africa to the Orient and from continental Europe to Latin America.

As for *The Passing Show*—described by Ewen as "vaudeville . . . dressed up with the splendor of a Broadway extravaganza"[16]—its major inspiration came from Paris, but with plenty of American ingredients, including a plantation dance in which "a dozen colored youths" participated. It was an elaborate hodgepodge, with something for everybody. As we shall see, the formula caught on.

A new era in the American musical extravaganza opened with the colorful career of Florenz Ziegfeld (1869–1932), born and raised in Chicago. There, in 1893, he gave a big fillip to the World's Columbian Exposition, especially by introducing the "strong man" of vaudeville, Eugene Sandow. Often clad with little more than a fig leaf, Sandow lifted anything from a Greek column to a grand piano, including two women riding bicycles. After a profitable tour with Sandow, Ziegfeld settled in New York City, where he scored the first of many sensational coups by presenting the glamorous Anna Held in a show called *The Parisian Model* (1906). Featuring her provocative song "I Can't Make My Eyes Behave," the show ran for thirty-three weeks on Broadway and then first went on tour.

Ziegfeld next moved to the rooftop garden of the New York Theater, calling it the "Jardin de Paris." It was there, in 1907, that the *Follies* which made him famous began. The formula was that of "a fast-paced collage of raucous, broad comedy, snappy production numbers, parodies of celebrities and fads, and lots of pretty women."[17] Ziegfeld rapidly enlarged the scope of the entertainment with every kind of extravagant presentation, including current topics, comedy routines, and, of course, the ever-present gorgeous girls, and by 1911 his show was proudly billed as the *Ziegfeld Follies*. Eventually its motto would be "Glorifying the American Girl"—but that was not until 1922, and we shall return later to that phase of the American musical extravaganza (chapter 29).

During the early years of the twentieth century, the most effective ethnic-demotic strain in American musical comedy was represented by the brash and versatile George M. Cohan (1878–1942). In 1924, when his agent persuaded him to write his autobiography, Cohan stated: "My idea in this story is to appeal to the general public. To me the college professor with the tall forehead is of no more importance than the ordinary buck dancer or dramatic critic."[18] One such critic had written in the *Dramatic Mirror:* "Precisely why these Cohan concoctions are so popular with the New York public is a mystery the critic has never succeeded in solving to his personal satisfaction."[19] But Cohan was interested only in the collective satisfaction of his public. An appropriate motto for him—fashioned after Admiral Farragut's exclamation at the battle of Mobile Bay—might have been: "Damn the critics—full speed ahead!"

George M. Cohan began his theatrical career as a boy, touring with his parents and sister on the vaudeville circuit. At sixteen he was the guiding spirit of the Four Cohans, and in 1898 he made his first big hit with the topical song "I Guess I'll Have to Telegraph My Baby." He was soon busy writing songs and sketches for Broadway, displaying both the industry and the facility that soon brought him fame and fortune. If he did not actually become "The Man Who Owns Broadway" (the title of his 1909 musical comedy), he fulfilled the wish expressed in his song "I Want to Be a Popular Millionaire."

Although "Give My Regards to Broadway" was surely his theme song, Cohan was also "a trooper known to the Broadways of a nation— Chicago, St. Louis, Kansas City, Atlanta, New Orleans, Denver, San Francisco." In at least one instance he owed his success to the hinterland. His musical comedy *Little Johnny Jones* had a lukewarm reception at New York in 1904 but made it big on the road. Revised and improved, it was a hit on Broadway a year later, with George M. in the title role of an American jockey who goes to England to compete in the Derby. It has some of his most typical and highly successful songs, including "The Yankee Doodle Boy," personifying his chosen image as the quintessential American. This was also emphasized by changing the correct date of his birth (July 3) to July 4, so that he could sing, with conviction,

> I'm a Yankee Doodle do or die,
> A real live nephew of my Uncle Sam's,
> Born on the Fourth of July.

Cohan's next show, *Forty-five Minutes from Broadway* (1906), which starred Fay Templeton and Victor Moore, was a spoof of suburban life that put New Rochelle in the limelight. It was followed in the same year by *George Washington, Jr.,* memorable mainly for its highly theatrical display of patriotism in "You're a Grand Old Flag." In 1914 he turned to the revue format with *Hello, Broadway.* The rest of his career, increasingly beset by disappointments, scarcely concerns us here—with one exception: in 1917 he wrote the favorite song of World War I, "Over There."

Prominent among musical showmen making their careers at this time were Jerome Kern (1885–1945) and Irving Berlin (b. 1888). The latter's chief contribution was popularizing so-called ragtime numbers—which actually meant almost any kind of tricky syncopation—and making the current novelty dances an integral part of the show. His big opportunity came when he was asked to write the music for Charles Dillingham's production of *Watch Your Step* (1914)—billed as a "syncopated musical show" and characterized as a "ragtime riot and dancing delirium." The stars of the show were Irene and Vernon Castle, who delighted the public with the superb quality of their dancing in novelty numbers, including a tango. A critic remarked, "Mr. Berlin knows how to put the 'go' in tango"—musically speaking. Another critic, with a quip that might seem equivocal in 1914, commented, "Berlin is now part of America."

His name was actually Israel Baline, and he was raised in New York City, where he and his Jewish immigrant parents had settled in 1893. But as Irving Berlin he was to continue embodying "the American mix" in popular musical shows for many decades, as we shall note in a later chapter.

Jerome Kern, also born in New York of Jewish parents, received a "proper" musical training in piano, harmony, and composition, including study in Europe. But from the beginning he was attracted to popular musical shows, and in 1904 he worked as rehearsal pianist in that milieu. This eventually led to interpolating his own songs in various productions, and in 1914 he made a big hit with "They Didn't Believe Me," written for a musical titled *The Girl from Utah*. The following year he obtained his first major success with a musical comedy, *Very Good Eddie*, produced at the intimate Princess Theatre (December 23, 1915), with a libretto by Guy Bolton based on a farce by Phillip Bartholomae (*Over Night*, 1911) and lyrics by Schuyler Greene.

The Princess Theatre was small, seating only one less than 300. Yet the musicals presented there in 1915–18 effectively demonstrated that small-scale comedies, with no more than two sets and a small chorus and cast, could compete favorably, in attendance and box-office receipts, with more lavish productions. *Very Good Eddie* was such a hit that it soon crossed the barrier by moving uptown to a much larger theater on Broadway. After a return run at the Princess Theatre, it went on the road for a nationwide tour that lasted two years.

Other highly successful musicals by Kern produced at the Princess Theatre were *Oh, Boy!* (1917) and *Oh, Lady! Lady!* (1918)—both with lyrics by P. G. Wodehouse. But *Very Good Eddie* has a special significance because of its 1975 revival at the Goodspeed Opera House in East Haddam, Connecticut, where it was presented with great verve and charm—as with all of that company's many revivals and premieres. On December 21, 1975, *Very Good Eddie* moved to the Booth Theater in New York City, where it was acclaimed by the critics and enjoyed by enthusiastic audiences (I was lucky to be in their number). We should add that several songs by Kern not originally written for this musical comedy were interpolated in the 1975 revival. On the other hand, one of the big hits, "I've Got to Dance," had been dropped from the Princess Theatre performances but proved to be a bonanza for the modern public.

The decades from 1910 through the 1920s were a prolific period for Kern. He had a resounding success in 1920 with *Sally*, lavishly produced by Ziegfeld with elaborate sets and costumes by Joseph Urban. It starred

Marilyn Miller in a rags-to-riches romance, with a sentimental duet, "Look for the Silver Lining," as the musical hit of the show. In 1923 came *Stepping Stones,* featuring the versatile dancing talent of the Stone family—Fred with his wife and daughter. The amiable *Sunny* premiered in 1925, but what followed will be told later in chapter 29.

Meanwhile, in 1913 a black revue, *Darktown Follies,* had opened at the Lafayette Theater in Harlem, with J. Leubrie Hill—"the colored George M. Cohan"—as the guiding spirit: composer, conductor, set designer, manager, producer. What made the show remarkable were the dances, especially the "Circle Dance" at the end of the second act, to the vocal accompaniment of Hill's "At the Ball, That's All." This was a shuffling dance, taking off from the "ring shout" and its African antecedents. Although the show did not make Broadway, it did move downtown to the Grand Opera House on Twenty-third Street, and its dances and songs soon became the talk of the town. A novelty dance that attracted much attention was the "Texas Tommy," a forerunner of the "Lindy Hop," with its basic step a kick and hopping three times on each foot.

"We're fighting to get on Broadway," said Leubrie Hill. But the only way any part of his show got there was when Florenz Ziegfeld bought the rights to "At the Ball, That's All" and introduced it in his own revue—without mentioning Hill in the program or hiring any of the original cast. Nevertheless, *Darktown Follies* had made its mark—and it opened the way for an all-black musical show that, seven years later, did make it on Broadway.

This historic event occurred on May 23, 1921, when *Shuffle Along* opened at the Sixty-third Street Theatre for a run of 594 performances—which in those days meant a big hit. The show was put together by Eubie Blake and Noble Sissle in partnership with the comedy-dancing team of Flourney Miller and Aubrey Lyles. Their only assets consisted of talent and determination, so on the financial side they had to produce the show in cooperation with a white manager. Their tryouts in New Jersey and Pennsylvania were disappointing, and they reached Manhattan with a deficit of $18,000. Although the opening-night reviews were mixed, enough were so highly favorable that success was assured. After the New York run came fifteen weeks in Boston, a run in Chicago, and a nationwide tour that lasted until the summer of 1923. Of course, it played to mixed audiences in white theaters—which was a triumph for the American people as well as for show business.

Billed as "A Musical Melange," *Shuffle Along* had the bare semblance of a plot. Basically it was a broad satire of small-town politics, with a three-cornered mayoralty election race. Two of the candidates are crooks who try to outsmart each other and end up in a hilarious fistfight. Eventually a reform candidate wins, and the two would-be politicians are ousted.

Dancing was a vital ingredient of the show, with Charlie Davis as a fast tap dancer specializing in the "Buck and Wing," and Tommy Woods expertly performing his original, slow-motion acrobatic dances. The chorus line was splendid, and it included the sensational Josephine Baker, later to be a star of the *Folies Bergères* in Paris. Sissle and Blake were highly effective entertainers, and their songs were the heart of the show. These included "Love Will Find a Way," "Bandana Days," "Low Down Blues," "Full of Jazz," "Baltimore Buzz," "Shuffle Along," and "I'm Just Wild about Harry"—which was later to appear as a campaign song for Harry Truman.

Kimball and Bolcom, the biographers of Sissle and Blake, regard *Shuffle Along* as the "most telling example of Negro influence on American show business at large. . . . From it the explosion of the black American musical style was to fan out in all directions beyond Broadway to permeate the spirit of the Jazz Age."[20] Marshall Stearns adds his encomium: "When *Shuffle Along* broke through to Broadway, a new trend was set, a new legend born. Negro musicals were in demand thereafter, and dancing in musical comedy finally took wing."[21]

Notes

1. Cecil Smith, *Musical Comedy in America*, p. 17.
2. Letter from Charles Burnham to *New York Sun*, Sept. 23, 1932; quoted in ibid., p. 16.
3. See, for example, Robert Toll's description of the 1887 revival of *The Black Crook* by the Kirafly Brothers—a truly "modern" extravaganza for that period—in *On with the Show*, pp. 175–76.
4. Smith, *Musical Comedy in America*, p. 19. See also Charles M. Barras, *The Black Crook, a Most Wonderful History*, 2d ed., with "A Graphic History of the Parisian Ballet Girls" (Philadelphia: Barclay and Co., 1882).
5. For comprehensive data on *The Black Crook, Humpty Dumpty,* and *Evangeline*, see Deane L. Root, *American Popular Stage Music, 1860–1880*.
6. Isaac Goldberg, *Tin Pan Alley*, p. 62.
7. Toll, *On with the Show*, p. 183.
8. Sigmund Spaeth, *A History of Popular Music in America*, p. 192. For the "team" of Harrigan and Hart, see pp. 179–95.
9. Eileen Southern, *The Music of Black Americans*, 2d ed., p. 297.

10. Will Marion Cook, "Clorindy, the Origin of the Cakewalk," in *Anthology of the Afro-American in the Theatre,* ed. Lindsay Patterson, p. 54.

11. Quoted in Tom Fletcher, *100 Years of the Negro in Show Business,* pp. 138, 139–40.

12. Southern, *The Music of Black Americans,* 2d ed., p. 298.

13. James Weldon Johnson, *Black Manhattan,* p. 170.

14. Spaeth, *A History of Popular Music in America,* p. 321.

15. Smith, *Musical Comedy in America,* p. 116.

16. David Ewen, *New Complete Book of the American Musical Theater,* p. 407.

17. Toll, *On with the Show,* p. 302.

18. George M. Cohan, *Twenty Years on Broadway, and the Years It Took to Get There,* p. 6.

19. Quoted in Smith, *Musical Comedy in America,* p. 150.

20. Robert Kimball and William Bolcom, *Reminiscing with Sissle and Blake,* p. 148.

21. Marshall W. Stearns and Jean Stearns, *Jazz Dance,* p. 132.

Chapter 21
New England Again

One truth you taught us outlived all the rest:
Music hath Brahms to soothe the savage breast.
—D. G. Mason, lines to Percy Goetschius, on his eighty-second birthday

On Thanksgiving Day in the year 1895, a young American composer wrote in his journal: "Thank God Wagner is dead, and thank God Brahms is alive. And here's to the great classical revival of the twentieth century in America."[1] The name of this ardent young classicist—he was then only twenty-two—was Daniel Gregory Mason. The reader is familiar with the name of Mason and what it stands for in America's music: the transition from the singing-school tradition of early New England to the "better music" movement of Lowell Mason and the aesthetic refinement of William Mason. Daniel Gregory was the nephew of William, and with him this New England dynasty reaches its culmination in an almost ecstatic surrender to the potent spell of the European Classic-Romantic tradition. In a volume of reminiscences Mason described the musical atmosphere of his early years: "Our whole view of music was based on the style of the classic and romantic symphonists, beginning with Haydn and Mozart and ending with Mendelssohn and Schumann. Even Bach was rather on the edge of the music we recognized, and the rhythmic freedom or unmetricality of, say, Gregorian chant was decidedly beyond our horizon."[2]

Mason essentially never changed his orientation, and later in the same volume of reminiscences he says: "One of my deepest convictions has always been a sense of the supreme value in art of balance, restraint, proportion—in a word of classic beauty."[3] Mason also felt, and expressed, "an instinctive antipathy" toward everything in American music that did not conform to this ideal of classical balance and restraint. This attitude was shared by most of the "proper" New England composers, from Paine to Parker. Although they have been called "Boston Classicists," a better label would be "Conservative Eclectics."

Horatio William Parker (1863–1919) personifies the concept of cultural elitism rooted in the richest soil of the New England heritage. He came from a highly cultured family of Auburndale, Massachusetts. His mother was not only a church organist and pianist who gave him his first lessons in music but also a lover of literature who knew Greek and Latin and imbued him with the spirit of the classics. After musical studies in Boston he went to Germany in 1882 and became a pupil of Rheinberger in Munich. Upon his return three years later, he began his career as a hard-working professional musician, active as church organist, choir director, teacher, and composer, achieving a respectable prosperity for himself and his family. He personified the Anglo-American work ethic, which resulted in his demise at the age of fifty-six. From 1893 until his death he was Battell Professor of Music at Yale.

At the age of eighteen Parker wrote in his diary: "Every man should contribute to the advancement of the human race, should train himself carefully for work, should do something better than it has ever been done before. . . ."[4] This last desideratum obviously presented a strong challenge to a young American composer in the 1880s. But if we add "by an American," the qualification becomes less formidable. This conciliatory position was evidently taken by some well-disposed critics commenting on Parker's oratorio *Hora Novissima* (1893). After its New York premiere a reviewer praised "its boldness, originality and merit," concluding that it should be honored as "an example of what an American musician can accomplish."[5] Another reviewer declared that it "took rank among the best works written on this side of the Atlantic."[6] In other words, Parker was doing very well *for an American*. The same reviewer, however, was not content to leave well enough alone; he predicted that Parker's oratorio would be "received with praise in England"—which proved to be only a half-truth.

In 1899 *Hora Novissima* was performed at the Three Choirs Festival in Worcester, England, and did indeed receive considerable praise. But a critic for the *London Daily Chronicle* took a negative view: "The music oscillates between Gounod and Dvořák, with a decided preference for the former, and occasionally there are suggestions of Mendelssohn. . . . From beginning to end the work lacks individuality."[7] Even at home the lack of "individuality" was noted by well-disposed critics, although they evidently disguised this under the cloak of laudable emulation. However, the important musical newspaper writer Philip Hale chose to display his high opinion of *Hora Novissima*, as follows:

I recognize his great talent, a talent that approaches genius, if it is not absolute genius. He has the natural gifts, he has the learning. He has the strength, the sensuousness of healthy youth. His strength is not coarseness; his sensuousness is not eroticism [a dig at Wagner?]. The conception of this impressive work is of noble proportions; the execution of which is an honor to our national art.

Nor is it perhaps foolish to predict that the future historian of music in America will point back to "Hora Novissima" as a proof that when there were croakers concerning the ability of Americans to produce any musical compositions save imitations of German models, a young man appeared with a choral work of long breath that showed not only a mastery of the technique of composition, but spontaneous, flowing, and warmly colored melody, a keen sense of values in rhythm and in instrumentation, and the imagination of the born, inspired poet.[8]

Who could ask for anything more? American musical criticism at this time was marked by the spirit of Advent—the coming of the Great American Composer. Edward MacDowell had appeared to answer that hope. Now Louis Elson ventured to predict that Horatio Parker "will be the greatest composer that America has produced"—with the proviso that he shed some of his "pedantic" proclivities.[9]

Parker is the prototype of the American Composer as Gentleman, without a taint of bohemianism or irregularities of any kind—and with no trace of the uncouthness associated with Americans, to judge by the impression he made on a provincial journalist in England: "Mr. Parker is not in appearance like the traditional American. Young looking, stoutly built, clean shaven, with black moustache, and gifted with a charming manner, he commended himself at once to the choir. . . ."[10]

Parker's identification with New England culture was both deep-rooted and strongly held. In one of his lectures he said: "New England is the centre from which has radiated thus far a great part of all progress in Art, Literature, and other intellectual pursuits in America, and it seems perfectly fair to say that an History of Music in New England would practically cover the subject of the History of Music in America."[11]

This cultural localism was closely allied to Parker's Anglo-Saxonism, about which he wrote:

On the whole, I am inclined to think that music among the Anglo-Saxons is built upon a more solid foundation, one better calculated to sustain the weight of an imposing super-structure, than the music of the Germans. The music of the Germans is now so colored by externals that it has hardly a separate existence. That of the French seems not to come from deep enough, not to go deep enough—superficial. That of the Italians is opera—a form with such manifest limitations that one may almost regard it as outside the sphere of reasonable activity among Anglo-Saxons.[12]

He then goes on to say that if American music "remains untainted" by these negative influences it "seems sure to bring forth results of great beauty and value." We may gather that he was against diversity and in favor of decorum, with "beauty" as the ultimate value.

Parker was industrious and prolific; hence his total output is impressive. He favored large choral works such as cantatas and oratorios, as well as odes, motets, and ballads. He also wrote copiously for organ, and for voice and piano. Typical titles are *The Dream-King and His Love* (cantata; 1893) and *King Gorm the Grim* (ballad with orchestra; 1908). These now strike us as period pieces—images of a vanished cult; but with the voracious revivalism in American music since the bicentennial they may yet reappear. Meanwhile, we should note that Parker also had contact with the more mundane aspects of American society. For example, he participated in the opening of the Wanamaker department store in Philadelphia (1911), for which he composed a cantata titled *A Song of Times*, extolling and idealizing the benefits of commerce and technology. The score includes sections for military band and for a bugle corps. Might this not be a welcome alternative to *Hora Novissima* in a presumptive Parker revival?

Arthur W. Foote (1853–1937) differed from his New England colleagues in one respect: he did not study in Europe. But the Atlantic Ocean was, of course, no barrier to the assimilation of musical traits and styles from that continent. As Rupert Hughes remarked about Foote's music: "I know of no modern composer who has come nearer to relighting the fires that beam in the old gavottes and fugues and preludes."[13] Hughes was writing about the Serenade for String Orchestra, op. 25, consisting of Prelude, Air, Intermezzo, Romance, and Gavotte. He went on to say that these pieces "are an example of what it is to be academic without being only a-rattle with dry bones." One could at least hope to cover the bones attractively.

Arthur Foote was born in Salem, Massachusetts, and as a concession to his musical inclination his parents permitted him to take piano lessons when he was fourteen. At Harvard he directed the Glee Club and studied music with Paine, but still had a business career in sight when he graduated. It was B. J. Lang, to whom he had gone for lessons on the organ, who persuaded him that music should be his profession. So Foote became an organist and pianist, opened a teaching studio in 1876, began to compose, and settled down to a productive and congenial career in Boston. Like most of his contemporaries he was a Brahmsian but was flexible enough to be also a devotee of Wagner. He also followed the lead of Liszt in his ambitious symphonic poem *Francesca da Rimini* (1893), after the famous episode in Dante's *Divine Comedy*. The Brahmsian influence appears in his chamber music, including three string quartets, a piano quintet, and two piano trios. He wrote several suites for strings, which continue to be performed, as well as a quantity of church music, piano pieces, works for organ, and more than 100 songs, of which the best known is "The Night Has a Thousand Eyes."

Among the adjectives variously applied to the music of Arthur Foote are *noble, pure, refined, dignified, earnest,* and *agreeable.* It seems to me that these not only characterize an individual production but also epitomize an era and an aspiration that culminated in *fin-de-siècle* Boston.

We should not, however, take leave of Foote without mentioning—and indeed, emphasizing—his cantatas with orchestra, especially *The Wreck of the Hesperus* (1888) and *The Skeleton in Armor* (1893). These may be regarded as a culmination of the long, productive tradition of the dramatic cantata in America, of which *The Wreck of the Hesperus,* in particular, is exemplary. It deserves to be rescued from the sea of oblivion.

The Bostonians were not exclusively a men's club. One of the distinctions of the New England musical movement was that it nurtured the emergence of the first American women to achieve wide professional recognition as composers in the larger orchestral forms. They were Margaret Ruthven Lang (1867–1972) and Amy Marcy Cheney (1867–1944), who preferred to be known by her married name, Mrs. H. H. A. Beach. The former was born into the club, so to speak, for she was the daughter of Benjamin J. Lang (1837–1909), the pianist, conductor, composer, and teacher who was long an important influence on the musical life of Boston. He taught his daughter, who also studied with Chadwick and MacDowell, as well as in Germany. She faithfully followed the path traced by Chadwick in such works as the overtures and the Ballade for Orchestra (1901); *Sappho's Prayer to Aphrodite,* for contralto with orchestra (1895); *Phoebus,* for baritone and orchestra; and other large vocal-symphonic compositions. She also wrote about 200 songs, for which she became widely known, including "The Grief of Love" and "Oh, What Comes over the Sea." Rupert Hughes wrote that he considered her "Lament" to be "one of the greatest of songs, and proof positive of woman's high capabilities for composition."[14]

Lang's *Dramatic* Overture was performed by the Boston Symphony Orchestra in 1893: the first time that it had presented the work of an American woman composer.

Amy Cheney Beach (as we now prefer to call her) illustrates in her career both the problems and the opportunities of being a woman composer in a man's world. Of a musical family, and precociously gifted, she was encouraged to take up the piano, for that instrument (unlike the cello or the flute) was considered perfectly proper for women. But her family considered marriage, social position, and financial security more important than a musical career. So in 1885 she became the wife of Dr. H. H. A. Beach, a prominent and wealthy physician, who was slightly older than her father. Thus her professional career, in any independent sense, was thwarted, even though she had already been acclaimed as a soloist with the Boston Symphony at age sixteen. In the words of a biographer: "She did continue to perform and compose, however, but in a more lady-like attitude, under the patronage of her cultured husband."[15] This perhaps does not do justice to her independent spirit, for on October 30, 1896, the Boston Symphony Orchestra gave the first performance of her *Gaelic* Symphony—the first work in that form to be composed by an American woman. Four years later it was followed by another "first" when her Piano Concerto was performed by the same orchestra on April 6, 1900, with the composer as soloist.

These are the only symphonic works Beach composed, although she wrote several works for chorus with orchestra, as well as chamber music, pieces for piano, some church music, and many songs. Official commissions confirmed her status: a *Festival Jubilate* for the dedication of the Women's Building at the Chicago World's Columbian Exposition in 1893; *A Song of Welcome* for the Trans-Mississippi Exposition in Omaha in 1898; and a *Panama Hymn* for the Panama-Pacific Exposition in San Francisco in 1915.

The death of her husband in 1910 made her a free woman, and she rekindled her career aspirations with a four-year sojourn in Europe, where she concertized widely, presenting much of her own music. A performance of her *Gaelic* Symphony in Germany enhanced her prestige at home. From 1914 she lived in New York City but spent her summers in New England. Some of her songs such as "Ah, Love, but a Day" and "The Year's at the Spring" retained a lasting popularity.

In spite of her success, Amy Cheney Beach was in some ways a victim both of her family's social ambitions and of the "sexual aesthetics" that prevailed when she began her career. Women in music were sex-typed, and since all the important critics were men, they fell victim to sexually biased judgments on what women could or should achieve in musical composition. Women as composers became a highly controversial issue, even though by 1902 a writer remarked that "it is no longer looked upon as an eccentricity for women to compose."[16] The question was *what* and *how* they should compose.

These attitudes are reflected in criticisms of Beach's *Gaelic* Symphony. For example, Philip Hale wrote: "Occasionally she is noisy rather than sonorous. Here she is eminently feminine. A woman who writes for orchestra thinks 'I must be virile at any cost.'. . . The only trace of woman I find in this symphony is this boisterousness. . . ."[17]

A reviewer in the *Musical Courier* (February 23, 1898) has some variations on this theme: "The symphony of Mrs. Beach is too long, too strenuously worked over and attempts too much. Almost every modern composer has left a trace in her score, which in its efforts to be Gaelic and masculine ends in being monotonous and spasmodic. . . . There is no gainsaying her industry, her gift for melody . . . or her lack of logic. Contrapuntally she is not strong. Of grace and delicacy there are evidences in the Siciliano, and there she is at her best: 'but yet a woman.' "[18]

The sexual bias of such criticism is obvious, and the message is clear: when she displays qualities that are sex-typed as feminine, such as a gift for melody, or grace and delicacy, there is condescending approbation. But efforts "to be masculine" are put down, with the implication that a woman has no business trying to write a symphony anyhow. It is true that Beach was "not strong contrapuntally," but had she striven to be strong in that masculine domain, she would have been faulted for attempting to be "virile at any cost." Is it any wonder that Beach wrote only one symphony and one concerto, but 150 songs?

May I add as a coda an experiment that I tried on a large undergraduate class at the University of Texas. Having played excerpts from string quintets by Beach and Foote, I asked for a show of hands on which sounded more "masculine." A large majority voted for Amy Cheney Beach.

Women were becoming important as patrons of the arts, and none more so than Isabella Stewart Gardner of Boston, whose lavish Italian-style villa, Fenway Court, was filled with famous paintings and often with the sound of music. Many musicians vied for her favor, but the one whom she most admired and befriended was the Alsatian-born violinist and composer Charles Martin Loeffler (1861–1935), who emigrated to the United States in 1881 and a year later became first violin of the Boston Symphony Orchestra. In 1903 he resigned and retired to a farm he had bought in Medfield, where he continued to compose until his last years, producing his most important works during this period. These include *A Pagan Poem,* for orchestra with piano obbligato (1901; rev. 1907); *Canticum Fratris Solis,* a setting for voice and chamber orchestra of St. Francis's "Canticle of the Sun" (1925); and *Evocation* (1931), for orchestra, women's chorus, and speaking voice. He combined impressionism with technical refinement and poetic feeling. His affinities were essentially French, and he set to music several poems by Baudelaire and Verlaine.

Gardner met Loeffler soon after his coming to Boston, and she was one of the first to recognize his talent as a composer. He often played for her musicales at her Beacon Street home, and later at Fenway Court. One can scarcely resist the quip that he was her court musician. But that, indeed, was very much a part of the Boston scene.[19]

Two other musical personages prominent in Mrs. Gardner's entourage were Henry Lee Higginson (1834–1919), who founded the Boston Symphony Orchestra in 1881, and the Austrian conductor Wilhelm Gericke, who led the orchestra in 1884–89 and again in 1898–1906. Except for its first conductor, George Henschel, who was of Polish-Jewish descent, all the leaders of the Boston Symphony appointed by Higginson were of Germanic origin or background. The line ended in 1918, when Karl Muck was arrested as an enemy alien. But it must be said that all these foreign-born conductors performed a considerable quantity of music by American composers.

If Loeffler led us to the sumptuous elitism of Mrs. Gardner's milieu, George Whitefield Chadwick (1854–1931) takes us not only to the antique world of classical mythology but also—more significantly—to the non–Anglo-Nordic aspect of Boston, as well as to the ethnic and social variety of the American scene. To begin with, he was born in the working-class district of the industrial town of Lowell, Massachusetts, where his father, who had begun as a farmer, worked as a machinist. His infancy and adolescence were spent with grandparents in rural New Hampshire—not only far from the madding crowd but also far from Beacon Hill, the Atheneum, Harvard College, and other symbols of New England high culture. He managed to learn some musical skills, including the piano and organ; but his formal education ended with two years of high school. Meanwhile, his

Horatio Parker   Arthur W. Foote

George Whitefield Chadwick   Mrs. H. H. A. Beach

father had come up in the world, with his own insurance business, where George was employed for a time. Much to his parent's dismay, he soon quit and decided to make music his life's work.

After some musical study in Boston, he got a job at Olivet College, Michigan, in 1876. But he was smart enough to know that this was not the road to fame. Musical renown was obtained in Germany, whither he went the following year to study with Reinecke and Jadassohn in Leipzig, then with Rheinberger in Munich. In Leipzig his *Rip Van Winkle* Overture won first prize at the conservatory and was publicly performed with acclaim.

Ambitious though he undoubtedly was, young Chadwick was no grad-grind. He was sociable and much attracted to the visual arts, hence he joined an artistic circle led by the German-American painter Frank Duveneck. Chadwick had probably become acquainted with Duveneck's work at an exhibition held in Boston in 1875. From Munich the "Duveneck Boys," as they were called, journeyed through France, with Chadwick in the group. Although much attracted to France, he decided to return to the Munich mill. What he retained were visual images, a delight in color and contrast, which were to be reflected in his most characteristic music, notably the *Symphonic Sketches*. There is much truth in Victor Yellin's remark that "the more we penetrate the history of nineteenth-century American culture, the more it is difficult to maintain an idea of an American music separated from literature and art."[20]

In 1880 Chadwick returned to Boston and two years later joined the faculty of the New England Conservatory of Music. Fifteen years later he became its director—a prestigious position he held until his death. He was also a member of the Boston Academy of Arts and Letters and was deeply interested in both fields. The wide range of his cultural, aesthetic, and social concerns is reflected in his copious and varied compositional output. Perhaps to compensate for his lack of a Harvard education, he went in rather heavily for classical subjects, as in a series of overtures dedicated to the Muses: *Thalia* (Comedy), *Melpomene* (Tragedy), *Euterpe* (Music); the cantata *Phoenix Expirans* (1892); and the symphonic poem *Aphrodite* (1913), concerning which we are told: "The idea of the work was suggested by a beautiful head of the goddess, found on the island of Cnidos, and now in the Boston Art Museum."[21] I once rather snidely described this as "a proper Bostonian flirtation with the shade of Aphrodite."[22] But not all Bostonian flirtations are "proper," and I imagine that Chadwick may have really been in love with Aphrodite. At all events, we should let the music speak both for itself and for him.

Chadwick's three symphonies, especially the Second Symphony (1886) and the Third Symphony (1894), should certainly be revived, as well as his chamber music, including five string quartets (1878–98) and a piano quintet (1888). There are also piano pieces, organ works, and many songs, including the well-known "Ballad of Trees and the Master."

Five of Chadwick's later symphonic works have proved so attractive that they tend to overshadow the rest of his large production. These are the four *Symphonic Sketches* (1895–1907) and the "symphonic ballad" *Tam O'Shanter* (1915), based on the poem by Robert Burns. The first *Sketch* dates from 1895 and marks a decisive turning point in his creative expression. Titled "Jubilee," it melds Chadwick's affinity for pictorial art and literary expression (especially poetry) with his inspired perception of the exuberant effects to be derived from what has been aptly described as "the idiosyncratic union of Anglo melody and Afro-Caribbean beat."[23] All this is also expressed verbally in the verses that he quotes:

> No cool gray tones for me!
> Give me the warmest red and green,
> A coronet and a tambourine,
> To paint my Jubilee!

To establish this mood, the *Sketch* (*Allegro molto vivace*) opens with a jovial theme proclaimed by the whole orchestra, *fortissimo*, followed soon by another striking theme stated in unison by bass clarinet, bassoons, violas, and cellos. Then the horns announce a phrase in C major, which Philip Hale describes as a "patting Juba horn call," referring to some lines from Richard Hovey's *More Songs from Vagabondia* (Boston, 1896):

> When the wind comes up from Cuba
> And the birds are on the wing,
> And our hearts are patting Juba
> to the banjo of the spring . . .

After a lyrical episode for woodwinds and horns, the *Sketch* ends excitingly with a coda marked *presto*.

The second and third *Sketches*, "Noël" and "Hobgoblin," are ingeniously expressive and resourceful; but it is the final number, "A Vagrom Ballad," that claims our attention here as representing Chadwick's major symphonic departure from the "proper Bostonian" atmosphere in which he lived and moved and had his social being. (Boston, of course, had its seamy side, and we shall encounter it again in Chadwick's music.) The "tramp" was then a ubiquitous character in America, both in real life and on stage, and the story is told that Chadwick's "Ballad" was prompted by "an encampment of tramps on the outskirts of Worcester, Massachusetts, which Chadwick habitually passed en route to directing the annual Music Festival there."[24] A headnote to the score, however, indicates Chadwick's penchant for blending realism with poetic expression:

> A tale of tramps and railway ties
> Of old clay pipes and rum
> Of broken heads and blackened eyes
> And the "thirty days" to come.

As perceived in American popular culture, the hobo is both victim and clown, put down by the established order, applauded by the public as a comic figure of the stage, perhaps envied by those chafing at convention and routine. In "A Vagrom Ballad" these multiple images are evoked and contrasted with vivid sequences of parody, pathos, exuberance, and humor. In the vast output of the Classic-Romantic New Englanders, Chadwick's "Ballad" stands out as a brilliantly effective example of *verismo* in American musical composition.

Chadwick's earthiness and sense of humor are also manifested in his two comic operas, *A Quiet Lodging* (1892) and especially *Tabasco* (1894). A lyric drama in three acts titled *Judith*, based on the biblical episode of Judith and Holofernes, dates from his classical period and fails to be effective either as opera or drama. It is otherwise with his unjustly neglected masterpiece of operatic *verismo*, *The Padrone* (1912), which was turned down when he submitted it to the Metropolitan Opera, then under the direction of the Italian impresario Giulio Gatti-Casazza. He is said to have rejected it because it dealt with "life among the humble Italians" and was "probably too true to life."[25] This, of course, was an indirect tribute to Chadwick's power of empathy and his pioneer achievement in creating a realistic American opera. The Padrone is the powerful boss who advances passage money for Italian immigrants seeking a better life in America and then exploits them brutally. In the end he is murdered by one of his victims, who becomes the heroine of the opera. This was the seamy side of Boston, and Chadwick was the first to dramatize it, musically and realistically.

A minor but not negligible figure of the Boston group was Arthur B. Whiting (1861–1936), who in many ways personified the cultural-aesthetic climate we have been discussing. He was born in Cambridge, which almost meant that Harvard was his cradle. Having decided to make music his career, he studied composition with Chadwick, then went to Germany for the prescribed academic polishing in Munich. He returned full of enthusiasm for Brahms, with what his friend D. G. Mason called "the classic spirit," sternly opposed to anything "slipshod or mawkish or inept."[26]

In this climate of idealistic austerity, Whiting sometimes went beyond the pale by setting to music Kipling's *Barrack Room Ballads,* or composing bagatelles and waltzes. His major works include a Concert Overture (1886), a Piano Concerto (1888), the Fantasia, op. 11, for piano and orchestra (1897), and Suite for Strings and Four Horns (1891). This music drew from Philip Hale a choice bit of critical sarcasm:

> Mr. Whiting had, no doubt has, high ideals. Sensuousness in music seemed to him as something intolerable, something against public morals, something that should be suppressed by the selectmen. Perhaps he never went so far as to petition for an injunction against sex in music; but rigorous intellectuality was his one aim. He might have written A Serious Call to Devout and Holy Composition, or A Practical Treatise upon Musical Perfection, to which is now added, by the same author, The Absolute Unlawfulness of the Stage Entertainment Fully Demonstrated.[27]

Why should anyone attempt a *post facto* dissection of the New England classical scene, when the irrepressible Philip Hale, who was on the spot, has done it for us?

As for Arthur Whiting, he once proposed that his epitaph should be: "Here lies one who did not compose enough." But surely a more grateful tribute from posterity would be: "Here lies one who did not compose too much."

Of the New England composers born in the 1870s, the most prominent were Frederick Shepherd Converse (1871–1940), Edward Burlingame Hill (1872–1960), and Daniel Gregory Mason (1873–1953), whom we have already met. All three were pupils of Paine at Harvard; Converse and Hill also studied with Chadwick. But a significant difference appears: while Converse continued his studies with Rheinberger in Munich, Hill and Mason went to Paris, where the former studied with Widor, the latter with Vincent d'Indy. The trend toward France was to have important consequences for American music, and something more should be said about its New England antecedents. It started with the fame and prestige of French organist-composers, beginning with Alexandre Guilmant (1837–1911), and continuing with Charles-Marie Widor, Louis Vierne, Marcel Bonnet, and Marcel Dupré. (Vierne taught Nadia Boulanger, who later became the leading teacher of several generations of American composers.) Some of these French organists toured widely in the United States and did much to turn the tide toward France, in both composition and performance. But Boston was the pivotal center of this trend, thus providing a broader dimension to the New England scene.

A minor figure who nevertheless personifies the Francophile pattern was the New England organist Homer A. Norris (1860–1920), who spent four years in Paris studying organ, theory, and composition. In 1896 he published in Boston his *Practical Harmony on a French Basis*—symbolic of things to come.

The New England musical movement that we have been discussing flourished from 1880 to 1920, give or take a few years. It was perhaps not so much a "movement" as an ingrained cultural and aesthetic climate that brought together a number of gifted individuals united by hereditary bonds and common ideals. It was evidently the most closely knit group to appear in American art music until that time. In spite of its culturally centripetal character, it had some impact abroad, and in the United States its prestige was far-reaching.

The Boston Symphony Orchestra, as we have noted, was loyal to the New England clan—and it did not stop with a "first performance" gesture. Of the older generation, Paine had seven works performed, nearly all more than once; the incidental music to *Oedipus Tyrannus* was presented five times. Foote did well with eight works, the Suite in E Major for strings being favored with four performances. Parker wrote little for orchestra, but his Organ Concerto and *Northern Ballad* were performed. Chadwick came off with the lion's share: eighteen works were played, with the "Dramatic Overture" *Melpomene* a favorite. Frederick S. Converse also did very well, with fifteen works—including his far-out novelty *Flivver Ten Million: A Joyous Epic* (1926). More characteristic of his home-ground milieu was the widely performed "Orchestral Fantasy" *The Mystic Trumpeter* (1904).

The question arises: How did the New Englanders fare beyond Boston? The answer is: Very well indeed. Without attempting to marshal comprehensive statistics for all the composers concerned, we can note that Chadwick had twenty-two works performed by twenty orchestras, ranging across the continent from New York to Seattle. Again, the *Melpomene* Overture proved popular, with thirteen performances in various cities. But most frequently performed of all were the *Symphonic Sketches,* with a steady record of performances by fifteen orchestras up to 1961, while *Tam O'Shanter* was also a favorite.[28]

Elliott Carter has remarked on "the tendency for each generation in America to wipe away the memory of the previous one."[29] Historians do what they can to remedy that situation—including a reminder that no culture can ultimately thrive on a concept of value that fails to acknowledge its debt to the past. When the past is ignored the present has no future.

Notes

1. Daniel Gregory Mason, *Music in My Time,* p. 101.

2. Ibid., p. 14.

3. Ibid., p. 101.

4. Horatio Parker, diary, Jan. 1, 1882; quoted in Isabel Parker Semler and Pierson Underwood, *Horatio Parker,* p. xx.

5. *Freund's Weekly,* May 6, 1894; quoted in William Kay Kearns, "Horatio Parker," p. 83.

6. *New York Times,* May 4, 1893; quoted in Kearns, "Horatio Parker," p. 84.

7. Quoted in Kearns, "Horatio Parker," p. 170.

8. *Boston Journal,* Feb. 5, 1894; quoted in ibid., pp. 85–86.

9. Unidentified clipping in Allan Brown Collection, Boston Public Library, Feb. 5, 1894; cited in Kearns, "Horatio Parker, p. 85.

10. *Worcester Chronicle,* Aug. 26, 1899; quoted in Kearns, "Horatio Parker," p. 167.

11. Parker, "Addresses, Essays, Lectures," in Library of the School of Music, Yale University, nos. 1–13; cited in Kearns, "Horatio Parker," pp. 87–88.

12. Parker, "Impressions of a Year in Europe" (1902); quoted in Semler and Underwood, *Horatio Parker,* pp. 164–65.

13. Rupert Hughes, *Famous American Composers,* p. 227.

14. Ibid., p. 434.

15. E. Lindsey Merrill, "Mrs. H. H. A. Beach: Her Life and Music," p. 5.

16. Otto Ebel, preface to *Women Composers: A Biographical Handbook of Women's Work in Music* (Brooklyn, N.Y.: F. H. Chandler, 1902), p. v; quoted in Judith Tick, "Women as Professional Musicians," p. 95.

17. Philip Hale, "Beach's Gaelic Symphony," *Boston Tribune,* Nov. 1, 1896; quoted in Tick, "Women as Professional Musicians," p. 114.

18. Quoted in Tick, "Women as Professional Musicians," p. 114.

19. Ralph P. Locke, "Charles Martin Loeffler: Composer at Court," pp. 30–37. Among other activities, Loeffler founded a female string quartet called the American Quartet.

20. Victor Fell Yellin, "Chadwick, American Musical Realist," p. 79.

21. Rupert Hughes, *American Composers: A Study of the Music of This Country, and of Its Future, with Biographies of the Leading Composers of the Present Time* [rev.

ed. of Hughes, *Famous American Composers,* with additional chapters by Arthur Elson] (1914; rpt., New York: AMS Press, 1973), p. 458.

22. Gilbert Chase, *America's Music: From the Pilgrims to the Present* (New York: McGraw-Hill, 1955), p. 371.

23. Yellin, "Chadwick, American Musical Realist," p. 90.

24. Ibid., p. 91.

25. Quoted in ibid., p. 94.

26. Mason, *Music in My Time,* pp. 65–66.

27. Quoted in Hughes, *Famous American Composers,* p. 289.

28. Data from Kate Hevner Mueller, *Twenty-seven Major American Symphony Orchestras.*

29. Elliott Carter, "Expressionism and American Music," p. 1.

Chapter 22
The Native Americans

To the Indian, song is the breath of the spirit
that consecrates the acts of life.
—Natalie Curtis, *The Indians' Book* (1907)

Competent observers have generally agreed on the importance of music in American Indian tribal cultures. In the words of pioneer ethnologist Alice C. Fletcher: "Music enveloped the Indian's individual and social life like an atmosphere. There was no important personal experience where it did not bear a part, nor any ceremonial where it was not essential to the expression of religious feeling. The songs of a tribe were coextensive with the life of the people."[1] Fletcher made this statement in 1900; eight decades later another ethnologist, Charlotte Heth, confirmed the view of her predecessor: "Indian music as a vital part of life and as an important art form remains essential to Indian identity in the twentieth century."[2] The problem of Indian tribal identity in a highly industrialized and mobile society will reappear in the course of this chapter.

The earliest accounts of music and dance among the aborigines of the newly discovered "Indies" date from 1496 and thereafter continued to accumulate in the writings of chroniclers, explorers, missionaries, travelers, and eventually the modern anthropologists, ethnologists, and ethnomusicologists who brought scientific training to their task. Thus the overall documentation is tremendous, attesting to the fascination of this indigenous culture in a New World that was also very old.[3] The eventual availability of the phonograph, and later the magnetic tape recorder, greatly advanced the preservation of tribal data.

The first quasi-scientific treatise on North American Indian music was compiled by a New Yorker named Theodore Baker (1851–1934). After preparing himself for a career in business, Baker switched to musical studies in Germany, at the University of Leipzig. There, in 1882, he published his dissertation, *Über die Musik der nordamerikanischen Wilden*, of which an English translation did not appear until 1976. Baker had done some fieldwork in the summer of 1880, gathering Iroquois harvest songs in western New York and a variety of songs from several tribes at the Training School for Indian Youth in Carlisle, Pennsylvania; others he took from printed sources.

But the most wide-ranging impact was made by two women: Alice Fletcher (1838–1923) and Frances Densmore (1867–1957)—the latter strongly motivated and "inspired" by the former. Unlike Densmore, who was trained in classical music, Fletcher opted for a career in anthropology and ethnology, and from 1886 she was on the staff of the Peabody Museum of American Archaeology and Ethnology at Harvard. She achieved eminence in her career, becoming president of the American Anthropological Society in 1903 and of the American Folklore Society in 1905. Her best-known works are *A Study of Omaha Indian Music* (Baltimore, 1893), *Indian Story and Song from North America* (Boston, 1900), *Indian Games and Dances with Native Songs* (Boston, 1915). In her fieldwork with the Omahas, she had the assistance of Francis La Flesche, an Omaha Indian, and John C. Fillmore (1843–98), a trained musician, who analyzed and harmonized the melodies.

Concerning the Pawnee of Oklahoma, Fletcher noted that "religious ceremonies were connected with the cosmic forces and the heavenly bodies. The dominating power was Tirawa. . . . The heavenly bodies, the winds, thunder, lightning, and rain were his messengers." Moreover: "The mythology of the Pawnee is remarkably rich in symbolism and poetic fancy, and their religious system is elaborate and cogent. The secret societies, of which there were several in each tribe, were connected with the belief in supernatural animals. The functions of these societies were to call the game, to heal diseases, and to give occult powers. Their rites were elaborate and their ceremonies dramatic."[4]

We are also told that the Pawnee personified the Evening Star as a woman, placing her next in power to Tirawa. From her garden in the west, with fields of ripening corn and many buffalo, sprang all forms of life. Her consort was the Morning Star, "a warrior who drove the other stars before him across the sky." From their union the first human being was created, and from his marriage to the daughter of the Sun and the Moon sprang the human race. The Morning Star ceremony was held early in the spring, for the purpose of securing good crops in the coming season.

Turning now to Frances Densmore, it would seem that her training in piano and composition at the Oberlin Conservatory of Music and with

John K. Paine in Boston was an unlikely preparation for fieldwork among Indian tribes. But, she tells us, an experience at the Chicago World's Columbian Exposition changed her life: "I heard Indians sing, saw them dance and heard them yell, and was scared almost to death."[5] She was also fascinated and felt that this was a crucial moment in her career. She then turned to Fletcher's book on the Omahas, and this was the main source for her highly successful lectures on Indian music, beginning in 1895. It was not until ten years later that she began her own fieldwork, commencing with the Chippewa in 1905. From 1907 she worked under the auspices of the Bureau of American Ethnology, which published many of her monographs, covering an immense area of tribal music. To give an idea of her industry and thoroughness, the two-volume monograph on Chippewa music (1910–13) contains 380 songs—the largest collection ever published from one tribe.[6]

Concentrating on the Plains-Pueblo area, Densmore went on to gather data from the Menominee, Pawnee, Teton Sioux, Mandan, Hidatsa, Cheyenne, Arapaho, Papago, and others. Among the Papago of southern Arizona, she collected war songs, hunting songs, dream songs, ceremonial songs, songs for the entertainment of children, and humorous songs. An example of the last is "The Pigeon and His Tiswin Lodge." Tiswin is a wine made from the fruit of the saguaro cactus. It was customary to construct a special lodge for the drinking of tiswin, and the wine was drunk during the ceremony for making rain. Hence the reference to a cloud: "The pigeon pretended that he was setting up a tiswin lodge. The frog doctor drank his wine, got drunk and shouted, and pulled out his cloud."[7]

The Papago ceremony for making rain was held early in August and was the occasion for a festival in which many rainmaking songs were sung. Another ceremony for obtaining rain and good crops was the Viikita, held every four years. This involved fasting and the carrying of an object representing the sun. In some communities the drinking of tiswin was part of the ritual. A song of the Viikita ceremony emphasizes the importance of clouds in the cosmic economy of these desert dwellers: "We see the light that brightens in the east,/It seems to turn to flame,/On the edge of it is something that looks like a white feather,/But we see that it is white clouds."[8]

The Pueblo Indians of New Mexico and Arizona were thus named by the Spaniards because they lived in cliff-side communities in houses made of stone and adobe. They were a peaceful agricultural people, skilled in handicrafts and with elaborate ceremonial rituals. Their best-known tribes are the Zuni and Hopi. The former settled near the Little Colorado River, among the buttes and mesas of New Mexico. Their daily occupations are reflected in their corn-grinding songs, sung by the women as they grind the corn, or maize, in stone troughs called *metates,* upon which the corn is placed and ground by another stone. One of these songs, which was recorded by Natalie Curtis, refers to the "sacred mountain" of the Zuni, the great mesa that they call *To'yallanne.*

Early Indian studies and fieldwork in this area owed much to Mrs. Mary Hemenway of Boston, who, from 1887 until her death in 1894, sponsored the Hemenway Southwestern Expedition. From 1889 this was directed by J. Walter Fewkes, an ethnologist who was the first to use the phonograph (an early Edison treadle-run machine) for the recording of Indian music and speech. The Hopi songs thus recorded were transcribed and analyzed, with a wealth of scientific apparatus, by Benjamin Ives Gilman, and the results were published in 1908.

Fewkes wrote copiously on his observations of the ceremonial dances and rituals of various Pueblo tribes, especially the Hopi, Walpi, and Zuni. The main rituals for obtaining the life-giving element of water for the crops occurred in summer, with the Sacred Dances. One of these, the *Kō-kō,* Fewkes describes in detail:

> Each *Kō-kō* wore a painted mask with a long horse-hair beard extending down on the breast, while his own hair, carefully dressed, fell down on the back. On the top of his head he wore two or three bright yellow feathers, while on a string weighted by a stone, which hung down over the hair, small, white, downy feathers were tied at intervals. The mask was of blue color, with two slits for the eyes, and a third with zigzag bars representing teeth. . . . Around the neck hung numerous chains of shell beads and worsted yarn, from which depended ornaments made of the abalone and other shells. The shoulders and body, down to the loins, were bare, but the shoulders were painted a pinkish color, with zigzag markings, said to be rain symbols. . . . In one hand he held a gourd rattle, and in the other a sprig of cedar. The body was thrown into a slightly stooping posture, the elbows bent so that the forearm was thrown forward. Some of the *Kō-kō,* in the first dance, carried in the hand a live turtle. . . . Around the loins each *Kō-kō* wore a Moqui [Hopi] dance-blanket, a sash with long, white, pendent strings knotted at the ends, and from behind hung a fox skin, with head uppermost, and tail extending to the ground. Empty turtle shells . . . were tied to the sash behind. The legs and feet were bare, with the exception of a black woolen garter tied on the left leg, and a turtle shell securely fastened on the right, inside the knee. The turtle shell . . . had small [deer] hoofs suspended by buckskin thongs on one side. The rattle of these hoofs on the empty turtle shells could be heard for a considerable dis-

tance as the dancers, settling back on one leg, raised their feet and then brought them down to the earth in accord with the song which they chanted.[9]

Another ceremonial dance of the Zuni was the *Hay-a-ma-she-que* (Dancers who wear the masks), in which thirty-four dancers participated, wearing elaborately painted masks and strings of ornaments, and with the upper part of the body painted a deep red or copper color. The peculiar feature was a tablet carried by each dancer. As described by Fewkes: "Their heads were wholly covered by cedar boughs, which formed a helmet with an extensive collar. The tablet which they carried on the head above the cedar was a thin flat board with three apical projections, each ornamented with a feather. On this tablet, which was about two feet high, there were gaudily painted figures in the form of crescents, birdlike outlines, and variegated circles. . . . In the hands they carried a gourd rattle with a sprig of cedar."[10]

Fewkes wrote his article in 1891; this chapter of *America's Music* was written nearly a hundred years later. What has been the changing "shape of time" in the ethnic cultures of American Indian tribes? What sociocultural configurations have resulted from the process of acculturation over this period? The rest of our survey will concentrate on finding answers to these questions.

To begin with, let us turn to a small but culturally significant tribe of the Plains area: the Flathead Indians of western Montana. Our main reason for doing so is the important study by Alan P. Merriam, *Ethnomusicology of the Flathead Indians* (1967), which presents a detailed investigation of their music in the contexts of ethnography and cultural anthropology, with a broad historical perspective that provides a firm basis for understanding twentieth-century patterns of "Acculturation and Cultural Change" (chapter 5). Acculturation is defined as the process of sociocultural changes that occur when groups of individuals having different cultures come into continuous contact.

Merriam cites an example of this process in his discussion of "Death Songs, Wakes, and Dirges" among the Flathead. It appears that they had no funeral songs as such (perhaps using war dance songs instead), but that a " 'funeral song' was formulated and urged upon the Flathead by Christian missionaries."[11] As an example of intertribal acculturation, Merriam notes that "in historic times one of the major influences upon the Flathead were the Iroquois Indians"—and it might well be that "the impact of the Iroquois was of such consequence as to change the entire course of Flathead history."[12] The Flathead were also proselytized by Methodist missionaries in the nineteenth century, as were many other Indian tribes by various Christian denominations. The Jesuit missionaries went beyond dogma, introducing Western musical instruments and choral singing.

Nevertheless, Merriam maintained that "the elements of structure of Flathead and Western music are incompatible and do not blend. . . . In the traditional songs there is not a single element of Western music to be discerned." But Merriam did his fieldwork in 1950; how much of the tribal heritage remains intact in the 1980s? Perhaps Merriam already anticipated the answer when he wrote: "Western culture's encroachment upon the Flathead . . . has substantially narrowed the number of situations in which traditional music was performed. With the loss of suitable occasions for music performance, the Flathead have slowly abandoned their music, and a reduced range of song types continues to shrink as Flathead culture changes and as those who remember the old occasions for music die."[13] As a young Flathead musician said to Merriam: "Well . . . the old timers are kickin' off fast, and that kind of song is gettin' to be old stuff nowadays."[14]

Thus the traditional continuity of tribal music appears to be literally a matter of life and death. Reformulating our earlier question, what is the ratio of change to survival? This is the perspective that ethnologist Naomi Ware delineates in her field study of the Pima Indian Salt River Reservation located near Phoenix, Arizona, undertaken in the summers of 1965–66. She was told that "curing songs" still existed, but that she would probably never hear one unless she "actually went to a singer/doctor for a cure, believing in his ability to effect it." (We are told that the last Salt River medicine man died in the spring of 1966.) What was left for public performance were the social dance songs, evidently done rather informally: "A group of singers sits on chairs or benches with an overturned cardboard box serving as a drum. The dancers form a circle around the singers, clasp hands or link arms, and dance. They use a sliding-jumping sideways step, mostly clockwise, but occasionally counter-clockwise, according to the song. Both the spatial relationship of singers to dancers and the number of dancers are extremely flexible."[15]

This is a far cry from the elaborate ritual of the *Kō-kō* Sacred Dance of the Zuni described by Fewkes! But the Pima did attempt to revive some of the traditional dances, with women participating prominently. As Ware remarks: "The important thing about the revival groups . . . is the concern for preservation of Pima ways." And the tribal council has an obligation "to cultivate and preserve native arts, crafts and culture."[16] The link with the past has not been severed.

Nevertheless, Ware questions the viability of tribal traditions as she asks: "What does the musical situation at Salt River indicate about the future of Pima music, and what light does it shed on problems of musical acculturation among North American Indians?" Her answer could apply to many other tribes: "In all probability traditional Pima music at Salt River will cease to be performed when the present singers die out: the singers have not taught their songs to younger people. Even the revival groups will probably die out, since they depend upon traditional singers for accompaniment."[17]

Certainly there are everywhere strong socioeconomic factors exerting pressures against the total preservation and continuity of Indian tribal music and its concomitant rituals. No doubt the strong attraction of American popular music on Indian youth is an important consideration. But acculturation does not necessarily involve extinction, even when one culture is immensely larger and more powerful than the other. In the case of the American Indians, the process has involved adaptation and continuity, as well as imitation and assimilation. The increasing interest of white Americans in Indian tribal ceremonies and dances that involve music and native paraphernalia provides various incentives for their preservation and expansion.

As a result, while tribal identities continue to exist, the movement known as Pan-Indianism has come to the fore as an expression of Native American identity and culture on a national basis. Robert K. Thomas, writing in the 1960s, stated: "One can legitimately define Pan-Indianism as the expression of a new identity and the institutions and symbols which are both an expression of that new identity and a fostering of it. It is the attempt to create a new ethnic group, the American Indian; it is also a vital social movement which is forever changing and growing."[18]

The final phrase in the above quotation holds true for the general situation of Pan-Americanism in the 1980s. The primary impulse, originating mainly in the Plains area, soon spread widely. As delineated by Thomas:

The extreme spatial mobility of the Plains Indians is a very important factor in the rise of Pan-Indianism. Plains Indians think nothing of traveling hundreds of miles to attend celebrations at other Indian communities. In modern times, this mobility has fostered Pan-Indianism.

I am suggesting two things: First, that modern Pan-Indianism had its roots in a developing commonality that American Indians began to conceive of particularly in the Plains area; Second, that this commonality was brought to a head by the reservation system, in the way whites related to different tribes as "Indians" and by the pressure for assimilation which pushed Indians closer together.

The result of all this was a Pan-Indian religion, the Ghost Dance, which swept the Plains area in the nineties. Somewhat later, the Peyote movement followed the same course.[19]

Before describing some typical dance contexts, let us turn first to the Peyote religion, which became a widespread and highly influential cult. The name comes from the peyote, a plant derived from a spineless, carrot-shaped cactus, of which the above-ground one or two inches are dried and chewed. Originating in Mexico, the Peyote cult was well established in the United States by 1870 and soon spread over a vast area, especially among the Apache, Comanche, and Kiowa. It was influenced by the music of a religious ritual called the Ghost Dance, which came to the fore in the late nineteenth century. As ethnologist David McAllester writes: "The wide spread of the Ghost Dance must have contributed to the receptivity of the Indians to peyote. After a brief currency of the former the Indians were again left with little sense of spiritual direction, although the conditions of radical change and insecurity that fostered the Ghost Dance were intensified after its collapse. The Ghost Dance had established the idea and practice of intertribal religious movements."[20]

The last sentence in the above is clearly the key to understanding the immense spread of the Peyote religion and its ultimate impact on Pan-Indianism. We should add that in its early development there was some input from Christian sources. Nevertheless, peyotism is basically an aboriginal American religion, operating in terms of fundamental Indian concepts about powers, visions, and native modes of doctoring.

McAllester also describes the musical aspect of Peyote practices:

During the ceremony a drum and rattle, both of special design, are passed, with other paraphernalia, clockwise among the circle of participants. When a member receives the rattle he is expected to sing a number of songs, usually four, after which he passes the rattle on to the next man. The rattle goes ahead of the drum so that, immediately after his turn to sing, each man is the drummer for the man on his left. Four times during the course of the ceremony the leader interrupts the progression to sing special songs which are always used at these times. At other times a participant sings whatever songs he chooses from the repertory at his command, or even extemporizes on the spur of the moment.

Fully half of the participating time, usually a good deal more, of the peyotist is spent listening to or performing this music.[21]

The Peyote ceremonies begin in the evening and continue until midnight, when there is a break, with praying and smoking and purification; then the singing continues until dawn. Women attend the meetings but do not participate very actively: "They eat peyote and help with some of the songs sung by the men, but do not sing songs of their own when it would be their turn."[22]

The Pan-Indian movement that came to the fore in the 1950s had antecedents that went back for several decades and was rooted in the persistent search for an American Indian identity. Hazel Hertzberg summarizes this search for a common Indian identity in a comprehensive study of the movement:

> The long and complex process of Indian resistance and adjustment carried out largely in tribal terms reflected the diversity of Indian societies and the differing and fragmented nature of Indian contacts with whites. But all the while another theme was at work, sometimes complementing, sometimes contradicting, sometimes overwhelming the tribal one. This was the effort to find a common ground beyond the tribe, a broader identity and unity based on shared cultural elements, shared experiences, shared needs, and a shared common fate. Most such attempts were confined to a few tribes and local areas, but the most important involved Indians from many tribes and localities.[23]

Interestingly, many of the leaders in the incipient Pan-Indian movement were trained at the schools for Indian Youth, notably in Pennsylvania and Virginia. Not only did they learn English as a common language, they also developed a large and lasting intertribal solidarity. And, as Hertzberg notes, "Many of them went on to lead or participate in Pan-Indian organizations." Among the leaders was Francis La Flesche, the Omaha Indian previously mentioned as an assistant to Alice Fletcher. He eventually became an eminent anthropologist, associated with the Bureau of American Ethnology, but also denounced the reservation system about which so many Indians bitterly complained.

While tribal identity was increasingly attenuated by modern social and economic factors, Pan-Indianism widened its appeal as a means of retaining and expanding the overall Indian image in American society. Although many ritualistic elements were retained, the tribal aspect was no longer paramount. The long process of acculturation now strongly affected not only the relation between Indians and whites but also the entire tribal network of the aboriginal Americans.

Whatever types of musical expression may be attributed to American Indian music, they do not include anything resembling the self-contained, formalistic structures of Western composition, which can stand as works of creative art per se. "On the whole," as Bruno Nettl observes, "North American Indian music is among the simpler musics of the world"—being mostly monophonic. But he notes that there is also considerable intricacy in Native American musical styles. Commenting specifically on the music of the Pueblo Indians, he states that it "is the most complex and varied among North American Indians: lengthy melodies use a variety of pentatonic, hexatonic and heptatonic scales, and many of their songs show the incomplete-repetition principle. . . . The singing style has vocal tension and pulsation. . . . Melodic contours tend to be series of broad, sweeping, descending lines."[24]

As we have already observed, vocal and instrumental modes of performances are almost invariably linked to ritualistic or social occasions, in which symbolic choreography is a vital factor. The essential musical expression is vocal, including "cries, shouts, animal imitations, rhythmic aspirated breathing and ululations (high-pitched, wordless, sustained cries)."[25]

As described by Charlotte Heth, the instrumental artifacts include the following:

> Types of hand-held vessel rattles (a vessel enclosing pebbles, fruit seeds, or other noisemakers with a handle) are those made of carved wood, baskets, gourds, bark, rawhide, moose feet, clay, metal salt shakers, turtles, cow horns, copper, coconut shells, or buffalo tails. Strung rattles attached to the bodies or clothing of dancers are made from cocoons, deer hoofs, tin cans, turtles, petrified wood, sea shells, or metal cones. . . . Shells, bird beaks, deer hoofs or cocoons may be strung on sticks or hoops and played by hand to accompany singing. Other instruments such as rasps, bull-roarers, flutes, whistles, musical bows, fiddles, and clapping sticks are less common.[26]

The Indian flute or flageolet has been romanticized because of its association with courtship.

In descriptions of Indian singing one frequently encounters the phrase "meaningless syllables." This has been rejected by many ethnologists, who regard it as misleading and perhaps derogatory. The preferred term is *vocables,* further identified as "nonlexical syllables." An example is *he ya ho wi yo.* Only recently has this practice received in-depth scholarly analysis, notably in Leanne Hinton's 1977 dissertation on Havasupai songs.[27]

Hinton's central question is, "What is the function of the vocable in song?" Her preliminary reply is to approach the song "as a communication event" and to "look at the vocables directly, as units of sound created not randomly but according to a certain pattern that functions to enhance sound quality and that can tell us some important things about the aesthetics of song."[28] She goes on to state: "Every Havasupai song has some vocables. Even in the fully worded songs, vocables are used as line-end codas and as spacing-out devices to fit the words to the meter. In other genres of song, vocables play a larger role, and in some genres, a text will consist primarily of vocables."[29] Hinton also notes that nasals and glides predominate among vocables, and a crucial statement is the following: "We find that meaning is present in wordless songs in general, but that it is not tied at all to language; it instead becomes fused with function."[30]

In conclusion, Hinton suggests that "the choice of nonhigh vowels and of glides and nasals in vocable formation is purposeful, not random, and based on aesthetic considerations. . . . When a song does not need to be linguistically communicative, it is free to concentrate more fully on the aesthetic ideal, and the use of vocables helps to achieve that end."[31] Hinton proposes to show that "linguistic communication becomes less useful in situations where social solidarity is being expressed, and where people are seeking a sensation of spirituality."[32]

The use of vocables is widespread in American Indian culture, and they are often used as a kind of brief repetitive chorus, as in a Creek "Gar Dance," where the vocables *we he hai yo ne* are sung after each line of the text. This is one of the many dances that refer to animals, and in which women participate with men.

Since we have mentioned the Creek Indians, it will be opportune to recall that they were one of the "Five Civilized Tribes," along with the Choctaw, Chickasaw, Cherokee, and Seminole, who in the 1830s were forcibly removed from their homelands in the East and painfully herded across the Mississippi to what was then the Indian Territory. In 1902 this became the state of Oklahoma (the name is derived from the Choctaw *okla homma,* "red people"). While the Five Tribes remained partial to most of their traditional culture, other Oklahoma tribes were active in promoting Pan-Indianism, which, as previously noted, was largely nourished by elements from the Prairie-Plains area. Robert K. Thomas notes that "because Plains Indians come in contact with many social groups other than Indians in their travels, they have become urbane and sophisticated tribal people. In this process not only is their identity as 'Indians' strengthened, but a conception of themselves as generalized human beings, in particular American, has developed."[33]

Moreover, as Indians have been moving to the cities in greater numbers, Pan-Indianism has developed an urban phase that is often characterized by the participation of whites. The term *powwow* is currently used to designate Pan-Indian celebrations (which should not be confused with the more traditional intertribal meetings that still continue to be held). The powwows feature both ritualistic and popular social dances, in which men and women participate, as well as various social activities that one might find at a fair, such as raffles and choosing a "princess." As described by Charlotte Heth:

> Round Dances are frequently used as warm-up dances before the formal opening of a powwow (after the Gourd Dance if it is performed) and may be interspersed among War Dances, Grass Dances, trick Songs (for contests), etc. These social dances, along with the Oklahoma Two-Step, Rabbit Dance, and Owl Dance, offer a chance for audience members to participate. At these times visitors are allowed to dance without observing all the formal costuming and etiquette requirements for the more serious dances. Special dances performed as crowd pleasers might include the Navajo Ribbon Dance, the Swan Dance, the Hoop Dance, the Shield Dance, and one of the Pueblo Buffalo Dances. These dances when performed in a powwow setting are strictly for show, and often the dancers are paid handsomely for demonstrating them.[34]

There are also dances that cater especially to young people, performed after the traditional powwow, as outright social entertainment. These are the Forty-nine Dances, "in which the costumes are not prescribed, and the drum, central to most Plains music, may even be replaced by a car-hood or a cardboard box. The dances and songs are mostly for fun and may contain words about love, sweethearts, and problems."[35] In the powwows there is something for everybody.

By the 1980s Pan-Indian powwows were widespread throughout North America, with increasing participation by whites and a growing trend toward homogeneity. James Howard summarizes this trend: "Although in some cases the adoption of Pan-Indian dance and ceremonial forms and their accompanying music represents an *addition* to a more strictly tribal tradition (that is, New York, Canadian, and Oklahoma Iroquois; Florida Seminole and Mikasuki; Oklahoma Creek and Seminole; Mississippi Choctaw; Navajo and various Pueblo groups), more commonly it represents the adoption of these forms by Native Americans who are largely or totally unacquainted with *any* American Indian music, dance, or costuming as practiced by their ancestors."[36]

In several communities, however, and especially along the eastern seaboard, there have been attempts to restore some elements of traditional tribal practices by getting advice from older Indians who have retained much of their cultural heritage. Restoring and reviving Indian dress and games is often part of the desired picture.

Pan-tribal gatherings and presentations have become an impressive type of entertainment as well as a ceremonial occasion. A news item from Lewes, Delaware, tells us that in 1980 the third annual Nanticoke powwow drew "8,000 people, including 33 tribes from as far north as Canada and as far south as Florida and as far west as Arizona, Texas, Oklahoma, and North Dakota. In addition to Sussex County's 500 Nanticokes, there were Rappahanocks from Virginia, Oneida from New York, Abenaki from Canada, and Navajo from Arizona."[37]

While Pan-Indianism will undoubtedly continue to spread and thereby to represent the most conspicuous popular image of the Native Americans, elements of traditional tribal culture persist in spite of external and internal pressures. This holds true especially among certain tribes of the Southwest, as delineated by Charlotte Frisbie:

> The Southwestern United States has attracted and fascinated anthropologists since the earliest days of the discipline. The region, populated by a large number of America's first inhabitants, is characterized by cultural pluralism. Despite a long and well-known history of contact with a variety of cultures, Southwestern Indians continue to be distinctive in a number of ways from others around them. They maintain autonomous languages, dress, cognition, beliefs, and ritual dramas. The continuing encroachment of outsiders, with their religions as well as technological, political, and economic interests, and their desires to control, seems to do no more than slightly perturb the existing systems.[38]

In the final decades of the twentieth century, American Indians have gone beyond the irreversible pattern of acculturation and are faced with the problem of encroachment by the dominant white society. To what extent is the preservation of tribal identity feasible? One view is that religion, with its concomitant factors of ritual, dance, and music, can play an important role in maintaining social and cultural identity. Anthropologist William K. Powers has made a detailed cultural-historical study of religion pertaining to the Oglalas, a group related to the Tetons of the Plains area. He begins by asking, "How is it possible that, despite overwhelming odds in favor of assimilation into the 'mainstream' of American society, the Oglalas maintain a distinct social and cultural identity?"[39] He deals with this problem in terms of the balance between continuity and change.

In spite of the technological and materialistic patterns imposed by the federal government, the Oglalas maintain their traditional belief in "the hereditary chiefs, the medicine men, and the common people whose primary allegiance is to kin and local communities. It is in these Oglala extremes of the scale that we find persistence in Oglala values. Here, one's felt needs are satisfied through the medium of a religious system. It is here in the local communities that we find social relationships reminiscent of those of bygone days, relationships that now manifest themselves in novel ways, but which are nevertheless more Oglala than they are Euro-American."[40] Powers adopts Anthony Wallace's definition of religion, which, in turn, conforms to the aboriginal Indian concept: "Religion is a set of rituals, rationalized by myth, which mobilizes supernatural powers for the purpose of achieving or preventing transformations of state in men and nature."[41] He adds that this relates well to the Oglalas, "who do not differentiate between supernatural beings and impersonal supernatural forces in terms of their own concept of religion."

In describing what he calls "Sacred Things," Powers delineates "The Supernatural," "The Intermediaries," "Cosmology," and "Ritual." These are basic types or themes that apply to American Indian culture in general. The first and last involve appropriate songs and dances. The intermediaries are "sacred persons" (both men and women) who mediate between supernatural beings and powers and the common people. Among the rituals, the most widespread are those of "The Sweat Lodge," "Girl's Puberty Ritual," and especially the "Sun Dance," a prolonged and elaborate ritual that usually lasts four days, taking place in the summer. The Sun Dance became a point of controversy because some of the male participants are pledged to undergo the ordeal of having their breasts pierced by wooden skewers attached to two rawhide ropes, resulting in extreme physical pain.

As an example of the complexities and incongruities involved in the contact of tribal rituals with exterior pressures and internal discrepancies, we are told that when the Oglala Sioux tribal council took over the administration of the Sun Dance presentations in 1934, it saw an opportunity to transform the popular ceremony into a tourist attraction. "This required advertising and promotion and a fixed calendrical date in order to entice tourists onto the reservation, particularly from the neighboring white towns and the Black Hills-Badlands area, which had already been established as a thriving tourist attraction."[42]

The attraction between ritual and curiosity, between participants and spectators, has long been a sociocultural factor in the public presentation

Two Choctaw dances (from top to bottom): War Dance, Stealing Partners Dance. Choctaw-Chickasaw Heritage Committee Dancers, Ardmore, Okla., May 1985. Photos courtesy of Victoria Lindsay-Levine.

of elaborate religious ceremonies everywhere. More important, in all sub-cultures religious rites have been a vital component in maintaining communal identity. Powers writes of the Oglala: "He wears a white man's clothing, lives in a white man's house, and works at a white man's job. But when he seeks to affirm his own identity as an Oglala, he moves along the continuum to the only institution available to him that is distinct from the white man. He seeks identity in a religious system whose structure has remained in many respects constant since European contact."[43]

It would be misleading to suggest that the Native Americans are exclusively, or even primarily, concerned only with their traditional tribal music. We have previously indicated their interest in various types of American popular music. And Charlotte Heth has pointed out that an increasing number of Native Americans have turned to such far-reaching styles as country and western, jazz-swing, rock, and folksong.[44] We are talking about performers and composers who are widely active in these contexts. The concept is that of a genuinely vital and comprehensive movement.

Concurrently the output of ethnic recordings derived directly from Indian tribal sources has achieved an ever-increasing momentum, as evinced by the New World Records series; the historic sets issued by the Library of Congress, sponsored by its newly created American Folklife Center; and the extensive series North American Indian music issued by Folkways Records, which goes back to early field recordings by Fewkes and Densmore. Folkways has also issued a collection of Eskimo songs of the Hudson Bay area and Alaska, recorded on location by Laura Boulton, and twenty songs from St. Lawrence Island, recorded by Miriam Stryker, including examples of contemporary acculturation with such numbers as "Cowboy Song," "Helicopter Song," and "Eskimo Rock and Roll."

Historically and ethnically, the vast continental impact of Indian tribal music and dance, with its related rituals and myths, will continue to be an enduring and distinctive cultural heritage of the United States of America.

Notes

1. Alice C. Fletcher, *Indian Story and Song*, p. 114.
2. Charlotte Heth, "Synthesis of Indian Music," author's typescript, p. 1.
3. See Robert Stevenson, "Written Sources for Indian Music until 1882," pp. 1–40; and Stevenson, "English Sources for Indian Music until 1882," pp. 399–442.
4. Alice C. Fletcher, *Handbook of American Indians*, Smithsonian Institution,

Bureau of American Ethnology Bulletin no. 30, pt. 2 (Washington, D.C., 1910), p. 215; quoted in Frances Densmore, *Pawnee Music*, p. 4.

5. Charles Hofmann, ed., *Frances Densmore and American Indian Music*, p. 2.
6. Frances Densmore, *Chippewa Music*.
7. Frances Densmore, *Papago Music*, p. 217.
8. Ibid., p. 148.
9. J. Walter Fewkes, "A Few Summer Ceremonials at Zuni Pueblo," pp. 27–28.
10. Ibid., pp. 38–39.
11. Alan P. Merriam, *Ethnomusicology of the Flathead Indians*, p. 69.
12. Ibid., p. 124.
13. Ibid., p. 137.
14. Ibid., p. 147.
15. Naomi Ware, "Survival and Change in Pima Indian Music," p. 103.
16. Ibid., p. 110.
17. Ibid., p. 111.
18. Robert K. Thomas, "Pan-Indianism," p. 739.
19. Ibid., p. 741.
20. David P. McAllester, *Peyote Music*, p. 85.
21. Ibid., pp. 11–12.
22. Ibid., p. 19.
23. Hazel W. Hertzberg, *The Search for an American Indian Identity*, p. 6.
24. Bruno Nettl, "North America—Indian Musical Style," *The New Grove Dictionary* 13:298, 300.
25. Heth, "Synthesis," pp. 2–3.
26. Ibid., p. 4
27. The essence of Hinton's analysis is more readily available in her study "Vocables in Havasupai Song," pp. 275–305.
28. Ibid., p. 275.
29. Ibid., p. 279.
30. Ibid., p. 294.
31. Ibid., pp. 298–99.
32. Ibid., p. 299.
33. Thomas, "Pan-Indianism," p. 721.
34. Charlotte Heth, "Update on Indian Music," pp. 93–94.
35. Ibid., p. 94.
36. James H. Howard, "Pan-Indianism in Native American Music," p. 74.
37. Ibid., p. 76.
38. Charlotte Frisbie, ed., *Southwestern Indian Ritual Drama*, p. 1. Frisbie also contributed to this volume the chapter "Ritual Drama in the Navajo Blessing Ceremony" (pp. 161–98). Another richly documented and analytically interpreted study is David P. McAllester's "Shootingway, an Epic Drama of the Navajos" (chapter 9, pp. 199–237). McAllester elucidates what he calls "ideational" and "structural" elements in "this massive work of religious art" that lasted nine nights and eight days. Its antecedents reach far into the past; its future course we cannot predict.

39. William K. Powers, *Oglala Religion*, p. xi.

40. Ibid., pp. xiii–xiv.

41. Anthony F. C. Wallace, *Religion: An Anthropological View* (New York: Random House, 1966), p. 107; quoted in ibid., p. xv.

42. Powers, *Oglala Religion*, p. 140.

43. Ibid., p. 204.

44. Heth, "Synthesis," p. 17.

Chapter 23
The Rise of Ragtime

I can't help feeling that a person who doesn't open
his heart to ragtime somehow isn't human.
—H. K. Moderwell, *New Republic,* October 16, 1915

When Moderwell made the statement quoted above, ragtime music was un-
dergoing a sweeping indictment. Typical of the highbrow reaction was an
article in the *Etude* titled "The Invasion of Vulgarity in Music." There were
also tirades prompted by racial attitudes and moral condemnation. The following is a typical example: "It is an evil music that has crept into the
homes and hearts of our American people regardless of race, and must be
wiped out as other bad and dangerous epidemics have been eliminated."[1]

But ragtime also had its champions, most notably Hiram Moderwell,
who in his article for the *New Republic* wrote: "You may take it as certain
that if many millions of people persist in liking something that has not
been recognized by the schools, there is vitality in that thing."[2] We who
view ragtime from the perspective of an entire century are well aware of its
imperishable vitality as "an Original Black American Art" purged of racial
discrimination.

Before going on to individuals and styles, let us delve further into the
antecedents of ragtime. Another early devotee of ragtime, the novelist Rupert Hughes, wrote in 1899 that "Negroes call their clog dancing 'ragging'
and the dance a 'rag,' a dance largely shuffling. The dance is a sort of frenzy
with frequent yelps of delight from the dancers and spectators, and accompanied by the latter with hand clapping and stomping of feet. Banjo figuration is very noticeable in ragtime music and division of one of the beats
into two short notes is traceable to the hand clapping."[3]

The central role of the banjo in early minstrel music is discussed at
length by musicologist Hans Nathan in his chapter "Early Banjo Tunes
and American Syncopation."[4] He cites, for example, *The Complete American Banjo School* (Philadelphia, 1887), referring specifically to a piece called

"Darkies' Pastime." The rhythm in this jig (we are told) "may be tapped with the foot, 4 taps to each measure—which is the method generally adopted in playing jigs."[5] Nathan presents evidence that this practice dated back to the early 1840s. He also shows that the usual method was to stamp with the heel without lifting the entire foot—exactly as called for in the "stop-time" dances of ragtime.

Nathan's conclusion is that "the principle of pitting highly irregular accentuations in the melody, chiefly produced by melodic rather than dynamic means, against a precise metrical accompaniment [in the bass] is anticipated by early banjo tunes and undoubtedly derives from them."[6]

Ben R. Harney (1871–1938), no musicologist but a ragtime pianist and entertainer from Kentucky, who was brashly billed as the "World Famous Creator of Ragtime," had this to say about the banjo-to-piano transition:

> Real ragtime on the piano, played in such a manner that it cannot be put in notes, is the contribution of the graduated Negro banjo-player who cannot read music. On the banjo there is a short string that is not fretted and that consequently is played with the open thumb. . . . The colored performer, strumming in his own cajoling way, likes to throw in a note at random, and his thumb ranges over this for effect. When he takes up the piano, the desire for the same effect dominates him, being almost second nature, and he reaches for the open banjo-string note with the little finger. Meanwhile he is keeping mechanically perfect time with his left hand. The hurdle with the right-hand little finger throws the tune off stride, resulting in syncopation. He is playing two different tunes at once.[7]

We are told by the pioneer historian of ragtime, Rudi Blesh, that in the urban underworld districts of the Midwest, "the joints rang with the archaic, jangling, jig-piano syncopations that in only a few years would be a developed music to be dubbed ragtime."[8] It was at the turn of the century, then, that another worldwide dimension of America's music definitively emerged.

St. Louis was the city that set the pace, with an upsurge of black musicians, all young and gifted and reaching for fame. Many of them frequented the "sporting" district of St. Louis, called Chestnut Valley, and gathered at the Silver Dollar Saloon, operated by the legendary "Honest John" Turpin. His son Tom Turpin became a fabulous "jig" pianist and the composer of early ragtime hits such as "Bowery Buck" (1899), "Ragtime Nightmare" (1900), "Harlem Rag" (1897), and "St. Louis Rag" (1903). Unable to read music, he played by ear (as did many others), and his piano rags were written down by someone else. Tom Turpin soon became owner of the Rosebud Cafe, which was quickly known as a favorite meeting place for other ragtime musicians whom he helped and encouraged.

About 1885 a talented youngster named Scott Joplin arrived in St. Louis and soon became one of the "regulars" at the Silver Dollar Saloon. He was to make his headquarters in St. Louis for the next eight years, while appearing as an itinerant pianist in many other places in the Midwest. Born on the Arkansas side of Texarkana, on November 24, 1868, he inherited a musical talent from both his parents. His mother played the banjo and sang; his father, an ex-slave, played the violin and knew popular nineteenth-century dance music as well as traditional fiddle tunes.

Scott concentrated his musical talent on the piano, encouraged by his mother, who saved enough money to buy him a used upright. He soon became known as a proficient pianist and obtained engagements to play in the neighborhood. With a brother and two friends he formed the Texas Medley Quartette, for which he wrote his first published songs. These are in the genteel sentimental tradition, especially "A Picture of Her Face" (1895).

He was evidently bent on making music his life's work and looked for a larger field of activity. So, from the relative gentility of a poor but respectable Negro family, he switched to the tough tenderloin district of St. Louis. There he made his mark—and it also left its mark on him. But in the long run, in spite of problems and vicissitudes, it was Scott Joplin who set his immensely creative stamp on that great body of music that came to be known as classic ragtime.

A major event during this period was Joplin's visit to the Chicago World's Fair (World's Columbian Exposition) in 1893. There he met many ragtime pianists from the Midwest and formed a close friendship with Otis Saunders, who returned to St. Louis with Joplin the following year. Saunders urged Joplin to write down the pieces he had been playing and to try to have them published. Joplin took the advice and in 1899 succeeded in having his "Original Rags" published in Kansas City. The cover illustration depicts an old "darkey" picking up rags in front of his cabin and stuffing them into his pockets. (Cultural historians may well interpret this as an allegory of ragtime: from rags to riches.)

By this time Joplin and Saunders had gone to Sedalia, Missouri, which proved to be a turning point in the former's career. (Joplin later had a falling-out with Saunders, who claimed that *he* had written some of Joplin's best-known rags.) While playing piano at the Maple Leaf Club in Sedalia, Joplin also took courses in music theory and composition at a local college for Negroes. His aspirations were evidently both professional and artistic.

Some years earlier an ex-farmer and pioneer by the name of John Still-well Stark had opened a music store in Sedalia and started a small music-publishing business. When he heard Joplin play his piano rags at the Maple Leaf Club (a respectable center for social and recreational activities), Stark's pioneer instinct sensed that something new and potentially sensational was emerging in American music. The immediate result was his publication of Joplin's "Maple Leaf Rag" (1899). It was a huge popular success, and since Stark had given Joplin a royalty contract, they both profited from the sales. Stark, now ready for bigger things, moved to St. Louis, where he set up his own printing press and continued to publish ragtime music by Joplin and others. Later he opened an office in New York, but he was not cut out for the Tin Pan Alley type of commercial competition. In 1912 he returned to St. Louis and continued to champion ragtime, insisting that it was both respectable and artistically important. John Stilwell Stark (he died in 1927) was truly a cultural pioneer, a man of principle and conviction, to be honored in the annals of American music.

The "Maple Leaf Rag" gave Joplin not only a passport to respectability and financial independence, with wide popularity, but also an incentive for further artistic achievement. He began to have students, of whom the first and most gifted were Arthur Marshall and James Sylvester Scott, and he collaborated with both men on several rags. He also moved toward more extended compositions such as "The Ragtime Dance" (1902), including a "caller" announcing the various figures.

Joplin went on to write an opera, *A Guest of Honor* (1903), which apparently had one performance in St. Louis and thereafter was never heard nor seen (the score has disappeared). At this time Joplin was married and living in St. Louis as a middle-class citizen. But by 1905 he was divorced and apparently led a nomadic life until he went to New York City in 1907. There, in 1908, Stark published an important didactic work by Joplin, *School of Ragtime*—a landmark in the development and diffusion of classic ragtime.

The term *classic* was used by Stark to counteract the notion, widely held in the popular mind and promoted by Tin Pan Alley publishers, that any conspicuously syncopated music was ipso facto ragtime. For Stark and the composers whom he promoted, a "rag," like a march, was a composition with definite formal structure, basically sectional, consisting of sixteen bar strains (usually three to five), with repeats. Schematically, the first section would be AA BB A; the second, CC DD. Often the first strain is preceded by a brief introduction. The formalism is not rigid, for it allows many variants in the number of strains and their sequence. In Joplin's "The Chrysanthemum" (1904), for example, the third strain is repeated at the end. A more unusual sequence is that of the Joplin-Hayden "Felicity Rag" (1911), which follows the scheme: Introduction AA BB / CC Transition AA.

The preface to Joplin's *School of Ragtime* (we must assume that Stark had a hand in it) begins with a defensive tone:

> What is scurrilously called ragtime is an invention that is here to stay. That is now conceded by all classes of musicians. That all publications masquerading under the name of ragtime are not the genuine article will be better known when these exercises are studied. That real ragtime of a higher class is rather difficult to play is a painful truth which most pianists have discovered. Syncopations are no indication of light or trashy music, and to shy bricks at "hateful ragtime" no longer passes for musical culture. To assist amateur players in giving the "Joplin Rags" that weird and intoxicating effect intended by the composer is the object of this work.[9]

What is rather startling here is the phrase "weird and intoxicating effect intended by the composer." Was there in Scott Joplin and his "classical" colleagues an atavistic strain that harks back to what Lafcadio Hearn witnessed and described as "Original Songs and Peculiar Dances" of the Negroes along the levees of Cincinnati in the 1870s? He notes in particular a "weird, wild, lively air" and "the intoxication of the dance."[10] The coincidence of "weird" and "intoxicating" is astonishing—unless we assume that Stark had read Hearn's article! Or does it perhaps point to the extraordinary effect—between the aesthetic and the ecstatic—that ragtime had on many enthusiasts in its post-1960 revival? But, as Charles Ives proved, great music often mysteriously contains an "Unanswered Question."

Joplin's treatise, subtitled *Six Exercises for Piano,* was evidently intended for beginners or amateurs, for it spells out the elementary dos and don'ts of piano ragtime technique. Anyhow, it was unlikely that any conservatory-trained pianists would take to that kind of music—*then.* One of his admonitions is to "Play slowly until you catch the swing, and never play ragtime fast at any time." The latter rule he emphasizes again and again. He warns the beginner that "very often good players lose the effect entirely, by playing too fast." As we shall see, eastern ragtime pianists would ignore that admonition, as did vaudeville entertainers and flashy barrelhouse performers. Meanwhile, the "classical" rags published by Stark ceaselessly reiterated: "Not fast, not fast, not fast."

At the time of his death in 1917, Joplin had written fifty-three pieces for piano, including several marches and waltzes, together with seven pieces in collaboration and some songs. Among his most celebrated rags (besides those already mentioned) are "The Easy Winners: A Ragtime Two Step" (1901), "Palm Leaf Rag" (1903), "The Cascades" (1904), "Pine Apple Rag" (1908), and "Solace: A Mexican Serenade" (1909).[11]

The challenge of classic ragtime composition was to achieve variety and continuity within a rigid, sectional-thematic formal structure. Working with such self-imposed restrictions, Joplin continued to explore and exemplify the potential of classic ragtime for stylistic and expressive variety. While the vast majority of piano rags were subtitled either "Two Step" or "March" (sometimes juxtaposed), Joplin and some of his colleagues experimented with the waltz, which presented the challenge of integrating a dance in 3/4 time with the duple-meter framework of ragtime.

Joplin's "Bethena: A Concert Waltz" (1905) is an ingenious and delightful example of such a stylistic accommodation. The left hand generally keeps to a steady 3/4, while the right hand carries a syncopated theme

throughout the piece. More than any of his contemporaries, Joplin combined tradition with innovation and consistency with invention. He was the adventurous classicist par excellence.

Since ragtime was to become a national music for all Americans—and soon to be shared with the world—it is symbolically appropriate that, of the two composers who were closest to Joplin both personally and artistically, one was black, the other white: James Sylvester Scott (1886–1938) and Joseph F. Lamb (1887–1960). The former was born in Neosha, Missouri, moved with his family to Kansas, and in his early teens became known as an accomplished pianist. Because his parents were black, poor, and nomadic, his early life lacked stability. But at the age of sixteen he got a job as window washer in the Dumars music store of Carthage, Missouri, and when his employer surprised him at the piano one day, things began to change. He became the house pianist, and Dumars soon published his music.

The big turning point came in 1906 when he met Joplin, who recommended him to Stark. The latter soon became his principal publisher, beginning with "Frog Legs Rag" in 1906, continuing with "Kansas City Rag" (1907), "Sunburst Rag" (1909), "Ragtime Oriole" (1911), and many others to follow. From 1914 Scott lived in Kansas City, where he taught music, played the organ in a movie theater, and, until 1922, continued to compose piano rags, as well as three waltzes and some songs.

Scott's ragtime pieces are marked by elegance and brilliancy; to be fully effective they require considerable virtuosity. He combined "Grace and Beauty" (the title of one of his rags, 1910) with resourceful inventiveness. One of his foremost interpreters, William Bolcom, speaks of "the piano-devouring pyrotechnics of Scott's later rags, which are among the most demanding of all published piano ragtime."[12] These later rags include "Efficiency Rag" (1917), "New Era Rag" (1919), "Troubadour Rag" (1919), and—one of the most brilliant—"Pegasus: A Classic Rag" (1919). (It should be noted that most titles were supplied by his publisher.)

Joseph Lamb was born in Montclair, New Jersey, and was raised in a respectable middle-class milieu, with two sisters who played classical music at the piano. He began his musical activity at the same genteel level, with "Celestine Waltzes," for piano, and the setting of various poems for voice with piano. His parents intended him to prepare for the priesthood, but he preferred electrical engineering. Soon, however, he quit college and got a job in the garment district of Manhattan that he kept for the rest of his working life.

Living and raising a family in Brooklyn, he deliberately cut himself off from the professional-commercial centers of music, thus remaining obscure as a person, while riding the crest of the ragtime wave as a composer. When that subsided he continued to compose piano rags for his own satisfaction, thereby leaving a rich legacy of music in manuscript. After his death in 1960, just as the ragtime revival was beginning, his posthumous compositions appeared in print, starting with the appropriately titled portfolio *Ragtime Treasures* (1964).

Lamb owed his beginnings as a ragtime composer to the friendship of Joplin and the cooperation of Stark, who in 1907 published the first rag by this unknown youngster. It was titled "Sensation" and bore the rubric "arranged by Scott Joplin"—actually, a friendly boost for Lamb.

In view of his cultural background and aloofness from professional entertainment, it is not surprising that his piano rags are among the most artistic of that genre. They are often marked by allusions to the lighter classics, as in "The Ragtime Nightingale" (1915), referring to an art song by

Ethelbert Nevin, evoked by appropriate ornamentation. Curiously, an allusion to Chopin's *Revolutionary* Etude appears in the opening measures—which could be characterized as "the storm before the song."

Although Lamb had some trouble naming his rags, he evidently did well with "Excelsior Rag" (1909) and "American Beauty Rag" (1913). But he explained (or complained?) that some of the names he had chosen were changed by Stark, notably "Top Liner Rag" (1916) and "Bohemia Rag" (1919). To the question "What's in a name?" we can only reply, "Something catchy, topical, humorous, or elegant." Joseph Lamb covered the field, but his forte was elegance—combined with originality.

Concerning the last-mentioned quality, we can refer to Lamb's "Arctic Sunset" (one of the posthumous pieces), about which Blesh remarks: "It is unique in Lamb's published work in explicitly prescribing different tempi for various of its themes," thus freeing classic ragtime from the " 'one fixed tempo' restriction that dated from the original use of ragtime to accompany social dancing."[13]

In this elite domain of classic ragtime, there was a "sleeper" awaiting to reveal to posterity his innovative impulse and creative genius. This was Artie Matthews (1888–1959), a black pianist raised in Springfield, Missouri, where he had formal training in music. But as a youngster he was lured by ragtime, and at age sixteen he went to the St. Louis World's Fair of 1904, where some ragtime players were congregating. When he returned to St. Louis three years later, he was an accomplished ragtime performer and headed for a successful career in the world of popular entertainment. He combined the atmosphere of the Rosebud Cafe with the show business milieu of the Booker T. Washington Theater and the black Theater Owners Booking Association—for both of which he wrote and arranged the music.

With a series of "Pastime Rags" for piano, published between 1913 and 1920 by the Stark Music Company in St. Louis, Matthews established his position as a memorable ragtime composer and performer of high rank. Each of the five "Pastime Rags" that he published has the subtitle "A Slow Drag," and his classical bent is indicated by the admonitions "don't fake" and "not fast." His rhythms and harmonies are generally more complex and varied than those of the standard classic rags. The tango rhythm is prominent, especially in number 5, where it predominates with brilliant effect. As summarized by William Bolcom: "Each of the five pieces depends on an extremely careful balance of phrase and counterphrase. . . . Stoptime, slow drag, barrelhouse, and tango are all here in a witty but profound mix that reveals new dimensions on each hearing."[14]

In previous chapters we have alluded to ragtime as popular entertainment in various contexts and guises, from band concerts to vaudeville acts. Before continuing to explore this phase of the ragtime boom, we should not overlook its flirtations with classical music. For example, "ragging the classics" became a fad with amateurs as well as with professional performers and arrangers. Typical among the latter was Mike Bernard, who in 1900 won the ragtime piano competition in New York City. He really went for the heavy stuff with his ragging arrangements of "The Finale to Rubenstein's E-Flat Concerto" and the "Fantasy on the Pilgrim's Chorus from Tannhauser." Other ragtime arrangers came out with such specimens as "Zam-a-Zam Rag" (based on the overture to Hérold's opera *Zampa*); "Hungarian Rag" (alluding to Liszt's second Hungarian Rhapsody); and "Coontown's Merry Widow—A Ragtime Arrangement of the Famous Opera."[15]

According to Ann Charters, "Popular song writers trying to cash in on the craze innundated America with ragtime, and usually the appeal lay more in the novelty titles than in the music."[16] Among the titles she cites are "Dish Rag (Dedicated to Our Cook)," "Turkish Towel Rag (A Rub Down)," and "Wagner Couldn't Write a Ragtime Song." Obviously these represent the nadir of Broadway commercialism.

Any touch of syncopation turned the trick for Tin Pan Alley, and there are enduring songs that remain from this popular ragtime craze. We think of Kerry Mills's "At a Georgia Camp Meeting" (1899), Ben Harney's "Mr. Johnson, Turn Me Loose" (1895), Hughie Cannon's "Bill Bailey, Won't You Please Come Home?" (1902), and especially "There'll Be a Hot Time in the Old Town Tonight" (1896), generally attributed to Joe Hayden for the words and Theodore A. Metz for the music.

Of the Tin Pan Alley songwriters none is more conspicuously representative than Irving Berlin, whose "Alexander's Ragtime Band" (1911) is a classic of its kind. It was a favorite of instrumental performers such as the vaudeville entertainer and banjoist Fred Van Eps, whose version for banjo with orchestra was a great hit. A close contender was Berlin's "When the Midnight Choo-Choo Leaves for Alabam'" (words by Collin and Harlan). Less known is "The International Rag" (1913), which he presented at the New York Hippodrome, where he was billed as "The King of Ragtime"—not a total misnomer if we add "white, commercial, synthetic."

One of the most delightfully appealing songs of the ragtime entertainment peak is "Those Ragtime Melodies" (Hodgkins). As sung by the truly Peerless Quartet, it conveys all the allure of what was in many ways a golden age of American popular song.

Ben Harney had a song called "The Cake Walk in the Sky" (1899), which he played and sang with a genuine "jig-time" chorus, including not only the raggy rhythm but also a kind of "slanguage" that went with it. The celebrated vaudeville entertainer and songwriter Gene Greene, who made a big hit with "King of the Bungaloos" (1909), which he recorded in 1911 and again in 1917, also gives us his authentic presentation of "jig-time."[17]

Scott Joplin's "The Ragtime Dance" (1902), for which he wrote both words and music, has a blend of ragtime rhythms duplicated in the voice and piano parts. The vocal text describes both the setting of the dances and the manner in which each should be performed: "Let me see you do the 'rag time dance,' Turn left and do the 'Cake walk prance'—Turn the other way and do the 'Slow drag.' . . ." The second section goes into "Stop Time," during which "the pianist will please *Stamp* the heel of one foot heavily upon the floor at every word 'Stamp.' Do not raise the toe of the foot from the floor while stamping." The verso of the title page informs us that "Complete directions for all the steps of the 'Ragtime Dance' are published by Scott Joplin—and can be obtained where ever this piece is for sale."[18]

Joplin wrote and published relatively few songs; but there are vocal versions of "Maple Leaf Rag" (1903), with words by Sydney Brown, and "Pine Apple Rag" (1910), words by Joe Snyder. The first of these has a stereotyped "coon" song-and-dance context, but the second is an absolute jewel. It is for solo voice and chorus, with some lines of "patter," spoken rhythmically over two light arpeggios and two staccato eighth notes in the piano part. The text is sophisticated, witty, colloquial, lively, and perfectly wedded to the entrancing "jig" style of classic ragtime in its vocal expression.[19] The second stanza opens with a good-natured plug for ragtime versus highbrow heavies:

> Some people rave about Wagnerian airs,
> Some say the Spring Song is divine,
> Talk like that is out of season,
> What I like is something pleasin',
> Pine Apple rag for mine.

We turn now to the presentation of traditional ragtime music in the context of orchestral performance, which once again brings Stark and Joplin into the foreground. About 1912 Stark published in St. Louis a collection of *Standard High-Class Rags,* arranged for small orchestra. Of the fifteen numbers, six were by Joplin, beginning with "Maple Leaf Rag" and ending with "The Entertainer"—as though symbolizing the alpha and omega of classical ragtime.

James Scott was well represented with four rags, including "Grace and Beauty," while Joseph Lamb and Arthur Marshall had one apiece. Scott Hayden figured in collaboration with Joplin on "Sunflower Slow Drag," while two numbers closer to the popular scene were Kirwin's "African Pas" and J. R. Robinson's "The Minstrel Man." The collection eventually became known as "The Red-Backed Book of Rags," and as such it was a wellspring of the 1970s ragtime revival.[20] The orchestrations are for small ensemble, allowing for various combinations, including trumpet, clarinet, trombone, flute, piccolo, tuba, piano, drums, violins, viola, cello, and bass.

Joplin had played cornet for a while as a member of the Queen City Concert Band in Sedalia, and several of his works, including the opera *Treemonisha* (see chapter 30), indicate his interest in the art of orchestration. As a link to Sedalia and its concert band, we may note that the latter included in its repertory a ragtime number, "Eli Green's Cakewalk" (1896). This was written by one of the few women ragtime composers whose names have come down to us, Sadie Koninski. She is by no means forgotten: three quarters of a century later, Eli Green cakewalked again with the Dawn of the Century Ragtime Orchestra, in an arrangement by its director, David E. Bourne, who also arranged and recorded Joe Lamb's "Bohemia Rag."[21] An enterprising arranger may come up with "Eli Green's Bohemian Ragtime Cakewalk"!

We should now take a look at the eastern ragtime scene, whose leading figures, unlike the Midwest exponents of classic ragtime, were more concerned with variety than with formality. They were involved with all kinds of popular music, including blues and jazz. They liked their ragtime fast, their rhythms tricky, and their melodies catchy; improvisation was also important for them. They were often involved with show business and wrote many songs. The three most representative eastern musicians are James P. Johnson (1891–1955), Charles Luckeyeth ("Luckey") Roberts (1890–1968), and Eubie Blake (1883–1983), whom we have already met as a partner of Noble Sissle.

James P. Johnson was born in Brunswick, New Jersey, but he retained some old southern customs, as revealed in the piano piece that made him famous, "Carolina Shout," which he is said to have written in 1914.[22] Eventually it would strongly influence such up-and-coming jazz youngsters as Fats Waller and Duke Ellington.

James P. (as he was familiarly called) was first turned on to ragtime as a teenager, when he heard a friend playing Joplin's "Gladiolus Rag" (1907). Eventually he broke through the sectional rigidity of classic ragtime by blending it with the blues, and he developed the propulsive left-hand rhythmic style known as stride piano. Among his early ragtime pieces are "Caprice Rag" (1914), "Daintiness Rag" (1916), and "Harlem Strut" (1917).

In contrast to Johnson, Eubie Blake was turned on by hearing James ("Jess") Pickett's "The Dream," a rag that has been called "a Spanish number because of its tango bass."[23] Eubie was then about fifteen but already familiar with the red-light district of Baltimore, where he was born and raised by a pious mother who thought that ragtime was the work of the Devil. But for Eubie it was entrancing music, and if the place to hear and play it was in a bawdy house, there he would go. His mother had bought him a small organ and paid for his piano lessons, hoping that he would become a respectable musician and perhaps play the organ at her church. Instead, he got a job as pianist in one of the fancier "houses" (five-dollar tips!). From there he went on to join a medicine show and a colored minstrel show, but was soon back in the Baltimore "district."

In 1899 he composed his first and most famous ragtime piece, the "Charleston Rag." This was followed by "Corner Chestnut and Low" (1903), "Eubie's Boogie" (1904), and "Novelty Rag" (1910). Two other rags of this period, "Chevy Chase" and "Fizz Water," were the first to be published, in 1914. By this time Eubie was playing in Atlantic City during the summer, where he formed a close friendship with Luckey Roberts and nursed his ambition to accomplish great things in music, not limiting himself to ragtime. We have already recounted his career in show business, and now he appears as a highly popular personification of the great ragtime revival—plus the only pianist ever to record one of his own compositions, "Charleston Rag," at an interval of fifty years (1921–71).

The best summary of Eubie Blake's style and significance is that of Kimball and Bolcom in their splendid book *Reminiscing with Sissle and Blake:* "Eubie's tricks were many and from varied sources, as befits his highly eclectic temperament, but the most immediately salient feature of all his playing and composition, without which the particular flavor of his music is lost, is *accent*. Eubie is master of the accent in all its forms: on-the-beat, off-the-beat, in-between. These accents, unlike many of the others' tricks, could be composed into the music, a fact of utmost importance."[24]

Perhaps it would have pleased Joplin to know that of the pianists immediately responsible for the revival of his classic rags, three were *professors* in the academic sense of the term (as contrasted with the colloquial use it re-

Noble Sissle and Eubie Blake (1973). Photo by Mary Velthoven.

ceived in the "sporting" districts). The pianist who first recorded *The Complete Piano Works of Scott Joplin* was a professor of English at Kentucky Wesleyan College, but in his role as a ragtime performer he was known as Professor John W. "Knocky" Parker—which could be interpreted as a rather sporty title. The jacket cover nevertheless announces that the music was "Presented in the Classic Form," and the liner notes are both copious and analytical, as befitted a doubly titled professor.[25]

Meanwhile another pianist-professor, Joshua Rifkin, with academic degrees in composition (Juilliard) and musicology (Princeton), made a recording in 1970 titled *Scott Joplin Piano Rags*. He was then twenty-six and had been playing ragtime and jazz since the age of ten. His first Joplin recording was immediately and widely successful, leading to volumes 2 and 3, issued in 1972 and 1974. Rifkin adhered to Joplin's admonition, "Never play ragtime fast," and his rags are classical in the fullest sense of the term.[26]

Concurrently, ragtime buff William Bolcom, also academically trained in piano and composition, and a professor at the University of Michigan in Ann Arbor, widened the scope of the classic ragtime revival by recording a selection of rags by Tom Turpin, Luckey Roberts, James Scott, Joseph Lamb, and, of course, Scott Joplin. (We have already mentioned his recording of the "Pastime Rags" by Artie Matthews.)[27]

In the realm of professional entertainment and mass-media popularization, pianist-composer Max Morath anticipated the ragtime revival in the early 1960s with his television series "The Ragtime Years." He also concertized and lectured widely on the ragtime circuit and contributed to the Joplin apotheosis with his 1972 Vanguard recording *The Best of Scott Joplin and Other Rag Classics*.[28]

Another aspect of the ragtime revival is represented in the neoragtime compositions by contemporary composers who can be identified as ragtime buffs. Among them are three already mentioned: John "Knocky" Parker, Joshua Rifkin, and William Bolcom. Closely associated with the last of these was William Albright; in 1969 they jointly composed and recorded a ragtime piece titled "Brass Knuckles." Typical of Bolcom's ragtime output are "Seabiscuits" (1967) and "Graceful Ghost" (1970), concerning which he has written: "In it I have tried to imagine an extension of Louis Chauvin's gentle French-Creole quality."[29] Max Morath and John Arpin were likewise prominent and influential in contributing to the compositional phase of ragtime in the 1970s. This development is also represented in print by a collection titled *The Ragtime Current*, compiled by Rudi Blesh.[30]

To conclude, it is fitting that the earliest and most dedicated champion of ragtime, Hiram Moderwell, should have the last say here. As he wrote in his 1915 article for the *New Republic:*

> It has carried the complexities of the rhythmic subdivision of the measure to a point never before reached in the history of music. It has established subtle conflicting rhythms to a degree never before attempted in any popular music or folk-music, and rarely enough in art-music. It has shown a definite and natural evolution—always a proof of vitality in a musical idea. It has gone far beyond most other popular music in the freedom of inner voices (yes, I mean polyphony) and of harmonic modulation. And it has proved its adaptability to the expression of many distinct moods.[31]

Notes

1. Arthur Weld, "Our Musical Condition," *Negro Music Journal* 1 (Mar. 1903): 138; quoted in Edward A. Berlin, *Ragtime,* p. 44.
2. Hiram K. Moderwell, "Ragtime," *New Republic,* Oct. 16, 1915, p. 284.
3. Rupert Hughes, "A Eulogy of Rag-Time."
4. Hans Nathan, *Dan Emmett and the Rise of Early Minstrelsy,* pp. 189–213.
5. Ibid., p. 190.
6. Ibid., p. 209.
7. *Ben Harney's Ragtime Instructor,* arr. Theodore H. Northrop (Chicago: Sol Bloom, 1897).
8. Rudi Blesh and Harriet Janis, *They All Played Ragtime,* pp. 39–40.
9. See *The Collected Works of Scott Joplin,* ed. Vera Brodsky Lawrence, vol. 1, *Works for Piano,* p. 284.
10. Lafcadio Hearn, "Levee Life: Haunts and Pastimes of the Roustabouts, Their Original Songs, and Peculiar Dances," *Cincinnati Commercial,* Mar. 17, 1876; reprinted in Hearn, *An American Miscellany,* ed. Albert Mordell, vol. 1, pp. 163, 164.
11. For the piano pieces, see *The Collected Works of Scott Joplin,* vol. 1.
12. William Bolcom, liner notes to *Pastimes & Piano Rags,* Nonesuch H-71299.
13. Rudi Blesh, liner notes to *The Classic Rags of Joe Lamb,* Golden Crest CRS 4127; Milton Kaye, piano.
14. Bolcom, liner notes to *Pastimes & Piano Rags.*
15. For other examples of "ragging the classics," see Berlin, *Ragtime,* pp. 66–71.
16. Ann Charters, *The Ragtime Songbook,* p. 33.
17. The 1917 recording is reproduced on *Ragtime Entertainment,* comp. David A. Jasen, RBF Records 22.
18. *The Collected Works of Scott Joplin,* ed. Vera Brodsky Lawrence, vol. 2, *Works for Voice,* pp. 291–301, passim.

19. "Pine Apple Rag" is recorded on the album *Classic Rags & Ragtime Songs,* Columbia P 12974; conducted by T. J. Anderson.

20. For a recording of this collection, see *Scott Joplin, the Red Back Book,* Angel S-36060; the New England Conservatory Ragtime Ensemble, Gunther Schuller, conductor.

21. See *Silk and Rags,* Arcane Records AR 602; Dawn of the Century Ragtime Orchestra, Prof. David E. Bourne, conductor.

22. For "Carolina Shout" and other "stride pieces" by Johnson, including "Mule-Walk Stomp" (ca. 1920), "Eccentricity—Syncopated Waltz" (ca. 1917), "Modernistic (You've Got to Be)" (1920), and "Snowy Morning Blues" (ca. 1925), see *Ragtime Back to Back,* University of Michigan School of Music Records SM 0004; performed by William Albright.

23. Blesh and Janis, *They All Played Ragtime,* p. 191.

24. Robert Kimball and William Bolcom, *Reminiscing with Sissle and Blake,* p. 48. For a comprehensive discography, see pp. 247–54.

25. See *The Complete Piano Works of Scott Joplin: The Greatest of Ragtime Composers,* Audiophile AP 71–72; interpreted and played by Prof. John W. "Knocky" Parker. Parker also had an earlier release (1963) of Joplin rags on Audiophile.

26. See Nonesuch H-71248, H-71264, and H-71305.

27. See *Heliotrope Bouquet: Piano Rags by Turpin, Joplin, Joplin-Chauvin, Lamb, Scott, Roberts, Bolcom, Bolcom-Albright,* Nonesuch H-71257; William Bolcom, piano.

28. See Vanguard VSD 39–40. In 1973 Morath also brought out *The World of Scott Joplin,* Vanguard SRV-310 SD and Quad VSQ-30031. This included rags by James Scott, Arthur Marshall, and Joseph Lamb.

29. William Bolcom, liner notes to *Heliotrope Bouquet.*

30. *The Ragtime Current,* comp. Rudi Blesh. Included are works by Albright, Ashwander, Bolcom, Morath, Waldo, and others.

31. Moderwell, "Ragtime," p. 285.

Chapter 24

Composer from Connecticut

Do you really think anybody would be fool enough
to try to play a thing like that?
—Edgar Stowell to Charles Ives, in the summer
of 1912 or 1913, referring to *The Fourth of July*

In the year 1894 Antonin Dvořák was teaching in New York and advocating
an American "national" music based on the use of Negro and Indian melodies. Edward MacDowell, "a glorious young figure" (so Hamlin Garland
saw him), wearing a derby hat and a curled mustache, walked in Boston
Common musing on Arthurian legends and Celtic lore. Horatio Parker, erudite, fastidious, Munich trained, fresh from the triumph of his cantata *Hora
Novissima,* had just assumed his duties as professor of music at Yale University. A youth of nineteen (going on twenty) from the town of Danbury, Connecticut, went to New Haven and matriculated in the class of '98 at Yale. His
name was Charles Edward Ives.

Young Ives was the son of George E. Ives, a band director and music
teacher in Danbury, where Charles was born on October 20, 1874. The Ives
family was of old New England stock and occupied a prominent place in
the town. In their position music was not regarded as a suitable profession
for male offspring. An education at Yale and a career in banking, law, or
business fulfilled the normal expectation. In this milieu George Ives was
somewhat of a maverick. He not only played cornet in the Danbury band
and performed on the violin at local musicales (which was perfectly
proper) but obtained the concession of studying theory with a German-
American professor in New York.

Then the Civil War broke out, and in 1862, at the age of seventeen,
George Ives recruited and organized a volunteer band that was attached to
the First Connecticut Artillery Regiment. After the war he made a brief try
at business but soon decided to make music his profession. Besides leading

the Danbury town band, he gave lessons, directed church choirs, and conducted or played with small theater orchestras.

Thus Charles Ives was the first of his lineage to be the son of a professional musician. But it was his father's character, openness of mind, and penchant for experiment, rather than his professionalism per se, that had the deepest and most enduring effect on the son. The basic factor was a many-sided, pluralistic view of music, in its social, creative, and functional aspects.

Among the technical devices with which George Ives experimented was that of producing quarter tones. As described by his son many years later:

> He rigged up a contrivance to stretch 24 or more violin strings and tuned them up to suit the dictates of his own curiosity. He would pick out quarter-tone tunes and try to get the family to sing them, but I remember he gave that up except as a means of punishment—though we got to like some of the tunes which kept to the usual scale and had quarter-tone notes thrown in. But after working for some time he became sure that some quarter-tone chords must be learned before quarter-tone melodies would make much sense and become natural to the ear, and so for the voice. He started to apply a system of bows to be released by weights, which would sustain the chords, but in this process he was suppressed by the family and a few of the neighbors. A little later on he did some experimenting with glasses and bells, and got some sounds as beautiful, sometimes, as they were funny—a complex that only children are old enough to appreciate.[1]

There were also exercises intended "to stretch our ears and strengthen our musical minds," as when "he would occasionally have us sing, for instance, a tune like *The Swanee River* in the key of E♭, but play the accompaniment in the key of C."[2] When Charles began to play the drum in his father's brass band, there was no objection to experimenting with unusual chords "if it was done with some musical sense—that is, if I would make some effort to find out what was going on, with some reason."[3]

George Ives repudiated conformity, but he believed in discipline. Charles later wrote, "Father had kept me on Bach and taught me harmony and counterpoint from a child until I went to college."[4] (He also used the standard textbooks of Jadassohn on harmony and counterpoint.) The main departures from academic standards were (1) that sound was a world of infinite possibilities to be explored and (2) that music was to be most valued when related to human events.

In later life Charles Ives reacted strongly to the criticism of a "routine-minded professor" who told him that gospel hymns and "street tunes" should have no place in a composer's music—certainly not in a symphony! Such an opinion, he declared, was based on something the professor had "probably never heard, seen, or experienced." For Ives, human experience was the basis of all creativity. He wrote in retrospect:

> I remember, when I was a boy—at the outdoor Camp Meeting services in Redding, all the farmers, their families and field hands, for miles around, would come afoot or in their farm wagons. I remember how the great waves of sound used to come through the trees—when things like *Beulah Land, Woodworth, Nearer My God to Thee, The Shining Shore, Nettleton, In the Sweet Bye and Bye* and the like were sung by thousands of "let out" souls. The music notes and words on paper were about as much like what they "were" (at those moments) as the monograms on a man's necktie may be like his face. Father, who led the singing, sometimes with his cornet or his voice, sometimes with both voice and arms, and sometimes in the quieter hymns with a French horn or violin, would always encourage the people to sing their own way. Most of them knew the words and music (theirs) by heart, and sang it that way. If they threw the poet or composer around a bit, so much the better for the poetry and the music. There was power and exaltation in these great conclaves of sound from humanity.[5]

The key word here is "humanity." We can indeed affirm that Charles Ives was our first great musical humanist, using the liberal definition of *humanism* as a philosophy or attitude concerned with human beings and their achievements and interests. Ives's humanism was to manifest itself not only musically but also philosophically, ideologically, and politically.[6]

Meanwhile, young Charlie was making an impression in Danbury as an up-and-coming composer and performer. In its issue of January 17, 1888, the local *Evening News* carried the following item, under the heading "Amusements":

> The feature of the evening, in the musical line, was the rendition of the "Holiday Quickstep," composed and arranged for an orchestra by Charlie Ives, a thirteen-year-old-son of George E. Ives. Master Ives is certainly a musical genius, being an accomplished performer on several instruments, as well as a composer and arranger. The "Holiday Quickstep" is worthy a place with productions of much older heads, and Master Charlie should be encouraged to further efforts in this line. We shall expect more from this talented youngster in the future.

What might have been merely a local puff proved to be a true prophecy that would eventually make the town of Danbury famous in the world of music.

Under normal circumstances such versatile precocity would be expected to lead to a professional career in music. Master Charlie was not merely a talented youngster to be shown off by his lady-teacher at some church benefit or at a genteel *soirée musicale*. At fourteen he was engaged as organist at the Congregational church and soon afterward at the Baptist church. After a concert at the latter in 1890, the *Evening News* predicted for him "a brilliant future as an organist." After Danbury he was indeed a church organist in New Haven and New York (from 1894 to 1902), but he certainly did not envisage that as a career.

Besides playing the organ in church and the drum in his father's band (as well as baseball and football!), Ives did considerable composing during these early years. His most remarkable juvenile work was the *Variations on America,* for organ, which he performed in 1891–92 in Danbury and elsewhere. He tells us that it was not played much in church concerts because "it made the boys laugh"—no doubt because of some unexpected sounds. As Ives explained: "One variation was the theme in canon, put in three keys together, B♭–E♭–A♭, and backwards A♭–E♭–B♭."[7] There are also short interludes between the variations, including one with the right hand in F, the left hand and pedal in G-flat, "as a kind of canon together." One of the variations is in the rhythm of a polonaise. It is sheer Ives, and delightfully so.

An earlier piece mentioned by Ives is an overture titled *The American Woods,* about which he later wrote: "The part suggesting a Steve Foster tune, while over it the old farmers fiddled a barn dance with all of its jigs, gallops, and reels, was played in Danbury on the old Wooster House bandstand in 1889."[8] Of interest here is the allusion not only to one of Ives's favorite composers but also to the barn dances and the fiddling tunes that were very much a part of his youthful environment and consequently woven into his compositions, notably in the Second Symphony.[9]

A typical early work is the *Fugal Song (for Harvest Season),* probably written and performed in 1893, for tuba, trombone, cornet, and voice. It is in four keys (C, F, B-flat, E-flat) and hence is a forerunner of the fugue in four keys on "The Shining Shore"—George F. Root's popular hymn— which is in C, G, D, A. This was the sort of thing that "got him in wrong" when he began to study with Parker at Yale—although the latter's reaction appears to have been relatively mild. According to Ives: "Parker took it as a joke (he was seldom mean). . . . He would just look at a measure or so, and hand it back with a smile, or joke about 'hogging all the keys at one meal.' . . ."[10]

It was not until his junior year, however, that academic regulations allowed Ives to take full-time (four-hour) courses with Parker. In the interim he attended some of the latter's general classes, even though he found that these were "governed too much by the German rule."[11] After the first two or three weeks of his freshman year, Ives tells us, "I didn't bother him with any of the experimental ideas that Father had been willing for me to think about, discuss, and try out."[12]

The distressing fact is that shortly after Ives began his first term at Yale, he was struck a terrible blow when his father died, at age forty-nine. We have only to read Ives's copious *Memos* to perceive that he idealized his father as the fountainhead of what he valued most in life and in music.

During his last two years of study with Parker, Ives composed his First Symphony, in four movements, to satisfy the academic requirements. He later explained that it was "supposed to be in D minor, but the first subject went through six or eight different keys, so Parker made me write another first movement. But it seemed no good to me, and I told him that I would much prefer to use the first draft. He smiled and let me do it, saying, 'But you must promise to end in D minor.' "[13]

Because we now think of Ives primarily as a composer, we tend to assume that his musical studies were the most important aspect of his four years at Yale. But it was his life-style that was more significantly influenced by the traditions, associations, and socioeconomic standards that he assimilated during his undergraduate years. College life, rather than academic courses (in which he did rather poorly), was the matrix of the Yale experience, in which Ives fully participated. He used his musical talent to write college songs, music for fraternity shows, and the lively marches that he loved—as well as entertaining at the piano. His status as a "Yale man" was fully recognized when, in his junior year, he was tapped for membership in Wolf's Head, the prestigious senior society.

Ives reveled in every kind of popular song, from Tin Pan Alley tunes to ragtime. He remembered having heard some "black-faced comedians . . . ragging their songs" at the Danbury Fair, including one that began, "I'm a-livin' easy/On pork chops greasy."[14] In New Haven he frequented a vaudeville house called Poli's and was much impressed by the pianist, George Felsberg: "I used to go down there and 'spell him' a little if he wanted to go out for five minutes and get a glass of beer, or a dozen glasses."[15] If Felsberg opted for the dozen, Ives would have plenty of time to experiment with ragtime—which was to be a consistently important factor in his compositional output, most notably in the First Piano Sonata (in seven movements, 1901–9) and the *Ragtime Dances* (or *Ragtime Pieces*, 1902–4).[16]

Much of the ragtime atmosphere was also developed and absorbed at the Hyperion Theater in New Haven, where the orchestra conductor, Frank Fichtl, would willingly perform any music offered by Ives. Ives later recalled:

> A kind of shuffle-dance-march (last century rag) was played on the piano—the violin, cornet, and clarinet taking turns in playing sometimes old songs, sometimes popular tunes of the day, as *After the Ball.* . . .
> Some similar things were tried in the D. K. E. shows [a Yale fraternity], but not very successfully, as I remember. Marches with college tunes in the trio against the original themes went better,—though Prof. Fichtl, in the theater orchestra, would get students in the audience whistling and beating time (sometimes) to the off-key and off-time tunes.[17]

Touches of ragtime as manipulated by Ives appear in several of his major compositions such as the "Hawthorne" movement of the *Concord* Sonata, the Trio for Piano, Violin, and Cello (1904–5; rev. 1911), and the utterly fantastic and fiendishly complex scherzo titled *Over the Pavements* (1906–13), for piccolo (optional), clarinet, bassoon (or saxophone), trumpet, three trombones (optional), bass drum, cymbal, and piano. It is interesting also that Ives brought some of his favorite hymn tunes such as "Bringing in the Sheaves," "O Happy Day," and "I Hear Thy Welcome Voice" into his ragtime pieces.

From what has been revealed thus far, it would seem that Ives was not headed for a professional career in music—which for composers in the larger classical forms generally meant obtaining an academic position. He wanted to be free to write his own kind of music, and for this he needed financial independence. Thus, after graduating from Yale he found employment with the Mutual Life Insurance Company of New York and was thereby on the way to becoming (in the words of William Brooks) "the most spectacular amateur in musical history."

In 1908 he married Harmony Twichell, daughter of a prominent clergyman from Hartford, and thereafter they divided their time between a town house in Manhattan and a home they built in West Redding, near Danbury. They had no children but eventually adopted a daughter. Ives composed assiduously in his spare time, on weekends and holidays, often working far into the night. Neither he nor his wife cared for the conventional social life of a successful business executive—which he soon became. In January 1907 he formed an agency called Ives and Company, which two years later became the firm of Ives and Myrick, operating as an agency of Mutual Life. For the next twenty years it was immensely successful, and Ives became a very wealthy man. But he was never ostentatious, and in his later years, especially after suffering his second heart attack in 1918, he lived a rather retired life.

With respect to his musical works—he had written about ninety compositions, large and small—few were heard publicly until many years later. According to Ives, "During the twenty years ending in 1919, only one conductor had seen any of my music." To which he added, with typical wry humor, that "not enough conductors have seen enough of my music to be able to get even a good impression of how bad it is."[18]

In 1910, when he showed his First Symphony to the distinguished conductor Walter Damrosch, who agreed to try it in rehearsal, the first reaction was "Charming!" But when "the music got a little more involved," that was the end of that venture. The last straw was Damrosch's patronizing remark: "You'll just have to make up your mind, young man! Which DO you want, a rhythm of two or a rhythm of three?"[19] For Ives it was never "either-or" but "both-and" (to borrow from the words of Kierkegaard's dichotomy).

This sort of put-down was repeated on many occasions, so that he was goaded into saying, "I began to feel that if I wanted to write music that was worth while (that is, to me), I must keep away from musicians."[20] He meant, of course, the academic, die-hard professionals. His problem was how to hear his own music, not only in his mind but as a sound-projecting entity to which an audience (or at least a listener!) could react. Now and then a receptive musical friend would play a piece for him, but it was not until the 1930s that a considerable number of dedicated professional musicians began to perform his music persistently and effectively. The two champions of Ives who were the first to make his music widely known were Henry Cowell and John Kirkpatrick, the latter a famous pianist.

Meanwhile, Ives was composing and revising (and interweaving) a vast quantity of music, of unprecedented variety and originality. We need only mention, as examples, such piano pieces as *The Anti-Abolitionist Riots* (1908), the *Three-Page* Sonata (1905), and *Some Southpaw Pitching* (ca. 1909), as well as the *Two Contemplations* for orchestra, consisting of *Central Park in the Dark* (1906) and *The Unanswered Question* (1906). The latter, presented as "A Cosmic Landscape," for trumpet, four flutes, treble woodwind, and string orchestra, represents the quintessence of Ives's spiritual search for the Unknown. The foregoing is only to sample the range of his themes; some larger works will be discussed later.

Ives's faith in the common man was rooted in his formative years in Danbury, nourished by his reading of Emerson and Thoreau, and strengthened by the neglect of, or scorn for, his music by professional highbrow musicians. We have already noted many of the ways in which Ives, following the example of his father, identified himself with the musical experience of the people, from the holiday festivities and marching bands to the hymn singing of the camp meetings. Referring to a tune that a group of people were singing, he wrote: "It wasn't a Broadway hit, it wasn't a musical comedy air, it wasn't a waltz tune or a dance tune. . . . It was (only) the refrain of an old Gospel Hymn that had stirred many people of past generations. It was nothing but—*In the Sweet Bye and Bye*. It wasn't a tune written to be sold, or written by a professor of music—but by a man who was but giving out an experience."[21]

Ives was especially receptive to popular hymn tunes because they represented for him the quintessence of a deeply felt human experience, both individual and collective. In all he quotes some fifty-four hymn tunes, the majority from American composers of the nineteenth century. Especially favored are Lowell Mason's "Nearer, My God, to Thee" (Bethany) and "From Greenland's Icy Mountains" (Missionary Hymn), Root's "The Shining Shore," Joseph Philbrick Webster's "The Sweet By and By," G. A. Minor's "Bringing in the Sheaves," and Asahel Nettleton's "Come, Thou Fount of Every Blessing" (also attributed to John Wyeth). But "quoting" for Ives becomes an intricate and complex process, woven into the deep structures of his creative expression.

Since we have brought up the fundamental process of quotation, we should also say something about the secular input, classified by John Kirkpatrick as "Patriotic Songs and Military Music," "Popular Songs," and "College Songs."[22] In the first category there are thirteen items, ranging from "Yankee Doodle" to "America," and from "Reveille" (bugle call) to "Semper Fidelis," not forgetting "Hail Columbia" and "The Star-Spangled Banner." The most often quoted are Root's "The Battle Cry of Freedom," Work's "Marching through Georgia," Shaw's "The Red, White and Blue" (or "Columbia, the Gem of the Ocean"), and "John Brown's Body" (or "Battle Hymn of the Republic"), the tune from a spiritual. Dan Emmett's "Dixie's Land" vies with George M. Cohan's "Over There," and "La Marseillaise" with "Maryland, My Maryland."

Thirty-six popular songs are listed, with Stephen Foster in the lead, joined by Root and Work, as well as James Bland and Paul Dresser. Included are such perennial favorites as "Little Annie Rooney," "The Girl I

Charles Ives

Left behind Me," and "A Son of a Gambolier." The college songs are less numerous and widespread, with Yale in the ascendancy, although Princeton and Harvard also are mentioned, the latter rather snidely in "Harvard Has Blue Stocking Girls."

To these categories are added other popular tunes, primarily instrumental, such as "Arkansas Traveller," "Money Musk," "Sailor's Hornpipe," and "Turkey in the Straw" (or "Old Zip Coon"). In sum, a widely fascinating spectrum of American popular tunes (with some international input), to which there is nothing comparable in the entire range of American composition. But the uniqueness resides less in the number and variety than in the intricate interweaving and creative juxtaposition of the tunes in Ives's music. (This will be further delineated when we come to discuss the great Fourth Symphony.)

Ives's use of borrowed material is both evocative and structural, both symbolic and functional. Far from relying mainly on literal quotation, it is an evocation by allusion and association, stirring roots of memory and recalling the collective experiences of Americans through remembrances creatively reinterpreted and transformed. Not a medley but a melding.

Except when referring to specific technical problems or details, Ives generally emphasized the associative or symbolic content rather than the compositional process when writing about his own music. He once wrote, "Maybe music was not intended to satisfy the curious definiteness of man." And he added, "Maybe it is better to hope that music may always be a transcendental language in the most extravagant sense." He would perhaps have liked music to be beyond analysis. In his own exegesis he either linked it to earthly humanity or let it soar toward the infinite. The latter was clearly the aim of his unfinished *Universe* Symphony, subtitled "The Universe, Past, Present, and Future," as he outlined it in the three projected sections: (1) Past: Formation of the waters and mountains; (2) Present: Earth, evolution in nature and humanity; (3) Future: Heaven, the rise of all to the spiritual.[23]

This project was perhaps linked to Ives's view of Emerson as "America's deepest explorer of the spiritual immensities. . . . We see him—standing on a summit at the door of the infinite, where many men do not dare to climb, peering into the mysteries of life, contemplating the eternities, hurling back whatever he discovers there—now thunderbolts, for us to grasp, if we can, and translate—now placing quietly, even tenderly, in our hands, things that we may see without effort. . . ."[24] This would do rather well, too, as a spiritual portrait of Ives, including his creative expression.

Ives also had a deep affinity with Thoreau, and in Hawthorne he found "a sensitiveness to supernatural sound-waves"[25] and a substance charged with "the phantasmal, the mystical . . . from the deeper picturesque to the illusive fantastic. . . ."[26] For the common touch he turned to Bronson Alcott (more famous for his daughters than for his philosophy), in whose home he discerned "a kind of common triad of the New England homestead . . . a value that seems to stir a deeper feeling, a stronger sense of being nearer some perfect truth than a Gothic cathedral or an Etruscan villa."[27]

In this theme of concord and the transcendentalists, Ives found "a conviction of the power of the common soul," which he expressed so profoundly and eloquently in his Second Piano Sonata, subtitled *Concord, Mass., 1840–60.* Its four movements are titled "Emerson," "Hawthorne," "The Alcotts," and "Thoreau." In 1912 Ives played the whole sonata for his friend Max Smith, who said the Alcott movement "was by far the best." As Ives wrote: "By 'best' Maxie meant (but didn't know it) the easiest to listen to—that is, for his nice ears."[28] For him, there was a chasm of incomprehension between the "nice ears" of the connoisseurs and the "static, rule-making do-as-I'm-told professors," and the music that moves "as the mountain does."[29] Privately (in his notebook), Ives reacted vehemently to the lack of understanding for what he was trying to accomplish in the sonata. For example: "And when the Nice Old Ladies [i.e., critics and professors] say 'no design—formless—all music should have design and form'— Yes, Sarah, but not your designs and forms—No, Sirree! In this Sonata they're spitting about, there is design—somewhat more than there should be, it seemed to me—and the form is obvious, but it isn't drabbed on every milestone on the way *up* or *to* or *on*—it takes care of itself, so to speak, and isn't yanked back every thirty-two measures by those nice apron strings hanging on the classroom scroll."[30]

Ives continues with one of his most truly transcendental and self-revealing statements on musical composition:

A natural procedure in a piece of music, be it a song or a week's symphony, may have something in common [with]—I won't say analogous to—a walk up a mountain. There's the mountain, its foot, its summit—there's the valley—the climber looks, turns, and looks down or up. He sees the valley, but not exactly the same angle he saw it at [in] the last look—and the summit is changing with every step—and the sky. Even if he stands on the same rock at the top and looks toward Heaven and Earth, he is not in just the same key he started in, or in the same moment of existence.[31]

Also illuminating is another comment on the *Concord* Sonata: "The continuity of this music is more a process of natural tonal diversification and distribution than of natural tonal repetition and resolution."[32] Both form and continuity are ever present. The "obscurity" was in the mind of the beholder, inhibited by habit, hence incapable of perceiving that "the world of tonal vibrations . . . has unthought of (because untried) possibilities for man to know and grow by."[33]

It was the perception and realization of these untried possibilities that separated Ives from the professional musical world of his creative years and condemned him to appear as an outcast of the mainstream. His alienation, however, was as many-sided as his musical output. It was not simply a matter of stylistic aberrations, but also of sympathies, affinities, and convictions incompatible with the ideals of genteel culture and aesthetic taste. The prevailing aesthetic stance was *exclusive,* whereas Ives's creative drive was *inclusive.*

We may note here that the meaning of *aesthetic* as having or showing refined taste or being in accordance with good taste came into English usage about 1870 and was widely accepted while Ives was growing to maturity. But it was precisely this cult of refined taste that Ives rejected. He had no use for what Carlyle called "a wash of quite fluid aesthetic tea." He wanted a stronger substance. He turned to Emerson because he saw him as rising "to almost perfect freedom of action, of thought and of soul, *in any direction and to any height*" (italics added).[34]

The variety and scope of Ives's music is astonishing. Yet, because it always bears his personal stamp, it must be regarded as a whole, as a system of interrelated elements—no matter how incongruous some of them may seem. Can such a song as "In the Alley" be regarded as compatible with the "Emerson" movement of the *Concord* Sonata? In the Ivesian canon, the answer is yes, because *compatible* means capable of existing together in the same subject. The "subject" here is not a corpus of compositions per se—a body of discrete objects—but rather the mental, affective, and imaginative world of humanity in which these musical expressions live, move, and have their being. One may, of course, select among them those that appear most impressive and designate these as masterpieces. This is an undeniable aesthetic practice and a critical prerogative. But to dismiss other pieces as trashy simply because they do not conform to a specified norm is like cutting off a man's toes simply because they are not as important as his arms. One can get a lot of satisfaction from wiggling one's toes!

When Ives published his volume of *114 Songs,* he said: "I have not written a book at all—I have merely cleaned house."³⁵ It was not an anthology but an *omnium gatherum*, unprecedented in its scope. To the collection he added a "Postface" that contains some of his most characteristic thoughts. For example: "Everything from a mule to an oak which nature has given life has a right to that life, and a right to throw into that life all the values it can."³⁶ Critics and pundits would attempt to separate the "mules" from the "oaks" and doubtless assign a greater value to the latter on aesthetic premises. But for Ives the value of any living entity—including a song or a symphony—is intrinsic to its being, not an attribute externally assigned or bestowed. A song, like a tree or a mule or a man, has its own "rights":

> If it feels like kicking over an ash can, a poet's castle, or the prosodic law, will you stop it? Must it always be a polite triad, a "breve gaudium," a ribbon to match the voice? Should it not be free at times from the dominion of the thorax, the diaphragm, the ear, and other points of interest? . . . If it happens to feel like trying to fly where humans cannot fly, to sing what cannot be sung, to walk in a cave on all fours, or to tighten up its girth in blind hope and faith and try to scale mountains that are not, Who shall stop it?³⁷

Charles Ives needed all the hope and faith that he could summon in order to continue believing that his music had a right to life, liberty, and the pursuit of appreciation. Barriers of antagonism or indifference vied with ridicule or distortion when Ives began to publish some of his music at his own expense. At times he was troubled by self-doubt, and then he asked himself: "Why is it that I like to use these different things and try out other ways etc. which nobody else evidently has any pleasure in hearing, seeing, or thinking about? Why do I like to do it? Is there some peculiar defect in me, or something worse that I'm afflicted with?" His ailment was congenital originality in a climate of conformity.

By 1918 Ives had composed four symphonies along with a work titled *Holidays*, consisting of four independent pieces: *Washington's Birthday, Decoration Day, The Fourth of July,* and *Thanksgiving* and/or *Forefather's Day* (the whole presented as "A Symphony"); *Three Places in New England* (First Orchestral Set; also *A New England* Symphony), for orchestra, consisting of three parts—"The St. Gaudens in Boston Common," "Putnam's Camp, Redding, Conn.," and "The Housatonic at Stockbridge"; four sonatas for violin and piano; two string quartets; three sonatas for piano; *Three Harvest Home Chorales* and other choral works; and a quantity of other music. Yet none of these had been publicly performed in a major concert hall, and almost nothing had been published.

Ives had suffered a heart attack in 1906, and again in 1918, complicated by diabetes. He became concerned about the fate of his music, with a huge quantity of manuscripts in disarray. Could anyone else cope with the confusion? He decided to undertake the task himself, beginning with the *Concord* Sonata, which he prepared for the press in 1918–19, along with the *Essays before a Sonata*. Both were printed, separately, at Ives's expense, and copies were mailed gratis to friends and others, including "teachers, professors, etc., in nice colleges and conservatwaties," who obviously did not understand "that this is not a nice sonata for a nice piano player, but something that the writer had long been thinking about."[38] The deeper the thought, the shallower the response.

The volume of *114 Songs,* privately printed in 1922 (about 1,500 copies), was mailed to a long list of individuals, institutions, and publications that Ives compiled from various sources, including *Who's Who in America.* The *New York Sun* ran an article with the heading "Here's the Chance to Get a Nice Song Book Free." For Ives this was like a stab in the back, as "nice" was the word he used to express scorn for the "sissies" who couldn't "take" his music. An editorial in the *Musical Courier* treated the *114 Songs* as a joke, and the opening sentence was: "Who is Ives? We have not the least idea."

Nevertheless, a few individuals responded to the publications, including the musician, educator, and writer Henry Bellamann and Clifton Furness, a younger musician and teacher. Both men became close friends of Ives and effective promoters of his music. After 1923 Ives virtually ceased to compose. Beset by ill health, he lived in semiretirement, and by January 1930 he had given up his insurance business. About this time he began to meet musicians who did much to make his music known, such as pianist E. Robert Schmitz, composer and theorist Henry Cowell, conductor Nicolas Slonimsky, and pianist-musicologist John Kirkpatrick, who gave the first complete performance of the *Concord* Sonata at Town Hall, New York City, on January 20, 1939. This was a turning point in the recognition of Ives as a great composer of unique genius.

Another important development was Ives's connection with the Pan-American Association of Composers (1928–34), largely promoted by Henry Cowell and Edgard Varèse. With financial support from Ives, Slonimsky undertook, on behalf of the association, two orchestral concert tours of Europe, in 1931 and 1932. The programs included Ives's *Three Places in New England,* which Slonimsky briefly characterized as "transcendental geography [and history!] by a Yankee of strange and intense genius." So now Ives was in the company of such American composers as Cowell, Ruggles, Riegger, Roy Harris, Ruth Crawford, and Varèse—even though

he was not yet acknowledged as *primus inter pares* by the conservative critics. Philip Hale of Boston blasted these "restless experimenters" and lamented that Slonimsky had not chosen such proper composers as E. B.
Hill, Deems Taylor, and Arthur Foote.

We conclude now with a summary of Ives's four symphonies (formally designated as such). Little need be said about the eclectic First Symphony of his student years, except that it is an attractive work with typical
Ivesian touches. It had to wait until 1965 for its first performance by a major symphony orchestra (Chicago).

The Second Symphony (1900–1902, with some earlier material), is in
five movements, with a duration of about thirty-five minutes. Of the first
movement, *Andante moderato,* Ives notes that it was "from an organ sonata
played in part at Centre Church," while the third movement, *Adagio
cantabile,* was originally an organ prelude played at the same church in
1896. The last movement, *Allegro molto vivace,* he describes as "partly from
an early overture called the *American Woods* (Brookfield)."[39]

The Third Symphony (1904), also using material from earlier organ
pieces, is in three movements: *Andante, Allegro, Largo.* It is scored for a
small orchestra, with bells ad libitum (or chimes). These are heard in the
last two measures of the symphony, "as distant church bells," marked with
a decrescendo sign from *ppp* to *ppppp*—the ultimate *pianissimo!* The bells
are heard as triads of B minor and G-sharp minor, floating above the
chords of B-flat major and F major in the strings.

The first and third movements are devotional in character, utilizing
material originally written for the Presbyterian church services, as well as
themes from familiar hymns. A section in the first movement, marked *Adagio cantabile,* is based on the hymn tune "O, What a Friend We Have in Jesus." We also find a reminiscence of the revival hymn "There Is a Fountain
Filled with Blood." Another well-known hymn, "Just As I Am without
One Plea," figures prominently as a main theme in the third movement,
treated contrapuntally with a subject derived from the first movement. The
contrasting middle movement, in ternary form (*ABA*), has for its principal
theme an attractive rhythmically flexible melody of folklike character, while
the middle section brings in one of the marching rhythms that were so dear
to Ives.

The Third Symphony had its first public performance by the New
York Little Symphony in the Carnegie Chamber Music Hall on April 5,
1946, with Lou Harrison conducting. A year later it was awarded a Pulitzer
Prize: the first big step toward national recognition. Thereafter perfor-

mances of major works came with increasing frequency. The Second Symphony was presented for the first time by the New York Philharmonic, with four performances conducted by Leonard Bernstein in February 1951. The extraordinary Fourth Symphony, however, had to wait until twelve years after Ives's death before its first complete public performance, on April 26, 1965, with Leopold Stokowski conducting the American Symphony Orchestra in Carnegie Hall. (Also participating were two assistant conductors, and the Schola Cantorum of New York, directed by Hugh Ross, performed the vocal parts in the first and last movements.)

The impact of this premiere was tremendous. (As a member of the enthusiastic audience, I can vouch for its extraordinary effect.) The Music Critics Circle of New York voted a special award to the symphony "for its originality and genius." Some months later it was presented on National Educational Television over more than 100 stations throughout the United States (and later, abroad).

Ives composed the Fourth Symphony in the years from 1909 to 1916, drawing as usual on much material from earlier compositions. The first movement (Prelude: *Maestoso*) is very short and has for its main theme a favorite hymn, "Watchman, Tell Us of the Night." There are selections from "Nearer, My God, to Thee," and at one point the flute and first violins play the latter hymn tune while the chorus enters with "Watchman." Ives manages to bring in one of his favorite tunes, "The Sweet By and By," which is also heard in the other movements.

According to Ives, the "aesthetic program" of the Fourth Symphony is "that of the searching questions of 'What?' and 'Why?' which the spirit of man asks of life. This is particularly the sense of the *Prelude*. The three succeeding movements are the diverse answers in which existence replies." Thus, concerning the second movement, *Allegretto,* Ives wrote that "it is not a scherzo in an accepted sense of the word, but rather a comedy—in which an exciting, easy, and worldly progress through life is contrasted with the trials of the Pilgrims in their journey through the swamps and rough country. The occasional slow episodes—Pilgrims' hymns—are constantly crowded out, overwhelmed by the former. The dream, or fantasy, ends with an interruption of reality—the Fourth of July in Concord—brass bands, drum corps, etc."[40]

As program annotator Leonard Marcus adds: "The 'comedy' is of the utmost complexity, superimposing complex rhythms with accelerandos, ritardandos and unbarred passages. Dozens of tunes are quoted, including *Marching Through Georgia; In the Sweet Bye and Bye; Turkey in the Straw;*

Camptown Races; Throw Out the Lifeline; Beulah Land; Yankee Doodle; Jesus, Lover of My Soul; and Ives' perennial favorite, *Columbia the Gem of the Ocean.*"⁴¹ The overall effect is fantastically impressive.

The third movement (Fugue: *Andante moderato*), taken from the first movement of Ives's First String Quartet ("From the Salvation Army," 1896), consists of a double fugue on the hymn tunes "From Greenland's Icy Mountains" and "All Hail the Power of Jesus' Name." The fourth movement (*Largo maestoso*) is described by Ives as "an apotheosis of the preceding content, in terms of something to do with the reality of existence and its religious experience."⁴² It derives from a "Memorial Slow March" that Ives composed in 1911. The predominant musical theme is that of "Nearer, My God, to Thee"—making a triple-header for the eminent Dr. Lowell Mason.

By the time the Fourth Symphony had its belated premiere, Ives had achieved international recognition as a greatly original, immensely creative composer, who gave new dimensions to the vast and varied heritage of America's music.

Notes

1. Charles E. Ives, *Essays before a Sonata,* pp. 110–11.
2. Charles E. Ives, *Memos,* ed. John Kirkpatrick, p. 115.
3. Ibid., pp. 42–43.
4. Ibid., p. 49.
5. Ibid., pp. 132–33.
6. Ives, *Essays before a Sonata,* pp. xiii–xxiv.
7. Ives, *Memos,* p. 38.
8. Ibid., p. 155.
9. See Sydney Robinson Charles, "The Use of Borrowed Material in Ives' Second Symphony," pp. 102–11.
10. Ives, *Memos,* p. 49.
11. Ibid.
12. Ibid., p. 116.
13. Ibid., p. 51.
14. Words and music by Irving Jones, an important black entertainer. See Isaac Goldberg, *Tin Pan Alley,* pp. 155–56.
15. Ives, *Memos,* p. 56.
16. See ibid., pp. 155–56.
17. Ibid., pp. 39–41.
18. Ibid., p. 29.
19. Henry Cowell and Sidney Cowell, *Charles Ives and His Music,* p. 68.
20. Ibid., p. 74.

21. Ives, *Memos,* p. 93. Kirkpatrick adds in a footnote to this passage that "The Sweet By and By" was "written about 1867, words by Dr. Sanford Filmore Bennett (1836–98), tune by Joseph Philbrick Webster (1819–75), best known as arranged by Hubert P. Main" (p. 93 n. 8).

22. John Kirkpatrick, comp., "A Temporary Mimeographed Catalogue of the Music Manuscripts and Related Materials of Charles Edward Ives, 1874–1954, Given by Mrs. Ives to the Library of the Yale School of Music, September, 1955" (John Kirkpatrick, 1960).

23. Ives, *Memos,* p. 106.

24. Ives, "Emerson," *Essays before a Sonata,* pp. 11–12.

25. Ives, "Hawthorne," *Essays before a Sonata,* p. 41.

26. Ibid., p. 39.

27. Ives, "The Alcotts," *Essays before a Sonata,* p. 47.

28. Ives, *Memos,* p. 186.

29. Ibid., pp. 191–92, 197.

30. Ibid., p. 196.

31. Ibid.

32. Ibid., p. 195.

33. Ibid., p. 197.

34. Ives, "Emerson," p. 35.

35. "Postface to 114 Songs," in Ives, *Essays before a Sonata,* p. 130.

36. Ibid., p. 128.

37. Ibid., pp. 130–31. The copy of *114 Songs* given to the author by Mrs. Ives has no preface, but in the two final pages (unnumbered), in fine print, there is a typically Ivesian dissertation ranging from "Greek philosophers, ward-politicians, unmasked laymen and others" to "Some of the songs in this book . . . cannot be sung, and if they could, perhaps might prefer, if they had a say, to remain as they are." Published by himself, the last page reads "C. E. Ives, Redding, Conn., 1922."

38. Ives, *Memos,* p. 188.

39. Ibid., appendix 3, p. 155. See also Charles, "The Use of Borrowed Material in Ives' Second Symphony."

40. Leonard Marcus, program annotator of the American Symphony Orchestra, in liner notes to Charles E. Ives, *Symphony No. 4,* Columbia ML 6175 (MS 6775).

41. Ibid.

42. Ibid.

PART FOUR

America and the World

Chapter 25

The Ultramodern Movement

I am ready to lay aside traditional work and march with you
and the ultra-modern group.
—John Becker, letter to Henry Cowell (1928)

Before the term *avant-garde* became fashionable, critics and proponents
called the movement it designated "ultramodern." The ultramodern movement had its heyday in the 1920s and 1930s, coinciding curiously with the
Jazz Age and the Great Depression. It was preceded by the movement
called futurism, which originated in Italy and had its immediate impact
from about 1908 to 1918—although the term itself continued to be used in
some circles thereafter, for its influence waned but did not cease. Futurism
most directly influenced the visual arts, but it also involved music, mainly
through the theories of Luigi Russolo and the work of the composer Francesco Pratella. In 1913 Russolo published *L'arte dei rumori* (The art of
noises), in which he viewed the evolution of modern music as parallel to
that of industrial machinery.[1] It was necessary, he declared, to break the narrow circle of pure sounds and to conquer the infinite variety of noise-
sounds. These were identified with technology and the urban-industrial environment, but not to the exclusion of human and animal sounds such as
cries, groans, howls, laughter, and sobs. The aim was increasingly to en-
large and enrich the domain of sounds in all categories.

While it is difficult to measure the immediate musical influence of futurism, there is abundant evidence that Russolo's manifesto did anticipate
many developments in experimental music of the twentieth century. According to the dictum of Renato Poggioli, "the futurist moment [*sic*] belongs to all the avant-gardes and not only to the one named for it."[2] This is
so because an avant-garde is by definition impelled to move forward in
time and to establish its outposts in the future.

Except in that general sense, we cannot say that there was a futurist
movement in America. But, adopting Poggioli's term, we can say that there

was a futurist *moment* in American music. In the 1910s the label of futurist was applied to music that seemed revolutionary, radically far-out, even anarchistic. In that decade its controversial exponent in the United States was a young Russian emigrant named Leo Ornstein (b. 1892),[3] who arrived in New York with his family in 1907. In 1911 Ornstein, who began his career as a child prodigy, made his first American appearance as a concert pianist and soon titillated the public with "terrific glissandos."[4]

But suddenly, for no reason that he could explain—perhaps a reaction against having to practice pieces like Liszt's twelfth Hungarian Rhapsody all day—he began to write some highly dissonant music, of the kind that would be called anarchistic. The first was *Dwarf Suite,* composed in one day in 1913. There followed *Suicide in an Airplane* and *Wild Men's Dance* (*Danse sauvage*), which became the most notorious of his early piano pieces. Many years later he stated these were written "by a young person with no experience whatever with modern music" (perhaps he just sniffed it in the air).[5]

Soon, however, he was including the most "advanced" modern music in his concert repertory, both in Europe (1913–14) and in a series of four programs at the Bandbox Theatre in New York (January–February 1915). Besides his own pieces, he played works by Scriabin, Schoenberg, Cyril Scott, and Ravel—much of it for the first time in America. Although there were the usual facetious remarks about the wild "Futurist," Ornstein had a following among the liberal intellectuals of that time, such as Waldo Frank, Edmund Wilson, and Paul Rosenfeld. Frank, for example, wrote an article titled "Leo Ornstein and Emancipated Music" for the *Onlooker* (1916), in which he went overboard by stating that Ornstein gave promise of being a greater composer than Schoenberg or Stravinsky!

Not every critic shared this enthusiasm. Charles L. Buchanan, writing in 1918, found Ornstein's music to be an "audacious experimentation rather than an accomplished beauty."[6] More specifically, Ornstein "eliminates a thematic continuity . . . gives us masses of shrill, hard dissonances, chords consisting of anywhere from eight to a dozen notes made up out of half tones heaped one upon the other."[7] This last device soon became known as tone clusters, and concerning their use and intended effect, Ornstein remarked many years later (referring, specifically, to *Wild Men's Dance*): "My rigid classical training was of but little use to me. The musical ideas germinated their own techniques and I found myself using clusters for the necessary percussion effects and to meet the much deeper need to project the dark brooding quality that intrigued me so much in contemplating prehistoric man."[8]

Among Ornstein's supporters the critic Paul Rosenfeld best summed up the impression that alert contemporaries got from Ornstein's innovations: "What was thrilling about his earlier pieces was their sensitivity, their approach toward a style expressive of the age of steel, their 'feeling of today.' . . ."[9]

Ornstein's American-born counterpart in the futurist domain was George Antheil (1900–1959), from Trenton, New Jersey, a child prodigy on the piano at age six and a precocious composer at twelve. Like Ornstein, he began to write piano pieces that were radically dissonant and daringly experimental, with modernistic titles such as *Airplane* Sonata (1922), *Death of the Machines* (1923), *Mechanisms* (1923–24), and *Sonata Sauvage* (1923). In 1922 he toured as a concert pianist in England and Central Europe and was billed as the "American Pianist-Futurist." A year later he settled in Paris, where he quickly achieved notoriety and was hailed as a rising star of the avant-garde, with Ezra Pound as his chief promoter. His circle also included such innovators as James Joyce, Fernand Léger, Pablo Picasso, and Erik Satie.

Pound and his mistress, the violinist Olga Rudge, commissioned Antheil to write two violin sonatas, which Rudge performed at the Salle Pleyel in November 1923. Antheil tells us in his memoirs, *Bad Boy of Music,* that the copyist, in preparing these pieces for the concert, edited out all the "discords" because he thought they were the mistakes of a tyro! While the First Violin Sonata was savagely "barbaric," the Second has been described as "a rollicking dialogue between the violin, which Antheil later said represents the banal music of the past and present, and the piano, which represents the music of the future."[10] It has snatches of American popular song, jazz rhythms, and folk dances, as well as a tango rhythm. There is also a section for drum—played at the premiere by Ezra Pound.

According to Pound, Antheil anticipated—at least in conversation— some of the far-out developments of the post-1950 avant-garde, such as " 'tuning up' whole cities [and] silences twenty minutes long in the form, etc."[11] He also planned to write an opera on the Cyclops episode in Joyce's *Ulysses,* with nonacting singers who "vocalize into receivers connected with loud speakers scattered through the auditorium."[12] To Joyce's disappointment, the opera was never completed—although its advent was widely publicized. Thus, Antheil may be said to have invented an avant-garde genre: a work that exists only in its description. An analogue would be the much-publicized "riots" that allegedly occurred at every concert given by Antheil but that were mostly verbal fabrications by Pound and his accomplices.

The work that made Antheil internationally notorious was the *Ballet mécanique* (1923–25), originally composed to accompany an abstract film by Fernand Léger and thereafter expanded as an independent composition for eight pianos, pianola, eight xylophones, two electric doorbells, percussion, wind machine, and "airplane propeller"—this last described by an eye-and-ear witness as "an adapted fan with a forty-eight-inch reach, six vicious blades, and a capacity of 4,000 revolutions per minute."[13]

This controversial opus was first performed privately at the lavish home of Mrs. Christian Gross, an American millionairess who aspired to be a proud patroness of the arts. The much-touted public premiere took place at the Théâtre des Champs-Elysées on June 19, 1926, in a concert conducted by Vladimir Golschmann. The reviews brought out the "riot" headlines—although the Paris *Tribune* qualified this as basically "a riot of laughter."

Ezra Pound, who fancied himself as a musical pundit, undertook to launch a sensational publicity campaign for Antheil in the United States. With the help of his publisher, Donald Friede, he touted Antheil as the "ultra-modernist leader" of American music. Notices and articles with eye-catching headlines appeared in newspapers and periodicals everywhere, announcing the imminent arrival of the young iconoclast who "Seeks a Technic to Express Skyscrapers and Subways in Tone while His Audiences Riot."

This was the promotional prelude to an all-Antheil concert to be given at Carnegie Hall in New York, on April 10, 1927, billed as "The Biggest Musical Event of the Year." A feature article in the *New York Herald Tribune* announced the upcoming event as "A Riot of Music"—in very large print. The program opened with the String Quartet no. 1 (1924), followed by the previously mentioned Sonata no. 2 for Violin, Piano, and Drum (a piece the composer associated with the Picasso 1918 cubist period—an artistic revolution of which few Americans were aware at that time). Building to its climax, the program next featured the world premiere of *A Jazz Symphony* of 1925, said to have been composed at the request of Paul Whiteman. Then came the presumptive pièce de résistance, the *Ballet mécanique,* which proved to be a colossal flop. The reviews were excoriating; one example will suffice: "Rarely has a public scandal been so expertly rehearsed, and never did one flop to earth with a more sickening and merited thud."[14] Knowing what crit-

ics have written of such great composers as Ives and Varèse, we can now ignore this and similarly biased obiter dicta. But for Antheil the shock was ap-
palling; he returned to Paris despondent and broke—a victim not so much
of publicity by the ton as by the Pound.

Nearly ten years later, in 1936, Antheil gave a *post facto* explanation of
his intentions in this controversial work: "I personally consider that the Ballet Mécanique was important in one particular and that it was conceived in
a new form . . . specifically the filling out of a certain time canvas with musical abstractions and sound material composed and contrasted against one
another with the thought of time values rather than tonal values. . . . I used
time as Picasso might have used the blank spaces of his canvas. . . . My
ideas were the most abstract of the abstract."[15]

Does this make Antheil a precursor of the "abstract composers"—as
Virgil Thomson called them—of the 1950s? He certainly anticipated some
of their ideas and procedures, notably the use of noise components characterized by differing degrees of pitch or nonpitch and the concept of a composition as a time-space canvas to be filled with musical abstractions—i.e.,
sounds divorced from tonal and thematic implications.

The use of long silences as an intrinsic part of the compositional form
(previously noted by Pound) is also a significant innovation of Antheil's
music. Charles Amirkhanian, an American avant-garde composer, radio
producer, and leading authority on Antheil, informs me that the score for
the original version of *Ballet mécanique,* which has a performance time of
about thirty-five minutes, contains silences for all instruments (*tutti*) of
quite long duration. He adds that, in the opinion of Nicolas Slonimsky (a
conductor much involved with the avant-garde movements of this period),
"this might be the first use of such silences within movements in the history of Western music."[16] Moreover, Antheil evidently regarded the *Ballet
mécanique* as a work in progress, for it exists in many versions, the last of
which (1953) was a drastic revision, reducing the number of pianos by half
and the total duration to about eighteen minutes.

Antheil soon ceased to be the "Bad Boy of Music," returning to the
United States in 1933 and establishing himself in Hollywood, where he
wrote film scores and composed several symphonies, an opera, *Volpone* (after Ben Jonson's play), and other works that were no longer controversial.
By the 1970s his earlier compositions, including *A Jazz Symphony* and especially the *Ballet mécanique,* were well established as enduring "period
pieces" in both America and Europe.[17]

Antheil, in his salad days, was a loner and an expatriate with a clique, but in the United States the ultramodern movement was promoted by organized group action, as represented notably by the International Composers' Guild (1921–27) and the Pan-American Association of Composers (1928–34). We should note that the primary aim of these organizations was not to promote a specific movement per se but rather to encourage the performance and publication of distinctively "new" music and thereby aid the "advanced" composer beset by indifference or hostility. The leading promoters and organizers of these associations were Edgard Varèse and Henry Cowell, the former from France, the latter from California, both meeting on common ground in New York City.

Edgard Varèse (1883–1965) was born in Paris of French and Italian parentage and had to overcome strong paternal opposition in order to take up a musical career.[18] Although his formative years were spent in Italy, his deepest cultural roots were in France, where he pursued his advanced musical training. But a sojourn in Berlin from 1907 to 1913 also had important consequences, particularly through his friendship with the composer, pianist, and theorist Ferruccio Busoni (1866–1924), whose advanced ideas, as set forth in the *Entwurf einer neuen Ästhetik der Tonkunst* (Sketch of a new aesthetic of music, 1907), had a decisive influence on Varèse.[19] He responded eagerly to such dicta as: "The function of the creative artist consists in making laws, not in following laws already made"; and "Music was born free; and to win freedom is its destiny."[20]

Another crucial experience came when he read a definition of music by the nineteenth-century philosopher, physicist, and mathematician Hoene Wronski, who postulated that the aesthetic object of music is "the corporealization of the intelligence that is in sounds." This was to him "the first perfectly intelligible conception of music" that he had encountered, and it caused him to start thinking about music as "spatial—as moving bodies of sound in space."[21] He also studied the work of Helmholtz (*On the Sensations of Tone*) and was fascinated by the description of experiments with sirens.[22] Later, he made experiments of his own and found that the "beautiful parabolas and hyperbolas of sound the sirens gave me and the haunting quality of the tones made me aware for the first time of the wealth of music outside the narrow limits imposed by keyboard instruments."[23]

Varèse's promising career as composer and conductor in Europe was interrupted by World War I. Discharged from the army because of poor health, he went to the United States at the end of 1915 and soon decided to make New York his permanent home (he became an American citizen in

1927). He had hoped for a position as conductor but failed to obtain one because of his insistence on performing ultramodern works. His own compositions were, of course, beyond the pale of acceptable symphonic fare. As he prophetically declared in 1917: "Our musical alphabet is poor and illogical. Music, which should be alive and vibrating, needs new means of expression and science alone can infuse it with youthful sap."[24] And he further stated, in the same article, "I dream of instruments obedient to my thought and which with their contribution of a whole new world of unsuspected sounds will lend themselves to the exigencies of my inner rhythm."[25]

Much of Varèse's music was inspired or stimulated by the dynamism of New York, which he loved. His most productive period was from 1918 to 1936, during which he composed *Amériques,* for large orchestra (1918–21; rev. 1927); *Offrandes,* for soprano, chamber orchestra, and percussion (1921); *Hyperprism,* for two woodwinds, seven brasses, and percussion (1922–23); *Octandre,* for chamber ensemble of winds and brasses, with four percussion players (1923); *Intégrales,* for wind and brass ensemble, with four percussion players (1924–25); *Arcana,* for symphony orchestra (1925–27); *Ionisation,* for percussion ensemble and two sirens (1929–31); and *Ecuatorial,* for bass voices with four trumpets, four trombones, piano, organ, ondes martenot, and fifteen percussion instruments (1933–34; rev. 1961).

Works of this kind were obviously not compatible with the standard concert repertory. Of the conductors heading major symphony orchestras, only Leopold Stokowski in Philadelphia ventured to perform ultramodern music. Eager as he was to perform Varèse's *Amériques,* it took him more than three years to overcome the resistance of his committee. Meanwhile, Varèse was not disposed to accept defeat—especially as he received financial support from Gertrude Vanderbilt Whitney. When some of his works, such as *Hyperprism,* were received with hissing and hooting, he reacted by repeating it! On this occasion W. J. Henderson of the *New York Herald* wrote what may be the most perceptive comment ever made by any music critic of his time: "Edgard Varèse will go down in musical history as the man who started something."[26]

Varèse went on creating his world of "organized sound," using a wide array of percussion instruments, including those of indeterminate pitch. *Timbre*—the quality or "color" of a tone—is a paramount element in his music and is largely dependent on the harmonics (overtones) produced by each instrument and the shifting combinations of the overtone series. Varèse envisaged new musical apparatuses capable of emitting "sounds of any number of frequencies" and of revealing the "harmonic possibilities of the overtones . . . in all their splendor":[27] "Just as the painter can obtain different intensities and gradations of color, the composer could then obtain different vibrations of sound, not necessarily conforming to the traditional half-tone, full-tone, but varying from vibration to vibration."[28] With respect to form Varèse said: "Form is a result—the result of a process. Each of my works discovers its own form."[29]

In his instrumentation Varèse generally avoided the strings, favoring brass and woodwind, with a large array of percussion effects. Thirty-two percussion instruments are used in *Intégrales,* including Chinese blocks, sleigh bells, slap stick, chains, string drum (or lion's roar), and twigs (to be played on shell of bass drum). All of these are deployed with great subtlety, clarity, and precision, achieving what has been aptly characterized as "an indivisible vertical structure, shimmering over the full extent of the delineated sound-space."

Varèse's astonishing achievement was the creation of "a whole world of unsuspected sounds" prior to the invention of the magnetic tape recorder and the electronic synthesizer. He lived to use these media also, notably in *Déserts* (ca. 1950–54) and *Poeme électronique* (1957–58). But we now turn to his last work, which is of special interest: *Nocturnal* (1961), commissioned by the Koussevitzky Music Foundation. For Varèse it remained an unfinished work, although it had its "world premiere" at a concert in New York's Town Hall (May 1, 1961). After the death of Varèse, *Nocturnal* was taken in hand by his young alter ego and close friend, Chou Wen-chung, who tells us that *Nocturnal* "is a world of sounds remembered and imagined, conjuring up sights and moods now personal, now Dantesque, now enigmatic." He then asks and concludes: "Could one, knowing Varèse's unique career, resist wondering about the line, 'I rise, I always rise after crucifixion'? . . . A phantasmagorial world? Yes, but as real as Varèse's own life."[30] The text of *Nocturnal* "includes words and phrases extracted from *The House of Incest* by Anaïs Nin and syllables devised by Varèse."[31] Both Nin and Varèse were full of surprises in their lifetime and will no doubt be remembered as such for many decades to come.

We turn now to a counterpart of Varèse in the promotion and creation of ultramodern music in America, Henry Cowell (1897–1965). He is a striking example of how beneficial it can be for a composer to be exposed, during his formative years, to experiences that open the way to uninhibited exploration of the varied and unorthodox means of musical expression. He grew up in and around San Francisco, with no regular exposure to European concert music. But during the impressionable years of adolescence, he became acquainted with the ecclesiastical modes (through a neighborhood organist), with oriental music (through Chinese neighbors), and with Irish-American songs (through his parents). He then began to compose at the piano, relying mainly on intuition and experimentation.

Thus, as a teenager, on March 5, 1914, at a concert sponsored by the San Francisco Musical Society (or Club), he performed a type of music for piano that had never been heard before. This was a big work, titled *Adventures in Harmony* (ca. 1911), now recognized as "his first piece with written-down tone-clusters."[32] Curiously enough, through most of his life Cowell had insisted that *The Tides of Manaunaun* was the first piece he performed using tone clusters. He believed this performance took place on March 10, 1912, but in the early 1960s, a skeptical truth seeker searched the San Francisco newspapers and convinced Cowell that his 1912 date was erroneous.

The Tides of Manaunaun (ca. 1912) was probably not performed until September 1917, but it soon became widely known as one of the most conspicuous works of his early years. In it he combined a modal melody, of the kind to which he was so partial, with tone clusters extending over one and two octaves, thus:[33]

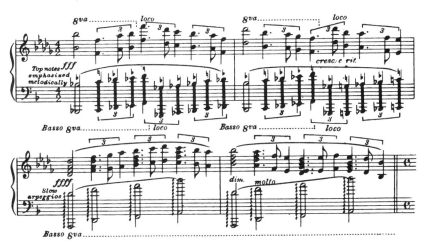

Cowell directs that the tone clusters are to be played with the forearm, with the flat of the hand, or with the fist, depending on the length of the cluster. In the piece called *Tiger* (1928) there are clusters so large that they must be played with both forearms together. But it is not a matter of "banging" the keyboard.

We are told that by 1917, when Cowell was twenty years old, he had composed, "according to his own records . . . one hundred and ninety-nine works for nearly all conventional combinations and many unconventional ones."[34] His rise to fame was extraordinary, considering that when he moved with his parents to Kansas his formal education ended with a third grade certificate and "he had been a gardener, a collector of wild plants, and a swineherd."[35]

Upon returning to California he worked as a school janitor while also attending classes at the University of California, Berkeley. This proved to be a turning point in his life, for he came under the influence of the remarkable teacher and innovative theorist Charles Seeger (1886–1979), who convinced him that systematic study was necessary to achieve further progress. Thus, while he studied theory and counterpoint at Berkeley, his experimental interests were also encouraged by Seeger, who urged him to establish a theoretical basis for his innovations. The result was a book titled *New Musical Resources,* which he had largely completed by 1919, although it was not published until 1930. Joscelyn Godwin calls it "probably the earliest comprehensive statement of intent by a 'modernistic' American composer" and "an indispensable document in the history of American music."[36]

Cowell's keyboard pieces of this early period are both varied and numerous—and, of course, totally sui generis. They include *Exultation* (1919), *The Harp of Life* (1924), *Lilt of the Reel* (1925), *Dynamic Motion* (1914), *The Trumpet of Angus Og* (1924), *The Voice of Lir* (1919), and many others. Of special interest is *Aeolian Harp* (1923), which is sounded entirely on the strings of the piano: "Chords are depressed silently on the keyboard to release their dampers so that when the strings are stroked only the tones so selected will sound. Single tones are plucked, *pizzicato,* as the proper key is depressed to free the string desired."[37] In *Sinister Resonance* (ca. 1930) the music is played on the piano keyboard, but the timbre is altered by the player's manipulation of the strings with his fingers, producing stopped tones, muted tones, and harmonics.

In 1927 Cowell took the initiative in founding the *New Music Quarterly,* with the announced purpose of publishing ultramodern works. He was, indeed, a precursor, with an infinite variety of sources, and many others would follow in his path. (He will reappear in chapter 33, "Innovation and Experiment.")

By the early 1930s the Pan-American Association of Composers in

Henry Cowell

New York was spreading the ultramodern movement in both the United States and Europe. With Nicolas Slonimsky conducting, two concert tours were made abroad in 1931 and 1932, both financed by Ives. Thus Europe had a taste of such up-and-coming composers as Cowell, Ives, Riegger, Rudhyar, Ruggles, and Ruth Crawford Seeger—much to the disgust of that proper Bostonian critic, Philip Hale, who vehemently deplored that the United States should be represented by such "wild-eyed anarchists."

Ruth Crawford (1901–53), who became the second wife of Charles Seeger, was the first American woman composer to be recognized as a significant member of the avant-garde. Her much-admired String Quartet (1931) anticipates serial techniques in the control of compositional parameters—especially in the last movement, where a contrapuntal line "is strictly organized according to a ten-note pitch series that is developed by a process of rotation."[38] The third movement employs a procedure that has been termed "contrapuntal dynamics," whereby each voice or part makes use of asymmetrically independent dynamic values.

Especially remarkable are her Three Songs on poems by Carl Sandburg, for contralto, oboe, piano, percussion, and optional chamber orchestra (1930–32). The second song, "Prayer of Steel," not only employs ordered pitch-sets in an original manner but also projects the dynamism of the industrial era more effectively—and more musically—than the futurists ever did. Other works include an *Etude in Mixed Accents*, for piano (1930); *Two Ricercari*, for voice and piano (1932); and three suites, for various chamber ensembles (1927, 1929, 1952).

With hindsight we can characterize many of the composers involved with the ultramodern movement as antiestablishment. This attitude was vehemently embodied in the Midwest composer John J. Becker (1886–1961), who in 1928 declared: "I hate all academic procedure. I think everything in American life and American education is too damned academic. (*Emphasis on the damned.*)"[39] This statement was made in a letter to Ezra Pound, with whom Becker began to correspond as the result of a highly favorable review he wrote on Pound's *Antheil and the Treatise on Harmony* (Chicago, 1927). The correspondence continued for several years and provided much fuel for Becker's antiestablishment stance.

Becker's extremism—someone called him "an artistic Bolshevik"—was exacerbated by his frustration in attempting to develop a modernist movement in the Midwest. The tide began to turn for him when, in October 1927, he received a note from Cowell asking him to subscribe to the *New Mu-*

sic Quarterly. Becker replied affirmatively, whereupon new horizons quickly opened up for him, as he formed a lasting friendship with Cowell, who not only published and promoted his music but also introduced him to avant-garde composers who welcomed him as a congenial colleague.

Of special importance was his contact with Ives, who unstintingly encouraged and assisted him in many ways. A very opportune moment for his rising career came when he was invited to conduct a performance of his *Concerto Arabesque* (1930), for piano and twelve solo instruments, at a concert of the Pan-American Association of Composers in New York. This event took place on February 16, 1932, and as a result Becker was more committed than ever to bringing ultramodernism to the Midwest (he was then living in St. Paul, Minnesota).

Thus, on May 25, 1933, with the St. Paul Chamber Orchestra, he presented and conducted a program billed as an "Ultra-Modern American Concert." The program consisted of Cowell's *Polyphonica,* Ives's *In the Night,* Riegger's *Scherzo,* Ruggles's *Lilacs,* and Becker's *Concerto Arabesque.* The critical reaction was predictably hostile. But the event was historic in that it brought to the Midwest the first presentation of an advancing trend in the creative originality of contemporary American music.[40]

Becker summed up his credo as a composer in the dictum: "Laws are made for imitators; creators make their own laws."[41] Describing some of his orchestral procedures, he mentioned "the juxtaposition of contrasting instruments, that is, instruments which have no relationship to each other as far as their orchestral color is concerned." Another device is that of "long sustained sections of seconds, scored for instruments of the same color."[42] In the *Symphonia Brevis* he produced "an effect like the cutting of steel" by having "the top line of a dissonant counterpoint or chordal movement in the orchestra . . . doubled in octaves by the piano played with a percussive stroke."[43]

Becker used the term *soundpiece* for a variety of compositions, mostly string quartets, including several with piano. His output as a whole was vast and varied, including a quantity of keyboard pieces, music for the dance, incidental stage music, and a great amount of choral and vocal music.

We are also reminded that Becker's association with Ezra Pound was not only epistolary but also closely musical. For example, he set to music Pound's translations of the Chinese poet Li Po's "Separation on the River Kiang" and "Taking Leave of a Friend" (1927). He also wrote a composition for full orchestra, voice, and dance titled *Dance Figure* (1932), based on a poem of that title by Pound.

The leading authority on Becker—musicologist and pianist Don Gillespie—reminds us that "Becker was the first person to promulgate the theory of the 'Ives group,' or 'The American Five,' as it is often called today." This included Ives, Ruggles, Riegger, and Cowell, along with Becker, as a "center of the experimental movement of his day." The basic summary by Gillespie is as follows: "The most significant outcome of his musical crusade is that, partly by design and partly by accident, Becker became the Midwestern spokesman for the group of early American composers and articulated what he considered its goal: the establishment of an American music with experimental tendencies drawn from the American experience rather than from Europe."[44]

Among the composers now designated as "The American Five," the oldest (next to Ives) was Carl Ruggles (1876–1971), also a New Englander. Born and raised near Boston, he eventually settled in Arlington, Vermont. As a youngster he studied the violin and soon had jobs playing for theater orchestras in Boston. He went on to study composition with Paine at Harvard—which did not prevent him from becoming a radical innovator. His first teaching job, in 1907, was at a private school of music in Winona, Minnesota. He soon quit this position to become conductor of the town's symphony orchestra. Meanwhile he had married a singer, Charlotte Harriet Snell, and was composing an opera, *The Sunken Bell,* which he worked on for thirteen years with no tangible results. His work on the opera gave him incentive, however, to go to New York in 1917, hoping to interest the Metropolitan Opera—with no success. The positive result was that New York became his home base, and he soon joined the ultramodern circle of that metropolis. There he met Varèse and later Cowell, who became congenial colleagues and strong supporters of his music.

The International Composers' Guild performed five of his major works from 1922 to 1926, and the Pan-American Association of Composers followed with five more performances in the 1930s, including those conducted by Slonimsky in Europe. The latter featured what has come to be regarded as Ruggles's most important composition, *Sun-treader* (1926–31), which I had the privilege (and the astonishment!) of hearing at the Salle Pleyel in Paris, on February 12, 1932, with Slonimsky conducting members of the Paris Symphony Orchestra. As we shall see, this great masterpiece had to wait thirty-four years before its first performance in the United States.

Meanwhile, we may quote John Kirkpatrick's perceptive description of *Sun-treader:* "It brings to definitive flowering all his previous ideas and techniques: consistency of melodic variation, variety of interval in dissonant counterpoint, variety of durations in free rhythm, vast pitch ranges, vast perspectives of melodic destination, even a monumental splendor of traditional sonata form (symphony in one movement) complete with dramatic contrast between the two themes."[45]

Before further discussing the music, it seems pertinent here to recall that Ruggles was also a visual artist, a painter of individual power and creativity, recognized as such by the wide and enduring tributes to his work. For example, in January 1951, the Detroit Institute of Arts (which owned five paintings by Ruggles) opened a show of his works with a piano recital that included arrangements of two orchestral compositions, *Angels* (1920–21) and *Marching Mountains* (1941), and two *Evocations,* originally written for piano (1935–43). In praise of the artist, the director of the Institute wrote: "He brings to his painting not only a highly developed musical sense of style but a very interesting creative mind."

Ruggles was also drawn to rhapsodic and mystical poets, as in *Vox Clamans in Deserto,* for soprano and small orchestra (1923), with settings from Robert Browning and Walt Whitman. The score of *Men and Mountains,* for orchestra (1924), has a quotation from William Blake: "Great things are done when men and mountains meet." The music critic Lawrence Gilman saw Ruggles as "a mystic, a rhapsodist, a composer who sees visions and dreams fantastic dreams." This is probably exaggerated: he was also a shrewd Yankee artisan who knew that it takes the right notes in the right places to move men and mountains with music.

Charles Seeger understood and delineated both aspects of Ruggles's creative personality: the intellectual and the rhapsodic, the interplay of calculation and intuition. In general, his music moves within a firmly defined and deliberately contained formal-aesthetic orbit. There are self-imposed limitations such as the nonrepetition of notes in the melodic line (not always strictly observed) and, in general, a considerable textural complexity. Nevertheless, Seeger concludes that in the ratio between organization and fantasy there is a preponderance of the latter.[46]

The composer Lou Harrison has written perceptively about the quality of Ruggles's counterpoint: "It is characterized by an absolute lack of negative spacing in the voices, which is to say that no voice is ever given over to repetitious arpeggiation or figuration of any kind. Each voice is a real melody, bound into a community of singing lines, living a life of its own with regard to phrasing and breathing, careful not to get ahead or behind in its rhythmic co-operation with the others, and sustaining a responsible independence in the whole polyphonic life."⁴⁷ The phrase "a community of singing lines" seems to me most felicitous in describing both the texture and the spirit of the music.

In addition to the compositions already mentioned, the deliberately limited catalogue of Ruggles's works includes *Toys* (1919), for voice and piano; *Portals* (1925), for string orchestra; *Organum* (1944–47), for orchestra; and *Exaltation* (1958), a hymn tune for congregation (or chorus) and organ (or brass), in memory of his wife's death. Some works appeared in more than one version. For example, the previously mentioned *Evocations*, originally consisting of four "chants" for piano (1937–43, rev. 1954), were arranged for orchestra in 1944–47. They contain much of Ruggles's most intricate and original music.

For the grand finale we turn to the belated but exalted American premiere of *Sun-treader*, on January 24, 1966—less than two months before the composer's ninetieth birthday. The event took place in Portland, Maine, sponsored by Bowdoin College as part of a three-day tribute to Ruggles. He was not well enough to attend the celebration—especially since there had been a near blizzard the night before. But this did not prevent the attendance of almost 2,000 persons from all over the United States.

The opening session began with a lecture-tribute to Ruggles by Virgil Thomson and a preview of an exhibition of his paintings. Six of his compositions preceded the epic performance of *Sun-treader* by the Boston Symphony Orchestra, with Jean Martinon as guest conductor. The occasion as a whole marked an ever-memorable event in the cultural stature of the United States.

In contrast to Ruggles, Wallingford Riegger (1885–1961) was prolific, eclectic, and somewhat academic in spite of his ultramodern phase. Unlike Ornstein and Antheil, who moved from the radical to the conservative, he reversed his course from a rather lush Romanticism to dissonant and dodecaphonic idioms. His use of the latter was personal and unorthodox, melded with traditional forms. He himself described his various styles as "non-dissonant (mostly)," "impressionistic," "partly dissonant," and "dissonant."

Riegger was born in Albany, Georgia, into a musical family, but received his main professional training in Germany and at the Institute of Musical Art in New York. From 1928 he lived in New York, where he participated in the Pan-American Association of Composers, which performed six of his works, including Three Canons for Woodwinds (1931), *Dichotomy* (1931–32), Trio for Harp, Flute, and Cello (1933)—also called

Divertissement—Trio for Piano, Violin, and Cello (1919–20; his op. 1), and *Frenetic Rhythms* (1933). This last, commissioned by Martha Graham, was one of many ballet scores that he wrote for her, as well as for other dancers such as Doris Humphrey, Hanya Helm, and Eric Hawkins.

Riegger was a prolific composer in many fields, from the orchestra to the band, with a large output of chamber music and vocal works, most notably a setting of Keats's *La Belle Dame sans merci* (1923), for four singers and chamber orchestra. But he was also bent on making his mark in the ultramodern movement. The story goes that his publisher, on the strength of the early works, accepted his *Study in Sonority* (1926–27), for ten violins or any multiple of ten, "sight unseen"—and was unspeakably shocked when he discovered that it was full of dissonances! Riegger had indeed altered course: the work was written in a strongly dissonant contrapuntal texture, for which he invented (as Cowell remarked) "a chord to play the part of the tonic, and another to play that of the dominant."[48]

Riegger's partial adoption of the serial technique is manifested in the orchestral work titled *Dichotomy* in which he used two unorthodox tone rows, one with eleven tones, the other with thirteen (ten different tones plus three that recur). Concerning some features of the work, he wrote:

> Among the special things I should like to point out is what I call "cumulative sequence," a device by no means original with me, but used perhaps more consciously and to a greater degree in my work than elsewhere. . . . This is the old Three Blind Mice idea, keeping the original motive and *adding* a sequence, above or below, instead of moving the motive itself. I also use something I call "organic stretto," e.g., the telescoping of different sections, instead of the subject with itself, as in the fugue. It is like beginning a subordinate theme before the principal theme is established.[49]

Years later, Henry Cowell wrote: "Renewed acquaintance with this piece convinces me that it is one of the very best orchestral works to come from the pen of an American." But the major large-scale work that definitively confirmed Riegger's stature was the Symphony no. 3 (1946–47), in which twelve-tone configurations are freely used in conjunction or contrast with classical elements. This concept was prefigured in the admirable String Quartet no. 1, composed in 1938–39. As Elliott Carter said, Riegger added "a new musical style to American tradition."

In 1917, soon after Varèse arrived in New York, another French-born musician came to the United States and quickly identified himself with the ultramodern movement. His name was originally Daniel Chennevière (b. 1895), but he adopted the pseudonym of Dane Rudhyar, by which he is generally known. Like Varèse, he was interested in philosophy, and, like Ruggles, he also painted. Poetry, psychology, and astrology were other interests that he cultivated, and he was strongly attracted to the culture of the Orient. He believed that "anything that breaks down the narrow idolatry of musicians with regard to European musical concepts is valuable." Hence he looked toward oriental music as a means of doing away with "cut-and-dried keyboard scales" and thereby achieving "melodic continuity between successive notes." About 1930 he made a prophecy: "The gateway to the Orient is through Occidental America. It is therefore natural to assume that it will be through America that the influence of Oriental music will be first felt in the Occident."[50]

Rudhyar's interest in the music of the Orient is reflected in the nine *Tetragrams* and four *Pentagrams* for piano that he wrote in the 1920s.[51] He invented the term *syntony*, which he used as a title for two orchestral works and a piano piece (1920–29). His aim was a "creative synthesis" of Eastern and Western elements.

Like Cowell, Rudhyar was much concerned with developing new musical resources for the age of technology, and his vision was prophetic. In the 1920s he endeavored to demonstrate that "everything is unstable and relative in our music," and that it would therefore "be imperative to make radical changes."[52] Observing that "the theory of Relativity is sweeping the intellectual world of to-day," he declared that in the "musical axioms which tyrannically rule over European music there lies no more absoluteness, no more certainty than in the axioms of physical science, which have so utterly vanished before a closer and more daring investigation lately."[53]

Rudhyar also anticipated Cage in proclaiming the omnipresence of sound:

> Sound is an element of the Universe. Every thing around us is sound, sound that oftentimes we do not hear because of the limitations of our ear, yet in some respect sound. Our music, however, does not use all this infinitude of sounds; it is too rich, too chaotic for our musical sense; we are lost in the profusion of audible vibrations. We, therefore, have selected some specific sounds produced by some almost invariable instruments, and have thus created a little cosmos of sounds in which we feel at home. We have expurgated Nature, we have encaged it, and thus rejoice in our easy mastery over this atrophied material.[54]

Was not Rudhyar truly a precursor of that cosmological demiurge from California who came to un-Cage the universe of sound for Man and Nature in the era of technology?

And if anyone wants something more specific, there is Rudhyar's insistence on the nonequivalence of the octave: another fundamental tenet of Cage's musical thought. Iconoclastically, Rudhyar declared: "We Occidentals, in spite of all our glorious musical repertoires, of our wondrous orchestras, *have not yet learned what a sound is*."[55] For that, we must turn to the Orient. Once we understand the meaning of *sounds* as contrasted with mere *notes*, we can harness Western technology to liberate the potential of sound: "What Music needs is, above all, a kind of electric instrument, conceived in a way similar to the basic idea of the 'Telharmonium' of Dr. Cahill which was experimented with some 15 years ago. Such an instrument will permit us to produce by combination *any sound* whatsoever.... A dazzling profusion of new materials will flood the imagination of future creators...."[56]

Obviously, the "electric instrument" invented by Dr. Thaddeus Cahill and first presented in 1900 fell far short of the results envisioned by Rudhyar. It was more like a huge machine consisting of a collection of dynamos operated by an alternating current and weighing 200 tons! It was, in plain terms, a huge, expensive flop. But it *did* point toward the time when, as Rudhyar (and Busoni also) foresaw, "a dazzling profusion" of electronic inventions would "flood the imagination of future creators."

Notes

1. Luigi Russolo, *L'arte dei rumori;* English translation by Robert Filliou, *The Art of Noise* (*Futurist Manifesto, 1913*).
2. Renato Poggioli, *The Theory of the Avant-Garde,* trans. Gerald Fitzgerald, p. 68.
3. Most reference works give his date of birth as 1895. But in an interview in 1972, Ornstein stated that this was an error and gave the correct date as 1892. See Vivian Perlis, "The Futurist Music of Leo Ornstein," p. 736 n. 1.
4. Ibid., p. 737.
5. Ibid.
6. Charles L. Buchanan, "Ornstein and Modern Music," pp. 180–81.
7. Ibid., p. 178.
8. Leo Ornstein, letter to author, July 28, 1963.
9. Paul Rosenfeld, *An Hour with American Music,* pp. 64–65.
10. Quoted in the *New York Herald* (Paris), Dec. 28, 1927.
11. Ezra Pound, "Antheil, 1924–1926," *Criterion,* Oct. 1926.
12. Robert Forrest Wilson, "Paris for Young Art," p. 410, describes the projected opera in detail.

13. Charles M. Praeger, "A Riot of Music," *New York Herald Tribune*, Apr. 10, 1927.

14. Review by Richard L. Stokes, *New York Evening World*, Apr. 11, 1927.

15. Letter to Nicolas Slonimsky, July 21, 1936; quoted in Slonimsky, *Music since 1900*, p. 288.

16. Charles Amirkhanian, letter to author, July 31, 1972.

17. The Antheil revival was especially active in West Germany and Holland, with a surge of concerts, radio broadcasts, and television programs.

18. Varèse's given name often appears without the final *d* in reference works and even in some of his published scores; he himself used the (French) form *Edgard*.

19. For the English translation of Busoni's *Entwurf einer neuen Ästhetik der Tonkunst*, see *Sketch of a New Esthetic of Music*, trans. Theodore Baker.

20. Busoni, *Sketch of a New Esthetic of Music*, pp. 22, 5.

21. Hoene Wronski (1778–1853) actually wrote as follows: "The aesthetic division of *time* being for the musical artist the means of arriving at the realization of his thought, the mode of *corporealization of intelligence in sounds*, it is necessary first to conceive the *scheme of time* in the musical works." See Anne Parks, "Freedom, Form, and Process in Varèse," pp. 10–20.

22. Hermann Ludwig Ferdinand von Helmholtz (1821–94) published in 1862 his great work known in English as *On the Sensations of Tone as a Physiological Basis for the Theory of Music*. See reprint of second English edition (New York: Dover Publications, 1954).

23. Louise Varèse, *Varèse*, p. 193.

24. In the French magazine *391*, no. 5 (June 1917), a short-lived, avant-garde periodical published in New York; quoted in ibid., p. 132.

25. As quoted in Elliott Schwartz and Barney Childs, eds., *Contemporary Composers on Contemporary Music*, p. 196.

26. Varèse, *Varèse*, p. 193.

27. Schwartz and Childs, eds., *Contemporary Composers on Contemporary Music*, p. 198.

28. Varèse, *Varèse*, p. 218.

29. Schwartz and Childs, eds., *Contemporary Composers on Contemporary Music*, p. 203.

30. Chou Wen-chung, preface to Edgard Varèse, *Nocturnal*, ed. Chou Wen-chung (New York: Colfranc Music Publishing Corp., 1969), p. iv.

31. Ibid., p. iii.

32. William Lichtenwanger, letter to author, Feb. 6, 1984. Mr. Lichtenwanger has the most comprehensive data on Cowell for this period.

33. Henry Cowell, *Piano Music of Henry Cowell*, vol. 2 (New York: Associated Music, 1982). See also liner notes to *Piano Music of Henry Cowell*, Folkways FM 3349, p. 4.

34. Joscelyn Godwin, preface to Henry Cowell, *New Musical Resources*, p. ix.

35. Ibid.

36. Ibid., p. xiii.

37. Liner notes to *Piano Music of Henry Cowell*, p. 5.

38. Robert P. Morgan, liner notes to Ruth Crawford Seeger, *String Quartet,* Nonesuch H-71280.

39. Letter from John Becker to Ezra Pound, Jan. 1, 1928; quoted in Don Chance Gillespie, "John Becker." I am much indebted to this authoritative source.

40. The "Ultra-Modern American Concert" was repeated at Alice Tully Hall in New York City by the Dennis Russell Davies Ensemble, on May 4, 1975.

41. John J. Becker, "Finding a Personal Orchestral Idiom," p. 256.

42. Ibid., p. 126.

43. Ibid., p. 256.

44. Gillespie, "John Becker," p. 279.

45. John Kirkpatrick, "The Evolution of Carl Ruggles," p. 157.

46. Charles Seeger, "Carl Ruggles," in *American Composers on American Music,* ed. Henry Cowell; previously published in *Musical Quarterly* 18 (Oct. 1932): 578–92.

47. Lou Harrison, *About Carl Ruggles,* pp. 7–8; and Harrison, "Carl Ruggles," p. 16.

48. Henry Cowell, "Wallingford Riegger," p. 9.

49. Ibid. For a comprehensive coverage of the man and his music, see Stephen Spackman, *Wallingford Riegger.*

50. Dane Rudhyar, "Oriental Influence in American Music," in *American Composers on American Music,* ed. Cowell, p. 185.

51. For a recording of the *Tetragrams,* first series, see Serenus SRS 12072.

52. Dane Rudhyar, "The Relativity of Our Musical Conceptions," p. 117.

53. Ibid., p. 108.

54. Ibid., p. 109.

55. Ibid., p. 113.

56. Ibid., p. 115. The "Telharmonium" (also called "Dynamophone") refers to an instrument invented by Dr. Thaddeus Cahill, which came to the attention of Busoni through an article by Ray Stannard Baker, "New Music for an Old World," *McClure's Magazine* 27 (July 1906): 291–301. Designed to transmit electrically generated musical sounds over the telephone system, it proved to be cumbersome and impractical. See Otto Luening, "Some Random Remarks about Electronic Music," pp. 89–98; and Busoni, *Sketch of a New Esthetic of Music,* p. 33.

Chapter 26

New American Mix

The philosophy of the Melting Pot has given way
to cultural pluralism.
—Américo Paredes, *A Texas-Mexican "Cancionero"*

Standard dictionaries define the noun *mix* as an act or process of mixing, and in American vernacular usage the term has the connotation of "something produced by mixing." In a democratic context the latter formulation epitomizes the national development of the United States of America, evoking the spirit of its official motto, *e pluribus unum*. As a nation we are one, but ethnically, as a people, we are many. And it might be pertinent to recall Louis Adamic's statement that "it is to Ellis Island rather than Plymouth Rock that a great part of the American people trace their history."

But even in the colonial period there was a confluence of contrasting cultures: British, Scotch-Irish, Dutch, French, Spanish, German, African—along with the native Indians. The Spaniards, who first discovered and colonized the New World, occupied vast areas of North America, from Florida to California. During the twentieth century, by continuous immigration (mostly from Mexico), they became the second largest ethnic group in the United States, surpassed only by the blacks. The Mexicans were "Spanish" chiefly by the language of the majority. Otherwise their ethnic origins were mixed, with a prominent Indian strain.

In the period from 1880 to 1920 the United States had become truly a nation of immigrants, on a scale that dwarfed the influx of the preceding hundred years. Twenty-three and a half million immigrants entered this country as compared with somewhat over ten million from 1820 to 1880. But numbers alone do not tell the whole story. The new immigration represented a drastic shift from northern and western to southern and eastern Europe. The nationalities most heavily involved were Russian, Polish, Austrian, Hungarian, Greek, Turkish, Portuguese, Spanish, and Balkan. Slavic, Semitic, and Latin elements were in the ascendant.

Alarmed by such heterogeneous multitudes, the "old Americans"—especially those of Anglo-Saxon stock—took measures to restrict immigration, beginning with the first Quota Act of 1921, so that during the next four decades total immigration was only a little over eight million. While the Nordic nations enjoying preferred status seldom filled their quotas, however, the "lesser breeds" kept clamoring at the gates.

These patterns of immigration had a strong impact on the American musical scene, ranging from composition in the larger forms to show-business entertainment, the popular song industry, and ethnic musical traditions that spread throughout the nation. In the first category, the list was headed by Aaron Copland (originally Kaplan) and George Gershwin (originally Gershovitz), whose parents were Russian-Jewish immigrants.

Each side had its champions and detractors, with Daniel Gregory Mason as the most vociferous defender of the Anglo-Celtic domain. He reacted strongly to what he regarded as "the insidiousness of the Jewish menace to our artistic integrity." For him the "integrity" of the truly American was enshrined in such works as Edgar Stillman Kelley's *New England* Symphony (1913) and John Powell's overture *In Old Virginia* (1921). The essential factor, he maintained, was "a kind of moderation" and "a tender sort of reticence." It puzzled and pained him that this Anglo-Saxon "reticence" [as in Shakespeare and Keats?!] was being overwhelmed by the Jewish influence, and he lamented: "Our whole contemporary aesthetic attitude toward instrumental music, especially in New York, is dominated by Jewish tastes and standards, with their Oriental extravagance, their sensuous brilliancy and intellectual facility and superficiality. . . . Our public taste is in danger of being permanently debauched, made lastingly insensitive to qualities most subtly and quintessentially our own, by the intoxication of what is, after all, an alien art."[1]

Mason picked on the Swiss-born, Jewish-American composer Ernest Bloch (1880–1959) as being "long the chief minister of that intoxication to our public." Disclaiming any "anti-Jewish propaganda," he avers that he is merely pointing out that our "subservience" to this kind of "alien art" makes us deaf to "the possibilities of another that is more peculiarly our own."[2]

To show that he was not an ivory-tower intellectualist (*highbrow* was the current term), Mason conceded that Anglo-Americanism could be expressed in such slogans as "Step lively" and "Keep smiling," which are related to the national trait called "American hustle." But he draws the line at jazz, because "it has no persuasiveness, no magic, no psychological truth."

He contrasts it unfavorably with "such a real American folksong" as "Turkey in the Straw," in David Guion's setting for orchestra. "Such animation is native to us," he asserts, and adds, "Genuinely American is this childlike innocence. . . ."[3]

But Mason was living in an ivory tower or perhaps in a cave strewn with ancestral bones. In the variegated strata of the New Americanism, Mason and his ilk were fossils, and, like all fossils, they reveal significant patterns of the past. Take, for example, this lamentation by Mason: "One hardly knows whether to laugh or cry when one hears young Bostonians striving to outdo Schönberg in sterile, ugly counterpoint, young New Yorkers vying with Stravinsky in brittle pseudo-classicism, young Californians trying to be more starkly primitive than Prokofieff!"[4]

The plague of barbarians had evidently spread from coast to coast. That some of them made a show of American patriotism was no palliative for Mason, as we judge from his denunciation of Bloch's symphonic-choral tribute to his adopted land, with which he "capped his dealings with us by the grim jest of presenting to us a long, brilliant, megalomaniac, and thoroughly Jewish symphony—entitled *America*."[5]

Bloch composed *America* in 1927 for a contest sponsored by *Musical America,* in which the piece won first prize. He stated in his dedication: "This Symphony has been written in love for this country/In reverence to its Past—In faith for its Future/It is dedicated to the memory of Abraham Lincoln and Walt Whitman, whose vision has upheld its inspiration."

In his preface, Bloch wrote of "a Union, in common purpose . . . of widely diversified races. . . ." This ethnic diversity was to be increasingly expressed in America's music during the decades that followed.

Although Bloch composed a quantity of nonethnic music, the works that first brought him international fame, and for which he continues to be best known, are of Hebraic character. He came to America in 1916, was active as teacher and conductor, and in 1924 acquired citizenship. He made an immediate impression with *Three Jewish Poems* (1913), followed by *Schelomo: Hebrew Rhapsody* (1916), for cello and orchestra, and *Israel* (1912–16), a symphony for orchestra and vocal quintet. These were all performed in New York in 1917, and together with *Baal shem* (1923), for violin and piano (later orchestrated, 1939), these works marked the crux of the Hebraic impact in America's art music. It was a rising tide that would not soon recede.

In a previous chapter we mentioned the Russian-born, Jewish composer Leo Ornstein, who after his fling at futurism turned to more eclectic and neoclassical modes of expression. His *Hebraic Fantasy,* for violin and piano (1929), was written to celebrate Albert Einstein's fiftieth birthday. The Five Songs for voice with orchestra (or piano) were written to texts by the Jewish-American author Waldo Frank. The neo-Romantic Quintette for Piano and Strings, op. 92 (1927), is described by Vivian Perlis as "charged with vitality, spontaneity, and passion while retaining not only an inner logic, but extraordinarily complicated harmonic and rhythmic structures. There are long, sweeping melodies, tunes reminiscent of Russian and Cossack songs, and driving rhythmic patterns."[6]

Lazare Saminsky (1882–1959), who immigrated to America in 1920, had a wide range of interests that included folklore and liturgy, metaphysics and philosophy, teaching and writing. He published six books, of which *Living Music of the Americas* (New York, 1949) was the first publication to cover the entire spectrum of musical composition in the Western Hemisphere. Although often eccentric and sometimes prejudiced, he was much more open-minded than Mason, and his judgments are not based on racial bias. He believed in the viability of a "dual loyalty—to America's culture and the Hebraic heritage."[7] This cultural dualism is reflected in his music.

The *Hebrew Folk Songs and Folk Dances,* for piano (1922), and *Songs of the Russian Orient,* for voice and piano or chamber orchestra (1925–26), were balanced by *Newfoundland Air,* for chorus with piano, on a text by Thoreau (1935), and *Pueblo, a Moon Rhapsody,* for orchestra (1936). The *Anthology of Hebrew Sacred and Traditional Songs,* for cantor, soloists, and organ (1946), had its counterpart in *From the American Poets,* for chorus, piano, and percussion *ad libitum* (1940–48).

Of the second-generation Jewish-American composers, born in the United States, the most prominent are Aaron Copland, Leonard Bernstein, and George Gershwin. Of these, only Bernstein appears to have retained a strong Hebraic link, combined with wide eclecticism. Copland, in his autobiographical sketch, "Composer from Brooklyn," makes no mention of a Jewish background. As the family name, Kaplan, was pronounced "Koplan," the transition to "Copland" was quickly made. The young Aaron heard Jewish music in the synagogue and at weddings and other social functions, but, unlike Bernstein, he was not much influenced by these contacts. Whatever Jewish traits may be detected in Copland's music, the only overt Hebraic expression is that of *Vitebsk: Study on a Jewish Theme* (1928), for piano, violin, and cello.

Copland's contributions to the "New American Mix" are so varied and far-reaching that they had best be left for a later section of this chapter.

Meanwhile, Leonard Bernstein appears on the scene—a situation that has conspicuously marked his entire career in a worldwide marathon of fame.

Born in Lawrence, Massachusetts, in 1918, he was brought up to revere the Hebrew religious tradition by his pious father. He was also influenced by the eloquent sermons of a rabbi whose synagogue he attended. As the family was well-to-do, he received a proper Bostonian education, from the Latin School to Harvard University. From playing the piano at home, he went on to study music at Harvard and at the Curtis Institute in Philadelphia, with additional summer studies at Tanglewood.

Bernstein is at once the most Hebraic and the most eclectic of the three composers we are discussing, both in the diversity of sources on which he has drawn and the variety of genres he has cultivated, ranging from opera and operetta to Broadway musicals (these are dealt with in other chapters).

His first important work of Hebraic character was the *Jeremiah* Symphony (1941–44), which evokes "adolescent memories of Jewish songs . . . prayer cadences, Bar Mitzvah cantillation, and traditional Biblical chant."[8] *Hashkivenu* (1945), for cantor solo, chorus, and organ, is more ecclesiastically oriented. The Symphony no. 3 (*Kaddish*, 1961–63), for woman narrator, soprano, boys' chorus, mixed chorus, and orchestra, juxtaposes a spoken text written by Bernstein and a Jewish prayer of mourning. Because of its existential angst, it can be regarded as a Hebraic sequel to Symphony no. 2 (*The Age of Anxiety*), for piano and orchestra (1947–49). This is based on W. H. Auden's poem of the same title—a kind of exposé of modern neurosis, much in vogue during this period.

Bernstein made use of jazz-related effects in several of his compositions such as the Serenade for Violin, Strings, and Percussion (1954). Said to have been "inspired" by Plato's *Symposium*, it might be regarded as an example of "planned incongruity"—a device not infrequent in Bernstein's output. A conspicuous example is the controversial *Mass* of 1971, described as "A Theatre Piece for Singers, Players, and Dancers." Here the rampant eclecticism ranges from liturgical chant to hard rock. It will probably be remembered as a unique period piece of the 1970s.

In contrast to Bernstein, George Gershwin (1898–1937) began his professional career on the Broadway–Tin Pan Alley circuit and became the first denizen of that milieu to compose enduring works of worldwide fame in the larger forms of classical music. While both men shared a Jewish heritage, this was not prominent in Gershwin's output. His biographer Charles Schwartz, however, postulates an "apparent duality in

Gershwin's musical style"—namely that of "Second Avenue Yiddish combined with native American"—and he supports this view with specific musical examples such as a comparison of " 'S Wonderful" with an excerpt from Abraham Goldfaden's "Noach's Teive."⁹ He emphasizes the recurrent minor third as characteristic of Jewish melody and notes "a resemblance between Gershwin's music and snappy Jewish folk-dance tunes called *frailachs*."¹⁰ The Yiddish musical theater was important in Manhattan during Gershwin's youth, and he was certainly familiar with the music of such composers as Joseph Rumshinsky, Abraham Goldfaden, and Shlomo Secunda.¹¹

It would be misleading to regard Gershwin's crossover from pop to classical as a late or sudden transition. His parents were moderately well-to-do, there was a piano in the parlor, and George was encouraged to take music lessons with well-qualified teachers. Most important was the influence of his piano teacher Charles Hambitzer, who introduced him to such composers as Bach, Beethoven, Liszt, Chopin, Debussy, and Ravel. To his sister Olive, Hambitzer wrote: "I have a new pupil who will make his mark if anybody will. The boy is a genius. . . ."¹²

But George was not single-minded: he did not have an either-or mentality. At age fifteen he entered the world of Tin Pan Alley as a song-plugger for Remick and began to write popular songs. Yet in 1915 he began to study harmony, theory, and orchestration with the distinguished pedagogue Edward Kilenyi. The next year he published his first popular song and collaborated with Sigmund Romberg in *The Passing Show of 1916*. The big breakthrough came in 1919, when his song "Swanee" made a tremendous hit as sung by blackface entertainer Al Jolson (1886–1950; originally Asa Yoelson, born in Russia).

In that same year Gershwin wrote a piece for string quartet with the principal theme in blues style. A year later he was engaged to write music for George White's *Scandals*—a connection that continued for the next four years. In 1923 he took some lessons from the celebrated composer and teacher Rubin Goldmark and also accompanied the renowned concert singer Eva Gauthier (1885–1958) in a recital that included some of his own songs, along with those by Bartók, Hindemith, Milhaud, and Schoenberg. I think we can agree with Carl Van Vechten that this was an important event in America's musical history. The cult barriers had been broken.

For George White's *Scandals of 1922*, Gershwin wrote a one-act "Negro Opera" titled *Blue Monday*, which was withdrawn after the opening night as too "grim" for the patrons of a "girlie" show.¹³ But the orchestra leader,

Paul Whiteman, was very much impressed by the score and as a result asked Gershwin to write a piece in "jazz style" to be performed in a concert he was preparing, billed as "An Experiment in Modern Music." Although Gershwin was extremely busy writing musical-comedy numbers, he accepted the commission and within three weeks wrote the piano part of the work that would soon be world famous as *Rhapsody in Blue*. The orchestration was done by Whiteman's arranger, Ferde Grofé (1892–1972).[14]

Although Gershwin's holograph score was inscribed "For Jazz Band and Piano," the completed version was inscribed "For Piano Solo and Orchestra." This was, in fact, more realistic, for, while Whiteman's orchestra included many outstanding jazzmen, it was far from being a *jazz band* in the basic meaning of that term.

In addition to the usual saxophones, trumpets, and trombones of a jazz band, Grofé's orchestration included two clarinets, oboe, tuba, two French horns, accordion, celesta, two pianos, string bass, banjo, timpani, traps, and eight violins divided in two stands. It was, in effect, an orchestral mix. In the original score the names of certain musicians are written beside their instruments, and various jazz effects are indicated, such as "Siegrist solo, muted kazoo," "Fly swatter or Brush," "Let string snap" (banjo and bass). At one point the tuba is directed to play with flutter tongue—"if possible." With these musicians, anything was possible!

The much-publicized and celebrity-studded "Experiment in Modern Music" took place in mid-Manhattan's Aeolian Hall on February 12, 1924, with a hodgepodge program that began with "Livery Stable Blues" and concluded with Sir Edward Elgar's *Pomp and Circumstance* March no. 1. The audience was suddenly aroused when it heard the opening clarinet glissando of *Rhapsody in Blue*—a special wailing effect produced by Russ Gorman, when "halfway up the 17-note run, he suddenly slid home on a long portamento." Gershwin himself exerted the charm and brio that always characterized his piano playing. The leap into fame was sudden and worldwide.[15]

A year later Walter Damrosch, then conductor of the New York Symphony, commissioned Gershwin to write a work of symphonic proportions. The result was the Piano Concerto in F, which Gershwin also orchestrated: he was now a "serious" composer, yet never without the popular touch. The work was first performed on December 3, 1925, and Gershwin at the piano was enthusiastically acclaimed. The concerto is in the three traditional movements, marked *Allegro, Andante con moto*, and *Allegro con brio*. It was not a transmutation of jazz, as Damrosch affirmed, but rather a post-Romantic work transformed by the verve and variety of American popular music, as brilliantly conceived by Gershwin.

Gershwin's next symphonic work was *An American in Paris,* first performed in New York on December 13, 1928. Effectively orchestrated, bright and brash, it is typically American both in its brio and its sentimentality, with a particularly attractive blues section. Here Gershwin projected the spirit of a decade in a period piece that retains its full vitality and vivacity. This *was* America in the 1920s—Paris included!

In 1932 Gershwin began to study orchestration with Schillinger, and a year later the results were evident in the controlled eclecticism of the Variations on "I Got Rhythm" for piano and orchestra. With the *Cuban* Overture (*Rumba;* 1932), he made one of several contributions to the Latin connection that was having an increasing impact on America's music. He wrote, "In my composition I have endeavored to combine the Cuban rhythms with my own thematic material." And he added, "The conclusion of the work is a coda featuring the Cuban instruments of percussion."[16] He had brought back instruments such as the maracas, bongos, claves, and güiro from a visit to Havana that he found very enticing.

Gershwin composed relatively little for piano solo. Most notable are the three Preludes (1926), designed to be performed in sequence: (1) *Allegro ben ritmico e deciso,* (2) *Andante con moto e poco rubato,* (3) same as title (1). These are miniatures that blend blues and jazz ingredients with the Romantic piano tradition, and they have been continually favored in concert performances. According to Schwartz, "Even the melody for his famous second 'Prelude,' the slow middle one . . . seems Jewish on account of its stress on the minor third."[17]

Also characteristic of Gershwin's compositional output were the improvisations on his own songs that he liked to perform at the keyboard. A sampling of eighteen such pieces was published in 1932 as *George Gershwin's Song-Book,* for which he wrote an introduction, beginning with the truism that "America, in the last twenty years, has become a veritable hotbed of popular music."[18]

He goes on to state that "the rhythms of American popular music are more or less brittle; they should be made to snap, and at times to cackle."[19] He also acknowledges the influence of popular piano entertainers such as Mike Bernard, Les Copeland, Luckey Roberts, Zez Confrey, Vic Arden, and Phil Ohman, each of whom "was responsible for the popularization of a new technique, or a new wrinkle in playing." For example: "There was the habit . . . Les Copeland had of thumping his left hand onto a blurred group of notes, from which he would slide into a regular chord; it made a rather interesting pulse in the bass, a sort of happy-go-lucky *sforzando* effect. Then there was Bernard's habit of playing the melody in the left hand, while he wove a filigree of counterpoint with the right; for a time this was all the rage, as it sounded pretty well to ears that were not accustomed to the higher musical processes."[20]

Although Gershwin had become fully accustomed to the "higher" spheres of music with respect to compositional styles, he never displayed any kind of cultural superiority. On the contrary he states that "to all of these predecessors I am indebted; some of the effects I use in my transcriptions derive from their style of playing the piano."[21]

Turning now to Aaron Copland (b. November 14, 1900), we begin with an autobiographical sketch that he wrote, titled "Composer from Brooklyn": "I was born on a street in Brooklyn that can only be described as drab. It had none of the garish color of the ghetto, none of the charm of an old New England thoroughfare, or even the rawness of a pioneer street. It was simply drab. It probably resembled one of the outer districts of lower middle-class London, except that it was peopled largely by Italians, Irish, and Negroes."[22]

The first twenty years of his life were spent in that mixed milieu, but evidently not much of it influenced him musically. His father ran a department store, and his mother, who was musical, encouraged her children to study violin and piano—but merely as a pastime or hobby. According to Copland, no one ever talked music to him or took him to a concert: "Music as an art was a discovery I made all by myself." And he added, "The idea of becoming a composer seems gradually to have dawned" upon him "sometime around 1916. . . ."[23] The next step was to study harmony with Rubin Goldmark, and to discover for himself "the literature of music." There followed three decisive years in Paris (1921–24), where his principal teacher in composition was Nadia Boulanger.

The turning point came shortly after his return from France, when he decided to write a work "that would immediately be recognized as American in character." And he added, "This desire to be 'American' was symptomatic of the period."[24] He soon decided that he "wanted frankly to adopt the jazz idiom and see what [he] could do with it in a symphonic way."[25] The sensational result came with the Concerto for Piano and Orchestra (1926), in one movement with two parts. It was first performed by the Boston Symphony Orchestra on January 28, 1927, with Serge Koussevitzky conducting and Copland at the piano. Objectively, we can say that it had verve and power and an unmistakable American tang. It was also the last of what Copland called his "experiments" with symphonic jazz.

In one of his many lectures, Copland stated that "he did not believe American composers could create a type of music distinctly national without a literature of folk music as a background." Strongly upholding that conviction, he made it tangible and enduring with his assimilation and presentation of American folklore, beginning with highly successful ballets. An immediate hit was *Billy the Kid* (1938), written for the Ballet Caravan. Its antihero is the legendary desperado of the trans–Pecos West, about whom many a ballad tells:

> I'll sing you a song of Billy the Kid,
> I'll sing you a song of the desperate deeds that he did,
> Way out in New Mexico long, long ago,
> When a man's only chance was his own fo'ty fo'.

The music of this ballet also became widely known as a concert suite arranged by Copland, including his versions of such traditional tunes as "Great Grandad," "The Old Chisholm Trail," "Goodby, Old Paint," and "The Dying Cowboy" ("Oh, Bury Me Not on the Lone Prairie"), plus a "Mexican Dance" (the *Jarabe*).[26]

The next ballet, *Rodeo,* was choreographed by Agnes de Mille and produced by the Ballet Russe de Monte Carlo in New York on October 16, 1942. It presents a cowgirl-cowboy competition that leads to romance and hence a happy ending. Along with more familiar cowboy songs, there are freely treated versions of "Sis Joe" and "If He'd Be a Buckaroo." From the score Copland extracted *Four Dance Episodes* for concert performance, consisting of "Corral Nocturne," "Buckaroo Holiday," "Saturday Night Waltz," and "Hoedown."

Then came *Appalachian Spring* (the title is from a poem by Hart Crane), first performed by Martha Graham and her company on October 30, 1944, at the Coolidge Auditorium in the Library of Congress. Originally written for a chamber orchestra of thirteen players, a concert version for medium large orchestra was made in 1945. The music evokes the pastoral mood of early America, with its scenes of tenderness between the Bride and her Intended, the folk-hymn atmosphere of the Revivalist and his Flock, the suggestion of country dances and fiddle tunes, and the sentiments of rural piety expressed in the Shaker song "Simple Gifts." The five variations on this tune, in a style that has been called "American Baroque" (with full credit to Copland), are immensely effective and have become a popular classic, especially with brass ensembles.

Copland then went on to write two sets of *Old American Songs* (1950–52), newly arranged for voice and piano accompaniment. The first set included "The Boatman's Dance," "The Dodger," "Long Time Ago," "Simple Gifts," and "I Bought Me a Cat." The second consists of "The Little Horses (Lullaby)," "Zion's Walls (Revivalist Song)," "The Golden Willow Tree (Anglo-American Ballad)," "At the River (Hymn Tune)," and "Ching-a-ring Chaw (Minstrel Song)." The added labels of the second set are evidently intended to remind the modern public of America's varied song styles and social contexts.

These traditional songs are balanced at the literary level by the *Twelve Poems of Emily Dickinson* (1949–50), a song cycle for mezzo-soprano with piano accompaniment. (This was later orchestrated and first performed as such in 1970.)

Copland's American vista obviously has a wide scope, from the folk-popular to the literary-classical. Historical presentations depicting American scenes and famous individuals are also involved. Most notable is the *Lincoln Portrait* (1942), for speaker and large orchestra, with its declamatory style, its quotation of the Gettysburg Address, its snatches of popular songs from the Civil War period, and its presentation of the folk ballad "Springfield Mountain" as a recurrent theme.

Copland was also the first North American composer since Gottschalk to form a far-reaching connection with Latin America, where he not only traveled and lectured widely but also became the leading teacher of its most important composers of the new generation, notably Alberto Ginastera (1916–83). In Mexico he formed a close friendship with Carlos Chávez, who conducted the first performance of Copland's spirited piece for large orchestra *El Salón México* (1933–36), with the Orquesta Sinfónica of Mexico City, on August 17, 1937.

Copland had conceived the idea of writing such a piece during his first visit to Mexico in 1932, when he was especially attracted by the vivacity of a popular dance hall, the Salón México. In that "hot spot," he later wrote, "one felt, in a very natural and unaffected way, a close contact with the Mexican people."[27] The *personal* "contact" was certainly very "close," but it also seems certain that the music in the dance hall had no rapport with the orchestral composition titled *El Salón México*. For that work he turned to the publications of two prominent folklorists: the *Cancionero mexicano* by

Frances Toor, and *El folklor y la música mexicana* by Rubén M. Campos. Among the melodies that he borrowed are the very typical and popular "El palo verde," "La jesucita," and "El mosco." But only a folklorist or an ethnomusicologist would know the difference, and the audience is always happy.

We turn now to the traditional and popular songs that have passed from Mexico to the bordering American states from Texas to California, beginning with the oldest and most widespread type of Hispanic-American narrative song, the *corrido*. Its roots extend far back in Spanish history, and it is the equivalent of what we call a ballad in English. While the old Spanish ballads dealt mainly with past events, the majority of *corridos* refer mostly to current events (which of course eventually become "historical"). Unlike the folk-popular songs called *canciones,* which are mostly in duple meter, the *corridos* display a prevalence of ternary rhythms, often in 3/8 and 6/8.[28]

The vicissitudes of immigrants and migrant workers who crossed the border from Mexico to the United States are frequently depicted in the *corridos*. Typical examples are "El deportado" (The deportee), who is sent back across the Rio Grande, and "El Chicano," who finds that his hope of making "mucho dinero" (lots of money) in the United States is only an illusion. The "Corrido Pensilvania" portrays the hardship of separation, as a Chicano laborer goes to work in Pennsylvania but his wife is not allowed to follow him. The *corridos* were generally performed by two singers with guitar accompaniment.[29]

The term *Chicano* is generally understood to mean Mexicans in the United States or Mexican Americans, and as such it will frequently be used here, in various contexts. In view of the widespread impact of what has been called "Tex-Mex" *conjunto* music, we shall concentrate mainly on the Texas scene. But for a wider cultural perspective we need to recall that in the 1840s a large number of Germans, Czechs, and Poles settled in Texas, bringing with them traditional dances such as the polka, mazurka, and redova—as well as their favorite instrument, the accordion. The latter had become widely popular by the turn of the century, especially among Mexican migrant laborers.

By the 1920s both the accordion and the guitar were basic to Chicano music, and a typical small group would often consist of these two instruments together with the *bajo sexto*, described as a large rhythm-bass guitar. At first the single-row accordion was used, later replaced by the three-row button type. The combination of *bajo sexto* and accordion provided the basic rhythms for *norteño-conjunto* music, which was generally for dancing—although singing was often included, customarily as a duo.

Beginning in the 1930s, accordionist Narciso Martínez came to the fore as a leading performer and songwriter, making a big hit with his polka titled "La chicharronera," recorded in 1935. Not only was it an instant and lasting success, but it also (in the words of Manuel Peña) "set the stage for the emergence of a definable and enduring conjunto style." Peña goes on to explain:

> The recording itself shows that style in its embryonic form. It paired up Martínez on accordion with Santiago Almeida on *bajo sexto;* the two instruments have since become staples in the conjunto. Martínez's technique is especially noteworthy with respect to the style's subsequent development. Like the accordionists who followed him until the late 1940s, Martínez played with a fluid legato which connected all the notes within a phrase. The polka, which became by far the most popular dancing tune, was played at a brisk 120–130 beats per minute. The sixteenth-note patterns common to the polkas of Martínez and his contemporaries made the phrases seem to run into each other in rapid succession. The overall articulation sounded rushed [and] the *bajo sexto,* serving as both harmony and bass line, tended to emphasize the bass notes over the upbeat strum.[30]

Another popular contemporary of Martínez was Santiago Jiménez, also an accordionist, and we are told that he was the first "to incorporate the contrabass, generally known as *tololoche,*" in the *conjunto* ensemble.[31] His father had been an accordionist, and the family tradition was further continued by Santiago's son, familiarly known as "Flaco" Jiménez. The latter updated the basic *norteño* style with input from blues and jazz, also getting into the rock scene.

Culturally and socially there was a distinction between the traditional *conjunto* music, identified with the lower working class, and that of the modern style called *orquesta texana,* intended for the higher-class Texas-Mexicans. Peña, however, points out that some *conjunto* groups, notably that of Roberto Pulido, have "achieved a remarkable synthesis between conjunto and *orquesta,* successfully integrating two alto saxophones into the ensemble to create a blended sound."[32] And, like Santiago Jiménez, he has also brought blues, jazz, and rock into his performances.

We have noted that Chicano music often began with a family group, and a case in point is that of the Mendoza family, which began to perform in the 1920s. The mother played guitar, the father tambourine, one daughter the mandolin, another the violin. It was this very young violinist, Lydia Mendoza, who would become the Lone Star prima donna of Tex-Mex music. At first the family sang as a group, but in the 1930s Lydia emerged as a solo singer, accompanying herself on the twelve-string guitar. She soon began to record and continued to do so throughout her brilliant career, which took her all over the United States and on many tours abroad. The twelve-string guitar was her vade mecum.

Her first big song hit was "Mal hombre," which she did not write but tells us she learned "from a chewing-gum wrapper that they sold in Monterrey." Of her own songs, the best known are probably "Amor bonito" and "Besando la cruz"—touching the basic Hispanic themes of love and piety. Lydia Mendoza has been hailed as "La Gloria de Texas." But beyond that, the glory of her songs, like that of all American popular music, is at once regional, national, and international.[33]

After a period of retirement (1940–47), Mendoza was persuaded to go on tour again by an impresario from California who proclaimed, "I'm going to revive Lydia Mendoza." Thirty years later she was a highly honored personality when she performed at the Conference on Ethnic Recordings in America, in the Coolidge Auditorium of the Library of Congress, on January 24, 1977.[34]

This event was sponsored by the American Folklife Center at the Library of Congress, directed by folklorist Alan Jabbour. An important outcome was the publication in 1982 of *Ethnic Recordings in America: A Neglected Heritage,* including such basic topics as ethnic, commercial, and field recordings, and concluding with a comprehensive "Guide to Resources," worldwide in scope. There is also an appendix on the archives of ethnic musics to be found in universities, folklore centers, state museums, and specialized libraries throughout the United States. To cite one example, the Rodgers and Hammerstein Archives of Recorded Sound in the New York Public Library at Lincoln Center include "The Benedict Stambler Collections of Jewish Music Recordings," with about 4,000 items, ranging from the cantorial repertory to the Yiddish "pop" theater. From the Library of Congress, the series of recordings titled *Folk Music in America* covers a wide scope, from early "Reels and Polkas" of the 1920s to ragtime and jazz.

Turning now to an urban context in New York City, we have Mark Slobin's excellent book, *Tenement Songs: The Popular Music of the Jewish Immigrants* (1982). Slobin notes that "many ethnic groups have produced their own sheet music," notably "Finnish presses in the Midwest . . . French-American printers in New England [and] Ukrainian firms in New York. . . ."³⁵ But, he writes, "the Jewish-American commercial repertoire has been badly overlooked," and it "is of central importance to the evolution of immigrant music."³⁶ Slobin traces the development of this repertory by distinguishing the variety of ethnic musical sources from the ubiquity of American popular music. Concentrating on the area of lower Manhattan, he moves with deep perception from "The Mythic Old World" to "Making a Music Culture" in the United States, followed by "The Graphic Side of Music"—with many sheet-cover illustrations, from Cantor Sirota's "Rachmono D'one" to Irving Berlin's "The Ragtime Violin."

In his final chapter, "Between the Sheet Music Covers: Style," Slobin asks: "If this Jewish music is unabashedly and exuberantly eclectic . . . how can we presume to define a basic ethnic style?" For him, the answer is simple: "Look to the musical situations where the group takes style most seriously. Seek the musical symbol."³⁷ The rest is up to the reader, who will find much to ponder and assimilate in this remarkable book.

What about the ethnic scene in the South? For this we turn to the Center for Southern Folklore, which in 1981 received a grant for developing its "Ethnic Heritage Project." As their bulletin states: "The Mid-South has a varied ethnic population which includes Jewish, Italian, Greek, Lebanese, Russian, Polish, Chinese, Laotian, German and Vietnamese people. By focusing attention on these communities the Center feels the project will help to strengthen ethnic identity."³⁸ These and other ethnic groups participated in the center's "Ethnic Heritage Festival," held in Memphis, Tennessee, in January 1982.

One of the featured artists was Tsilya Sadetsky, a Jewish-American singer who in 1976 migrated to Memphis together with her son Igor, who accompanied her on the piano. Many of the Yiddish and Russian folksongs that she presents were learned from older family members. Other performers in the festival included "Israeli, Greek, Scottish and Laotian folk dance groups, an Irish accordionist, a Scottish bagpiper, a Chinese folk singer, a Polish polka band, and Greek bouzouki players."³⁹ Who could ask for anything more?

Still in the Midwest, but moving toward the North, we find the Popovich Brothers of South Chicago, four in number, with Serbian antecedents and a deep feeling for the traditional music of their ancestral land. Like many others with Serbo-Croatian backgrounds, their basic musical style was that of the *tamburitza* tradition, which became widely popular

Lydia Mendoza

The Popovich Brothers. Photo courtesy of the Ethnic Folk Arts Center Archive, New York, N.Y.

throughout the United States. Their stringed instruments ranged from the very largest to the very smallest, and in their community they were immensely popular. They had begun their professional career in 1925, and fifty years later they sprang into sudden fame that soon became worldwide. This occurred when filmmaker Jill Godmilow, in September 1975, decided to produce a motion picture titled *The Popovich Brothers of South Chicago,* done in collaboration with Ethel Raim and Martin Koenig, codirectors of what was then the Balkan Arts Center in New York City (it later became the Ethnic Folk Arts Center, with a wide range of musical and social activities). The film was completed on January 15, 1977, and quickly achieved both national and international acclaim.

"In the 1970's," Raim and Koenig state, "America discovered *ethnicity*—'roots' were suddenly something to be proud of. But for tens of millions of Americans ethnicity is and always has been a fact of life . . . a primary source of sustenance and a means of survival."[40] And music has always been a permanent feature of that life.

Notes

1. Daniel Gregory Mason, *Tune In, America,* pp. 160–61.
2. Ibid., pp. 161–62.
3. Ibid., pp. 162, 164, 165.
4. Ibid., pp. 167–68.
5. Ibid., pp. 161–62.
6. Vivian Perlis, liner notes to *American Contemporary: First Recording of Music by Leo Ornstein,* Composers Recordings (CRI) SD 339.
7. Lazare Saminsky, *Living Music of the Americas,* p. 119.
8. Jack Gottlieb, "Bernstein, Leonard," in *Dictionary of Contemporary Music,* ed. John Vinton, p. 81.
9. Charles Schwartz, *Gershwin,* pp. 28–29.
10. Ibid., p. 325.
11. For this connection, see also Mark Slobin, *Tenement Songs.*
12. Schwartz, *Gershwin,* p. 16.
13. For comprehensive data on *Blue Monday,* see David Ewen, *George Gershwin,* pp. 63–65.
14. Grofé's given names were Ferdinand Rudolf. Born in New York City, he studied piano, viola, and composition at the Leipzig Conservatory. Besides being Whiteman's pianist and arranger (1919–33), he composed a variety of works on American scenes, notably the *Grand Canyon* Suite (1931).
15. For a comprehensive description of this famous event, see Thornton Hagert,

liner notes to *An Experiment in Modern Music: Paul Whiteman at Aeolian Hall,* Smithsonian Institution and RCA Special Products R 028, pp. 1–10.

16. Schwartz, *Gershwin,* pp. 222, 224.

17. Ibid., p. 323.

18. *George Gershwin's Song-Book* was originally published by Simon and Schuster (New York, 1930). As "Gershwin at the Keyboard," it is included in the *New York Times Gershwin Years in Song,* with an introduction by Edward Jablonski and Lawrence D. Stewart, pp. 279–322.

19. Ibid., p. 280.

20. Ibid., p. 279.

21. Ibid., p. 280.

22. Aaron Copland, *Our New Music,* p. 212.

23. Ibid., p. 213.

24. Ibid., p. 225.

25. Ibid., p. 216.

26. Excerpts from *Billy the Kid* were arranged for piano solo by Lukas Foss.

27. Quoted in program notes, Boston Symphony Orchestra, Oct. 14, 1938.

28. See John Holmes McDowell, "The *Corrido* of Greater Mexico as Discourse, Music, and Event," in *"And Other Neighborly Names,"* ed. Richard Bauman and Roger D. Abrahams, pp. 44–75.

29. See Américo Paredes, *A Texas-Mexican "Cancionero,"* especially part 2, "Songs of Border Conflict," with extensive historical data. Recordings of Texas-Mexican border music, with copious historical notes by Chris Strachwitz and Philip Sonnichsen, can be obtained from Arhoolie Records of El Cerrito, Calif.

30. Manuel H. Peña, "The Emergence of Conjunto Music, 1935–1955," in *"And Other Neighborly Names,"* ed. Bauman and Abrahams, pp. 283–84.

31. Ibid., p. 284.

32. Ibid., p. 290.

33. For representative recordings by Lydia Mendoza, from 1928 to the 1950s, see *Lydia Mendoza,* parts 1 and 2, Texas-Mexican Border Music, vols. 15–16, Folklyric Records (Arhoolie Records) 9023–24.

34. See James S. Griffith, "Lydia Mendoza," pp. 102–31. Included are Mendoza's biographical recollections, as "La alondra de la frontera," also translated into English.

35. Slobin, *Tenement Songs,* p. 122.

36. Ibid., p. 120.

37. Ibid., p. 182.

38. *Center Update* (Center for Southern Folklore, Memphis, Tenn.), Dec. 1981, p. 1.

39. Ibid.

40. Ethel Raim and Martin Koenig, "The Popovich Brothers of South Chicago," *Ethnic Folk Arts Bulletin,* Sept. 1983, p. 1.

Chapter 27
Everywhere the Blues

"Got de blues, but too damn mean to cry."
—Traditional

They began in the Deep South, emerging after Emancipation, but nobody knows exactly when or how, except that they are rooted in the folklore and the sociocultural condition of American blacks. John and Alan Lomax conjecture that "when a lonely Negro man plowing in some hot, silent river bottom" raised his voice in a wailing "cornfield holler," he was heralding the birth of the blues.[1]

John W. Work also writes of the "holler" as a precursor of the blues, describing the former as "a fragmentary bit of yodel, half sung, half yelled, by which the Negro was known all over the country side." He goes on to say: "In these 'hollers' the idiomatic material found in the blues is readily seen; the excessive portament, the slow time, the preference for the flatted third, the melancholy type of tune, the characteristic cadence."[2]

There were also "dance hollers" (not "melancholy"!), in which a leader might shout, "Swing your partners!"—a reminder to us (so imbued with the notion of melancholy or self-pity) that the blues, with various types of instrumental accompaniment, came to be widely used for dancing in many areas of the rural South. Harry Oster, writing of an "old-time dance and blues fiddler" from Mississippi, draws attention to "the liveliness and gaiety with which the blues (and other types of folk-songs) are performed. . . ."[3] Thus the blues had an outgoing social aspect (as antidote to the harsh, grueling farm labor of rural blacks) as well as an introspective, negative aspect, emphasizing frustration and suffering (ranging from sexual relationships to imprisonment and forced labor). The overall context of the blues may be characterized as a blending of realism and imagination, sadness and humor, satire and sexuality, with a matrix of repetition and spontaneity.

When a roustabout on the Mississippi levee sang

> Gwine down de river befo' long,
> Gwine down de river befo' long,
> Gwine down de river befo' long,

the repetitive three-line stanza prefigured the basic verse pattern of the blues. When the last line was varied to bring home the particular message or mood, the characteristic type of the blues was born:

> I've never seen such real hard times before,
> I've never seen such real hard times before,
> The wolf keeps walkin' all 'round my door.

While the verses are highly idiosyncratic, it is the interplay of words and music (both vocal and instrumental) that reveals the quintessence of the blues. Here, for example, is a stanza of "Levee Camp Blues":

> Oh, that ole gal o'mine, stays out all night long;
> Oh, that ole gal o'mine, she stays out all night long;
> Oh, I can't do nothing with you, woman, no matter
>   what the pore boy do.

A version sung by Robert Pete Williams with guitar accompaniment was recorded by Harry Oster, who thus describes the effect: "Each verse begins with a long drawn out cry which suggests the influence of the holler. The singer sometimes sustains a syllable and runs it through a short melodic phrase. . . . There are frequent slurs, and usually at the ends of lines the last note tapers off downward into nontonal grunts—survivals of African style. The effect is to intensify the emotion and to sustain it beyond the limits of the words."[4]

The sociocultural context of the rural blues (also called "country" or "downhome") is delineated in the demographic pattern of the Mississippi Delta—a fertile plane bounded by the Mississippi River on the west and the Yazoo River on the east, and extending northward and southward from Vicksburg to Memphis. Many blacks, lured by illusive prospects of better wages, began migrating to this area in the 1890s, and within a few decades they largely outnumbered the white population. Blacks with musical aptitude (and there were many) soon found they could make extra money—sometimes enough to avoid the hardship of farm labor in a hot, humid climate—with their music. If they were lucky they might have the patronage of whites, as was the case of "Big Bill" Broonzy, who tells us that he and his brother "would be playing and sitting under screened porches while the other Negroes had to work in the hot sun. . . ."[5] Eventually, Broonzy would be one of many bluesmen from the Delta who were to gain wide recognition and considerable good fortune when the recording industry brought the blues to the rest of America, where it emerged as one of the three main currents of Afro-American popular music, along with ragtime and jazz.[6] It was not very long until the sound of the blues would be heard around the world.

According to Samuel Charters: "Even with the confusion of sources and influences . . . it does seem clear that it was in the Mississippi delta counties that the first blues were sung, and of all the southern areas where the blues became a deeply rooted folk style, it was in the delta where there was the richest creative growth."[7]

Whether or not the blues were first sung in the Delta remains a matter of conjecture. What can be documented are early written accounts of blues in the Delta, such as those given in the autobiography of the black bandleader and composer W. C. Handy. While stopping in the town of Tutwiler, Handy heard "a lean, loose-jointed Negro [who] had commenced plunking a guitar. . . . As he played, he pressed a knife on the strings of the guitar. . . ." His song consisted of the line "Goin' where the Southern cross' the Dog" twice repeated, and the accompaniment was "the weirdest music I had ever heard."[8]

Further travel in the Delta soon brought to Handy's attention the AAB form of the blues, including an example that was to become widely familiar:

> Boll weevil, where you been so long?
> Boll weevil, where you been so long?
> You stole my cotton, now you want my corn.

Handy was immediately fascinated by the form and the style, and, as we shall see, he adapted them to his own purposes as a professional composer, with immense success.

Now we must get down to the grass roots of the blues scene and then trace its impact on the outside world. Let us begin with a famous old-timer, Charley Patton (1887–1934), of whom Samuel Charters has written this vivid sketch: "Patton's music was as much a part of the delta as the mud on the banks of the Sunflower River or the smell of the fields back of Belzoni. He sang in cabins, in ramshackle road houses, in country dance halls, even in gardens and plantation house back yards. He sang for everybody in the delta, white and colored, and he had songs for every kind of audience. Nearly half of the songs that he recorded were play party songs or folk songs, country ballads or gospel songs. He could be thought of almost as a songster, rather than a blues singer. . . ."⁹

The term *songster* was applied in the rural South to local musicians whose repertory was so varied that it could not be contained in a single category. Besides, the country folk were not fussing with categories—a system of classification that concerns scholars and logicians. If the blues came to be literally everywhere, then it follows that they drew from many sources in the broad nexus of Afro-American folklore and culture.

Patton's best-known and most frequently performed blues is "Pony Blues," of which the first stanza plays on the sexual meaning of "rider":

> Hitch up my pony, saddl' up my black mare;
> Hitch up my pony, saddl' up my black mare;
> I'm gon' find a rider, ooh, baby in the world somewhere.

Jeff Titon points out that "Patton's idiosyncratic 'gallop' rhythms are apparent in the accompaniment."¹⁰ He also lists the following derivations from "Pony Blues": Big Joe Williams, "My Grey Pony"; Johnny Temple, "My Pony"; Son House, "Pony Blues"; and Howlin' Wolf, "Saddle My Pony." These equine tributes to Charley Patton (all recorded) attest his enduring and widespread influence and perhaps justify the album title of his collected recordings, *Charley Patton: Founder of the Delta Blues*.¹¹ Although he was certainly not "the onlie begetter" of the blues, Patton has a much stronger claim to the title "Father of the Blues" than did the Broadwaybound W. C. Handy, who adopted it for his autobiography.

Having previously mentioned "Big Bill" (William Lee) Broonzy (1893–1959), we should add that he was one of seventeen children born to poverty and hardship in a small Mississippi town. Finding his own style through trial and persistence, he was soon able to perform successfully in the 1930s, often with piano accompaniment or with a small jazz group. His main instrument was a large guitar, and he also sang. Using a more freely developed and varied type of blues stanza (as did many other performers), he recorded such numbers as "Big Bill Blues," "Bull Cow Blues," and "Mistreatin' Mama Blues."

As he rose in fame, he became a big figure in Chicago and is said to have copyrighted more than 300 blues of various kinds. What a giant step forward when a black man from the Mississippi Delta could have the opportunity to copyright the blues that he played and sang! We should add that Broonzy wrote a great many songs of many kinds that carried significance for the blacks. An example would be "Sun Gonna Shine in My Door." What he meant can be expressed in what he said: "Blues is a natural fact, something that a fellow lives. If you don't live it, you don't have it."[12]

The life of Robert Johnson, "King of the Delta Blues Singers," was short, violent, and tormented. As summarized by Richard Middleton: "Perpetually pursued by trouble, riven by extreme alienation and persecution-mania, murdered at twenty-one, with a history of drink, women and conflict behind him, Johnson looms large in blues history as the quintessential country singer."[13] The extraordinary recordings that he made were crowded into a few years preceding his death in 1937, yet they exerted a powerful influence not only on such blues innovators as Muddy Waters and Elmore James but also on many rock musicians of the next generation.

From his native habitat in the Delta, Johnson traveled widely—including Louisiana, Texas, and Arkansas—and was active in Memphis, St. Louis, and Chicago. Absorbing many influences, he transformed them into a unique personal style—as guitarist, singer, and poet of the blues: the Rimbaud of the Delta. His verses are often marked by vivid imagery and a surrealistic quality, as in "Hellhound on My Trail":

> I got to keep movin', Blues fallin' down like hail;
> I got to keep movin', Blues fallin' down like hail;
> I can't keep no money with a hellhound on my trail.

It might be said that Johnson disintegrated all the traditional elements of the blues and re-created them in his own tormented image. The result is both disturbing and powerfully effective. The range and variety of his instrumental and vocal effects is astonishing. With his voice he will use falsetto or humming or talking; the vocal quality can be rough and gritty or smooth and delicate. On the guitar he can use subtle plucking techniques, and he can push for hard-driving boogie rhythms. At times his singing turns into shrieks, as of a soul in torment. While seemingly on the verge of disaster, he unfailingly continues to weave his magic spell. He is both fearful and defiant, as in this allusion to a voodoo spell:

> You sprinkled hot-foot powder all around my door,
> You sprinkled hot-foot powder all around my door,
> It keeps me with a ramblin' mind, Rider, every old place I go.

Seldom if ever has symbolic expression in poetry and music been so deeply rooted in the life experience of its creator.

Dozens of Delta bluesmen deserve mention if only space permitted, among them Francis "Scrapper" Blackwell, "Blind" Blake, Willie Brown, Tommy Johnson, and especially Eddie "Son" House. Many have come from small towns of the Delta, for example, Bo Diddley, Little Walter, Muddy Waters, and Howlin' Wolf—to mention those who preferred not to use their given names. Others such as Sam Cooke, John Lee Hooker, and Otis Spann stood by their surnames *and* given names.

Although the importance of the Delta in the emergence of the blues is indisputable, any unilateral view should be avoided. We need only look toward Texas, for example, to find one of the most important and influential of the early bluesmen in the person of Blind Lemon Jefferson (1897–1930). Born and raised on a farm not far from Dallas, he was blind from birth and turned toward music as his only chance to make a living. Going to Dallas, he soon became a familiar figure as a street musician and honky-tonk performer. He also traveled throughout Texas, as well as Mississippi, Alabama, and Georgia, picking up traditional tunes that he adapted to his own manner of singing and his extraordinary guitar style. As described by Peter Welding:

> The conceptual richness of the vocal-instrumental interaction, the great fluency with which the instrumental passages are ripped off, as well as the strongly improvisatory character of many of the accompaniments—all evidence a thorough-going mastery of the guitar that is the hard-won result of endless hours of practice. Lemon's accompaniments are marvels of invention, light and brilliant. They are not so much responsorial comments on the vocal lines (the standard blues guitar role) as they are totally independent yet interactive lines with a complementary motion of their own. . . .[14]

In 1925 Jefferson went to Chicago to make his first recordings for Paramount, which billed him as "a real old-fashioned blues singer" (no innovators need apply!).[15] His first release, which included "Booster Blues" and "Dry Southern Blues," was a big success. He lived in Chicago off and on for his remaining years and recorded about eighty releases, but he made little money and is reputed to have spent that on women and booze. The story goes that he froze to death on a bitterly cold night in the streets of Chicago.

Lemon's "Black Snake Moan," with its overt sexual imagery, is highly characteristic of his style, as are "Rabbit Foot Blues," "Hangman Blues," and "Low-Down Mojo Blues." As Tony Russell remarked, bluesmen who grew up in the 1920s "nearly always cite Jefferson as the great formative influence. . . ."[16]

As a coda to Blind Lemon's recording career and a reminder of the contextual diversity of the blues, let us note that he was the first to record and to widely popularize a spiritual-to-blues number called "See That My Grave Is Kept Clean" (1928). In subsequent decades it was recorded by various bluesmen, with different titles such as "Two White Horses," "One Kind Favor," and "Dig My Grave with a Silver Spade":

> Well, dig my grave with a silver spade,
> Well, dig my grave with a silver spade,
> You may let me down with a golden chain.

Among the bluesmen directly influenced by Blind Lemon Jefferson was Huddie Ledbetter (1885–1949), better known as "Leadbelly." Born on a farm in Louisiana, he learned at an early age to play both the concertina and the guitar. He picked up all kinds of music from many sources and was much in demand to play for neighborhood parties called "sukey jumps." In Shreveport he earned some money by attracting customers to local stores—a kind of live-music, commercial come-on. He then moved to Texas, where he worked in the cotton fields (an experience evoked in "Pick a Bale of Cotton"). The turning point was his meeting with Blind Lemon, who not only gave him valuable musical advice but showed him the way to easier money in the streets and brothels of East Dallas. He also became enamored of the twelve-string guitar, which he soon remarkably mastered.

Leadbelly became notorious for his violent outbursts, including murder, for which he did time at penitentiaries in Texas and Louisiana. In 1934 he was pardoned and released, largely through the intervention of Texas folklorist John A. Lomax—and then it was on to New York for fame and fortune. He not only achieved popular success as a performer and songwriter—notably the best-selling "Irene, Goodnight"—but also became a kind of cult figure among the elite, as demonstrated by his appearance at Harvard College. Ledbetter's repertory ranged from ballads to bawdy; he put his special stamp on such blues as "Easy Rider," "Roberta" (barrelhouse blues), "Alberta," and "I'm on My Last Go-Round" (also known as "Fannin Street"—a memento of the Shreveport red-light district).

Of the Texas bluesmen from a later generation, the most widely acclaimed was Sam "Lightnin' " Hopkins (1912–82), who, like many of his contemporaries, rode the crest of the "second wave" of the blues-recording and personal-appearance boom that began in the 1950s.

For the first wave of the recording boom, we must return to the 1920s and to the initial predominance of women in this phase of professional blues history. The prime motivation was commercial, for the recording companies perceived the opportunity of opening up the "black market" with issues of so-called race records that had a particular appeal for blacks. In 1920 a black composer, Perry Bradford, persuaded the General Phonograph Company to use the black singer Mamie Smith, instead of the very popular white entertainer Sophie Tucker, to record two of his songs. The result was so successful that another recording by Mamie Smith, which included "Crazy Blues," soon followed (August 1920). "Crazy Blues" was among the first blues songs to be recorded, and it became a hit with blacks. Others followed in quick order, notably, in November of the same year, "Jazz Me Blues" and "Everybody's Blues," sung by Lucille Hegamin (a light-skin entertainer), accompanied by a seven-piece jazz band. Thus a pattern was established that prevailed for the next decade in both the recording industry and commercial entertainment (primarily vaudeville). Small jazz combos were standard, although pianists and some country musicians also had their fling. The audiences were predominantly black.

By the edict of later blues historians, this phase of the blues as vaudeville entertainment with a predominance of black female singers and musicians came to be labeled "classic." Its most famous exponents were Gertrude "Ma" Rainey (1886–1939) and Bessie Smith (1894–1937), the former from Georgia, the latter from Tennessee. Rainey acquired both her surname and her nickname when, at age eighteen, she married William "Pa" Rainey, a professional entertainer. With him she joined the celebrated Rabbit Foot Minstrels and later the Tolliver Circus and Musical Extravaganza, where they were billed as "Assassinators of the Blues"—an ambiguous phrase that has been variously interpreted. It probably meant "killers" or "knockouts."[17]

Before long, Ma Rainey was off on her own, a star attraction of the notorious Theater Owners Booking Association (T.O.B.A.—often referred to as "Tough on Black Artists"). She featured the blues that made her famous, which she also recorded for Paramount beginning in December 1923 and continuing until 1928. When her contract was not renewed, the explanation given was that "her down-home material had gone out of fashion."[18]

Rainey was far from beautiful, but she had a magnetic stage presence, enhanced by her lavish costumes and adornments, including a necklace of diamonds and gold pieces. She was both flamboyant and earthy, and her feeling for the blues was deep and strong. The power and expressiveness of her style is revealed in such numbers as "Victim of the Blues," "Deep

Moaning Blues," and "New Bo-weevil Blues." The scope and variety of accompaniments ranged from her "Tub Jug Washboard Band" and the duo of "Georgia Tom" Dorsey on piano and Tampa Red on guitar to various jazz combos and piano solos. One of her most impressive recordings is "See See River Blues," with Louis Armstrong on trumpet, deliberately slow paced and immensely impressive. Her qualities as a classic blues singer were eloquently described by Rudi Blesh:

> Ma Rainey's singing, monumental and simple, is by no means primitive. It is extremely conscious in its use of her full expressive means, definitely classic in purity of line and its rigid avoidance of the decorative.
> Rainey's voice is somber but never harsh, and its sad and mellow richness strikes to the heart. Her vibrato, slow, controlled and broad, is one of the important and characteristic elements in her tone production, and her tones are projected by sheer power with an organlike fullness and ease. The deepest and most genuine feeling fills her every note and phrase with gusty humor or with an elegiac and sometimes almost gentle sadness.[19]

Then came the Depression, and in 1933 Ma Rainey retired, leaving behind a living legend and a priceless legacy of recordings.[20] Her successor was Bessie Smith, who became known as "Empress of the Blues." Born in Chattanooga, she was raised in sordid conditions of abject poverty. Gifted with a good voice, she began to sing for coins on street corners, and in 1912 she joined the Moses Stokes Minstrel Company and went on the road. Ma Rainey was then a member of the troupe, and Bessie may have learned from her—but not to the exaggerated extent that has been claimed. A year later she was appearing on her own in Atlanta, and thereafter with several touring companies. By 1922 her home base was Philadelphia, where her recording auditions found no favor with Thomas Edison. But a year later an executive of Columbia Records in New York was tipped off by a more perceptive scout and immediately sent the black pianist Clarence Williams to fetch her. So it was that on February 15, 1923, Bessie Smith, with Williams at the piano, made her first successful recording, with "Down Hearted Blues" and "Gulf Coast Blues." The result was sensational. Within a year it sold more than ten million copies, catapulting Bessie into sudden fame.

Bessie became a star of the black vaudeville circuit and "was soon established as the biggest selling blues artist of the period."[21] She traveled in her own railroad car, lavishly equipped and ample enough to accommodate her entire company. She was truly the "Empress." But she had married a man who seemed mainly concerned with profiting by her success. As her marital misfortune increased, so did Bessie's craving for alcohol and a walloping spree, which eventually led to her decline and fall. It might be said that Jimmie Cox's song of 1922, "Nobody Knows You When You're Down and Out," became a symbol of her last years (it was one of her big numbers). She attempted a comeback in 1937, but within a few months she was the victim of a fatal traffic accident while driving from Memphis to Mississippi. With her death the world lost a great artist and a vibrant personality.

Although Bessie Smith occasionally recorded with a juke-style band, most of her recordings were made with outstanding jazz musicians such as Fletcher Henderson, Coleman Hawkins, Buster Bailey, Jack Teagarden, and Louis Armstrong. In 1925, with Armstrong on cornet and Fred Longshaw on harmonium, she recorded the most famous of all "composed" blues: Handy's "St. Louis Blues." In the same year, she recorded another number by Handy, "The Yellow Dog Blues," with a jazz combo that included Buster Bailey on clarinet, Coleman Hawkins on tenor sax, and Fletcher Henderson on piano. This was coupled with a splendidly evocative New Orleans number, "Cake Walking Babies," and what George Avakian wrote about these two sides applies to all of Bessie's best recordings: "The sides recorded that day [May 5, 1925] are fantastic in their integration and emotional impact. Bessie has seldom performed with such vitality, imagination, expressive power, and rhythmic swing. Almost every word contains subtle inflections which heighten the artistic appeal of her interpretations."[22] My only quibble with this tribute is over the word "seldom."

Bessie Smith is credited with having written both words and music for many of her songs, including "Back Water Blues" (a dramatic evocation of the Mississippi floods), "In the House Blues," and "Shipwreck Blues." Other classic blues singers also made their mark as songwriters. Ida Cox (ca. 1900–1967), billed as "The Uncrowned Queen of the Blues," wrote many successful blues, of which the best known is "Wild Women Don't Have the Blues." Victoria Spivey, from Texas, was boosted as "a blues shouter with a turn for sorrowin' talk" and nicknamed "Queen Victoria."[23] One of her later recordings, made with bluesmen Lonnie Johnson and Memphis Slim, was titled *The Queen and Her Knights*—a far cry from the old honky-tonks! Spivey's best-known numbers are "T-B Blues" and "Black Snake Blues."

At this point it seems pertinent to ask why black women held center stage in the first popular-commercial surge of the blues. The background is set forth by LeRoi Jones: "Most of the best-known country singers were wanderers, migratory farm workers, or men who went from place to place seeking employment. In those times, unless she traveled with her family it was almost impossible for a [black] woman to move about like a man. It was also unnecessary since women could almost always obtain domestic employment."[24]

The rise of the Negro theater turned the tide and offered new opportunities for gifted black women outside the household and the church. Jones writes: "Minstrelsy and vaudeville not only provided employment for a great many women blues singers but helped to develop the concept of the professional Negro female entertainer."[25] As we saw in the careers of Ma Rainey and Bessie Smith, the blues expanded the professional horizons for black female entertainers and impelled them toward permanent success in the lucrative entertainment field, aided and abetted by the recording industry.

We mentioned that Bessie Smith sang several blues by the black Alabama composer W. C. (William Christopher) Handy (1873–1958), including the world-famous "St. Louis Blues." Handy also wrote and published "Memphis Blues," "Joe Turner Blues," "Beale Street Blues," "Yellow Dog Blues," and many others. That several of these were written before 1914 certainly justifies his claim as the initiator of *composed* blues in the professional meaning of the term. Although Handy had a rural background and was in close touch with black communities of the South as a traveling bandleader, he had some training in musical theory and composition, so that he was able to give a rather sophisticated polish to the blues that he derived and arranged from traditional sources. Eventually he moved to New York City, where he established himself as a music publisher. Compared with the Tin Pan Alley songwriters who cashed in on the commercial novelty of the blues, Handy was a genuine composer of the blues, whose origins and development he had observed and absorbed.

We noted in the case of Blind Lemon Jefferson that black rural bluesmen did not lag far behind the classic female blues singers in achieving national popularity and some degree of financial benefit via the recording industry. This also involved a trend toward the cities, so that urban centers such as Memphis, St. Louis, Kansas City, Chicago, Detroit, and New York became important for the expansion and diffusion of the blues in their various developments and transformations.

One of these developments was the increasing significance of the piano, either alone or with other instruments. For example, the innovative and influential blues singer and pianist Leroy Carr (1899–1934) was often joined by a remarkable guitarist called Scrapper Blackwell. Paul Oliver summarizes the effect: "Leroy Carr and his guitarist-partner Scrapper Blackwell were in the vanguard of a smoother, more obviously city-sounding trend in the music. The bittersweet combination of Scrapper's guitar and Carr's piano and melancholy voice rejected Country parochialisms while retaining traditional blues color."[26]

From 1928 until his death, Carr recorded more than 100 blues for Vocalion, beginning with his first big success, "How Long, How Long Blues." Among the many numbers recorded with Scrapper Blackwell were "Kokomo Blues," "Trouble Blues," and "Midnight Hour Blues."

Another development was the boogie-woogie style of piano blues, pioneered by Jimmy Yancey (1898–1951), whose wife, "Mama" Yancey, was a fine blues singer. Boogie-woogie transfers to the piano the standard harmonic sequence of the twelve-bar blues (tonic–subdominant–dominant seventh–tonic) and a persistent rhythmic figure in the left hand, embroidered by rhythmic-melodic configurations in the right hand. The typical Yancey bass has a powerful, hard-driving rhythm. Examples are "Five o'Clock Blues" (or "Yancey Stomp"), "Midnight Blues" (fast stomp), and "How Long Blues" (slow stomp). Yancey was also partial to the dotted habanera rhythm popularized by Handy.

Among those who continued the boogie-woogie style were Clarence "Pine Top" Smith (1900–1928), Meade Lux Lewis (1905–64), and Albert Ammons (1907–49). Smith made a big hit with "Pine Top's Boogie-Woogie," followed by "Jump Steady Blues." Lewis's masterpiece is "Honky-Tonk Train Blues," with its chromatic harmonies and compelling cross-rhythms. Ammons's version of "St. Louis Blues" displays the tremendous drive of his style.

To these names should be added that of Pete Johnson, active in Kansas City together with the singing bartender Joe Turner, one of the so-called blues shouters. Together they recorded a hard-driving number called "Roll 'Em, Pete," to which Paul Oliver calls our attention as marking the beginning of what came to be known as rhythm and blues, the forerunner of rock and roll.

These various trends and styles pointed toward the transition from country blues, basically characterized by the self-accompanied singer-guitarist, to city blues, characterized by group accompaniments that eventually relied heavily on electric amplification. It is true that country blues had utilized various instrumental combos—especially for social occasions—such as the fiddle, mandolin, harmonica, and string bass, as well as jugs, kazoos, and washboards. But, with the exception of the harmonica and the string bass, these instruments were supplanted by others in the new urban milieu.

W. C. Handy. Photo courtesy of the Music Division, The New York Public Library at Lincoln Center, Astor, Lenox and Tilden Foundations.

The harmonica had come to the fore in the late 1930s, when the blind harmonica player Sonny Terry began to accompany the blind blues singer Fulton Allen, better known as Blind Boy Fuller, from North Carolina. After the latter's death in 1940, Sonny Terry teamed up with Carolina bluesman Brownie McGhee, thus pointing to the growing importance of bluesmen from the eastern seaboard.

Another harmonica player, Sonny Boy Williamson, from Tennessee, was influential in making this instrument an important factor in the incipient Chicago blues trend. He developed a technique of playing the harmonica, known as "cross harp," that influenced many other bluesmen.

Prominent in the development of urban blues was McKinley Morganfield (1915–83), better known as Muddy Waters, from Mississippi, whose Chicago-based blues band was enhanced by the piano playing of Otis Spann, later to become an important blues-and-soul exponent. Muddy Waters exercised a seminal influence not only as a bandleader but also as a blues singer and guitarist, specializing in the bottleneck "slide" technique, and as a songwriter and arranger.

The dynamic growth of the blues in Chicago was due to the large influx of blacks from the South between 1930 and 1950. This migration per se, however, does not account for the characteristic development of the Chicago blues scene. Mike Rowe points out that "at a time when blacks were leaving the South in their thousands to swell the urban populations of the North and West it's interesting that two only of the host areas, Chicago and California, should develop a discrete regional postwar style. What was so special about these areas?"[27]

Why did this innovation not occur, for instance, in New York, or in a number of other northern cities with a large concentration of blacks? In Rowe's view the existence of a flourishing "race" recording industry in Chicago is an important consideration, but not conclusive because New York was in a similar situation. He believes that both in California, where the Texas style predominated, and in Chicago, where the Mississippi influence prevailed, it was the regional factor that became decisive. In New York the largest influx of blacks came from the southeastern states; hence:

> The most reasonable explanation must be a musical one: that the very nature of the South Eastern style, with its gentle picked melodies, inhibited its modernisation, which in the case of Mississippi was effected by heavy amplification and adaptation to a band style. It seems certain that the Delta blues, harsh, rhythmic and aggressive, were more in tune with the feelings and aspirations of the new generation of urban dwellers, who, though mindful of

their past, had set their sights firmly on the future. This seems to be borne out by the popularity of the Chicago artists throughout the country . . . during the heyday of the style.[28]

Charles Keil appears to support this view when he writes that "the distinguishing features of Delta country blues—drones, moans, the bottleneck guitar techniques, constant repetition of melodic figures, harmonica tremolos, a heavy sound and rough intensity—are usually intensified in the city context."[29] That is exactly what happened in Chicago.

Similar developments were taking place in Kansas City and Memphis. But it should be noted that these cities, drawing on much the same sources from the Deep South, also provided a dynamic input for the Chicago movement. This is personified in the career of B. B. (Riley) King (b. 1925), raised on a plantation in Mississippi. Gravitating to Memphis, he worked as a disc jockey and began to record a hard-driving type of blues, influenced by both jazz and gospel. He was known on the radio as "The Boy from Beale Street," whence originated the initials B. B. that stuck to his name.

King's instrument was the amplified guitar, with which he fashioned a highly personal style from diverse influences such as the music of Bukka White and Charlie Christian. His vocals reveal his background as a singer of spirituals and gospel hymns. Moving to Chicago, he continued to record and perform with a group that included trumpet, tenor sax, organ, string bass, and drums—with King's amplified guitar (which he named Lucille) as the queen of the consort. He soon became known as "King of the Blues" (an ambiguous sobriquet), duly accredited by the high exponent of urban blues, Charles Keil, who in 1965 wrote: "If the adjectives 'unique,' 'pure,' and 'authentic' apply to any blues singer alive today, they certainly apply to B. B. King."[30]

The troublesome question is whether such eulogistic adjectives are valid in the current musical climate of our fin-de-siècle superhype and clamorous turnover. If *unique* is freely interpreted to signify a strongly assertive personal style, its validity might be allowed. But *purity* and *authenticity* are variables that do not necessarily conform with a relentless drive toward superstardom and the frenzied momentum of a charismatic personality. At any rate, in the 1970s B. B. King was strenuously moving toward soul—the new synthesis of blues, gospel, and jazz.

The blues are unquestionably a deeply rooted and widely influential type of Afro-American musical and verbal expression. While ragtime and jazz were readily assimilated by white musicians, the blues became essentially an expression of black Americans. True, they have had their Tin Pan Alley projections as well as their impact on white musicians, including outstanding composers, both American and foreign, from Copland to Ravel and Thomson to Stravinsky.

Writing in the 1960s, LeRoi Jones declared that such creative black musicians as Cecil Taylor and Ornette Coleman had "restored the hegemony of blues as the most important basic form in Afro-American music."[31] On the other hand, it has been argued by some cultural anthropologists that many urban blacks regard the blues as relating to the past and associated with hardships and deprivations that they do not care to recall.[32] We may readily concede that no single musical idiom will exert a permanent "hegemony" in the fast-changing cultural, technical, and demographic patterns of the supermodern world. Synthesis and innovation reflect the irreversible dynamism of contemporary society, as well as its lack of telic motivation.

A Detroit bluesman was quoted as saying: "I don't play blues much now. Got to change with the times."[33] That was in 1968. Almost ten years later, an article in the *New York Times* announced "A New Trend in Basic Blues." Hegemonies disappear; renovative trends continue.

Notes

1. John Avery Lomax and Alan Lomax, *American Ballads and Folk Songs*, p. 191.
2. John Wesley Work, ed., *American Negro Songs and Spirituals*, pp. 34–35.
3. Harry Oster, *Living Country Blues*, p. 7.
4. Ibid., p. 13.
5. William Ferris, *Blues from the Delta*, p. 35.
6. See Robert M. W. Dixon and John Godrich, *Recording the Blues*.
7. Samuel B. Charters, *The Bluesmen*, p. 22.
8. W. C. Handy, *Father of the Blues*, p. 74.
9. Charters, *The Bluesmen*, p. 38.
10. Jeff Todd Titon, *Early Downhome Blues*, p. 69.
11. Yazoo Records L-1020.
12. Quoted in Harold Courlander, *Negro Folk Music, U.S.A.*, p. 124.
13. Richard Middleton, *Pop Music and the Blues*, p. 64.
14. Peter Welding, liner notes to *The Immortal Blind Lemon Jefferson*, Milestone MLP 2004.
15. See Dixon and Godrich, *Recording the Blues*, p. 34.
16. Tony Russell, *Blacks, Whites, and Blues*, p. 49.

17. Titon, *Early Downhome Blues*, pp. 103–4.

18. *Chicago Defender*, Nov. 24, 1928, pt. 1, p. 7; quoted in Sandra R. Lieb, *Mother of the Blues*, p. 41.

19. Rudi Blesh, *Shining Trumpets*, p. 125.

20. The most comprehensive presentation of Ma Rainey as "The Mother of the Blues" will be found in the two-record set *Ma Rainey*, Milestone Records 47021, with a very extensive and highly personal estimation by Dan Morgenstern.

21. Dixon and Godrich, *Recording the Blues*, p. 21.

22. George Avakian, liner notes to *The Bessie Smith Story* 3, Columbia CL 857.

23. Derrick Stewart-Baxter, *Ma Rainey and the Classic Blues Singers*, p. 63.

24. LeRoi Jones, *Blues People*, p. 91.

25. Ibid., p. 93.

26. Paul Oliver, liner notes to *The Story of the Blues*, Columbia G 30008.

27. Mike Rowe, *Chicago Breakdown*, p. 211.

28. Ibid., p. 213.

29. Charles Keil, *Urban Blues*, p. 59.

30. Ibid., p. 102.

31. Jones, *Blues People*, p. 225.

32. Michael Haralambos, "Soul Music and Blues: Their Meaning and Relevance in Northern United States Ghettos," in *Afro-American Anthropology*, ed. Whitten and Szwed, pp. 367–83.

33. Ibid., p. 373.

Chapter 28

Jazz: Tradition and Transformation

Jazz is the expression of America's self, its sensual
potency, its lyrical force.
—Anaïs Nin, *Diary,* vol. 6

The music that came to be called jazz had its matrix in the strongly distinctive traditions of Afro-American music, including the propulsive dynamism of African dancing, the hot rhythm of gospel hymns, the form and in-
flection of the blues, and the syncopated rhythms of ragtime. As etymolo-
gists differ on the origin of the term *jazz,*[1] we can simply accept its common usage and proceed at once to the heart of the matter; the *music*—with
its creators and performers.

New Orleans has a strong claim to being the cradle and nursery of
jazz. In the aftermath of the Civil War, marching bands with black musicians abounded in the Crescent City, playing for parades, picnics, and every kind of public entertainment or celebration. These bands had an important role in the development and diffusion of jazz and have continued to represent the communal spirit of New Orleans, both in lively street marches
and impressive funeral dirges.[2]

About the turn of the twentieth century, small instrumental combos,
of five to seven pieces, were much in demand for dances. These generally
consisted of cornet, clarinet, and trombone for the melody section, with
guitar, bass, and drums for the rhythm—and optional piano. Later, the cornet was generally replaced by the trumpet. Such combinations continued
to be widely popular in New Orleans and soon spread to many other centers. A pioneer figure was Charles "Buddy" Bolden, and when he was
struck down by insanity in 1907, there were many contenders for his
crown.

Prominent among them was Freddie Keppard (1889–1933), who took over the Olympia Band about 1906 and soon established his reputation both as leader and performer. Having started his musical career on the cornet at age sixteen, he later switched to trumpet—a trend soon followed by many other jazz players. According to his contemporary Ferdinand Morton, "There was no end to his ideas; he could play one chorus eight or ten different ways."[3]

Although most of the precursors and pioneers of jazz were black, some white musicians also got on the bandwagon that was evidently going places. Several of them, including Nick LaRocca (cornet) and Alcide Nunez (clarinet), played with Jack Laine's Reliance Band in New Orleans. In 1915–16 both were playing at the Haymarket Cafe with a quintet that included Johnny Stein on drums and Henry Ragas on piano. There they were heard by an impresario from Chicago, who offered them a contract to play at his nightclub. By the time the musicians arrived, the club had been closed by the police! But they obtained an engagement at Schiller's Cafe, billed as "Stein's Band from Dixie." According to one account, after someone shouted "Jass it up, boys," the group was billed as "Stein's Dixie Jass Band."

Finding their salaries inadequate, four of the group quit, leaving Stein holding the bag. With Tony Sbarbaro replacing Stein on drums, the group was reorganized as the Original Dixieland Jazz Band. This was in June 1916, and their success was sensational, both at the Casino Gardens and in vaudeville, where (according to *Billboard*) "the way the five of them tear away at their instruments bought down the house."[4] At the end of October, Nunez was replaced on clarinet by Larry Shields, who came to be regarded as the most important member of the group. So the band that was soon to make jazz history in New York now consisted of Shields, LaRocca, Edwards, Sbarbaro, and Ragas.

In New York they made "jazz" instantly notorious, although nobody seemed to know how it was spelled—*jass, jas, jaz,* and *jasz* all appeared in print. The patrons who flocked to the "Paradise" Supper Club and Ballroom in the new Reisenweber Building on Eighth Avenue and Fifty-eight Street could not have cared less about the spelling. They came to see, hear, and dance to "The Jasz Band"—billed as "The First Sensational Amusement Novelty of 1917." The punch line was: "You've Just Got to Dance When You Hear It."[5]

That held good not only for the crowds at Reisenweber's but also for the million or two who bought the first recordings of "The Original Dixieland Jass Band" (so advertised on March 7, 1917), issued by Victor. The first two releases were "Dixie Jass Band One Step (Introducing 'That Teasin' Rag')" and "Livery Stable Blues." The latter selection (also known as "Barnyard Blues") soon became a symbol for the kind of raucous Dixieland jazz characterized by so-called barnyard-breaks, imitating such animal sounds as a donkey braying, a horse whinnying, and a rooster crowing.

Although Freddie Keppard had appeared at the New York Winter Garden for three weeks in January and February 1916, with a group billed as "That Creole Band," he is reputed to have refused a recording offer made in 1917, "because that would make it too easy to steal."[6] So it was the Original Dixieland Jazz Band that hit the jackpot, both with its recordings and its sensationally successful appearances in the United States and in England, where the group had a tremendous vogue. By 1924, however, they were finished as an effective force in jazz, partly because of personal problems, but also because of rising competition.

The immediate impact and historical significance of the Original Dixieland Jazz Band have been aptly summarized by Gunther Schuller:

> The ODJB reduced New Orleans Negro music to a simplified formula. It took a new idea, an innovation, and reduced it to the kind of compressed, rigid format that could appeal to a mass audience. As such it had a number of sure-fire ingredients, the foremost being a rhythmic momentum that had a physical, even visceral, appeal. Moreover, this rhythmic drive was cast in the most unsubtle terms, as was the ODJB's melodic and harmonic language, with none of the flexibility and occasional subtlety shown by the best Negro bands of the period. But in its rigid substitution of sheer energy for expressive power, of rigid formula for inspiration, the ODJB had found the key to mass appeal.[7]

By far the most significant and influential of the early white jazz bands was the New Orleans Rhythm Kings, originally known as the Friar's Society Orchestra—from the name of the Chicago nightclub where they performed, beginning in 1921. The group consisted of Paul Mares (cornet), George Brunies (trombone), Leon Rappolo (clarinet), Elmer Schoebel (piano), Louis Black (banjo), Frank Snyder (drums), and Arnold Loyocano (bass). In 1922–23 they made a number of recordings for Gennett that had a direct impact on the young white musicians who developed what came to be known as the "Chicago Style." They certainly influenced the most gifted exponent of that style, Bix Beiderbecke, who was only eighteen when he first heard them.

At this time the fabulous New Orleans jazz pianist, composer, and arranger known as "Jelly Roll" Morton (1890–1941) was in Chicago, and in the summer of 1923 he made some recordings together with the New Orleans Rhythm Kings at the Gennett studio in Richmond, Indiana. This was evidently the first racially mixed recording date, and it produced such notable sides as the celebrated "Clarinet Marmalade" and the Morton specialties "Mr. Jelly Lord" and "Milenberg Joys."

Morton, like many other New Orleans musicians, had played much ragtime in his early years, but he was the first to perceive and define the distinction between ragtime and jazz, insisting that the latter, whatever its sources or borrowings, was a new type of music that transformed what it absorbed. In his later years he told Alan Lomax: "You have the finest ideas from the greatest operas, symphonies and overtures in jazz music. . . . I transformed a lot of those numbers into jazz time. . . . The *Tiger Rag*, for an instance, I happened to transform from an old quadrille, which was originally in many different tempos."[8]

When Gunther Schuller ventured the opinion that Morton "must have been greatly impressed by the way opera composers like Verdi and Donizetti managed to organize their larger ensemble pieces,"[9] he probably had in mind the recordings, mostly of Morton's own compositions, that Jelly Roll had made for Victor in 1926, "where contrasting individual lines attain a degree of complexity and unity that jazz had not experienced before."[10]

The Red Hot Peppers, with whom Morton made these recordings, was formed mostly by black musicians from New Orleans, including Edward "Kid" Ory on trombone, Omer Simeon on clarinet, and Johnny St. Cyr on banjo and guitar. The pieces by Morton were "Black Bottom Stomp," "Dead Man Blues," "Grandpa's Spells," and "Doctor Jazz." These alone would justify the title that Schuller bestowed on Morton as "The First Great Composer" in the realm of jazz.

The next development in both Chicago and the surrounding areas of the Midwest brings on the scene a number of young whites who were fascinated by the novelty of the New Orleans jazz they heard as teenagers. The one who made the most enduring mark, as both performer and composer, was Leon Bix Beiderbecke (1903–31), who came from Davenport, Iowa. Having first learned to play the piano, he was attracted to the cornet after hearing Louis Armstrong perform on a Mississippi River steamboat. Soon afterward he was sent to study at an academy near Chicago, and from there he quickly gravitated toward the ongoing jazz movement.

In 1924 he joined the very successful Wolverine Orchestra, with which he made his first recordings—soon to be followed by others performed with his own Rhythm Jugglers, as well as many more for Jean Goldkette and his orchestra and Paul Whiteman's orchestra. Throughout his career he preferred playing the cornet to the trumpet. As described by George Avakian: "This gave him a rounder, warmer, more intimate tone, as opposed to the more penetrating trumpet tone. There is always a reserved quality to Bix's cornet sound; it's as though he never lets himself go all-out emotionally, even on a barrelhouse Dixieland performance like *At the Jazz Band Ball*. He was one of the most exciting musicians who ever lived, but he did it by the individuality of his tone and the imaginativeness of his improvisations."[11]

Bix Beiderbecke also loved to play the piano, which provided a more intimate medium for expressing his ingrained artistic aspirations. Musically, he had a divided allegiance: to jazz and to art music, for he came under the spell of Debussy, Ravel, Delius—even MacDowell! However, he never mastered the techniques of formal composition; he improvised at the piano, and someone else did the written notation for him. The titles of his best-known piano pieces, such as "Candlelights" and "In a Mist," are indicative of this dual affinity.

As we have observed, many black musicians from New Orleans were active in Chicago during the 1920s, and several of them made recordings that stand as landmarks in the history of jazz. When the young cornet player Louis Armstrong (1909–71), who had left "King" Oliver's band in 1924 to join Fletcher Henderson's in New York, returned to Chicago in 1925, he formed a group of his own for studio recording. Known as either the Hot Five or the Hot Seven, depending on the number of players, the recordings they made from November 1925 to December 1928 were widely and decisively influential. The emergence of the solo as a major creative element in jazz was Armstrong's particular achievement. (During this period he switched from cornet to trumpet.)

The personnel varied, but at first the Hot Five consisted of Armstrong as leader, Johnny Dodds on clarinet (and occasionally alto sax), Kid Ory on trombone, Johnny St. Cyr on banjo, and Lil Armstrong on piano. (In 1928 she was replaced by Earl Hines, who soon gained renown as one of the great masters of jazz piano.) Among the outstanding numbers recorded during this three-year period are "Cornet Chop Suey," "Potato Head Blues," "Hotter Than That," "West End Blues," and "Big Butter and Egg Man."

Armstrong's recording of "Big Butter and Egg Man" became a *locus classicus* of jazz history because of the transcendent importance given to it by the influential French critic André Hodeir. About Armstrong's solo chorus in this recording, Hodeir wrote: "This astonishing chorus is a perfect example of the phenomenon of '*transformation without sacrifice of fidelity*' in which subsequent jazz has abounded. Even more important, it is perhaps the first example of a typically individual esthetic conception to be found in the history of recorded jazz. . . . It is not unreasonable to believe that this improvisation of a genius opened a new chapter in the evolution of jazz" (italics added).[12]

The italicized phrase above is related to the idea embodied in Gunther Schuller's praise of Armstrong's performance in "Big Butter and Egg Man," as revealing an "intuitive grasp of musical logic and continuity, coupled with an imaginative sense of variation."[13] Schuller also has a very perceptive analysis of Armstrong's performance in "West End Blues," which he regards as "certainly the crowning achievement of this date [1928], and perhaps of Armstrong's recorded output." For him, the essence of the achievement is the combination of "two ideas—the occasionally used opening break . . . and the extended stop-time chorus—into a cadenza that is free in tempo." The gist of Schuller's insight is contained in the remark that "Louis had found the perfect jazz counterpart to the hundreds of popular cornet cadenzas that were such an integral aspect of the American musical tradition."[14] Thus we discover another facet of America's vast musical heritage, ranging from hymns to march tunes, that jazz adopted and transformed.

The world's tribute to Louis Armstrong made him the most widely popular and beloved personality in the realm of jazz. Hailed by his nickname as "Satchmo the Great" ("Satchmo" being a contraction of "Satchel Mouth"), he was truly a legend in his own lifetime.

The 1930s have been tagged by jazz historians as the beginning of the *swing* era, and many pundits have since offered varying definitions of that elusive term. The simplest was that proposed by Hodeir: "a certain way of making rhythm come to life."[15] This is a description rather than a definition, and it is probably best to leave it at that. For our purpose it will suffice to note that *swing* was the vogue term for jazz in the 1930s. Duke Ellington said it with music in 1931, in a number called "It Don't Mean a Thing if It Ain't Got That Swing." A year later Bennie Moten and his Kansas City orchestra recorded a piece called "Moten Swing," about which Martin Williams has written: "Here . . . was a large jazz orchestra which could *swing* cleanly and precisely according to the manner of Louis Armstrong—a group which had grasped his innovative ideas of jazz rhythm and had realized and developed them in an ensemble style."[16]

Actually, when Armstrong published his first autobiography in 1936, he argued that swing was the basic ingredient of New Orleans jazz and that the main differences in the newer music was that it used scored orchestrations, more sophisticated harmonies, and more professionally trained musicians.

Thus far we have spoken of black jazz musicians who were the innovators of swing, and we should also include Fletcher Henderson and Chick Webb, among others. Yet it was indicative of the trend during this period that a white band picked up the swing tag and gave it nationwide impact via radio broadcasts and disc recordings. The Benny Goodman band, formed in New York, toured from coast to coast, with increasing success, between 1935 and 1937. Goodman (1909–86) began his career as a clarinetist in his native Chicago and was internationally acclaimed as both solo performer and bandleader. He benefited greatly by featuring the arrangements of Fletcher Henderson in such numbers as "When Budda Smiles," "King Porter Stomp," "Blue Skies," and "Down South Camp Meeting."

Having mentioned Benny Moten (1894–1935) in connection with swing, we should add that when he died his band was taken over by William "Count" Basie (1904–84), who in 1937–38 made path-breaking recordings with Decca, including such numbers as "Swinging the Blues," "Jive at Five," and "Jumpin' at the Woodside." These reveal the powerful drive, impelled by Basie's tremendous piano style and inexhaustible inventiveness, that the group achieved, with Lester Young on tenor sax as a prime innovator.

On the saxophone, what Lester Young (1909–59) was to the Count Basie orchestra, Coleman Hawkins (1904–69) was to the Fletcher Henderson orchestra. Between them they made the sax a major force in modern jazz, each with a unique style that was widely emulated. Hawkins's "Body and Soul" became a jazz classic.

Meanwhile, a black musician from Washington, D.C., who came to be known as "Duke" Ellington (1899–1974), was pursuing a creative career that could not be circumscribed by any particular movement or trend. Eventually he would become a great jazz composer in the classical meaning of the term, while maintaining the group participation and collaborative effort that constitute the core of jazz. He was also a pianist of stature, initially influenced by the stride piano style of such innovative performers as James P. Johnson and Willie "The Lion" Smith.

After his Washington apprenticeship Ellington went to New York in 1922 and soon formed his own band, with which he began to record in 1924. The personnel included trumpet player James "Bubber" Miley, a key figure in the development of the Ellington sound, especially through his use of the plunger mute and so-called growl effects. As Ellington recalled: "He [Bubber] used to growl all night long, playing gutbucket on his horn. That was when we decided to forget all about the sweet music."[17] This meant going back to the early New Orleans jazz and taking off from there in a series of unprecedented transformations.

We have spoken of "the Ellington sound" as a collaborative effort, and this must be understood to mean not only the stylistic input of the players but also, in some cases, their creative contributions. With regard to Miley, for example, Gunther Schuller writes: "He was not only the band's most significant soloist but actually wrote, alone or with Ellington, many of the compositions in the band's book between 1927 and 1929. . . . There seems little doubt that those compositions that bear Bubber's name along with Ellington's were primarily created by Miley. These include the three most important works of the period—recorded in late 1926 and early 1927— *East St. Louis Toodle-Oo, Black and Tan Fantasy,* and *Creole Love Call.*"[18]

The "Black and Tan Fantasy" was originally written for a floor show at the famous Cotton Club in Harlem, where Ellington was featured from 1927 to 1932. Yet it is recognized as one of the great jazz creations, about which a critic wrote: "This challenging masterpiece has the weird imagery of a Blake poem and the macabre sense of a Fritz Lang film of the late 'twenties."[19] Indeed, it proved to be a much-recorded masterpiece; but, as each recording is different, it contradicts the concept of a *masterpiece* as an inviolable, unchanging entity.

Key sidemen with Ellington at this time included Joe "Tricky Sam" Nanton on trombone, Barney Bigard on clarinet, Johnny Hodges on alto and soprano sax, and "Cootie" Williams on trumpet—a great master of the growl effects identified with the "jungle" numbers that the orchestra developed during this period. Typical of this genre is "Echoes of the Jungle" (1931), which has as its urban counterpart "Echoes of Harlem." Williams was the featured soloist in both. Later, Cootie and Ellington came into full glory with that masterpiece in miniature the "Concerto for Cootie" (1940)—the first real concerto in the jazz idiom.

Beginning with "Mood Indigo" in 1930, Ellington became increasingly innovative, particularly in his use of chromaticism and bitonal harmonies, as well as in the temporal extension of his compositions. The first step was to transcend the three-minute duration—one side of a 78 RPM recording—that generally determined the timing of a piece. He began with "Creole Rhapsody" (1931), which filled both sides of a ten-inch record. With "Reminiscing in Tempo" (1935) he used two ten-inch records, for a total of twelve minutes on four sides. These were also significant as independent compositions, not intended for dancing or floor-show entertainment.

Taking a big step forward in extended time, Ellington in 1942 completed a tone poem for jazz orchestra and vocal soloist, with a duration of fifty minutes. The title refers to "people of color" and their cultural role in the New World: *Black, Brown, and Beige*. The premiere was at Carnegie Hall on January 23, 1943.[20]

Ellington went on to write many tone poems and orchestral suites, several in collaboration with his gifted arranger and faithful alter ego Billy Strayhorn (1915–67), who had been his associate since 1939. The long list of suites includes *Such Sweet Thunder* (or *Shakespearean* Suite, 1957) and *Toot Suite*—a French pun that shows that Duke never lost his sense of humor.

Consistently aspiring to compose in the larger forms, Ellington accepted a commission from the NBC Symphony to write a piece titled *Harlem* (1950), described as a "concerto grosso for jazz band and symphony orchestra." A suite in three movements, *The Golden Broom and the Green Apple* (1965) was also written for symphony orchestra. In his later years he was much concerned with religion and a religious view of life, resulting in three *Sacred Concerts* (1965, 1968, 1973) composed in the last decade of his career. Written for his own jazz orchestra, augmented by vocal soloists and chorus, these were enthusiastically acclaimed when performed in various cathedrals, in both the United States and Europe.

From such popular tunes as "In a Sentimental Mood," "Sophisticated Lady," and "Solitude," through the instrumental masterpieces of the middle period and the classically oriented later works, Ellington demonstrated the extraordinary range of his creative versatility. A tribute by Vic Bellerby is well deserved: "With the possible exception of Charles Ives, it is doubtful if America has produced a musician of such originality as Duke Ellington. For over thirty years [as of 1960] he has succeeded in translating the changing patterns of society around him into hundreds of compositions, which show a mixture and a range of moods not seen before in American music."[21]

Duke Ellington. Photo courtesy of the Music Division, The New York Public Library at Lincoln Center, Astor, Lenox and Tilden Foundations.

In the 1940s jazz was in a potentially explosive period. Gifted jazzmen with original ideas were restless under the hegemony of big-band swing and rampant commercialism. In August 1942 a nationwide ban on recording was imposed by the musicians' union in a dispute with the licensing agencies. The ban, which lasted until November 1944, put a lid on this explosive situation. Jazz innovators went on developing their new ideas but could not reach large sectors of the public that got their jazz chiefly through recordings. When the lid was off, the new music that came to be known as "bebop" (or simply "bop") seemed to come with disconcerting suddenness. Critical reaction was largely hostile. The idea of jazz as a transformational process had not yet caught on.

The trends of bebop coalesced in New York, beginning with several innovative jazzmen who about 1940 gathered at a nightclub in upper Manhattan called Minton's Playhouse. The musicians came from all parts of the United States, but a strong case has been made for the crucial impact of Kansas City jazz, particularly through the influence of creative soloists such as Lester Young and Charlie Parker on saxophone and the dynamic riff-style developed by the Count Basie orchestra.[22] Parker (1920–55), born in Kansas City, became the most influential figure not only in bebop but in the whole development of postswing jazz. He was closely associated with John Birks "Dizzy" Gillespie (b. 1917), a trumpet player from South Carolina who soon developed a style as distinctive as that of Parker. In 1945 Gillespie formed his All Star Quintet, with Parker on alto saxophone: a brilliant duo.

The style of drumming was an important factor in bebop, as demonstrated particularly by Kenny Clarke, Jo Jones, and Max Roach. They emphasized a light, subtle use of the top cymbal instead of the persistent use of the "sock" cymbal. As described by Ross Russell: "The vibration of the cymbal, once set in motion, is maintained throughout the number, producing a shimmering texture of sound that supports, agitates, and inspires the line men."[23]

The increasing importance of the string bass, both rhythmically and melodically, is another feature of bebop that had significant results for modern jazz. The pioneers in this area were Jimmy Blanton (1881–1942) and Oscar Pettiford (1922–60). The great guitarist whom everyone aspired to emulate was Charlie Christian (1916–66), while the piano pacesetters were Earl "Bud" Powell (1924–66) and Thelonious Monk (1917–82).

Soaring to new heights of invention and imagination, the great Charlie Parker, whom Hodeir characterized as "an improviser of genius," also had roots in the basic New Orleans jazz tradition, notably his affinity with Armstrong. Like the latter, he favored and adopted the classic five-man group, with saxophone and trumpet plus rhythm section. Often called by his nicknames "Yardbird" or "Bird," he was a unique character, unpredictable, frequently surprising in his unprecedented innovations. Hodeir credits Parker with being "the first to bring off the feat of introducing into jazz a certain melodic discontinuity that yet avoids incoherence."[24] Parker's incomparable forte was improvising on familiar tunes such as Gershwin's "Embraceable You" and "Lady Be Good," which always resulted in a highly personal expression. But there are also his typical masterpieces such as "Parker's Mood," "Ornithology," and "Scrapple from the Apple."

Pianist-composer and leader Thelonious Monk transformed eccentricity into an artistic component that is both immensely original and intensely communicative. Besides performing with the most prestigious combos, he formed his own groups (a quartet in the 1940s, a quintet in the 1950s), with which he recorded many of his own masterpieces such as "Misterioso," "Evidence," and "Criss-Cross." Concerning "Criss-Cross," Schuller notes its "radical aspect" as "an abstraction [that] simply states and develops certain musical ideas, in much the same way that an abstract painter will work with specific nonobjective patterns."[25] Martin Williams praises Monk's version of "Smoke Gets in Your Eyes" (with the quintet, 1954), as "a superb example of the Monkian alchemy. . . ."[26]

Among many other outstanding black pianist-composers were Thomas "Fats" Waller (1904–43) and Art Tatum (1910–56). The former, raised in Harlem, began his professional career as a theater organist. He was the first jazz musician to master both the pipe organ and the Hammond organ, which he effectively adapted to a uniquely personal jazz style. He also had great success as a singer and wrote many song hits such as "Ain't Misbehavin' " and "Honeysuckle Rose."

Tatum, almost totally blind, developed a distinctive style that blended European classical influences with the Afro-American heritage. He could take a popular song such as "Too Marvelous for Words" and make it into a miniature masterpiece of jazz.

Just as bebop was a reaction against big-band swing, so the next development was a reaction against the frenetic pace of bebop. A cooling-off period was evidently due—and the key word of the new order was in fact *cool*. Many of its leading exponents, such as Gil Evans and Gerry Mulligan, were white, but they worked in close cooperation with such black musicians as Miles Davis, Max Roach, and John Lewis. What several of them had in common was some degree of classical training.

The collaboration of Miles Davis and Gil Evans in "Miles Ahead" (1957) marked a significant development in the use of a large orchestra (twenty players) to expand the scope of the cool. The instrumentation consisted of solo flügelhorn, five trumpets, four trombones, two French horns, tuba, alto sax, bass clarinet, flute, string bass, and drums. Concerning the creative results, English critic Max Harrison wrote: "In elaboration and richness of resource they surpass anything previously attempted in big-band jazz and constitute the only wholly original departure in the field outside Ellington's work."

John Lewis (b. 1920) is a prototype of the classically trained and oriented composer in jazz. Also active as pianist and arranger, Lewis's main impact was as founder and leader of the Modern Jazz Quartet (1952–75), which performed many of his compositions blending classical forms with a distinctly personal style of jazz. Miles Davis (b. 1926), from St. Louis, was sent to New York to study music at the Juilliard School. But he soon discovered Fifty-second Street, where jazz combos abounded, and quickly decided that it was more satisfying to learn from jazz musicians than to study formally at Juilliard. After playing with Charlie Parker, he formed his own nine-piece band in 1948, with which he made a set of recordings in 1949–50 that would later be known as *Birth of the Cool*.

In the mid-1950s the "cool" movement was challenged by a new trend that came to be called "hard bop" or "funky." This involved a quasi-primitive emotional drive, with strong injections of hot gospel and rhythm-and-blues styles. The pianist-composer-arranger Horace Silver, first with tenor saxophonist Stan Getz, later with bandleader and drummer Art Blakey— called by Nat Hentoff "the most emotionally unbridled drummer in jazz"—set the pace for the funky trend in 1955, relying heavily on blues riffs. Blakey's Jazz Messengers and the band led by the brothers Nat and Julian "Cannonball" Adderley were probably the most representative bands of the funky movement. This involved exploiting the melodic and rhythmic complexities of bop while reverting to a more traditional harmonic framework. Several musicians associated with hard bop, notably tenor saxophonists John Coltrane and Sonny Rollins, were to emerge as influential figures of the next decade.

This was a period of experimental innovation, and among the white jazzmen who had an important role was the blind pianist, composer, and bandleader "Lennie" (Leonard Joseph) Tristano (1919–78). He was active in Chicago with a progressive group that included alto saxophonist Lee Konitz (b. 1927), and in 1949–50 they made some recordings that broke new ground and "offered the most advanced harmonic and contrapuntal sounds employed in jazz to that date." (Examples are "Crosscurrents" and "Tautology.") Soon afterward (April 1952), Konitz joined the Charles Mingus ensemble in making recordings whose titles symbolize the esoteric trend, while moving "in the direction of decreased redundancy and increased complexity."

Charles Mingus (1922–79) and Ornette Coleman (b. 1930) were among the most progressive jazzmen on the scene at this time. The former was raised in the black suburb of Los Angeles called Watts and was early exposed to blues and gospel singing. Having decided to make the string bass his major instrument, he soon developed a remarkable virtuosity and versatility. After participating in both the bop and funky phases with great effect, Mingus in the 1950s established in New York City a jazz workshop to experiment with compositional techniques. His aim was to avoid using a musical score while maintaining a formal framework for each composition.

His solution was to work out the lines of the composition mentally and then play the framework on the piano for his musicians to assimilate. In this way he could project his own creative individuality while allowing a maximum of individual freedom to the musicians. His works based on collective improvisation have been characterized as achieving "order on the brink of chaos." A major work is *Meditations of Integration* (1964), of nearly thirty minutes' duration, which passes from melancholy lyricism to wild cacophony, held together by expressive dialogues and strongly defined rhythms. And, in another mood, who but Mingus could have invented a title such as "All the Things You Could Be by Now if Sigmund Freud's Wife Was Your Mother"!

Ornette Coleman was born in Texas, lived for a while in New Orleans, then studied theory and composition while working as an elevator operator in Los Angeles. In the summer of 1959 the sponsorship of a recording company enabled him to study at the short-lived Lenox School of Jazz in Massachusetts. He then settled in New York City, where he and his friend Don Cherry (a trumpet player), with bassist Charlie Haden and drummer Billy Higgins, formed a quartet that appeared at the Five Spot Cage—with results that were explosively controversial.

While it cannot be categorically stated that this marked the beginning of "free jazz," it was certainly a breakthrough in that direction. An album by the Coleman quartet issued at this time was prophetic as *The Shape of Jazz to Come* (1959), and it was followed by the also indicative *Change of the Century* (1959). As a further irritant to the traditionalists, Coleman for a while used a plastic saxophone, and Cherry played a pocket trumpet.

Such irritants amid apparent chaos evidently obscured the fact that "the division into three four-bar periods—the groundwork of the blues form—is observed by Coleman to a far greater extent than was usual in post-bebop jazz improvisation."[27] Nevertheless, Coleman was bent on a radical departure from the harmonic underpinning of jazz improvisation, as emphasized by the title of his next recording, *Free Jazz* (1960).

Semantics aside, Coleman was certainly not the only begetter of free jazz. This began with the undermining of tonality and functional harmony, which had hitherto served as the foundation for jazz improvisation based on chord changes. An important step in this direction was the emphasis on *modality* rather than *tonality*. As expressed by Miles Davis: "There will be fewer chords but infinite possibilities as to what to do with them."[28] The emphasis would be on melodic rather than harmonic variation. Davis and John Coltrane (1926–67) were pioneers in this development.

In 1959 Coltrane (saxophone) formed his own quartet, with which he recorded an album appropriately titled *Giant Steps*. A year later, with *My Favorite Things*, he expanded the modal concept in the improvisations. Then, in a recording of "India" Coltrane, joined by Eric Dolphy on alto sax, used the theme merely to establish "the emotional mood, without providing a rhythmic, harmonic or formal foundation."[29] This elicited a critical reaction that spoke of "anarchy" and "anti-jazz"—an infallible sign of effective innovation.

Coltrane, with his first large-scale composition, *A Love Supreme* (1964)—a suite in four movements—emerged not only as a technical innovator but also a spiritual leader, the acknowledged guru of what LeRoi Jones called "Now Black Music." Thereafter, until his untimely death, Coltrane produced seven albums, beginning with *Ascension* and ending with *Expression*.

Cecil Taylor (b. 1933) might be called the John Lewis of free jazz, insofar as he was trained in classical music, felt strongly attracted toward European composers, and aspired to combine classical forms with jazz idioms. As pianist, arranger, and composer, he found his own way of fusing contemporary art music with innovative jazz creations. His occasional use of tone clusters and excursions into atonality, along with structural complexity, identified him with the avant-garde wing of the new jazz, and he stated that his aim was to create a kind of music with "improvisation, content, and shape becoming one."[30]

Yet Taylor's innovations were not entirely divorced from the New Orleans tradition. In spite of his conservatory training, he was not bound to sight-reading from a definitive score. He told an interviewer: "I had found out that you get more from the musicians if you teach them the tunes by ear, if they have to listen for changes instead of reading them off the page, which again has something to do with the whole jazz tradition, with how the cats in New Orleans at the turn of the century made their tunes."[31]

At this point we must risk a historical hiatus in order to look at the role of women in jazz. Hitherto their fame has rested largely on their singing and piano playing. Mildred Bailey (1907–51) is tagged as "the first female to sing with a band" and "the first white female to be completely accepted in jazz circles." The others who became famous were all black, including Ella Fitzgerald (b. 1918), who at age sixteen began to sing with Chick Webb's band. At his death in 1939 she took over the band for a short period. Her first big hit was with "A-Tisket, A-Tasket," recorded in 1938. Eventually she developed a large and varied repertory that included "high-class" popular songs such as those by Gershwin, Cole Porter, and Harold Arlen. With a dynamic personality, she attracted large audiences everywhere and was hailed as "the public's singer."

Billie Holiday (1915–59), who experienced both fame and personal tragedy, began as a nightclub singer in New York and immediately displayed a highly individual style. It has been said that "her distortions of pitch are wedded, welded rather, to her manipulations of the beat," and her "incessant modifications of the pulse are the most expressive devices in her art."[32] Typical numbers are "He's Funny That Way" and "All of Me," both recorded with strong support from saxophonist Lester Young.

Sarah Vaughan (b. 1924), both singer and pianist, launched her brilliant career performing with Earl Hines's orchestra in 1943. She had wide versatility, and in the 1950s she recorded both for a large studio orchestra in Hollywood and with a trumpet and piano duo in New York. The songs were, respectively, "Dancing in the Dark" and "Ain't No Use." She was highly successful, from Europe to Latin America, and was dubbed "the Divine Sarah."

What is less known is the role of women in jazz bands, playing such instruments as trumpet, saxophone, string bass, vibes, and so on. Often they formed all-female groups such as the International Sweethearts of Rhythm, a big band active in the 1940s, featuring saxophonist Vi Burnside. The Hip Chicks included Margie Hyams on vibes and Marion Gange on guitar. Hyams also played with Woody Herman's band. Other women who played with mostly male bands were saxophonist L'Ana Webster Hyams, trumpet player and singer Valaida Snow, bassist June Rotenberg, and pianists Beryl Booker and Terry Pollard. As Rotenberg said, "My greatest concern . . . was not to be playing with women only—but just to be playing." And she added, "Why should there be a distinction made to begin with?"[33]

Finally, we come to a very famous jazz pianist and composer, Mary Lou Williams (1910–81), who from 1920 to 1942 was associated with Andy Kirk's band, Clouds of Joy, as performer and arranger. She is credited with having composed over 300 pieces, including an orchestral score, the *Zodiac Suite*, performed by the New York Philharmonic in 1946. Her popular pieces include "Roll 'Em," "Camel Hop," "Cloudy," "Froggy Bottom," and "What's Your Story Morning Glory." In a more serious vein is "Mary Lou's Mass," a jazz composition first performed at Saint Patrick's Cathedral of New York in 1975.

Turning to a later generation and a whole new scene characterized by exoticism in scope and overdubbing in technique, we find pianist-composer-conductor Carla Bley (b. 1938) assuming a prominent role. Born in Oakland, California, she went to New York City as a nightclub pianist and in 1964 formed the Jazz Composer's Orchestra with Mike Mantel as coleader. But it was in the 1970s that she achieved wide acclaim with *Escalator over the Hill* (1971), a three-record set described as an "opera," with text by poet Paul Haines. Labeled "A Chronotransduction," it relied greatly on overdubbing.[34]

This was followed by *Tropic Appetites* (1974), also with words by Haines, which reached out toward the ambience of the Far East. It calls for eight performers, who play twenty-one instruments plus miscellaneous percussion. Bley herself plays piano, electric piano, clarinet, organ, marimba, celeste, recorders, and percussion.[35] All this, of course, is achieved by synthesizing techniques, as jazz gets into electronics. Robert Palmer described the composition as "kaleidoscopic, at times sinuously modal, at others convoluted and atonal. Brass bands collide with scaled-down chamber orchestras and tribal music invades the ballroom of a grand hotel."[36] Eclecticism is the stamp of such compositions, repudiating the separation of styles and genres.

The trend toward eclecticism, also characterized as the "New Synthesis" of the 1970s, had its forerunners in such innovative compositions as George Russell's "Jazz in the Space Age" (1960), and before that the vogue for Afro-Cuban music launched by Gillespie with cult-drummer Chano Pozo, among others, and the increasing interest in African rhythms and modal configurations of the Far East.

Max Harrison remarks that jazz was no longer merely entertainment but had assimilated all the compositional forms of world music, for "the abandonment of repeating chord sequences as a basis for improvisation left jazz open to a variety of alliances with other music."[37] Moreover, referring to Miles Davis's extraordinary concoction titled "Bitches' Brew" (1969) as a forerunner of this trend, he writes: "This music, sometimes called ELECTRIC JAZZ, showed that it was possible to use some rock procedures in a more sensitive, complex and more consistently inventive way, although this in itself minimized the rock and maximized the jazz character of the result."[38]

As we have observed throughout this chapter, jazz has been largely assimilative and eclectic in its various permutations and phases. Moreover, its impact has been consistently international, in both popular and classical composition, so that by the 1980s we definitely discern its global character on a vastly impressive scale. Musicians of northern Europe have set the pace for large-scale, inventive, and progressive jazz composition and performance, and other nations are forging ahead. Perhaps the most symbolic title is that of Pedro Iturralde's flamenco-flavored opus "Jazz Meets the World."

Notes

1. See Robert S. Gold, *A Jazz Lexicon*, pp. 162–65.
2. William J. Schafer, *Brass Bands and New Orleans Jazz*, including bibliography, discography, and musical examples.
3. Alan Lomax, *Mister Jelly Roll*, p. 126.
4. *Billboard*, Sept. 1, 1916; quoted in H. O. Brunn, *The Story of the Original Dixieland Jazz Band*, p. 44.
5. Advertisement quoted in Brunn, *The Story of the Original Dixieland Jazz Band*, p. 51.
6. Martin Williams, *Jazz Masters of New Orleans*, p. 21.
7. Gunther Schuller, *Early Jazz*, pp. 179–80.
8. Lomax, *Mister Jelly Roll*, p. 66.

9. Schuller, *Early Jazz,* p. 148.

10. Ibid., p. 149. See also James Dapogny, ed., *Ferdinand "Jelly Roll" Morton: The Collected Piano Music,* for comprehensive data on Morton's compositional principles and performance practices.

11. George Avakian, "Bix Beiderbecke," in *The Art of Jazz,* ed. Martin Williams, pp. 60–61. See also Avakian, liner notes to *Chicago Style Jazz,* Columbia CL 632.

12. André Hodeir, *Jazz,* pp. 57–58.

13. Schuller, *Early Jazz,* p. 103.

14. Ibid., p. 115.

15. Hodeir, *Jazz,* p. 103.

16. Martin Williams, liner notes to *Count Basie in Kansas City; Bennie Moten's Great Band of 1930–1932,* RCA Victor Vintage LPV-514. The recording is included in *The Smithsonian Collection of Classic Jazz,* ed. Martin Williams (Washington, D.C.: Smithsonian Institution, 1973).

17. Nat Shapiro and Nat Hentoff, eds., *Hear Me Talkin' to Ya,* p. 231.

18. Schuller, *Early Jazz,* p. 326.

19. Vic Bellerby, "Duke Ellington," in *The Art of Jazz,* ed. Williams, p. 147.

20. *Black, Brown, and Beige* was recorded with Mahalia Jackson as vocalist in 1958. See Columbia Special Products (CSP) JCS-8015.

21. Bellerby, "Duke Ellington," p. 158.

22. See Ross Russell, *Jazz Style in Kansas City and the Southwest,* especially chapters 14, 15, and 20.

23. Ross Russell, "Bebop," in *The Art of Jazz,* ed. Williams, p. 190.

24. Hodeir, *Jazz,* pp. 104–5.

25. Gunther Schuller, "Thelonious Monk," in *Jazz Panorama,* ed. Martin Williams, p. 220; quoted in *The Smithsonian Collection of Classical Jazz,* ed. Williams, pp. 36–37.

26. Martin Williams, liner notes to *The Golden Monk, Thelonious Monk,* Prestige 7363; quoted in *The Smithsonian Collection of Classic Jazz,* ed. Williams, p. 38.

27. Ekkehard Jost, *Free Jazz,* p. 47.

28. As quoted in Jack Chambers, *Milestones I,* p. 280.

29. Jost, *Free Jazz,* p. 28.

30. A. B. Spellman, *Black Music: Four Lives,* p. 38.

31. Ibid., pp. 70–71.

32. Glenn Coulter, "Billie Holiday," in *The Art of Jazz,* ed. Williams, p. 162.

33. Art Napoleon, liner notes to *Women in Jazz: All Women Groups,* Stash ST-111.

34. *Escalator over the Hill,* Jazz Composers of America (JCOA) 3LP EOTH.

35. *Tropic Appetites,* Watt Works (BMI) WATT/1.

36. Robert Palmer, "Musicians in Pursuit of Exotic Jazz," *New York Times,* Oct. 13, 1974, sec. 2, p. 36.

37. Max Harrison, "Jazz: The 1970s—New Synthesis," *New Grove Dictionary of Music and Musicians* 9:577.

38. Ibid.

Chapter 29

The Pit and the Proscenium

A Broadway musical needs an orchestra pit capable
of an occasional brassy sassiness [and] the specific
scenic conventions that the proscenium offers.
—Clive Barnes, *New York Times,* June 1976

After a brief postwar depression, by 1924 the American economy was
booming. Prosperity and plenty were "just around the corner," within
reach of anyone smart enough to cut corners. "Like the old legend of the
Fountain of Youth, a new belief arose that we had discovered the way to
eternal prosperity. If that were so, why wait until one had saved the money
for anything one wanted?"[1] Take the cash and let the credit go: *now* is the
time to live it up. The symbolic name of Broadway epitomized the prevailing climate of euphoria and illusion: the enticing escapism of operetta, the
swashbuckling romance or entertaining nonsense of comic opera, the fun
and games of musical comedy, the lavish display of spectacular revues.

The established revues simply adjusted the dates on their billboards to
catch up with the calendar: *Artists and Models of 1924,* Earl Carroll's *Vanities of 1924,* George White's *Scandals of 1924, Grand Street Follies of 1924,
Ziegfeld Follies of 1924.* Some shows were on the way out, others were coming up. The Shuberts's *Passing Show of 1924* was the last of that twelve-year
cycle, while Flo Ziegfeld's *Follies* were sporadic after the 1924–25 season,
and Irving Berlin's lavish *Music Box Revue* ended with its 1924 edition.
But Earl Carroll's *Vanities*—a glorified girlie show—lasted until 1932, and
George White's *Scandals,* which began in 1919, survived sporadically into
the twenties.

The spectacular revues could be characterized as lavish variety shows,
including some topical humor. The *Ziegfeld Follies,* for example, featured
both the sing-song repartee of comedians Gallagher and Shean and the
topical patter of Will Rogers and his lariat. Moreover, the rise of the "little
revue," with its emphasis on satire and topical takeoffs (as contrasted with

seminude displays), gave a new and more sophisticated dimension to this type of show. For example, the *Greenwich Village Follies,* produced by John Murray Anderson from 1919 to 1928, began by evoking—and lampooning—the bohemian atmosphere of the Village, with numbers such as "I'm the Hostess of a Bum Cabaret," and made a bow to comic-strip culture with "The Krazy Kat's Ball." But eventually it yielded to the lures of the flesh, pursuing delusions of grandeur at the fashionable Winter Garden and other uptown theaters. With hindsight, the 1924 edition becomes nostalgically memorable by its presentation of five Cole Porter songs, including "I'm in Love Again," as sung by the popular Dolly Sisters.

The *Grand Street Follies,* another Greenwich Village enterprise, launched in 1922, was more faithful to the format of an "intimate" revue (although it did move uptown to the Booth Theatre for its last two shows). Literate, sophisticated, witty, amusing, satirical, and topical, its first edition was self-characterized as a "low-brow show for high-grade morons."[2] It was also the first revue to be controlled largely by women, for it was directed by Agnes Morgan (who also wrote the book and lyrics), and much of the music was by Lily Hyland. Its chief targets of satire were exponents of highbrow culture, such as tragedians, classical ballet dancers, opera singers, artistic recitalists, serious drama (Ibsen, Shaw), the Russian Art Theater (then much in vogue), and literary coteries, notably that of the highly touted "round table" luncheons at the Algonquin Hotel in midtown Manhattan. Popular culture was not immune to feminine satire, as musical comedies and personalities of the entertainment world were lampooned—and on occasion harpooned.

By 1929 the *Grand Street Follies* had run its course; but it had established a genre—the intimate revue—that was to flourish during the Depression, not only because it was inexpensive to produce but also because it provided a forum for political positions and social causes that came to the fore during that period of agitation and propaganda. But before going on to discuss the politically motivated theater of the 1930s, let us see how musical comedy was faring on the eve of the Great Depression, triggered by the financial crash of 1929.

We begin with the up-and-coming team of George Gershwin and his brother Ira (writer of the lyrics), for whom 1924 was a turning point, with their first big hit, *Lady, Be Good!* This included immediately appealing and enduring numbers such as "Fascinating Rhythm," "So Am I," "Oh, Lady, Be Good," and the very topical "I'd Rather Charleston." The youthful brother-and-sister dancing and singing team of Fred and Adele Astaire were the stars of the show, which also had a successful run in London.

Some decades later it became fashionable to put down these early musical comedies because of their inane plots and frivolous character. But after all, they were meant to be comedies, with music and dancing and occasional dialogue interspersed with jokes. Who needs plausible characters or dramatic consistency in order to be entertained? Personally, I believe that the classical period of American musical comedy was from about 1915 to 1934—from Jerome Kern's *Very Good Eddie* to Cole Porter's *Anything Goes.* Wacky, zany, silly—whatever you like—but musically and choreographically delightful. I had the good fortune of catching up with the revival of *Very Good Eddie,* which after its summer presentation by the Goodspeed Opera House in East Haddam, Connecticut, became a hit of the New York season in 1975–76. This was but one of the many revivals presented by the Goodspeed Opera House that have converted the past into a present joy.

From 1920 to 1924 Gershwin wrote musical numbers for George White's *Scandals,* producing about thirty-five songs, many with lyrics by G. B. "Buddy" De Sylva. One of the most delightful and enduring was "I'll Build a Stairway to Paradise," written for the *Scandals of 1922.* The orchestra on that occasion was led by Paul Whiteman, and this marked the beginning of an association with Gershwin that was to have very important results. Probably the best known of Gershwin's songs for the *Scandals* is "Somebody Loves Me" (1924), with lyrics by De Sylva and Arthur Francis.

In 1925 Gershwin had another theatrical success with *Tip-Toes,* which again featured his favorite piano duo, Phil Oman and Victor Arden, in the pit. The songs included "These Charming People" (trio), "Looking for a Boy," "That Certain Feeling," and the lively and very popular ensemble "Sweet and Low-Down"—accompanied by an array of kazoos!

With their next two shows, *Oh, Kay!* (November 8, 1926) and *Funny Face* (November 22, 1927), the Gershwins went well over the 200 mark in number of performances (256 and 244, respectively), which in those days meant a hit. *Oh, Kay!* starring Gertrude Lawrence, included such memorable numbers as "Someone to Watch Over Me," "Clap Yo' Hands," and "Fidgety Feet." *Funny Face* featured Fred and Adele Astaire, for whom Ira wrote the words of the colloquial patter song "The Babbitt and the Bromide." The score included one of Gershwin's best-loved songs, " 'S Wonderful," as well as "My One and Only" and "He Loves and She Loves."

The year 1927 also brought a fiasco for the Gershwins, when *Strike Up the Band* flopped in its Philadelphia tryouts. But that is a story that had better wait for the "political" phase of their productions that surfaced in the 1930s.

Meanwhile, to get a cross section of developments in the 1920s, let us turn to an immensely successful operetta that marked a turning point in the American musical theater. In an earlier chapter ("On with the Show"), it was remarked that operetta "never became truly Americanized." But now we are dealing with an extraordinary exception: the operetta *Rose-Marie* (1924), by the Czech-American composer Rudolf Friml (1879–1972), who from 1906 made his home in the United States.

The setting of *Rose-Marie* is actually in the Canadian Rockies, and the Canadian Mounted Police have an important role in the plot, which concerns the triumph of virtue over villainy, with an Indian theme thrown in for good measure. The latter involves a duet of lovers and an "Indian Love Call," a big and enduring hit. The lyrics are by Otto Harbach and Oscar Hammerstein II.

It is not so much the plot that concerns us as the quality of the music, which presents several dramatic styles in the context of a musical show, while generally breaking away from the ubiquitous clichés of the Viennese tradition. One critic wrote: "There is drama and melodrama, musical comedy, grand opera, and opéra-comique [with] the most entrancing music it has long been our privilege to hear."[3] Was this not a recipe for—or at least an anticipation of—the kind of American show that would eventually be known as a musical?

Rose-Marie had an opening run of 557 performances in New York—which was extraordinary for that time. Soon it had four companies touring on the road, and in 1927 it returned to Broadway for another long run. It was financially "the biggest grosser of the decade. In fact, nothing surpassed its multimillion dollar take until *Oklahoma!*, over twenty years later."[4]

Three years after *Rose-Marie* came Jerome Kern's *Show Boat*, based on the popular novel by Edna Ferber, with the book and lyrics by Oscar Hammerstein II. Produced at the Ziegfeld Theater on December 27, 1927, it had an initial run of 572 performances and received superlative praise from many sources. Thereafter it was repeatedly revived on stage and made into several motion-picture versions. On April 8, 1954, it had its operatic accolade with a performance by the New York City Opera. Its status and durability as a classic of the American musical theater cannot be questioned.

What can be questioned are its "artistic entity, dramatic truth, authentic characterizations [and] logical story line"—to quote a typical panegyric.[5] Even Lehman Engel, who admits that it marked a "milestone" in the American musical theater, has nothing good to say about the libretto: "The characters are two-dimensional, the proportions are outrageous, the plot development is predictable and corny, and the ending is unbearably sweet." Furthermore, "The element of coincidence in the book is not only silly but sloppy, for the action could have been motivated without resorting to nonsense."[6]

All of this is true enough; but it misses the whole point, which is that—granting the effective quality of the tunes and lyrics—*Show Boat* nevertheless owes its immense popularity precisely to its make-believe characters, its corny and predictable plot, its very bearable sentimentality, and its silly use of coincidence.

Actually, it all began with Ferber's best-selling novel, of which a critic remarked, "From beginning to end her story reeks with melodrama far less convincing than the worst ever acted on a showboat stage."[7] It may be objected that we are dealing with a *musical* play, and that the music transcends the shallowness of the plot. Most of the songs are indeed above average quality, including "Why Do I Love You?" "Can't Help Lovin' Dat Man," and especially the most memorable "Ol' Man River," sung by the black baritone Jules Bledsoe.

We return now to what was still called musical comedy, although in some aspects it was shedding the insouciance of the early twenties. The added ingredient was political and social satire, as in the Gershwins' previously mentioned *Strike Up the Band*. Its libretto was by George S. Kaufman, a playwright with political leanings to the Left and a slashing satirical vein directed at such targets as militarism, automatic patriotism, bumbling diplomacy, big-business imperialism, and chauvinism. The show had some good, catchy tunes, notably "Strike Up the Band!" "Yankee Doodle Rhythm," and "The Man I Love."[8] But such "loaded" numbers as "Fletcher's American Cheese Society," "The Unofficial Spokesman," and "The War That Ended War," smacked more of propaganda than of entertainment. The public that opened its arms to Cap'n Andy and Magnolia in *Show Boat* was not disposed to embrace Horace J. Fletcher, wheeler-dealer mogul of the American Cheese Company.

Nevertheless, an attempt was made to make the show more palatable, and a popular writer, Morris Ryskind, was called to perform the operation.

In its much-revised form *Strike Up the Band* opened on Broadway (January 14, 1930) and had a moderate run of 191 performances. While targets of satire remained, more comedians were thrown into the plot, new songs were added, and the public was entertained, if not enchanted.

Hence the Gershwins were encouraged to pursue the political-satirical genre, resulting in one big success, *Of Thee I Sing* (1931), and a semifailure, *Let 'Em Eat Cake* (1933), both with books by Kaufman and Ryskind and lyrics by Ira Gershwin. The first show was a spoof of the big American election circus, and it demonstrated that good-humored political satire could prove popular when blended with such catchy songs as "Love Is Sweeping the Country," "Of Thee I Sing," and "Wintergreen for President." But the poor response to *Let 'Em Eat Cake,* with its bitter satire and repetitious propaganda that quickly became boring, simply proves that sometimes the public knows best.

Still in the political vein, the unsinkable Kaufman joined forces with Moss Hart to concoct a libretto for *I'd Rather Be Right* (1937), with music by Richard Rodgers, who already had a long list of successes to his credit. These included *Dearest Enemy* (1925), *A Connecticut Yankee* (1927), and *Present Arms* (1928). Lured by the political vogue of the 1930s, Kaufman based his new comedy on Franklin D. Roosevelt's New Deal and set his plot in the nation's capital. (The role of Roosevelt was taken by George M. Cohan.) The show had a moderate run of 290 performances; but the absence of revivals suggests that the public was unwilling to be continually entertained with such topical songs as "A Homogeneous Cabinet" or "We're Going to Balance the Budget"—the latter surely pertaining to the never-never land of operetta.

The topical revue was also a medium for sociopolitical satire. For example, in *As Thousands Cheer* (1933), music and lyrics by Irving Berlin, an actress impersonating the Statue of Liberty sang, "We'll all be in heaven when the dollar goes to hell." The show's format was that of building scenes around newspaper headlines, and this included a banner whose social realism broke with the taboo of show business: "Unknown Negro Lynched by Frenzied Mob," with Ethel Waters singing the deeply moving "Supper Time," a meal that her husband would never share again. Waters later remarked, "I had stopped the show with a type of song never heard before in a revue."[9]

An entire musical show based on such a theme would doubtless have turned audiences away. The advantage of a revue was that it offered variety, so that the bitter pill could be taken with the sweet, the pleasant with the sour. Steering a course between these poles was a revue called *New Americana,* which featured in 1932 a number that not only became an instant hit but has remained in our popular folklore as the theme song of the Depression: "Brother, Can You Spare a Dime?" The words are by Edgar Yipsel Harburg, nicknamed "Yip," who also wrote the lyrics for such enduring songs as "It's Only a Paper Moon" (1933) and "Over the Rainbow" (1939). The writer of the tune was Jay Gorney (of Russian origin), composer of scores for many musical comedies in the 1920s and 1930s.

By far the most notable of the Depression revues with a sociopolitical content was *Pins and Needles,* which owed its phenomenal success largely to the talents of Harold Rome (b. 1908). With an upper middle-class background and an excellent education at Yale, he became an economic casualty of the Depression and turned to songwriting to augment the illusory benefits of a nonsalaried job. Obviously, he was aware of the problems of the working class and gave voice to these troubles in his topical songs. His songs attracted the attention of the head of the International Ladies Garment Workers Union, who proposed that he write the words and music for a revue that the union's members were planning to produce, combining recreation with propaganda. The cast was to consist entirely of union members, and the production would be in the Labor Stage Theatre (formerly the Princess Theater), with a seating capacity of 300.

Rome accepted the challenge, and after a year of preparation and rehearsal—these were amateurs, remember!—the show called *Pins and Needles* opened on November 27, 1937. All seats cost one dollar. It proved to be a terrific success, with an unprecedented run of over 1,000 performances. Intended primarily as social recreation for union members, it attracted all sections of the population, including those of the "carriage trade"—the privileged class—at whom much of the satire was directed. After three years at the Labor Stage it moved uptown to the larger Windsor Theater and went through several "editions" with continual changes to keep it up-to-date.

The keynote number of *Pins and Needles* was "Sing Me a Song of Social Significance," which could be taken as a theme song of the Depression, with tongue in cheek. Others were "Doin' the Reactionary," "It's Better with a Union Man," "It's Not Cricket to Picket," and "Big Union for Two," which linked unionism to wedded bliss.

Rome continued in the topical-satirical vein with *Sing Out the News* (1938), memorable mainly for the song "Franklin D. Roosevelt Jones," sung by Hazel Scott. Then came *Let Freedom Ring,* notable only as an instant flop (eight performances!). The times were changing, with the United States being drawn into World War II and pressures shifting from the Left to the Right. After the war Rome tried again with *Call Me Mister* (1946), which had a successful run. It dealt with the difficulty of adjusting to civilian life ("Little Surplus Me"), as well as with political and racial issues in numbers such as "The Senator's Songs" and "The Red Ball Express"—the latter an indictment of race prejudice affecting a former black G.I. Significantly, however, the big hit of the show was a frivolous number, "South America, Take It Away," burlesquing the current vogue for Latin-American popular songs and dances. This was a signal that people wanted, not propaganda and "social significance," but entertainment and distraction.

Meanwhile, black musicians were also on the scene, most notably with Eubie Blake and Noble Sissle, who after the triumph of *Shuffle Along* were eager to make their mark again. Their aim now was to present an elaborate show combining musical comedy with elements of the revue and extravaganza—a dazzling and expensive production with a cast of 125, including gorgeous Josephine Baker. Titled *The Chocolate Dandies,* it opened in New York on September 1, 1924, and had a mixed critical reception.

On the positive side, a reviewer for the *Tribune* wrote: "New York never has seen a colored show to compare with the rip-roaring revue . . . brought to the Colonial Theater last night. . . . There is plenty of good, clean comedy, good dancing, remarkable music and more pep in two hours than any show has brought to this town in many, many months." In his opinion, it was "far and away ahead of 'Shuffle Along.' "[10]

This opinion was shared by the critic of the *Telegraph:* "There never was a colored show like 'The Chocolate Dandies.' It is the 'Ziegfeld Follies' or 'Music Box Revue' done in brownskin. . . . There is not a dull moment in the entertainment. It is at least 50 per cent better than 'Shuffle Along.' That's high enough praise for any show."[11]

The show combined fantasy with realism, humor with sentiment, in the setting of a mythical southern town called "Banville," on the last day of the local fair and horse races. (There were actually three live horses and their jockeys simulating a track race by the device of a treadmill.)

The critics who took a negative view were obviously motivated by racial prejudice. The show was too elaborate, too pretentious, to be genuinely "Negro." One critic complained that it was "both sophisticated and conventional. . . . You feel the arresting, the civilizing hand of Julian Mitchell in the direction. Nobody seems to go out of his head. . . . There is, in a word, too much 'art' and not enough Africa."[12] How pretentious of blacks to aim at artistic achievement!

Eubie Blake was well aware of the situation. He commented that "people who went to a colored show . . . expected only fast dancing and Negroid humor, and when they got something else they put it down."[13] He was convinced that *The Chocolate Dandies* was a better show than *Shuffle Along*, with superior songs such as "Dixie," "Jassamine Lane," and "Manda."

The problem of *The Chocolate Dandies* was that it required an immense cast, lavish costumes, and elaborate sets: hence it was very costly to produce. It had only ninety-six performances in New York before undertaking a tour of sixty weeks in other cities.

While musical comedy in the pristine mold of an entertaining show with singing, dancing, and dialogue continued to proliferate, there was a growing trend toward more consistent plots, fuller characterization, and a wider range of musical styles. A trendsetter in this direction was *The Cat and the Fiddle* (1931), with book and lyrics by Otto Harbach and music by Jerome Kern, who stated that he was attempting "to explore new paths." Instead of chorus girls, comedy routines, and production numbers, there would be "a strong motivation for the music throughout."[14]

By making the leading lady an American composer of popular music, and her male counterpart a European composer of "serious" music—thus complicating their romance by a conflict of musical tastes—Harbach gave Kern the opportunity to introduce a wide range of musical styles. The situation also provided an opportunity to exploit what was then a current topic: the conflict between highbrow and lowbrow attitudes. The hit song of the show was "The Night Was Made for Love," whose melody keeps reappearing like an operatic leitmotiv.

When Kern's next musical show, *Music in the Air*, appeared in the following year, theater critic Brooks Atkinson of the *New York Times* declared that "at last the musical drama has been emancipated."[15] The "emancipation" would continue apace.

Any search for new landmarks of the American musical show must certainly focus on the innovative features of *On Your Toes* (1936), with music by Richard Rodgers, book by Lorenz Hart and George Abbott, and choreography by Balanchine—whose presence obviously indicates that something different was afoot. In fact, the entire plot is built around two ballets, one satirical, the other sinister. The central male character is a young man, with vaudeville antecedents, who aspires to a career in classical ballet. He gets his first chance when he appears as a last-minute substitute in the minor role (a Nubian slave) in the ballet *La Princesse Zenobia*, brilliantly concocted by Balanchine with tongue in cheek.

The big dramatic-choreographic breakthrough is in the last act, with the "gangster" ballet titled *Slaughter on Tenth Avenue*, in which the three principal characters are the Hoofer, the Stripper, and Big Boss. The scene is a disreputable nightclub. A triangle situation develops, as Big Boss becomes jealous of the Hoofer, who has been dancing and drinking with the Stripper. The really original twist comes when the main plot suddenly gets entangled with that of the ballet. Some gangsters, mistaking the identity of the dancer taking the part of the Hoofer (who is also the main lead in the show), appear in the nightclub with intent to murder him as a double-crosser. In the resulting gunfire the Stripper and Big Boss are killed, while the police arrive in the nick of time to save the Hoofer, who has been dancing all the time to avoid the gangster's bullets. Not only had the integration of ballet and musical comedy been achieved with great success, but also a brilliant satire on the gangster films that proliferated in the 1930s had been produced.

Meanwhile, Cole Porter (1892–1965) brought a new literary and melodic sophistication to the pristine period of American musical comedy, with a combination of wit and wackiness, of finesse and farce, and of elegance and bawdiness (he was even called "the genteel pornographer"). A Yale graduate and a man of wealth who moved in the international circles of high society, he succeeded in writing shows that became immensely popular in spite of making few concessions to the mass market. Eventually, he even made Shakespeare everybody's cup of tea, with *Kiss Me, Kate* (1948), an adaptation of *The Taming of the Shrew*.

Following *Fifty Million Frenchmen* in 1929 (which survived the stock-market crash) and the *Gay Divorce* in 1932 (notable above all for the highly detachable "Night and Day"), Porter proved even more convincingly with the show *Anything Goes* (1934) that he could infuse new life into old musical comedy formulas. True, like all Broadway shows, it was a cooperative enterprise, involving a diversity of top-notch talent. The original book, by Guy Bolton and P. G. Wodehouse, was revised by the up-and-coming team of Howard Lindsay and Russel Crouse. The settings were by Donald Oenslager, the dances by Robert Alton, the orchestration by Robert Russell Bennett. The performing stars were Ethel Merman, Bettina Hall, William Caxton, and comedian Victor Moore.

But what made everything *go* were the lyrics and tunes of Cole Porter,

Scene from the ballet *Slaughter on Tenth Avenue* in *On Your Toes* (1936). Pictured (from left to right): Tamara Geva, George Church, Ray Bolger, and Basil Galahoff. Photo courtesy of the Billy Rose Theatre Collection, The New York Public Library at Lincoln Center, Astor, Lenox and Tilden Foundations.

such as "I Get a Kick Out of You," "All through the Night," "Anything Goes," "The Gypsy in Me," and, most memorably, "You're the Top"—that rare tour de force of invention and wit applied to rhyme and simile—which is also a catalogue of the modern age in America.

The 1940s began with an innovative musical, *Pal Joey,* by Richard Rodgers and Lorenz Hart, based on stories by John O'Hara dealing with disreputable characters in Chicago's tough South Side. With no concessions to sentimentality, romantic love, or happy endings, the libretto presents an antihero named Joey, a nightclub hoofer on the make. He sees his chance for the big time when a wealthy society woman falls for him, showering gifts and luxuries, including a nightclub where he can strut as Mr. Big. This also provides an opportunity for stylistic dancing, including a ballet scene. Complications ensue when blackmailers threaten trouble, but the society dame proves to be pretty hard-boiled herself. She outwits the blackmailers and rids herself of Pal Joey, too.

Brooks Atkinson summed up the controversy raised by the show when he asked rhetorically if it was possible "to make an entertaining musical comedy out of an odious story."[16] The answer is that the show broke with the conventions of musical comedy and assumed a premise whereby *entertainment* was not necessarily synonymous with *amusement.* Taken on its own terms, it was a success as well as an innovation. Twelve years later the serious or realistic musical was an accepted fact of American show business. When *Pal Joey* was revived in 1952, it had a run of 542 performances—a record for revivals at that time. The critics were enthusiastic, the public receptive, and the awards impressive. We might say that Pal Joey was the apotheosis of an antihero in spite of himself.

The 1940s also brought the consolidation of the American musical through the collaboration of Richard Rodgers and his new lyric writer Oscar Hammerstein II, beginning with the unprecedented triumph of *Oklahoma!* Produced by the Theatre Guild in New York on March 31, 1943, it broke all previous records with a run of 2,212 performances. Based on the play *Green Grow the Lilacs* by Lynn Riggs, it combined rural Americana with believable characters and a modicum of "corn," plus elaborate but dramatically consistent ballets choreographed by Agnes de Mille.

That Hammerstein was aware of having broken new ground is attested by his remark that what he and Rodgers had done amounted "almost to a breach of implied contract with a musical-comedy audience."[17] What he had in mind is best illustrated by a remark concerning *Oklahoma!,* generally attributed to Mike Todd: "No legs, no jokes, no chance." That simply underestimated the capacity of the public to respond to attractive innovations, especially when combined with sentiment, humor, and a touch of evil, adorned with alluring lyrics and enticing tunes.

Rodgers and Hammerstein went on to establish the enduring prestige and popularity of the dramatic musical with such shows as *Carousel* (1945), *Allegro* (1947), *South Pacific* (1949), and *The King and I* (1951). We should note, however, that *Allegro,* critically acclaimed as a "stunning blending of beauty, integrity, imagination, taste and skill," and as possessing "the lyric rapture of a musical masterpiece," was not a box-office success.[18] So there is a limit to public tolerance of creative innovation. Conversely, the most conventional and tritely predictable of the Rodgers and Hammerstein musicals, *The Sound of Music* (1959), based on the story of the Trapp Family Singers, was a runaway best-seller, in the theater, in the movies, and in recordings.

Rodgers and Hammerstein were also active as theatrical producers, and one of their projects was for a show built around the life story of Annie Oakley, the sharpshooting star of Buffalo Bill's Wild West Show. Titled *Annie Get Your Gun,* with music by Irving Berlin and a book by Herbert and Dorothy Fields, the show opened on May 16, 1946, and had a run of 1,147 performances. It was far and away Berlin's greatest hit, as well as a triumph for Ethel Merman, who learns that "You Can't Get a Man with a Gun"—especially the man she wants, who happens to be the sharpshooter for Pawnee Bill's rival show. The final rousing number, "Show Business," could be regarded as a symbolic tribute to Berlin's own remarkable career (he celebrated his ninety-fifth birthday on May 11, 1983).

The 1950s opened with an immediate hit that also proved to be enduring: *Guys and Dolls,* with music and lyrics by Frank Loesser (1910–69), based on stories by Damon Runyon. This could be called "a fable of Broadway," for the would-be tough guys and small-time gamblers it depicts actually have hearts of (human) gold, and they do the right thing by the Salvation Army lass—which is to save her romance at any cost. With George S. Kaufman's staging, Michael Kid's dances, and Jo Mielziner's settings all enhancing the catchy songs by Loesser, *Guys and Dolls* fully merited the citation for its "originality and its avoidance of the usual musical comedy patterns."[19]

Loesser's versatility is demonstrated by a comparison of two later musicals: *The Most Happy Fella* (1956) and *How to Succeed in Business without Really Trying* (1961). The former is based on a play by dramatist Sidney Howard, *They Knew What They Wanted,* about an aging winegrower in

California who has persuaded, by mail, a young waitress from San Francisco to marry him. He had deceived her by sending a photograph, not of himself, but of his handsome young foreman, and his deception leads to foreseeable consequences, as the young bride soon finds herself with child by the younger man. A violent outcome threatens but is averted when the older man decides to forgive if not to forget. So, with his contrite wife and bastard child, the reconciled winegrower becomes a "Most Happy Fella."

As viewed by drama critic Brooks Atkinson of the *New York Times,* Loesser "has told everything of vital importance in terms of dramatic music." Moreover: "His music drama . . . goes so much deeper into the souls of its leading characters than most Broadway shows and it has such an abundant and virtuoso score . . . that it has to be taken on the level of theater."[20] If we are actually dealing with a "music drama," then Atkinson's description comes very close to the concept of opera, and at least one authority (Lehman Engel) has placed *The Most Happy Fella* in a category that he calls the "Broadway Opera."[21]

With *How to Succeed in Business without Really Trying,* Loesser and his writers undertook the challenging task of putting across a farcical satire of American big business while adhering to the principle of a fully integrated musical show. As the librettist, Abe Burrows, remarked: "We promised ourselves that every song would make a point and that no one would stop dead, center stage, in order to sing a song that had no purpose in the story."

While they were about it, they might have written a number à la Gilbert and Sullivan: "Every Little Song Must Have a Purpose." Instead, they produced a hilariously funny and enormously successful musical commentary on American manners, morals, and money that had an initial run of 1,417 performances and thereafter promised to go on forever without really trying too hard.

Leonard Bernstein made his mark on the Broadway scene with *On the Town* (1944), *Wonderful Town* (1953), *Candide* (1956), and, most impressively, *West Side Story* (1957). This last is a resetting of the tragedy of Romeo and Juliet in a twentieth-century context of gang warfare and ethnic animosity in upper Manhattan. The idea was suggested by Jerome Robbins, who also created the choreography that has such a vital part in the action. Bernstein's score is dynamic, eclectic, resourceful, by turns lyrical and dramatic, and tender and menacing.

The team of Frederick Loewe as composer and Alan Jay Lerner as lyricist hit the all-time jackpot with *My Fair Lady* (1956), based on George Bernard Shaw's *Pygmalion,* having an unprecedented first run of 2,717 performances. The revivals thereafter never ceased, both on stage and on the screen. Its combination of humor, satire, and elegance, with ever-memorable songs such as "I Could Have Danced All Night" and "I've Grown Accustomed to Her Face," have proved to be irresistible.

By the 1960s popular musical shows were truly big business. For example, Jerry Herman's *Hello, Dolly!* (1964) broke the record with 2,844 performances, while Jerry Bock's *Fiddler on the Roof* (1964) set a new high with a first run of 3,242. A year later, Mitch Leigh's *Man of La Mancha* did very well with its initial run of 2,328. There was also the enormous diffusion of musicals through the mass media of motion pictures and television.

Of the new generation, Stephen Sondheim (b. 1939) soon made an impression with his versatility and inventiveness. He went into show business after graduating from Williams College and studying composition with Milton Babbitt. His first big success was with *A Funny Thing Happened on the Way to the Forum* (Alvin Theatre, May 8, 1962), which proved to be both funny and profitable, with Zero Mostel as the star comedian. There followed *Anyone Can Whistle* (1964), *Do I Hear a Waltz* (1965), *Company* (1970), and his first "serious" (but enchanting) masterpiece, *A Little Night Music* (February 25, 1973), based on Ingmar Bergman's film *Smiles of a Summer Night.* Its run of 600 performances was modest, but touring companies followed, both in the United States and abroad. The critical response was enthusiastic.

Sondheim broke new ground with *Pacific Overtures* (January 11, 1976), libretto by John Weldman. It deals with Commodore Perry's opening of Japan to the Western world—but from a Japanese point of view. The entire cast was Asian, and only oriental instruments were used. But "the show made no concession to the tired businessman, so its run was modest and its profits nil."[22]

The 1970s also saw a resurgence of musical shows by blacks, beginning with *The Wiz* (January 1975), which proved to be a smash hit. Based on the children's book by Frank L. Baum, *The Wizard of Oz,* it was no child's play but rather a weird extravaganza that rocked through outer space with Charlie Smalls's dynamic score and lots of vivacious dancing.

The all-black version of *Guys and Dolls* opened at the Broadway Theater on July 21, 1976, and was directed by Billy Wilson, who also did the highly effective choreography. A drastic switch in ethnic identity was definitely visible. As Wilson said: "It was like taking chicken soup and making it a little more gumbo"—not so "little," either! He was also bent on substituting Afro-American expressions for the Jewish idioms that appeared in the original version by Loesser.

With *Ain't Misbehavin'* (May 9, 1978), Fats Waller reappeared in spirit thirty-five years after his death, stamping his vivid personality on the show. This was built around a medley of favorite songs that he had either written or made his own with unique performances. Two of the songs, "I Can't Give You Anything but Love" and "Sunny Side of the Street," were previously accredited to Jimmy McHugh, to whom Fats had sold the rights when he needed money.

The fourth black hit of the decade was *Eubie!* (1978), based mainly on songs that Blake and Sissle had written for their shows and vaudeville acts. Eubie, at ninety-five, was only a spectator; but he could listen to the theme song, "Everybody's Just Wild about Eubie!" with a zest that he never lost.

On April 29, 1968, a revolutionary event took place at the Biltmore Theater in midtown Manhattan. This was the first Broadway production of *Hair* ("The American Tribal Love-Rock Musical"), with music by Galt MacDermot, book and lyrics by Gerome Ragni and James Rado. Its impact was explosive and marked a new era for American musicals. Oddly enough, it was presented at the Public Theater of the New York Shakespeare Festival and was produced by Joseph Papp. The Broadway version, revised and refurbished, would soon be heard around the world.

Hair was an outburst of the counterculture, a repudiation of the status quo in the context of Vietnam, with its ritual burning of draft cards. All conventional theatrics and traditional staging were discarded, as a well-planned chaos made direct personal contact with the audience. The less tight the plot, the more meaningful the message. This was most effectively conveyed by such memorable songs as "Aquarius," "I Got Life," and "Good Morning, Starshine."

The success of *Hair* opened the way for other rock musicals, including an import from England, *Jesus Christ Superstar,* presented at the Mark Hellinger in Manhattan on October 12, 1971. (The first English production was in London on August 9, 1972.) The authors were Tim Rice for the lyrics and Andrew Lloyd Webber for the music. It has been called a "rock opera," and it does have a true dramatic quality. This does not preclude colloquial speech, as in a dialogue between the Apostles and Jesus, "What's the Buzz?" At least one critic called the rock opera "a triumph" and its songs "marvelous." It was translated into many languages, presented in concert performances, and the recording was a best-seller.

For a drastic contrast we have the boisterous bravado and antiestablishment stance of the rock-and-roll scene of the 1950s as nostalgically depicted in *Grease,* which opened in New York's Eden Theater on February 14, 1972. The libretto and the lyrics were the joint work of two theater men, Jim Jacobs and Warren Casey, who had grown up during the rock-and-roll craze. The animators of the main action are two freewheeling high-school groups, the Burger Palace Boys and the Pink Ladies. They are tough, bad-mouthed, promiscuous—and partial to Chuck Berry's guitar style. Typical songs are "Greased Lightnin'," "Born to Hand-Jive," and "Rock 'n' Roll Party Queen." Its popularity has not ceased to ride the nostalgia circuit.

Originality and defiance of tradition, rather than any popular vogue, motivated the presentation of *A Chorus Line,* first shown at Joseph Papp's Public Theater on April 15, 1975. It made such an impression that on July 25 it switched to the Broadway circuit at the Shubert Theatre, where it has enjoyed an immensely long run into the 1980s. With lyrics by Edward Kleban, music by Marvin Hamlisch, choreography by Michael Bennett, and an utterly unconventional stage design by Robin Wagner, the show abandons the traditional libretto in favor of a highly original idea.

The core of the action consists of a director whose job it is to select a chorus of eight dancers from seventeen applicants; so we witness the ordeal of tryouts, with successes and failures. Probing interviews by the director reveal personal problems and hang-ups, which constitute the serious side of the show. An original touch is that the director remains unseen. Between the visual display of dancing and the psychological revelations of the probing, undisturbed by the conventional character of the songs and music, audiences are both titillated and fascinated.

The last-mentioned effects are, of course, what makes musical comedy perennially attractive, whether in the dancing or the dialogue, the tapping or the singing. Very little has changed since the beginning of the 1980s. Repetitions of the past are still in vogue, while performers give a new twist to this or that. For example, when *On Your Toes* became an "Award-Winning Musical Hit" in 1983, it was hailed as "a musical smash" largely because of the "spectacular dancing" by the ballerina Galina Panova, who (in the words of Gene Shalit) "dances up a storm."

Much the same happened with "The New Gershwin Musical" titled *My One and Only* (after the song that he wrote for *Funny Face*), featuring the dancing duo of Twiggy and Tommy Tune at the St. James Theatre. They were touted as entertainers "with the easy look of absolute elegance that comes from being wrapped in the very latest of Tony Award-winning Broadway hits."

Dream Girls, featuring three black female singers at the Imperial Theatre, got both Tony and Grammy awards, while *The Tao Dance Kid* at the Broadhurst Theatre "kicks up a storm in musical comedy heaven" (according to the *New York Times*). At the Majestic Theatre, *42nd Street* is presented as a "Song and Dance Extravaganza," with choreography by Gower Champion. And finally there is *Cats,* based on *Old Possum's Book of Practical Cats* by T. S. Eliot, having a long run at the Winter Garden Theatre. Advertised as "Now and Forever," it could just happen that this might be true.

Notes

1. James Truslow Adams, *The March of Democracy,* vol. 4, *America—a World Power,* p. 280.
2. David Ewen, *New Complete Book of the American Musical Theater,* p. 191.
3. Charles Belmont Davis, " 'Rose-Marie' Scores with Mary Ellis and Her Strong Support," *New York Tribune,* Sept. 3, 1924, p. 12; quoted in ibid., p. 459.
4. Gerald Bordman, *American Musical Theatre,* p. 391.
5. Ewen, *New Complete Book of the American Musical Theater,* p. 473.
6. Lehman Engel, *The American Musical Theater,* pp. 13, 14.
7. For a comprehensive critique of *Show Boat,* see Philip Graham, *Showboats,* pp. 190–96.
8. "The Man I Love" was originally written for *Lady, Be Good!* but was dropped after the play's tryout. It was also dropped from the revised 1930 version of *Strike Up the Band* but became a hit as an independent song.
9. Quoted in Ewen, *New Complete Book of the American Musical Theater,* p. 26.
10. Quoted in Robert Kimball and William Bolcom, *Reminiscing with Sissle and Blake,* pp. 172–73.
11. Quoted in ibid., p. 178.
12. Quoted in ibid., p. 180.
13. Ibid., p. 181.
14. Ewen, *New Complete Book of the American Musical Theater,* p. 83.
15. Ibid., p. 353.
16. Quoted in ibid., p. 403.
17. Quoted in ibid., p. 380.
18. Ibid., p. 6.
19. Ibid., p. 199.
20. Quoted in ibid., p. 346.
21. Engel, *The American Musical Theater,* pp. 132–54, especially pp. 151–54.
22. Bordman, *American Musical Theatre,* p. 682.

Chapter 30
Toward an American Opera

For a long time there has existed a strong desire
for somebody to write a real American opera.
—Aaron Copland, *Our New Music* (1941)

Unlike Eugene O'Neill in *Desire under the Elms,* Copland did not specify
the locus of that alleged "strong desire" for "a real American opera." Obviously, it was not a desire felt very strongly under the chandelier of the Metropolitan Opera House. To be sure, during the long regime (1908–35) of
Giulio Gatti-Casazza, the "Met" was decently hospitable to operas by
American composers, beginning with *The Pipe of Desire* by Frederick S.
Converse, produced in 1910. This evidently had nothing to do with
O'Neill's brand of desire, for we are told that the would-be lovers are only
"part human," while the other characters are "creatures of the land of
fancy." Nevertheless, posterity is impressively informed that " 'The Pipe of
Desire' has the distinction for all time of having been not only the first
American Opera to be presented at the Metropolitan Opera House but
also the first opera to be sung there in English during the regular season.'"
A doubleheader!

The next American event at the Met was even more impressive, for it
involved a competition for the "best" opera in English by an American
composer, with a prize of $10,000. The winner was the distinguished New
England composer Horatio Parker, whose opera *Mona,* with a libretto by
Brian Hooker, was produced at the Met on March 14, 1912. The plot turns
on love versus patriotism, for Mona is a princess of Britain at the time of
the Roman conquest, who falls in love with the son of the Roman governor yet cannot stifle her hatred of the haughty invaders. Its survival value is
negligible.

In the same year that *Mona* was produced at the Met, another New England composer, George Chadwick, completed his realistic opera *The
Padrone,* dealing with the exploitation of Italian immigrants by their boss.

When he submitted it to the Met, it was turned down. We may surmise that Gatti-Casazza was not disposed to having his countrymen displayed in a bad light. Besides, he knew that realism of the here-and-now type was bad for the box office—not to speak of bounties from the boxholders of the Diamond Horseshoe.

Significantly, the two most successful American operas produced at the Met during this period had settings very remote from the American scene. These were *The King's Henchman* (February 17, 1927) and *Peter Ibbetson* (February 7, 1931), both by Deems Taylor (1885–1966). The former had a libretto by Edna St. Vincent Millay; the latter was based on the novel by Gerald du Maurier. The first received fourteen performances in three seasons, the second, sixteen performances in four seasons. These records surpassed those of any other American opera produced at the Met. Yet neither *The King's Henchman* nor *Peter Ibbetson* became part of the repertory, and neither opera had musical traits or dramatic contexts that could be characterized as distinctively American.

Meanwhile, on the West Coast, a woman composer by the name of Mary Carr Moore (1873–1957) was writing a quantity of operas that gained considerable attention. She was a native of Tennessee, and her mother, Sarah Pratt Carr, was a literary bluestocking who wrote the libretto for her daughter's best-known opera, *Narcissa* (1911). This has been described as "very likely the first grand opera to have been composed, scored, and then conducted by an American woman."[2] The first performance took place in Seattle on April 22, 1912, and it was later presented in San Francisco (1925) and Los Angeles (1945)—all conducted by the composer.

Narcissa is a historical opera built around the missionary spirit that swept through America in the early nineteenth century. The central male character, Dr. Marcus Whitman, was historically one of the missionaries who made the trek to Oregon in the 1830s. He combined intense patriotism with missionary zeal, shared by his devoted wife, Narcissa. But the Indians regarded this as encroachment of their territory, resulting in violence and terror, with the killing of Marcus and Narcissa in a massacre that took place in 1847. We should note, by the way, that the cast of characters included five Native Americans, among them two women, who performed an "Indian Chorus with Dance," using Indian syllables.

Moore wrote two other full-length operas that were produced: *Los rubios* (1931) and *David Rizzio* (1927–28), as well as two operettas, *The Oracle* (1894) and *Flutes of Jade Happiness* (1932–33; performed 1934), plus over 200 songs, many larger vocal pieces, and a quantity of instrumental works.[3]

Even though it may have been largely ephemeral, the widespread vogue for Indianist operas during this period should not be ignored in a cultural context. The most notable example is that of Charles Wakefield Cadman's *Shanewis,* produced at the Met on March 23, 1918. It had a total of eight performances in two seasons—the record for an American opera until that time. In discussing his compositional approach for this work, Cadman said he "felt that Bizet, Gounod, Verdi and Puccini were models worth taking."[4] But they did not take him very far toward a really *American* opera. Yet Cadman did use some diluted Indian themes in his score, and *Shanewis* reached a wider public when it was presented on the National Broadcasting Company network in 1928 and 1933.

Encouraged by his success, Cadman went on to write another Indianist opera, *The Sunset Trail,* which took him to the Far West, with its premiere in Denver, Colorado, in 1922. Thereafter he became less interested in Native American themes and turned to the early New England scene with his two-act opera *A Witch of Salem* (1926).

Henry T. Finck, a rather finicky and influential critic, stated that *Shanewis* was "worth preserving for future seasons inasmuch as Cadman's theatrical sense is strong." A number of American operas have been considered worthy of preservation for posterity. There is, however, no consensus as to whether they should be embalmed, congealed, or mummified.

American operas of the past have generally been preserved in a silent limbo called "print," located in tombs of learning called "libraries." There, in stacks seldom disturbed by a curious hand, are the heroes and villains, the happy or tragic lovers, the adventurers and plotters, the leaders and the followers that inhabit the alluring land of opera. Of course, the music is there too—for those who know how to read it. But opera is meant to be both seen and heard; the theater is its vital ground, the stage its showcase. The annals of American opera offer at least one instance whereby a work long resting in the limbo of print suddenly came to life and bestowed its creative vitality and moral message upon many thousands of delighted listeners and viewers. Such was the semimiracle of *Treemonisha,* the only surviving opera by the great ragtime composer Scott Joplin.

When Joplin arrived in New York in 1907, he was imbued with the idea of writing an opera that would be both "serious" and entertaining, drawing on the ragtime idiom when appropriate—as in the various dance episodes (with singing)—but otherwise adhering to the general style of opera while avoiding delusions of grandeur through the inflation of vocal and dramatic gestures. This was not what producers expected from the "King of Ragtime." When the *New York Age,* in its issue of August 7, 1913, announced that an opera by Joplin would be performed the following year at the Lafayette Theater in Manhattan, the news proved to be premature—by about sixty years—at least with regard to a theatrical production of the work.

What actually happened was that Joplin, discouraged and despondent over his lack of success, published the vocal score of his opera, at his own expense, in 1911. It thus came to the attention of a perceptive and prophetic reviewer, who in the *American Musician* of June 14, 1911, wrote that Joplin had "created an entirely new phase of musical art and has produced a thoroughly American opera."⁵

Obsessed by his operatic idea, and in failing health that aggravated his despair, Joplin, in 1915, arranged for a kind of run-through of *Treemonisha* at an obscure hall in Harlem, for an invited audience. Unable to afford an orchestra, Joplin presided at the piano. There was no scenery or staging of any kind. The work was received with indifference or incomprehension. It was the end of the line for Joplin; two years later he was dead.

Here the curtain comes down for the end of the first act in the historical drama of Scott Joplin and *Treemonisha*. The temporal continuity of the classical theater (so dear to historians also) is interrupted by a long hiatus, as we await the triumphant reappearance of *Treemonisha* after six decades of indifference and neglect. The story of her resurrection will then be told in full.

In the interim, let us note that whereas about 1940 Aaron Copland was stating that for a long time there had existed "a strong desire for somebody to write a real American opera," by 1910 that desire had already been fulfilled, although only one solitary voice proclaimed it amid a desert of indifference.

Treemonisha is an extreme case, but we have more than once failed to recognize the scope and ultimate significance of "a real American opera" when it has appeared. This is because in order for American opera to be truly *American,* it must necessarily be different from the standard models established by the European tradition. The most conspicuous example of this confusion is the case of Gershwin's *Porgy and Bess.* After its premiere at the Alvin Theatre in New York on October 10, 1935, the critical reception was mixed and in some instances obviously confused. Olin Downes of the *New York Times* stated his opinion that Gershwin had not "completely formed his style as an opera composer." What kind of style did he expect?

A clue may be found in what follows: "The style is at one moment of opera and another of operetta or sheer Broadway entertainment."⁶ It was evidently this mixture of styles to which Downes objected. The operatic style was distinct and separate from the style of the Broadway musical shows, and never the twain should meet. With hindsight we can perceive that it was precisely this musico-theatrical synthesis that gave its specific character to what we have come to recognize as "a real American opera."

An objective evaluation of *Porgy and Bess* was made difficult not only by the operatic expectations it aroused but also by the drastic cuts of the initial production and the several productions that followed, thus obscuring some of the operatic features while emphasizing the "Broadway" aspect. It is a curious fact, indicative of the eccentricities in American operatic history, that *Porgy and Bess* had to wait until the 1970s before it was produced in its complete form—not only as "a real *American* opera" but also as a *real* opera. There is an analogy between *Treemonisha*, which arose like the phoenix from the ashes of oblivion, and *Porgy and Bess*, which suddenly appeared in its full dramatic stature some four decades after its initial production. This is also an encouraging comment on our cultural maturity, even though one is tempted to add, "Better late than never."

Gershwin's opera had been in gestation for a long time, and he completed it only two years before his untimely death. In the fall of 1926 he read a novel called *Porgy*, by DuBose Heyward, dealing with a community of blacks in Charleston, South Carolina, where the author himself lived. Gershwin was immediately attracted to the story, built around a local character called "Goat Sammy," a cripple who traveled about in a small goat-drawn cart. Heyward also turned the novel into a play, which was produced by the Theater Guild in 1927. After seeing the play, Gershwin was convinced that an effective opera libretto could be fashioned from it. He was in correspondence with Heyward, who offered his full cooperation. But there were delays and snags, the latter arising from Al Jolson's interest in making a musical out of *Porgy*, in collaboration with Jerome Kern and Oscar Hammerstein. By 1934 this trio had lost interest in the project, and Heyward's libretto became available to Gershwin, whose brother Ira contributed the lyrics.

Meanwhile, Gershwin was doing his "fieldwork" quite seriously, in addition to writing and orchestrating a full-scale opera in three acts and nine scenes, of which the manuscript score contains 700 pages of closely written music. He spent the summer of 1934 on Folly Island, near Charleston, absorbing as much as he could of the character, the manners, the music, and the speech of the blacks in this isolated area. He attended religious services of the Gullah Negroes and took part in their singing. He noted the cries of the street vendors in Charleston, with their fascinating melodic inflections. These—the cries of the Strawberry Woman, the Honey Man, the Crab Man—are the folklore gems of the opera. Some of the songs, such as "It Ain't Necessarily So" and "There's a Boat Dat's Leavin' Soon for New York," are patently Broadway show tunes. But who would wish to emulate the fastidiousness of the highbrow critic (Lawrence Gilman) who objected to the song hits in Gershwin's score as "blemishes upon its musical integrity."[7] History shows that an exclusively aesthetic "integrity" has never made a successful opera, but many a good tune has.

As conceived and written by Gershwin, *Porgy and Bess* was a grand opera in both its musical and dramatic dimensions. It contained three hours of music, including arias and recitatives. Neither the arias and recitatives nor the length were considered suitable for a Broadway production; hence, extensive cuts were made. In all, seven numbers were omitted from the original production, including the introductory "Jasbo Brown Blues," the "Buzzard Song" (a dramatic aria), and a spiritual, "Sure to Go to Heaven."

Measured by Broadway box office standards, the original run of *Porgy and Bess*—sixteen weeks in New York followed by two months on the road—was disappointing. But for an American opera, this was unprecedented. Later productions achieved a wider popularity but at the expense of drastic cuts, amounting in one case to nearly forty-five minutes of music, as well as a reduced orchestra and cast. As music director Alexander Steinert remarked of *Porgy and Bess:* "It belongs in an opera house, played by a large orchestra, for which it was written." And in the 1950s Gershwin's opera, although still truncated, was produced at some of the world's most famous opera houses, in Europe and South America, thanks to sponsorship by the United States State Department. In 1959 *Porgy and Bess* was seen and heard by millions of people in a technicolor film version produced by Samuel Goldwyn.

But the complete and authentic *Porgy and Bess* had to wait until 1975 for its full revelation to the public. It then received a splendid production by the Houston Grand Opera Company, which demonstrated beyond a shadow of doubt that Gershwin's opus was not only really American but also truly operatic. In September 1976 this production was brought to New York, where it achieved both critical acclaim and box office success. As if to doubly certify the operatic stature of Gershwin's great work, in that same year the first complete recording of *Porgy and Bess,* in its full symphonic-vocal-dramatic dimensions, was made by the Cleveland Orchestra and Chorus, with an all-black cast of highly trained singers (the Houston Opera production also featured an all-black cast).[8]

When Copland wrote of the desire for "a real American opera," he did not spell out in detail what he meant by that designation. He did, however, mention two composers—Virgil Thomson and Marc Blitzstein—who "seem to have set us on our way toward having our own kind of operatic piece." He was not sure that "what they write is to be called opera, but it certainly is a form of musical drama that is thoroughly absorbing and attacks the primary operatic problem of the natural setting of English to music."[9] He remarked that previous American operas had "made English sound like 'translationese.' " He might have added that the stilted librettos did not help.

Thomson's first opera, *Four Saints in Three Acts,* had in common with *Porgy and Bess* a performance by an all-Negro cast; but there the similarity ends. Thomson's background and aims were very different from those of Gershwin, although he, too, had the distinction of having his opera performed in a Broadway theater rather than at the Met. This meant that it qualified as "entertainment," even though it was certainly not everybody's cup of tea.

It all began when Gertrude Stein, whom Thomson had known in Paris, agreed to write a libretto about saints in Spain, principally St. Teresa and St. Ignatius, in her inimitable prose style, as crystal clear as it was cryptic, carrying complete conviction with a minimum of logical syntax. Thomson, on his part, felt that contemporary music in the 1930s had become needlessly difficult and pointlessly complex, especially as a setting for speech.

Thomson's delightful and deliberately "simplistic" music greatly facilitates our participation in the nonlogical verbal landscape of images and metaphors, characters and rituals, created by Stein's untrammeled text. The score incorporates elements from a variety of religious traditions, ranging from Gregorian chant to American folk hymnody. There is also a charming tango. But why a Negro cast for an opera about (mostly) European saints? In a letter to Stein, Thomson wrote: "My negro singers, after all, are a purely musical desideratum, because of their rhythm, their style and especially their diction."[10] In his autobiography he stated: "The Negroes proved in every way rewarding. Not only could they enunciate and sing; they seemed to understand because they sang. They resisted not at all

Stein's obscure language, adopted it for theirs, conversed in quotations from it. They moved, sang, spoke with grace and with alacrity, took on roles without self-consciousness, as if they were the saints they said they were. . . . [They] gave meaning to both words and music by making the Stein text easy to accept."[11]

The opera, moreover, was choreographed throughout. In Thomson's words: "It was thanks to the choreography, indeed, and to our cast that the production's major quality shone out—a unity of concept and performance that no one had seen before in opera."[12] Another "first" for the American lyric theater!

After opening in Hartford, Connecticut, on February 8, 1934, sponsored by "The Friends and Enemies of Modern Music," *Four Saints* had a run of several weeks on Broadway, after which it moved to Chicago. Much of its effect was due to the extraordinary decors and costumes by Florine Stettheimer and the skillful choreography by Frederick Ashton. This unique Stein-Thomson opus lives on with no delusions of grandeur yet is an imperishable landmark in America's musical theater.

More than twenty years were to pass before Thomson's next opera, also with a libretto by Gertrude Stein. This was *The Mother of Us All*, produced at the Brander Matthews Theater of Columbia University on May 7, 1947—a locus that might be described as "off-Broadway north." The central figure of the opera is Susan B. Anthony, pioneer leader in the struggle for women's suffrage in the nineteenth century. The cast includes many other historical characters, anachronistically distributed, among them John Adams, Daniel Webster, Ulysses S. Grant, Anthony Comstock, Andrew Johnson, Thaddeus Stevens, and Lillian Russell.

In the last scene all gather around the statue of Susan B. and her comrades in the suffrage fight. Suddenly her voice is heard as she attempts to explain what it is all about (previously she had said, "I am not puzzled but it is all very puzzling"). She sums it up thus: "Life is strife, I was a martyr all my life not to what I won but to what was done." If this is still puzzling, try listening to the music; then all becomes crystal clear.

The same qualities of clarity and felicity in setting English to music that characterized Thomson's earlier opera are evident in this score. The musical ingredients consist largely of heterogeneous Americana, stylistically evoked rather than literally quoted: revival hymnody, gospel songs à la Salvation Army street bands, modal folk melodies, popular song idioms, and so forth. Thomson employs the calculated cliché and the deliberate commonplace with amazing freshness.

Robert Indiana, who designed the elaborate sets and costumes for the first full-scale and decisively impressive production of *The Mother of Us All*, by the Santa Fe (New Mexico) Opera Company, in the summer of 1976, considered the work the most American of all operas. As Peter G. Davis wrote of that occasion: "A great American opera has finally received the kind of exciting and imaginative major production that it has always deserved."[13]

Marc Blitzstein (1905–64), the second composer mentioned in Copland's discussion of "a real American opera," came from an upper middle-class family of Philadelphia, where he studied at the Curtis Institute of Music. Following two trends of the time, he also studied with Boulanger in Paris and with Schoenberg in Berlin. Although he paid tribute to the fashionable neoclassicism of the moment with a piano concerto, it was the "opera-farce" *Triple Sec* (1928) that signaled his overriding dedication to the musical theater. His work in that medium coincided with, and was conditioned by, his radical sociopolitical stance.

In the midst of the Great Depression, Blitzstein published an article titled "Coming—the Mass Audience!" wherein he proclaimed: "There is a crisis on; and music is in a state of crisis no less than economics or politics." For him the issue was not whether "first-rate works are being written," but rather that "no new work is having any direct or alive contact with the public." On the contrary, "the music seems to be aimed away from the public."[14] In his view the "Sacred Repertoire of the Classics" was served out to audiences "in the form of pathos and narcosis, solace and wish-titillation."[15] His partisan commitment evidently prevented him from accepting the cynical view that this was pretty much what the public wanted.

In any case his populist convictions induced him to repudiate "the exalted heroism of grand opera," which "is not for our twentieth-century American ears."[16] What were the alternatives? These might include a blend of realism and satire, of popular-song style and traditional aria style, of original music and quoted material for its associative effect, of speech passing into song, and especially the use of the vernacular, never any high-flown diction. Influences could come from many sources, including those of jazz and blues, the Broadway revue and musical comedy, and the "new realism" of the American theater, with its emphasis on social issues.

Blitzstein was from an early age fascinated by the Broadway musical theater, and in particular by the musical comedies of Gershwin. Like Gershwin, he mastered the popular piano styles of the twenties and thirties. He was also familiar with the popular-satirical musical style of Kurt Weill and the "agit-prop" ("agitation and propaganda") theater of Bertold Brecht. Drawing on all of these sources, but with a distinctively personal approach, Blitzstein, in 1937, wrote the words and music for what he called "a play in music" titled *The Cradle Will Rock*. The action takes place in "Steeltown, U.S.A." during the 1930s and revolves around an organizational drive by the local steelworkers' union. But the time is by no means simply a confrontation between labor and management. It is rather the corruption of society by the power of big money, and the "prostitution" of the middle-class leaders—editors, college presidents, clergymen, doctors— as they succumb to bribes and threats from the local big boss. The "good guys" are clearly the workers, including an honest prostitute who must work for a precarious living. While the workers are depicted as "real" human beings, the representatives of the Establishment are broadly caricatured, appearing as both farcical and sinister. If there is a "hero," he is Larry Foreman, the union organizer.

In keeping with Blitzstein's affinity for the Broadway theater, *The Cradle Will Rock* was originally scored for a small pit orchestra including tenor saxophone, accordion, and guitar. The libretto contains considerable spoken dialogue, and none of the vocal numbers is conventionally operatic. Nevertheless, I would not hesitate to call it "a real *American* opera"— with the emphasis as indicated. In any case, *The Cradle Will Rock* in 1960 was elevated to a full-scale production by the New York City Opera, which presumably certified its operatic status.

Blitzstein's *The Cradle Will Rock* was first presented to the public in June 1937, under circumstances that can only be described as chaotic. It was scheduled to be produced at the Maxine Elliott Theatre in New York under the sponsorship of the Federal Theatre Project, and there was an advance sale of 14,000 tickets. Complications arose because the act authorizing the W.P.A. Theatre Project was due to expire on June 30, whereupon the actors and musicians went on strike in protest. The W.P.A. ordered the cancellation of the show, and union members were forbidden to appear in any performance. Another theater had to be found, and in that theater the actors sat in the house and walked to the edge of the stage to play and sing their scenes, while Blitzstein presided at the piano. The result was a sort of "happening" that captured headlines and achieved enduring notoriety. But it also set a false precedent, as some later productions deliberately imitated this improvised, helter-skelter model when there was no longer any justification for it.

Blitzstein continued in a similar vein with his next important stage work, *No for an Answer* (1938–40), produced in New York's Mecca Auditorium on January 5, 1941. It, too, deals with unionism and the class struggle, but in a less acerbic manner, involving waiters and other resort-hotel employees who face unemployment during the winter months. It was hailed as "a true people's opera" by the *Daily Worker,* while a reviewer in *Opera News* (organ of the Metropolitan Opera Guild) raised some pertinent questions: "Can an opera be written today on a burning issue of the times? Can it be sung in the modern American vernacular, staged without benefit of scenery, played without benefit of orchestra, and still hold a capacity audience spellbound on the edge of their very uncomfortable chairs?" His reply to these questions: "Yes for an answer."

The same reviewer went on to assess the significance of Blitzstein's achievement: "In his affirmation of the operatic tradition, his demonstration of the belief that singing reinforces the drive of the spoken line, Mr. Blitzstein has made a definite contribution to the world of opera today. Does opera belong to the past? No, for an Answer!"[17]

So, whatever the circumstances of the class struggle or the confrontation between conservatives and radicals, there was evidently no clash of critical judgment in this instance. Yet one could ask just how far the Establishment would be prepared to go in sponsoring operas "on a burning issue of the times." It might depend on who was feeling the heat.

The question might have been put to the test had Blitzstein lived to complete his opera on the once-burning and still-smoldering issue of the trial and execution of Sacco and Vanzetti. Astonishingly, to begin with, this was commissioned by the Ford Foundation for production by the Metropolitan Opera. At Blitzstein's death in 1964, only the first two acts were substantially completed. The task of finishing the score was entrusted to his friend and emulator Leonard Bernstein, but neither the completed work nor the production has materialized.

In 1948–49 Blitzstein wrote what in all respects qualifies as "a real American opera." Based on Lillian Hellman's play *The Little Foxes,* it was titled *Regina,* after the selfish, domineering, and utterly unscrupulous main character. Its Boston opening in 1949 was followed by a run of fifty-six performances in New York. It continued to make operatic history with a revival by the New York City Opera in April 1953. It also puzzled the critics, who did not know how to classify it. One labeled it a "jazz opera." True, the score calls for a dance band on stage to play for the party given by Regina. But one might just as well call Mozart's *Don Giovanni* a "dance opera" because it, too, employs a dance band on stage. Not so, the jazz labeler might object, because Blitzstein's score is full of syncopated rhythms, and some of its songs have the cut of Broadway ballads. One also finds a Negro spiritual and a revival hymn sung by the black servants and an intermezzo for piano, in the style of Gottschalk, played on stage, symbolizing, perhaps, the genteel veneer that covers the corruption of these people. Who is to say that these ingredients are not operatic? The composer decides, in the context of time, place, and circumstance. Blitzstein simply chose an "American mix" that suited his purpose both musically and dramatically.

Leonard Bernstein first presented *The Cradle Will Rock* with full orchestra, when he conducted it in a concert performance with the New York Symphony in 1947. And when Bernstein wrote his satirical one-act opera *Trouble in Tahiti* (1952), he dedicated it to Blitzstein. What the two composers had in common was a theatrical flair, an impulse toward social commentary, and a gift for assimilating the idioms of American popular music.

With *Trouble in Tahiti* (to his own libretto), Bernstein exposed the troubled psyche of suburban America, bombarded by chamber-of-commerce patter ("Sweet in the spring, healthful in winter") and the come-ons of real-estate agents ("Out of the hubbub, less than an hour by train"). The atmosphere of suburbia is established by "The Trio" (two men and a girl), described as "a Greek chorus born of the radio commercial," who sing generally "in a whispering, breathy *pianissimo,* which comes over the amplifying system as crooning."[18]

The protagonists are a youngish couple with one child, whose marriage has ill withstood the ravages of routine and the withering of early illusions. In an aria the wife sings in a shop, she tells about "a terrible, awful movie" she has just seen, called *Trouble in Tahiti.* Although she begins by denouncing it as "escapist technicolor twaddle," she is soon carried away by the lush mood of the theme song, "Island Magic"—a captive of escapism in spite of herself. In the end, the couple can think of nothing better to do than to go to the movies. Although they have already seen the picture, it is still "the bought-and-paid-for magic, waiting on a Silver Screen."

What now of the more traditional American opera since 1950? With emphasis on American subject matter, the most consistently impressive contribution is that of Douglas Moore (1893–1969). After writing a considerable quantity of instrumental Americana, he made his mark in the theater with a "folk opera," *The Devil and Daniel Webster* (1938), on a libretto by Stephen Vincent Benét. In 1950 he completed the tragic opera *Giants in the Earth,* after the somber novel by O. E. Rolvaag, depicting the hardships and spiritual conflicts of a Swedish pioneer family in the Dakota Territory. It won a Pulitzer Prize, and the cultural historian Vernon Parrington cited it as "the effective beginning of realism in American opera." (Moore revised it in 1963.) Another opera, *The Wings of the Dove* (1961), after the novel by Henry James, was commissioned by the Ford Foundation and was produced by the New York City Opera in 1961. The conservative critic Winthrop Sargeant called it "the most artistically successful American opera thus far written." Moore's last opera, *Carrie Nation* (1966), dealt with the colorful and militant temperance crusader (1846–1911), who wielded a hatchet to smash bottles in the saloons.

The opera by Moore that made the strongest and most lasting impression is *The Ballad of Baby Doe,* produced at the Central Opera Festival of Colorado in 1956. The libretto, by John La Touche, tells the true story of Baby Doe Tabor, with its main setting in Leadville, Colorado, from 1880 to 1935. In that year the aged and impoverished Baby Doe froze to death in a shack near the "Matchless Mine," which had brought sudden wealth to her husband and which she had promised him never to abandon. Tabor himself, after becoming the richest man in Colorado and divorcing his first wife to marry the young and beautiful Baby Doe, lost all his wealth in the silver crisis of 1895 and died four years later.

There is an episode of glitter and glamor when Tabor, as interim senator takes his new wife to Washington; but the scandal of divorce ruined his political career. These are all good operatic ingredients, and Moore made the most of them. Working within a traditional framework of arias and set pieces, he skillfully deployed his musical resources for the best dramatic effects and delineation of character. He also drew on elements of America's demotic music to evoke local atmosphere. *The Ballad of Baby Doe* is unquestionably the most successful grand opera by an American to deal with the historical past of the United States.

From Eduard Sobolewski's *Mohega* in 1859 to *Baby Doe* in 1956, we can trace a remarkable succession of feminine protagonists in American opera. True, they abound in European opera also. But the sequence of American heroines offers some interesting patterns. In the operas we have discussed, Narcissa and Shanewis are sacrificial victims of antagonisms they cannot control, although Shanewis sacrifices her happiness rather than her life. While Baby Doe had her moment of triumph, she became a victim of social prejudice and—more remarkable for an operatic plot—of the defeat of the "free silver" policy advocated by William Jennings Bryan (who appears as a character in the opera) that ruined her husband.

Regina, in Blitzstein's opera, embodies a dominant spirit of evil who makes victims of those around her. But here, again, money becomes a crucial consideration, for greed and power are her basic motives. On a lesser scale, one might compare her with Vanessa, in Samuel Barber's opera of that name (1958), whose overbearing selfishness makes a sacrificial victim of her daughter. Obviously, Carrie Nation, in Moore's opera, and Susan B. Anthony, in *The Mother of Us All,* are dominant personalities also, but they devote themselves to a cause that they regard as worthy. The subject of personal causes brings us back to the last of our operatic heroines, one who emerges as the leader and savior of her people—the cause for which she was evidently predestined.

Scott Joplin's *Treemonisha,* as we have noted, slumbered in oblivion for six decades, until the ragtime revival of the 1970s brought her to the attention of the public. The opera was first produced in a semiprofessional performance in Atlanta (January 1972) and was presented again the following summer at the Filene Center (Wolftrap Farm Park), near Washington, D.C. The first full-scale professional production was given by the Houston Grand Opera in May 1975, using an orchestration by Gunther Schuller, who conducted, and featuring an all-black cast.[19] This production also had a successful run in New York.

The opera is in three acts, corresponding to morning, noon, and evening of the same day, although the retrospective time span is from 1866 to 1884. The setting is a plantation in Arkansas, surrounded by a dense forest. Ned and Monisha, a childless black couple, find a baby girl abandoned under a tree in front of their cabin. They adopt her and are able to give her an education with the help of a neighboring white family. As the opera opens, Treemonisha is eighteen and the only member of the black community who can read and write. She dedicates herself to freeing her people from the ignorance and superstition that lets them be cowed and exploited by the conjurers—the "bad guys" of the plot. So there is a confrontation, and Treemonisha is in danger of her life. Her rescue provides a climactic moment, after which she forgives her enemies, and the people acclaim her as their leader.

Treemonisha is a didactic opera, intended to teach a moral as well as to adorn a tale with music, singing, and dancing. Its outright preaching is counterbalanced by such fantastic touches as the "Frolic of the Bears" and the highly spirited dances with singing, culminating in the grand finale:

Marching onward, marching onward,
Marching to that lovely tune.

Except for the dance numbers, *Treemonisha* is not a "ragtime opera," but rather a moralistic and fantastic opera that blends the natural with the supernatural and pits good against evil, in the manner of a black American *Magic Flute*. Whether Joplin knew it or not, the plot is deeply rooted in mythology: the theme of the foundling child as savior. Whatever its antecedents or its shortcomings (particularly in the libretto), many of us will agree with Carman Moore that "the obvious vital ingredient in *Treemonisha* is the musical genius of Scott Joplin."[20]

Taking the bicentennial as a marker, we can now ask: What is the status of opera in America as we enter the final decades of the twentieth century? Viewing the scene as a whole, regardless of national origin, the answer would be that it is flourishing. In the season of 1975–76, for example, there were 477 opera companies, large and small, professional and amateur, together with 436 opera departments in colleges and universities, which altogether accounted for 7,109 performances.[21] Of the 229 "contemporary" works performed, the "top ten" were all by Americans, native-born or naturalized. The former were represented by George Gershwin, Douglas Moore, and Carlisle Floyd; the latter by Gian-Carlo Menotti and Kurt Weill. Doubtless due to the bicentennial impetus, there were 2,323 performances of American operas, including such "oldies" as *The King's Henchman* and *Merry Mount*.

Menotti (b. 1911), a native of Italy, came to the United States in 1928 and by 1937 made his mark with a one-act comic opera, *Amelia Goes to the Ball*. A year later this was produced at the Met, leading to a commission from the National Broadcasting Company for a radio opera, *The Old Maid and the Thief* (1939). The work that made him famous was *The Medium* (1945; performed 1946), a "musical tragedy" in two acts that had an unprecedented run on Broadway and thereafter became a national and international success. Other highly successful operas were *The Consul* (1949; performed 1950) and *The Saint of Bleecker Street* (1954), both with tragic subjects. An opera written especially for television in 1951, *Amahl and the Night Visitors,* suggested by Hieronymus Bosch's painting "The Adoration of the Magi," became a permanent presentation for the celebration of Christmas.

Carlisle Floyd (b. 1926) achieved instant recognition when his realistic opera *Susannah* won the New York Music Critics' Circle award following

558 America's Music

its New York premiere in 1956. Set in the rural South, with the fervor of religious revivalism leading to a tragic denouement, it was dramatically effective. Floyd continued his career with such dramatic operas as *Wuthering Heights* (performed 1958), *The Passion of Jonathan Wade* (performed 1962), and *Of Mice and Men* (performed 1970).

American composers of opera can be classified in two categories: the professional and the incidental. Composers of the latter category would typically write one or two operas as a digression from their basic output. Such was the case with Aaron Copland's *The Tender Land* (1952–54), which eschews the style of grand opera, concentrating instead on a lower middle-class family living on a farm in the Midwest. Samuel Barber aspired toward conventional grand opera with *Vanessa* (1957), performed at the Met in January 1958 with considerable success (the libretto was by Menotti). But a more ambitious attempt with *Antony and Cleopatra* (1965–66) proved to be more superficially grandiose than operatically impressive.

On the consistently professional side, Menotti and Floyd had a flamboyant successor in Thomas Pasatieri (b. 1945), who became a front-runner in pleasing the public and making money (which is what Rossini and Donizetti did). His career has been described as "meteoric," with at least fifteen successful operas to his credit by his late thirties, and commissions coming from all parts of the United States, from Austin to Seattle. Pasatieri's formula of success is that his "operas all deal with highly emotional characters caught in strong theatrical situations."[22] We should also note that his libretti are often drawn from literary masterpieces, as with *Black Widow* (1972), based on a novel by Unamuno; *The Seagull* (1974), from Chekhov's play; and *Washington Square* (1976), after the novel by Henry James. Later operas include *Three Sisters* (1979), *Before Breakfast* (1980), *The Goose Girl* (1981), and *Maria Elena* (1983).

To cap this almost incredible career, we are told that, "most astonishing of all, Pasatieri actually makes a living solely by writing operas—the first American-born and trained composer to accomplish this improbable feat in a country that has yet to develop a firmly grounded operatic tradition of its own."[23]

While the standard operas are inevitably predominant, there are also various nonconformist and experimental types that may be compared to the exploration of outer space. There is, for example, an opera by Paul Earls titled *The Death of King Phillip* (1976)—referring to the American Indian Chief who was given that name—that utilizes various sound-and-sight sources. Andrew Porter described it as "an adventurous, exciting, and

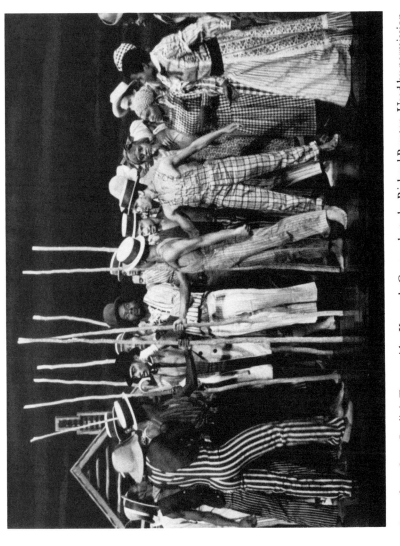

Scene from Scott Joplin's *Treemonisha*. Kennedy Center photo by Richard Braaten. Used by permission.

very accomplished opera, enhanced by astonishing light effects [such as] laser-projected images. . . ."[24]

On a much larger scale we have the freewheeling operas of Philip Glass (b. 1937), such as *Einstein on the Beach* (1975) and *Satyagraha,* with their immense durations and their rejection of conventional operatic standards. The first of these had its American premiere on November 21, 1976—using the facilities of the Met without its formal imprimatur. Written in collaboration with playwright Robert Wilson, it had a small musical ensemble consisting of three wind instruments, two electric organs, violin, and female voice—all relying heavily on amplification. The total duration was nearly five hours. Much publicized, it had a second performance before a full house.

Satyagraha had its premiere in Rotterdam and in November 1981 was given five performances at the Brooklyn Academy of Music. As described by Joseph Roddy:

> *Satyagraha* is in three acts and depicts the young *Mahatma* Gandhi's first use of organized passive resistance against state-sanctioned race prejudice in South Africa from 1893–1914. Its vocal text, sung in Sanskrit, is a set of texts culled from the Bhagavad-Gita section of the ancient Hindu poem Mahabharata. The action on stage is witnessed in each act by a figurative counterpart, representing the past, present and future of Satyagraha. With its words and plot paralleled or layered, instead of linked or interlocked as they are in other operas, *Satyagraha*'s vocal text provides a moral commentary on the stage without being a narrative part of the production.[25]

The instrumentation is influenced by the composer's deep affinity with the music of the Far East, especially that of India. (See chapter 33 for a description of this affinity.)

Satyagraha is a historical opera without the customary histrionic trappings, and with a moral message for the modern world, including the advocacy of nonviolence and civil rights. It is not an opera for which one goes to applaud and cheer the world-famous tenor or the leading soprano.

The primary meaning of *opera,* in Italian, is "work" (noun). But in English *work* is also a verb, and in that sense lies its primary significance for American opera as the space age approaches the twenty-first century. If it is an impressive theater piece with music that *works,* why not call it an *opera,* with more emphasis on the message than the form?

Notes

1. Edward Ellsworth Hipsher, *American Opera and Its Composers,* p. 123. *The Pipe of Desire,* in one act, with libretto by George Edward Burton, had its first performance in Boston on Jan. 31, 1906.

2. Cynthia S. Richardson, *"Narcissa,* by Mary Carr Moore," p. 15.

3. For data on the operas and other works by Mary Carr Moore, see the *Sonneck Society Newsletter* 7 (Summer 1981): 14–16.

4. Quoted in Hipsher, *American Opera and Its Composers,* p. 100.

5. Quoted in Carman Moore, "Notes on Treemonisha," *The Collected Works of Scott Joplin,* ed. Vera Brodsky Lawrence, vol. 2, p. xli.

6. Olin Downes, *New York Times,* Oct. 11, 1935.

7. Quoted in Charles Schwartz, *Gershwin,* p. 266.

8. *Porgy and Bess,* London Records OSA 13116; Lorin Maazel, music director and conductor; Robert Page directing the Cleveland Orchestra Chorus, and Becky Seredick the Children's Chorus.

9. Aaron Copland, *Our New Music,* p. 188.

10. Letter of May 30, 1933; quoted in Virgil Thomson, *Virgil Thomson,* p. 231.

11. Thomson, *Virgil Thomson,* p. 239.

12. Ibid., p. 242.

13. Peter G. Davis, "Opera: 'Mother' of the Mesas," *New York Times,* Aug. 13, 1976.

14. Marc Blitzstein, "Coming—the Mass Audience!" p. 23.

15. Ibid., pp. 29, 24.

16. Marc Blitzstein, "On Writing Music for the Theatre," p. 82.

17. *Opera News* 5 (Jan. 13, 1941): 28.

18. See Leonard Bernstein, *Trouble in Tahiti: An Opera in Seven Scenes,* piano-vocal score (New York: G. Schirmer, 1953).

19. *Scott Joplin's Treemonisha,* DGG 2707083.

20. Moore, "Notes on Treemonisha," p. xliv.

21. Maria F. Rich, "U.S. Opera Survey, 1975–76," pp. 34–40.

22. Peter G. Davis, "They Love Him in Seattle," *New York Times Magazine,* Mar. 21, 1976, p. 42.

23. Ibid.

24. Andrew Porter, "The Matter of Mexico," p. 120.

25. Joseph Roddy, "Listening to Glass," *In Performance* (Brooklyn Academy of Music), Nov. 1981, p. 6.

Chapter 31

The Grand Tradition

Will you seek afar off? You surely come back at last,
In things best known to you finding the best, or as good as the best.
—Walt Whitman, "A Song for Occupations"

The composer Ernst Krenek defined *tradition* as "the continuity of ideas expressed through the repetition of procedures. If we apply the term to the creative aspect of music, it designates adherence to compositional procedures of the past, especially of the immediate past. It is the continuation of things created in the past, but still alive in the present."[1]

As we have observed in tracing the course of artistic musical composition in the United States, composers on this side of the Atlantic generally followed the formulas and procedures established by the acknowledged masters of European art music. These were the "things best known" to aspiring American composers, whose ambition apparently was to achieve what might be considered "as good as the best"—or at least, almost as good. The training of composers emphasized the "compositional procedures of the past" as an immutable ideal that might evolve but should never be subjected to the trauma of discontinuity.

By the 1920s a new generation of American composers came to the fore who generally respected—we might even say, admired and cherished—the formal patterns of the Grand Tradition, such as the sonata, the concerto, and the symphony, while nevertheless seeking (in varying degrees) idiosyncratic elements of expression. The composer and critic Robert Evett published in 1955 an article discussing the works of several of these composers, such as Samuel Barber, Peter Mennin, Robert Palmer, and Vincent Persichetti, "whose aesthetic and technical standards are basically traditional."[2] Delineating a model for the "broad principles" they shared, he listed the following:

1. A fundamental allegiance to tonality.
2. A concern for counterpoint and conventionally "correct" part-writing.

3. A tendency to build their work on expansive melodic materials.
4. A striving for the Grand Manner and extreme seriousness of mood, especially in their more protracted works.

Turning first to the older generation, we find an example in Howard Hanson (1896–1981), whose seven symphonies fully correspond to the basic schema set forth by Evett, including "extreme seriousness of mood." His modern prototype is Sibelius—an affinity probably related to Hanson's Scandinavian antecedents. This connection is reflected in his First Symphony (1922), titled *Nordic,* which "sings of the solemnity, austerity and grandeur of the North, of its restless surging and strife, of its somberness and melancholy."[3] The title of the Second Symphony (1930), *Romantic,* speaks for itself, while the Third Symphony (1937–38) was conceived as an encomium to the epic qualities of the Swedish pioneers in America. The *Requiem* Symphony (no. 4, 1943) is dedicated to the memory of his father, and the religious mood is continued in the *Sinfonia Sacra* (no. 5, 1954). The Seventh Symphony (1977), *The Sea,* is for orchestra with chorus.

According to Nicolas Slonimsky, "Hanson's individuality reveals itself in the peculiarly American spaciousness of his melodic structures, a grandeur of symphonic design in the cyclic formation of thematic materials, and the vivacity of rhythmic patterns that naturally yield themselves to fugal developments."[4] It will not, I trust, be considered unduly cynical to regard skeptically the notion of a "peculiarly *American* spaciousness" in the symphonies of Hanson. Similar claims have been made for other American composers, and one wonders if this view is not perhaps based on the persistent image of America's wide open spaces as perpetuated in the saga of the prairies.

Hanson, like many of his American predecessors, favored the symphonic poem, as in *Lux Aeterna* (1923, with viola obbligato) and *Pan and the Priest* (1926, with piano obbligato). He continued the tradition of the cantata with *The Lament of Beowulf* (1925) and of grand opera with *Merry Mount* (1933), based on a notorious episode in Puritan New England. As director of the Eastman School of Music in Rochester, New York, and conductor of its Philharmonia Orchestra, he did much to promote the cultivation and acceptance of American music.

Other composers belonging to the so-called Generation of 1920 and who were equally dedicated to the symphony as a heritage of the Grand Tradition were Walter Piston, Roger Sessions, Aaron Copland, and Roy Harris. Of these, Piston (1894–1976) and Sessions had in common not only a New England background and a Harvard education but also a concept of the symphony as a self-contained formal structure, not related to, or dependent on, external or associative factors.

A native of Rockland, Maine, Piston came to Boston with his family in 1905 and in 1912 was enrolled in the Massachusetts Normal Art School to study architectural drawing. In the meantime he taught himself to play the violin and piano, whereby he earned some money playing with dance bands and theater orchestras, as well as later (having taken up the saxophone) making a living by performing in dance halls and other places of entertainment. He began his more "serious" career as an artist but soon decided to enroll as a special student at Harvard, in 1919. There his musical talents were recognized by Professor Archibald T. Davison, who guided him toward a career in composition. Having matriculated in 1920, he graduated summa cum laude in 1924 and soon afterward received a Paine Fellowship for further study in Paris, with Nadia Boulanger and Paul Dukas. Upon returning to the United States two years later, he joined the music faculty at Harvard, where he continued a highly influential and productive career until his retirement in 1960. Deploring "the standardized academic routine which taught harmony and counterpoint according to outmoded and unimaginative textbooks,"[5] he remedied that situation by publishing three widely used textbooks of his own: *Harmony* (1941), *Counterpoint* (1947), and *Orchestration* (1955).

As with many American composers of his generation (and later), Piston's professional career was launched when Serge Koussevitzky performed several of his works with the Boston Symphony Orchestra, beginning with the *Symphonic Piece* in 1928, followed by the Suite for Orchestra (no. 1) in 1930.

In our context of the Grand Tradition, we have every reason to agree with the Harvard colleague, G. Wallace Woodworth, who stated that "the backbone of Piston's output is his set of eight symphonies." (Use of the term "set" in this context is intriguing.) Nevertheless, we must acknowledge the importance and expressive character of the five string quartets. Whatever the form, we may agree with Professor Woodworth that "Piston's style derives from a disciplined technique in harmony, counterpoint, and orchestration, and it emphasizes the manipulation of musical ideas, embracing both the contrapuntal patterns of Bach and the developmental practices of Mozart and Beethoven."[6]

Clifford Taylor confirms the essential elements of tonality and structure in the creative process:

Piston's work is essentially tonal in this sense of implied triadic structure and its association of root and fifth. The traditional corollary of root function, particularly in the large structural sense, is clearly at work; local occurrences of major and minor thirds, especially in melodic context, serve to imply triadic structure, with the lower tones in each configuration taking on the appearance of root structure and function. Texture, too, is essentially conceived in terms of a harmonic order of this general kind, in varying degrees of vertical or diversionary linear projection.[7]

Piston combined allegiance to classical values and configurations with an affinity for neoclassicism, especially as exemplified by Stravinsky. To his eight symphonies, composed between 1937 and 1965, and five string quartets, we should add the two violin concertos (1939 and 1960), the Viola Concerto (1957), and the Piano Concerto of 1959, summing up Piston's impressive contribution to the continuity of the Grand Tradition.

Roger Sessions (1896–1985) was born in Brooklyn, New York, but his parents were of New England stock, and their son evidently inherited the intellectual precocity attributed to that hotbed of culture, for he wrote an opera at the age of twelve and enrolled in Harvard at fourteen. After graduating he studied composition with Parker at Yale (1915–17) and became a teacher at Smith College in Northampton, Massachusetts, where he proceeded to compose in his spare time—the usual pattern for American composers of "serious" music. But something was lacking: he felt the need to strike a deeper vein of creativity. The opportunity came when he met Ernest Bloch and undertook further study in composition with him. This "shock of recognition"—the answer to what he had been seeking—proved to be decisive in his life. When Bloch went to Cleveland in 1921, Sessions followed. Four years later, when Bloch left, Sessions pulled up roots and went to Europe, where he spent most of the next eight years in Florence, Rome, and Berlin.

Before that time, however, he had written his first important score as incidental music for a performance of Andreyev's symbolic tragedy *The Black Masters,* at Smith College, in June 1923. From this music he made in 1928 a symphonic suite of dramatic impact, which became his most frequently performed work.

One critic assures us that Sessions's music owed much to Stravinsky, while another hailed him as "an American Brahms"—a comparison that would probably make the latter turn over in his grave. Yet there was an affinity with Brahms, if we agree with Mark Schubart that Sessions is "an intensely serious composer."[8] This view is reinforced by such a work as the String Quartet no. 2 (1951), which may be regarded as a modern extension of the quartet tradition of Beethoven and Brahms. As Andrew Imbrie stated: "His unique musical sensibility expresses itself in line, continuity, and the large gesture. . . . Sessions is neither a system builder nor a preserver of inherited values."[9] Large, yes, but never merely grandiose in the manner of those who ape the Grand Tradition without revitalizing it.

Except for the years he spent in Europe, Sessions developed his professional career mostly in the context of teaching at several universities, chiefly at Princeton and the University of California at Berkeley, as well as a year at Harvard (1968–69), holding the Charles Eliot Norton professorship. This involved a series of six lectures, subsequently published in book form, which contain the essence of Sessions's views on all aspects of music from understanding and hearing to performing and composing. His concept of composition is expressed as follows: "For although all of the genuine composer's vital experiences undoubtedly find their way to his musical imagination, and are transmuted and synthesized there in terms of musical materials, it is in the realm of musical imagination, and there alone, that musical criteria are to be found."[10]

By the 1950s Sessions had assimilated and freely adapted the elements of Schoenberg's twelve-tone method, beginning with the Violin Sonata of 1953. According to Imbrie, "As his style became more chromatic, he found 12-tone technique helpful in solving problems of texture," and he continued to use it in subsequent works, including all the symphonies after the Second (1946).[11] A considerable gap followed the latter, with Symphony no. 3 appearing in 1957 and four others in succession until 1968. Not until a decade later did Sessions complete his Symphony no. 9, which had its premiere by the Syracuse Symphony Orchestra on March 22, 1980. (The performance took place in New York's Carnegie Hall.)

Sessions seldom adheres to formal patterns and divisions of the traditional symphony. He comes closest to this in Symphony no. 6 (1966), "in celebration of the 200th anniversary of the state of New Jersey," which is in three distinct movements: *Allegro, Adagio e tranquillo, Allegro moderato.* It ends, exceptionally, with a finale *a tutti, fortissimo.* More typical is the connecting of one movement to another, as in Symphonies nos. 5, 8, and 9 (1964, 1968, 1980). Of special character is the Symphony no. 4 (1958), with its three descriptive movements: "Burlesque" (*Allegro giocoso*), "Elegy"

(*Adagio*), "Pastorale" (*Andante tranquillo e grazioso*). As is usual with Sessions, changes of tempo within movements are frequent. This is particularly notable in the Symphony no. 8 (1968), consisting of two movements: *Adagio e mesto* and *Allegro con brio*. Also contributing to textural variety are many transitions in tempo combined with a great diversity of instrumental patterns.[12]

Aaron Copland's greatest impact, as noted in chapter 26, came from the variety, versatility, and communicative quality of his major works ranging from ballets to film scores. But there is another aspect of his creative achievement that significantly relates to the orbit of the Grand Tradition.

In one of the earliest appraisals of Copland's music (1920), the perceptive and opinionated critic Paul Rosenfeld observed that "the earmark of Copland's music is leanness, slenderness of sound, sharpened by the fact that it is found in connection with a strain of grandiosity."[13] Obviously, it is this last quality with which we are now primarily concerned. Could it be said, for example, that Copland was "straining for effect" in some aspects of his major symphonic work, the Symphony no. 3 for large orchestra (1944–46)?

In this context we note that Copland's first biographer, Arthur Berger (also an important composer), picked up from Rosenfeld's comment: "Though Copland's style has undergone many changes since this statement was made, the combination of leanness and a certain grandiosity is still one of the things that invest his music with a quite special and intriguing quality." And he adds: "In the case of the massive Third Symphony, this Romantic element seems to stem from Mahler rather than Wagner."[14] Copland was indeed an admirer of Mahler, whose works, he said, had in them "the stuff of living music."[15]

Concerning the modern symphony in general, Berger writes: "Along with grandness of conception, the broad symphonic pattern as it has survived in this century, brings certain features of grandiloquence and flashiness. We observe them in the way rather obvious sentiments are driven at times and forced on audience attention by over-repetition."[16] Judging by audience reaction, there appears to be little objection, if any, toward a repetition of "obvious sentiments" in standard symphonies. While the critic may object to a "protracted sequential development" or the "brassy insistence" on a prolonged fanfare, the public enjoys it all, and the symphony as a grandiose statement just keeps rolling along.

Copland's Symphony no. 3, which is in four movements, has many fine qualities, including a distinctively personal style and an impressive mastery of the orchestral devices at his command. He had previously written two shorter symphonies, the First in 1928, the Second in 1932–33; but after the Third he wrote no more.

In all, Copland wrote some twenty major works pertaining to classical forms of the Grand Tradition, representing about one quarter of his total output. The Piano Concerto, in one movement (1926), may be regarded as marginal because of its strong emphasis on jazz. The Concerto for Clarinet and String Orchestra (with harp and piano, 1948), was written for jazzman Benny Goodman.

The most important works for piano solo are the Variations of 1930, the Sonata of 1941, and the Fantasy of 1957. These are more classical in their titles than in their contents. Traditional devices are of course used but are often twisted and decomposed beyond recognition, especially in the brilliantly original Variations. In contrast the Piano Sonata, in three movements, is more openly classical in form and spirit, for "in this beautiful work Copland is more overtly diatonic, using key signatures and fairly definite key centres."[17] With the Piano Fantasy, Copland turned to chromatic serialism, using a twelve-tone row, but without repudiating diatonic associations.

During this period Copland also composed the Sonata for Violin and Piano (1942–43) and the Piano Quartet (1950), followed by the *Orchestral Variations* (1957), Nonet for Strings (1960), and two impressive orchestral works: *Connotations* (1962) and *Inscape* (1967). The former is the first "purely" symphonic work he had written since the Third Symphony; it was also the first orchestral composition in which he made use of twelve-tone principles. As described by Copland: "Structurally the composition comes closest to a free treatment of the Baroque form of the chaconne. A succession of variations, based on the opening chords and their implied melodic intervals, supplies the basic framework."[18]

Connotations was written by request to celebrate the New York Philharmonic's move to Lincoln Center for the Performing Arts in 1962 and was the only work by an American composer included on the concert program.

Aaron Copland, Roger Sessions, and Roy Harris are the three composers of their generation who achieved the most personal creative extensions of the Grand Tradition. And it is to Harris that we now turn.

"Gentlemen, a genius—but keep your hats on!" With this paraphrase of Robert Schumann's excited tribute to Chopin's op. 1, Arthur Farwell be-

Aaron Copland. Photo courtesy of the Music Division, The New York Public Library at Lincoln Center, Astor, Lenox and Tilden Foundations.

gan an article on Roy Harris published in the *Musical Quarterly* of January 1932—the year in which the latter's op. 1, a sonata for piano, appeared in print. Farwell went on to proclaim that Harris might well "prove to be the protagonist of the time-spirit"—a prophecy that was to be especially confirmed in his fourteen symphonies.[19]

Roy Harris (1898–1979) was born in a log cabin, on Lincoln's birthday, in Lincoln County, Oklahoma. The circumstances of his birth and early childhood had the makings of a legend that would have him appear as a rugged, pioneer son of the Midwest. But, in fact, his family moved to California while he was still a child and settled on a farm in the San Gabriel Valley. With an ear for music, he played piano and clarinet, listened to recordings, and went to concerts whenever he could. After some general musical studies in Los Angeles, he went to the University of California at Berkeley for two years of formal training. But the decisive turning point in his life came when he returned to Los Angeles and studied privately with Farwell, for whom he developed a deep affinity.

By age twenty-four he had begun composing, and his first encouraging recognition came in 1924, when his *Andante* for orchestra, having won first prize in a competition, was performed by Hanson in Rochester. He then went on to study with Nadia Boulanger in Paris and delved deeply into the classics, especially Bach and Beethoven.

Although Harris composed music in many genres, including chamber pieces (such as the Piano Quintet of 1936), sonatas, concertos, cantatas, and other vocal works (notably *Abraham Lincoln Walks at Midnight*, 1953), his major contributions are the fourteen symphonies he wrote between 1933 and 1976. The First Symphony (1933) was commissioned and performed by the Boston Symphony Orchestra on January 26, 1934, under the direction of Koussevitzky, who called it "the first truly tragic symphony by an American."[20] In keeping with his conviction that "the creative impulse is a desire to capture and communicate feeling," Harris gave this summary of his symphony: "In the first movement I have tried to capture the mood of adventure and physical exuberance; in the second, of the pathos which seems to underly all human existence; in the third, the will to power and action."[21]

The Symphony no. 2 (1935), also commissioned and performed by the Boston Symphony (Richard Burgin conducting), is likewise in three movements. The first is a sort of bravura introduction; the second (*Molto cantabile*) is a "study in canons," and the third a "study in rhythmic developments," which is again intended to convey "a feeling of power." The emphasis on canonic writing is characteristic of Harris, with whom canon and fugue are favorite devices.

With the performance of Symphony no. 3 (1937) by Koussevitzky and the Boston Symphony (final revision, February 24, 1939), Harris achieved a resounding triumph. Within a year it had ten performances by the Boston Symphony alone, in various cities. During the 1941–42 season it had thirty-three performances by American orchestras, besides several performances abroad.

The Symphony no. 3, as outlined by the composer, is in one movement, which in turn consists of five sections:

I. Tragic—low string sonorities.
II. Lyric—strings, horns, woodwinds.
III. Pastoral—woodwinds with a polytonal string background.
IV. Fugue—dramatic.
    A. Brass and percussion predominating.
    B. Canonic development of materials from Section II, constituting background for further development of fugue.
    C. Brass climax, rhythmic motive derived from fugue subject.
V. Dramatic—Tragic.
    A. Restatement of violin theme of Section I: *tutti* strings in canon with *tutti* woodwinds against brass and percussion developing rhythmic motive from climax of Section IV.
    B. Coda—Development of materials from Sections I and II over pedal timpani.[22]

In his subsequent symphonies Harris alternated between works of primarily formal character (nondescriptive contexts) and compositions based on contextual associations, such as the *Abraham Lincoln* Symphony (no. 10, 1965), which moreover tend to include vocal elements. It would be misleading to assume, however, that the symphonies with only a formal designation are unrelated to the American scene and the character of its people. In the Symphony no. 5 (1942; rev. 1946), for example, which is in three movements (sometimes identified as Prelude, Chorale, and Fugue), Harris stated that he wanted to portray qualities that "our popular dance music . . . cannot reveal. Our people are more than pleasure-loving. We also have qualities of heroic strength—determination—will to struggle—faith in our destiny."[23] This might be characterized as his "Sinfonia Eroica"—at least symbolically. (The overtly Americanist symphonies will be discussed later.)

Among composers of the next generation, William Schuman (b. 1910) most dramatically and consistently expanded the heritage of the Grand Tradition within an essentially American context. Born and raised in New York City, he was headed for a commercial career, but from an early age he took a keen interest in popular music. While in high school he organized and performed with a jazz band, and later he wrote a large number of popular songs for the commercial trade. But after hearing his first symphonic concert with the New York Philharmonic in 1930, he decided that *this* was the kind of music he wanted to compose. He then enrolled in the Malkin Conservatory and by 1935 had written his First Symphony. The following year he contacted Roy Harris, who was then teaching at the Juilliard School of Music and with whom he formed an immediate and lasting rapport. He went on to study privately with Harris, and by 1937 he had written his Symphony no. 2, which Koussevitzky performed with the Boston Symphony in February 1939. It was not well received (too far-out for Boston!), but he did better with Symphony no. 3 (1941), also performed by Koussevitzky—then the great and good promoter of the up-and-coming American composers.[24]

Meanwhile, Schuman was also busy writing chamber music and choral works, which he was to continue throughout his career, along with such successful choreographic scores as *Undertow* (1945), *Night Journey* (1947), *Judith* (1949), and *The Witch of Endor* (1965). His orchestral Americana would include an *American Festival* Overture (1939) and *New England Triptych* (1956), the latter on music by Billings. But in his output as a whole, the ten symphonies he wrote are basic to his production.

Bruce Saylor states that "the core of Schuman's output is formed by his orchestral music, of which the symphonies are the most significant part. From Harris he inherited a broad, nonrepetitive cantilena, non-functional triadic and polytonal harmony, and expansive gestures."[25] To this Vincent Persichetti adds that "melodic implication seems always at the source" of Schuman's music.[26] In his view: "This is our clue to understanding his music. Each idea pivots on the melodic. The rhythmic structure is implied in the thematic outlines and the harmonies are suggested by the characteristic melodic skips and general textural feeling. Even form ideas are generated by the physical needs and implications of the primary melody."[27]

William Brooks has suggested that a distinction might be made (a matter of emphasis) between the "*American* Symphony" and the "American *Symphony*." For example, Hanson, Piston, and Sessions would be more concerned with emphasizing the latter, while Ives, Harris, and Schuman would tend toward the former. In each case it is a matter of degree; but the general concept has validity, with Hanson at one end of the spectrum and Ives at the other.

Schuman's exact contemporary Samuel Barber (1910–81) was conspicuously loyal to the Grand Tradition yet paradoxically reluctant to cultivate the symphony as its prime symbol. Very early in his career (1936) he wrote a symphony in one movement, and his Symphony no. 2 appeared in 1944. But many years later he destroyed all of the latter except the second movement, which he used for a piece titled *Night Flight* (1964). His classical bent is manifested in such works as the Violin Concerto (1939–40), Cello Concerto (1945), and Piano Concerto (1962); the Sonata for Cello and Piano (1932) and the Piano Sonata (1949); and the String Quartet in B Minor (1930). On the whole he blends or contrasts traditional tonality with modern dissonances, and in at least one work for piano, *Excursions* (1944), he draws on American folk-popular music. Because his compositions are so generally accessible, it may be said that Barber popularized the Grand Tradition during this period.

In the decades from 1920 to 1970, the symphony was undoubtedly a symbol of prestige in America, and the goal appears to have been that of attaining—or, better still, surpassing—the magic number nine. Vincent Persichetti (b. 1915) achieved the desired pinnacle with Symphony no. 9 (1971), appropriately subtitled *Janiculum* (one of the Seven Hills of Rome), for it meant that he had reached the summit.

Peter Mennin (1923–83), utterly loyal to the Grand Tradition, has been earmarked as "primarily a symphonist," although he had also written choral music, cantatas, and a quantity of chamber music. He was off to a conspicuous start when his Second Symphony (1944) obtained the first Gershwin Memorial Award in 1945. His Symphony no. 6 (1953), commissioned by the Louisville Philharmonic Society, was hailed at its premiere by a local critic in glowing terms: "The new Symphony compels attention from the portentous introduction through the triumphant finale." To proceed from the portentous to the triumphant was indeed the most impressive identification with the Grand Tradition.

Mennin's last symphony—which was also his Ninth, the magic number—was commissioned by the National Symphony Orchestra of Washington, D.C., for the celebration of its fiftieth anniversary in the spring of 1983.

Not to be overlooked is the many-sided composer and critic Virgil Thomson, who will be more conspicuously delineated in a later chapter.

His concern for the Grand Tradition was not paramount, and he wrote only two symphonies, of which the more characteristic is the *Symphony on a Hymn Tune* (1928), which does borrow some traditional traits. He describes the work as "a set of variations on the hymn 'How Firm a Foundation'; each movement consists of a further set of variations tightened up in various ways, the first in the manner of a sonata, the second as a Bach chorale-prelude, the third as a passacaglia. The fourth is twice tightened up, once as a fugato, once as a rondo."[28] He alternates between classical genres, such as two string quartets (1931, 1932) and a Cello Concerto (1950), and such personal idiosyncrasies as the *Sonata da chiesa* (1926)—consisting of Chorale, Tango, and Fugue, for clarinet, horn, trumpet, trombone, and violin—and the *Variations and Fugues on Sunday School Tunes*, for organ (1926).

We turn now to the great American symphonic saga as represented by Roy Harris, beginning with *An American Portrait* (1929)—his first full-scale orchestral work (following the *Andante* of 1926). It was originally designated as his First Symphony, but when he came to write the *Symphony 1933*, he decided to call that the "First," so that the earlier composition became known only by its descriptive name. Nevertheless, we can regard *An American Portrait* as a symbolic harbinger of the vast tableau of symphonic Americana that Roy Harris would produce throughout his prolific career.

Paradoxically, the first acknowledged Americanist symphony that Harris wrote has no intrinsic relation to the formal type of the Grand Tradition but is more like a "songfest" with orchestra—or, as Henry Simon aptly said, "not so much a symphony as a little concert of Americana."[29] Listed as Symphony no. 4 and subtitled *Folksong* Symphony, it was first written in 1940 and revised in 1942. With this work the composer sought to promote musical cooperation and understanding between local high school, college, and community choruses and the symphony orchestras of their cities.[30] The definitive version was first performed by Dimitri Mitropoulos with the New York Philharmonic-Symphony Orchestra and New York High School Choruses, on December 31, 1942. Considering the forces involved and a duration of thirty-seven minutes, it does not seem so "little." The overall configuration is that of five choral sections and two instrumental interludes.

The first choral section, "Welcome Party," is based on the Civil War song "When Johnny Comes Marching Home" (upon which Harris composed an overture in 1934). The second, titled "Western Cowboy," brings in "The Dying Cowboy" (or, "Bury Me Not on the Lone Prairie") and "As I Walked Out in the Streets of Laredo." Then comes the first interlude, "Dance Tunes," for strings and percussion, reminiscent of traditional fiddle tunes. The next choral section, "Mountaineer Love Song," is followed by the second interlude, for full orchestra, with a medley of lively tunes. After that comes the choral "Negro Fantasy," featuring the camp-meeting hymn "De Trumpet Sounds It in My Soul," and the finale returns to cowboy lore with "The Gal I Left behind Me."

We turn now to the impressive Symphony no. 6 (1944), written in time of war and subtitled *Gettysburg*. It is dedicated to "the Armed Forces of Our Nation," and its four movements are titled "Awakening," "Conflict," "Dedication," and "Affirmation." Harris conceived these experiences as constituting "that great cycle which always attends any progress in the intellectual or spiritual growth of the people,"[31] and he felt that this had its "classic expression" in Lincoln's Gettysburg Address, to which the symphony refers.

The Symphony no. 7 in one movement (1952; rev. 1955) offers a complete contrast to the foregoing. Although it opens rather solemnly, it soon becomes a richly orchestrated ragout, with bits of varied Americana, ranging from pastoral evocations and hymnlike tunes to country dances and bits of ragtime, plus a rumba rhythm. An admonition to the orchestra stated that "the snare-drum player should really play his little solo like Fred Astaire dances!" When the symphony was performed in October 1955 by Ormandy with the Philadelphia Orchestra, a reviewer remarked that it "seemed to relate to a movie story rather than to reality."[32] But is this not precisely what constitutes the popular epic of America in the twentieth century?

All of Harris's symphonies were commissioned, and the next in line came from the San Francisco Symphony Orchestra, with no. 8 (1962), which is in one movement with five interconnected parts. The *San Francisco* Symphony had its premiere on January 17, 1962, in the city for which it was named, with Enrique Jorda conducting and Johana Harris playing the important parts for piano. It might be described as a pictorial evocation of San Francisco in sound.

The next commission was from Eugene Ormandy for the Philadelphia Orchestra, and Harris expressed some qualms about coming abreast of Beethoven: "It could be considered an act of presumption to write a 9th Symphony. But, if a composer reaches the time of life when he has already written eight symphonies, and yet another symphony is commanded, what is he to do? He must either turn back in acknowledged defeat or test his strength to swim the strong tide of traditional skepticism."[33] As far as we know, he was the only American composer to express publicly his qualms about emulating Beethoven numerically. But perhaps he felt protected by his spirit of dedication to the American nation, with support from Walt Whitman.

The Symphony no. 9 is in three movements, and from their formal context one would not assume the preponderance of a strong underlying symbolic expression. But each movement represents a phrase from the Preamble to the Constitution of the United States: (1) Prelude: "We, the People. . . ." (2) Chorale: "to form a more perfect Union. . . ." (3) Contrapuntal Structures: "promote the general welfare. . . ." When the symphony was premiered by Ormandy with the Philadelphia Orchestra on January 18, 1963 (it was completed in August 1962), Harris wrote some program notes from which we quote:

> As I went to work, "We the People" became in my mind the beginning, a Prelude, a swift moving panorama of all kinds of people in their basic drives and emotions—a kind of quick Dance of Life, of rhythms, melodies, dynamics, and instrumental colors."To form a more perfect Union" became a long, flowing chorale in which the harmony was emphasized. "To promote the general welfare" meant a more formal planning of clearly interrelated functions. I found the contrapuntal structure of Fugue, Canon and Stretto most clearly stated such purpose. Consequently, I selected three mottos from the inscriptions of Walt Whitman, who spent the last years of his life in Camden.
> (1) "Of Life Immense in Passion, Pulse, Power";
> (2) "Cheerful for Freest Action Formed";
> (3) "The Modern Man I Sing."
> Three subjects were conceived to express the musical counterpoint of those three mottos. The third movement was built in three sections of the development of all three subjects.[34]

This was not the only occasion on which Harris had turned to Walt Whitman for inspiration. In 1934 he made a setting of "A Song for Occupations" for eight-part mixed chorus, and in 1935 he wrote the *Symphony for Voices,* for chorus a cappella, in three movements, using texts by Whitman: (1) "Song for All Seas, All Ships," (2) "Tears," (3) "Inscription." (Originally this had included "I Hear America Singing" as the first movement, which was later dropped.)

With the Symphony no. 10 (1965), titled *Abraham Lincoln,* Harris turned again to his great American culture-hero. The symphony is in five movements: (1) "Lonesome Boy," (2) "The Young Wrestler," (3) "Abraham Lincoln's Convictions," (4) "Civil War—Brother against Brother," (5) "Praise and Thanksgiving for Peace." Commissioned by the Music Educators National Conference, and written for speaker with four-part mixed chorus, plus brass, two pianos, and percussion, it was intended for direct communication with young people as both performers and listeners.

The Symphony no. 11, in one movement (1967), had no programmatic context; but with Symphony no. 12 (1968; rev. 1969), the *Père Marquette* Symphony, Harris again turned to his dominant theme: the making of America, and especially its westward expansion. (The work was commissioned by the Father Marquette Tercentenary Commission.) The symphony has two main parts: (1) "The Old World," (2) "The New World." But part 1 has two separate movements, and part 2 has three interconnected movements. The work calls for a tenor solo and a speaker, with full orchestra. The original and the revised versions had their premieres in 1968 and 1969 respectively, with Harris conducting the Milwaukee Symphony Orchestra.

Then came the grand finale, with the *Bicentennial* Symphony (1975; originally called Symphony no. 14, but rather disconcertingly changed to no. 13—or was that meant as a tribute to the original thirteen states?). Commissioned by the University of California at Los Angeles, and written for chorus and orchestra, the symphony had its premiere in Washington, D.C., on February 10, 1976, with Murry Sidlin conducting the National Symphony Orchestra and the All-Texas Chorus.

The five movements are as follows: Introduction ("Revolution for Freedom"), (1) "Preamble to the Constitution," (2) "Freedom versus Slavery 1976," (3) "Civil War: Brothers Kill Brothers," (4) "Emancipation Proclamation," (5) "Freedom." More literal than symbolic, more documentary than formalistic, the *Bicentennial* Symphony is consistent with the role of Roy Harris as interpreter and musical chronicler of the great American saga.

Very early in his career, Harris made a crucial statement regarding his convictions as a composer: "Musical literature never has been and never will be valuable to society as a whole until it is created as an authentic and characteristic culture of and from the people it expresses. History reveals that the great music has been produced only by staunch individuals who sank their roots deeply into the social soil which they accepted as their own."[35]

Even though we may not completely agree with all the implications of that statement, it nevertheless befits Roy Harris, the leading exponent of the "time spirit" in American musical composition and the first to delineate the historical and regional aspects of the American nation and its people from coast to coast. We may therefore venture to postulate that Roy Harris is, in himself, both the creator and the protagonist of his great American musical saga.

For a literary analogy we turn to the first American epic poem, *The Conquest of Canaan* (1776–85), written by the New England author Timothy Dwight, who drew on the Grand Tradition of narrative poetry from Homer to Milton and Pope. Although its ostensible subject is the war between the Israelites and the Canaanites, "most of Dwight's contemporaries read the poem as an allegory of the Revolution, with Washington represented by Joshua."[36] My point, however, is not so much concerned with the subject of the poem as with Dwight's achievement in having written the first epic poem by an American, and one which could be, and was, understood as an allegory of American freedom and victory. In the words of historian Kenneth Silverman:

> Dwight translated into the events of ancient history an ideal of American character, a sense of the personality appropriate to republicans. To be an American, he and others felt, was to have new feelings; he filled his poem with unembodied but representative emotional states, with pictures usually declaring benevolence plus courage, reason plus endurance, democracy plus righteousness. But the true hero of the poem is Dwight himself, the epic poet. . . . *The Conquest of Canaan* is a gesture of cultural maturity whose inmost subject is the writing of an epic poem by an American.[37]

Similarly, Roy Harris filled his numerous symphonies with "unembodied but representative emotional states" intended to proclaim that certain qualities he perceived and admired were deeply rooted in the culture and character of the American people. It might be objected that Harris presented *embodied* figures of great Americans in his symphonies. Yet the musical context in which they are portrayed is determined by the personal vision of the composer. Therefore we may paraphrase Silverman by saying that the symphonic-choral works of Roy Harris as a whole represent a cultural gesture whose inmost subject is the writing of a national epic by an American composer. It follows that the true hero is Harris himself, as both the creator and the symbolic protagonist of his twentieth-century epic of American democracy.

Notes

1. Ernst Krenek, "Tradition in Perspective," p. 27.
2. Robert Evett, "How Right Is Right?" p. 33.
3. Quoted in Arthur Cohn and Arthur Loesser, liner notes to Howard Hanson, *Symphonies Nos. 1 "Nordic" and 3,* Mercury Golden Imports SRI 75112; Eastman-Rochester Orchestra, Howard Hanson, conductor.
4. Nicolas Slonimsky, "Hanson, Howard," *Dictionary of Contemporary Music,* ed. John Vinton, p. 299.
5. Elliott Carter, "Walter Piston," p. 359.
6. G. Wallace Woodworth, "Piston, Walter," *Dictionary of Contemporary Music,* ed. Vinton, p. 576.
7. Clifford Taylor, "Walter Piston: For His Seventieth Birthday," p. 104.
8. Mark A. Schubart, "Roger Sessions: Portrait of an American Composer," p. 197.
9. Andrew W. Imbrie, "Sessions, Roger," *Dictionary of Contemporary Music,* ed. Vinton, p. 675.
10. Roger Sessions, *Questions about Music,* p. 127.
11. Imbrie, "Sessions, Roger," p. 675.
12. See Edward Downes, *The New York Philharmonic Guide to the Symphony,* pp. 850–52.
13. Paul Rosenfeld, *An Hour with American Music,* p. 128.
14. Arthur Berger, *Aaron Copland,* p. 40.
15. Ibid.
16. Ibid., p. 76.
17. Douglas Young, "The Piano Music," pp. 18–21, especially p. 18.
18. Quoted in Downes, *The New York Philharmonic Guide to the Symphony,* p. 270.
19. Arthur Farwell, "Roy Harris," p. 19.
20. Quoted in Hugo Leichtentritt, *Serge Koussevitzky,* p. 130.
21. Quoted in ibid.
22. See Downes, *The New York Philharmonic Guide to the Symphony,* pp. 380–81.
23. Quoted in Leichtentritt, *Serge Koussevitzky,* p. 135.
24. As Leichtentritt shows, Koussevitzky did more than any other conductor of his time to promote the recognition of American composers.
25. Bruce Saylor, "Schuman, William (Howard)," *New Grove Dictionary of Music and Musicians* 16:826.
26. Flora Rheta Schreiber and Vincent Persichetti, *William Schuman,* p. 52.
27. Ibid., p. 51.
28. Quoted in Kathleen Hoover and John Cage, *Virgil Thomson: His Life and Music,* pp. 153–54.
29. Quoted in Lowell M. Durham, liner notes to Roy Harris, *Folk-Song Symphony,* Angel S-36091; Utah Symphony and Utah Chorale, Maurice Abravenel, conductor.
30. See Harris's "historico-biographical note" to this symphony in liner notes to

Roy Harris, *Folksong Symphony 1940,* Vanguard SRV 347; American Festival Chorus and Orchestra, Vladimir Golschmann, conductor; and Robert Strassburg, comp., *Roy Harris,* p. 13.

31. Quoted in David Ewen, *The World of Twentieth-Century Music,* p. 343.
32. Quoted in *Time,* Oct. 31, 1955, p. 40.
33. Roy Harris, in program notes for the Philadelphia Orchestra, Jan. 18, 1963.
34. Quoted in Ewen, *The World of Twentieth-Century Music,* p. 346.
35. See Henry Cowell, ed., *American Composers on American Music,* p. 165.
36. Kenneth Silverman, *A Cultural History of the American Revolution,* p. 501.
37. Ibid., p. 503.

Chapter 32

Creative Systems

The construction of the system has itself become an essential
and inseparable component of the creative act.
—Robert P. Morgan, in *Critical Inquiry* (Autumn 1977)

On April 11, 1941, Arnold Schoenberg, Viennese-born composer and theorist, creator of "the method of composing with twelve tones," became an
American citizen. Until 1925 he had taught and composed in Vienna, building his reputation on works of post-Romantic tendency, such as *Verklärte
Nacht* (Transfigured night). But as he drew away from the safe base of traditional tonality he became a controversial figure, often arousing violent
opposition by his alleged undermining of the "eternal" laws of music.
Withal, his reputation and prestige were such that in 1925 he was appointed
to succeed Busoni as professor of advanced composition at the Prussian
Academy of Fine Arts in Berlin.

But as a Jew his situation in Berlin became precarious after Hitler
seized power, and in 1933 he was dismissed by the Ministry of Education
under pressure from the Nazis. He went first to Paris with his family and
then to the United States, where he was invited to teach a master class at
the Malkin Conservatory in Boston. In 1935 he taught at the University of
Southern California, and the following year he moved to the University of
California at Los Angeles, where he remained until his retirement in 1944,
having had a strong impact on many of the younger American composers.
He died on July 13, 1951, at age seventy-six.

Before he formulated the method of composing with twelve tones,
Schoenberg had achieved what he called "the emancipation of the dissonance" in several compositions written between 1906 and 1911, such as the
Chamber Symphony, op. 9 (1906), Second String Quartet (1907–8), and the
two sets of Piano Pieces. In these works, he said, "the overwhelming multitude of dissonances cannot be counterbalanced any longer by occasional returns to such tonal triads as represent a key."[1] This procedure came to be

known as *atonality*, although Schoenberg himself disliked the term. Faced with the problems that his experiment had unleashed, he sought a new principle of organization that would provide unity and coherence along with variety and flexibility, while not rescinding the freedom of dissonance—that is, the free circulation of all twelve tones of the chromatic scale on an equal basis.

Thus, in the Five Piano Pieces, op. 23 (1920–23), he began "working with tones." Then, in the Piano Suite, op. 25 (1921–23), and the Wind Quintet, op. 26 (1924), the material is organized entirely on the basis of tone rows, and the *"Method of Composing with Twelve Tones Which Are Related Only with One Another"* (as Schoenberg called it) takes definite shape.[2]

Schoenberg's formulation of the twelve-tone method could be interpreted as a defensive reaction against the anarchy of atonality. Another Viennese-born composer, Ernst Krenek, did indeed view this as "a form of reaction against the bold, shocking, initial ventures into the atonal territory around 1910."[3] In any event, it is important to remember, in relation to the developments dealt with in this chapter, that Schoenberg always felt a deep affinity for the values of the Grand Tradition in Western European art music. He was an innovator rather than a revolutionist; in later years he often returned to tonal-harmonic composition, and he firmly asserted that the great Classic and Romantic composers were his best teachers.

Krenek points out that Schoenberg held fast to the basic "classical compositional procedures of thematic statement, motivic relationship and development (which Schönberg called 'progressive variation')" and to "traditional structural schemes of the sonata and rondo forms, the variations cycle, and the various characters of the pre-Classical suite."[4] Krenek's further remarks on the conservative factors in twelve-tone composition (which he refers to as "dodecaphony") are also pertinent to our topic:

> The conservative tendency in dodecaphony is tied up with the adherence to classical structural concepts, which in turn is a consequence of the persistent belief in the indispensability of thematic development. As long as the essential nature of the twelve-tone row is seen in its unifying power, whereby all and any parts of the musical design are brought into the closest possible motivic relationships, the twelve-tone technique remains the most efficient way of applying classical methods of design in a changed, nonclassical idiom.[5]

As we shall see, twelve-tone composition, in its many variants and transformations, became in America a means of reaffirming rather than repudiating the basic values of traditional tonal music. The process was one of liberation, with both a radical change and an underlying continuity. What developed eventually was a network of transformational systems.

Before going on to trace the transition from "method" to "system," it would be well to say more about the development of twelve-tone composition in the United States. Of the immediate followers of Schoenberg, the one who exerted the greatest influence in America was Anton Webern (1883–1945). This was accomplished through his music and his ideas, for he never came to this continent; moreover, his widest impact was posthumous. The composer Mel Powell, writing in 1959, declared: "The recent impact of Anton Webern's musical thought on that of the younger American composers has implied as violent a shaking up as any musical point of view can experience."[6] The term "violent" seems excessive; the effect appears to have been one of discovery and revelation. As summarized by Wallace McKenzie: "What was discovered in Webern's music at that time was a purity of conception and consistency of style that seemed to lead from a traditional base to a completely new sound world; it seemed to contain in its structure the roots of new levels of organization (i.e., serialism)."[7]

Of course, certain American composers such as Sessions, Carter, and Babbitt had become acquainted with Webern's music long before the so-called post-Webern period of the 1950s. Nor should we overlook the less radical yet nonetheless significant influence of Alban Berg (1885–1935), the third member of the Viennese twelve-tone triumvirate. His concern with adapting twelve-tone procedures to large symphonic forms related to the Grand Tradition appealed particularly to those American composers torn between conservative inclinations and innovative promptings.

Such was the case, for example, with the Midwest composer Ross Lee Finney (b. 1906), who, having first studied with Nadia Boulanger in Paris, went to work with Berg in Vienna (1931–32). But because of Finney's deep commitment to tonality, it was many years before he came to accept the view that "the twelve-tone technique is not actually in opposition to functionalism but is a technique concerned with chromatic integration."[8] He then took the step from highly chromatic dissonant textures to twelve-tone structural organizations, in works after 1950.

In 1952 Finney composed the *Variations on a Theme of Alban Berg* for piano, taking his theme from the beginning of Berg's Concerto for Violin and Orchestra, which he regarded as "a wonderful example of an eventfully planned musical statement." However, Finney's first twelve-tone composition was the String Quartet no. 6 in E (1950), expressing more of an affinity with Berg than with Schoenberg or Webern. Berg, for example, in his Violin Concerto of 1935 had utilized a tone row deliberately constructed to include major and minor triads as well as the whole-tone scale.

Concerning his own music, Finney wrote: "No work that I have ever written has sprung from logic; music springs, I am sure, from musical ideas and gestures. The real problem, therefore, and the one that concerns me more and more, is to find a *lyric* expression within the bounds of organization that seem to me important."[9]

Other works in which Finney used twelve-tone configurations in accordance with his flexible criteria are the Symphonies no. 2 (1959) and no. 3 (1963), the String Quartets no. 7 (1955) and no. 8 (1960), and the Piano Quintet no. 2 (1961). In a 1975 interview he stated: "I believe that twelve-tone technique concerns primarily the minutiae of a style, and that pitch polarity determines the large design."[10]

Of the older, established composers, Roger Sessions—who expressed great admiration for Schoenberg—turned to twelve-tone writing with his Violin Sonata (1953), followed by the String Quintet of 1958 and the Third and Fourth symphonies of the same decade. Sessions actually developed his own method of composing with twelve tones as he wrote in 1958: "The series [tone row] will determine the composer's vocabulary; but once the vocabulary has been so determined, the larger questions of tonal organization remain. My own strong feeling is that, while these questions must certainly be answered in terms not alien to the series, it is not serialism as such that can ever be made to account for them."[11]

On the occasion of the first performance of his Symphony no. 8, Sessions wrote in the program notes:

> I have purposely avoided matters of technique, including the dodecaphonic principle which underlies the vocabulary and the structure of the work. The dodecaphonic principle has been now [1968] in existence for forty years, and its basic principles are available for those who are curious about it. Some composers, of which I am one, find it helpful in gaining the musical results that they want. But it can never be strongly enough emphasized that it is the musical result, and not the technical means by which it is accomplished, that matters, and which is the composer's article of faith.[12]

Sessions was willing to adopt twelve-tone configurations as a component of his creative work but not as a determining factor. He viewed them as a *method* rather than a *system*. The *American Heritage Dictionary* makes the following distinction between these two concepts: "*Method* emphasizes procedures according to a detailed, logically ordered plan. *System,* broader in scope, stresses order and regularity *affecting all parts of a relatively complex procedure*" (italics added). The consequent delineations of this chapter will be mainly concerned with the transition from method to system in the American development of twelve-tone composition.

For a key statement on this development, we turn first to the composer, theorist, and critic Benjamin Boretz (b. 1934), who discusses the fundamental role of his colleague Milton Babbitt:

> Babbitt, with all of the developments of 20th-century scientific, philosophical, and linguistic study at his disposal, was the first to recognize the relativistic nature of such constructs as tonal functions and 12-tone relations. From this followed the further recognition that a musical composition might be understood as representing a set of interdependent empirical-rational choices out of a vast domain of possibility (and hence as representing a potential for uniqueness in musical identity far greater than had ever before been envisioned). In being so understood, moreover, a composition could come to be perceived, in a more than metaphorical or honorific way, as a unique and complex instance of rational thought within an empirical domain. Thus for Babbitt the force of any "musical systems" was not as universal constraints for all music, but as alternative theoretical constructs, rooted in a community of shared empirical principles and assumptions validated by tradition, experience, and experiment.[13]

The concept of musical systems as "alternative theoretical constructs" leads directly to the conclusion that "the invention of musical systems themselves becomes an act of composition" (Boretz). Before going on to trace the development and impact of this concept, let us say something about Milton Babbitt's background and interests.

Babbitt was born in Philadelphia (in 1916) but was raised in Jackson, Mississippi, where from a very early age he displayed an equal addiction to music and to mathematics. At New York University he studied both subjects, and their combination became the foundation of his creative and theoretical achievements. He also studied composition with Sessions, both privately and at Princeton University. His musical interests were by no means narrow: for a time in the 1940s he alternated theoretical research with a fling at writing musical comedies and popular songs. From 1948 he was professor of composition at Princeton, where he trained and influenced many of the younger composers attracted by twelve-tone music. A growing interest in electronics led to his appointment, in 1959, as one of the four codirectors of the Columbia–Princeton Electronic Music Center. Thereafter he composed consistently, but not exclusively, with electronic media, notably in such works as *Composition for Synthesizer* (1961–63) and *Philomel* (1964), the latter for soprano and synthesized accompaniment on tape. He has also written chamber and orchestral works and a piece in jazz style titled *All Set* (1957). The title is a pun on his preferred term for the tone row, which he calls the "twelve-pitch set."

Babbitt was attracted to twelve-tone writing because with it "we can structuralize rhythm as we cannot in tonality,"[14] and he regarded rhythm as the central problem of contemporary composition. He also aimed to achieve the "total structuralization" of a composition by serial means, stating that "the twelve-tone set must absolutely determine *every* aspect of the piece."[15] He further explained: "My new works . . . were concerned with embodying the extensions, generalizations, and fusions of certain techniques contained in the music of Schoenberg, Webern and Berg, and above all with applying the pitch operations of the twelve-tone system to non-pitch elements: durational rhythms, dynamics, phrase rhythm, timbre, and register, in such a manner as to preserve the most significant properties associated with these operations in the pitch domain when they are applied in these other domains."[16] Babbitt stated in a later article that "the first explicit steps in the direction of a 'totally organized' twelve-tone music were taken here [i.e., in America] some fifteen years ago, motivated positively by the desire for a completely autonomous conception of the twelve-tone system, and for works in which all components, in all dimensions, would be determined by the relations and operations of the system."[17]

The time span indicated by Babbitt would place the beginnings of the American initiative about 1940. Elsewhere he affirms that "the specific base . . . for achieving a total twelve-tone work" were arrived at by 1945.[18] These dates are important in establishing the transformational contribution of American composers to twelve-tone theory and practice. On this point it is pertinent to quote the words of Brian Fennelly, referring to "the extensions of serial controls to nonpitch elements that occurred in Europe in the 1950s." Although superficially similar, these are "of an essentially different nature," because the European movement "does not display the consistency of interacting systematic relationships that characterizes the corresponding developments in the U.S."[19]

To spell out in detail all the "interacting systematic relationships," from "set combinatoriality" to rhythmic "time-points," would take us far beyond the scope of a cultural interpretation concerned primarily with ideas and trends. Hence we shall continue with some representative composers who have developed individual systems of composition, ranging from specific twelve-tone (or serial) practice to freer, more open concepts.

George Perle (b. 1915) "was among the first American composers to be attracted by the music and thought of Schoenberg, Berg, and Webern."[20] But he very soon developed his own systems, and in his widely known book *Serial Composition and Atonality: An Introduction to the Music of Schoenberg, Berg, and Webern,* concentrating on the possibilities of serial composition, he aimed at finding a "dodecaphonic functionality" to replace the diatonic functionality of tonal music. This led to the development of his "twelve-tone modal system," which he used in most of his compositions from 1950 on. Typical examples are *Three Movements,* for orchestra (1960), String Quartet no. 5 (1960; rev. 1967), and the Cello Concerto (1966).

As described by his former pupil Paul Lansky: "Basically this creates a hierarchy among the notes of the chromatic scale so that they are all referentially related to one or two pitches which then function as a tonic note or chord in tonality. The system similarly creates a hierarchy among intervals and finally among larger collections of notes, 'chords.' The main debt of this system to the 12-tone system lies in its use of an ordered set to structure its relations. This set, however, does not necessarily control linear succession in the same way that a 12-tone set does."[21]

The reiterated emphasis on *system* in the foregoing passages should make clear the importance of this concept in contemporary American musical thought. A system is formally defined as "a set of objects together with relationships between the objects and their attributes." In a musical composition the "objects" are such properties as pitch, duration, timbre, and texture. The "relationships" established by the composer constitute the "composition." But in the case of Perle we can also note that "his work is an example of how a musician can create strong and beautiful works of art amid a distracted age."[22]

The creative continuity and the transformational potential of twelve-tone composition are strikingly exemplified in the creative output and theoretical stance of Charles Wuorinen (b. 1938), the most prolific and articulate latter-day disciple of Schoenberg and Babbitt.

Both in theory and practice, Wuorinen has maintained the fundamental importance of what is technically described as the "twelve-pitch-class system." In a 1962 interview he asserted that, while "most of the Europeans say that they have 'gone beyond' and 'exhausted' the twelve-tone system," in America "the twelve-tone system has been carefully studied and generalized into an edifice more impressive than any hitherto known."[23]

Wuorinen studied composition at Columbia University, where he graduated with a master of arts degree in 1963 and taught until 1971. His principal teachers were Otto Luening and Vladimir Ussachevsky, both pioneers in composing with magnetic tape and other electronic devices. They were also codirectors of the Columbia–Princeton Electronic Music Center, so that Wuorinen was soon drawn into this orbit, with such works as *Orchestral and Electronic Exchanges,* for orchestra and synthesized sound (1964–65), and *Time's Encomium* (1968–69), for synthesized and processed-synthesized sound. Concerning the latter he tells us that he "employed primarily the RCA Synthesizer, and therefore (because of that device's characteristics) the basic materials are the twelve tempered pitch classes and pitch-derived time relations." He then "made the large-scale structure by processing the synthesized material in one of the Center's analog studios."[24]

As an accomplished pianist and conductor, Wuorinen gave much importance to the composer-performer relationship. Realizing that the new music required specially trained and dedicated performers, in 1962 he co-founded, with the composer and flutist Harvey Sollberger, the Group for Contemporary Music. By the same token, many of his works were written for chamber ensembles rather than full orchestra. For example, one of his most effective scores, *Speculum Speculi* (1972), was written especially for the Speculum Musicae ensemble, a group dedicated to performing music, new and old, not favored in the standard concert repertory.

Wuorinen's orchestral works include *Contrafactum* (1969) and two piano concertos, of which the Second (for amplified piano) was composed in 1974. A critic commented on "the great diversity co-existent with consistency" in the latter, and many such examples of coexistence are found both in his music and his intellectual convictions. With respect to the compositions, it has been remarked that "no amount of familiarity will enable the listener to predict the 'sound' of a new work." Actually, the personal imprint is always there, but it is continually transformed by an apparently inexhaustible capacity for recombining the components at various levels (such as foreground and background) and in ever-changing configurations.

What Wuorinen has to say about his own music, of course, conveys the most direct message (an "inside track") for the listener. Take for example the piece for string orchestra titled *Grand Bamboula* (1971), about which he writes: "The title is from Gottschalk, but no other relation is intended, and I confess that I used it mainly for what the sound of its words evokes." To which he helpfully adds, "The work is composed in a variant of my characteristic manner." Then comes the nitty-gritty of components and configurations:

The locations of events in it, and thus the larger pace by which the work proceeds, are all determined by translating the pitch-intervals of the composition's twelve-tone set into time-intervals—lengths that separate events from each other. Normally in my practice, I would consider these "events" to be single notes and the time-intervals the distances among them. But here the "events" are actually motivic in themselves; they are short musical gestures, phrases, textures, juxtaposed to make the composition's totality. It may be this that makes the work seem "lighter" than other compositions of mine—this, as well as my intent.[25]

At this point I would hope that the reader might be enticed into hearing the *Grand Bamboula* (even though it might make Gottschalk turn over in his grave!). We must, in any case, turn now to Wuorinen's crucial peroration, which is strongly pertinent to the basic context of this chapter:

In a way, the *Grand Bamboula* demonstrates as clearly as any work my present attitude toward the organizing powers of the twelve-tone system. It has become for me a musical system of such encompassing size that it seems to merge into a yet larger organism that embraces Western tonal music too. In the *Bamboula,* the set can never be heard in the foreground; rather it is shape-defining, harmony-determining, and gesture-unleashing. At the same time, it is truly generative of foreground detail. But many of the concerns that are presumed basic to twelve-tone music (aggregate formation, clear presentation of sets or segments of them in the foreground, etc.), have no place here, and seem to me to be contextual matters, perhaps essential to a given work, but not to the Schoenbergian universe as a whole. And to repeat: what strikes me most is the sense that different though their classic expositions may be, the tonal and twelve-tone systems are non-dichotomous and complementary—overlapping, moreover, and converging in the kind of musical continuity that may be said to underlie all Western music. *Credo in unam musicam.*

While Wuorinen's unifying credo may ultimately prevail as a future "shape of time" in musical composition, during the presumed transitional period many listeners will probably continue to experience difficulty in coming to terms with the plethora of accelerating innovations and technical advances as we approach the twenty-first century. The problem is by no means limited to twelve-tone composition, for the urge to innovate, to invent new systems, is widespread and has many aspects. Take, for example, Elliott Carter (b. 1908), who at a certain point in his career said, "I want to invent something I haven't heard before." The statement was not only subversive but risky, for what most listeners (and some professional musicians) want and cling to is precisely what they *have* heard before.

Carter, who was born in New York and raised in an atmosphere of high culture, majored in literature at Harvard, and that influence pervades much of his thought. It was not until his senior year that he began to study composition with Walter Piston, after which he went to Paris for further study with Nadia Boulanger. While acknowledging the high standards of coherence and meaning in the classical heritage of Western music, he nevertheless decided to make a path of his own and to formulate experimentally his personal concepts of form and style, of coherence and meaning. This "crucial experience," as he called it, began with his String Quartet no. 1 (1951), about which he later said: "I decided for once to write a work very interesting to myself. . . . I wanted to write a work that carried out completely the various ideas I had at that time about the form of music, about texture and harmony—about everything."[26] Although Carter has not actually elaborated a formal system in the manner of Babbitt, his many statements concerning his compositional procedures and their motivating ideas undoubtedly define a systematic approach.

When Carter, referring to his First String Quartet, said, "From that point on I decided that I would just write whatever interested me, whatever expressed the conceptions and feelings that I had, without concern for the existing public,"[27] he came rather close to the position taken by Babbitt in the latter's notorious article "Who Cares If You Listen?"[28] But there the similarity ends, for Carter has expressed a negative attitude toward twelve-tone composition. Nevertheless, there is a connection, insofar as certain analogies can be drawn. For example, in discussing the importance of Carter's rhythmic innovations, Robert Morgan remarks that these are "to some extent comparable to the innovations made in the pitch domain by Schoenberg and his followers." He goes on to explain:

> Just as Schoenberg broke away from the idea of a single fundamental pitch to which all others were hierarchically related, relying instead upon a system in which pitches were related equally to one another through the disposition of a series or row, so Carter has broken away from the idea of a single fundamental pulse or grouping of pulses, to which all other durations are subordinate, using instead a system of rhythmic proportions relating many different pulses, or tempos, equally to one another. The two phenomena are, at root, surprisingly analogous: in both cases the elements in question—pitch and speed (the latter including individual durations as well as longer spans of time)—are correlated within a unified multi-dimensional field of mutual relationships. In both instances, however, what is essential is not so much the specific *system* as a matter of thinking in a new way about pitch and durational relationships in general, a way that in the pitch area has already had an influence extending far

beyond Schoenberg's own particular "twelve-tone" procedures. . . . And I would not be surprised if the ultimate ramifications of Carter's rhythmic ideas may prove to be almost as widespread.[29]

The foregoing obviously takes the view that we are not dealing with closed systems but with creative systems capable of many ramifications and extensions.

Allen Edwards, in his conversations with Carter, posed the question: "How have you dealt with the matter of pitch structure in your works, and what functional role has this played in relation to the other dimensions of musical rhetoric with which you are involved?[30] From Carter's long and detailed response, I quote some of the most pertinent passages. To begin with, he said that in all his works from the Cello Sonata (1948) up through the *Double Concerto for Harpsichord and Piano with Two Chamber Orchestras* (1961), he "used specific chords mainly as unifying factors in the musical rhetoric—that is, as frequently recurring central sounds from which the different material of the pieces was derived." The First String Quartet, for example, "is based on an 'all-interval' four-note chord, which is used constantly, both vertically and occasionally as a motive to join all the intervals of the work into a characteristic sound whose presence is felt 'through' all the very different kinds of linear intervallic writing."[31]

Carter attaches great importance to the principle of coordination. As he told Edwards: "I believe there are an infinite number of possible new convincing coordinations, and in my music the harmonic sounds are closely related to tempos and rhythmic ideas to form characteristic kinds of events that are distinct and followable, not only because of their pitch-structure but because of their other coordinated aspects."[32]

Carter has been as prolific in his writing as in his music. For example, in many of his recordings, such as those of the String Quartets nos. 1 and 2 (1951 and 1959), explanatory writings can cover as much as both sides of the record jacket. The same is true for the Sonata for Flute, Oboe, Cello and Harpsichord (1952) and the Sonata for Cello and Piano (1948).[33] Concerning the Variations for Orchestra (1955), Carter tells us that "each variation has its own shape, since shape, too, as a mode of musical behavior, helps define character," and he "was eager to put into concrete musical terms a number of ideas I had had about the old form of the variation." The result was hailed by a critic of the *Boston Globe* as "an astounding imaginative feat of virtuoso orchestral writing."[34]

Perhaps because he is aware that technicalities and systematic concepts may be a hindrance rather than an incentive to the appreciation of complex musical compositions, or simply because he is extremely well read and has a deep interest in ideas and analogies, Carter, in describing his own compositions, often resorts to literary comparisons and allusions. For example, concerning the *Double Concerto for Harpsichord and Piano with Two Chamber Orchestras,* he begins by stating that "a concept had to be found that made this instrumental confrontation vivid and meaningful."[35]

This was, of course, worked out in musical terms to begin with, involving "various relationships of pitched and non-pitched instruments, with the soloists as mediators, and the fragmentary contributions of the many kinds of tone colors to the progress of the sound events were fundamental." But soon he began to think of "a literary analog to the concerto's expected form," which he found in *De rerum natura,* a work by the Roman poet Lucretius, "which describes the formation of the physical universe by the random swervings of atoms, its flourishing and its destruction." Not content with that, he goes on to a further analogy with Alexander Pope's *Dunciad,* of which he remarks: "The beautiful end of Pope's poem seemed to articulate in words the end of the work I had already composed." The passage to which he refers is a parody of Lucretius, which ends thus:

> Nor public flame, nor private, dares to shine;
> Nor human spark is left, nor glimpse divine!
> Lo! thy dread empire, Chaos! is restor'd;
> Light dies before thy uncreating word:
> Thy hand, great Anarch! lets the curtain fall;
> And universal Darkness buries all.[36]

Those persons to whom *De rerum natura* is a closed book and the *Dunciad* a relic of outmoded wit may find little or no satisfaction in such analogies. They might, indeed, regard the innovative-experimental composer as a prototype of the "great Anarch" ruling over a "dread empire" of musical "Chaos." But why should a composer's mind not range over as vast a range of images and ideas as that of a poet or philosopher? And, if so, should this not be regarded as an integral factor—a creative component—of his compositional system? This view has certainly been amply displayed in the musical-literary universe of Elliott Carter, and it will again be represented in the many-sided interests of the composer to whom we now turn.

George Crumb (b. 1929) was born and raised in West Virginia—a state better known for its coal mines than for its composers. He studied composition with Ross Lee Finney at the University of Michigan and with Boris Blacher at the Hochschule für Musik in Berlin. In 1965 he joined the music faculty at the University of Pennsylvania. From such a routine situation he has soared imaginatively and creatively into a uniquely personal atmosphere replete with poetic imagery and symbolic idiosyncrasies.

With the tragic sense of life as a kind of ostinato to his poetic vision, he has developed a quasi-surrealistic concept of musical expression and performance, which in some of his major works involves a semitheatrical presentation, including prescribed costumes, nonmelodic speech, and ritualistic movements on stage. His imagination roams far and wide, from moon flights in outer space to the song of the humpback whales in arctic seas.

Crumb has been consistently partial to the poetry of the ill-fated Spanish writer Federico García Lorca (1898–1936), and he has set much of it to music, notably in the four "Books" of *Madrigals* (1965–69), the *Songs, Drones, and Refrains of Death* (1968), and in one of his most characteristic works, *Ancient Voices of Children* (1970). (His Lorca texts are always to be sung in Spanish.)[37]

As a reminder that Crumb does not repudiate his West Virginia background, the score of the last-mentioned work calls for a musical saw and a mandolin to be played with bottleneck. A banjo appears in *Night of the Four Moons* (1969), and a stone "jug" in *Music for a Summer Evening (Makrokosmos III)* (1974), scored for two amplified pianos and percussion.

In *Echoes of Time and the River (Echoes II)* (1967)—the work that immediately established his reputation when performed by the Chicago Symphony Orchestra—the score calls for groups of musicians to walk around the stage at various times, in keeping with the subtitle *Four Processionals for Orchestra*. This is, in effect, an audiovisual ceremony, in which the players are called upon to whisper and shout, to whistle chords, and tap out the composer's name in Morse code. There is also a gong whose pitch is "bent" by immersion in a bucket of water.[38]

Crumb's scores—usually of very large dimensions—constitute a kind of time-space scenario, in which actions and movements, as well as sounds, are precisely indicated. Symbols and gestures are important; exits and entrances are significant. We are told that *Night of the Four Moons* "might be enhanced by a discreet use of stage lighting effects." Moreover, "if the work is performed in a quasi-theatrical manner, the singer might be dressed in Spanish cabaret costume."[39] The vocal factor is the antithesis of bel canto and rejects all conventional effects. It may be shouted or whispered, hummed or spoken or hissed, and when necessary sung—but never

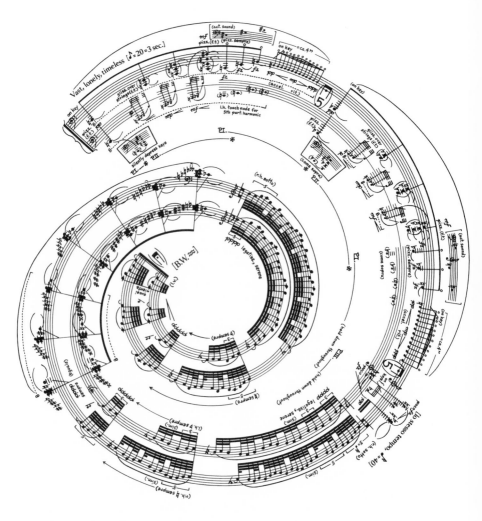

"Spiral Galaxy," from George Crumb, *Makrokosmos*, vol. 1. © 1974 by C. F. Peters Corporation. Used by permission.

merely for vocal display. The result is expressive, symbolic, visceral, incantatory.[40] In *Black Angels (Images I)*, for electric string quartet (1970), Crumb tells us that "the amplication of the stringed instrument . . . is intended to produce a highly surrealistic effect." Furthermore, "the performers also play maracas, tam-tams, and water-tuned crystal glasses, the latter played with the bow for the 'glass-harmonica' effect in GOD-MUSIC."[41]

While it would be misleading to tag Crumb as a musical surrealist—his achievement is too varied and original for that limitation—there is nevertheless an underlying affinity, and no composer has explored and exemplified more deeply and imaginatively the hidden sources of surrealistic expression than this mystic superrealist from West Virginia.

When asked to formulate his credo, Crumb replied: "Music might be defined as a system of proportions in the service of a spiritual impulse."[42] This is a far cry from the mathematical basis of composition based on the twelve-pitch set as practiced by Babbitt and his followers. Yet the concept of a system—however symbolic—remains valid in terms of structure and expression, coordination and impulse, form and spirit. These are shaping forces in creative art that persist through the changes of time and place.

Notes

1. Arnold Schoenberg, "My Evolution," in *Style and Idea*, ed. Leonard Stein, p. 86.

2. Arnold Schoenberg, "Composition with Twelve Tones (1)," in ibid., p. 218.

3. Ernst Krenek, "Tradition in Perspective," p. 34.

4. Ibid., pp. 32–33.

5. Ibid., p. 34.

6. Mel Powell, "Webern's Influence on Our Young Composers," *New York Times*, May 3, 1959; quoted in Gilbert Chase, "Webern in America," p. 154.

7. Wallace McKenzie, "Webern, Anton," in *Dictionary of Contemporary Music*, ed. John Vinton, p. 808.

8. Ross Lee Finney, letter to author, Feb. 22, 1954.

9. Ibid.

10. See Cole Gagne and Tracy Caras, *Soundpieces*, p. 184.

11. Roger Sessions, letter to the editor, *Score: A Music Magazine*, no. 23 (July 1958): 63; reprinted in Andrew Imbrie, "The Symphonies of Roger Sessions," p. 25.

12. New York Philharmonic Society, program notes, May 2, 1968.

13. Benjamin Boretz, "Babbitt, Milton," in *Dictionary of Contemporary Music*, ed. Vinton, p. 44.

14. Anthony Bruno, "Two American Twelve-Tone Composers," p. 22.

15. Ibid., p. 170.

16. Quoted in liner notes to Milton Babbitt, *Composition for Four Instruments . . .*, Composers Recordings CRI-138.

17. Milton Babbitt, "Some Aspects of Twelve-Tone Composition," p. 55.

18. Ibid.

19. Brian Fennelly, "12-Tone Techniques," in *Dictionary of Contemporary Music*, ed. Vinton, p. 780.

20. Paul Lansky, "Perle, George," in ibid., p. 568.

21. Ibid.

22. Leo Kraft, "The Music of George Perle," p. 463.

23. "Charles Wuorinen: An Interview with Barney Childs, 1962," in *Contemporary Composers on Contemporary Music*, ed. Elliott Schwartz and Barney Childs, p. 370.

24. Charles Wuorinen, liner notes to Charles Wuorinen, *Time's Encomium for Synthesized & Processed Synthesized Sound*, Nonesuch H-71225.

25. Charles Wuorinen, liner notes to *Grand Bamboula for String Orchestra* (*1971*), Nonesuch H-71319; the Light Fantastic Players, Daniel Shulman, conductor.

26. See Allen Edwards, *Flawed Words and Stubborn Sounds*, p. 35.

27. Ibid., p. 36.

28. Milton Babbitt, "Who Cares If You Listen?" *High Fidelity* 8 (Feb. 1958): 38–40, 126–27; reprinted in *The American Composer Speaks*, ed. Gilbert Chase, pp. 234–44.

29. Robert P. Morgan, "Elliott Carter's String Quartets," pp. 3–4.

30. Edwards, *Flawed Words and Stubborn Sounds*, p. 106.

31. Ibid., pp. 106–7.

32. Ibid., p. 109.

33. Elliott Carter, *Sonata for Flute, Oboe, Cello & Harpsichord . . . Sonata for Cello & Piano . . .*, Nonesuch H-71234.

34. Elliott Carter, liner notes to Elliott Carter, *Variations for Orchestra . . . Double Concerto . . .*, Columbia Records MS 7191.

35. Ibid.

36. Ibid.

37. See Crumb's copious liner notes to George Crumb, *Ancient Voices of Children*, Nonesuch H-71255.

38. For a recording, see the Louisville Orchestra First Edition Records LS-711 (Louisville, 1971).

39. George Crumb, *Night of the Four Moons* (New York: C. F. Peters Corp., 1971), p. [3].

40. For a recording, see Columbia Records M-32739.

41. George Crumb, *Black Angels* (*Images I*) (New York: C. F. Peters Corp., 1971).

42. *Contemporary Music Catalogue* (New York: C. F. Peters Corp., 1975), p. 16.

Chapter 33
Innovation and Experiment

Why with the time do I not glance aside
To new-found methods and to compounds strange?
—Shakespeare, Sonnet LXXXVI

In 1937 John Cage delivered a lecture on "The Future of Music: Credo," in which he predicted that "the use of noise . . . to make music . . . will continue and increase until we reach a music produced through the aid of electrical instruments . . . which will make available for musical purposes any and all sounds that can be heard."[1] Instead of the opposition between consonance and dissonance, the point of disagreement in the immediate future would be "between noise and so-called musical sound." Percussion music he regarded as "a contemporary transition from keyboard-influenced music to the all-sound music of the future," because "any sound is acceptable to the composer of percussion music; he explores the academically forbidden 'non-musical' field of sound insofar as is manually possible."[2]

That prophetic vision came from the mind of a composer who was born and raised in California, which was also the birthplace of two other innovative-experimental composers: Harry Partch and Henry Cowell. Not only did they explore new methods and open up new vistas and values, they also created the image of California as a fertile ground for nourishing avant-garde visions and activities. True, Cage and Cowell eventually moved eastward and settled in New York, but what they brought with them was a California heritage. With time there would be a trend in the other direction, as experimental centers and activities took root in California.

Henry Cowell (1897–1965) was the oldest of this West Coast trio, and his innovative use of tone clusters, particularly in his piano pieces, was discussed in chapter 25 ("The Ultramodern Movement"). We should now mention two of his early experimental works, the *Romantic* and *Euphometric* quartets, the first composed in 1915–17 (for two flutes, violin, viola), the second in 1916–19 (two violins, viola, cello). Cowell thought of these as

"rhythm-harmony" pieces because they were based on the relationship between harmonic and rhythmic ratios. His point of departure was "the possibility of a demonstrable physical identity between rhythm and harmony"—a hypothesis that he and a fellow student in physics (at the University of California) verified by experimenting with a pair of sirens: "Our experiments with two simultaneous sirens showed that if they are tuned in
the relationship 3:2, they will sound the *interval* of a perfect fifth; if they are
both slowed down, keeping the same 3:2 relationship, they arrive at a
rhythm of 3 against 2, heard as gentle bumps but also visible in tiny puffs of
air through the holes in the sirens. . . . Tuned to any other harmonic ratio,
of course, the same thing happens, proving that these ratios express a single physical relationship which is heard as rhythm when slow and as pitch
when fast."[3]

Obviously to counteract any impression of abstract experimentation,
Cowell stated: "In both quartets the musical intention was flowing and lyrical, not severe or harsh. . . ." Also: "Both quartets are polyphonic, and
each melodic strand has its own rhythm." As Cowell went on to experiment with this type of "rhythm-harmony" piece, he realized that "the meters for the most part were necessarily so complex that they were obviously
unperformable by any known human agency. . . ."[4] How frustrating!

Nevertheless, he cherished the hope that "an instrument could be devised that would put under human control even more complex rhythms
by means of comparatively simple performance on a keyboard." Sketches
for such an instrument were made in 1916, but there were no funds for its
construction. Later it occurred to Cowell that "the principle of the 'electronic eye' might be applied to such a device." So in 1929 he approached
the inventor Leon Theremin, then living in New York, who agreed to
build a keyboard that could produce one to sixteen rhythms—"either any
number together, or all of them at once, or one after the other." The resulting instrument, which was called "rhythmicon," was "tuned to match
the overtone series, so that all the ratios in rhythm and pitch, up to the
sixteenth," might be given, and pitched high or low. There was, however,
a catch: "Since there was no way of giving melodic freedom by varying
the note-lengths in a single part, and no method of accenting, these early
quartets still could not be played on it."[5]

Disappointed but not discouraged, Cowell composed other rhythmic-
harmonic pieces for the new instrument, most notably a work titled
Rhythmicana (1931), for rhythmicon and orchestra, in four movements. Ac-

cording to Nicolas Slonimsky, "A new musical wonder, provisionally christened 'rhythmicon,' was presented to the world for the first time on January 19, 1932, at the New School for Social Research [New York], where
Cowell is in charge of musical activities."[6]

But *Rhythmicana* was not performed on that occasion—nor indeed
was it performed at all during Cowell's lifetime, for it was impossible to co-
ordinate efficiently the rhythmicon with the orchestra. Instead, the premiere took place in Palo Alto, California, on December 3, 1971, with the
Stanford Symphony Orchestra, and we are told that it was "greeted with
considerable enthusiasm by the audience."[7]

To tell how this came about is to anticipate the electronic era that
Cowell foresaw. Briefly, the rhythmicon attracted the attention of Leland
Smith, a composer and computer specialist at Stanford University in Palo
Alto. After tracking down the original score and parts of *Rhythmicana,* he
decided that it could be effectively performed if "programmed" in advance
through a computer. With some modifications designed to take full advantage of the technical possibilities of the computer—particularly with respect to timbre, tempo, and rhythm—the new version was realized at the
Stanford Artificial Intelligence Project Center, and the public performance
followed. Cowell had truly become a prophet of the electronic era![8]

We turn now to Harry Partch (1901–74), who was born in Oakland,
California. He moved to Arizona with his parents as a young boy but eventually returned to California and became identified with that state in many
ways. Self-taught in composition, Partch also learned to play a variety of instruments. But he was destined to be a loner, going his own way, formulating his own philosophical-aesthetic-social system. He later recalled, "Having decided to follow my own intuitive path I began to write music on the
basis of harmonized spoken words, for new instruments and in new
scales."[9] This type of music he designated as *corporeal,* in contrast to *abstract*—his term for formal composition.

Corporeal music is essentially monophonic, based on the premise that
"of all the tonal ingredients a creative man can put into his music, his voice
is at once the most dramatically potent and the most intimate."[10] This "essentially vocal and verbal music" is characterized as being "vital to a time
and place." Moreover, "Corporeal music is emotionally 'tactile.' It does not
grow from the root of 'pure form.' It cannot be characterized as either mental or spiritual."[11] The barriers between expression and reality would no

longer exist in this music. With hindsight we can see that this is an intuitive preview of certain types of pop singing that developed in the 1960s, wherein the effect of intimacy before huge crowds is achieved by the potency of the microphone and electronic amplification.

Partch was in some ways a precursor of the beatnik. When the Great Depression came, he took to the road as a hobo. From this brief experience he drew such corporeal pieces as *U.S. Highball: A Musical Account of a Transcontinental Hobo Trip* (1943); *Barstow: Eight Hitchhiker Inscriptions from a Highway Railing at Barstow, California* (1941); *San Francisco: A Setting of the Cries of Two Newsboys on a Foggy Night in the 'Twenties* (1943); and *The Letter: A Depression Message from a Hobo Friend* (1943). All of these pieces were composed between 1941 and 1943, and they can be aptly characterized as period pieces.

In his musical system Partch rejected the twelve-tone tempered scale and substituted a division of the octave into forty-three microtones. He invented and constructed (or, in some cases, adapted) instruments to play the music of his microtonal system, based on just intonation. In 1933 he made his first experimental model of a keyboard, and in 1941 he constructed the chromelodeon, a reed organ retuned to his microtonal scales. In 1938 he built a kithara, with seventy-two strings in chords of six each. The harmonic canon, with forty-four strings and a movable bridge for each string, was rebuilt in 1945.

In all, Partch created an array of percussive instruments that were visually as well as acoustically striking. Various types of marimbas were built from 1946 to 1963, culminating in the marimba eroica, originally made of vertical redwood blocks, later rebuilt with Sitta-spruce blocks. The marvelous cloud-chamber bowls were made from the tops and bottoms of pyrex carboys, suspended on a frame. Other instruments followed, even more original and beautiful as unique works of art.

As such, they became visual elements in various stage works, choreographic and dramatic, that loom large in Partch's output. These include *Plectra and Percussion Dances* (1949–52), in three sections: "Castor and Pollux," "Ring around the Moon," "Even Wild Horses." This last is subtitled "Dance Music for an Absent Drama" and consists of three acts, freely based on Arthur Rimbaud's macabre poem *A Season in Hell*. Musically, it is an ethnic potpourri, including Partched versions of the samba, rumba, *naniga*, conga, "Tahitian Dance," and "Afro-Chinese Minuet"! This was followed by *Oedipus: A Music-Dance Drama* (1951; rewritten 1952–54), and *The Bewitched: A Dance Satire* (1955), both highly typical of his stage presen-

Harry Partch performing on the cloud-chamber bowls. Photo courtesy of Danlee Mitchell.

tations. He used the term *theater pieces* for his sixteen stage works and explained his concept as follows:

> My idea has been to present the drama expressed by language, not to obscure it either by operatic aria or symphonic instrumentation. Hence, in critical dialogue, music enters almost insidiously, as tensions enter. The words of the players continue as before, spoken, not sung, but are a *harmonic part* of the music. . . . Tone of spoken word and tone of instrument are intended to combine in a compact emotional or dramatic expression, each providing its singular ingredient. My intention is to bring human drama, made of words, movement, and music, to a level that a mind with average capacity for sensitivity and logic can understand and therefore evaluate.[12]

This obviously repudiates contemporary concepts of opera and goes back to the *dramma per musica* as conceived by the Florentine *camerata* in the seventeenth century. The culmination of this aspect of Partch's musical theater comes with two works in which even the instrumentalists become part of the stage ritual. These are *Revelation in the Courthouse Park* (1960; after *The Bacchae* of Euripides) and *Delusion of the Fury: A Ritual of Drama and Delusion* (1965–66).[13]

The most original and important of Partch's purely instrumental works is *And on the Seventh Day Petals Fell on Petaluma*, begun in 1963, with the final version completed in 1966. We are told that this was "conceived as a study for, and to be used with," *Delusion of the Fury*, and that "the work includes the entire gamut of Partchian instruments." The definitive 1966 version consists of eleven "Verses" for quartets and quintets, and twenty-three "Verses" for twenty-four of the unique instruments invented by Partch, from "Zymo-Xyl" to "Blue Rainbow."[14]

Partch tells us that his purpose was to "exploit the instrumental resources to the full," including "untried rhythms and polyrhythms." As he explained the procedure: "Each of the first twenty-three verses is exactly one minute long, not counting the final beat. These are duets and trios. Then, by electronic synthesizing, pairs of verses are combined in numbers twenty-four through thirty-three. . . . The electronic syntheses result in quartets and quintets starting with number twenty-four, and with a septet at the end. . . ."[15]

Partch's main concern was always with "the quality of vitality that makes a culture significant." In a way, he embodied the counterculture in his repudiation of mass production, commercial opportunism, and social conformity. His last composition is characteristically titled *The Dreamer That Remains: A Study in Loving* (1972). We are told by the composer that "in its entirety, the work is predeterminedly dramatic."[16] The same could be said of Partch's life as a whole.

Our third Californian, John Cage, was born in Los Angeles in 1912. Early in his career he was significantly influenced by Cowell, with whom he studied for a year in New York (1933–34). He was fascinated by Cowell's unorthodox methods of extracting strange sounds from a piano, as well as by the non-European musical cultures Cowell taught at the New School for Social Research. Returning to California, Cage continued to study composition with Schoenberg but soon concluded that composing with twelve tones was "no longer necessary." So he went on to something else—a process that was to continue for the rest of his career. He became involved with painting, the dance, writing and lecturing, Zen Buddhism, and the liberation of music from the weight of the past.

As a percussion composer Cage began to explore the "academically forbidden" domain of sounds with *Construction in Metal* (1939), scored for orchestral bells, five thundersheets, twelve-gong gamelan, eight cowbells, three Japanese temple gongs, four automobile brake drums, eight anvils, four Turkish and four Chinese cymbals, four muted gongs, water gong, suspended gong and tantam, plus a piano muted by metal cylinders on the strings by an assistant to the pianist (the latter also sweeps the bass strings with a timpani stick). Structurally the work is based on a rhythmic method analogous to the Indian *tala,* in which "the whole has as many parts as each unit has small parts, and these, large and small, are in the same proportion."[17]

In 1938 Cage—taking a tip from Cowell—developed his own version of the prepared piano, using basically a bolt or large wooden screw inserted between two strings, whereby he developed a whole new gamut of sounds. The piano had become, in effect, "a percussion ensemble under the control of a single player." He further explained: "All the factors of the piano preparation, objects and their positions, were found experimentally. They represent a choice determined by taste rather than reasoned relations. . . . The result is a gamut of sounds moving from lower to higher octaves without the correspondances of pitch characteristic of scales and modes."[18]

These devices were applied with great creative ingenuity in the set of sixteen Sonatas and Interludes (1946–48), which were first performed by pianist Maro Ajemian at the Twenty-five Year Retrospective Concert of the Music of John Cage that took place at Town Hall, New York City, on

May 15, 1958, marking a turning point in Cage's career. But with Cage it was never a matter of "devices" or innovations per se: he tells us that the Sonatas and Interludes were written when he "first became seriously aware of Oriental philosophy," and after reading the work of Ananda K. Coomaraswamy, he "decided to attempt the expression in music of the 'permanent emotions' of Indian traditions."[19]

In 1951 Cage completed the Concerto for Prepared Piano and Orchestra, in three parts, which we are told "was composed with the help of a set of large charts on which rhythmic structures were drawn up." Cage stated: "I let the pianist express the opinion that music should be improvised or felt, while the orchestra expressed only the chart, with no personal taste involved. In the second movement I made large concentric moves on the chart for both pianist and orchestra, with the idea of the pianist beginning to give up personal taste. The third movement had only one set of moves on the chart for both, and a lot of silences. . . ." Then follows a statement that is quintessential Cage: "Until that time, my music had been based on the traditional idea that you had to say something. The charts gave me my first indication of the possibility of saying nothing."[20] The paradigm of this concept is the piece titled *4' 33''* (1952), designated as "tacet, any instrument or combination of instruments." Cage explained, "This is a piece in three movements during all three of which no sounds are intentially produced. The lengths of time were determined by chance operations but could be any others."[21] It has been frequently performed, notably by Cage's inseparable colleague David Tudor; but as far as we know it has not been recorded.

About this time Cage was developing a view that went "away from ideas of order towards no ideas of order." He wanted a composition to be free—not only from preconceived norms but also from the personal taste and volition of the composer. The first step in this direction was the use of chance operations. This occurred in *Music of Changes* (1951), for piano, in which "the note-to-note procedure, the method, is the function of chance operations." Moreover, "at each small structural division . . . chance operations determined stability or change of tempo." Hence the structure itself became indeterminate, because "it was not possible to know the total time-length of the piece until the final chance operation, the last toss of coins affecting the rate of tempo, had been made."[22] The "toss of coins" refers to the chance operations set forth in the Chinese *I-Ching* (Book of changes), by which three coins are tossed six times (originally used for obtaining oracles).

Music of Changes was a turning point for Cage because it demonstrated that structure could be indeterminate. Thus, in *Music for Piano* (1953–56), "structure is no longer a part of the composition means." For Cage, then, composition became "an activity characterized by process and essentially purposeless."[23] (I take this to mean that its "purpose" is in its *being.*)

Cage also developed other methods for chance operations, notably the use of charts. Here the sound elements are classified according to five characteristics: frequency, amplitude, duration, timbre, and order of succession. Once classified, they can be manipulated by a number of ingenious chance operations to yield many unpredictable combinations. The aim is "to make a musical composition the continuity of which is free of individual taste and memory (psychology) and also of the literature and 'traditions' of the art. The sounds enter the time-space centered within themselves, unimpeded by service to any abstraction. . . ."[24]

A model would be the Concert for Piano and Orchestra (1957–58), which has no master score and which Cage regards as a work continually "in progress," even though he finds "each performance definitive." He writes: "Each part is written in detail, both specific directives and specific freedoms being given to each player, including the conductor. . . . The pianist's part is a 'book' containing 84 different kinds of composition, some, varieties of the same species, others, altogether different. The pianist is free to play any elements of his choice, wholly or in part and in any sequence."[25] Thus there is freedom without anarchy, selection without repetition.

The availability of the magnetic tape recorder in the early 1950s was to have far-reaching effects on musical composition. Working with Earle Brown and David Tudor, Cage in 1952 conceived the *Imaginary Landscape* no. 5, described as "a score for making a recording on tape, using as material any 48 phonograph records." Its composition involved chance operations derived from the *I-Ching*. This was followed by *Williams Mix,* which used some 600 recordings as "raw material." Then came *Fontana Mix* (1958), with "parts to be prepared from the score for the production of any number of tracks of magnetic tape, or for any number of players, any kind and number of instruments." The work is described as a composition "indeterminate of its performance," with graphically complex ingredients and mixtures, and we are surprisingly told that "the use of this material is not limited to tape music but may be used freely for instrumental, vocal and theatrical purposes."[26] The electronic age was in the offing; but freedom of choice remained, and the imagination would come to terms with the machine.

The most important development in electronic composition came through the use of voltage-controlled synthesizers and digital computers. The first computer-generated composition was realized in 1955, when Lejaren A. Hiller (b. 1924) and Leonard M. Isaacson "proposed that the composition of music could be treated by the Monte Carlo method."[27] This may have been a gamble—but not with the roulette wheel! It referred to the use of a mathematical procedure for solving certain types of complex problems. The result was the *Illiac Suite* for string quartet, which they frankly presented as a product of experimental research rather than a work of creative art.[28]

In 1958 Hiller joined the music faculty of the University of Illinois at Urbana-Champaign, where he greatly stimulated the development of computer-generated music. A notable example was the *Computer Cantata* (1963), done in collaboration with Robert A. Baker. The big breakthrough came in 1967–68, when Cage joined Hiller in creating a large work titled *HPSCHD*—obviously an acronym for *harpsichord*, reduced to six input units that the computer could handle. One of the most elaborately random and scholastically complex compositions ever conceived, *HPSCHD* would require a whole chapter for its full description. Its primary source is a piece attributed to Mozart, the *Introduction to the Composition of Waltzes by Means of Dice* (K. Anh. C 30.01). Cage, lured by any type of chance operation, picked this up, combined it with the *I-Ching*, and, with Hiller at the controls, put it through the computer-programming system known as digital-to-analog conversion.[29]

Although it was mostly a "Mozart Mix," each of the seven harpsichordists involved in the performance played something different, to achieve the effect of calculated chaos. But, as Cage explained, "When you use the word 'chaos,' it means there is no chaos, because everything is equally related—there is an extremely complex interpenetration of an unknowable number of centers."[30] Cage will certainly go down in history as the Grand Master of Chaos.

Nevertheless, the performance dimensions of *HPSCHD* are flexible, ranging from the full complement of fifty-one magnetic tapes and seven "live" harpsichordists to merely one of each, or any number in between. Its premiere at the Illinois campus on May 16, 1969, was a huge audiovisual, multimedia, superelectronic bash.

Emphasis on visual and environmental factors involving multimedia activities became a feature of the avant-garde during the 1950s. A typical event was the so-called happening, which could consist of almost any kind of activity in any designated environment. Credit for the prototype happenings has been given to John Cage and ballet dancer-choreographer Merce Cunningham, who at Black Mountain College, North Carolina, along with pianist David Tudor and painter Robert Rauschenberg, conceived and produced an event of this kind.[31]

In the 1960s an important center for multimedia flourished in Ann Arbor, Michigan, with the ONCE Group, consisting of filmmakers, theatrical designers, visual artists, musical performers, and composers. Among the last mentioned, Robert Ashley (b. 1930) and Gordon Mumma (b. 1935) were much involved with electronics. Mumma adopted the term *cybersonics* to designate his system of electronically controlled composition, as in *Megathon for William Burroughs* (1963), for ten electronic, acoustical, and communication channels.

Ashley, in collaboration with painter-sculptor Milton Cohen, developed a series of electronic music-theater pieces and was increasingly influenced by film techniques and forms. In the 1970s he turned to video as another visual medium that was rapidly becoming attractive to avant-garde composers. He took the initiative, in 1977, for putting together a work titled *Music with Roots in the Ether,* described as "video portraits of composers and their music." The composers were all Americans identified with the current avant-garde movement: David Behrman, Philip Glass, Gordon Mumma, Pauline Oliveros, Alvin Lucier, Terry Riley, and Ashley himself. Ashley regards the whole series as "one big theatre piece." As such, it is a collaborative work, with a cameraman and an art director, along with eight other assistants. Hence the question arises: What price video composition? The medium may be the message—but who pays the piper?

While videotape is an effective audiovisual medium, it is not physically "alive," and for this we must turn to the mixed-media works that feature live performers. An outstanding example is *The Emperor of Ice Cream* (1962; rev. 1974) by Roger Reynolds (b. 1934), based on the poem by Wallace Stevens. As described by Reynolds: In this work my central concern for the spatial organization of sounds, for the expressive and structural potential of this musical dimension first emerged. The glossing of text, both vocally, theatrically, and through instrumental emulation of the voices is practiced throughout."[32] The score—in itself a fascinating work of graphic art—indicates not only the sounds but also the movements of the singers and instrumentalists on stage. The scoring is for four male and four female vocalists, piano, vibraphone, percussion, and double bass.

In 1969 Reynolds joined the music faculty of the University of California at San Diego and three years later was appointed director of the newly created Project for Music Experiment, which brought together a rotation of experimental composers and research specialists, including audiovisual technicians.

A typical work by Reynolds during this period is *I/O: A Ritual for 23 Performers* (1970), based on R. Buckminster Fuller's concept of complementary opposites, "and in particular upon the wealth of relationships that exist between male and female."[33] As usual with Reynolds, the whole presentation is elaborately complex, including electronics, lighting, and theatrical effects.

Reynolds has often been attracted to literary sources, as in ". . . *from behind the unreasoning mask*" (1975), which draws on Melville's *Moby Dick*, and *Compass* (1972–73), from a story by Jorge Luis Borges. In the latter the key idea is thus expressed: "Everything becomes a word in a language in which something or someone, day and night, goes on writing that infinite GIBBERISH, the history of the world." A middle section of the score, "Experimental Bridge," is subtitled "Gibberish," which leads to "Dis-Harmony," followed by the concluding "Agony"—all vocally as well as instrumentally and electronically expressed (plus black-and-white screen projections). We are told that "a conductor is required." Why not a magician-technician?

From the 1960s the influences of the Far East, as well as Africa, became increasingly significant in American avant-garde circles. One of Cowell's students, Lou Harrison (b. 1917), was strongly attracted to the music of the Orient, and while traveling mainly in Japan, Korea, and Taiwan, he mastered most of the instruments pertaining to those cultures. Making his home base in California, he worked for a time with Partch and adopted the methods of just intonation, while also creating scale patterns of his own. He came into prominence with a piece for percussion titled *Canticle No. III,* concerning which Virgil Thomson wrote: "Lou Harrison's Canticle No. III, for flute, guitar and seven percussion players, is one of those delicate and delicious symphonies masterfully sustained that are a unique achievement of the composer. The most instantaneously recognizable effects come from the Far East. . . . [But] it is Western in its drama and structure. . . . The work is subtle, lovely to listen to and powerful in expression, a memorable experience."[34]

The foregoing is typical of the many accolades bestowed on Harrison's highly personal yet immediately expressive compositions, of which an outstanding example is the Suite for Solo Violin, Piano, and Small Orchestra (1951). And it is these instruments that manage to evoke the sounds of Indonesian gamelan music, mainly by featuring piano, celesta, and harp. The combination of Eastern and Western musics is typical of these compositions, including the *Concerto in Slendro* (1961), *Pacifica Rondo* (1963), and the Symphony no. 3 (1982), which had its premiere at the Cabrillo Music Festival, conducted by Dennis Russell Davies.[35]

Philip Glass, from Baltimore (b. 1937), had a conventional beginning for his musical career. He graduated from the University of Chicago, received a degree from the Juilliard School of Music, and studied with Nadia Boulanger in Paris. But there the standard pattern ends: he learned more of "the tricks of the trade" from Milhaud—yet the crucial turning point came when Ravi Shankar, grand master of the sitar, revealed to him a new concept of rhythm "based on completely different ways of thinking."[36] This involved building a composition from small units that are continually regrouped according to predetermined patterns. The next step was to study the tabla with another Indian master, Alla Rakha.

All of this led to the radical concept of musical composition as a process of performance, which required the collaboration of a performing group able and willing to work over long periods of time with total dedication. This was indeed an unprecedented situation, for Glass and his group of performers worked for an entire year to rehearse and construct his *Music in Changing Parts* (1970). There was, moreover, the problem of renting a concert hall for a work that might last from four to six hours, as did another magnum opus, titled *Music in Twelve Parts* (1971–74). Although the latter had its premiere at New York's Town Hall, it is not surprising that most performances took place in museums, art schools, or a loft in Manhattan's Soho district.

In 1972 Glass told an interviewer, "I began listening to the 'sound' of the music and I found that had become more interesting than the structure." Hence he became increasingly involved in "the kind of almost psycho-acoustical experiences that happened while listening to the music."[37] In the 1970s he also ventured into the realm of "progressive rock" with a piece called "North Star," whereby he 'discovered the wonderful world of over-dubbing."[38] This was, in effect, another mode of structuring sound.

Steve Reich (b. 1936) was a New Yorker who eventually made his way to California before returning to Manhattan. At Cornell University he majored in philosophy, but his musical interests were encouraged by Professor William Austin. So he went on to study composition at Juilliard and at Mills College in Oakland, California. He became interested in electronics at the San Francisco Tape Music Center but soon decided that this did not communicate in a way that was meaningful to him, so he went in other directions.

Reich's essential innovations began through experimenting with "gradually shifting phase relationships between two or more identical repeating patterns" (as in *Piano Phase,* 1967, for two pianos). His aim was to develop a type of performance "that was both completely worked out beforehand and yet free of actually reading the notation." Explaining his preference for "live" performance rather than electronics, he stated: "In any music which depends on a steady pulse, as my music does, it is actually tiny micro-variations of that pulse created by human beings, playing instruments or singing, that gives life to the music."[39] His concept of music is that of "a particular liberating and impersonal kind of ritual,"[40] relating to what human beings experience both in Nature and in their own minds and feelings.

Because of the special character of his music, it became necessary for Reich to have his own ensemble of performers, beginning with three musicians in 1966, later increased to twelve. For some larger works such as *Work in Progress for 18 Musicians and Singers* (begun in 1974), the number of performers could vary according to the time and circumstance. About this work Reich has said: "The opening eleven-chord cycle . . . is a kind of pulsing cantus for the entire piece." He explains:

> The structure of this piece is based on a cycle of eleven chords played at the very beginning of the piece. All the instruments and voices play and sing pulsing notes within each chord. Each chord is held for the duration of two breaths, and the next chord is gradually introduced, and so on, until all eleven are played and the ensemble returns to the first chord. This first pulsing chord is then maintained by two pianos and two marimbas with one piano and marimba playing on the quarter-note pulse, and the other two playing on the off beat, an eighth away. While this pulsing chord is held for about five minutes a small piece is constructed on it. When this piece is completed there is a sudden switch to the second chord, and a second small piece is constructed. This

means that each chord that might have taken 15 or 29 seconds to play in the opening section is then stretched out as the basic pulsing melody for a five-minute piece very much as a single note in *cantus firmus,* or Gregorian chant melody of a 12th-century four-part Organum by Perotin might be stretched out for several minutes as the harmonic center for a section of the Organum.[41]

Thus, the avant-garde is often closer to a remote past than to a more proximate tradition. Temporal remoteness becomes a kind of novelty.

An important factor in Reich's compositional process is his involvement with music of the Orient and Africa. He became interested in African music in 1962 and in 1970 studied drumming with a master drummer of the Ewe tribe in Ghana. He was attracted to Balinese music, and in 1973 he worked with the Balinese Gamelan Semar Pegulingan in Seattle. We can think of him as an eclectic for whom the entire universe of controlled sounds is potentially creative. He is partial to mallet instruments such as the marimba and glockenspiel, as well as to the small Cuban clapping sticks called claves (as in *Music for Pieces of Wood,* 1973) and to the clapping of hands (*Clapping Music,* 1972).

Reich tells us that back in the United States he was turned on to jazz as a teenager, and when he went to Cornell University, he played drums with a campus combo. While at Mills College he listened to Coltrane at the Jazz Workshop in San Francisco, and he recently told an interviewer: "John Coltrane's music between 1961 and 1964 made a tremendous impression on me. You can hear it." He also added: "My music has a beat, and perhaps you can dance to it."[42]

Maybe that accounts for the response to Reich's music by young people. They may or may not be dancing in the aisles, but they are taking it all in with great gusto. Is there a primal instinct that responds to the sound of drumming and clapping, and the visceral impact of slowly persisting and changing rhythms that work like an incantation? Not only do you hear it, but you can feel it—atavistically.

The influence of Partch continued to have an impact on many of the younger American composers, including Ben Johnston (b. 1926), from Macon, Georgia. While studying piano and composition at the Cincinnati College Conservatory of Music, he came across a copy of Partch's *Genesis of a Music,* which immediately opened up new vistas. He got in touch with Partch, who was then living on a ranch in Gualala, California, and received an invitation to go out there and work as an apprentice-assistant—especially to tune the microtonal instruments. This was a decisive move for Johnston, although he probably did not realize it until later. After six months with Partch he went on to study with Darius Milhaud at Mills College and in 1951 joined the music faculty at the University of Illinois.

There he succeeded in bringing Partch to the campus as a "composer in residence," and as a consequence Johnston became irrevocably involved with microtonal composition—which meant years of patient and persistent labor. The crucial turning point was the Sonata for Microtonal Piano, on which he worked for five years (completed in 1965). Like other works to follow, it was based on his conviction of the need "to reopen doors closed by the acceptance of the twelve-tone equal-tempered scale as the norm of pitch usage." He explained: "My *Sonata for Microtonal Piano* deploys chains of just-tuned (untempered) triadic intervals over the whole piano range in interlocked consonant patterns. Only seven of the eighty-eight white and black keys of the piano have octave equivalents, one pair encompassing the distance of a double octave and the remaining six pairs separated by almost the entire length of the keyboard. Thus there are eighty-one different pitches, providing a piano with almost no consonant octaves."[43]

In a later microtonal work we find a fusion with the Asiatic tradition: *Two Oboes and Two Tablas and Two Banyas* (1969–70), with a just-intonation scale of 142 tones. He has also experimented with vocal techniques, notably in an improvisational piece, *Visions and Spells* (1975), for the New Verbal Workshop; and *Two Sonnets of Shakespeare* (1979), for solo voice, requiring a three and a half octave of male vocal range. He returns to his great mentor with *In Memory, Harry Partch* (1975), for soprano, computer tape, string quartet, eight percussionists, and slide show.

Conlon Nancarrow (b. 1912), born in Texarkana, Arkansas, appeared to be headed for a conventional career in composition when he went to the Cincinnati College-Conservatory, followed by study in Boston with Piston and Sessions. (He also played the trumpet in jazz bands.) When the Spanish Civil War broke out, he joined the Abraham Lincoln Brigade, to fight on the republican side against the fascists (May 1937). As a result, when he returned to the United States, his passport was revoked. He then went to Mexico and made his permanent home in a suburb of the capital.

Nancarrow soon became fascinated with the possibilities of composing music directly for the player piano (also known as the pianola). As described by Charles Hamm: "The essence of the operation of all player pianos is that a perforated paper roll passes over a vacuum; each perforation activates a mechanism that depresses a hammer, which strikes a string and thus produces a note. The perforations on the horizontal axis of the roll determine which notes are to be struck; the vertical arrangement controls the timing—the sequence in which the notes are to be struck and the time intervals between notes. Thus it is possible to create music—to compose—directly on the piano roll."⁴⁴

Quite so! But what patience and fortitude, what technical skill and persistent determination are required in the process. Thus Nancarrow, with immense dedication, became the first composer to produce works of original character through the medium of the player piano. But it was not until the 1970s that this music came to be widely known and admired, thanks to the interest and enthusiasm of such American composers as James Tenney, Charles Amirkhanian, John Cage, Gordon Mumma, and Roger Reynolds. Then recordings of Nancarrow's music began to appear, including the *Complete Studies for Player Piano*, recorded in the composer's home studio, with a brilliant analysis and interpretation by Tenney.⁴⁵ Volume 1 opens with Study no. 3 (1949), subtitled "Boogie-Woogie Suite." Because of its roots in jazz, blues, and ragtime, this is an excellent introduction to the music of Nancarrow.

"The two most distinctive characteristics of Nancarrow's work as a whole," Tenney writes, "are his *rhythmic procedures* and his exploration of manifold varieties of *polyphonic textures*—and polyphonic perception."⁴⁶ Moreover, the *Studies for Player Piano* "constitute a virtually exhaustive investigation and creative realization of countless new possibilities in the areas of rhythm, tempo, texture, polyphonic perception, and form, all of which will provide exciting challenges to composers, theorists, and listeners alike for many decades to come."⁴⁷

Women have become increasingly involved with contemporary "advanced" musical composition and performance, including a variety of experimental trends. Conspicuous in this area is Pauline Oliveros (b. 1932), who from her early training at the University of Houston, was involved with developing a combination of sound imagery and instrumental colors. In 1952 she moved to San Francisco, where she studied with Robert Erickson for a period of six years. From him she derived the concept of organic rhythm, "that is rhythm which shifts, expands, contracts, and is not periodic in the metrical sense." Instead, "there is a sense of simultaneous fast and slow tempos."⁴⁸

In 1961 she became a cofounder of the San Francisco Tape Music Center, with Morton Subotnick and Ramon Sender. A typical work of this period is *Sound Patterns* (1962), a textless piece for mixed chorus that gave the impression of an "overall electronic/orchestral sound produced by vocal sounds of an abstract nature." Thus she "abandoned precise control of pitch . . . in order to gain the possibility of complex clusters of sound."[49]

Her compositional interests continued to be flexible and exploratory, with both electronic and instrumental-vocal features. She also became "increasingly concerned with theatrical and visual materials as a part of the music." Thus, in such works as *Aeolian Partitions* and *The Wheel of Fortune*, "the musicians' actions as performers are as important as the sounds produced." These are, in effect, "theater pieces," as they require that the musicians "play" a role as well as an instrument. Her main concern is with "the total act and environment of performance."[50]

In *Aeolian Partitions* (1970), for example, commissioned by Bowdoin College and "Conditioned by the Aeolian Players for Flute, Clarinet, Violin, Cello, and Piano," we find that the "score" consists mainly of directions for the musicians to "perform" this or that gesture or movement on cue. For instance: "Violinist turns back to audience, begins to draw bow soundlessly across string (fingering A 880 on the E string), and begins to walk slowly to the back wall, pacing himself for one minute." The cellist "then launches into a virtuoso cadenza from the existing literature (double stops, fast passages, etc.), stops abruptly before the resolution, exits to his left briskly, returns with a broom, sweeps around chair then exits again."[51]

With two brief exceptions the score consists of similar directions, and at the end we are told that "the audience may be invited to join in the telepathic improvisation" and to "see if you can influence the performer to play your pitch by mental telepathy." But we are not told how many responded when it was performed at Bowdoin College. Presumably the invitation is always open.

We turn now to the remarkable career of Barbara Kolb (b. 1939), who—in the words of Donal Henahan—"has become . . . one of the most frequently performed of contemporary composers."[52] Born and raised in Hartford, Connecticut, she studied at the Hart College of Music (1957–64) and with Lukas Foss and Gunther Schuller at Tanglewood. It was Foss who drew attention to her music when he performed the *Three Place Settings* (1968), for narrator, clarinet, violin, double bass, and percussion. Further recognition came with such highly characteristic works as *Trobar Clus* (1970), commissioned by the Fromm Foundation in cooperation with the Berkshire Music Center, and *Soundings* (1972), commissioned by the Koussevitzky Music Foundation. The piece for piano titled *Appello* (1976) proved to be widely popular, with a string of performances ranging from Colorado to California, Maryland to Minnesota, Montreal to Paris, and London to Luxembourg.

Regarding *Appello,* Kolb explains: "An appello in Italian is an imperative call, an alarm, a call to a lost child, the word you put at the top of an advertisement: attention. Each of the four movements is suggestive of a different kind of call." Henahan described *Appello* "as a highly organized piece, employing serial structure in both melodic and harmonic writing, and the tone-row used in all four movements is taken, as a kind of homage, from Book 1A of Pierre Boulez's 'Structures.' "[53]

It was Boulez who gave the New York premiere of *Soundings* (it required two conductors), and in February 1978 Seiji Ozawa performed it with the Boston Symphony Orchestra, followed a month later by his tour of Japan. Meanwhile, Kolb had received the *Prix de Rome* for music composition (1969–71), thus becoming the first American woman to have earned this prestigious prize. Her international acceptance was clearly established.

Between 1965 (beginning with a piece for two clarinets titled *Rebuttal*) and 1983, Kolb had written twenty-five compositions, of which at least ten were widely performed and acclaimed. In October 1983 she was assigned to a year's residence at the Institut de Recherche et Coordination Acoustique / Musique in Paris, where she would compose a work for chamber orchestra and tape.

In discussing one of her most characteristic compositions, *Soundings,* Kolb describes it as being, "in some strange way," related to "the influence of jazz; it's a certain type of repetition of sounds with very slow changing harmonies and rhythms that kind of weld together, rather than being kept separate, to create different characters."[54]

The *Chromatic Fantasy,* for narrator and six instruments (1979), with a text by poet Howard Stern, she describes as "fanciful, witty and surreal," while noting "the bizarre yet colorful selection of instruments," ranging from soprano saxophone to electric guitar. After six performances throughout the United States, it received further acclaim when presented by the New York Philharmonic on June 4, 1983. Kolb tells us of the "many factors [that] entered the creative process of this work":

> First, the diversity of instruments brought *L'Histoire du Soldat* to mind. With its emphasis on jazz (ragtime in Stravinsky's case), blending of colors, and story-telling nature, *Chromatic Fantasy* seemed to already fit into a mold. In addition, I had recently completed a large orchestral work, *Grisaille,* which emphasized the development of texture and color evolving from having analyzed

Boulez's *Rituel.* Although the structure and content of my works have little to do with that of *Rituel,* both *Grisaille* and *Chromatic Fantasy* utilize sonorities which are reminiscent of this extraordinary work in a way which relates more to gesture and the stylistic character of *Rituel* rather than to any specific or detailed aspect of his technique. Also, the title bears conscious homage to the musical meaning of "chromatic" and to that archetypal D minor *Chromatic Fantasy* of J. S. Bach.

The text is divided into three parts which all interrelate. The poem in its entirety is expressed in the second section, whereas the first section, a condensed variation of the poem, and the third, an impressionistic extract of phrases and ideas from the poem, were written expressly for the musical rendition.

Finally, as in the case of Stravinsky's *L'Histoire du Soldat, Chromatic Fantasy's* main intent is to entertain.[55]

Who could ask for anything more? Creative entertainment, originally conceived and effectively presented, is Kolb's forte. Many other women composers are going her way, but with their own idiosyncrasies and creative achievements.

Notes

1. John Cage, *Silence,* pp. 3–4.
2. Ibid., p. 5.
3. Henry Cowell, Preface (Jan. 1964); reprinted in Cowell, *Quartet Romantic, 2 Flutes, Violin, Viola; Quartet Euphometric, 2 Violins, Viola, Violoncello* (New York: C. F. Peters Corp., 1974).
4. Ibid.
5. Ibid.
6. Nicolas Slonimsky, "Henry Cowell," in *American Composers on American Music,* ed. Henry Cowell, p. 60.
7. Leland Smith, "Henry Cowell's *Rhythmicana,*" p. 141.
8. Ibid., pp. 134–47.
9. Harry Partch, *Genesis of a Music,* p. 6.
10. Ibid., p. 7.
11. Ibid., p. 8.
12. Ibid., p. 332.
13. See Harry Partch, *Delusion of the Fury: A Ritual of Drama and Delusion,* Columbia Records M2 30576; conducted by Danlee Mitchell, under the supervision of Partch. Included is a booklet illustrating Partch's self-made instruments, in full color.
14. Paul Earls, "Harry Partch: Verses in Preparation for 'Delusion of the Fury,'" pp. 3, 7, and passim.

15. Partch, *Genesis of a Music,* pp. 348–49.

16. A recording of *The Dreamer That Remains* (titled *Harry Partch, John Cage,* New World Records NW 214) has Partch as "Intoning Voice and Narrator." Also included are excellent descriptive and biographical data by Ben Johnston.

17. John Cage, liner notes to *The 25-Year Retrospective Concert of John Cage,* recorded in performance, Town Hall, New York, May 15, 1958; produced and distributed by George Avakian (New York, 1959).

18. Ibid.; also quoted in John Cage, *Sonatas and Interludes for Prepared Piano* (*1946–48*), Composers Recordings CRI 199; performed by Maro Ajemian.

19. Cage, brochure notes to *The 25-Year Retrospective Concert.*

20. Quoted in Bernard Jacobson, liner notes to John Cage, *Concerto for Prepared Piano & Orchestra (in 3 Parts) (1951)* . . . , Nonesuch H-71202.

21. Robert Dunn, ed., *John Cage,* p. 25.

22. Cage, *Silence,* p. 20.

23. Ibid., p. 22.

24. Ibid., p. 59.

25. Cage, brochure notes to *The 25-Year Retrospective Concert.*

26. Dunn, ed., *John Cage,* pp. 39–40.

27. Lejaren Hiller and Leonard M. Isaacson, *Experimental Music,* p. 3.

28. For a complete score, see ibid., pp. 181–97. See also Hiller, liner notes to *Computer Music from the University of Illinois,* Heliodor (MGM Records) HS 25053. This recording includes the *Computer Cantata.*

29. See Peter Yates, liner notes to John Cage and Lejaren Hiller, *HPSCHD for Harpsichords & Computer* . . . , Nonesuch H-71224.

30. Quoted in Richard Kostelanetz, "They All Came to Cage's Circus," *New York Times,* May 25, 1969, sec. 2, p. 23.

31. Ellsworth J. Snyder, "Chronological Table of John Cage's Life," in *John Cage,* ed. Richard Kostelanetz, p. 39.

32. *Roger Reynolds: Profile of a Composer,* p. 45.

33. Ibid., p. 47.

34. Virgil Thomson, "American Music," *New York Herald Tribune,* Feb. 23, 1953.

35. The earlier *Elegiac* Symphony (1975), commissioned by the Koussevitzky Foundation in the Library of Congress, was rerecorded by Arch Records S-1772.

36. Willoughby Sharp and Liza Béar, "Phil Glass: An Interview in Two Parts," p. 29.

37. Ibid., p. 28.

38. John Rockwell, "Space Rock—into the Weird Blue Yonder," *New York Times,* Feb. 13, 1977, sec. 2, p. 29.

39. Steve Reich, *Writings about Music,* p. 25.

40. Ibid., p. 11.

41. Steve Reich, notes for performances of his music at "The Kitchen" in New York City, May 1975.

42. Cole Gagne and Tracy Caras, *Soundpieces,* p. 316.

43. Quoted in Charles Hamm, liner notes to *Sound Forms for Piano,* New World Records NW 203, p. 5.

44. Ibid., p. 4.

45. See *Complete Studies for Player Piano: The Music of Conlon Nancarrow*, vol. 1, with a historical-analytical essay by James Tenney, Arch Records S-1768; produced by Charles Amirkhanian.

46. Tenney, essay (courtesy of Soundings Press), in ibid., p. 2.

47. Ibid., p. 1.

48. Pauline Oliveros, "Career Narrative," typescript sent to the author, p. 1.

49. Ibid., p. 2. See also Heidi Von Gunden, *The Music of Pauline Oliveros*, for a comprehensive coverage, including a catalog of works, bibliography of her writings, and musical examples.

50. Oliveros, "Career Narrative."

51. Pauline Oliveros, *Aeolian Partitions*, in *Scores: An Anthology of New Music*, comp. Roger Johnson, pp. 316–19.

52. Donal Henahan, "Rebel Who Found a Cause," *New York Times*, Nov. 17, 1976, sec. C, p. 21.

53. Ibid.

54. Gagne and Caras, *Soundpieces*, p. 276.

55. Barbara Kolb, program note in *Chromatic Fantasy for Narrator and Six Instruments* (New York: Boosey and Hawkes, 1983).

Chapter 34

Country to Rock—with Soul

Country music cannot be studied as a purely rural phenomenon.
It must always be considered in relation to the dominant society
that lies around it, the industrial-technical-urban society that
has modified and transformed all American values.
—Bill C. Malone, *Country Music, U.S.A.*

On June 14, 1923, an enterprising recording director for OKeh Records
named Ralph Peer, with acoustical equipment set up in a rented loft on
Nassau Street in Atlanta, recorded the singing and playing of a southern
"hillbilly" musician known as Fiddlin' John Carson.[1] The two songs he recorded were "The Little Old Log Cabin in the Lane" and "The Old Hen
Cackled and the Rooster's Going to Crow." We are told that Peer
"thought the singing was awful and insisted that only Carson's fiddle tunes
be recorded."[2] It took a while to get accustomed to the nasal sound of an
old-time hillbilly folksinger from the southern uplands. But a local record
dealer persuaded Peer to let him market 500 copies of the Carson recording
in the Atlanta area. Within a few weeks they were all sold, and the dealer
was ready for another shipment.

Peer got the message: he brought Carson to New York, signed him
up for an exclusive contract, and recorded twelve more of his songs. "With
the recording of Fiddlin' John," writes historian Bill Malone, "the hillbilly
music industry began its real existence"[3]—harbinger of the multibillion-dol-
lar country-and-western entertainment business that was to sweep the
United States (and a large part of the world) during the next half-century.

In his authoritative book *Country Music, U.S.A.*, Malone sums up the
two main developments of the 1920s:

> Essentially, two forms of music developed within hillbilly music during the
> early period, two forms that dominated it until the emergence of "western"
> music in the 1930's. These . . . can be called "country" and "mountain." Both

were country, or rural, in origin, but mountain music came to be identified in the minds of many people as the type that originated in the Appalachians. Country music was that type which stressed more individual solo singing, utilized more nontraditional instruments, and was influenced by popular music and Negro blues music. . . . Mountain music tended to be more conservative and to rely more on the traditional songs and instruments, and it was performed in the traditional, high-nasal harmony.[4]

These two trends were personified by Jimmie Rodgers for "country" and the Carter Family for "mountain" style. (Both were first recorded by Peer in 1927.) The performing members of the original Carter Family, who were from Virginia, consisted of Alvin Pleasant Carter, who played fiddle; his wife, Sara, who sang and played the autoharp; and Sara's sister Maybelle, who married into the family. She also played the autoharp, as well as the banjo, but was most remarkable and influential for her guitar playing, which became known as the "Carter style." This involved "bass melody or harmony notes along with interspersed chords produced by brushing across the higher strings."[5] Maybelle told an interviewer that she had learned this way of playing from her brothers; hence it was probably traditional. It has since been widely imitated.

The Carter Family, including its many talented descendants and members by marriage, did more than any other pioneer group to bring to mass audiences the songs, ballads, and hymns of the Anglo-American folk tradition—eventually blended with other types of popular country music.[6]

Jimmie Rodgers (1897–1933) was the most influential figure in shaping and popularizing the hillbilly trend and anticipating what came to be known as country and western. He was no hillbilly himself, for he came from Meridian, Mississippi, and the first music he absorbed was from the deep South. The son of a railroad worker, he became a train brakeman, riding the rails in Mississippi and Louisiana. He learned to sing the blues from the blacks and picked up their banjo and guitar styles. But he was also close to the Anglo-American folksong tradition, blended with popular currents. Utterly distinctive was his "blue yodel" effect, with its falsetto on a higher octave. The first yodel that he recorded, in "T for Texas," was an instant success.[7]

Again it was the enterprising Ralph Peer who first recorded the songs of Jimmie Rodgers, for Victor in 1927, mostly with guitar. The early titles indicate the wide variety of his repertory: "The Soldier's Sweetheart," "Blue Yodel," "The Brakeman's Blues," "In the Jailhouse Now," and "My

Carolina Sunshine Girl."[8] Many of his songs were written in collaboration with his sister-in-law Elsie McWilliams, including "Mississippi Moon" and "Lullaby Yodel."

Jimmie had only a perfunctory training in music and often had to rely on the help of others for his performances. But by the 1930s he had become a superstar celebrity, from Texas to New York and far beyond. He made his last home in Texas, where he boosted the popular cowboy image that was in vogue, with such songs as "The Yodeling Cowboy" and "When the Cactus Is in Bloom."

The variety and range of Jimmie Rodgers's repertory is impressive: from blues to ballads, from folk to pop, from humor to sentiment. The unifying factor is an unmistakable personal style, at once sentimental and sincere, folkish and artful, rowdy and refined. Toward the end, when he sang the "TB Blues," he must have known that tuberculosis would send him to an untimely grave.

Hillbilly and country music—the latter outpacing the former—was soon highly popularized by the radio, the recording industry, and by perennial shows such as the Grand Ole Opry, National Barn Dance, and Louisiana Hayride. Nashville, Tennessee, became a dominant center with the Grand Ole Opry, and by the 1960s the "Nashville Sound" was widely tagged as "country-pop." This was characterized by electric guitars, piano, and background choruses, with input from rock and roll. In this high-powered atmosphere, such popular entertainers as Roy Acuff and Gene Autry were also capitalist entrepreneurs.

About Acuff (b. 1903), we are told that he has written "close to one hundred songs, the most famous of which is 'Precious Jewel' "—doubtless very well named for one who had the equivalent of many "precious jewels" in his vast coffers.[9] Other typical Acuff songs are "Just to Ease My Worried Mind," "Not a Word from Home," and "Branded Wherever I Go"—a typical batch of country music sentimentality.

Gene Autry, born in Tioga, Texas, in 1907, began by emulating the Jimmie Rodgers blue-yodel style and reached into fame as the "Oklahoma Singing Cowboy" on the WLS radio Barn Dance program in Chicago. We are told that "before long, Sears (then owner of WLS) was selling literally millions of Gene Autry records and thousands of songbooks. . . ." Moreover, "his vocal style developed and matured into something distinctly his own [and] his voice expressed a sincerity and unaffected honesty which created a feeling of immediacy between the singer and his listeners. . . ."[10] He was equally effective in both his radio and stage shows, the latter featuring the "Gene Autry Rodeo."

Typical Autry songs are "Tumbling Tumbleweeds," "South of the Border," and "Be Honest with Me." But perhaps many readers are not aware that he also wrote two best-sellers for children: "Here Comes Santa Claus" and "Rudolph the Red Nosed Reindeer." He appeared in many motion pictures that included his own songs such as "Rainbow on the Rio Colorado" and "Back in the Saddle Again." In sum: "He helped bring hillbilly music out of its backwater, gave it a new life, a deserved and long-needed dignity, and a national exposure. The fact that he became a millionaire in the process should no longer impede our acknowledgment of this tremendous achievement."[11]

Songwriter and singer Hank Williams (1923–53), from Alabama, remained solely an entertainer during his brief career, and after his untimely death from alcoholism, he became an imperishable legend. Moreover, "his were the first songs firmly to bridge the gulf between country and pop music," beginning with his great hit "Cold, Cold Heart."[12] As recorded by Tony Bennett in 1951, it sold over a million copies. Other big successes included "Your Cheatin' Heart," the hymn "I Saw the Light," and the bouncy "Move It on Over."

Meanwhile, the country sound was being enhanced by a type of instrumental music with traditional roots that came to be known as "bluegrass." The name has no geographical connotation, although it is true that Bill Monroe, who set the style with his string band, the Blue Grass Boys, came from Kentucky. It all began when Monroe decided to concentrate on the mandolin, developing a hard-driving style that emulated the old-time fiddling of the hoedowns and barn dances.

Together with his brother Charlie on guitar—who featured the bass-guitar runs that became identified with bluegrass—Bill Monroe in 1938 formed the Blue Grass Boys, with whom he continued to make country-music history, mainly with his mandolin innovations but also as singer, arranger, and composer. The typical bluegrass band consisted of fiddle, guitar, mandolin, string bass, and five-string banjo. This last, however, was not included in Monroe's band until 1945, when Earl Scruggs joined the group—and then its effect was sensational. In the words of Malone, Scruggs "rejuvenated the five-string banjo, made his own name preeminent among country and folk musicians, and established bluegrass music as a national phenomenon."[13]

Also with the Blue Grass Boys at this time was Lester Flatt, famous

Roy Acuff and his band shortly after they arrived at WSM from Knoxville in 1938. (Left to right) Oswald Kirby, Jess Easterday, Acuff, Little Rachel Veach, Lonnie (Pap) Wilson. Photo courtesy of the Center for Popular Music, Middle Tennessee State University, Murfreesboro, Tennessee.

Bill Monroe in 1974. (Left to right) Kenny Baker (fiddle), Bill Monroe (mandolin), unknown guitarist (possibly Joe Stuart), Jack Hicks (banjo), bass player not visible or known. Photo by Charles K. Wolfe. Used through the courtesy of the Center for Popular Music, Middle Tennessee State University, Murfreesboro, Tennessee.

for his guitar runs, especially the one known as the "Lester Flatt G-run" (N.B.—the *G* is *not* flatted!). This was a traditional technique that he enhanced and popularized. Flatt and Scruggs, who formed a band called the Foggy Mountain Boys in 1948, became the two most influential figures in bluegrass music during the following decades.

The impact of this folk-rooted country music—Alan Lomax called it "folk music with over-drive"—was strong and far-reaching. It stimulated the appreciation of traditional values while appealing to youth with its innovations and independent assimilation of elements from jazz and rock music.

If bluegrass bands and the Nashville sound could be said to represent "folk music with over-drive," it should also be noted that, along with its impact as popular entertainment, folk-popular music in the 1930s acquired strong overtones of social protest and ideological involvement. Thus there was a two-way input to the performance arena: from singers who had inherited and grown up with the folk tradition, such as the Carter Family and Almeda Riddle,[14] and from "outsiders" who were attracted to it both intrinsically and because it provided a medium of communication for their social ideas. Pete Seeger, Phil Ochs, and Joan Baez were typical of the latter approach.

But who were the "people," and who were the "folk"? To view the latter solely in the context of isolated rural enclaves was no longer realistic after the communications explosion of the 1920s. Other demographic pressures came from industrial expansion, which demanded mobility to supply its labor force. This prompted John Greenway to assert that " 'folk' in our culture is an economic term." Modern civilization, he maintained, was "educating the old agricultural folk out of existence, but a new folk, the industrial community, is taking its place."[15]

Another pragmatic folklorist, Archie Green, confronted a similar problem in his study of miners' songs. He began by formulating a broader definition of folksong as "a piece received aurally by listeners and singers which is accepted by them and which is also altered in the process of movement over time."[16] To the question "Can an industrial song become a folksong?" Green replies in the affirmative, because "folklore was found in all strata of society."[17] He also defines his specific criteria: "An industrial folksong describes work itself and portrays the life, diversions, and struggles of men on the job."[18] He cites the ballad of "John Henry" as an example.

What could be described as a sociocultural crossover is represented in the career of Sarah Ogan Gunning, "the daughter, sister, and wife of Kentucky coal miners," whose repertory included hundreds of traditional ballads and folksongs that she sang in authentic Appalachian folk style.[19] During the depression of the 1930s she became actively involved in the struggle of the miners for unionization and wrote such militant songs as "Down on the Picket Line" and "I Hate the Company Bosses." Although Green repudiates these as folksongs because they are not in the folk tradition, we might say that they are neofolksongs—a type that was to proliferate as songs of protest in the troubled decades to come.[20]

The combination of the Great Depression and attempts by the Establishment to suppress the rise of unionism led many liberal members of the upper middle class to champion the cause of the workers. An outstanding example is that of Charles Seeger (1886–1979), an eminent folklorist and musicologist and the father of Pete Seeger, who, along with singer-composer Lee Hays, played a prominent role in the neofolksong movement of social protest.

It has been argued that "the American Left was basically the starting point of the urban folk music movement because the only audiences available during that period were generally part of this ideologically isolated community."[21] Of special significance in this context was a benefit concert for rural migratory workers that took place in New York City (March 1940), at which Pete Seeger and Woody Guthrie met for the first time. Also present was folklorist, singer, and scholar Alan Lomax, who later referred to this event as the beginning of the folksong revival in America.

Woody Guthrie (1912–67) is credited with having written more than 1,000 songs. At least 100 have become classics of grass-roots Americana, including "This Land Is Your Land," "Pastures of Plenty," "Dust Bowl Refugee," "Reuben James," and "This Train Is Bound for Glory." Pete Seeger wrote: "His music stayed rooted in the blues, ballads and breakdowns he'd been raised on in the Oklahoma Dust bowl. . . . Woody was a national folk poet. . . . A generation of songwriters learned from him."[22] Pete Seeger was among the first to pass on the message of Woody Guthrie to the American people.

In 1941 Pete Seeger took the initiative in founding the Almanac Singers, who aimed at bringing the informal, directly communicative appeal of folk-type music into the urban middle-class milieu. Then came the Weavers (1949–52), who made it big on radio and television, in theaters and nightclubs, and on recordings that are said to have sold over four million copies.

Pete Seeger had to pay dearly for what a congressional committee regarded as "un-American" views; but eventually he was exonerated and became a great favorite of the campus circuit, as well as the dedicated promoter of worthy causes such as environmental protection and civil rights. He said it with music and confirmed it with deeds. His fame was worldwide.[23]

The 1950s and 1960s brought a great surge of what came to be known as "folk-pop"—the commercial popularization of folk music by professional entertainers. For example, the "Ballad of Davy Crockett" sold more than seven million records in one year and became a national craze. The highly successful Kingston Trio, doing the campus circuit, made a tremendous hit with "Tom Dooley," a ballad involving a passionate love triangle, culminating in murder and retribution by hanging. Another vocal trio, Peter, Paul, and Mary, had great acclaim with their versions of traditional folksongs. Whatever the source or the style, mass communication was the keynote, popularity the proof.

Nevertheless, for large sectors of the folk-pop audience, it was not only the music but also the "cause" that counted, involving such issues as civil rights, nonconformist life-style, and the war in Vietnam. Thus, folk-pop inevitably merged with the protest movements—a trend that is personified in three contrasting personalities: Phil Ochs, Joan Baez, and Bob Dylan.

Phil Ochs (1940–76) was drawn into the neofolksong movement as an undergraduate at Ohio State University. More interested in his guitar than his grades, he soon dropped out and made his way to that Mecca of the urban folksinger, Greenwich Village in Manhattan. Dylan's defection from the protest movement in 1964 provided an opening for Ochs, who seized the opportunity with a head full of timely topical songs. His first album, *All the News That's Fit to Sing* (1964), emphasized civil rights for blacks. The next, *I Ain't Marching Anymore* (1965), featured antiwar statements such as the title song and "Draft Dodger Rag." From his third album the song "Love Me, I'm a Liberal" made a mockery of what he regarded as hypocritical, middle-of-the-road liberalism.

By the end of the 1960s, rock music was sweeping the nation, and Ochs was left behind, floundering in a receding tide. Seeking terra firma, he resorted to orchestral accompaniments, accepted the electric guitar, and got into folk rock with his 1969 album *Rehearsals for Retirement*. Forebodingly, the cover depicted a tombstone with his own obituary. Two years later he brought out *Phil Ochs's Greatest Hits*. Yet he could not come to terms with the 1970s: at age thirty-five he committed suicide. Perhaps he was "the most talented political songwriter of the decade"—but, unlike Dylan, he was unable to change with the times.[24]

Bob Dylan (b. 1941) was a college dropout from Duluth who found the neofolksingers more interesting than his professors. His great idol was Woody Guthrie, and an incentive for going to New York was to visit his hero, for whom he wrote the "Song to Woody." He then went hunting for jobs in the cabarets and coffeehouses of Greenwich Village, and at one place he was told "he sounded like a hillbilly and they were interested only in real folk singers."[25] It is true that he *could* sing like a hillbilly—but also like bluesmen from Texas or the Delta, or the stars of country music, or the established neofolksingers. What soon became evident was that his eclecticism was creative, his basic style distinctively personal—especially his accompaniments on guitar and harmonica.

These qualities were quickly perceived by John Hammond of Columbia Records, who brought out in November 1961 the recording titled simply *Bob Dylan*. Most of the numbers were traditional: the Negro spirituals "In My Time of Dyin' " and "Gospel Plow"; the southern mountaineer folksong "Man of Constant Sorrow"; the "Freight Train Blues," adapted from old recording by Roy Acuff; and one of Blind Lemon Jefferson's great blues, "See That My Grave Is Kept Clean." The autobiographical sketch "Talkin' New York Blues" revealed his versatility, inventiveness, and sense of humor.

With his next album, *The Free-Wheelin' Bob Dylan* (1963), he assumed his role as "one of the living bridges between beat bohemianism and the radical counter culture."[26] Most of the songs were his own and included such social messages as "Blowin' in the Wind," "Masters of War," and "A Hard Rain's A-Gonna Fall." Then came *The Times They Are A-Changin'* (1964), with its prophetic message ("Your sons and daughters are beyond your command") and its antiwar manifesto ("With God on Our Side"). The same year he brought out *Another Side of Bob Dylan,* with the usual mix and a trend toward rock. This anticipated a crucial point in his career, when he made an overt transition to rock at the 1965 Newport Festival. This shocked and angered his cult followers, but his aim was to exploit the potential power of the folk-rock combination. The three milestones in this direction were *Bringing It All Back Home, Highway 61 Revisited* (both 1965), and *Blonde on Blonde* (1966).

The second of these made the strongest impact. The title song, "Highway 61 Revisited," is a tour de force of surrealist imagery, all converging on

Highway 61 as if this were the sacrificial-penitential hub of the universe. For example: "God said to Abraham, kill me a son. . . . Where you want this killin' done?—God said, Down on Highway 61." The mood continues with "Tombstone Blues" and "Desolation Row." Poetically, Dylan was the Rimbaud of the rock counterculture.

In 1966 Dylan had a close brush with death in a motorcycle accident, and his long convalescence may be seen as a symbolic enactment of his withdrawal from the self-destructive world of dropouts and drugs. His 1968 album *John Wesley Harding*, which reverted to featuring the harmonica and acoustic guitar, carried a message of renewed confidence, in a low-keyed southern country style—with a touch of rock. The surrealist setting reappears in such songs as "Frankie Lee and Judas Priest" and "As I Walked Out One Morning." The following year, with *Nashville Skyline*, he moved into the country-and-western scene.

It is not our purpose here to cover Dylan's entire career, with its many changes, but rather to delineate the highlights of his most productive and influential period, during which he personified basic ideologies and lifestyles of the 1960s, translating and transcending them in his lyrics, his music, and his adventurous versatility.

Joan Baez, born in the same year as Dylan, was briefly associated with him in the protest movement of the early 1960s, notably at the 1963 Newport Folk Festival, where she sang his song "With God on Our Side." Baez was born in New York City, of Scotch-Irish and Mexican parentage, and was raised in California. Gifted with a good voice, she learned to play the guitar, quickly dropped out of college, and achieved instant success with her first appearance at the Newport Festival in 1959.

While Dylan withdrew from the protest movement, she persisted in her crusade for peace and justice, becoming an active leader of campus demonstrations. But she also remained faithful to the traditional folksong repertory and included some light classical numbers. With this versatility she was able to survive the decline of the protest movement while remaining faithful to its principles, especially in her campaign against war and militarism. In 1965 she established in California the Institute for the Study of Non-Violence, supported by her earnings as a world-famous singer.

From her first recording (*Joan Baez*, 1960) she was on the way to international fame, and thereafter her albums appeared regularly, featuring traditional songs of every kind and in several languages. She was, of course, especially fluent in Spanish. She had a flair for blending the folkish and the traditional and was eclectic in her choices while consistent in her aims.

Among her albums are *Joan Baez in Concert* (1962), *Farewell Angelina* (1965), *Baptism: A Journey through Our Times* (1968), and *Any Day Now* (1969).

The rocking 1960s also brought to popularity the music called soul, rooted in gospel and blues. Its precursors were such great black gospel singers as Clara Ward, Sister Rosetta Tharpe, and the incomparable Mahalia Jackson (1911–72). They took their gospel out of the storefront churches and into the mainstream of America's music. Country gospel singing by both blacks and whites had become increasingly popular since the 1920s, and with wide radio broadcasting available in the 1930s, many groups and individuals, such as the Carter Family, Ernest Phipps and His Holiness Singers, Uncle Dave Macon, and Rev. J. M. Gates and Congregation, reached large sections of the population.[27]

Tony Heilbut writes: "In the 1930's, a new kind of gospel appeared, provoked by the Depression. Much more dynamic and stylized, the artists performed newly composed material in a striking new way. . . ."[28] Mahalia Jackson went on to be the star of black gospel singing for several decades, culminating in the 1950s with such numbers as "I Will Move On Up a Little Higher," "When I Wake Up in Glory," and "Just a Little While to Stay Here." Marion Williams made her mark as group leader of the Clara Ward Singers and then achieved lasting fame as a soloist, projecting strong emotional moods as evidenced especially in the great gospel hymn "The Day Is Past and Done," accompanied by piano and organ.

Among outstanding groups of the 1950s and 1960s were the Angelic Gospel Singers, the Dixie Hummingbirds, the Staple Singers, and the Abyssinian Gospel Choir.[29]

James Cleveland, the black singer who became known as the "Crown Prince of Gospel," tells us that he "grew up in Chicago completely fascinated by Mahalia Jackson." He in turn taught and influenced Aretha Franklin, who became "Lady Soul" of the pop charts. Cleveland had his first big success in 1960 with "The Love of God," a soulfully transfigured banality that became a smash hit. Typically, he exploited the emotional impact of the high, piercing falsetto identified with gospel singing.

The music of the fabulous blind musician from Georgia Ray Charles (b. 1930)—pianist, singer, composer, songwriter, arranger, bandleader, popular entertainer—spans a wide range of musical styles, from jazz to rock, folk to pop, and rhythm and blues to country and western. Here we shall view him primarily as an exponent of soul and as the audacious iconoclast who transmuted gospel into sex. His 1955 song "I've Got a Woman" was a remake of the gospel hymn "My Jesus Is All the World to Me." Its companion piece, "This Little Girl of Mine," came out of the gospel song "This Little Light of Mine."

In his own inimitable style, Ray Charles went on to mix gospel style with sex appeal in his low-keyed song "What'd I Say," which moved to the top as a single in 1959. Gospel traits such as moaning and "speaking in tongues" were parodied for the benefit of Eros. Yet the emotional fervor and intensity of feeling were retained and reinforced by the beat of rhythm and blues, which gave such a strong impetus to soul music. To draw on the semantics of album titles, the transmutation of gospel to soul is delineated in such Ray Charles albums as *Ingredients in a Recipe for Soul, A Man and His Soul,* and *Volcanic Action of My Soul.* Whatever he did, in any direction, is epitomized in the title of another album: *A Portrait of Ray—Doing His Thing.*[30]

James Brown (b. 1933), from the Georgia hill country, felt that he had earned the right to call himself "Soul Brother No. 1" after he had struggled from poverty and hardship to achieve wealth and fame. Starting with a road-show group called the Famous Flames, by the 1960s he was widely known as "Mr. Dynamite." Frenzied dynamism was his forte, sex the source of his charisma. Building on a base of gospel and blues, with his band playing a heavy, jagged beat, he let go with dramatically emotional vocals, punctuated by shrieking and screaming, and provoking what has been called a "mass erotic frenzy." His appeal was largely to blacks, and he maintained a strong sense of black identity, as expressed in his 1968 hit "Say It Loud—I'm Black and I'm Proud." With such early hits as "Night Train" and "Shout and Shimmy," he set a trend that other soul shouters would follow.

Aretha Franklin (b. 1942) began by singing in her father's church choir and got off to a poor start professionally when a recording executive decided she should be groomed as a pop star for the cabaret circuit. Six years later she switched to another company and the liberation of gospel music. Her 1967 album *Aretha Arrives* was aptly named, for then came *Aretha: Lady Soul* (1968), which made number 2 on the charts. Her gospel background and intense temperament had a contagious effect on audiences: "Where the 'girl groups' of the early Sixties had been sweet and cutesy, Aretha and her backup singers were strong and fierce, combining decades of gospel techniques in their interplay."[31]

Aretha Franklin had deep personal problems, which she expressed in her albums *Spirit in the Dark* (1971) and *Young, Gifted and Black* (1972). But these were followed by her great album (with James Cleveland) *Amazing Grace* (1972), proving that the old gospel fervor was alive in her soul. The term *soul* has many meanings, but for blacks it came to be an assertion of their cultural and personal identity.

This spirit was strongly embodied in the person of Otis Redding (1941–67), who said: "Soul is something that you really have to bring up from your heart." Influenced by Little Richard and linked to the Memphis sound, he came to the fore with such ballads as "Pain in My Heart," "That's How Strong My Love Is," and "Respect." In 1966 he brought out *The Otis Redding Dictionary of Soul,* including ballads, blues, and gospel. This proved to be his living monument: a year later he was killed in a plane crash.

Wilson Pickett (b. 1941) switched from spirituals to sex appeal, maintaining the driving power of gospel with a strong rhythm-and-blues beat. He made his mark as a songwriter with "If You Need Me" (1963) and "In the Midnight Hour" (1965), the latter hailed as "one of the biggest soul hits of all time."[32]

While country-and-western music continued to flourish as the basic type of popular entertainment for millions of Americans, a more controversial—and for many a more exciting—kind of music came on the scene. It began as "rockabilly," described by one of its practitioners (Carl Perkins) as "blues with a country beat."[33] Thus it blended bluegrass style with urban blues—particularly of the jazz-influenced sort that came to be known as rhythm and blues. The basic instrumentation consisted of rhythm guitar, lead guitar, string bass, and drums, with piano optional.

The electrically amplified guitar had a crucial role in this development, eventually extending to the whole rock scene of the 1960s. Its antecedents date from the late 1930s with the innovations of black guitarist Aaron "T-Bone" Walker. As described by Robert Palmer: "By using his amplifier's volume control to sustain pitches, and combining this technique with the string-bending and finger vibrato practiced by traditional bluesmen, Walker in effect invented a new instrument. . . . In addition, he developed a chordal style on fast numbers, a pumping guitar shuffle which led eventually to the archetypal rock 'n' roll guitar style of Chuck Berry."[34]

Charles Edward "Chuck" Berry (b. 1926) was both a great guitarist and a highly talented songwriter and singer who moved on stage with vim and vigor. His "Back in the U.S.A." became a classic, and he achieved wide popularity with such big hits as "Maybellene," "Roll Over Beethoven," and "Johnny B. Good."

Although a white group—Bill Haley and His Comets—achieved the first international rock-and-roll hit with "Rock Around the Clock" (1955), black musicians such as Chuck Berry, Fats Domino, Bo Diddley, and Little Richard exerted the strongest influence on the rise of rock, especially on British groups such as the Rolling Stones and the Beatles.

Nonetheless, it was a white rockabilly youngster from Mississippi named Elvis Presley (1935–77) who was heading toward worldwide fame. Raised in Memphis from the age of thirteen, he absorbed its blues and hill-billy styles through every pore. His big chance was when Sam Philips, of Sun Records, came to Memphis, reputedly on the lookout for a white per-former "who had the Negro sound and the Negro feel."[35] Philips's quest ended when Presley cut his first disc for Sun Records in the summer of 1954. He featured the song "Good Rockin' Tonight," written by the black musician Roy Brown.

So it was the "Hillbilly Cat" from Mississippi who brought the news of "Good Rockin' " to millions of fans, illustrating it with gyrations that earned him the nickname of "Elvis the Pelvis." There followed a lucrative career in Hollywood films, a spate of recordings, and the posthumous aura of a tarnished but probably imperishable legend. He is best remembered by such early numbers as "Heartbreak Hotel," "Jailhouse Rock," and "Love Me Tender."

California was the scene of a music that came to be known as rock, largely concentrated in the Haight-Ashbury section of San Francisco, noto-rious for its hippies—the dropouts of a new generation. Prominent among the rising rock bands were Big Brother and the Holding Company and Jef-ferson Airplane. The former owed its success to a singer from Texas named Janis Joplin (1943–70), who leaped into stardom at the Monterey Pop Fes-tival. Among her best-known numbers are "Ball and Chain," "Me and Bobby McGee," and "Piece of My Heart." Her fame and power are imper-ishable.

Jefferson Airplane had a talented singer and songwriter in Grace Slick, who in their album *Surrealistic Pillow* (1967) made a big hit with "White Rabbit," the "psychedelic anthem" of the beat generation. Another band, the Grateful Dead, got into the psychedelic scene through the mysterious LSD chemist Stanley Ousley, who convinced them that *very* high amplifica-tion was the shot in the arm they needed to get their message across. Typical of this approach was their 1968 album *Anthem of the Sun,* a lush array of studio-manipulated sonorities in which six musicians perform on twenty-nine instruments, including kazoo, guïro, claves, gong, chimes, finger cymbals, and prepared piano.

Jimi Hendrix (1941–70) was a black singer and guitarist from Seattle who erupted into sudden fame when he came on like a fiery volcano at the Monterey Festival in 1967, topping his frenzy by setting fire to his guitar—a gesture of destructive bravado that became his trademark. When his first album, *Are You Experienced,* appeared, it marked a high peak in hard rock. Such pieces as "Manic Depression," "I Don't Live Today," and "Love or Confusion" were both symptomatic and creatively expressive. Three years later, Jimi Hendrix was dead in London, a victim of drugs and the tensions of a madly creative superstar who had to conquer by excess.

In Los Angeles the Doors symbolized both the rebellion of the counterculture and the self-destructive pressures of the acid-rock scene, as personified in their leader, Jim Morrison. A dropout from U.C.L.A, his Venice was a Pacific beach and its acid trips. With a facile poetic gift and an urge for action, he took his group to the night spots of the Strip, where they were discovered by an alert impresario. The result was an album titled *The Doors,* which made number 2 on the 1967 charts, while its most famous song, "Light My Fire," reached number 1 as a single. This has been called "the anthem of a generation"[36]—but the fire soon burned out. The final number on the album, prophetically named "The End," was a macabre, neo-Gothic, pseudo-Freudian, quasi-realistic ode to disillusion and dissolution:

> The end of laughter and soft lies,
> The end of night we tried to die.
> This is the End.

Four years and seven albums later, ravaged by drugs and alcohol, Morrison was dead in Paris at the age of twenty-seven. Posterity may remember him as the poet who put the Oedipus complex into rock music.

In a less hectic context the Los Angeles group called the Beach Boys exploited the natural resources of the Pacific Ocean and the challenge of surfing. They quickly had the youth of America on their side, and in 1962 they made a national hit with "Surfin' Safari," soon followed by "Surfin' U.S.A." As a result, they created a powerful youth cult that was to spread around the world. Under the ambivalent guidance of producer-vocalist Brian Wilson, the euphoria was meshed with themes of insecurity and disillusion. Nevertheless, they played both sides of the game, and their 1966 single "Good Vibrations" was number 1 on the pop charts.

The leading exponents of folk rock in Los Angeles were the Byrds, who in 1965 made an immediate and lasting success with their version of Dylan's "Mr. Tambourine Man." This was followed by Pete Seeger's "Turn, Turn, Turn," which also made it to the top of the charts. Their guiding spirit was Roger McGuinn, who played an electric twelve-string guitar and aimed at a synthesis of neofolk, hard rock, and free jazz as exemplified by Coltrane. Their big deal came with "Eight Miles High"—which they claimed was about aircraft overhead!

What could be called "the Counterculture Put-On" was grotesquely and cynically personified by Frank Zappa and the Mothers of Invention. Their first album, *Freak Out* (1966), was followed by *Lumpy Gravy* (1967) and *Cruisin' with Ruben and the Jets* (1968). Regarding this last, Carl Belz, in *The Story of Rock,* maintains that it "involves a conscious return to earlier rock music, particularly the ballad style of the 1950s and the early 1960s."[37]

The fact remains that the "Put-On" became for Zappa and his cohorts their ultimate source for turning it "All The Way UP!!"—as they did in *Lumpy Gravy,* described as "a curiously inconsistent piece which started out to be a ballet but probably didn't make it."[38] It did, however, present something exceptional with the "ABNUCEALS EMUUKHA electric SYMPHONY orchestra & chorus."

We conclude with the Mothers of Invention presenting *Absolutely Free,* "A Series Of UNDERGROUND ORATORIOS" that include such numbers as "Plastic People," "The Duke of Prunes," and "Invocation & Ritual Dance of the Young Pumpkin." Although it may all seem wacky, the verve and the invention make it truly incomparable.[39]

The Zappa satire was mild compared with that of the Fugs, a New York group that embodied the underground movement in lower Manhattan, hurling every kind of insult at the Establishment, from blasphemy to obscenity. The result has been described as a blend of Lenny Bruce and Henry Miller set to music. There were touches of Swinburne and Verlaine for added decadence, and contemporary input from such poets as Allen Ginsberg and Gregory Corso. Typical songs were "New Amphet Amine Shriek," "Hallucination Horrors," and "Swineburne Stomp." Paradoxically, their offensive notoriety led to their being featured "on the cover of Establishment publications like *Life* and the *Saturday Evening Post.*"[40]

In the 1970s the term *rock and roll* came to be applied to almost any kind of pop music with a strong beat and a presumably powerful message for its devotees, who were mostly young and out of step with the dominant sociocultural and economic patterns of the Establishment. Musically, verbally, and socially these attitudes erupted in what came to be called punk rock, which had its first explosion in Great Britain among lower-class teenagers fed up with frustration, poverty, and the pressures of conformity. The most outrageous and belligerent group were the Sex Pistols, whose lead singer called himself Johnny Rotten.

A British journalist described punk as "music, clothes, style, small magazines called 'fanzines.' Punk is kids coming together to play rock 'n' roll, edit their papers and get them onto the streets for other kids to read."[41] The past was repudiated: "No Elvis, Beatles, or the Rolling Stones." As a punk spokesman said: "We're not about destroying ourselves or other people. . . . We want to destroy ideas and attitudes."

With appropriate incongruity, the big breakthrough in American punk rock occurred in the bicentennial year of 1976. The term *new wave* also came into vogue, as favored by the recording industry and the mass media. The basic impulse was still anti-Establishment, but gestures of defiance were more outrageous than destructive. Groups flaunted weird or provocative names such as Avengers, Screamers, Weirdos, Nuns, Nervous Eaters, Suicide, and Talking Heads.

From its launchpad in New York City, with bands such as the Ramones and the Dictators flaunting their hard-driving "garage" style—the primitive phase of punk rock—the new wave spread rapidly throughout the United States (and Canada), with San Francisco notable for both performing and recording. Prominent groups in the Bay Area were Chrome, MX-80, Tuxedo-Moon, and the Residents, whose first album was an outrageous parody of the Beatles and the Rolling Stones.

The Residents took a giant step forward with their 1979 album *Eskimo,* five years in the making. Viewed by one critic: *"Eskimo* is music arranged according to non-musical principles. The songs are actually stories 'as told with organized sound.' "[42] The "stories" portray ethnic rituals of the Polar Eskimos, such as "The Walrus Hunt," "Arctic Hysteria," "The Angry Angakok," "A Spirit Steals a Child," and "The Festival of Death." The Residents designed and built the "Ceremonial Band Instruments" that accompany the printed stories that are not actually included with the recording. There is also an underlying social message, for we are reminded that the Polar Eskimo "has been relocated entirely into government housing, and now spends most of the day watching reruns on TV."[43]

Punk rock represents a great deal more than a far-out freakish fad. For example, it became an integral part of the new-wave trends in the visual arts, as we learn from the following description: "Artists all over America picked up on punk. . . . The grafitti, collage, and fashion, all elements of punk, have a neo-Dada flavor. . . . The first punk bands in New York used to play the Mercer Arts Center; in Toronto, Cleveland, and San Francisco, art schools added musicians and audiences to the local scenes. . . . *Talking Heads* met in art school, Amo Poe mixes punk and film, there's lots of video, and everybody's got cameras—punk is so photogenic."[44]

Whether it be a pose or a fad or a defiant stance, some new wavers proclaim that they are "artists." In the words of Johnny Ramone: "All artists gotta establish a base. Picasso, The Beatles, Fellini; all them guys. We ain't no different from them."[45] The outrageously flamboyant Tonio K. (1980 album, *Life in the Foodchain*), when asked about his influences, mentioned the dadaists Hugo Ball and Kurt Schwitters, along with Thomas Mann, Bob Dylan, James Brown, and the Rolling Stones.[46] The great eclectic put-on? Whatever the pose, in much the same way that many of the visual arts have gone pop, punk and new wave have given as much priority to visual effects and symbols as to the sounds they produce.

These sounds rely heavily on synthesizing techniques, and in recording sessions the sound-mixing technician has a paramount function. The typical performing group consists of four musicians, but more may be added as needed. The usual instrumentation comprises drums and other percussion, keyboards, and bass, with guitar, violin, and sax often added. Synthesizers are of course essential, and vocals are prominent, if not always intelligible.

Many of the punk groups started by playing in garages; then the new wave was brought into the recording studios and thence into concert halls and arenas. But much of the live music performances went on as a social activity, in towns, cities, and campuses, with dancing as a counterpart.

Until recently little attention had been given to the impact of contemporary popular music on industrial laborers. But David A. Spurr, in his article "Industrial Rock 'n' Roll: New Music for a New Breed of Worker," demonstrates one way "in which rock music—Punk, New Wave, or just old-time rock 'n' roll—attempts to come to terms with the day-to-day reality of an industrial environment."[47]

Taking an automobile factory in Detroit as an example, Spurr cites a working-class rock band that converted a tune of the Rolling Stones, "Miss You," into the following industrial ditty (the "Flintoid" refers to the android or human automaton):

I work Buick all day long,
Building car doors makes ya strong,
I'm a Flintoid.
Then I go out in my ride,
Got my buddies by my side,
We're all Flintoids, yeah!

Here we have traveled from Fiddlin' John Carson's hillbilly tunes to the new wave that spread from the Atlantic to the Pacific, thus confirming Bill Malone's dictum that "the industrial-technological-urban society has modified and transformed all American values."

Notes

1. Concerning the term *hillbilly*, see Archie Green, "Hillbilly Music: Source and Symbol," pp. 204–28.
2. Bill C. Malone, *Country Music, U.S.A.*, rev. ed., p. 37.
3. Ibid., p. 38.
4. Malone, *Country Music, U.S.A.* (1968), p. 62.
5. Larry Sandberg and Dick Weissman, *The Folk Music Sourcebook*, pp. 63–64.
6. See John Atkins, "The Carter Family," in *Stars of Country Music*, ed. Bill C. Malone and Judith McCulloh, pp. 95–120.
7. See John Greenway, "Jimmie Rodgers—a Folksong Catalyst," pp. 231–34.
8. For information on the recordings of Jimmie Rodgers, see Nolan Porterfield, *Jimmie Rodgers*, pp. 379–429.
9. Elizabeth Schlappi, "Roy Acuff," in *Stars of Country Music*, ed. Malone and McCulloh, p. 194.
10. Douglas B. Green, "Gene Autry," in ibid., pp. 144–45.
11. Ibid., pp. 154–55.
12. Roger M. Williams, "Hank Williams," in ibid., p. 237.
13. Malone, *Country Music, U.S.A.*, rev. ed., p. 314.
14. Roger D. Abrahams, ed., *A Singer and Her Songs: Almeda Riddle's Book of Ballads.*
15. John Greenway, *American Folksongs of Protest*, p. 9.
16. Archie Green, *Only a Miner*, p. 5.
17. Ibid., p. 6.
18. Ibid., p. 8.
19. Gunning's Appalachian-style songs are recorded on *Sarah Ogan Gunning "Girl of Constant Sorrow,"* Folk-Legacy FSA-26. For her talking and singing about the miners' union, see the videotape *Coalfield Music*, Broadside TV, Johnson City, Tenn.
20. See R. Serge Denisoff, *Great Day Coming*, including a "Selected Discography of American Protest Songs," pp. 198–200.

21. Ibid., p. 148.

22. Pete Seeger, foreword to Woody Guthrie, *Bound for Glory*, pp. x–xi.

23. See the excellent biography by David King Dunaway, *How Can I Keep from Singing: Pete Seeger*, with a comprehensive discography.

24. Jerome L. Rodnitzky, *Minstrels of the Dawn*, p. 82.

25. Anthony Scaduto, *Bob Dylan*, p. 93.

26. Rodnitzky, *Minstrels of the Dawn*, p. 106.

27. For early examples and antecedents, see *An Introduction to Gospel Song*, comp. and ed. Samuel B. Charters, RBF Records RF 5.

28. Tony Heilbut, liner notes to *The Gospel Sound*, Columbia Records G-31086.

29. For a comprehensive discography, see Tony Heilbut, *The Gospel Sound: Good News and Bad Times*, pp. 327–37.

30. For an extensive discography, see *A 25th Anniversary in Show Business to Ray Charles*, ABC Records ABC(s) 731.

31. Russell Gersten, "Aretha Franklin," in *The Rolling Stone Illustrated History of Rock & Roll*, ed. Jim Miller, p. 236. He also sees her album *Young, Gifted, and Black* as taking its place "alongside the disillusioned, confessional work of such writers as Doris Lessing and Anais Nin."

32. Peter Guralnick, "Soul," in ibid., p. 196.

33. Peter Guralnick, "Rockabilly," in ibid., p. 64.

34. Robert Palmer, "Rock Begins," in ibid., p. 18.

35. Peter Guralnick, "Elvis Presley," in ibid., p. 34.

36. Lester Bangs, "The Doors," in ibid., p. 262.

37. Carl Belz, *The Story of Rock*, p. 211.

38. Frank Zappa, *Lumpy Gravy*, Verve 8741.

39. *Absolutely Free*, Verve V/V6-5013x.

40. Lillian Roxon, *Rock Encyclopedia*, p. 199.

41. Dike Blair and Isabelle Anscombe, *Punk*, p. 7.

42. Glenn O'Brien, *New Musical Express* (San Francisco).

43. Liner notes to *Eskimo*, Ralph Records RPH 7906.

44. Blair and Anscombe, *Punk*, p. 97.

45. Ibid.

46. Quoted in Steve Simels, "Tonio K," p. 73.

47. David A. Spurr, "Industrial Rock 'n' Roll: New Music for a New Breed of Worker," *Pacific News Service* (San Francisco).

American Music on Record

William Brooks

Introduction

America's Music is devoted in part to elucidating the ways in which the *interactions* between different genres and traditions have generated the American musical experience. America's recording industry, however, has generally worked differently: most companies have found it profitable to concentrate on a single, identifiable repertory. Thus the structure of the industry has both mirrored and exacerbated the perception that America's music is a collection of separate traditions.

For a time the 1970s seemed to offer a truly integrated view of America's musical history, and a surge of noteworthy recording followed. Two such efforts stand out as landmarks. The first was the series Recorded Anthology of American Music: 100 discs issued by New World Records with funds provided by the Rockefeller Foundation. For the first time a single set of recordings attempted to encompass America's entire musical domain, from commercial music to field recordings to opera, and spanning the eighteenth century to the present. The series is an essential resource for the teaching of American music and remains the best starting point for the study of many genres and periods. It is available in libraries throughout the country, and its use has been greatly facilitated by an excellent *Index to the New World Recorded Anthology of American Music* prepared by Elizabeth A. Davis (New York: W. W. Norton and Co., 1981). The recordings can also serve as references, since most include detailed notes, often containing discographies.

The second paradigmatic recording of the 1970s was *Scott Joplin Piano Rags,* played by Joshua Rifkin (Nonesuch H-71248), which startled everyone by climbing to the eighteenth spot on *Billboard's* "classical LP" chart. Suddenly it seemed that American music might bring commercial success, and several companies rushed to issue wide-ranging albums or anthologies.

This effort was led by Teresa Sterne; under her guidance Nonesuch issued dozens of excellent discs, including Joan Morris and William Bolcom's *After the Ball* (H-71304), original instruments playing *19th-Century American Ballroom Music* (H-71313), a superb recording of *Stephen Foster Songs* (H-71268), a five-volume anthology offering a *Spectrum [of] New American Music* (H 71219–21, 71302–3), and albums containing works by Ives, Griffes, Varèse, Cage, Carter, and many others.

Other companies scrambled to catch up. Within a year of Rifkin's Nonesuch release, Vanguard produced its own ragtime album, a landmark two-record set by Max Morath (VSD 39–40); it followed this with art-music albums devoted to Gottschalk, Heinrich, Varèse, Rzewski, and others. Vox Productions concentrated on an excellent series of anthologies, all issued in three-record sets: a nineteenth-century popular potpourri (SVBX 5309); four sets of vocal music (SVBX 5350, 5304, 5353, 5354); two of piano music (SVBX 5302–3); three of string quartets (SVBX 5301, 5305, 5306); and a collection titled *Avant Garde Woodwind Quintets* (SVBX 5307). For all these genres the "Vox Boxes" are an exceptionally valuable resource. Desto issued a similarly useful *Anthology of American Piano Music* (Desto 6445–47) and a four-disc Gottschalk collection (Desto DC 6470–73).

The integrative impulse, represented on the one hand by New World Records and on the other by the flurry of mixed releases in the 1970s, seems to have spent itself. Indeed, it may have been false from the outset, a temporary consequence of the cultural ferment of the 1960s and bicentennial fervor. In recent years companies have become increasingly specialized, and the discography of American music remains primarily a discography by genre. The following brief overview of four major areas reflects this situation without endorsing it.

Concert ("art") music

Works by America's twentieth-century composers have been exhaustively cataloged in *American Music Recordings* (Brooklyn, N.Y.: Institute for Studies in American Music, 1982), which includes composers born as early as the 1870s and lists all recordings issued before June 1980. Recordings of composers active before 1865 are listed in another I.S.A.M. publication, *American Music before 1865 in Print and on Records* (Brooklyn, N.Y., 1976); this includes not only "art" music but any music for which pre-1865 printed sources exist: parlor songs, mission music, hymns and anthems, and so on. The listings have been extended to 1980 in two supplements by James R. Heintze in *Notes* (March 1978 and September 1980).

For composers active between 1865 and 1900, there is no single reference tool. *American Music Recordings* is worth checking, however, since it stretched its criteria to include composers like Horatio Parker, George Chadwick, and Arthur Foote. For a few other figures, specialized discographies can be found in Michael H. Gray and Gerald D. Gibson, *Bibliography of Discographies,* volume 1, *Classical Music, 1925–1975* (New York: R. R. Bowker Co., 1977), *The New Grove Dictionary of Music and Musicians,* ed. Stanley Sadie (London: Macmillan, 1980), or *The New Grove Dictionary of American Music,* ed. H. Wiley Hitchcock and Stanley Sadie (London: Macmillan, 1986). Other recordings can be located, somewhat tediously, by checking scattered issues of *Schwann*. The journal *American Music* and the newsletters issued by the Institute for Studies in American Music and by the Sonneck Society also contain lists and brief reviews on an irregular basis.

To sample American art music without reference to particular composers, one might usefully begin with the Recorded Anthology of American Music or with the Nonesuch, Vox, or Desto releases described above. The Society for the Preservation of the American Heritage also has an extensive series called Music in America, devoted primarily to repertory from the eighteenth and nineteenth centuries. Similarly, scattered among the several thousand issues of the Musical Heritage Society are a number containing American music, including a three-disc survey of organ music (MHS 262K, 263F, 264Z). CMS (Desto) has focused on the early and middle twentieth century; its issues include albums first released by the American Recording Society. Eastman Rochester Archives has reissued many recordings of mid-twentieth-century music made by Mercury in the 1950s. And the catalog of CRI (Composers Recordings, Inc.) includes several hundred recordings of recent music overseen by the composers themselves; in addition CRI acts as a distributor for historically important series such as the Louisville Orchestra First Editions and for present-day avant-garde labels like 1750 Arch.

Folk music

The single most important collection of field recordings in America is the Archive of Folk Culture at the Library of Congress. Much of the archive can only be consulted in person, but from time to time the library has issued LP discs containing some of the most interesting material. A bicentennial collection of fifteen discs titled *Folk Music in America* (LBC 1–15) is excellent, although it includes as much commercial material as archival. The library's other seventy-odd discs range from field recordings to mid-nineteenth-century music newly recorded on original instruments (OMP 101–2) to an illustrated set of lectures by John Lomax (AAFS L:49–53).

The other major source for folk music is the catalog of Folkways Records. Of special interest is the old (1951–52) Harry Smith *Anthology of American Folk Music* (FA 2951–53); although more recent collections have surpassed it in quality and diversity, it remains a model anthology and exerted a great influence on performers and scholars in the 1950s and 1960s.

To find other recordings the best starting point is Dean Tudor's *Popular Music: An Annotated Guide to Recordings* (Littleton, Colo.: Libraries Unlimited, 1983). (Indeed, Tudor's book is the single best guide to recordings of nearly *all* Americana except art music.) An excellent but more narrow volume is *Ethnic Recordings in America* (Washington, D.C.: American Folklife Center, 1982), which combines history, criticism, and a detailed "Guide to Resources." Yet more specialized is *Native North American Music and Oral Data* (Bloomington: Indiana University Press, 1979), which catalogs the holdings (through 1976) of the Archives of Traditional Music at Indiana University. Ray Lawless's *Folksingers and Folksongs in America* (1960; rev. ed. New York: Duell, Sloan and Pearce, 1965), although thoroughly out-of-date by now, contains some very useful analytical lists of early recordings. Larry Sandberg and Dick Weston's *Folk Music Source-Book* (New York: Alfred A. Knopf, 1976) offers a somewhat more recent discographic overview that extends to commercial music and the folk revival. Finally, the Library of Congress offers a range of finding aids and guides, including a brochure listing the contents of its own offerings and an annual "Selected List of Recordings" issued by the American Folklife Center since 1983.

Commercial music (blues, pop, rock, country, etc.)

Commercial music is, by definition, profit making; copyright restrictions make systematic, wide-ranging anthologies rare. Two excellent collections have been issued by the Smithsonian Institution: *The Smithsonian Collection of Classic Country Music* and *American Popular Song*. Scattered through the Recorded Anthology of American Music are several discs of commercial music, with generous notes and discographies. Most commercially produced anthologies are topical, organized either by style (e.g., *His-*

tory of Rhythm & Blues, Atlantic SD 8161–64, 8193–94, 8208–9), by label (*The Sun Box,* Charly Sun Box 100), or by decade (*Encores from the 30s,* Epic L2N 6072). Some of the best of these have been produced abroad, notably in Britain and Japan; still others were marketed originally as companion sets for books. Time-Life records has issued (by subscription only) some excellent three-disc anthologies, notably of country music; some of these are topical (*The Women,* TLCW 02; *Duets,* TLCW 05), but most are devoted to individual performers, from the Carter Family (TLCW 06) to Willie Nelson (TLCW 11).

For reissues (primarily of pre-1960 material), a few labels are particularly useful. Folkways has reissued (often on its "RBF" subsidiary) many "folk" recordings of marginal commercial standing. Arhoolie is especially helpful for southern and western regional musics; Historical Records offers well-annotated discs of rarities and oddities, particularly in blues and early jazz. Many excellent reissues of country ("old-time," "hillbilly") music have appeared on the County, Rounder, and Old Timey labels; all three companies have also produced very useful anthologies such as *Early Days of Bluegrass* (Rounder 1013–17, 1019–20) and *Western Swing* (Old Timey OT 105, 116–17, 119–23). Earlier black music is well represented on Yazoo and Blues Classics; Savoy has issued a good collection of rhythm-and-blues anthologies. More recently even the largest companies have joined in marketing reissues; Columbia's ten discs of Bessie Smith (GP 33, G 30126, 30450, 30818, 31093) are a fine example.

The subgenre of stage and screen music is well represented on Time-Life records and among the Smithsonian releases; the latter include several reconstructions of early musicals from original recordings. Columbia has also assembled or reissued several noteworthy "original cast" albums. Labels in related areas include DRG Records (a mix of "star" recordings, reissued cast albums, and sound tracks), Entr'acte Recording Society (primarily film scores), and Mark56 Records (vintage radio). Recent waves of cinematic nostalgia (*American Graffiti, Back to the Future,* and so on) have generated sound-track recordings that are essentially anthologies from a particular period. Finally, for nearly any performer of stature there is at least one "Greatest Hits" or "Best of . . ." album; a sample of these, strategically chosen, can yield a good overview of a particular era.

To this great welter of material there are two especially useful guides. The first is Dean Tudor's volume, described above; the second is Michael H. Gray's *Bibliography of Discographies,* volume 3, *Popular Music* (New York: R. R. Bowker Co., 1983). The former is especially useful when trying to gain an overview of a genre; the latter is designed primarily to locate detailed discographies of particular musicians. Beyond these, one must turn to studies of particular genres.

David Hummel's *Collector's Guide to the American Musical Theatre* (Metuchen, N.J.: Scarecrow Press, 1984) is an exhaustive discography, arranged by show and indexed by personal names; Jack Raymond's *Show Music on Record* (New York: Frederick Ungar Publishing Co., 1982) is less thorough but usefully cross-indexed. *Hollywood on Record,* by Michael R. Pitts and Louis H. Harrison (Metuchen, N.J.: Scarecrow Press, 1978), offers a thorough discography of film music but is indexed only by performers.

Bill Malone's landmark history *Country Music, U.S.A.* (1968; rev. ed. Austin: University of Texas Press, 1985) contains valuable discographic information; and one should also consult Malone's and Judith McCulloh's *Stars of Country Music* (Urbana: University of Illinois Press, 1975). Robert K. Oermann's *The Listener's Guide to Country Music* (New York: Facts on File, 1983) offers brief but useful annotated discographies on a variety of subtopics.

Similarly, Peter Guralnick's *The Listener's Guide to the Blues* (New York: Facts on File, 1982) contains useful annotated discographies; in *Deep Blues* (New York: Viking Press, 1981), Robert Palmer compactly describes a more narrow repertory. Many biographical dictionaries include discographical information with each entry; among these are Brock Helander, *The Rock Who's Who* (New York: Schirmer Books, 1982), and a series of *Illustrated Encyclopedias* (of black music, jazz, country music, rock).

In *Stranded* (New York: Alfred A. Knopf, 1979), Greil Marcus published a lengthy annotated list of personal rock-and-roll favorites; the discography to Arnold Shaw's *Honkers and Shouters* (New York: Macmillan, 1978) contains a useful index to anthologies by performer. *The Rock Critics' Choice,* ed. Paul Giambaccini (New York: Quick Fox, 1978) compares the "top ten" choices of forty-eight critics. Both *The Rolling Stone Record Guide* (New York: Random House, 1979) and *Christgau's Record Guide* (New Haven: Ticknor and Fields, 1981) rate and review a large number of albums, although Christgau's tastes are highly idiosyncratic. Terry Hounsome's *New Rock Record,* 3d ed. (Poole, England: Blandford Press Link House, 1983) lists 40,000 LPs, indexed by group and performer.

For the musicologically minded there are also many retrospective discographies, like Brian Rust's *Complete Entertainment Discography* (New Rochelle, N.Y.: Arlington House, 1973) or John Godrich and R. M. W. Dixon's *Blues and Gospel Records, 1902–1942* (London: Storyville Publications, 1969); these, however, are usually of little help in locating recordings currently available. Finally, Joel Whitburn's variously titled compilations of *Billboard* charts (*Top Pop Artists and Singles, Top LP Records,* and so on) are extremely helpful guides to postwar popular taste.

Jazz

Most jazz is commercial music, of course; but the two categories tend to have been separated by discographers and historians and hence are discussed separately here. Probably the best overall introduction to the genre is *The Smithsonian Collection of Classic Jazz* (SI R2100). To some extent this has supplanted the eleven-disc history brought out by Folkways in the 1950s (FJ 2801–11), although the Folkways set remains excellent for music before 1940. Both Folkways and the Smithsonian have also produced many other notable reissues. Certain early Folkways releases concentrated on geographical areas such as New Orleans (Folkways 2461–65) or New York (RBF RF3). Most Smithsonian recordings are devoted to particular artists; especially outstanding are albums on King Oliver (SI 2001), Fletcher Henderson (SI 2006), and Duke Ellington (SI 2003, 2010, 2015, 2027).

Some anthologies are restricted to particular labels. *Blue Note's Three Decades of Jazz* (United Artists BN LA 158–60) is very useful; Columbia's *Jazz Odyssey* (JC3L 30, 32, 33) is somewhat uneven, although a later *Thesaurus of Classic Jazz* (C4L 18) is more consistent. Time-Life's subscription series Giants of Jazz (STLJ 01, etc.) includes about thirty, three-disc sets, each devoted to a single performer. The Recorded Anthology of American Music contains several discs covering certain aspects of jazz history in a roughly chronological fashion. Some very good collections have been released abroad, especially in France and Germany; *Jazz* (Opus Musicum OM 128–30) is a three-disc set that includes much recent material. And some jazz collections have been assembled to accompany books; Leonard Feather's *Encyclopedia of Jazz on Records* (MCA 2-4061-2) is a good example, although it is limited to Decca/MCA releases.

Certain companies have traditionally specialized in jazz: Biograph, Blue Note, Delmark, Herwin, Historical, Commodore, Origin Jazz Library, Prestige, Impulse, Milestone, Savoy, Jazz Archives. Several excellent guides offer a variety of opinions about the best of the albums available. Tudor's *Popular Music* (see above) is less authoritative in jazz than in other areas, but its organization (especially the lists of anthologies) is a virtue. In 1980 Len Lyons described *The 101 Best Jazz Albums* then available (New

York: William Morrow and Co., 1980), with detailed and informative anno-
tations. Max Harrison, Charles Fox, and Eric Thacker combined to select
The Essential Jazz Records, volume 1 (Westport, Conn.: Greenwood Press,
1984), in which they annotate over 250 records compactly and clearly, with
many useful cross-references. Walter Bruyninckx's exhaustive *60 Years of Recorded Jazz, 1917–77* was issued privately, on 8,000 hand-typed pages. Daniel
Allen, *Bibliography of Discographies,* volume 2, *Jazz* (New York: R. R.
Bowker Co., 1981), cites discographical studies of individual musicians as
well as of styles and areas. David Horn's excellent *Literature of American
Music* (Metuchen, N.J.: Scarecrow Press, 1977) contains an extensive section on jazz discographies, as well as occasional listings in other genres.
Nearly every history of jazz contains discographical recommendations, as
do dozens of biographies of individual musicians. Finally, for specialists,
there is a growing collection of historical discographies by label or period;
especially notable are those issued by Brian Rust and by Michel Ruppli.

Selected Bibliography

The Bibliography to the revised third edition of *America's Music* supplements with complete bibliographic data the abbreviated references given in the chapter notes. To facilitate this purpose, it has been arranged alphabetically in a unified listing. Comprehensive rather than exhaustive with respect to the vast and ever-expanding literature pertaining to America's music, the titles listed below represent both the range and types of sources used in preparing this study. The Bibliography is intended as a guide to the reader who may wish to pursue further special phases of the rich variety that is America's music.

Abrahams, Roger D. *Positively Black*. Englewood Cliffs, N.J.: Prentice-Hall, 1970.
———, ed. *A Singer and Her Songs: Almeda Riddle's Book of Ballads*. Music edited by George Foss. Baton Rouge: Louisiana State University Press, 1970.
Abrahams, Roger D., and George Foss. *Anglo-American Folksong Style*. Englewood Cliffs, N.J.: Prentice-Hall, 1968.
Adams, James Truslow. *The March of Democracy: A History of the United States*. 4 vols. 1932–33. Rpt. New York: Charles Scribner's Sons, 1965.
Adams, John. *Diary and Autobiography of John Adams*. Edited by L. H. Butterfield. 4 vols. Cambridge: Belknap Press of Harvard University, 1961.
Ahlstrom, Sydney E. *A Religious History of the American People*. New Haven: Yale University Press, 1972.
Aikin, Jesse B. *The True Principles of the Science of Music, with a Rare Collection of the Best Tunes That Are Published*. Philadelphia: J. B. Aikin, 1891.
Allen, William Francis, Charles Pickard Ware, and Lucy McKim Garrison, comps. *Slave Songs of the United States*. 1867. Rpt. New York: Peter Smith, 1951.
American Music before 1865 in Print and on Records: A Biblio-Discography. Preface by H. Wiley Hitchcock. I.S.A.M. Monographs, no. 6. Brooklyn, N.Y.: Institute for Studies in American Music, 1976.
Ammer, Christine. *Unsung: A History of Women in American Music*. Contributions in Women's Studies, no. 14. Westport, Conn.: Greenwood Press, 1980.
Anderson, Donna K. *The Works of Charles T. Griffes: A Descriptive Catalogue*. Studies in Musicology, no. 68. Ann Arbor, Mich.: UMI Research Press, 1983.
Anderson, Gillian B. " 'Samuel the Priest Gave Up the Ghost' and *The Temple of Minerva:* Two Broadsides." *Notes* 31 (Mar. 1975): 493–516.

————. " 'The Temple of Minerva' and Francis Hopkinson: A Reappraisal of America's First Poet-Composer." *Proceedings of the American Philosophical Society* 120 (June 1976): 166–77.

Andrews, Edward D. *The Gift to Be Simple: Songs, Dances and Rituals of the American Shakers.* 1940. Rpt. New York: Dover Publications, 1962.

Antheil, George. *Bad Boy of Music.* 1945. Rpt., with a new introduction by Charles Amirkhanian. New York: Da Capo Press, 1981.

Appel, Richard G. *The Music of the Bay Psalm Book, 9th Edition (1698).* I.S.A.M. Monographs, no. 5. Brooklyn, N.Y.: Institute for Studies in American Music, 1975.

Apthorp, William F. "Music." *Atlantic Monthly* 33 (Feb. 1874): 252–56.

Armitage, Merle. *George Gershwin: Man and Legend.* New York: Duell, Sloan and Pearce, 1958.

Armstrong, Louis. *Satchmo: My Life in New Orleans.* New York: Prentice-Hall, 1954.

————. *Swing That Music.* New York: Longmans, Green and Co., 1936.

Asbury, Samuel E., and Henry E. Meyer. *Old-Time White Camp-Meeting Spirituals.* Austin: Texas Folk-Lore Society, 1932.

Asch, Moses, and Alan Lomax, eds. *The Leadbelly Songbook: The Ballads, Blues, and Folksongs of Huddie Ledbetter.* New York: Oak Publications, 1962.

Atkins, John. "The Carter Family." In *Stars of Country Music: Uncle Dave Macon to Johnny Rodriguez.* Edited by Bill C. Malone and Judith McCulloh, 95–120. Urbana: University of Illinois Press, 1975.

Austin, William W. *"Susanna," "Jeanie," and "The Old Folks at Home": The Songs of Stephen Foster from His Time to Ours.* New York: Macmillan, 1975.

Avakian, George. Liner notes to *The Bessie Smith Story.* Vol. 3. Columbia CL 857. 1951.

————. Liner notes to *Chicago Style Jazz.* Columbia CL 632. N.d.

Babbitt, Milton. "Some Aspects of Twelve-Tone Composition." *Score and I.M.A. Magazine* 12 (June 1955): 53–61.

Baker, David N., Lida M. Belt, and Herman C. Hudson, eds. *The Black Composer Speaks.* Metuchen, N.J.: Scarecrow Press, 1978.

Baker, Theodore. *Über die Musik der nordamerikanischen Wilden.* Leipzig: Breitkopf & Härtel, 1882. Rpt., with an English translation by Ann Buckley, as *On the Music of the North American Indians.* New York: Da Capo Press, 1978.

Ballanta-(Taylor), Nicholas George Julius. *Saint Helena Island Spirituals.* New York: G. Schirmer, 1925.

Balliett, Whitney. *The Sound of Surprise: 46 Pieces on Jazz.* 1959. Rpt. New York: Da Capo Press, 1978.

Barbour, J. Murray. *The Church Music of William Billings.* 1960. Rpt. New York: Da Capo Press, 1972.

Barras, Charles M. *The Black Crook, a Most Wonderful History.* 2d ed., with "A Graphic History of the Parisian Ballet Girls." Philadelphia: Barclay and Co., 1882.

Barron, David Milton. "The Early Vocal Works of Anthony Philip Heinrich Based on American Themes." Ph.D. diss., University of Illinois at Urbana-Champaign, 1972.

Barton, William E. *Old Plantation Hymns: A Collection of Hitherto Unpublished Melodies of the Slave and the Freedman with Historical and Descriptive Notes.* 1899. Rpt. New York: AMS Press, 1972.

Bauman, Richard, and Roger D. Abrahams, eds. *And Other Neighborly Names: Social Process and Cultural Image in Texas Folklore.* Austin: University of Texas Press, 1981.

Becker, John J. "Finding a Personal Orchestral Idiom." *Musical America* 70 (Feb. 1950): 126–27, 256.

Belcher, Supply. *The Harmony of Maine.* 1794. Rpt. Earlier American Music, no. 6. New York: Da Capo Press, 1972.

Belden, Albert D. *George Whitefield—the Awakener: A Modern Study of the Evangelical Revival.* New York: Macmillan, 1953.

Bellinger, Lucius. *Stray Leaves from the Port-folio of a Methodist Local Preacher.* Macon, Ga.: J. W. Burke and Co., 1870.

Belz, Carl. *The Story of Rock.* 2d ed. New York: Oxford University Press, 1972.

Benson, Louis F. *The English Hymn: Its Development and Use in Worship.* 1915. Rpt. Richmond, Va.: John Knox Press, 1962.

Berger, Arthur. *Aaron Copland.* 1953. Rpt. Westport, Conn.: Greenwood Press, 1971.

Berlin, Edward A. *Ragtime: A Musical and Cultural History.* Berkeley and Los Angeles: University of California Press, 1980.

Berman, Eleanor Davidson. *Thomas Jefferson among the Arts: An Essay in Early American Esthetics.* New York: Philosophical Library, 1947.

Bernard, Kenneth A. *Lincoln and the Music of the Civil War.* Caldwell, Idaho: Caxton Printers, 1966.

Bierley, Paul E. *John Philip Sousa: American Phenomenon.* New York: Appleton-Century-Crofts, Education Division, Meredith Corp., 1973.

———. *John Philip Sousa: A Descriptive Catalog of His Works.* Music in American Life. Urbana: University of Illinois Press, 1973.

Billings, William. *The Continental Harmony.* Edited by Hans Nathan. Cambridge: Belknap Press of Harvard University Press, 1961.

Birge, Edward Bailey. *History of Public School Music in the United States.* Boston: Oliver Ditson Co., 1928.

Blair, Dike, and Isabelle Anscombe. *Punk.* New York: Urizen Books, 1978.

Blesh, Rudi. Liner notes to *The Classic Rags of Joe Lamb.* Milton Kaye, piano. Golden Crest CRS 4127. N.d.

———. *Shining Trumpets: A History of Jazz.* 2d rev. ed. 1958. Rpt. New York: Da Capo Press, 1975.

———, comp. *The Ragtime Current: Piano Solos by a Mainstream of Today's Ragtime Composers.* New York: Edward B. Marks, 1976.

Blesh, Rudi, and Harriet Janis. *They All Played Ragtime: The True Story of an American Music.* 4th rev. ed. New York: Oak Publications, 1971.

Blitzstein, Marc. "Coming—the Mass Audience!" *Modern Music* 13 (May-June 1936): 23–29.

———. "On Writing Music for the Theatre." *Modern Music* 15 (Jan.-Feb. 1938): 81–85.

Bolcom, William. Liner notes to *Heliotrope Boucquet: Piano Rags by Turpin, Joplin, Joplin-Chauvin, Lamb, Scott, Roberts, Bolcom, Bolcom-Albright.* William Bolcom, piano. Nonesuch H-71257. 1971.

———. Liner notes to *Pastimes & Piano Rags.* Nonesuch H-71299. 1974.

Bordman, Gerald. *American Musical Comedy: From "Adonis" to "Dreamgirls."* New York: Oxford University Press, 1982.

———. *American Musical Theatre: A Chronicle.* New York: Oxford University Press, 1978.

Borneman, Ernest. *A Critic Looks at Jazz.* London: Jazz Music Books, 1946.

Bost, George H. "Samuel Davies: Colonial Revivalist and Champion of Religious Tolerance." Ph.D. diss., University of Chicago, 1942.

Botkin, B. A. *A Treasury of Southern Folklore: Stories, Ballads, Traditions, and Folkways of the South.* 1949. Rpt. New York: Bonanza Books, 1980.

Bridenbaugh, Carl. *Cities in Revolt: Urban Life in America, 1743–1766.* New York: Alfred A. Knopf, 1955.

Bridenbaugh, Carl, and Jessica Bridenbaugh. *Rebels and Gentlemen: Philadelphia in the Age of Franklin.* New York: Reynal and Hitchcock, 1942.

Briggs, John. *Leonard Bernstein: The Man, His Work, and His World.* Cleveland: World Publishing Co., 1961.

Brink, Carol. *Harps in the Wind: The Story of the Singing Hutchinsons.* 1947. Rpt. New York: Da Capo Press, 1980.

Britton, Allen. "Theoretical Introductions in American Tune-Books to 1800." Ph.D. diss., University of Michigan, 1950.

Broder, Nathan. *Samuel Barber.* New York: G. Schirmer, 1954.

Brokaw, John W. "The Minstrel Show in the Hoblitzelle Theatre Arts Library." *Library Chronicle of the University of Texas,* n.s. 4 (Feb. 1972): 23–30.

Brooks, Edward. *The Bessie Smith Companion.* New York: Da Capo Press, 1983.

Brooks, Henry M. *Olden-Time Music: A Compilation from Newspapers and Books.* 1888. Rpt. New York: AMS Press, 1973.

Broonzy, William. *Big Bill Blues: William Broonzy's Story As Told to Yannick Bruynoghe.* 1955. Rpt. New York: Oak Publications, 1964.

Browne, Ray B., ed. *Popular Culture and the Expanding Consciousness.* New York: John Wiley and Sons, 1973.

Bruce, Dickson D., Jr. *And They All Sang Hallelujah: Plain-Folk Camp-Meeting Religion, 1800–1845.* Knoxville: University of Tennessee Press, 1974.

Bruce, Frank Neely. Liner notes to *The Dawning of Music in Kentucky.* Vanguard VSD 71178 (stereo) and VSQ 30023 (quad). 1973.

———. "The Piano Pieces of Anthony Philip Heinrich Contained in *The Dawning of Music in Kentucky* and *The Western Minstrel.*" D.M.A. thesis, University of Illinois at Urbana-Champaign, 1971.

Brunn, H. O. *The Story of the Original Dixieland Jazz Band.* 1960. Rpt. New York: Da Capo Press, 1977.

Bruno, Anthony. "Two American Twelve-Tone Composers: Milton Babbitt and

Ben Weber Represent Opposing Views." *Musical America* 71 (Feb. 1951): 22, 170.

Buchanan, Annabel Morris. *Folk Hymns of America*. New York: J. Fischer and Brother, 1938.

Buchanan, Charles L. "Ornstein and Modern Music." *Musical Quarterly* 4 (Apr. 1918): 174–83.

Buechner, Alan C. Brochure notes to *The New England Harmony*. Folkways FA 2377 (FS 3 2377). 1964.

———. "Yankee Singing Schools and the Golden Age of Choral Music in New England, 1760–1800." Ph.D. diss., Harvard University, 1960.

Buerkle, Jack V., and Danny Barker. *Bourbon Street Black: The New Orleans Black Jazzman*. New York: Oxford University Press, 1973.

Burkholder, J. Peter. *Charles Ives: The Ideas behind the Music*. New Haven, Conn.: Yale University Press, 1985.

Burleigh, Henry Thacker, ed. *Negro Minstrel Melodies: A Collection of Twenty-one Songs with Piano Accompaniment by Stephen C. Foster and Others*. New York: G. Schirmer, 1909.

Burton, Frederick R. *American Primitive Music, with Especial Attention to the Songs of the Ojibways*. 1909. Rpt. Port Washington, N.Y.: Kennikat Press, 1969.

Burton, Thomas G., ed. *Tom Ashley, Sam McGee, Bukka White: Tennessee Traditional Singers*. Knoxville: University of Tennessee Press, 1981.

Busoni, Ferruccio. *Sketch of a New Esthetic of Music*. Translated from the German by Theodore Baker. New York: G. Schirmer, 1911.

Byrd, William. *The Great American Gentleman: William Byrd of Westover in Virginia, His Secret Diary for the Years 1709–1712*. Edited by Louis B. Wright and Marion Tinling. New York: G. P. Putnam's Sons, 1963.

———. *The Writings of Colonel William Byrd of Westover in Virginia Esq'*. Edited by John Spencer Bassett. 1901. Rpt. New York: Burt Franklin, 1970.

Cage, John. Brochure notes to *The 25-Year Retrospective Concert of John Cage*. Recorded in performance, Town Hall, New York, May 15, 1958. Produced and distributed by George Avakian. 1959.

———. *M: Writings '67–'72*. Middletown, Conn.: Wesleyan University Press, 1973.

———. *Silence*. Middletown, Conn.: Wesleyan University Press, 1961.

———, comp. *Notations*. New York: Something Else Press, 1969.

Carawan, Guy, and Candie Carawan. *Voices from the Mountains*. 1975. Rpt. Urbana: University of Illinois Press, 1982.

Carlson, Joyce Mangler. "Early Music in Rhode Island, V: Oliver Shaw and the Psallonian Society." *Rhode Island History* 23 (Apr. 1964): 35–50.

Carr, Ian. *Miles Davis: A Critical Biography*. London: Quartet Books, 1982.

Carrell, James P., and David L. Clayton, comps. *The Virginia Harmony: A New and Choice Selection of Psalm & Hymn Tunes, Anthems, & Set Pieces*. 1831. 2d rev. ed. Winchester, Va.: Robinson and Hollis, 1836.

Carse, Adam. *The Life of Jullien: Adventurer, Showman-Conductor and Establisher of the Promenade Concerts in England, together with a History of Those Concerts up to 1895*. Cambridge: W. Heffer and Sons, 1951.

Carter, Elliott. "American Figure, with Landscape." *Modern Music* 20 (May-June 1943): 219–25.

———. "Expressionism and American Music." *Perspectives of New Music* 4 (Fall-Winter 1965): 1–13.

———. Liner notes to Elliott Carter, *Variations for Orchestra . . . Double Concerto. . . .* Columbia Records MS 7191.

———. "Walter Piston." *Musical Quarterly* 32 (July 1946): 354–75.

———. *The Writings of Elliott Carter: An American Composer Looks at Modern Music*. Compiled, edited, and annotated by Else Stone and Kurt Stone. Bloomington: Indiana University Press, 1977.

Cartwright, Peter. *Autobiography of Peter Cartwright, the Backwoods Preacher*. Edited by W. P. Strickland. Cincinnati: Cranston and Curts, 1856.

Castle, Irene, and Vernon Castle. *Modern Dancing*. 1914. Rpt. New York: Da Capo Press, 1980.

Caulkins, Frances Manwaring. *History of Norwich, Connecticut: From Its Possession by the Indians, to the Year 1866*. Hartford, Conn.: Author, 1866.

Cazden, Norman, Herbert Haufrecht, and Norman Studer, eds. *Folk Songs of the Catskills*. Albany: State University of New York Press, 1982.

Chambers, Jack. *Milestones I: The Music and Times of Miles Davis to 1960*. Toronto: University of Toronto Press, 1983.

Chappell, William. *The Ballad Literature and Popular Music of the Olden Time: A History of the Ancient Songs, Ballads, and of the Dance Tunes of England, with Numerous Anecdotes and Entire Ballads*. 2 vols. 1859. Rpt. New York: Dover Publications, 1965.

Charles, Sydney Robinson. "The Use of Borrowed Material in Ives' Second Symphony." *Music Review* 28 (May 1967): 102–11.

Charters, Ann, ed. *The Ragtime Songbook: Songs of the Ragtime Era by Scott Joplin, Hughie Cannon, Ben Harney, Will Marion Cook, Alex Rogers and Others*. New York: Oak Publications, 1965.

Charters, Samuel B. *The Bluesmen: The Story and Music of the Men Who Made the Blues*. New York: Oak Publications, 1967.

———. *The Country Blues*. 1959. Rpt. New York: Da Capo Press, 1975.

———. *Jazz: New Orleans, 1885–1963: An Index to the Negro Musicians of New Orleans*. 1963. Rpt. New York: Da Capo Press, 1983.

———. *The Legacy of the Blues: Art and Lives of Twelve Great Bluesmen*. 1975. Rpt. New York: Da Capo Press, 1977.

Charters, Samuel B., and Leonard Kunstadt. *Jazz: A History of the New York Scene*. 1962. Rpt., with a new introduction by Samuel Charters. New York: Da Capo Press, 1981.

Chase, Gilbert. "American Music and American Musicology." *Journal of Musicology* 1 (Jan. 1982): 59–62.

———. *America's Music: From the Pilgrims to the Present*. New York: McGraw-Hill, 1955; 2d rev. ed. 1966.

————. "The Shape of Time in America's Music." *Journal of American Culture* 4, no. 4 (1981): 92–106.

————. *Two Lectures in the Form of a Pair: Music, Culture, and History; Structuralism and Music.* I.S.A.M. Monographs, no. 2. Brooklyn, N.Y.: Institute for Studies in American Music, 1973.

————. "Webern in America: The Growth of an Influence." In Osterreichische Gesellschaft für Musik, *Beiträge '72/73* [5th International Webern Congress], 153–66. Kassel: Barenreiter, 1973.

————, ed. *The American Composer Speaks: A Historical Anthology, 1770–1965.* Baton Rouge: Louisiana State University Press, 1966.

Cheney, Simeon Pease. *The American Singing Book.* 1879. Rpt., with a new introduction by Karl Kroeger. Earlier American Music, no. 17. New York: Da Capo Press, 1980.

————. *Brother Cheney's Collection of Old Folks' Concert Music.* Boston: White, Smith and Co., 1879.

Church Music and Musical Life in Pennsylvania in the Eighteenth Century. 3 vols. Publications of the Pennsylvania Society of the Colonial Dames of America, no. 4. Philadelphia: Printed for the Society, 1926–47.

Cipolla, Wilma Reid. *A Catalog of the Works of Arthur Foote, 1853–1937.* Bibliographies in American Music, no. 6. Detroit: Information Coordinators, for the College Music Society, 1980.

Clarke, Garry E. *Essays on American Music.* Contributions in American History, no. 62. Westport, Conn.: Greenwood Press, 1977.

Cobb, Buell E. *The Sacred Harp: A Tradition and Its Music.* Athens: University of Georgia Press, 1978.

Cohan, George M. *Twenty Years on Broadway, and the Years It Took to Get There: The True Story of a Trouper's Life from the Cradle to the "Closed Shop."* 1924. Rpt. Ann Arbor, Mich.: University Microfilms, 1968.

Collins, Lee. *Oh, Didn't He Ramble: The Life and Story of Lee Collins As Told to Mary Collins.* Edited by Frank J. Gillis and John W. Miner. Music in American Life. Urbana: University of Illinois Press, 1974.

Combs, Josiah H. *Folksongs of the Southern United States (Folk-Songs du Midi des Etats-Unis).* Edited by D. K. Wilgus. Publications of the American Folklore Society, Bibliographical and Special Series, vol. 19. Austin: University of Texas Press, 1967.

Condon, Eddie, and Thomas Sugrue. *We Called It Music: A Generation of Jazz.* New York: Henry Holt and Co., 1947.

Confrey, Zez. *Zez Confrey's Modern Course in Novelty Piano Playing.* New York: J. Mills, 1923.

Cook, Harold E. *Shaker Music: A Manifestation of American Folk Culture.* Lewisburg: Bucknell University Press, 1973.

Cooke, George Willis. *John Sullivan Dwight: Brook-Farmer, Editor, and Critic of Music.* 1898. Rpt. New York: Da Capo Press, 1969.

Coon, Caroline. *1988: The New Wave Punk Rock Explosion.* New York: Hawthorn Books, 1977.

Copland, Aaron. *Copland on Music*. Garden City, N.Y.: Doubleday and Co., 1960.
———. *Music and Imagination*. Cambridge: Harvard University Press, 1952.
———. *Our New Music: Leading Composers in Europe and America*. 1941. Rev. ed., as *The New Music, 1900–1960*. New York: W. W. Norton and Co., 1968.
Copland, Aaron, and Vivian Perlis. *Copland: 1900 through 1942*. New York: St. Martin's/Marek, 1984.
Coulter, Glenn. "Billie Holliday." In *The Art of Jazz*. Edited by Martin Williams, 161–72. 1959. Rpt. New York: Da Capo Press, 1979.
Courlander, Harold. *Negro Folk Music, U.S.A.* New York: Columbia University Press, 1963.
Cowell, Henry. *New Musical Resources*. Preface and notes by Joscelyn Godwin. New York: Something Else Press, 1969.
———. "Wallingford Riegger . . . 'a Romantic Who Admires Strict Forms.' " *Musical America* 68 (Dec. 1948): 9, 29.
———, ed. *American Composers on American Music: A Symposium*. 1933. Rpt. New York: Frederick Ungar Publishing Co., 1962.
Cowell, Henry, and Sidney Cowell. *Charles Ives and His Music*. New York: Oxford University Press, 1969.
Crawford, Richard. *American Studies and American Musicology: A Point of View and a Case in Point*. I.S.A.M. Monographs, no. 4. Brooklyn, N.Y.: Institute for Studies in American Music, 1975.
———. *Andrew Law, American Psalmodist*. Evanston, Ill.: Northwestern University Press, 1968.
———, ed. *The Core Repertory of Early American Psalmody*. Recent Researches in Early American Music, nos. 11–12. Madison: A-R Editions, 1984.
Crèvecoeur, J. Hector John de. *Letters from an American Farmer*. Edited by Albert E. Stone, Jr. New York: New American Library, 1963.
Cripe, Helen. *Thomas Jefferson and Music*. Charlottesville: University Press of Virginia, 1974.
Cross, Lowell M., comp. *A Bibliography of Electronic Music*. Toronto: University of Toronto Press, 1967.
Crumb, George. Liner notes to George Crumb, *Ancient Voices of Children*. Nonesuch H-71255. 1971.
Curtis, Natalie [Mrs. Natalie Curtis Burlin]. *The Indians' Book: An Offering by the American Indians of Indian Lore, Musical and Narrative, to Form a Record of the Songs and Legends of Their Race*. 2d ed. 1923. Rpt. New York: Dover Publications, 1968.
Curwen, John Spencer. *Studies in Worship Music*. Ser. 1, 2d ed. London: J. Curwen and Sons, 1888.

Damon, S. Foster, ed. *Series of Old American Songs Reproduced in Facsimile from Original or Early Editions in the Harris Collection of American Poetry and Plays, Brown University*. Providence: Brown University Library, 1936.
Dance, Stanley. *The World of Duke Ellington*. New York: Charles Scribner's Sons, 1970.

Daniel, Ralph T. *The Anthem in New England before 1800.* Evanston, Ill.: Northwestern University Press, 1966.

Dart, Thurston. "The Cittern and Its English Music." *Galpin Society Journal* 1 (Mar. 1948): 46–63.

David, Hans T. *Musical Life in the Pennsylvania Settlements of the Unitas Fratrum.* Foreword by Donald M. McCorkle. Moravian Music Foundation Publications, no. 6. Winston-Salem, N.C.: Moravian Music Foundation, 1959.

Davidson, Robert. *History of the Presbyterian Church in the State of Kentucky, with a Preliminary Sketch of the Churches in the Valley of Virginia.* New York: Robert Carter, 1847.

Davis, Ronald L. *A History of Opera in the American West.* Englewood Cliffs, N.J.: Prentice-Hall, 1965.

Delaunay, Charles. *Django Reinhardt.* Translated from the French by Michael James. 1961. Rpt. New York: Da Capo Press, 1981.

De Lerma, Dominique-René. *Bibliography of Black Music.* 4 vols. Westport, Conn.: Greenwood Press, 1981–84.

Denisoff, R. Serge. *Great Day Coming: Folk Music and the American Left.* Music in American Life. Urbana: University of Illinois Press, 1971.

———. *Sing a Song of Social Significance.* Bowling Green, Ohio: Bowling Green University Popular Press, 1972.

Denisoff, R. Serge, and Richard A. Peterson, eds. *The Sounds of Social Change: Studies in Popular Culture.* Chicago: Rand McNally, 1972.

Densmore, Frances. *The American Indians and Their Music.* 1926. Rpt. New York: Johnson Reprint Corp., 1970.

———. *Chippewa Music.* 2 vols. 1910–13. Rpt. New York: Da Capo Press, 1972.

———. *Papago Music.* 1929. Rpt. New York: Da Capo Press, 1972.

———. *Pawnee Music.* 1929. Rpt. New York: Da Capo Press, 1972.

De Turk, David A., and A. Poulin, Jr., eds. *The American Folk Scene: Dimensions of the Folksong Revival.* New York: Dell Publishing Co., 1967.

Dictionary of American Biography. 20 vols., with supplements. New York: Charles Scribner's Sons, 1946.

Dietz, Robert James. "The Operatic Style of Marc Blitzstein in the American 'Agit-Prop' Era." Ph.D diss., University of Iowa, 1970.

DiMeglio, John E. *Vaudeville, U.S.A.* Bowling Green, Ohio: Bowling Green University Popular Press, 1973.

Dixon, Robert M. W., and John Godrich. *Recording the Blues.* New York: Stein and Day, 1970.

Dooley, James Edward. "Thomas Hastings: American Church Musician." Ph.D. diss., Florida State University, 1963.

Dorson, Richard M. *Buying the Wind: Regional Folklore in the United States.* Chicago: University of Chicago Press, 1964.

Dow, Lorenzo. *History of Cosmopolite; or, The Four Volumes of Lorenzo's Journal.* New York: J. C. Totten, 1814.

Downes, Edward. *The New York Philharmonic Guide to the Symphony.* New York: Walker and Co., 1976.

Downey, James Cecil. "The Music of American Revivalism, 1740–1800." Ph.D. diss., Tulane University, 1968.

Doyle, David Noel, and Owen Dudley Edwards, eds. *America and Ireland, 1776– 1976: The American Identity and the Irish Connection; The Proceedings of the United States Bicentennial Conference of Cumann Merriman, Ennis, August, 1976.* Westport, Conn.: Greenwood Press, 1980.

Doyle, John G. *Louis Moreau Gottschalk, 1829–1869: A Bibliographical Study and Catalog of Works.* Detroit: Information Coordinators, for the College Music Society, 1983.

Dreiser, Theodore. "Concerning the Author of These Songs." In *The Songs of Paul Dresser.* New York: Boni and Liveright, 1927.

Dunaway, David King. *How Can I Keep from Singing: Pete Seeger.* New York: McGraw-Hill, 1981.

Dunn, Robert, ed. *John Cage.* New York: Henmar Press, 1962.

Dwight, John Sullivan, ed. *Dwight's Journal of Music.* 41 vols. 1852–81. Rpt. New York: Johnson Reprint Corp., Arno Press, 1967.

Earls, Paul. "Harry Partch: Verses in Preparation for 'Delusion of the Fury.'" *Yearbook for Inter-American Musical Research* 3 (1967): 1–32.

Edwards, Allen. *Flawed Words and Stubborn Sounds: A Conversation with Elliott Carter.* New York: W. W. Norton and Co., 1971.

Eggleston, Edward. *The Circuit Rider: A Tale of the Heroic Age.* 1874. Rpt., with an introduction by Holman Hamilton. Lexington: University Press of Kentucky, 1970.

Ellington, Edward Kennedy ("Duke"). *Music Is My Mistress.* Garden City, N.Y.: Doubleday and Co., 1973.

Ellington, Mercer, with Stanley Dance. *Duke Ellington in Person: An Intimate Memoir.* Boston: Houghton Mifflin Co., 1978.

Elson, Louis C. *The History of American Music.* Rev. ed. 1925. Rpt. New York: Burt Franklin, 1971.

Emerson, Ralph Waldo. *An Oration Delivered before the Literary Societies of Dartmouth College, July 24, 1838.* Boston: Charles C. Little and James Brown, 1838.

Engel, Lehman. *The American Musical Theater: A Consideration.* Rev. ed. New York: Macmillan, 1975.

Epstein, Dena J. *Sinful Tunes and Spirituals: Black Folk Music to the Civil War.* Music in American Life. Urbana: University of Illinois Press, 1977.

Erskine, John. *The Philharmonic-Symphony Society of New York: Its First Hundred Years.* New York: Macmillan, 1943.

Eskew, Harry. "Joseph Funk's 'Allgemein nutzliche Choral-Music' (1816)." In Society for the History of the Germans in Maryland. *Thirty-second Report.* Edited by Klaus G. Wust, 38–46. Baltimore, 1966.

Ethnic Recordings in America: A Neglected Heritage. Foreword by Alan Jabbour. Studies in American Folklife, no. 1. Washington, D.C.: American Folklife Center, Library of Congress, 1982.

Euterpeiad; or, Musical Intelligencer. 1820–23. Rpt. New York: Da Capo Press, 1977.

Evans, David. *Big Road Blues: Tradition and Creativity in the Folk Blues.* Berkeley and Los Angeles: University of California Press, 1982.

Everett, Lemuel C., and A. B. Everett. *The New Thesaurus Musicus; or, United States Collection of Church Music.* Richmond, Va.: Published by the authors, 1858.

———. *The Progressive Church Vocalist.* 3d ed. New York: Mason Brothers, 1855.

Evett, Robert, "How Right Is Right?" *Score and I.M.A. Magazine* 12 (June 1955): 33–37.

Ewen, David. *George Gershwin: His Journey to Greatness.* Englewood Cliffs, N.J.: Prentice-Hall, 1970.

———. *New Complete Book of the American Musical Theater.* New York: Holt, Rinehart and Winston, 1970.

———. *Richard Rodgers.* New York: Henry Holt and Co., 1957.

———. *The Story of Irving Berlin.* New York: Henry Holt and Co., 1950.

———. *The World of Jerome Kern: A Biography.* New York: Holt, Rinehart and Winston, 1960.

———. *The World of Twentieth-Century Music.* Englewood Cliffs, N.J.: Prentice-Hall, 1968.

Ewing, George W. *The Well-Tempered Lyre: Songs & Verse of the Temperance Movement.* Bicentennial Series in American Studies, no. 5. Dallas: Southern Methodist University Press, 1977.

Farwell, Arthur. "Roy Harris." *Musical Quarterly* 18 (Jan. 1932): 18–32.

———. "Story of Rudolph Gott." *Musical America* 22 (Aug. 14, 21, and 28, 1915): 9; 9–10; 21.

Farwell, Arthur, and W. Dermot Darby, eds. *Music in America.* Vol. 4 of *The Art of Music.* Edited by Daniel Gregory Mason et al. New York: National Society of Music, 1915.

Farwell, Brice, ed. *A Guide to the Music of Arthur Farwell and to the Microfilm Collection of His Work.* Briarcliff Manor, N.Y.: Issued by B. Farwell for the estate of Arthur Farwell, 1972.

Feather, Leonard. *The Encyclopedia of Jazz in the Sixties.* New York: Horizon Press, 1966.

———. *Inside Jazz (Inside Bebop).* 1949. Rpt. New York: Da Capo Press, 1977.

Feather, Leonard, and Ira Gitler. *The Encyclopedia of Jazz in the Seventies.* New York: Horizon Press, 1976

Fenner, Thomas Putnam, comp. *Cabin and Plantation Songs As Sung by the Hampton Students.* New York: G. P. Putnam's Sons, 1874.

Ferris, William, Jr. *Blues from the Delta.* 1979. Rpt., with a new introduction by Billy Taylor. New York: Da Capo Press, 1984.

———. *Mississippi Black Folklore: A Research Bibliography and Discography.* Hattiesburg: University and College Press of Mississippi, 1971.

Ferris, William, Jr., and Mary L. Hart, eds. *Folk Music and Modern Sound.* Jackson: University Press of Mississippi, 1982.

Fewkes, J. Walter. "A Few Summer Ceremonials at Zuni Pueblo." *Journal of American Ethnology and Archaeology* 1 (1891): 1–61.

Fillmore, John C. *The Harmonic Structure of Indian Music.* New York: G. P. Putnam's Sons, 1899.

Finck, Henry T. *Songs and Song Writers.* New York: Charles Scribner's Sons, 1900.

Fisher, Miles Mark. *Negro Slave Songs in the United States.* 1953. Rpt. New York: Russell and Russell, 1968.

Fisher, William Arms. *One Hundred and Fifty Years of Music Publishing in the United States: An Historical Sketch with Special Reference to Pioneer Publisher, Oliver Ditson Company, Inc., 1783–1933.* Boston: Oliver Ditson Co., 1933.

Fithian, Philip Vickers. *Journal & Letters of Philip Vickers Fithian, 1773–1774: A Plantation Tutor of the Old Dominion.* Edited by Hunter Dickinson Farish. Williamsburg, Va.: Colonial Williamsburg, 1957.

Fletcher, Alice C. *Indian Story and Song from North America.* 1900. Rpt. New York: Johnson Reprint Corp., 1970.

Fletcher, Alice C., and Francis La Flesche. *A Study of Omaha Indian Music.* 1893. Rpt. New York: Kraus Reprint Co., 1967.

Fletcher, Tom. *100 Years of the Negro in Show Business.* 1954. Rpt. New York: Da Capo Press, 1984.

Flexner, James Thomas. *That Wilder Image: The Painting of America's Native School from Thomas Cole to Winslow Homer.* Boston: Little, Brown and Co., 1962.

Foote, Arthur. *Arthur Foote, 1853–1937: An Autobiography.* 1946. Rpt., with a new introduction, chronology, and index of names and compositions by Wilma Reid Cipolla. New York: Da Capo Press, 1979.

Foote, Henry Wilder. *Three Centuries of American Hymnody.* 1940. Rpt. Hamden, Conn.: Archon Books, 1968.

Foote, William Henry. *Sketches of Virginia, Historical and Biographical (First Series).* 1850. Rpt. Richmond, Va.: John Knox Press, 1966.

Ford, Ira W. *Traditional Music of America.* 1940. Rpt. New York: Da Capo Press, 1978.

Foster, George Murphy. *Pops Foster: The Autobiography of a New Orleans Jazzman As Told to Tom Stoddard.* Berkeley and Los Angeles: University of California Press, 1971.

Foster, Morrison. *My Brother Stephen.* Indianapolis: Privately printed for the Foster Hall Collection, 1932.

Foster, Stephen Collins. *The Social Orchestra.* 1854. Rpt., with an introduction by H. Wiley Hitchcock. Earlier American Music, no. 13. New York: Da Capo Press, 1973.

———. *Stephen Foster Song Book: Original Sheet Music of 40 Songs by Stephen Collins Foster.* Edited by Richard Jackson. New York: Dover Publications, 1974.

Franklin, Benjamin. *Complete Works of Benjamin Franklin.* 10 vols. Compiled and edited by John Bigelow. New York: G. P. Putnam's Sons, 1887–88.

———. *Papers of Benjamin Franklin.* 24 vols. Edited by Leonard W. Labaree et al. New Haven: Yale University Press, 1959–84.

Frazier, E. Franklin. *The Negro Church in America.* New York: Schocken Books, 1963.

Frisbie, Charlotte J. *Music and Dance Research of Southwestern United States Indians: Past Trends, Present Activities, and Suggestions for Future Research.* Studies in Music Bibliography, no. 36. Detroit: Information Coordinators, 1977.

———. "Ritual Drama in the Navajo Blessing Ceremony." In *Southwestern Indian Ritual Drama.* Edited by Charlotte Frisbie, 161–98. Albuquerque: University of New Mexico Press, 1980.

———, ed. *Southwestern Indian Ritual Drama.* School of American Research Advanced Seminar Series. Albuquerque: University of New Mexico Press, 1980.

Fuld, James J. *American Popular Music (Reference Book), 1875–1950.* Philadelphia: Musical Americana, 1955.

———. *A Pictorial Bibliography of the First Editions of Stephen C. Foster.* Philadelphia: Musical Americana, 1957.

Gagne, Cole, and Tracy Caras. *Soundpieces: Interviews with American Composers.* Metuchen, N.J.: Scarecrow Press, 1982.

Galbraith, Charles Burleigh. *Daniel Decatur Emmett: Author of "Dixie."* Columbus, Ohio: Press of Fredrick J. Heer, 1904.

Gallo, William K. "The Life and Church Music of Dudley Buck (1839–1909)." Ph.D. diss., Catholic University, 1968.

Gammond, Peter, ed. *Duke Ellington: His Life and Music.* 1958. Rpt. New York: Da Capo Press, 1977.

Garrison, Lucy McKim. "Songs of the Port Royal 'Contrabands.' " *Dwight's Journal of Music* 22 (Nov. 8, 1862): 254–55.

Gena, Peter, and Jonathan Brent, eds., with supplementary editing by Don Gillespie. *A John Cage Reader in Celebration of His 70th Birthday.* New York: C. F. Peters Corp., 1982.

Gershwin, George. *The New York Times Gershwin Years in Song.* Introduction by Edward Jablonski and Lawrence D. Stewart. New York: Quadrangle, New York Times Book Co., 1973.

Gerson, Robert A. *Music in Philadelphia.* 1940. Rpt. Westport, Conn.: Greenwood Press, 1970.

Gillespie, Don Chance. "John Becker: Midwestern Musical Crusader." Ph.D. diss., University of North Carolina, 1977.

———, comp. and ed. *George Crumb: Profile of a Composer.* Introduction by Gilbert Chase. New York: C. F. Peters Corp., 1986.

Gillett, Charlie. *The Sound of the City: The Rise of Rock and Roll.* 1970. Rpt. London: Souvenir Press, 1983.

Gillis, Frank J., and John W. Miner. See Collins, Lee.

Gilman, Benjamin Ives. *Hopi Songs.* Boston: Houghton Mifflin Co., 1908.

Gilman, Lawrence. *Edward MacDowell: A Study.* 2d ed. 1908. Rpt., with a new introduction by Margery L. Morgan [Margery Lowens]. New York: Da Capo Press, 1969.

Gilman, Samuel. *Memoirs of a New England Village Choir.* 1829. Rpt., with a new introduction by Karl Kroeger. New York: Da Capo Press, 1984.

Goen, C. C. *Revivalism and Separatism in New England, 1740–1800: Strict Congregationalists and Separate Baptists in the Great Awakening.* Yale Publications in Religion, no. 2. New Haven: Yale University Press, 1962.

Goetzmann, William H. *Exploration and Empire: The Explorer and the Scientist in the Winning of the American West.* New York: Alfred A. Knopf, 1966.

Gold, Robert S. *A Jazz Lexicon.* New York: Alfred A. Knopf, 1964.

Goldberg, Isaac. *George Gershwin: A Study in American Music.* Rev. ed. New York: Frederick Ungar Publishing Co., 1958.

———. *Tin Pan Alley: A Chronicle of American Popular Music.* New York: Frederick Ungar Publishing Co., 1961.

Goldman, Richard Franko, ed. *Landmarks of Early American Music, 1760–1800: A Collection of Thirty-two Compositions.* New York: G. Schirmer, 1943.

Gombosi, Marilyn. *A Day of Solemn Thanksgiving: Moravian Music for the Fourth of July, 1783, in Salem, North Carolina.* Chapel Hill: University of North Carolina Press, 1977.

Goodman, Benny, and Irving Kolodin. *The Kingdom of Swing.* 1939. Rpt. New York: Frederick Ungar Publishing Co., 1961.

Gottschalk, Louis Moreau. *Notes of a Pianist.* Edited, with a prelude, postlude, and explanatory notes by Jeanne Behrend. 1964. Rpt. New York: Da Capo Press, 1979.

———. *Piano Music of Louis Moreau Gottschalk: 26 Complete Pieces from Original Editions.* Compiled by Richard Jackson. New York: Dover Publications, 1973.

———. *The Piano Works of Louis Moreau Gottschalk.* Edited by Vera Brodsky Lawrence. 5 vols. New York: Arno Press, New York Times, 1969.

Gould, Nathaniel D. *History of Church Music in America, Comprising Its History and Its Peculiarities at Different Periods, with Cursory Remarks on Its Legitimate Use and Its Abuse; with Notices of the Schools, Composers, Teachers, and Societies.* 1853. Rpt. New York: AMS Press, 1972.

Graf, Herbert. *Opera for the People.* 1951. Rpt., with a new introduction by the author. New York: Da Capo Press, 1973.

Graham, Philip. *Showboats: The History of an American Institution.* Austin: University of Texas Press, 1951.

Green, Archie. "Hillbilly Music: Source and Symbol." *Journal of American Folklore* 78 (July-Sept. 1965): 204–28.

———. *Only a Miner: Studies in Recorded Coal-Mining Songs.* Music in American Life. Urbana: University of Illinois Press, 1972.

Green, Douglas B. "Gene Autry." In *Stars of Country Music: Uncle Dave Macon to Johnny Rodriguez.* Edited by Bill C. Malone and Judith McCulloh, 142–56. Urbana: University of Illinois Press, 1975.

Green, Stanley. *The World of Musical Comedy: The Story of the American Musical*

Stage As Told through the Careers of Its Foremost Composers and Lyricists. 4th rev. ed. San Diego: A. S. Barnes and Co., 1980.

Greenway, John. *American Folksongs of Protest.* Philadelphia: University of Pennsylvania Press, 1953.

———. "Jimmie Rodgers—a Folksong Catalyst." *Journal of American Folklore* 70 (July-Sept. 1957): 231–34.

Grenander, M. E. "Reflections on the String Quartet(s) Attributed to Franklin." *American Quarterly* 27 (Mar. 1975): 73–87.

Grider, Rufus A. *Historical Notes on Music in Bethlehem, Pa. (from 1741–1871).* 1873. Rpt., with a foreword by Donald M. McCorkle. Moravian Music Foundation Publications, no. 4. Winston-Salem, N.C.: Moravian Music Foundation, 1957.

Griffith, James S. "Lydia Mendoza: An Enduring Mexican-American Singer." In *Ethnic Recordings in America: A Neglected Heritage,* 102–31. Washington, D.C.: American Folklife Center, Library of Congress, 1982.

Grissom, Mary Allen. *The Negro Sings a New Heaven.* 1930. Rpt. New York: Dover Publications, 1969.

Guthrie, Woody. *Bound for Glory.* Foreword by Pete Seeger. New York: E. P. Dutton and Co., 1968.

Haas, Robert Bartlett, ed. *William Grant Still and the Fusion of Cultures in American Music.* Los Angeles: Black Sparrow Press, 1972.

Hagert, Thornton. Brochure notes to *An Experiment in Modern Music: Paul Whiteman at Aeolian Hall.* Smithsonian Institution and RCA Special Products R 028. 1981.

Hague, Eleanor, comp. *Spanish-American Folk-Songs.* 1917. Rpt. New York: Kraus Reprint Co., 1969.

Hall, James William, Jr. "The Tune-Book in American Culture, 1800–1820." Ph.D. diss., University of Pennsylvania, 1967.

Hall, Thomas Cuming. *The Religious Background of American Culture.* New York: Frederick Ungar Publishing Co., 1959.

Hallowell, Emily, ed. *Calhoun Plantation Songs.* Boston: C. W. Thompson and Co., 1901.

Hamm, Charles. Liner notes to *Sound Forms for Piano.* New World Records NW 203. N.d.

———. *Music in the New World.* New York: W. W. Norton and Co., 1983.

———. *Yesterdays: Popular Song in America.* New York: W. W. Norton and Co., 1979.

Handy, W. C. *Father of the Blues: An Autobiography by W. C. Handy.* Edited by Arna Bontemps. 1941. Rpt. New York: Collier Books, 1970.

———. *A Treasury of the Blues.* 1949. Reprinted and revised by Jerry Silverman as *Blues: An Anthology.* 1972. Rpt. New York: Da Capo Press, 1985.

Haralambos, Michael. *Right On: From Blues to Soul in Black America.* 1974. Rpt. New York: Da Capo Press, 1979.

————. "Soul Music and Blues: Their Meaning and Relevance in Northern United States Ghettos." In *Afro-American Anthropology.* Edited by Norman E. Whitten, Jr., and John F. Szwed, 367–83. New York: Free Press, 1970.

Haraszti, Zoltán. *The Enigma of the Bay Psalm Book.* Chicago: University of Chicago Press, 1956.

Hare, Maud (Cuney). *Negro Musicians and Their Music.* Washington, D.C.: Associated Publishers, 1936.

Harrison, Lou. *About Carl Ruggles.* Yonkers, N.Y.: Oscar Baradinsky, 1946.

————. "Carl Ruggles." *Score and I.M.A. Magazine* 12 (June 1955): 15–26.

Harrison, Max. *Charlie Parker.* New York: A. S. Barnes and Co., 1961.

Harrison, William P., comp. and ed. *The Gospel among the Slaves: A Short Account of Missionary Operations among the African Slaves of the Southern States.* 1893. Rpt. New York: AMS Press, 1973.

Harwell, Richard B. *Confederate Music.* Chapel Hill: University of North Carolina Press, 1950.

Hasse, John Edward, ed. *Ragtime: Its History, Composers, and Music.* New York: Schirmer Books, 1985.

Hastings, George E. *The Life and Works of Francis Hopkinson.* Chicago: University of Chicago Press, 1926.

Hastings, Thomas. *Dissertation on Musical Taste; or, General Principles of Taste Applied to the Art of Music.* 1822. Rpt. New York: Da Capo Press, 1974.

————. *Dissertation on Musical Taste.* [2d rev. ed.] 1853. Rpt. New York: Johnson Reprint Corp., 1968.

Hatfield, Edwin F., comp. *Freedom's Lyre; or, Psalms, Hymns and Sacred Songs, for the Slave and His Friends.* 1840. Rpt. Miami, Fla.: Mnemosyne Publishing Co., 1969.

Hauser, William. *The Olive Leaf: A Collection of Beautiful Tunes, New and Old.* Wadley, Ga.: W. Hauser and B. Turner, 1878.

Haywood, Charles. *A Bibliography of North American Folklore and Folksong.* 2 vols. 2d rev. ed. New York: Dover Publications, 1961.

————, ed. *The James A. Bland Album of Outstanding Songs.* New York: Edward B. Marks Music Corp., 1946.

Heaps, Willard A., and Porter W. Heaps. *The Singing Sixties: The Spirit of Civil War Days Drawn from the Music of the Times.* Norman: University of Oklahoma Press, 1960.

Hearn, Lafcadio. *An American Miscellany.* Edited by Albert Mordell. 2 vols. New York: Dodd, Mead and Co., 1924.

————. *Two Years in the French West Indies.* New York: Harper and Brothers, 1890.

Heilbut, Tony. *The Gospel Sound: Good News and Bad Times.* New York: Simon and Schuster, 1971.

————. Liner notes to *The Gospel Sound.* Vol. 1. Columbia Records G31086. N.d.

Heinrich, Anthony Philip. *The Dawning of Music in Kentucky; or, The Pleasures of Harmony in the Solitudes of Nature* (*opera prima*)/*The Western Minstrel* (*opera seconda*). Earlier American Music, no. 10. New York: Da Capo Press, 1972.

Helmholtz, Hermann Ludwig Ferdinand von. *On the Sensations of Tone as a Physiological Basis for the Theory of Music.* 2d ed. 1885. Rpt. New York: Dover Publications, 1954.

Hendler, Herb. *Year by Year in the Rock Era: Events and Conditions Shaping the Rock Generations That Reshaped America.* Westport, Conn.: Greenwood Press, 1983.

Hensel, Octavia [Mrs. Mary Alice Ives Seymour]. *Life and Letters of Louis Moreau Gottschalk.* Boston: Oliver Ditson and Co., 1870.

Hentoff, Nat, and Albert J. McCarthy, eds. *Jazz: New Perspectives on the History of Jazz by Twelve of the World's Foremost Jazz Critics and Scholars.* 1959. Rpt. New York: Da Capo Press, 1974.

Herndon, Marcia. *Native American Music.* Norwood, Pa.: Norwood Editions, 1980.

Hertzberg, Hazel W. *The Search for an American Indian Identity: Modern Pan-Indian Movements.* Syracuse: Syracuse University Press, 1971.

Heth, Charlotte. "Update on Indian Music: Contemporary Trends." In *Sharing a Heritage: Indian Arts.* Edited by Charlotte Heth, 89–100. Los Angeles: U.C.L.A. American Indian Studies Center, 1984.

———, ed. *Sharing a Heritage: American Indian Arts.* Contemporary American Indian Issues, no. 5. Los Angeles: U.C.L.A. American Indian Studies Center, 1984.

Hewitt, John Hill. *Shadows on the Wall; or, Glimpses of the Past.* 1877. Rpt. New York: AMS Press, 1971.

Higginson, J. Vincent. *Hymnody in the American Indian Missions.* Papers of the Hymn Society, no. 18. New York: Hymn Society of America, 1954.

Higginson, Thomas W. "Negro Spirituals." *Atlantic Monthly* 19 (June 1867): 685–94.

Hiller, Lejaren A., Jr. Liner notes to *Computer Music from the University of Illinois.* Heliodor (MGM Records) HS 25053. N.d.

Hiller, Lejaren A., Jr., and Leonard M. Isaacson. *Experimental Music: Composition with an Electric Computer.* 1959. Rpt. Westport, Conn.: Greenwood Press, 1979.

Hines, Robert Stephan, ed. *The Orchestral Composer's Point of View: Essays on Twentieth-Century Music by Those Who Wrote It.* Norman: University of Oklahoma Press, 1970.

Hinton, Leanne. "Vocables in Havasupai Song." In *Southwestern Indian Ritual Drama.* Edited by Charlotte Frisbie, 275–305. Albuquerque: University of New Mexico Press, 1980.

Hipsher, Edward Ellsworth. *American Opera and Its Composers.* 1927. Rpt., with a new introduction by H. Earle Johnson. New York: Da Capo Press, 1978.

History of the Handel and Haydn Society. 2 vols. in 3 parts. 1911, 1913, 1914. Rpt., with new descriptive content by Judith Tick. New York: Da Capo Press, 1977–79.

Hitchcock, H. Wiley. *Ives: A Survey of the Music.* I.S.A.M. Monographs, no. 19. Brooklyn, N.Y.: Institute for Studies in American Music, 1977.

———. *Music in the United States: A Historical Introduction.* 2d ed. Englewood Cliffs, N.J.: Prentice-Hall, 1974.

———, ed. *American Music before 1865 in Print and on Records: A Biblio-Discography.* I.S.A.M. Monographs, no. 6. Brooklyn, N.Y.: Institute for Studies in American Music, 1973.

———, ed. *The Phonograph and Our Musical Life: Proceedings of a Centennial Conference, 7–10 December 1977.* I.S.A.M. Monographs, no. 14. Brooklyn, N.Y.: Institute for Studies in American Music, 1980.

Hitchcock, H. Wiley, and Vivian Perlis, eds. *An Ives Celebration: Papers and Panels of the Charles Ives Centennial Festival-Conference.* Music in American Life. Urbana: University of Illinois Press, 1977.

Hixon, Donald L. *Music in Early America: A Bibliography of Music in Evans.* Metuchen, N.J.: Scarecrow Press, 1970.

Hobson, Wilder. *American Jazz Music.* 1939. Rpt. New York: Da Capo Press, 1976.

Hodeir, André. *Jazz: Its Evolution and Essence.* Translated from the French by David Noakes. 1956. Rpt. New York: Da Capo Press, 1975.

Hoffmann, Frank. *The Literature of Rock, 1954–1978.* Metuchen, N.J.: Scarecrow Press, 1981.

Hofmann, Charles, ed. *Frances Densmore and American Indian Music: A Memorial Volume.* Contributions from the Museum of the American Indian Heye Foundation, vol. 23. New York: Museum of the American Indian, Heye Foundation, 1968.

Holl, Herbert. "Some Versions of Pastoral in American Music." Ph.D. diss., University of Texas at Austin, 1980.

Hood, George. *A History of Music in New England, with Biographical Sketches of Reformers and Psalmists.* 1846. Rpt., with a new introduction by Johannes Riedel. New York: Johnson Reprint Corp., 1970.

Hoogerwerf, Frank W. *Confederate Sheet-Music Imprints.* I.S.A.M. Monographs, no. 21. Brooklyn, N.Y.: Institute for Studies in American Music, 1984.

Hoover, Kathleen, and John Cage. *Virgil Thomson: His Life and Music.* New York: Thomas Yoseloff, 1959.

Horn, David. *The Literature of American Music in Books and Folk Music Collections: A Fully Annotated Bibliography.* Metuchen, N.J.: Scarecrow Press, 1977.

Horn, Dorothy D. *Sing to Me of Heaven: A Study of Folk and Early American Materials in Three Old Harp Books.* Gainesville: University of Florida Press, 1970.

Horricks, Raymond. *Count Basie and His Orchestra: Its Music and Its Musicians.* Discography by Alun Morgan. 1957. Rpt. Westport, Conn.: Negro Universities Press, 1971.

Howard, James H. "Pan-Indianism in Native American Music." *Ethnomusicology* 27 (Jan. 1983): 71–82.

Howard, John Tasker. *Stephen Foster, America's Troubadour.* New York: Thomas Y. Crowell Co., 1953.

Howe, M. A. De Wolfe. *The Boston Symphony Orchestra, 1881–1931.* 1931. Revised and extended in collaboration with John N. Burk. Rpt. New York: Da Capo Press, 1978.

Huggins, Coy Elliott. "John Hill Hewitt: Bard of the Confederacy." Ph.D. diss., Florida State University, 1964.

Hughes, Rupert. "A Eulogy of Rag-Time." *Musical Record,* Apr. 1, 1899.

————. *Famous American Composers, Being a Study of the Music of This Country, and of Its Future, with Biographies of the Leading Composers of the Present Time.* Boston: L. C. Page and Co., 1900.

Hutchinson, John Wallace. *Story of the Hutchinsons (Tribe of Jesse).* Edited by Charles E. Mann, with an introduction by Frederick Douglass. 2 vols. 1896. Rpt. New York: Da Capo Press, 1977.

Imbrie, Andrew. "The Symphonies of Roger Sessions." *Tempo* 103 (1972): 24–32.

Ingalls, Jeremiah. *The Christian Harmony; or, Songster's Companion.* 1805. Rpt., with a new introduction by David Klocko. Earlier American Music, no. 22. New York: Da Capo Press, 1981.

Inserra, Lorraine, and H. Wiley Hitchcock. *The Music of Henry Ainsworth's Psalter (Amsterdam 1612).* I.S.A.M. Monographs, no. 15. Brooklyn, N.Y.: Institute for Studies in American Music, 1981.

Ives, Charles E. *Essays before a Sonata and Other Writings.* Edited by Howard Boatwright. New York: W. W. Norton and Co., 1962.

————. *Memos.* Edited by John Kirkpatrick. New York: W. W. Norton and Co., 1972.

Jablonski, Edward, and Lawrence D. Stewart. *The Gershwin Years.* 2d ed. Garden City, N.Y.: Doubleday and Co., 1973.

Jackson, Bruce, ed. *Folklore and Society: Essays in Honor of Benj. A. Botkin.* Hatboro, Pa.: Folklore Associates, 1966.

————, ed. *The Negro and His Folklore in Nineteenth Century Periodicals.* Publications of the American Folklore Society, Bibliographical and Special Series, vol. 18. Austin: University of Texas Press, for the American Folklore Society, 1967.

Jackson, George Pullen. *The Story of the Sacred Harp, 1844–1944: A Book of Religious Folk Songs as an American Institution.* Nashville: Vanderbilt University Press, 1944.

————. *White and Negro Spirituals: Their Life Span and Kinship.* Locust Valley, N.Y.: J. J. Augustin, 1943.

————. *White Spirituals in the Southern Uplands: The Story of the Fasola Folk, Their Songs, Singings, and "Buckwheat Notes."* 1933. New ed., with an introduction by Don Yoder. Hatboro, Pa.: Folklore Associates, 1964.

————, comp. and ed. *Another Sheaf of White Spirituals.* 1952. Rpt., with a preface by Don Yoder. New York: Folklorica Press, 1981.

————, comp. *Spiritual Folk Songs of Early America: Two Hundred and Fifty Tunes and Texts with an Introduction and Notes.* 1937. Rpt. Locust Valley, N.Y.: J. J. Augustin, 1953.

Jackson, Irene. *Afro-American Religious Music: A Bibliography and a Catalogue of Gospel Music.* Westport, Conn.: Greenwood Press, 1979.

Jackson, Richard. *United States Music: Sources of Bibliography and Collective Biography*. I.S.A.M. Monographs, no. 1. Brooklyn, N.Y.: Institute for Studies in American Music, 1973.

————, comp. *Popular Songs of Nineteenth-Century America: Complete Original Sheet Music for 64 Songs*. New York: Dover Publications, 1976.

Jacobson, Bernard. Liner notes to John Cage, *Concerto for Prepared Piano & Orchestra (in 3 Parts) (1951)*. . . . Nonesuch H-71202. N.d.

Jasen, David A., and Trebor Jay Tichenor. *Rags and Ragtime: A Musical History*. New York: Seabury Press, 1978.

Jefferson, Thomas. *Notes on the State of Virginia*. Edited by William Peden. Chapel Hill: University of North Carolina Press, 1955.

————. *The Papers of Thomas Jefferson*. 21 vols. Edited by Julian P. Boyd. Princeton, N.J.: Princeton University Press, 1950–83.

————. *The Writings of Thomas Jefferson*. 10 vols. Edited by Paul Leicester Ford. New York: G. P. Putnam's Sons, 1892–99.

Johnson, Charles Albert. *The Frontier Camp Meeting: Religion's Harvest Time*. Dallas: Southern Methodist University Press, 1955.

Johnson, Guy B. *Folk Culture on St. Helena Island, South Carolina*. 1930. Rpt., with a foreword by Don Yoder. Hatboro, Pa.: Folklore Associates, 1968.

Johnson, H. Earle. *Hallelujah, Amen! The Story of the Handel and Haydn Society of Boston*. 1965. Rpt., with a new introduction by Richard Crawford. New York: Da Capo Press, 1981.

————. *Musical Interludes in Boston, 1795–1830*. 1943. Rpt. New York: AMS Press, 1967.

————. *Operas on American Subjects*. New York: Coleman-Ross Co., 1964.

Johnson, James Weldon. *Black Manhattan*. New York: Arno Press, 1968.

Johnson, Roger, comp. *Scores: An Anthology of New Music*. New York: Schirmer Books, 1981.

Jones, Charles C. *The Religious Instruction of the Negroes*. 1842. Rpt. New York: Negro Universities Press, 1969.

Jones, LeRoi [Imamu Amiri Baraka]. *Black Music*. 1967. Rpt. Westport, Conn.: Greenwood Press, 1980.

————. *Blues People: Negro Music in White America*. 1963. Rpt. Westport, Conn.: Greenwood Press, 1980.

Joplin, Scott. *The Collected Works of Scott Joplin*. Edited by Vera Brodsky Lawrence. Editorial consultant, Richard Jackson. 2 vols. New York: New York Public Library, 1971.

Jordan, Philip D. *Singin' Yankees*. Minneapolis: University of Minnesota Press, 1946.

Jost, Ekkehard. *Free Jazz*. 1974. Rpt. New York: Da Capo Press, 1981.

Kahn, E. J., Jr. *The Merry Partners: The Age and Stage of Harrigan and Hart*. New York: Random House, 1955.

Kanter, Kenneth Aaron. *The Jews on Tin Pan Alley: The Jewish Contribution to American Popular Music, 1830–1940.* New York: Ktav Publishing House; Cincinnati: American Jewish Archives, 1982.

Katz, Bernard, ed. *The Social Implications of Early Negro Music in the United States.* New York: Arno Press, New York Times, 1969.

Kearns, William Kay. "Horatio Parker, 1863–1919: A Study of His Life and Music." Ph.D. diss., University of Illinois at Urbana-Champaign, 1965.

Keil, Charles. *Urban Blues.* Chicago: University of Chicago Press, 1966.

Keller, Charles Roy. *The Second Great Awakening in Connecticut.* New Haven: Yale University Press, 1942.

Kemble, Frances Anne. *Fanny, the American Kemble: Her Journals and Unpublished Letters.* Edited by Fanny Kemble Wister. Tallahassee, Fla.: South Pass Press, 1972.

———. *Journal of a Residence on a Georgian Plantation in 1838–1839.* 1863. Edited, with an introduction, by John A. Scott. New York: Alfred A. Knopf, 1961.

Kennington, Donald, and Danny L. Read. *The Literature of Jazz: A Critical Guide.* 2d rev. ed. Chicago: American Library Association, 1980.

Kimball, Robert, and William Bolcom. *Reminiscing with Sissle and Blake.* New York: Viking Press, 1973.

King, A. Hyatt. "The Musical Glasses and Glass Harmonica." *Proceedings of the Royal Musical Association* 72 (1945–46): 97–122.

Kirkeby, Ed. *Ain't Misbehavin': The Story of Fats Waller.* 1966. Rpt. New York: Da Capo Press, 1975.

Kirkpatrick, John. "The Evolution of Carl Ruggles: A Chronicle Largely in His Own Words." *Perspectives of New Music* 6 (Spring-Summer 1968): 146–66.

———, comp. "A Temporary Mimeographed Catalogue of the Music Manuscripts and Related Materials of Charles Edward Ives, 1874–1954, Given by Mrs. Ives to the Library of the Yale School of Music, September, 1955." John Kirkpatrick, 1960.

Klein, Joe. *Woody Guthrie: A Life.* New York: Alfred A. Knopf, 1980.

Klotzman, Dorothy, ed. *Richard Franko Goldman: Selected Essays and Reviews, 1948–1968.* I.S.A.M. Monographs, no. 13. Brooklyn, N.Y.: Institute for Studies in American Music, 1980.

Kmen, Henry A. *Music in New Orleans: The Formative Years, 1791–1841.* Baton Rouge: Louisiana State University Press, 1966.

———. "The Roots of Jazz and the Dance in Place Congo: A Re-Appraisal." *Yearbook for Inter-American Musical Research* 8 (1972): 5–16.

Koch, Lawrence O. *Yardbird Suite: A Compendium of the Music and Life of Charlie Parker.* Bowling Green, Ohio: Bowling Green University Popular Press, 1983.

Kofsky, Frank. *Black Nationalism and the Revolution in Music.* New York: Pathfinder Press, 1970.

Konkle, Burton Alva. *Joseph Hopkinson, 1770–1842: Jurist—Scholar—Inspirer of the Arts, Author of Hail Columbia.* Philadelphia: University of Pennsylvania Press, 1931.

Koon, George William. *Hank Williams: A Bio-Bibliography.* Westport, Conn.: Greenwood Press, 1983.

Korf, William E. *The Orchestral Music of Louis Moreau Gottschalk.* Musicological Studies, vol. 37. Henryville, Pa.: Institute of Mediaeval Music, 1983.

Korn, Bertram W. "A Note on the Jewish Ancestry of Louis Moreau Gottschalk, American Pianist and Composer." *American Jewish Archives* 15 (Nov. 1963): 117–19.

Kostelanetz, Richard, ed., *John Cage.* New York: Praeger Publishers, 1970.

Kraft, Leo. "The Music of George Perle." *Musical Quarterly* 57 (July 1971): 444–65.

Krehbiel, Henry Edward. *Afro-American Folksongs: A Study in Racial and National Music.* 1914. New York: Frederick Ungar Publishing Co., 1962.

———. *Notes on the Cultivation of Choral Music and the Oratorio Society in New York.* 1884. Rpt. New York: AMS Press, 1970.

———. *The Philharmonic Society of New York: A Memorial.* New York: Novello, Ewer and Co., 1892.

Krenek, Ernst. "Tradition in Perspective." *Perspectives of New Music* 1 (Fall 1962): 27–38.

Kreuger, Miles. *Show Boat: The Story of a Classic American Musical.* New York: Oxford University Press, 1977.

Kroeger, Karl. Liner notes to *A Psalm of Joy,* Moravian Music Foundation MMF 001. 1975.

Krohn Ernst C. "Alexander Reinagle as Sonatist." *Musical Quarterly* 18 (Jan. 1932): 140–49.

———. "Nelson Kneass: Minstrel Singer and Composer." *Yearbook for Inter-American Musical Research* 7 (1971): 17–41.

Krummel, D. W., Jean Geil, Doris J. Dyen, and Deane L. Root, eds. *Resources of American Music History: A Directory of Source Materials from Colonial Times to World War II.* Music in American Life. Urbana: University of Illinois Press, 1981.

Labat, Jean-Baptiste. *Nouveau voyage aux isles de l'Amérique contenant l'histoire naturelle de ces pays, l'origine, les moeurs, la religion & le gouvernement des habitans anciens & modernes. . . .* 2 vols. The Hague: P. Husson et al., 1724.

Lahee, Henry Charles. *Grand Opera in America.* 1902. Rpt. New York: AMS Press, 1973.

Lambert, Barbara. "The Musical Puritans." *Bulletin of the Society for the Preservation of New England Antiquities* 62 (1972): 66–75.

Lambert, G. E. *Duke Ellington.* New York: A. S. Barnes and Co., 1961.

Lang, Paul Henry, ed. *One Hundred Years of Music in America.* New York: G. Schirmer, 1961.

Langdon, George D., Jr. *Pilgrim Colony: A History of New Plymouth, 1620–1691.* Yale Publications in American Studies, no. 12. New Haven: Yale University Press, 1966.

Lanier, Sidney. *Music and Poetry: Essays upon Some Aspects and Inter-Relations of the Two Arts.* 1898. Rpt. Westport, Conn.: Greenwood Press, 1969.

————. *The Science of English Verse.* New York: Charles Scribner's Sons, 1911.

Latrobe, Benjamin Henry Boneval. *Impressions Respecting New Orleans: Diary & Sketches, 1818–1820.* 1821. Edited, with an introduction and notes, by Samuel Wilson, Jr. New York: Columbia University Press, 1951.

Laurie, Joseph, Jr. *Vaudeville: From the Honky-Tonks to the Palace.* 1953. Rpt. Port Washington, N.Y.: Kennikat Press, 1972.

Lawless, Ray M. *Folksingers and Folksongs in America: A Handbook of Biography, Bibliography, and Discography.* Rev. ed. 1968. Rpt. Westport, Conn.: Greenwood Press, 1981.

Lawrence, Vera Brodsky. *Music for Patriots, Politicians, and Presidents: Harmonies and Discords of the First Hundred Years.* New York: Macmillan, 1975.

————, ed. *The Wa-Wan Press, 1901–1911.* 5 vols. New York: Arno Press, New York Times, 1970.

Lederman, Minna. *The Life and Death of a Small Magazine (Modern Music, 1924–1946).* I.S.A.M. Monographs, no. 18. Brooklyn, N.Y.: Institute for Studies in American Music, 1983.

Lee, Dorothy Sara. *Native North American Music and Oral Data: A Catalogue of Sound Recordings, 1893–1976.* Bloomington: Indiana University Press, 1979.

Leichtentritt, Hugo. *Serge Koussevitzky: The Boston Symphony Orchestra and the New American Music.* Cambridge: Harvard University Press, 1946.

Leonard, Neil. *Jazz and the White Americans: The Acceptance of a New Art Form.* Chicago: University of Chicago Press, 1962.

Lichtenwanger, William, ed. *Oscar Sonneck and American Music.* Music in American Life. Urbana: University of Illinois Press, 1983.

Lieb, Sandra R. *Mother of the Blues: A Study of Ma Rainey.* Amherst: University of Massachusetts Press, 1981.

Locke, Alain L. *The Negro and His Music.* 1936. Rpt. Port Washington, N.Y.: Kennikat Press, 1968.

Locke, Ralph P. "Charles Martin Loeffler: Composer at Court." *Fenway Court: Annual Report of the Isabella Stewart Gardner Museum.* Boston, 1974.

Loesser, Arthur. *Humor in American Song.* New York: Howell, Soskin, 1942.

Loggins, Vernon. *Where the World Ends: The Life of Louis Moreau Gottschalk.* Baton Rouge: Louisiana State University Press, 1958.

Lomax, Alan. *Folk Song Style and Culture.* Washington, D.C.: American Association for the Advancement of Science, 1968.

————. *The Folk Songs of North America in the English Language.* Garden City, N.Y.: Doubleday and Co., 1960.

————. "The Homogeneity of African-Afro-American Musical Style." In *Afro-American Anthropology: Contemporary Perspectives.* Edited by Norman E. Whitten, Jr., and John F. Szwed, 181–201. New York: Free Press, 1970.

————. *Mister Jelly Roll: The Fortunes of Jelly Roll Morton, New Orleans Creole and "Inventor of Jazz."* 2d ed. Berkeley and Los Angeles: University of California Press, 1973.

————, comp. *Hard Hitting Songs for Hard-Hit People.* New York: Oak Publications, 1967.

Lomax, John Avery. *Songs of the Cattle Trail and Cow Camp*. 1919. Rpt. Great Neck, N.Y.: Granger, 1979.

Lomax, John Avery, and Alan Lomax, comps. *American Ballads and Folk Songs*. New York: Macmillan, 1934.

———. *Cowboy Songs and Other Frontier Ballads*. Rev. ed. New York: Macmillan, 1938.

———. *Negro Folk Songs As Sung by Lead Belly, "King of the Twelve-String Guitar Players of the World," Long-Time Convict in the Penitentiaries of Texas and Louisiana*. New York: Macmillan, 1936.

———. *Our Singing Country: A Second Volume of American Ballads and Folk Songs*. New York: Macmillan, 1941.

Longyear, Katherine Marie Eide. "Henry F. Gilbert, His Life and Works." Ph.D. diss., Eastman School of Music, University of Rochester, 1968.

Lowens, Irving. *Music and Musicians in Early America*. New York: W. W. Norton and Co., 1964.

———. *Music in America and American Music: Two Views of the Scene*. I.S.A.M. Monographs, no. 8. Brooklyn, N.Y.: Institute for Studies in American Music, 1978.

Lucas, G. W. *Remarks on the Musical Conventions in Boston*. Northampton, Mass.: Printed for the author, 1844.

Luening, Otto. "Some Random Remarks about Electronic Music." *Journal of Music Theory* 8 (1964): 89–98.

Lyell, Charles. *A Second Visit to the United States of North America*. 2 vols. New York: Harper and Brothers, 1849.

Lyon, James, comp. *Urania: A Choice Collection of Psalm-Tunes, Anthems, and Hymns*. 1761. Rpt., with a new preface by Richard Crawford. New York: Da Capo Press, 1974.

McAllester, David P. *Enemy Way Music: A Study of Social and Esthetic Values As Seen in Navaho Music*. Papers of the Peabody Museum of American Archaeology and Ethnology, Harvard University, vol. 41, no. 3. Cambridge: Peabody Museum, Harvard University, 1954.

———. *Indian Music of the Southwest*. Colorado Springs: Taylor Museum of the Colorado Springs Fine Arts Center, 1961.

———. *Peyote Music*. Viking Fund Publications in Anthropology, no. 13. 1949. Rpt. New York: Johnson Reprint Corp., 1964.

———. "Shootingway, an Epic Drama of the Navajos." In *Southwestern Indian Ritual Drama*. Edited by Charlotte Frisbie, 199–237. Albuquerque: University of New Mexico Press, 1980.

McCarthy, Albert J. *Louis Armstrong*. New York: A. S. Barnes and Co., 1961.

McCurry, John Gordon. *The Social Harp*. 1855. Rpt., edited by Daniel W. Patterson and John F. Garst. Athens: University of Georgia Press, 1973.

MacDougall, Hamilton C. *Early New England Psalmody: An Historical Appreciation, 1620–1820*. Brattleboro, N.H.: Stephen Daye Press, 1940.

MacDowell, Edward. *Critical and Historical Essays*. Edited by W. J. Baltzell. 1912. Rpt. New York: Da Capo Press, 1969.

McDowell, John Holmes. "The *Corrido* of Greater Mexico as Discourse, Music, and Event." In *"And Other Neighborly Names": Social Process and Cultural Image in Texas Folklore*. Edited by Richard Bauman and Roger D. Abrahams, 44–75. Austin: University of Texas Press, 1981.

McDowell, Lucien L., comp. *Songs of the Old Camp Ground*. Ann Arbor, Mich.: Edwards Brothers, 1937.

McIlhenny, Edward A., comp. *Befo' de War Spirituals*. Boston: Christopher Publishing House, 1933.

McIntosh, Rigdon M., comp. *Light and Life: A Collection of New Hymns and Tunes for Sunday-Schools, Prayer Meetings, and Revival Meetings*. Boston: Oliver Ditson Co., 1881.

McKay, David. "William Selby, Musical Emigré in Colonial Boston." *Musical Quarterly* 57 (Oct. 1971): 609–27.

McKay, David, and Richard Crawford. *William Billings of Boston: Eighteenth-Century Composer*. Princeton, N.J.: Princeton University Press, 1975.

Macken, Bob, Peter Fornatale, and Bill Ayres. *The Rock Music Source Book*. Garden City, N.Y.: Anchor Books, 1980.

McLean, Albert, Jr. *American Vaudeville as Ritual*. Lexington: University Press of Kentucky, 1965.

Madeira, Louis Cephas, comp. *Annals of Music in Philadelphia and History of the Musical Fund Society from Its Organization in 1820 to the Year 1858*. 1896. Rpt. New York: Da Capo Press, 1973.

Mainzer, Joseph. *The Gaelic Psalm Tunes of Ross-shire, and the Neighbouring Counties*. Edinburgh: J. Johnstone, 1844.

Maisel, Edward M. *Charles T. Griffes: The Life of an American Composer*. New York: Alfred A. Knopf, 1943.

Malone, Bill C. *Country Music, U.S.A.* Rev. ed. Austin: University of Texas Press, 1985.

———. *Southern Music / American Music*. Lexington: University Press of Kentucky, 1979.

Malone, Bill C., and Judith McCulloh, eds. *Stars of Country Music: Uncle Dave Macon to Johnny Rodriguez*. Music in American Life. Urbana: University of Illinois Press, 1975.

Manion, Martha L. *Writings about Henry Cowell: An Annotated Bibliography*. I.S.A.M. Monographs, no. 16. Brooklyn, N.Y.: Institute for Studies in American Music, 1982.

Marcus, Greil. *Mystery Train: Images of America in Rock 'n' Roll Music*. Rev. ed. New York: E. P. Dutton and Co., 1982.

Marcus, Leonard. Liner notes to Charles E. Ives, *Symphony No. 4*. Columbia ML 6175 and MS 6775. N.d.

Marks, Edward B. *They All Had Glamour: From the Swedish Nightingale to the Naked Lady*. New York: Julian Messner, 1944.

Marquis, Donald M. *In Search of Buddy Bolden: First Man of Jazz.* Baton Rouge: Louisiana State University Press, 1978.

Marrocco, W. Thomas. "The String Quartet Attributed to Benjamin Franklin." *Proceedings of the American Philosophical Society* 116 (Dec. 1972): 477–85.

Marsh, J. B. T. *The Story of the Jubilee Singers, with Their Songs.* Rev. ed. 1881. Rpt. New York: Negro Universities Press, 1969.

Martin, Marianne W. *Futurist Art and Theory, 1909–1915.* Oxford: Clarendon Press, 1968.

Marx, Leo. *The Machine in the Garden: Technology and the Pastoral Ideal in America.* New York: Oxford University Press, 1964.

Mason, Daniel Gregory. *The Dilemma of American Music and Other Essays.* 1928. Rpt. Westport, Conn.: Greenwood Press, 1969.

———. *Music in My Time and Other Reminiscences.* 1938. Rpt. Westport, Conn.: Greenwood Press, 1970.

———. *Tune In, America: A Study of Our Coming Musical Independence.* 1931. Rpt. Freeport, N.Y.: Books for Libraries Press, 1969.

Mason, Henry Lowell. *Lowell Mason: An Appreciation of His Life and Work.* Papers of the Hymn Society, no. 8. New York: Hymn Society of America, 1941.

Mason, Lowell, comp. *The Boston Handel and Haydn Society Collection of Church Music.* 1822. Rpt. Earlier American Music, no. 15. New York: Da Capo Press, 1973.

Mason, William. *Memories of a Musical Life.* 1901. Rpt. New York: AMS Press, 1970.

Mates, Julian. *The American Musical Stage before 1800.* New Brunswick, N.J.: Rutgers University Press, 1962.

Mather, Cotton. *Diary of Cotton Mather.* Edited by W. C. Ford. 2 vols. 1911–12. Rpt. New York: Frederick Ungar Publishing Co., 1957.

Mathews, Max V., et al. *The Technology of Computer Music.* Cambridge: MIT Press, 1969.

Mathews, W. S. B., ed. *A Hundred Years of Music in America.* 1889. Rpt. New York: AMS Press, 1970.

Mattfeld, Julius. *A Handbook of American Operatic Premieres.* Detroit Studies in Music Bibliography, no. 5. Detroit: Information Service, 1963.

Maurer, Maurer. "The Library of a Colonial Musician, 1755." *William and Mary Quarterly* 7 (Jan. 1950): 39–52.

Maust, Wilbur Richard. "The Symphonies of Anthony Philip Heinrich Based on American Themes." Ph.D. diss., Indiana University, 1973.

Maxson, Charles Hartshorn. *The Great Awakening in the Middle Colonies.* Chicago: University of Chicago Press, 1920.

May, Henry. *The End of American Innocence: A Study of the First Years of Our Own Time, 1912–1917.* New York: Alfred A. Knopf, 1959.

Mead, Rita H. *Doctoral Dissertations in American Music: A Classified Bibliography.* I.S.A.M. Monographs, no. 3. Brooklyn, N.Y.: Institute for Studies in American Music, 1974.

———. *Henry Cowell's New Music, 1935–1936: The Society, the Music Editions, and the*

Recordings. Studies in Musicology, no. 40. Ann Arbor, Mich.: UMI Research Press, 1981.

Meeker, David. *Jazz in the Movies.* New York: Da Capo Press, 1982.

Mellers, Wilfrid. *Music in a New Found Land: Themes and Developments in the History of American Music.* New York: Alfred A. Knopf, 1965.

Mellquist, Jerome, and Lucie Wiese, eds. *Paul Rosenfeld: Voyager in the Arts.* New York: Creative Age Press, 1948.

Merriam, Alan P. *The Anthropology of Music.* Evanston, Ill.: Northwestern University Press, 1964.

———. *Ethnomusicology of the Flathead Indians.* Viking Fund Publications in Anthropology, no. 44. Chicago: Aldine Publishing Co., 1967.

Merriam, Alan P., and Robert J. Brenford. *A Bibliography of Jazz.* 1954. Rpt. New York: Da Capo Press, 1970.

Merrill, E. Lindsey. "Mrs. H. H. A. Beach: Her Life and Music." Ph.D. diss., Eastman School of Music, University of Rochester, 1963.

Metcalf, Frank J. *American Writers and Compilers of Sacred Music.* 1925. Rpt. New York: Russell and Russell, 1967.

Mezzrow, Milton "Mezz," and Bernard Wolfe. *Really the Blues.* New York: Random House, 1946.

Middleton, Richard. *Pop Music and the Blues: A Study of the Relationship and Its Significance.* London: Victor Gollancz, 1972.

Miller, Jim, ed. *The Rolling Stone Illustrated History of Rock & Roll.* New York: Rolling Stone Press, Random House, 1976.

Milligan, Harold Vincent. *Stephen Collins Foster: A Biography of America's Folk-Song Composer.* New York: G. Schirmer, 1920.

Molner, John W. "Art Music in Colonial Virginia." In *Art and Music in the South.* Edited by Francis B. Simkins, 63–108. Farmville, Va.: Longwood College, 1961.

Moore, John W. *A Dictionary of Musical Information, Containing Also a Vocabulary of Musical Terms and a List of Modern Musical Works Published in the United States from 1640 to 1875.* 1876. Rpt. New York: Burt Franklin, 1971.

Mordecai, Samuel. *Virginia, Especially Richmond, in By-Gone Days; with a Glance at the Present: Being Reminiscences and Last Words of an Old Citizen.* 2d ed. Richmond, Va.: West and Johnston, 1860.

Moreau de Saint-Méry, [Médéric Louis Elie]. *Description topographique, physique, civile, politique et historique de la partie française de l'Isle Saint-Domingue.* 2 vols. Philadelphia: Author, 1797–98.

Morehouse, Ward. *George M. Cohan: Prince of the American Theater.* Philadelphia: J. B. Lippincott Co., 1943.

Morgan, Robert P. "Elliott Carter's String Quartets." *Musical Newsletter* 4 (Summer 1974): 3–11.

———. Liner notes to Ruth Crawford Seeger, *String Quartet;* George Perle, *String Quartet No. 5;* Milton Babbitt, *String Quartet No. 2.* Nonesuch H-71280. 1973.

Morison, Samuel Eliot. *Harvard College in the Seventeenth Century.* Cambridge: Harvard University Press, 1936.

Morneweck, Evelyn Foster. *Chronicles of Stephen Foster's Family.* 2 vols. 1944. Rpt. Port Washington, N.Y.: Kennikat Press, 1973.

Morton, Ferdinand "Jelly Roll." *Ferdinand "Jelly Roll" Morton: The Collected Piano Music.* Edited by James Dapogny. Washington, D.C.: Smithsonian Institution Press; New York: G. Schirmer, 1982.

Morton, Louis. *Robert Carter of Nomini Hall: A Virginia Tobacco Planter of the Eighteenth Century.* 2d ed. Williamsburg, Va.: Colonial Williamsburg, 1945.

Mueller, Kate Hevner. *Twenty-seven Major American Symphony Orchestras: A History and Analysis of Their Repertoires, Seasons 1842–43 through 1969–70.* Bloomington: Indiana University Studies, 1973; distributed by Indiana University Press.

Murie, James R. *Ceremonies of the Pawnee.* Edited by Douglas R. Parks. 2 vols. Washington, D.C.: Smithsonian Institution Press, 1980–81.

Mussulman, Joseph A. *Music in the Cultured Generation: A Social History of Music in America, 1870–1900.* Evanston, Ill.: Northwestern University Press, 1971.

Napoleon, Art. Liner notes to *Women in Jazz: All Women Groups.* Stash St-111–13. 1978.

Nash, Roderick. *Wilderness and the American Mind.* New Haven, Conn.: Yale University Press, 1967.

Nathan, Hans. *Dan Emmett and the Rise of Early Negro Minstrelsy.* Norman: University of Oklahoma Press, 1962.

———. *William Billings: Data and Documents.* Bibliographies in American Music, no. 2. Detroit: Information Coordinators, for the College Music Society, 1976.

Nettl, Bruno. *North American Indian Musical Styles.* Memoirs of the American Folklore Society, vol. 45. Austin: University of Texas Press, 1954.

The New Grove Dictionary of American Music. Edited by H. Wiley Hitchcock and Stanley Sadie. 4 vols. London: Macmillan, 1986.

The New Grove Dictionary of Music and Musicians. Edited by Stanley Sadie. 20 vols. London: Macmillan, 1980.

Nketia, J. H. Kwabena. *African Music in Ghana.* Evanston, Ill.: Northwestern University Press, 1963.

———. *The Music of Africa.* New York: W. W. Norton and Co., 1974.

Northrop, Theodore H., arr. *Ben Harney's Ragtime Instructor.* Chicago: Sol Bloom, 1897.

Nye, Russel Blaine. *Society and Culture in America, 1830–1860.* New York: Harper and Row, 1974.

———. *This Almost Chosen People: Essays in the History of American Ideas.* East Lansing: Michigan State University Press, 1966.

———. *The Unembarrassed Muse: The Popular Arts in America.* New York: Dial Press, 1970.

Odell, George C. D. *Annals of the New York Stage*. 15 vols. 1927–49. Rpt. New York: AMS Press, 1970.

Odum, Howard W., and Guy B. Johnson. *The Negro and His Songs: A Study of Typical Negro Songs in the South*. 1925. Rpt. Hatboro, Pa.: Folklore Associates, 1964.

———. *Negro Workaday Songs*. 1926. Rpt. New York: Negro Universities Press, 1977.

Offergeld, Robert. *The Centennial Catalogue of the Published and Unpublished Compositions of Louis Moreau Gottschalk*. New York: Ziff-Davis Publishing Co., 1970.

Oliver, Paul. *Bessie Smith*. 1959. Rpt. New York: A. S. Barnes and Co., 1961.

———. *Blues Fell This Morning*. 1960. Reprinted as *The Meaning of the Blues*. New York: Collier Books, 1963.

———. Liner notes to *The Story of the Blues*. Columbia G 30008. 1969.

———. *Savannah Syncopators: African Retentions in the Blues*. New York: Stein and Day, 1970.

———. *Screening the Blues: Aspects of the Blues Tradition*. London: Cassell, 1968.

———. *The Story of the Blues*. 1969. Rpt. New York: Chilton Books, 1974.

Olmsted, Frederick Law. *A Journey in the Back Country in the Winter 1853-4*. 2 vols. New York: G. P. Putnam's Sons, 1907.

———. *A Journey in the Seaboard Slave States, with Remarks on Their Economy*. 1856. Rpt. New York: Negro Universities Press, 1968.

Olson, Kenneth E. *Music and Musket: Bands and Bandsmen of the American Civil War*. Contributions to the Study of Music and Dance, no. 1. Westport, Conn.: Greenwood Press, 1981.

Olsson, Bengt. *Memphis Blues and Jug Bands*. London: Studio Vista, 1970.

O'Neill, Francis, ed. and comp. *The Dance Music of Ireland*. Chicago: Lyon and Healy, 1907.

Oster, Harry. *Living Country Blues*. Detroit: Folklore Associates, 1969.

Ostrander, Gilman M. *American Civilization in the First Machine Age: 1890–1940*. New York: Harper and Row, 1970.

Ostransky, Leroy. *The Anatomy of Jazz*. 1960. Rpt. Westport, Conn.: Greenwood Press, 1973.

Owen, Barbara. *The Organ in New England: An Account of Its Use and Manufacture to the End of the Nineteenth Century*. Raleigh, N.C.: Sunbury Press, 1979.

Owen, Earl McClain, Jr. "The Life and Music of Supply Belcher (1751–1836), 'Handel of Maine.' " D.M.A. thesis, Southern Baptist Theological Seminary, 1969.

Oyer, Mary. *Exploring the Mennonite Hymnal: Essays*. Newton, Kans.: Faith and Life Press; Scottdale, Pa.: Mennonite Publishing House, 1980.

Palmer, Robert. *Deep Blues*. New York: Viking Press, 1981.

———. *A Tale of Two Cities: Memphis Rock and New Orleans Roll*. I.S.A.M. Monographs, no. 12. Brooklyn, N.Y.: Institute for Studies in American Music, 1979.

Paredes, Américo. *"With His Pistol in His Hand": A Border Ballad and Its Hero*. Austin: University of Texas Press, 1958.

———. *A Texas-Mexican "Cancionero": Folksongs of the Lower Border*. Music in American Life. Urbana: University of Illinois Press, 1976.

Parker, John Rowe. *Musical Biography; or, Sketches of the Lives and Writings of Eminent Musical Characters*. 1824. Rpt. Detroit: Detroit Reprints in Music, Information Coordinators, 1975.

Parks, Anne. "Freedom, Form, and Process in Varèse." Ph.D. diss., Cornell University, 1974.

Parrington, Vernon Louis, ed. *The Connecticut Wits*. New York: Harcourt, Brace and Co., 1926.

Parrish, Lydia. *Slave Songs of the Georgia Sea Islands*. Music transcribed by Creighton Churchill and Robert MacGimsey. 1942. Rpt., with an introduction by Olin Downes and a foreword by Bruce Jackson. Hatboro, Pa.: Folklore Associates, 1965.

Parsons, Elsie Worthington Clews. *Folk-Lore of the Sea Islands*. Memoirs of the American Folklore Society, no. 16. Cambridge, Mass.: American Folklore Society, 1923.

Partch, Harry. *Genesis of a Music: An Account of a Creative Work, Its Roots and Its Fulfillments*. 2d rev. ed. New York: Da Capo Press, 1974.

Paskman, Dailey, and Sigmund Spaeth. *"Gentlemen, Be Seated!" A Parade of the Old-Time Minstrels*. New York: Doubleday, Doran, and Co., 1928.

Patterson, Daniel W. *The Shaker Spiritual*. Princeton, N.J.: Princeton University Press, 1979.

Patterson, Lindsay, ed. *Anthology of the Afro-American in the Theatre: A Critical Approach*. International Library of Afro-American Life and History. 1967. Rpt. Cornwells Heights, Pa.: Publishers Agency, 1976.

Payton, Rodney J. "The Music of Futurism: Concerts and Polemics." *Musical Quarterly* 62 (1976): 25–45.

Peña, Manuel H. "The Emergence of Conjunto Music, 1935–1955." In *"And Other Neighborly Names."* Edited by Richard Bauman and Roger D. Abrahams, 280–99. Austin: University of Texas Press, 1981.

Perle, George. *Serial Composition and Atonality: An Introduction to the Music of Schoenberg, Berg and Webern*. Berkeley and Los Angeles: University of California Press, 1962, 1968, 1972.

Perlis, Vivian. *Charles Ives Remembered: An Oral History*. New Haven: Yale University Press, 1974.

———. "The Futurist Music of Leo Ornstein." *Notes* 31 (June 1975): 735–50.

———. Liner notes to *American Contemporary: First Recording of Music by Leo Ornstein*. Composers Recordings (CRI) SD 339. 1975.

———. *Two Men for Modern Music: E. Robert Schmitz and Herman Laninger*. I.S.A.M. Monographs, no. 9. Brooklyn, N.Y.: Institute for Studies in American Music, 1978.

Perry, Rosalie Sandra. *Charles Ives and the American Mind*. Kent, Ohio: Kent State University Press, 1974.

Peterson, Clara Gottschalk. *Creole Songs from New Orleans in the Negro-Dialect.* New Orleans: L. Grunewald Co., 1902.

Phillips, Ulrich B. *American Negro Slavery: A Survey of the Supply, Employment and Control of Negro Labor As Determined by the Plantation Regime.* 1918. Rpt. Baton Rouge: Louisiana State University Press, 1966.

Placksin, Sally. *American Women in Jazz—1900 to the Present: Their Words, Lives and Music.* New York: Seaview Books, 1982.

Playford, John. *An Introduction to the Skill of Musick.* 12th ed. 1694. Rpt., with a new introduction, glossary, and index by Franklin B. Zimmerman. New York: Da Capo Press, 1972.

Pleasants, Henry. *The Greatest American Popular Singers.* New York: Simon and Schuster, 1974.

Poggioli, Renato. *The Theory of the Avant-Garde.* Translated from the Italian by Gerald Fitzgerald. Cambridge: Belknap Press, Harvard University Press, 1968.

Pollack, Howard. *Walter Piston.* Studies in Musicology, no. 50. Ann Arbor, Mich.: UMI Research Press, 1982.

Porter, Andrew. "The Matter of Mexico." *New Yorker,* Apr. 19, 1976, pp. 115–20.

Porterfield, Nolan. *Jimmie Rodgers: The Life and Times of America's Blue Yodeler.* Music in American Life. Urbana: University of Illinois Press, 1979.

Pound, Ezra Loomis. *Ezra Pound and Music: The Complete Criticism.* Edited by R. Murray Schafer. New York: New Directions Publishing Corp., 1977.

Powers, William K. *Indians of the Southern Plains.* New York: G. P. Putnam's Sons, 1971.

———. *Oglala Religion.* Lincoln: University of Nebraska Press, 1977.

Pratt, Waldo Selden. *The Music of the French Psalter of 1562: A Historical Survey and Analysis, with the Music in Modern Notation.* Columbia University Studies in Musicology, no. 3. New York: Columbia University Press, 1939.

———. *The Music of the Pilgrims: A Description of the Psalm-book Brought to Plymouth in 1620.* 1921. Rpt. New York: Russell and Russell, 1971.

Publications of the Colonial Society of Massachusetts: Collections. Vols. 22–23, *Plymouth Church Records, 1620–1859.* Boston: Colonial Society of Massachusetts, 1920–23.

Quincy, Josiah. "Journal of Josiah Quincy, Junior, 1773." *Massachusetts Historical Society Proceedings* 49 (1915–16): 424–81.

Rau, Albert G., and Hans T. David, comps. *A Catalogue of Music by American Moravians, 1742–1842: From the Archives of the Moravian Church of Bethlehem, Pa.* Bethlehem, Pa.: Moravian Seminary and College for Women, 1938.

Read, Oliver, and Walter L. Welch. *From Tin Foil to Stereo: Evolution of the Phonograph.* 2d ed. Indianapolis: Bobbs-Merrill Co., 1976.

Redway, Virginia Larkin. *Music Directory of Early New York City: A File of Musicians, Music Publishers and Musical Instrument-Makers in New York Directories from 1786 through 1835, together with the Most Important New York Music Publishers from 1836 through 1875.* New York: New York Public Library, 1941.

Reich, Steve. *Writings about Music.* Halifax: Press of the Nova Scotia College of Art and Design; New York: New York University Press, 1974.

Reis, Claire R. *Composers in America.* 1947. Rpt., with a new introduction by William Schuman. New York: Da Capo Press, 1977.

Reynolds, Roger. *Mind Models: New Forms of Musical Experience.* New York: Praeger Publishers, 1975.

Rice, Edward Le Roy. *Monarchs of Minstrelsy, from "Daddy" Rice to Date.* New York: Kenney Publishing Co., 1911.

Rich, Arthur Lowndes. *Lowell Mason: "The Father of Singing among the Children."* Chapel Hill: University of North Carolina Press, 1946.

Rich, Maria F. "U.S. Opera Survey, 1975–76: More of Everything." *Opera News* 41 (Nov. 1976): 34–40.

Richardson, Cynthia S. *"Narcissa,* by Mary Carr Moore: A Singular Contribution to American Opera." Abstract of author's master's thesis. *Sonneck Society Newsletter* 7 (Summer 1981): 15–16.

Ritter, Frédéric Louis. *Music in America.* 1890. Rpt., with a new introduction by Johannes Riedel. New York: Johnson Reprint Corp., 1970.

Rochberg, George. *The Hexachord and Its Relation to the 12-Tone Row.* Bryn Mawr, Pa.: Theodore Presser Co., 1955.

Rockwell, John. *All American Music: Composition in the Late Twentieth Century.* New York: Alfred A. Knopf, 1983.

Rodnitzky, Jerome L. *Minstrels of the Dawn: The Folk-Protest Singer as a Cultural Hero.* Chicago: Nelson-Hall, 1976.

Roger Reynolds: Profile of a Composer. Introduction by Gilbert Chase. New York: C. F. Peters Corp., 1982.

Rogers, Delmer D. "Nineteenth-Century Music in New York City As Reflected in the Career of George Frederick Bristow." Ph.D. diss., University of Michigan, 1967.

Rohrer, Gertrude M., comp. *Music and Musicians of Pennsylvania.* 1940. Rpt. Port Washington, N.Y.: Kennikat Press, 1970.

Root, Deane L. *American Popular Stage Music, 1860–1880.* Studies in Musicology, no. 44. Ann Arbor, Mich.: UMI Research Press, 1981.

Root, George Frederick. *The Story of a Musical Life: An Autobiography by George F. Root.* 1891. Rpt. New York: Da Capo Press, 1970.

Rosenberg, Bruce A. *The Art of the American Folk Preacher.* New York: Oxford University Press, 1970.

Rosenberg, Neil V. *Bluegrass: A History.* Music in American Life. Urbana: University of Illinois Press, 1985.

Rosenfeld, Paul. *Discoveries of a Music Critic.* New York: Harcourt, Brace and Co., 1936.

———. *An Hour with American Music.* Philadelphia: J. B. Lippincott Co., 1929.

———. *Musical Chronicle (1917–1923).* New York: Harcourt, Brace and Co., 1923.

Rossiter, Frank R. *Charles Ives and His America.* New York: Liveright, 1975.

Roszak, Theodore. *The Making of a Counter Culture: Reflections on the Technocratic*

Society and Its Youthful Opposition. Garden City, N.Y.: Doubleday and Co., 1969.

Routley, Erik. *The Musical Wesleys*. 1968. Rpt. Westport, Conn.: Greenwood Press, 1976.

Rowe, Mike. *Chicago Breakdown*. 1973. Rpt. New York: Da Capo Press, 1979.

Roxon, Lillian. *Rock Encyclopedia*. New York: Grosset and Dunlap, 1969.

Rudhyar, Dane. "The Relativity of Our Musical Conceptions." *Musical Quarterly* 8 (Jan. 1922): 108–18.

Rushton, William Faulkner. *The Cajuns: From Acadia to Louisiana*. New York: Farrar Straus Giroux, 1979.

Russcol, Herbert. *The Liberation of Sound: An Introduction to Electronic Music*. Englewood Cliffs, N.J.: Prentice-Hall, 1972.

Russell, Charles Edward. *The American Orchestra and Theodore Thomas*. 1927. Rpt. Westport, Conn.: Greenwood Press, 1971.

Russell, Henry. *Cheer! Boys, Cheer! Memories of Men & Music*. London: John Macqueen, 1895.

Russell, Ross. *Bird Lives! The High Life and Hard Times of Charlie (Yardbird) Parker*. New York: Charterhouse, 1973.

———. *Jazz Style in Kansas City and the Southwest*. Berkeley and Los Angeles: University of California Press, 1971.

Russell, Tony. *Blacks, Whites, and Blues*. New York: Stein and Day, 1970.

Russell, William Howard. *My Diary, North and South*. Boston: T. O. H. P. Burnham, 1863.

Russolo, Luigi. *L'arte dei rumori: Manifesto futurista*. Milan: Direzione del movimento futurista, 1913. English translation by Robert Filliou as *The Art of Noise* (*Futurist Manifesto, 1913*). New York: Something Else Press, 1967.

Rutman, Darrett B. *Husbandmen of Plymouth: Farms and Villages in the Old Colony, 1620–1692*. Boston: Beacon Press, 1967.

Sachse, Julius F. *The German Pietists of Provincial Pennsylvania, 1694–1708*. 1895. Rpt. New York: AMS Press, 1970.

———. *Music of the Ephrata Cloister: Also Conrad Beissel's Treatise on Music As Set Forth in a Preface to the "Turtle Taube" of 1747. . . .* 1903. Rpt. New York: AMS Press, 1971.

Salzman, Eric. *Twentieth-Century Music: An Introduction*. 2d ed. Englewood Cliffs, N.J.: Prentice-Hall, 1974.

Saminsky, Lazare. *Living Music of the Americas*. New York: Howell, Soskin and Crown Publishers, 1949.

Sandberg, Larry, and Dick Weissman. *The Folk Music Sourcebook*. New York: Alfred A. Knopf, 1976.

Sandburg, Carl. *Abraham Lincoln: The War Years*. 4 vols. New York: Harcourt, Brace and Co., 1939.

Sanjek, Russell. *From Print to Plastic: Publishing and Promoting America's Popular*

Music (1900–1980). I.S.A.M. Monographs, no. 20. Brooklyn, N.Y.: Institute for Studies in American Music, 1983.

Sankey, Ira D., et al. *Gospel Hymns Nos. 1 to 6 Complete*. 1895. Rpt., with a new introduction by H. Wiley Hitchcock. Earlier American Music, no. 5. New York: Da Capo Press, 1972.

Sargeant, Winthrop. *Jazz: Hot and Hybrid*. 1938. Revised as *Jazz: A History*. New York: McGraw-Hill, 1964.

Sawyer, Charles. *The Arrival of B. B. King: The Authorized Biography*. Garden City, N.Y.: Doubleday and Co., 1980.

Saylor, Bruce. *The Writings of Henry Cowell: A Descriptive Bibliography*. I.S.A.M. Monographs, no. 7. Brooklyn, N.Y.: Institute for Studies in American Music, 1977.

Scaduto, Anthony. *Bob Dylan*. Rev. ed. New York: New American Library, 1979.

Scarborough, Dorothy. *On the Trail of Negro Folk-Songs*. 1925. Rpt., with a foreword by Roger D. Abrahams. Hatboro, Pa.: Folklore Associates, 1963.

Schafer, William J., with assistance from Richard B. Allen. *Brass Bands and New Orleans Jazz*. Baton Rouge: Louisiana State University Press, 1977.

Schaffner, Nicholas. *The British Invasion: From the First Wave to the New Wave*. New York: McGraw-Hill, 1983.

Schiff, David. *The Music of Elliott Carter*. London: Eulenburg Books; New York: Da Capo Press, 1983.

Schillinger, Frances. *Joseph Schillinger: A Memoir*. 1949. Rpt. New York: Da Capo Press, 1976.

Schillinger, Joseph. *The Mathematical Basis of the Arts*. 1948. Rpt. New York: Da Capo Press, 1976.

———. *The Schillinger System of Musical Composition*. 1941. Rpt. New York: Da Capo Press, 1978.

Schlappi, Elizabeth. "Roy Acuff." In *Stars of Country Music: Uncle Dave Macon to Johnny Rodriguez*. Edited by Bill C. Malone and Judith McCulloh, 179–201. Urbana: University of Illinois Press, 1975.

Schmidt, John C. *The Life and Works of John Knowles Paine*. Studies in Musicology, no. 34. Ann Arbor, Mich.: UMI Research Press, 1980.

Schoenberg, Arnold. *Style and Idea: Selected Writings of Arnold Schoenberg*. Edited by Leonard Stein, with translations by Leo Black. New York: St. Martin's Press, 1975.

Scholes, Percy A. *The Puritans and Music in England and New England: A Contribution to the Cultural History of Two Nations*. 1944. Rpt. New York: Russell and Russell, 1962.

Schreiber, Flora Rheta, and Vincent Persichetti. *William Schuman*. New York: G. Schirmer, 1954.

Schubart, Mark A. "Roger Sessions: Portrait of an American Composer." *Musical Quarterly* 32 (Apr. 1946): 196–214.

Schuller, Gunther. *Early Jazz: Its Roots and Musical Development*. New York: Oxford University Press, 1968.

Schultz, Christian. *Travels on an Island Voyage through the States of New-York, Pennsylvania, Virginia, Ohio, Kentucky and Tennessee, and through the Territories of Indiana, Louisiana, Mississippi, and New Orleans; Performed in the Years 1807 and 1808, Including a Tour of Nearly Six Thousand Miles.* New York: Isaac Riley, 1810.

Schwab, Arnold T. "Edward MacDowell's Birthdate: A Correction." *Musical Quarterly* 61 (Apr. 1975): 233–39.

Schwartz, Charles. *George Gershwin: A Selective Bibliography and Discography.* Bibliographies in American Music, no. 1. Detroit: Information Coordinators, for the College Music Society, 1974.

———. *Gershwin: His Life and Music.* Indianapolis: Bobbs-Merrill, 1973.

Schwartz, Elliott, and Barney Childs, eds. *Contemporary Composers on Contemporary Music.* 1967. Rpt. New York: Da Capo Press, 1978.

Schwartz, Harry Wayne. *Bands of America.* 1957. Rpt. New York: Da Capo Press, 1975.

Sears, Priscilla. *A Pillar of Fire to Follow: American Indian Dramas, 1808–1859.* Bowling Green, Ohio: Bowling Green University Popular Press, 1983.

Seeger, Charles. "Contrapuntal Style in the Three-Voice Shape-Note Hymns." *Musical Quarterly* 26 (Oct. 1940): 483–93.

Seeger, Pete. *The Incompleat Folksinger.* Edited by Jo Metcalf Schwartz. New York: Simon and Schuster, 1972.

Sellers, Charles Coleman. *Lorenzo Dow: The Bearer of the Word.* New York: Minton, Balch and Co., 1928.

Semler, Isabel Parker, and Pierson Underwood. *Horatio Parker: A Memoir for His Grandchildren, Compiled from Letters and Papers.* 1942. Rpt. New York: Da Capo Press, 1973.

Sessions, Roger. *Questions about Music.* New York: W. W. Norton and Co., 1971.

———. *Reflections on the Music Life in the United States.* New York: Merlin Press, 1956.

Sewall, Samuel. *The Diary of Samuel Sewall, 1674–1729.* 2 vols. Edited by M. Halsey Thomas. New York: Farrar Straus Giroux, 1973.

Seward, Theodore F., ed. *Jubilee Songs As Sung by the Jubilee Singers of Fisk University.* New York: Bigelow and Main, 1872.

Shanet, Howard. *Philharmonic: A History of New York's Orchestra.* Garden City, N.Y.: Doubleday and Co., 1975.

Shapiro, Nat, and Nat Hentoff, eds. *Hear Me Talkin' to Ya.* New York: Rinehart and Co., 1955.

———. *The Jazz Makers.* 1957. Rpt. Westport, Conn.: Greenwood Press, 1975.

Sharp, Willoughby, and Liza Béar. "Phil Glass: An Interview in Two Parts." *Avalanche* 5 (Summer 1972): 27–35.

Shaw, Arnold. *The Rockin' '50s: The Decade That Transformed the Pop Music Scene.* New York: Hawthorn Books, 1974.

Silber, Irwin, ed. *Songs of the Civil War.* New York: Columbia University Press, 1960.

Silverman, Kenneth. *A Cultural History of the American Revolution: Painting, Music,*

Literature, and the Theatre in the Colonies and the United States from the Treaty of Paris to the Inauguration of George Washington, 1763–1789. New York: Thomas Y. Crowell Co., 1976.

Simels, Steve. "Tonio K: Just What the Eighties Needed, a Dadaist Get Ready Man." *Stereo Review* 45 (Oct. 1980): 72–74.

Simkins, Francis B., ed. *Art and Music in the South: Institute of Southern Culture Lectures at Longwood College, 1960*. Farmville, Va.: Longwood College, 1961.

Simpson, Claude M. *The British Broadside Ballad and Its Music*. New Brunswick, N.J.: Rutgers University Press, 1966.

Simpson, Ralph Ricardo. "William Grant Still: The Man and His Music." Ph.D. diss., Michigan State University, 1964.

Sizer, Sandra S. *Gospel Hymns and Social Religion: The Rhetoric of Nineteenth-Century Revivalism*. Philadelphia: Temple University Press, 1978.

Skowronski, JoAnn. *Black Music in America: A Bibliography*. Metuchen, N.J.: Scarecrow Press, 1981.

Slobin, Mark. *Tenement Songs: The Popular Music of the Jewish Immigrants*. Music in American Life. Urbana: University of Illinois Press, 1982.

Slonimsky, Nicolas. *Music since 1900*. 3d ed. New York: Coleman-Ross, 1949.

Smith, Cecil. *Musical Comedy in America*. New York: Theatre Arts Books, 1950.

Smith, Julia. *Aaron Copland: His Work and Contribution to American Music*. New York: E. P. Dutton and Co., 1955.

Smith, Leland. "Henry Cowell's *Rhythmicana*." *Yearbook for Inter-American Musical Research* 9 (1973): 134–47.

Smith, Timothy L. *Revivalism and Social Reform in Mid-Nineteenth-Century America*. New York: Abingdon Press, 1957.

Smithsonian Collection of Classic Jazz. 6 discs. Selected and annotated by Martin Williams. Washington, D.C.: Smithsonian Institution, distributed by W. W. Norton and Co., 1973.

Society for the Preservation of Spirituals. *The Carolina Low-Country*. New York: Macmillan, 1931.

Sonneck, Oscar G. *A Bibliography of Early Secular American Music (18th Century)*. Revised and enlarged by William Treat Upton. 1945. Rpt., with a new preface by Irving Lowens. New York: Da Capo Press, 1964.

———. *Early Concert-Life in America (1731–1800)*. 1907. Rpt. New York: Da Capo Press, 1978.

———. *Early Opera in America*. 1915. Rpt. New York: Benjamin Blom, 1963.

———. *Francis Hopkinson: The First American Poet-Composer (1737–1791), and James Lyon: Patriot, Preacher, Psalmodist (1735–1794)*. 1905. Rpt., with a new introduction by Richard Crawford. New York: Da Capo Press, 1966.

———. "The Star Spangled Banner." 1914. Rpt. New York: Da Capo Press, 1969.

Sounds and Words: A Critical Celebration of Milton Babbitt at 60. Perspectives of New Music 14 (Spring-Summer 1976) and 15 (Fall-Winter 1976).

Sousa, John Philip. *Marching Along: Recollection of Men, Women, and Music*. Boston: Hale, Cushman and Flint, 1928.

Southern, Eileen. *The Music of Black Americans: A History.* 2d ed. New York: W. W. Norton and Co., 1983.

———, ed. *Biographical Dictionary of Afro-American and African Musicians.* Greenwood Encyclopedia of Black Music. Westport, Conn.: Greenwood Press, 1982.

———, ed. *Readings in Black American Music.* 2d ed. New York: W. W. Norton and Co., 1983.

Spackman, Stephen. *Wallingford Riegger: Two Essays in Musical Biography.* I.S.A.M. Monographs, no. 17. Brooklyn, N.Y.: Institute for Studies in American Music, 1982.

Spaeth, Sigmund. *A History of Popular Music in America.* New York: Random House, 1948.

———. *Read 'Em and Weep: The Songs You Forgot to Remember.* 1926. Rpt. New York: Da Capo Press, 1979.

———. *Weep Some More, My Lady.* 1927. Rpt. New York: Da Capo Press, 1980.

Spalding, Walter Raymond. *Music at Harvard: A Historical Review of Men and Events.* 1935. Rpt. New York: Da Capo Press, 1977.

Spaulding, Henry G. "Under the Palmetto." *Continental Monthly* 4 (Aug. 1863): 188–203.

Speck, Frank G. *Oklahoma Delaware Ceremonies, Feasts and Dances.* 1937. Rpt. New York: AMS Press, 1980.

Spellman, A. B. *Black Music: Four Lives.* New York: Schocken Books, 1970.

Spencer, Katherine. *Mythology and Values: An Analysis of Navaho Chantway Myths.* Memoirs of the American Folklore Society, vol. 48. 1957. Austin: University of Texas Press, 1975.

Spillane, Daniel. *History of the American Pianoforte.* 1890. Rpt., with a new introduction by Rita Benton. New York: Da Capo Press, 1969.

Stambler, Irwin. *Encyclopedia of Popular Music.* New York: St. Martin's Press, 1965.

Stampp, Kenneth M. *The Peculiar Institution: Slavery in the Ante-Bellum South.* New York: Alfred A. Knopf, 1956.

Standish, Lemuel Wilbur. *The Old Stoughton Music Society: An Historical and Informative Record of the Oldest Choral Society in America, together with Interesting Data of Its Organization, Meetings, Reunions and Outings, and a Complete List of Past and Present Officers and Members.* Stoughton, Mass.: Stoughton Printing Co., 1929.

Stanislaw, Richard J. *A Checklist of Four-Shape Shape-Note Tunebooks.* I.S.A.M. Monographs, no. 10. Brooklyn, N.Y.: Institute for Studies in American Music, 1978.

Stanley, Lana, comp. *Folk-rock: A Bibliography on Music of the Sixties.* San José State College Library, Bibliography series, no. 3. San José, Calif.: San José State College Library, 1970.

Starke, Aubrey Harrison. *Sidney Lanier: A Biographical and Critical Study.* 1933. Rpt. New York: Russell and Russell, 1964.

———. "Sidney Lanier as a Musician." *Musical Quarterly* 20 (Oct. 1934): 384–400.

Stearns, Marshall W. *The Story of Jazz.* New York: Oxford University Press, 1956.

Stearns, Marshall W., and Jean Stearns. *Jazz Dance: The Story of American Vernacular Dance.* New York: Macmillan, 1968.

Steinberg, Judith T. See Tick, Judith.

Stetzel, Ronald Delbert. "John Christopher Moller (1755–1803) and His Role in Early American Music." Ph.D. diss., University of Iowa, 1965.

Stevenson, Robert. "English Sources for Indian Music until 1882." *Ethnomusicology* 17 (Sept. 1973): 339–442.

———. "Gottschalk in Buenos Aires." *Inter-American Music Bulletin* 74 (Nov. 1969): 1–7.

———. *Protestant Church Music in America: A Short Survey of Men and Movements from 1564 to the Present.* New York: W. W. Norton and Co., 1966.

———. "Written Sources for Indian Music until 1882." *Ethnomusicology* 17 (Jan. 1973): 1–40.

Stewart, Rex. *Jazz Masters of the Thirties.* 1972. Rpt. New York: Da Capo Press, 1980.

Stewart-Baxter, Derrick. *Ma Rainey and the Classic Blues Singers.* New York: Stein and Day, 1970.

Sudhalter, Richard M., and Philip R. Evans, with William Dean-Myatt. *Bix, Man & Legend.* New Rochelle, N.Y.: Arlington House, 1974.

Sweet, William Warren. *Revivalism in America: Its Origin, Growth, and Decline.* New York: Charles Scribner's Sons, 1944.

Tallmadge, William H. "Baptist Monophonic and Heterophonic Hymnody in Southern Appalachia." *Yearbook for Inter-American Musical Research* 11 (1975): 106–36.

Tawa, Nicholas E. "The Performance of Parlor Songs in America, 1790–1860." *Yearbook for Inter-American Musical Research* 11 (1975): 69–81.

———. *Serenading the Reluctant Eagle: American Musical Life, 1925–1945.* New York: Schirmer Books, 1984.

———. *A Sound of Strangers: Musical Culture, Acculturation, and the Post–Civil War Ethnic American.* Metuchen, N.J.: Scarecrow Press, 1982.

———. *Sweet Songs for Gentle Americans: The Parlor Song in America, 1790–1860.* Bowling Green, Ohio: Bowling Green University Popular Press, 1980.

Tax, Sol, ed. *Acculturation in the Americas.* Vol. 2 of *Selected Papers of the XXIXth International Congress of Americanists.* Chicago: University of Chicago Press, 1952.

Taylor, Clifford. "Walter Piston: For His Seventieth Birthday." *Perspectives of New Music* 3 (Fall-Winter 1964): 102–14.

Taylor, Deems. *Some Enchanted Evenings: The Story of Rodgers and Hammerstein.* New York: Harper and Brothers, 1953.

Temperley, Nicholas. *The Music of the English Parish Church.* 2 vols. London: Cambridge University Press, 1979.

———. "The Old Way of Singing." *Journal of the American Musicological Society* 34 (Fall 1981): 511–44.

Temperley, Nicholas, and Charles G. Manns. *Fuging Tunes in the Eighteenth Century.* Detroit Studies in Music Bibliography, no. 49. Detroit: Information Coordinators, 1983.

Tenney, James. Liner notes to *Complete Studies for Player Piano: The Music of Conlon Nancarrow, vol. 1.* Arch Records S-1768. 1977.

———. *META-HODOS: A Phenomenology of Twentieth-Century Musical Materials and an Approach to the Study of Form.* New Orleans: Inter-American Institute for Musical Research, Tulane University, 1964.

Thomas, Robert K. "Pan-Indianism." In *The Emergent Native American: A Reader in Culture Contact.* Edited by Deward E. Walker, 739–46. Boston: Little, Brown and Co., 1972.

Thomson, Virgil. *Music, Right and Left.* 1951. Rpt. Westport, Conn.: Greenwood Press, 1969.

———. *The Musical Scene.* 1945. Rpt. Westport, Conn.: Greenwood Press, 1968.

———. *The State of Music.* 1939. Rpt. Westport, Conn.: Greenwood Press, 1974.

———. *Virgil Thomson.* New York: Alfred A. Knopf, 1966.

Tick, Judith. *American Women Composers before 1870.* Studies in Musicology, no. 57. Ann Arbor, Mich.: UMI Research Press, 1983.

———[Steinberg, Judith T.]. "Old Folks Concerts and the Revival of New England Psalmody." *Musical Quarterly* 59 (Oct. 1973): 602–19.

———. "Women as Professional Musicians in the United States, 1870–1900." *Yearbook for Inter-American Musical Research* 9 (1973): 95–133.

Tirro, Frank. *Jazz: A History.* New York: W. W. Norton and Co., 1977.

Titon, Jeff Todd. *Downhome Blues Lyrics: An Anthology from the Post–World War II Era.* Boston: Twayne Publishers, 1981.

———. *Early Downhome Blues: A Musical and Cultural Analysis.* Music in American Life. Urbana: University of Illinois Press, 1977.

Toll, Robert C. *Blacking Up: The Minstrel Show in Nineteenth-Century America.* New York: Oxford University Press, 1974.

———. *On with the Show: The First Century of Show Business in America.* New York: Oxford University Press, 1976.

Trollope, Frances. *Domestic Manners of the American People.* London: Whittaker, Treacher and Co., 1832.

Trotter, James M. *Music and Some Highly Musical People.* 1878. Rpt. New York: Johnson Reprint Corp., 1968.

Tufts, John. *An Introduction to the Singing of Psalm-Tunes, in a Plain & Easy Method, with a Collection of Tunes in Three Parts.* 5th ed. 1726. Rpt., with a foreword by Irving Lowens. Philadelphia: Albert Saifer for Musical Americana, 1954.

Turner, Frederick. *Remembering Song: Encounters with the New Orleans Jazz Tradition.* New York: Viking Press, 1982.

Ulanov, Barry. *Duke Ellington.* 1946. Rpt. New York: Da Capo Press, 1975.

———. *A Handbook of Jazz.* New York: Viking Press, 1957.

———. *A History of Jazz in America.* New York: Viking Press, 1952.

Upton, William Treat. *Anthony Philip Heinrich: A Nineteenth-Century Composer in America*. 1939. Rpt. New York: AMS Press, 1967.

————. *The Musical Works of William Henry Fry in the Collections of the Library Company of Philadelphia*. Philadelphia: Free Library, 1946.

————. *William Henry Fry: American Journalist and Composer-Critic*. New York: Thomas Y. Crowell Co., 1954.

Van Solkema, Sherman, ed. *The New Worlds of Edgard Varèse: A Symposium*. I.S.A.M. Monographs, no. 11. Brooklyn, N.Y.: Institute for Studies in American Music, 1979.

Varèse, Louise. *Varèse: A Looking-Glass Diary*. Vol. 1, *1883-1928*. New York: W. W. Norton and Co., 1972.

Velie, Alan R., ed. *American Indian Literature: An Anthology*. Norman: University of Oklahoma Press, 1979.

Vinton, John, ed. *Dictionary of Contemporary Music*. New York: E. P. Dutton and Co., 1974.

Virga, Patricia H. *The American Opera to 1790*. Studies in Musicology, no. 61. Ann Arbor, Mich.: UMI Research Press, 1982.

Von Gunden, Heidi. *The Music of Pauline Oliveros*. Metuchen, N.J.: Scarecrow Press, 1983.

Walker, Deward E., ed. *The Emergent Native American: A Reader in Culture Contact*. Boston: Little, Brown and Co., 1972.

Walker, William, comp. *The Southern Harmony, and Musical Companion*. 1854. Rpt., edited by Glenn C. Wilcox. Los Angeles: Pro Musicamericana, 1966.

Ward, William E. "Music of the Gold Coast." *Musical Times* 73 (Aug., Sept., and Oct. 1932): 707–10; 797–99; 901–2.

Ware, Naomi. "Survival and Change in Pima Indian Music." *Ethnomusicology* 14 (Jan. 1970): 100–13.

Waterman, Richard A. "African Influence on the Music of the Americas." In *Acculturation in the Americas*. Edited by Sol Tax, 207–18. Chicago: University of Chicago Press, 1952.

————. " 'Hot' Rhythm in Negro Music." *Journal of the American Musicological Society* 1 (1948): 24–37.

Waters, Edward N. *Victor Herbert: A Life in Music*. New York: Macmillan, 1955.

Weisberger, Bernard A. *They Gathered at the River: The Story of the Great Revivalists and Their Impact upon Religion in America*. Boston: Little, Brown and Co., 1958.

Welding, Peter. Liner notes to *The Immortal Blind Lemon Jefferson*. Milestone MLP 2004. 1967.

Wells, Frederic P. *History of Newbury, Vermont, from the Discovery of the Coös Country to Present Time*. St. Johnsbury, Vt.: Caledonian Co., 1902.

Wesley, John. *A Collection of Psalms and Hymns.* Charlestown, S.C.: L. Timothy, 1837.

——. *The Journal of the Rev. John Wesley, A.M.* Edited by Nehemiah Curnock. 8 vols. London: R. Culley, 1909–16.

Wetzel, Richard D. *Frontier Musicians on the Connoquenessing, Wabash, and Ohio: A History of the Music and Musicians of George Rapp's Harmony Society (1805–1906).* Athens: Ohio University Press, 1976.

White, B. F., and E. J. King. *The Sacred Harp.* 3d ed. 1859. Rpt., with a historical introduction by George Pullen Jackson. Nashville: Broadman Press, 1968.

White, Newman I. *American Negro Folk-Songs.* 1928. Rpt., with a foreword by Bruce Jackson. Hatboro, Pa.: Folklore Associates, 1965.

Whitfield, Irène Thérèse, ed. *Louisiana French Folk Songs.* 3d ed. Eunice, La.: Hebert Publications, 1981.

Whitten, Norman E., Jr., and John F. Szwed, eds. *Afro-American Anthropology: Contemporary Perspectives.* New York: Free Press, 1970.

Whittlesey, Walter R., and Oscar G. Sonneck. *Catalogue of First Editions of Stephen C. Foster (1826–1864).* 1915. Rpt. New York: Da Capo Press, 1971.

Wiggins, Gene. *Fiddlin' Georgia Crazy: Fiddlin' John Carson, His Real World, and the World of His Songs.* Music in American Life. Urbana: University of Illinois Press, 1987.

Wilder, Alec. *American Popular Song: The Great Innovators, 1900–1950.* Edited, with an introduction, by James T. Maher. New York: Oxford University Press, 1972.

Wilgus, D. K. *Anglo-American Folksong Scholarship since 1898.* 1959. Rpt. Westport, Conn.: Greenwood Press, 1982.

Williams, Martin. *Jazz Masters in Transition, 1957–69.* 1970. Rpt. New York: Da Capo Press, 1980.

——. *Jazz Masters of New Orleans.* 1967. Rpt. New York: Da Capo Press, 1978.

——. *Jelly Roll Morton.* New York: A. S. Barnes and Co., 1963.

——. *King Oliver.* New York: A. S. Barnes and Co., 1961.

——. Liner notes to *Count Basie in Kansas City; Bennie Moten's Great Band of 1930–1932.* RCA Victor Vintage LPV-514. N.d.

——. Liner notes to *The Golden Monk, Thelonious Monk.* Prestige 7363. N.d.

——, ed. *The Art of Jazz: Essays on the Nature and Development of Jazz.* 1959. Rpt. New York: Da Capo Press, 1979.

——, ed. *Jazz Panorama: From the Pages of the Jazz Review.* 1962. Rpt. New York: Da Capo Press, 1979.

Williams, Roger M. "Hank Williams." In *Stars of Country Music: Uncle Dave Macon to Johnny Rodriguez.* Edited by Bill C. Malone and Judith McCulloh, 237–54. Urbana: University of Illinois Press, 1975.

Willis, Richard Storrs. *Our Church Music: A Book for Pastors and People.* 1856. Rpt. New York: AMS Press, 1973.

Wilson, Alexander. *American Ornithology.* 9 vols. Philadelphia: Bradford and Inskeep, 1808–14.

Wilson, Robert Forrest. "Paris for Young Art." *Bookman* 61 (June 1925): 403–12.

Witmark, Isidore, and Isaac Goldberg. *From Ragtime to Swingtime: The Story of the House of Witmark*. New York: Lee Furman, 1939.

Wittke, Carl. *Tambo and Bones: A History of the American Minstrel Stage*. Durham, N.C.: Duke University Press, 1930.

Wolf, Edwin. *American Song Sheets, Slip Ballads and Political Broadsides, 1850–1870: A Catalogue of the Collection of the Library Company of Philadelphia*. Philadelphia: Library Company of Philadelphia, 1963.

Wolfe, Richard J. *Early American Music Engraving and Printing: A History of Music Publishing in America from 1787 to 1825 with Commentary on Earlier and Later Practices*. Music in American Life. Urbana: University of Illinois Press, in cooperation with the Bibliographical Society of America, 1980.

———. *Secular Music in America, 1801–1825: A Bibliography*. 3 vols. New York: New York Public Library, 1964.

Wolfe, Tom. *The Electric Kool-Aid Acid Test*. New York: Farrar Straus Giroux, 1968.

Woodforde, James. *The Diary of a Country Parson, the Reverend James Woodforde*. Edited by John Beresford. 5 vols. 1924–31. Rpt. Oxford: Clarendon Press, 1968.

Work, John Wesley, ed. *American Negro Songs and Spirituals: A Comprehensive Collection of 230 Folk Songs, Religious and Secular*. New York: Crown Publishers, 1940.

———. *Folk Song of the American Negro*. 1915. Rpt. New York: Negro Universities Press, 1969.

Wuorinen, Charles. Liner notes to Charles Wuorinen, *Time's Encomium for Synthesized & Processed Synthesized Sound*. Nonesuch H-71225. N.d.

Wyeth, John. *Wyeth's Repository of Sacred Music*. 5th ed. 1820. Rpt., with a new introduction by Irving Lowens. New York: Da Capo Press, 1975.

———. *Wyeth's Repository of Sacred Music, Part Second*. 2d ed. 1820. Rpt., with an introduction by Irving Lowens. New York: Da Capo Press, 1964.

Yates, Peter. Liner notes to John Cage and Lejaren Hiller, *HPSCHD for Harpsichords & Computer*. . . . Nonesuch H-71224. N.d.

———. *Twentieth-Century Music: Its Evolution from the End of the Harmonic Era into the Present Era of Sound*. 1967. Rpt. Westport, Conn.: Greenwood Press, 1980.

Yellin, Victor Fell. "Chadwick, American Musical Realist." *Musical Quarterly* 61 (Jan. 1975): 77–97.

———. "Rayner Taylor." *American Music* (Fall 1983): 48–71.

Yerbury, Grace D. *Song in America: From Early Times to about 1850*. Metuchen, N.J.: Scarecrow Press, 1971.

Young, Douglas. "The Piano Music." *Tempo* 95 (Winter 1970–71): 18–21.

Index

A Note on the Author

Gilbert Chase was born in 1906 in Havana, Cuba, where his father served as an officer in the United States Navy. Raised and educated in the United States, he attended Columbia University and graduated from the University of North Carolina, Chapel Hill. A prolific writer and distinguished scholar, critic, editor, and lecturer, he has taught at numerous institutions, including the Institute for Studies in American Music, the University of Oklahoma, University of Texas at Austin, State University of New York at Buffalo, University of Washington at Seattle, and Tulane University, where he founded and directed the Inter-American Institute for Musical Research and edited the institute's *Yearbook*. He has written extensively on Spanish and American topics. Among his publications are *The Music of Spain* (1941; 2d rev. ed. 1959), *A Guide to the Music of Latin America* (1945; 2d rev. ed. 1962), *The American Composer Speaks: A Historical Anthology, 1770–1965* (1966), and over 200 articles in English, French, Spanish, Italian, and Portuguese on art, literature, history, anthropology, folklore, music, and international affairs. Professor Chase retired in 1979 to devote his time to writing and lecturing.